I0836931

TESTIMONIALS.

The author is a lawyer, very learned in his profession, acute, critical, and used to raising and meeting practical doubts. Author of a treatise on the law of evidence, which has become a classic in the hands of the profession which he adorns, and teacher in one of the Law Seminaries which do honor to our country in the eyes of Europe, he brings rare qualifications for the task he assumes. * * * Such are our views of this work which we commend to all; to the legal profession, from the character of its topics and the rank of its author: to men desirous of knowledge, in every rank in life, because of its presenting this subject under such treatment as is applied to every day practical questions. It does not touch the intrinsic evidences of the Gospel: those which to the believer are, after all, the highest proofs. But it is to be remembered, that these are proofs which are not satisfactory until an examination of the outward evidence has led men to the conviction, that the Gospels cannot be false.—*Extract from the New York Observer*

It is the production of an able and profound lawyer, a man who has grown grey in the halls of justice and the schools of jurisprudence; a writer of the highest authority on legal subjects, whose life has been spent in weighing testimony and sifting evidence, and whose published opinions on the rules of evidence are received as authoritative in all the English and American tribunals; for fourteen years the highly respected colleague of the late Mr. Justice Story, and also the honored head of the most distinguished and prosperous school of English law in the world.—*North American Review.*

It is no mean honor to America that her schools of jurisprudence have produced two of the first writers and best esteemed legal authorities of this century—the great and good man, Judge Story, and his worthy and eminent associate Professor Greenleaf. Upon the existing Law of Evidence (by Greenleaf), more light has shone from the New World than from all the lawyers who adorn the courts of Europe.—*London Law Magazine.*

THE

TESTIMONY OF THE EVANGELISTS

THE

TESTIMONY OF THE EVANGELISTS

EXAMINED BY THE RULES OF EVIDENCE

ADMINISTERED IN COURTS OF JUSTICE

BY

SIMON GREENLEAF, LL.D.

LATE DANE PROFESSOR OF LAW IN HARVARD UNIVERSITY, AUTHOR OF "TREATISE ON THE LAW OF EVIDENCE"

WITH AN APPENDIX

CONTAINING A HISTORY OF THE MOST ANCIENT MANUSCRIPT COPIES OF THE NEW TESTAMENT, AND A COMPARISON OF THEIR TEXT WITH THAT OF THE KING JAMES' BIBLE

BY CONSTANTINE TISCHENDORFF

ALSO

A REVIEW OF THE TRIAL OF JESUS

NEW YORK

JAMES COCKCROFT & COMPANY

1874

PRESS OF
TOBITT
N.Y.
Nº 90
& BUNCE
FULTON ST.

TO THE

MEMBERS OF THE LEGAL PROFESSION.

GENTLEMEN,

THE subject of the following work I hope will not be deemed so foreign to our professional pursuits, as to render it improper for me to dedicate it, as I now respectfully do, to you. If a close examination of the evidences of Christianity may be expected of one class of men more than another, it would seem incumbent on us, who make the law of evidence one of our peculiar studies. Our profession leads us to explore the mazes of falsehood, to detect its artifices, to pierce its thickest veils, to follow and expose its sophistries, to compare the statements of different witnesses with severity, to discover truth and separate it from error. Our fellow-men are well aware of this; and probably they act upon this knowledge more generally, and with a more profound repose, than we are in the habit of considering. The influence, too, of the legal profession upon the community is unquestionably great; conversant, as it daily is, with all classes and grades of men, in their domestic and social relations, and in all the affairs of life, from the cradle to the grave. This influence we are constantly exerting for good or ill; and hence, to refuse to acquaint ourselves with the evidences of the Christian religion, or to act as though, having fully examined, we lightly esteemed them, is to assume an appalling amount of responsibility.

The things related by the Evangelists are certainly of the most momentous character, affecting the principles of our conduct here, and our happiness for ever. The religion of Jesus Christ aims at nothing less than the utter overthow of all other systems of religion in the world; denouncing them as inadequate to the wants of man, false in their foundations, and dangerous in their tendency. It not only solicits the grave attention of all, to whom its doctrines are presented, but it demands their cordial belief, as a matter of vital concernment. These are no ordinary claims; and it seems hardly possible for a rational being to regard them with even a subdued interest; much less to treat them with mere indifference and contempt. If not true, they are little else than the pretensions of a bold imposture, which, not satisfied with having already enslaved millions of the human race, seeks to continue its encroachments upon human liberty, until all nations shall be subjugated under its iron rule. But if they are well founded and just, they can be no less than the high requirements of Heaven, addressed by the voice of God to the reason and understanding of man, concerning things deeply affecting his relations to his sovereign, and essential to the formation of his character and of course to his destiny, both for this life and for the life to come. Such was the estimate taken of religion, even the religion of pagan Rome, by one of the greatest lawyers of antiquity, when he argued that it was either nothing at all, or was everything. *Aut undique religionem tolle, aut usquequaque conserva.**

With this view of the importance of the subject, and in the hope that the present work may in some degree aid or at least incite others to a more successful pursuit of this interesting study, it is submitted to your kind regard, by

Your obedient servant,

SIMON GREENLEAF.

* Cicero, Philip. II. § 43.

CONTENTS

AND

SYNOPSIS OF THE HARMONY.

	CONTENTS.	MATT.	MARK.	LUKE.	JOHN.
Sect.					
	PART I.				
	EVENTS CONNECTED WITH THE BIRTH AND CHILDHOOD OF OUR LORD.				
	TIME: *About thirteen and a half years.*				
1	Preface to Luke's Gospel.			1, 1–4	
2	An Angel appears to Zacharias. *Jerusalem.*			1, 5–25	
3	An Angel appears to Mary. *Nazareth.*			1, 26–38	
4	Mary visits Elizabeth. *Juttah.*			1, 39–56	
5	Birth of John the Baptist. *Juttah.*			1, 57–80	
6	An Angel appears to Joseph. *Nazareth.*	1, 18–25			
7	The Birth of Jesus. *Bethlehem.*			2, 1–7	
8	An Angel appears to the Shepherds. *Near Bethlehem.*			2, 8–20	
9	The Circumcision of Jesus, and his Presentation in the Temple. *Bethlehem. Jerusalem.*			2. 21–38	
10	The Magi. *Jerusalem. Bethlehem.*	2, 1–12			
11	The Flight into Egypt. Herod's cruelty. The Return. *Bethlehem. Nazareth.*	2, 13–23		2, 39–40	
12	At twelve years of age Jesus goes to the Passover. *Jerusalem.*			2, 41–52	
13	The Genealogies.	1, 1–17		3, 28–38	

Sect.	CONTENTS.	MATT.	MARK.	LUKE.	JOHN.
	PART II. ANNOUNCEMENT AND INTRODUCTION OF OUR LORD'S PUBLIC MINISTRY. TIME: *About one year.*				
14	The Ministry of John the Baptist. *The Desert. The Jordan.*	3, 1–12	.1, 1–8	3, 1–18	
15	The Baptism of Jesus. *The Jordan.*	3, 1–12	1, 1–8	3, 1–18	
16	The Temptation. *Desert of Judea.*	4, 1–11	1, 12–13	4, 1–13	
17	Preface to John's Gospel.				1, 1–18
18	Testimony of John the Baptist to Jesus. *Bethany beyond Jordan.*				1, 19–34
19	Jesus gains Disciples. *The Jordan Galilee?*				1, 35–52
20	The Marriage at Cana of Galilee.				2, 1–12
	PART III. OUR LORD'S FIRST PASSOVER, AND THE SUBSEQUENT TRANSACTIONS UNTIL THE SECOND. TIME: *One Year.*				
21	At the Passover Jesus drives the Traders out of the Temple. *Jerusalem.*				2, 13–25
22	Our Lord's Discourse with Nicodemus. *Jerusalem.*				3, 1–21
23	Jesus remains in Judea and baptizes. Further testimony of John the Baptist.				3, 22–36
24	Jesus departs into Galilee after John's imprisonment.	4, 12 14, 3–5	1, 14 6, 17–20	4, 14 3, 19–20	4, 1–3
25	Our Lord's Discourse with the Samaritan Woman. Many of the Samaritans believe on him. *Shechem* or *Neapolis.*				4, 4–42
26	Jesus teaches publicly in Galilee.	4, 17	1, 14, 15	4, 14–15	4, 43–45
27	Jesus again at Cana, where he heals the son of a nobleman lying ill at Capernaum. *Cana of Galilee.*				4 46–54
28	Jesus at Nazareth; he is there rejected, and fixes his abode at Capernaum.	4, 13–16		4–16–31	
29	The call of Simon Peter and Andrew, and of James and John, with the miraculous draught of fishes. *Near Capernaum.*	4, 18–22	1, 16–20	5, 1–11	
30	The healing of a Demoniac				

Sect.	CONTENTS.	MATT.	MARK.	LUKE.	JOHN.
	in the Synagogue. *Capernaum.*		1, 21–28	4, 31–37	
31	The healing of Peter's wife's mother, and many others. *Capernaum.*	8, 14–17	1, 29–34	4, 38–41	
32	Jesus with his Disciples goes from Capernaum throughout Galilee.	4, 23–25	1, 35–39	4, 42–44	
33	The healing of a Leper. *Galilee.*	8, 2–4	1, 40–45	5, 12–16	
34	The healing of a Paralytic. *Capernaum.*	9, 2–8	2, 1–12	5, 17–26	
35	The call of Matthew. *Capernaum.*	9, 9	2, 13, 14	5, 27, 28	
	PART IV.				
	OUR LORD'S SECOND PASSOVER, AND THE SUBSEQUENT TRANSACTIONS UNTIL THE THIRD.				
	TIME: *One Year.*				
36	The Pool of Bethesda; the healing of the infirm man; and our Lord's subsequent discourse. *Jerusalem.*				5, 1–47
37	The Disciples pluck ears of grain on the Sabbath. *On the way to Galilee?*	12, 1–8	2, 23–28	6, 1–5	
38	The healing of the withered hand on the Sabbath. *Galilee.*	12, 9–14	3, 1–6	6, 6–11	
39	Jesus arrives at the sea of Tiberias, and is followed by multitudes. *Lake of Galilee.*	12, 15–21	3, 7–12		
40	Jesus withdraws to the Mountain, and chooses the Twelve; the multitudes follow him. *Near Capernaum.*	10, 2–4	2 13–19	6, 12–19	
41	The Sermon on the Mount. *Near Capernaum.*	5, 1,—8, 1		6, 20–49	
42	The healing of the Centurion's servant. *Capernaum.*	8, 5–13		7, 1–10	
43	The raising of the Widow's son. *Nain.*			7, 11–17	
44	John the Baptist in prison sends Disciples to Jesus. *Galilee. Capernaum?*	11, 2–19		7, 18–35	
45	Reflections of Jesus on appealing to his mighty Works. *Capernaum.*	11, 20–30			
46	While sitting at meat with a Pharisee, Jesus is anointed by a woman who had been a sinner. *Capernaum?*			7, 36–50	
47	Jesus, with the Twelve, makes a second circuit in Galilee.			8, 1–3	
48	The healing of a Demoniac. The Scribes and Pharisees blaspheme. *Galilee.*	12, 22–37	3, 19–30	11, 14, 15 17–23	

Sect.	CONTENTS.	MATT.	MARK.	LUKE.	JOHN.
49	The Scribes and Pharisees seek a sign. Our Lord's reflections. *Galilee.*	12, 38–45		11, 16 24–36	
50	The true Disciples of Christ his nearest relatives. *Galilee.*	12, 46–50	3, 31–35	8, 19–21	
51	At a Pharisee's table, Jesus denounces woes against the Pharisees and others. *Galilee.*			11, 37–54	
52	Jesus discourses to his Disciples and the multitude. *Galilee.*			12, 1–59	
53	The slaughter of certain Galileans. Parable of the barren Fig tree. *Galilee.*			13, 1–9	
54	Parable of the Sower. *Lake of Galilee. Near Capernaum.*	13, 1–23	4, 1–25	8, 4–18	
55	Parable of the Tares. Other Parables. *Near Capernaum.*	13, 24–53	4, 26–34		
56	Jesus directs to cross the Lake. Incidents. The tempest stilled. *Lake of Galilee.*	8, 18–27	4, 35–41	8, 22–25 9, 57–62	
57	The two Demoniacs of Gadara. *S. E. coast of the Lake Galilee.*	8, 28–34 9, 1	5, 1–21	8, 26–40	
58	Levi's Feast. *Capernaum.*	9, 10–17	2, 15–22	5, 29–39	
59	The raising of Jairus's daughter. The woman with a bloody flux. *Capernaum.*	9, 18–26	5, 22–43	8, 41–56	
60	Two blind men healed, and a dumb spirit cast out. *Capernaum.*	9, 27–34			
61	Jesus again at Nazareth, and again rejected.	13, 54–58	6, 1–6		
62	A third circuit in Galilee. The Twelve instructed and sent forth. *Galilee.*	9, 35–38 10, 1. 5–42 11, 1	6, 6–13	9, 1–6	
63	Herod holds Jesus to be John the Baptist, whom he had just before beheaded. *Galilee? Perea.*	14, 1, 2 6–12	6, 14–16 21–29	9, 7–9	
64	The Twelve return, and Jesus retires with them across the Lake. Five thousand are fed. *Capernaum. N. E. coast of the Lake of Galilee.*	14, 13–21	6, 30–44	9, 10–17	6, 1–14
65	Jesus walks upon the water. *Lake of Galilee. Gennesareth.*	14, 22–36	6, 45–56		6, 15–21
66	Our Lord's discourse to the multitude in the Synagogue at Capernaum. Many Disciples turn back. Peter's profession of faith. *Capernaum.*				6, 22–71 7, 1

Sect.	CONTENTS.	MATT.	MARK.	LUKE.	JOHN.
	PART V. FROM OUR LORD'S THIRD PASSOVER UNTIL HIS FINAL DEPARTURE FROM GALILEE AT THE FESTIVAL OF TABERNACLES. TIME: *Six months.*				
67	Our Lord justifies his disciples for eating with unwashen hands. Pharisaic Traditions. *Capernaum.*	15, 1–20	7, 1–23		
68	The daughter of a Syrophenician woman is healed. *Region of Tyre and Sidon.*	15, 21–28	7, 24–30		
69	A deaf and dumb man healed; also many others. Four thousand are fed. *The Decapolis.*	15, 29–38	7, 31–37 8, 1–9		
70	The Pharisees and Sadducees again require a sign. [See § 49.] *Near Magdala.*	15, 39 16, 1–4	8, 10–12		
71	The Disciples cautioned against the leaven of the Pharisees, etc. *N. E. coast of the Lake of Galilee.*	16, 4–12	8, 13–21		
72	A blind man healed. *Bethsaida. (Julias.)*		8, 22–26		
73	Peter and the rest again profess their faith in Christ. [See § 66.] *Region of Cesarea Philippi.*	16, 13–20	8, 27–30	9, 18–21	
74	Our Lord foretells his own death and resurrection, and the trials of his followers. *Region of Cesarea Philippi.*	16, 21–28	8, 31–38 9, 1	9, 22–27	
75	The Transfiguration. Our Lord's subsequent discourse with the three Disciples. *Region of Cesarea Philippi.*	17, 1–13	9, 2–13	9, 28–36	
76	The healing of a Demoniac, whom the Disciples could not heal. *Region of Cesarea Philippi.*	17, 14–21	9, 14–29	9, 37–43	
77	Jesus again foretells his own death and resurrection. [See § 74.] *Galilee.*	17, 22, 23	9, 30–32	9, 43–45	
78	The tribute money miraculously provided. *Capernaum.*	17, 24–27	9, 33		
79	The Disciples contend who should be greatest. Jesus exhorts to humility, forbearance, and brotherly love. *Capernaum.*	18, 1–35	9, 33–50	9, 46–50	
80	The Seventy instructed and sent out. *Capernaum.*				

Sect.	CONTENTS.	MATT.	MARK.	LUKE.	JOHN.
81	Jesus goes up to the Festival of Tabernacles. His final departure from Galilee. Incidents in Samaria.			9, 51–56	7, 2–10
82	Ten Lepers cleansed. *Samaria.*			17, 11–19	
	PART VI.				
	THE FESTIVAL OF TABERNACLES, AND THE SUBSEQUENT TRANSACTIONS UNTIL OUR LORD'S ARRIVAL AT BETHANY, SIX DAYS BEFORE THE FOURTH PASSOVER.				
	TIME: *Six months less one week.*				
83	Jesus at the Festival of Tabernacles. His public teaching. *Jerusalem.*				7, 11–53 8, 1
84	The woman taken in Adultery. *Jerusalem.*				8, 2–11
85	Further public teaching of our Lord. He reproves the unbelieving Jews, and escapes from their hands. *Jerusalem.*				8, 12–59
86	A lawyer instructed. Love to our neighbor defined. Parable of the Good Samaritan. *Near Jerusalem.*			10, 25–37	
87	Jesus in the house of Martha and Mary. *Bethany.*			10, 38–42	
88	The Disciples again taught how to pray. *Near Jerusalem.*			11, 1–13	
89	The Seventy Return. *Jerusalem?*			10, 17–24	
90	A man born blind is healed on the Sabbath. Our Lord's subsequent discourses. *Jerusalem.*				9, 1–41 10, 1–21
91	Jesus in Jerusalem at the Festival of Dedication. He retires beyond Jordan. *Jerusalem. Bethany beyond Jordan.*				10, 22–42
92	The raising of Lazarus. *Bethany.*				11, 1–46
93	The counsel of Caiaphas against Jesus. He retires from Jerusalem. *Jerusalem. Ephraim.*				11, 47–54
94	Jesus beyond Jordan is followed by multitudes. The healing of the infirm woman on the Sabbath. *Valley of Jordan. Perea.*	19, 1, 2	10, 1	13, 10–21	
95	Our Lord goes teaching and journeying towards Jerusa-				

Sect.	CONTENTS.	MATT.	MARK.	LUKE.	JOHN.
	lem. He is warned against Herod. *Perea.*			13, 22–35	
96	Our Lord dines with a chief Pharisee on the Sabbath. Incidents. *Perea.*			14, 1–24	
97	What is required of true Disciples. *Perea.*			14, 22–35	
98	Parable of the Lost Sheep, etc. Parable of the Prodigal Son. *Perea.*			15, 1–32	
99	Parable of the Unjust Steward. *Perea.*			16, 1–13	
100	The Pharisee reproved. Parable of the Rich Man and Lazarus. *Perea.*			16, 14–31	
101	Jesus inculcates forbearance, faith, humility. *Perea.*			17, 1–10	
102	Christ's coming will be sudden. *Perea.*			17, 20–37	
103	Parables. The importunate Widow. The Pharisee and Publican. *Perea.*			18, 1–14	
104	Precepts respecting divorce. *Perea.*	19, 3–12	10, 2–12		
105	Jesus receives and blesses little Children. *Perea.*	19, 13–15	10, 13–16	18, 15–17	
106	The rich Young Man. Parable of the Laborers in the Vineyard. *Perea.*	19, 16–30 20, 1–16	10, 17–31	18, 18–30	
107	Jesus a third time foretells his Death and Resurrection. [See § 74, § 77.] *Perea.*	20, 17–19	10, 32–34	18, 31–34	
108	James and John prefer their ambitious request. *Perea.*	20, 20–28	10, 35–45		
109	The healing of two blind men near Jericho.	20, 29–34	10, 46–52	18, 35–43 19, 1	
110	The visit to Zaccheus. Parable of the ten Minae. *Jericho.*			19, 2–28	
111	Jesus arrives at Bethany six days before the Passover. *Bethany.*				11, 55–77 12, 1, 9–11
	PART VII.				
	OUR LORD'S PUBLIC ENTRY INTO JERUSALEM, AND THE SUBSEQUENT TRANSACTIONS BEFORE THE FOURTH PASSOVER.				
	TIME: *Five days.*				
112	Our Lord's public Entry into Jerusalem. *Bethany, Jerusalem.*	21, 1–11 14–17	11, 1–11	19, 29–44	12, 12–19
113	The barren Fig-tree. The cleansing of the Temple. *Bethany, Jerusalem.*	21, 12, 13 18, 19	11, 12–19	19, 45–48 21, 37, 38	

Sect.	CONTENTS.	MATT.	MARK.	LUKE.	JOHN.
114	The barren Fig-tree withers away. *Between Bethany and Jerusalem.*	21, 20–22	11, 20–26		
115	Christ's authority questioned. Parable of the Two Sons. *Jerusalem.*	21, 23–32	11, 27–33	20, 1–8	
116	Parable of the wicked husbandmen. *Jerusalem.*	21, 33–46	12, 1–12	20, 9–19	
117	Parable of the Marriage of the King's Son. *Jerusalem.*	22, 1–14			
118	Insidious question of the Pharisees: Tribute to Cæsar. *Jerusalem.*	22, 15–22	12, 13–17	20, 20–26	
119	Insidious question of the Sadducees: The Resurrection. *Jerusalem.*	22, 23–33	12, 18–27	20, 27–40	
120	A lawyer questions Jesus. The two great Commandments. *Jerusalem.*	22, 34–40	12, 28–34		
121	How is Christ the son of David? *Jerusalem.*	22, 41–46	12, 35–37	20, 41–44	
122	Warnings against the evil example of the Scribes and Pharisees. *Jerusalem.*	23, 1–12	12, 38–39	20, 45–46	
123	Woes against the Scribes and Pharisees. Lamentation over Jerusalem. *Jerusalem.*	23, 13–39	12, 40	20, 47	
124	The Widow's mite. *Jerusalem.*		12, 41–44	21, 1–4	
125	Certain Greeks desire to see Jesus. *Jerusalem.*				12, 20–36
126	Reflections on the unbelief of the Jews. *Jerusalem.*				12, 37–50
127	Jesus, on taking leave of the Temple, foretells its destrnction and the persecution of his Disciples. *Jerusalem. Mount of Olives.*	24, 1–14	13, 1–13	21, 5–19	
128	The signs of Christ's coming to destroy Jerusalem, and put an end to the Jewish State and Dispensation. *Mount of Olives.*	24, 15–42	13, 14–37	21, 20–36	
129	Transition to Christ's final coming at the Day of Judgment. Exhortation to watchfulness. Parables: The ten Virgins. The five Talents. *Mount of Olives.*	24, 43–51 25, 1–30			
130	Scenes of the Judgment Day. *Mount of Olives.*	25, 31–46			
131	The Rulers conspire. The supper at Bethany. Treachery of Judas. *Jerusalem. Bethany.*	26, 1–16	14, 1–11	22, 1–6	12, 2–8
132	Preparation for the Passover. *Bethany. Jerusalem.*	26, 17–19	14, 12–16		

Sect.	CONTENTS.	MATT.	MARK.	LUKE.	JOHN.
	PART VIII. THE FOURTH PASSOVER; OUR LORD'S PASSION; AND THE ACCOMPANYING EVENTS UNTIL THE END OF THE JEWISH SABBATH. TIME: *Two days.*				
133	The Passover Meal. Contention among the Twelve. *Jerusalem.*	26, 20	14, 17	22, 14–18 24–30	
134	Jesus washes the feet of his disciples. *Jerusalem.*				13, 1–20
135	Jesus points out the Traitor. Judas withdraws. *Jerusalem.*	26, 21–25	14, 18–21	22, 21–23	13, 21–35
136	Jesus foretells the fall of Peter, and the dispersion of the Twelve. *Jerusalem.*	26, 31–35	14, 27–31	22, 31–38	13, 36–38
137	The Lord's Supper. *Jerusalem.*	26, 26–29	14, 22–25	22, 19–20	
138	Jesus comforts his Disciples. The Holy Spirit promised. *Jerusalem.*				14, 1–31
139	Christ the true Vine. His Disciples hated by the world. *Jerusalem.*				15, 1–27
140	Persecution foretold. Further promise of the Holy Spirit. Prayer in the name of Christ. *Jerusalem.*				16, 1–33
141	Christ's last prayer with his disciples. *Jerusalem.*				17, 1–26
142	The agony in Gethsemane. *Mount of Olives.*	26, 30 36–46	11, 26 32–42	22, 39–46	18, 1
143	Jesus betrayed and made prisoner. *Mount of Olives.*	26, 47–56	14, 43–52	22, 47–53	18, 2-12
144	Jesus before Caiaphas. Peter thrice denies him. *Jerusalem.*	26, 57–58 69–75	14, 53–54 66–72	22, 54–62	18, 13–18 25–27
145	Jesus before Caiaphas and the Sanhedrim. He declares himself to be the Christ; is condemned and mocked. *Jerusalem.*	26, 59–68	14 55–65	22, 63–71	18, 19–24
146	The Sanhedrim lead Jesus away to Pilate.	27, 1–2 11–14	15, 1–5	23, 1–5	18, 28–38
147	Jesus before Herod. *Jerusalem.*			23, 6–12	
148	Pilate seeks to release Jesus. The Jews demand Barabbas. *Jerusalem.*	27, 15–26	15, 6–15	23, 13–25	18, 39–40
149	Pilate delivers up Jesus to death. He is scourged and mocked. *Jerusalem.*	27, 26–30	15, 15–19		19, 1–3
150	Pilate again seeks to release Jesus. *Jerusalem.*				

Sect.	CONTENTS.	MATT.	MARK.	LUKE.	JOHN.
151	Judas repents and hangs himself. *Jerusalem.*	27, 3–10			
152	Jesus is led away to be crucified. *Jerusaiem.*	27, 31–34	15, 20–23	23, 26–33	19, 16–17
153	The Crucifixion. *Jerusalem.*	27, 35–38	15, 24–28	23, 33–34	19, 18–24
154	The Jews mock at Jesus on the Cross. He commends his mother to John. *Jerusalem.*	27, 39–44	15, 29–32 15, 33–37	23, 35–37 39–43	19, 25–27
155	Darkness prevails. Christ expires on the Cross. *Jerusalem.*	27, 45–50		23 44–46	19, 28–30
156	The vail of the Temple rent, and graves opened. Judgment of the Centurion. The Women at the Cross. *Jerusalem.*	27, 51–56	15, 38–41	23, 45 47–49	
157	The taking down from the Cross. The burial. *Jerusalem.*	27, 57–61	15, 42–47	23, 50–56	19, 31–42
158	The Watch at the Sepulchre. *Jerusalem.*	27, 62–66			

PART IX.

OUR LORD'S RESURRECTION, HIS SUBSEQUENT APPEARANCES, AND HIS ASCENSION.

TIME : *Forty days.*

Sect.	CONTENTS.	MATT.	MARK.	LUKE.	JOHN.
159	The Morning of the Resurrection. *Jerusalem.*	28, 2–4	16, 1		
160	Visit of the Women to the Sepulchre. Mary Magdalene returns. *Jerusalem.*	28, 1	16, 2–4	24, 1–3	20, 1–2
161	Vision of Angels in the Sepulchre. *Jerusalem.*	28, 5–7	16, 5–7	25, 4–8	
162	The Women return to the City. Jesus meets them. *Jerusalem.*	28, 8–10	16, 8	24, 9–11	
163	Peter and John run to the Sepulchre. *Jerusalem.*			24, 12	20, 3–10
164	Our Lord is seen by Mary Magdalene at the Sepulchre. *Jerusalem.*		16, 9–11		20, 11–18
165	Report of the Watch. *Jerusalem.*	28, 11–15			
166	Our Lord is seen of Peter. Then by two Disciples on the way to Emmaus. *Jerusalem. Emmaus.*		16, 12–13	24, 13–25	
167	Jesus appears in the midst of the Apostles, Thomas being absent. *Jerusalem.*		16, 14–18	24, 36–49	20, 19–23
168	Jesus appears in the midst of the Apostles, Thomas being present. *Jerusalem.*				20–24–29

Sect.	CONTENTS.	MATT.	MARK.	LUKE.	JOHN.
169	The Apostles go away into Galilee. Jesus shows himself to seven of them at the Sea of Tiberias. *Galilee.*	28, 16			21, 1–24
170	Jesus meets the Apostles and above five hundred Brethren on a mountain in Galilee. *Galilee.*	28, 16–20			
171	Our Lord is seen of James; then of all the Apostles. *Jerusalem.*		16, 19–20	24, 50–53	
172	The Ascension. *Bethany.*				20, 30–31
173	Conclusion of John's Gospel.				21, 25

TABLE

FOR

FINDING ANY PASSAGE IN THE HARMONY.

MATTHEW.

Chap.	Verse.	Sect.	Chap.	Verse.	Sect.	Chap.	Verse.	Sect.
i.	1–17	13	xiii.	1–23	54	xxii.	41–46	121
	18–25	6		24–53	55	xxiii.	1–12	122
ii.	1–12	10		54–58	61		13–39	123
	13–23	11	xiv.	1–2	63	xxiv.	1–24	127
iii.	1–12	14		3–5	24		15–42	128
	13–17	15		6–12	63		43–51	129
iv-	1–11	16		13–21	64	xxv.	1–30	129
	12	24		22–36	65		31–46	130
	13–16	28	v.	1–20	67	xxvi.	1–16	131
	17	26		21–28	68		17–19	132
	18–22	29		29–38	69		20	133
	23–25	32		39	70		21–25	135
v.	1–48	41	xvi.	1–4	70		26–29	137
vi.	1–34	41		4–12	71		30	142
vii.	1–29	41		13–20	73		31–35	136
viii.	1	41		21–28	74		36–46	142
	2–4	33	xvii.	1–13	75		47–56	143
	5–13	42		14–21	76		57–58	144
	14–17	31		22–23	77		59–68	145
	18–27	56		24–27	78		69–75	144
	28–34	57	xviii.	1–35	79	xxvii.	1–2	146
ix.	1	57	xix.	1–2	94		3–10	151
	2–8	34		3–12	104		11–14	146
	9	35		13–15	105		15–26	148
	10–17	58		16–30	106		26–30	149
	18–26	59	xx.	1–16	106		31–34	152
	27–34	60		17–19	107		35–38	153
	35–38	62		20–28	108		39–44	154
x.	1	62		29–34	109		45–50	155
	2–4	40	xxi.	1–11	112		51–56	156
	5–42	62		12–13	113		57–61	157
xi.	1	62		14–17	112		62–66	158
	2–19	44		18–19	113	xxviii.	1	160
	20–30	45		20–22	114		2–4	159
xii.	1– 8	37		23–32	115		5–7	161
	9–14	38		33–46	116		8–10	162
	15–21	39	xxii.	1–14	117		11–15	165
	22–37	48		15–22	118		16	169
	38–45	49		23–33	119		16–20	170
	46–50	50		34–40	120			

MARK.

Chap.	Verse.	Sect.	Chap.	Verse.	Sect.	Chap.	Verse.	Sect.
i.	1–8	14	vii.	24–30	68	xii.	41–44	124
	9–11	15		31–37	69	xiii.	1–13	127
	12–13	16	viii.	1–9	69		14–37	128
	14	24		10–12	70	xiv.	1–11	131
	14–15	26		13–21	71		12–16	132
	16–20	29		22–26	72		17	133
	21–28	30		27–30	73		18–21	135
	29–34	31		31–38	74		22–25	137
	35–39	32	ix.	1	74		26	142
	40–45	33		2–13	75		27–31	136
ii.	1–12	34		14–29	76		32–42	142
	13–14	35		30–32	77		43–52	143
	15–22	58		33	78		53–54	144
	23–28	37		33–50	79		55–65	145
iii.	1–6	38	x.	1	94		66–72	144
	7–12	39		2–12	104	xv.	1–5	146
	13–19	40		13–16	105		6–15	148
	19–30	48		17–31	106		15–19	149
	31–35	50		32–34	107		20–23	152
iv.	1–25	54		35–45	108		24–28	153
	26–34	55		46–52	109		29–32	154
	35–41	56	xi.	1–11	112		33–37	155
v.	1–21	57		12–19	113		38–41	156
	22–43	59		20–26	114		32–47	157
vi.	1–6	61	xii.	27–33	115	xvi.	1	159
	6–13	62		1–12	116		2–4	160
	14–16	63		13–17	118		5–7	161
	17–20	24		18–27	119		8	162
	21–29	63		28–34	120		9–11	164
	30–44	64		35–37	121		12–13	166
	45–56	65		38–39	122		14–18	167
vii.	1–23	67		40	123		19–20	172

LUKE.

Chap.	Verse.	Sect.	Chap.	Verse.	Sect.	Chap.	Verse.	Sect.
i.	1–4	1	iv.	31–37	30	vii.	18–35	44
	5–25	2		38–41	31		36–50	46
	26–38	3		42–44	32	viii.	1–3	47
	39–56	4	v.	1–11	29		4–18	54
	57–80	5		12–16	33		19–21	50
ii.	1–7	7		17–26	34		22–25	56
	8–20	8		27–28	35		26–40	57
	21–38	9		29–39	58		41–56	59
	39–40	11	vi.	1–5	37	ix.	1–6	62
	41–52	12		6–11	38		7–9	63
iii.	1–18	14		12–19	40		10–17	64
	19–20	24		20–26	41		18–21	73
	21–23	15		27–30	41		22–27	74
	23–38	13		31	41		28–36	75
iv.	1–13	16		32–36	41		37–43	76
	14	24		37–49	41		43–45	77
	14–15	26	vii.	1–10	42		46–50	79
	16–31	28		11–17	43		51–56	81

LUKE—*continued.*

Chap.	Verse.	Sect.	Chap.	Verse.	Sect.	Chap.	Verse.	Sect.
ix.	57–62	56	xviii.	15–17	105	xxii.	31–38	136
x.	1–16	80		18–30	106		39–46	142
	17–24	89		31–34	107		47–53	143
	25–37	86		35–43	109		54–62	144
	38–42	87	xix.	1	109		63–71	145
xi.	1–13	88		2–28	110	xxiii.	1–5	146
	14–15	48		29–44	112		6–12	147
	16	49		45–48	113		13–25	148
	17–23	48	xx.	1–8	115		26–33	152
	24–28	49		9–19	116		33–34	153
	29–36	49		20–26	118		35–37	154
	37–54	51		27–40	119		38	153
xii.	1–59	52		41–44	121		39–43	154
xiii.	1–9	53		45–46	122		44–46	155
	10–21	94		47	123		45	156
	22–35	95	xxi.	1–4	124		47–49	156
xiv.	1–24	96		5–19	127		50–56	157
	25–35	97		20–36	128	xxiv.	1–3	160
xv.	1–32	98		37–38	113		4–8	161
xvi.	1–13	99	xxii.	1–6	131		9–11	162
	14–31	100		7–13	132		12	163
xvii.	1–10	101		14–18	133		13–35	166
	11–19	82		19–20	137		36–49	167
	20–37	102		21–23	135		50–53	172
xviii.	1–14	103		24–30	133			

JOHN.

Chap.	Verse.	Sect.	Chap.	Verse.	Sect.	Chap.	Verse.	Sect.
i.	1–18	17	ix.	1–41	90	xviii.	13–18	144
	19–34	18	x.	1–21	90		19–24	145
	35–52	19		22–42	91		25–27	144
ii.	1–12	20	xi.	1–46	92		28–38	146
	13–25	21		47–54	93		39–40	148
iii.	1–21	22		55–57	111	xix.	1–3	149
	22–36	23	xii.	1	111		4–16	150
iv.	1–3	24		2–8	131		16–17	152
	4–42	25		9–11	111		18–24	153
	43–45	26		12–19	112		25–27	154
	46–54	27		20–36	125		28–30	155
v.	1–47	36		37–50	126		31–42	157
vi.	1–14	64	xiii.	1–20	134	xx.	1–2	160
	15–21	65		21–35	135		3–10	163
	22–71	66		36–38	136		11–18	164
vii.	1	66	xiv.	1–31	138		19–23	167
	2–10	81	xv.	1–27	139		24–29	168
	11–53	83	xvi.	1–33	140		30–31	173
viii.	1	83	xvii.	1–26	141	xxi.	1–24	169
	2–11	84	xviii.	1	142		25	173
	12–50	85		2–12	143			

AN EXAMINATION

OF THE

TESTIMONY OF THE EVANGELISTS.

§ 1. In examining the evidences of the Christian religion, it is essential to the discovery of truth that we bring to the investigation a mind freed, as far as possible, from existing prejudice, and open to conviction. There should be a readiness, on our part, to investigate with candor, to follow the truth wherever it may lead us, and to submit, without reserve or objection, to all the teachings of this religion, if it be found to be of divine origin. "There is no other entrance," says Lord Bacon, "to the kingdom of man, which is founded in the sciences, than to the kingdom of heaven, into which no one can enter but in the character of a little child."[1] The docility which true philosophy requires of her disciples is not a spirit of servility, or the surrender of the reason and judgment to whatsoever the teacher may inculcate; but it is a mind free from all pride of opinion, not hostile to the truth sought for, willing to pursue the inquiry, and impartially to weigh the arguments and evidence, and to acquiesce in the judgment of right reason. The investigation, moreover, should be pursued with the serious earnestness which becomes the greatness of the sub-

[1] Nov. Org. l. 68. "Ut non alius fere sit aditus ad regnum hominis, quod fundatur in scientiis, quam ad regnum cœlorum in quod, nisi sub persona infantis, intrare non datur."

ject—a subject fraught with such momentous consequences to man. It should be pursued as in the presence of God, and under the solemn sanctions created by a lively sense of his omniscience, and of our accountability to him for the right use of the faculties which he has bestowed.

§ 2. In requiring this candor and simplicity of mind in those who would investigate the truth of our religion, Christianity demands nothing more than is readily conceded to every branch of human science. All these have their data, and their axioms; and Christianity, too, has her first principles, the admission of which is essential to any real progress in knowledge. "Christianity," says Bishop Wilson, "inscribes on the portal of her dominion 'Whosoever shall not receive the kingdom of God as a little child, shall in nowise enter therein.' Christianity does not profess to convince the perverse and headstrong, to bring irresistible evidence to the daring and profane, to vanquish the proud scorner, and afford evidences from which the careless and perverse cannot possibly escape. This might go to destroy man's responsibility. All that Christianity professes, is to propose such evidences as may satisfy the meek, the tractable, the candid, the serious inquirer."[1]

§ 3. The present design, however, is not to enter upon any general examination of the evidences of Christianity, but to confine the inquiry to the testimony of the Four Evangelists, bringing their narratives to the tests to which other evidence is subjected in human tribunals. The foundation of our religion is a basis of fact—the fact of the birth, ministry, miracles, death, resurrection, and ascension of Jesus Christ. These are related by the Evangelists as having actually occurred, within their own personal knowledge. Our religion, then, rests on the credit due to these witnesses. Are they worthy of implicit belief, in the matters which they relate? This is the question, in all human tri-

[1] Bishop Wilson's Evidences, p. 38.

bunals, in regard to persons testifying before them ; and we propose to test the veracity of these witnesses, by the same rules and means which are there employed. The importance of the facts testified, and their relations to the affairs of the soul, and the life to come, can make no difference in the principles or the mode of weighing the evidence. It is still the evidence of matters of fact, capable of being seen and known and related, as well by one man as by another. And if the testimony of the Evangelist, supposing it to be relevant and material to the issue in a question of property or of personal right, between man and man, in a court of justice, ought to be believed and have weight; then, upon the like principles, it ought to receive our entire credit here. But if, on the other hand, we should be justified in rejecting it, if there testified on oath, then, supposing our rules of evidence to be sound, we may be excused if we hesitate elsewhere to give it credence.

§ 4. The proof that God has revealed himself to man by special and express communications, and that Christianity constitutes that revelation, is no part of these inquiries. This has already been shown, in the most satisfactory manner, by others, who have written expressly upon this subject.[1] Referring therefore to their writings for the arguments and proofs, the fact will here be assumed as true. That man is a religious being, is universally conceded, for it has been seen to be universally true. He is everywhere a worshiper. In every age and country, and in every stage, from the highest intellectual culture to the darkest stupidity, he bows with homage to a superior Being. Be it the rude-carved idol of his own fabrication, or the unseen divinity that stirs within him, it is still the object of his adoration. This trait in the character of man is so uniform,

[1] See Dr. Hopkins's Lowell Lectures, particularly Lect. 2. Bp. Wilson's Evidences of Christianity, Vol. i. pp. 45–61. Horne's Introduction, Vol. i. pp. 1–39. Mr. Horne having cited all the best English writers on this subject, it is sufficient to refer to his work alone.

that it may safely be assumed, either as one of the original attributes of his nature, or as necessarily resulting from the action of one or more of those attributes.

§ 5. The object of man's worship, whatever it be, will naturally be his standard of perfection. He clothes it with every attribute, belonging, in his view, to a perfect character; and this character he himself endeavors to attain. He may not, directly and consciously, aim to acquire every virtue of his deity, and to avoid the opposite vices; but still this will be the inevitable consequence of sincere and constant worship. As in human society men become assimilated, both in manners and in moral principles, to their chosen associates, so in the worship of whatever deity men adore, they "form to him the relish of their souls." To suppose, then, that God made man capable of religion, and requiring it in order to the development of the highest part of his nature, without communicating with him, as a father, in those revelations which alone could perfect that nature, would be a reproach upon God, and a contradiction.[1]

§ 6. How it came to pass that man, originally taught, as we doubt not he was, to know and to worship the true Jehovah, is found, at so early a period of his history, a worshiper of baser objects, it is foreign to our present purpose to inquire. But the fact is lamentably true, that he soon became an idolator, a worshiper of moral abominations. The Scythians and Northmen adored the impersonations of heroic valor and of bloodthirsty and cruel revenge. The mythology of Greece and of Rome, though it exhibited a few examples of virtue and goodness, abounded in others of gross licentiousness and vice. The gods of Egypt were reptiles, and beasts and birds. The religion of Central and Eastern Asia was polluted with lust and cruelty, and smeared with blood, rioting, in deadly triumph, over all the tender affections of the human heart and all the convictions

[1] Hopkins's Lowell Lect., p. 48.

of the human understanding. Western and Southern Africa and Polynesia are, to this day, the abodes of frightful idolatry, cannibalism, and cruelty; and the aborigines of both the Americas are examples of the depths of superstition to which the human mind may be debased. In every quarter of the world, however, there is a striking uniformity seen in all the features of paganism. The ruling principle of her religion is terror, and her deity is lewd and cruel. Whatever of purity the earlier forms of paganism may have possessed, it is evident from history that it was of brief duration. Every form, which history has preserved, grew rapidly and steadily worse and more corrupt, until the entire heathen world, before the coming of Christ, was infected with that loathsome leprosy of pollution, described with revolting vividness by St. Paul, in the beginning of his Epistle to the Romans.

§ 7. So general and decided was this proclivity to the worship of strange gods, that, at the time of the deluge, only one family remained faithful to Jehovah; and this was a family which had been favored with his special revelation. Indeed it is evident that nothing but a revelation from God could raise men from the degradation of pagan idolatry, because nothing else has ever had that effect. If man could achieve his own freedom from this bondage, he would long since have been free. But instead of this, the increase of light and civilization and refinement in the pagan world has but multiplied the objects of his worship, added voluptuous refinements to its ritual, and thus increased the number and weight of his chains. In this respect there is no difference in their moral condition, between the barbarous Scythian and the learned Egyptian or Roman of ancient times, nor between the ignorant African and the polished Hindu of our own day. The only method, which has been successfully employed to deliver man from idolatry, is that of presenting to the eye of his soul an object of worship perfectly holy and pure, directly opposite, in moral character, to the gods he had formerly adored. He could not transfer to his deities a better character than he himself possessed. He must for ever remain enslaved to his idols, unless a new and pure object of worship were revealed to him, with a display of superior power sufficient to overcome his former faith and present fears, to detach his affections from grosser objects, and to fix them upon that which alone is worthy.[1] This is precisely what God, as stated in the Holy Scriptures, has done. He rescued one family from idolatry in the Old World, by the revelation of himself to Noah; he called a distinct branch of this family to the knowledge of himself, in the person of Abraham and his sons; he extended this favor to a whole nation, through the ministry of Moses; but it was through that of Jesus Christ alone that it was communicated to the whole world. In Egypt, by the destruction of all the objects of the popular worship, God taught the Israelites that he alone was the self-existent Almighty. At the Red Sea, he emphatically showed them that he was the Protector and Saviour of his people. At Sinai, he revealed himself as the righteous Governor, who required implicit obedience for men, and taught them, by the strongly-marked distinctions of the ceremonial law, that he was a holy Being, of purer eyes than to behold evil, and that could not look upon iniquity. The demerit of sin was inculcated by the solemn infliction of death upon every animal, offered as a propitiatory sacrifice. And when, by this system of instruction, he had prepared a people to receive the perfect revelation of the character of God, of the nature of his worship, and of the way of restoration to his image and favor, this also was expressly revealed by the mission of his Son.[2]

[1] It has been well remarked, that, if we regard man as in a state of innocence, we should naturally expect that God would hold communications with him; that if we regard him as guilty, and as having lost the knowledge and moral image of God, such a communication would be absolutely necessary, if man was to be restored. Dr. Hopkins's Lowell Lect., p. 62.

[2] The argument here briefly sketched, is stated more at large, and with

§ 8. That the books of the Old Testament, as we now have them, are genuine; that they existed in the time of our Saviour, and were commonly received and referred to among the Jews, as the sacred books of their religion;[1] and that the text of the Four Evangelists has been handed down to us in the state in which it was originally written, that is, without having been materially corrupted or falsified, either by heretics or Christians; are facts which we are entitled to assume as true, until the contrary is shown.

The genuineness of these writings really admits of as little doubt, and is susceptible of as ready proof, as that of any ancient writings whatever. The rule of municipal law on this subject is familiar, and applies with equal force to all ancient writings, whether documentary or otherwise; and as it comes first in order, in the prosecution of these inquiries, it may, for the sake of mere convenience, be designated as our first rule.

Every document, apparently ancient, coming from the proper repository or custody, and bearing on its face no evident marks of forgery, the law presumes to be genuine, and devolves on the opposing party the burden of proving it to be otherwise.

§ 9. An ancient document, offered in evidence in our courts, is said to come from the proper repository, when it is found in the place where, and under the care of persons with whom, such writings might naturally and reasonably be expected to be found; for it is this custody which gives authenticity to documents found within it.[2] If they come

great clearness and force, in an essay entitled "The Philosophy of the Plan of Salvation," pp. 13–107.

[1] See Professor Stuart's Critical History and Defense of the Old Testament Canon, where this is abundantly proved.

[2] Per TINDAL, Ch. J., in the case of Bishop of Meath *v.* Marquis of Winchester, 3 Bing. N. C. 183, 200, 201. "It is when documents are found in other than their proper places of deposit," observed the Chief

from such a place, and bear no evident marks of forgery, the law presumes that they are genuine, and they are permitted to be read in evidence, unless the opposing party is able successfully to impeach them.[1] The burden of showing them to be false and unworthy of credit, is devolved on the party who makes that objection. The presumption of law is the judgment of charity. It presumes that every man is innocent until he is proved guilty; that everything has been done fairly and legally, until it is proved to have been otherwise; and that every document, found in its proper repository, and not bearing marks of forgery, is genuine. Now this is precisely the case with the Sacred Writings. They have been used in the church from time immemorial, and thus are found in the place where alone they ought to be looked for. They come to us, and challenge our reception of them as genuine writings, precisely as Domesday Book, the Ancient Statutes of Wales, or any other of the ancient documents which have recently been published under the British Record Commission, are received. They are found in familiar use in all the churches of Christendom, as the sacred books to which all denominations of Christians refer, as the standard of their faith. There is no pretense that they were engraven on plates of

Justice, "that the investigation commences, whether it was reasonable and natural, under the circumstances of the particular case, to expect that they should have been in the place where they are actually found; for it is obvious, that, while there can be only one place of deposit strictly and absolutely proper, there may be many and various, that are reasonable and probable, though differing in degree, some being more so, some less; and in these cases the proposition to be determined is, whether the actual custody is so reasonably and probably accounted for, that it impresses the mind with the conviction that the instrument found in such custody must be genuine." See the cases cited in Greenl. on Ev. § 142; see also 1 Stark. on Ev. pp. 332–335, 381–386; Croughton *v.* Blake, 12 Mees. & W. 205, 208; Doe *v.* Phillips, 10 Jur. 34. It is this defect, namely, that they do not come from the proper or natural repository, which shows the fabulous character of many pretended revelations, from the Gospel of the Infancy to the Book of Mormon.

[1] 1 Greenl. on Ev. §§ 34, 142, 570.

gold and discovered in a cave, nor that they were brought from heaven by angels; but they are received as the plain narratives and writings of the men whose names they respectively bear, made public at the time they were written; and though there are some slight discrepancies among the copies subsequently made, there is no pretense that the originals were anywhere corrupted. If it be objected that the orginals are lost, and that copies alone are now produced, the principles of the municipal law here also afford a satisfactory answer. For the multiplication of copies was a public fact, in the faithfulness of which all the Christian community had an interest; and it is a rule of law, that,—

In matters of public and general interest, all persons must be presumed to be conversant, on the principle that individuals are presumed to be conversant with their own affairs.

Therefore it is that, in such matters, the prevailing current of assertion is resorted to as evidence, for it is to this that every member of the community is supposed to be privy.[1] The persons, moreover, who multiplied these copies, may be regarded, in some manner, as the agents of the Christian public, for whose use and benefit the copies were made; and on the ground of the credit due to such agents, and of the public nature of the facts themselves, the copies thus made are entitled to an extraordinary degree of confidence, and, as in the case of official registers and other public books, it is not necessary that they should be confirmed and sanctioned by the ordinary tests of truth.[2] If any ancient document concerning our public rights were lost, copies which had been as universally received and acted

[1] Morewood *v.* Wood, 14 East, 329, n., per Lord KENYON; Weeks *v.* Sparke, 1 M. & S. 686; Berkeley Peerage Case, 4 Campb. 416, per MANSFIELD, Ch. J.; see 1 Greenl. on Ev. § 128.

[2] 1 Stark. on Ev. pp. 195, 230; 2 Greenl. on Ev. § 483.

upon as the Four Gospels have been, would have been received in evidence in any of our courts of justice, without the slightest hesitation. The entire text of the Corpus Juris Civilis is received as authority in all the courts of continental Europe, upon much weaker evidence of its genuineness; for the integrity of the Sacred Text has been preserved by the jealousy of opposing sects, beyond any moral possibility of corruption; while that of the Roman Civil Law has been preserved by tacit consent, without the interest of any opposing school, to watch over and preserve it from alteration.

§ 10 These copies of the Holy Scriptures having thus been in familiar use in the churches, from the time when the text was committed to writing; having been watched with vigilance by so many sects, opposed to each other in doctrine, yet all appealing to these Scriptures for the correctness of their faith; and having in all ages, down to this day, been respected as the authoritative source of all ecclesiastical power and government, and submitted to, and acted under in regard to so many claims of right, on the one hand, and so many obligations of duty, on the other; it is quite erroneous to suppose that the Christian is bound to offer any further proof of their genuineness or authenticity. It is for the objector to show them spurious; for on him, by the plainest rules of law, lies the burden of proof.[1] If it were the case of a claim to a franchise, and a copy of an ancient deed or charter were produced in support of the title, under parallel circumstances on which to presume its genuineness, no lawyer, it is believed, would venture to

[1] The arguments for the genuineness and authenticity of the books of the Holy Scriptures are briefly, yet very fully stated, and almost all the writers of authority are referred to by Mr. Horne, in his Introduction to the Study of the Holy Scriptures, vol. i., *passim*. The same subject is discussed in a more popular manner in the Lectures of Bishop Wilson, and of Bishop Sumner of Chester, on the Evidences of Christianity; and, in America, the same question, as it relates to the Gospels, has been argued by Bishop McIlvaine, in his Lectures.

deny either its admissibility in evidence, or the satisfactory character of the proof. In a recent case in the House of Lords, precisely such a document, being an old manuscript copy, purporting to have been extracted from ancient Journals of the House, which were lost, and to have been made by an officer whose duty it was to prepare lists of the Peers, was held admissible in a claim of peerage.[1]

§ 11. Supposing, therefore, that it is not irrational, nor inconsistent with sound phiiosophy, to believe that God has made a special and express revelation of his character and will to man, and that the sacred books of our religion are genuine, as we now have them; we proceed to examine and compare the testimony of Four Evangelists, as witnesses to the life and doctrines of Jesus Christ; in order to determine the degree of credit, to which, by the rules of evidence applied in human tribunals, they are justly entitled. Our attention will naturally be first directed to the witnesses themselves, to see who and what manner of men they were; and we shall take them in the order of their writings; stating the prominent traits only in their lives and characters, as they are handed down to us by credible historians.

§ 12. MATTHEW, called also LEVI, was a Jew of Galilee, but of what city is uncertain. He held the place of publican, or tax-gatherer, under the Roman government, and his office seems to have consisted in collecting the taxes within his district, as well as the duties and customs levied on goods and persons, passing in and out of his district or province, across the lake of Genesareth. While engaged in this business, at the office or usual place of collection, he was required by Jesus to follow him, as one of his disciples; a command which he immediately obeyed. Soon afterwards, he appears to have given a great entertainment

[1] See the case of the Slane Peerage, 5 Clark & F. 24. See also the case of the Fitzwalter Peerage, 10 Id. 948.

to his fellow-publicans and friends, at which Jesus was present; intending probably both to celebrate his own change of profession, and to give them an opportunity to profit by the teaching of his new Master.[1] He was constituted one of the twelve apostles, and constantly attended the person of Jesus as a faithful follower, until the crucifixion; and after the ascension of his Master he preached the gospel for some time, with other apostles, in Judea, and afterwards in Ethiopia, where he died.

He is generally allowed to have written first, of all the evangelists; but whether in the Hebrew or the Greek language, or in both, the learned are not agreed, nor is it material to our purpose to inquire; the genuineness of our present Greek gospel being sustained by satisfactory evidence.[2] The precise time when he wrote is also uncertain, the several dates given to it among learned men, varying from A.D. 37 to A.D. 64. The earlier date, however, is argued with greater force, from the improbability that the Christians would be left for several years without a general and authentic history of our Saviour's ministry; from the evident allusions which it contains to a state of persecution in the church at the time it was written; from the titles of sanctity ascribed to Jerusalem, and a higher veneration testified for the temple than is found in the other and later evangelists; from the comparative gentleness with which Herod's character and conduct are dealt with, that bad prince probably being still in power; and from the frequent mention of Pilate, as still governor of Judea.[3]

§ 13. That Matthew was himself a native Jew, familiar with the opinions, ceremonies, and customs of his countrymen; that he was conversant with the Sacred Writings, and habituated to their idiom; a man of plain sense, but of

[1] Matt. ix. 10; Mark ii. 14, 15; Luke v. 29.

[2] The authorities on this subject are collected in Horne's Introduction, vol. iv. pp. 234–238, part 2, chap. ii. sec. 2.

[3] See Horne's Introduction, vol. iv. pp. 229–232.

little learning, except what he derived from the Scriptures of the Old Testament; that he wrote seriously and from conviction, and had, on most occasions, been present, and attended closely, to the transactions which he relates, and relates, too, without any view of applause to himself; are facts which we may consider established by internal evidence, as strong as the nature of the case will admit. It is deemed equally well proved, both by internal evidence and the aid of history, that he wrote for the use of his countrymen the Jews. Every circumstance is noticed which might conciliate their belief, and every unnecessary expression is avoided which might obstruct it. They looked for the Messiah, of the lineage of David, and born in Bethlehem, in the circumstances of whose life the prophecies should find fulfillment, a matter, in their estimation, of peculiar value: and to all these this evangelist has directed their especial attention.[1]

§ 14. Allusion has been already made to his employment as a collector of taxes and customs; but the subject is too important to be passed over without further notice. The tribute imposed by the Romans upon countries conquered by their arms was enormous. In the time of Pompey, the sums annually exacted from their Asiatic provinces, of which Judea was one, amounted to about four millions and a half of sterling, or about twenty-two millions of dollars. These exactions were made in the usual forms of direct and indirect taxation; the rate of the customs on merchandise varying from an eighth to a fortieth part of the value of the commodity; and the tariff including all the principal articles of the commerce of the East, much of which, as is well known, still found its way to Italy through Palestine, as well as by the way of Damascus and of Egypt. The direct taxes consisted of a capitation-tax, and a land-tax,

[1] See Campbell on the Four Gospels, vol. iii. pp. 35, 36; Preface to St. Matthew's Gospel, §§ 22, 23.

assessed upon a valuation or census, periodically taken, under the oath of the individual, with heavy penal sanctions.[1] It is natural to suppose that these taxes were not voluntarily paid, especially since they were imposed by the conqueror upon a conquered people, and by a heathen, too, upon the people of the house of Israel. The increase of taxes has generally been found to multiply discontents, evasions and frauds on the one hand, and, on the other, to increase vigilance, suspicion, close scrutiny, and severity of exaction. The penal code, as revised by Theodosius, will give us some notion of the difficulties in the way of the revenue officers, in the earlier times of which we are speaking. These difficulties must have been increased by the fact that, at this period, a considerable portion of the commerce of that part of the world was carried on by the Greeks, whose ingenuity and want of faith were proverbial. It was to such an employment and under such circumstances, that Matthew was educated; an employment which must have made him acquainted with the Greek language, and extensively conversant with the public affairs and the men of business of his time; thus entitling him to our confidence, as an experienced and intelligent observer of events passing before him. And if the men of that day were, as in truth they appear to have been, as much disposed as those of the present time, to evade the payment of public taxes and duties, and to elude, by all possible means, the vigilance of the revenue officers, Matthew must have been familiar with a great variety of forms of fraud, imposture, cunning, and deception, and must have become habitually distrustful, scrutinizing, and cautious; and, of course, much less likely

[1] See Gibbon's Rome, vol. i. ch. vi. and vol. iii. ch. xvii. and authorities there cited. Cod. Theod. Lib. xi. tit. 1–28, with the notes of Gothofred. Gibbon treats particularly of the revenues of a latter period than our Saviour's time; but the general course of proceeding, in the levy and collection of taxes, is not known to have been changed since the beginning of the empire.

to have been deceived in regard to many of the facts in our Lord's ministry, extraordinary as they were, which fell under his observation. This circumstance shows both the sincerity and the wisdom of Jesus, in selecting him for an eye-witness of his conduct, and adds great weight to the value of the testimony of this evangelist.

§ 15. MARK was the son of a pious sister of Barnabas, named Mary, who dwelt at Jerusalem, and at whose house the early Christians often assembled. His Hebrew name was John; the surname of Mark having been adopted, as is supposed, when he left Judea to preach the gospel in foreign countries; a practice not unusual among the Jews of that age, who frequently, upon such occasions, assumed a name more familiar than their own to the people whom they visited. He is supposed to have been converted to the Christian faith by the ministry of Peter. He traveled from Jerusalem to Antioch with Paul and Barnabas, and afterwards accompanied them elsewhere. When they landed at Perga in Pamphylia, he left them and returned to Jerusalem; for which reason, when he afterwards would have gone with them, Paul refused to take him. Upon this, a difference of opinion arose between the two apostles, and they separated, Barnabas taking Mark with him to Cyprus. Subsequently he accompanied Timothy to Rome, at the express desire of Paul. From this city he probably went into Asia, where he found Peter, with whom he returned to Rome, in which city he is supposed to have written and published his Gospel. Such is the outline of his history, as it is furnished by the New Testament.[1] The early historians add, that after this he went into Egypt and planted a church in Alexandria, where he died.[2]

§ 16. It is agreed that Mark wrote his Gospel for the

[1] Acts xii. 12, 25; xiii. 5, 13; and xv. 36-41; 2 Tim. iv. 11; Phil. 24; Col. iv. 10; 1 Pet. v. 13.

[2] Horne's Introduction, vol. iv. pp. 252, 253.

use of Gentile converts; an opinion deriving great force from the explanations introduced into it, which would have been useless to a Jew;[1] and that it was composed for those at Rome, is believed, not only from the numerous Latinisms it contains, but from the unanimous testimony of ancient writers, and from the internal evidence afforded by the Gospel itself.

§ 17. Some have entertained the opinion that Mark compiled his account from that of Matthew, of which they supposed it an abridgment. But this notion has been refuted by Koppe, and others,[2] and is now generally regarded as untenable. For Mark frequently deviates from Matthew in the order of time, in his arrangement of facts; and he adds many things not related by the other evangelists; neither of which a mere epitomizer would probably have done. He also omits several things related by Matthew, and imperfectly describes others, especially the transactions of Christ with the apostles after the resurrection; giving no account whatever of his appearance in Galilee; omissions irreconcilable with any previous knowledge of the Gospel according to Matthew. To these proofs we may add, that in several places there are discrepancies between the accounts of Matthew and Mark, not, indeed, irreconcilable, but sufficient to destroy the probability that the latter copied from the former.[3] The striking coincidences between them, in style, words, and things, in other places, may be accounted for by considering that Peter, who is supposed to have dictated this Gospel to Mark, was quite as intimately acquainted as Matthew with the miracles and discourses of our Lord; which, therefore, he would naturally recite in his preaching; and that the same things might very

[1] Mark vii. 3, 11; and ix. 43, and elsewhere.

[2] Mr. Norton has conclusively disposed of this objection, in his Evidences of the Genuineness of the Gospels, vol. i. Additional Notes, sec. 2, pp. cxv—cxxxii.

[3] Compare Mark x. 46, and xiv. 69, and iv. 35, and i. 35, and ix. 28, with Matthew's narrative of the same events.

naturally be related in the same manner, by men who sought not after excellency of speech. Peter's agency in the narative of Mark is asserted by all ancient writers, and is confirmed by the fact, that his humility is conspicuous in every part of it, where anything is or might be related of him; his weaknesses and fall being fully exposed, while things which might redound to his honor, are either omitted or but slightly mentioned; that scarcely any transaction of Jesus is related, at which Peter was not present, and that all are related with that circumstantial minuteness which belongs to the testimony of an eye-witness.[1] We may, therefore, regard the Gospel of Mark as an original composition, written at the dictation of Peter, and consequently as another original narrative of the life, miracles, and doctrines of our Lord.

§ 18. LUKE, according to Eusebius, was a native of Antioch, by profession a physician, and for a considerable period a companion of the apostle Paul. From the casual notices of him in the Scriptures, and from the early Christian writers, it has been collected, that his parents were Gentiles, but that he in his youth embraced Judaism, from which he was converted to Christianity. The first mention of him is that he was with Paul at Troas;[2] whence he appears to have attended him to Jerusalem; continued with him in all his troubles in Judea; and sailed with him when he was sent a prisoner from Cæsarea to Rome, where he remained with him during his two years' confinement. As none of the ancient fathers have mentioned his having suffered martyrdom, it is generally supposed that he died a natural death.

§ 19. That he wrote his Gospel for the benefit of Gentile converts is affirmed by the unanimous voice of Christian antiquity; and it may also be inferred from its dedication

[1] See Horne's Introd. vol. iv. pp. 252–259.

[2] Acts xvi. 10, 11.

to a Gentile. He is particularly careful to specify various circumstances conducive to the information of strangers, but not so to the Jews; he gives the lineage of Jesus upwards, after the manner of the Gentiles, instead of downwards, as Matthew had done; tracing it up to Adam, and thus showing that Jesus was the promised seed of the woman; and he marks the eras of his birth, and of the ministry of John, by the reigns of the Roman emperors. He also has introduced several things, not mentioned by the other evangelists, but highly encouraging to the Gentiles to turn to God in the hope of pardon and acceptance; of which description are the parables of the publican and pharisee, in the temple; the lost piece of silver; and the prodigal son; and the fact of Christ's visit to Zaccheus the publican, and the pardon of the penitent thief.

§ 20. That Luke was a physician, appears not only from the testimony of Paul,[1] but from the internal marks in his Gospel, showing that he was both an acute observer, and had given particular and even professional attention to all our Saviour's miracles of healing. Thus, the man whom Matthew and Mark describe simply as a leper, Luke describes as *full* of leprosy;[2] he, whom they mention as having *a* withered hand, Luke says had his *right* hand withered;[3] and of the maid, of whom the others say that Jesus took her by the hand and she arose, he adds, that *her spirit came to her again.*[4] He alone, with professional accuracy of observation, says that *virtue went out* of Jesus, and healed the sick;[5] he alone states the fact that the sleep of the disciples in Gethsemane was *induced by extreme sorrow;* and mentions the blood-like sweat of Jesus, as occasioned by the *intensity of his agony;* and he alone relates the miraculous healing of Malchus's ear.[6] That he

[1] Col. iv. 14. Luke, the beloved physician.

[2] Luke v. 12; Matt. viii. 2; Mark i. 40.

[3] Luke vi. 6; Matt. xii. 10; Mark iii. 1.

[4] Luke viii. 55; Matt. ix. 25; Mark v. 42.

[5] Luke vi. 19.

[6] Luke xxii. 44, 45, 51.

was also a man of a liberal education, the comparative elegance of his writings sufficiently shows.[1]

§ 21. The design of Luke's Gospel was to supersede the defective and inaccurate narratives then in circulation, and to deliver to Theophilus, to whom it is addressed, a full and authentic account of the life, doctrines, miracles, death and resurrection of our Saviour. Who Theophilus was, the learned are not perfectly agreed; but the most probable opinion is that of Dr. Lardner, now generally adopted, that, as Luke wrote his Gospel in Greece, Theophilus was a man of rank in that country.[2] Either the relations subsisting between him and Luke, or the dignity and power of his rank, or both, induced the evangelist, who himself also "had perfect understanding of all things from the first," to devote the utmost care to the drawing up of a complete and authentic narrative of these great events. He does not affirm himself to have been an eye-witness; though his personal knowledge of some of the transactions may well be inferred from the "perfect understanding" which he says he possessed. Some of the learned seem to have drawn this inference as to them all, and to have placed him in the class of original witnesses; but this opinion, though maintained on strong and plausible grounds, is not generally adopted. If, then, he did not write from his own personal knowledge, the question is, what is the legal character of his testimony?

§ 22. If it were "the result of inquiries, made under competent public authority, concerning matters in which the public are concerned,"[3] it would possess every legal attribute of an inquisition, and, as such, would be legally admissible in evidence, in a court of justice. To entitle such results, however, to our full confidence, it is not neces-

[1] See Horne's Introd. vol. iv, pp. 260–272, where references may be found to earlier writers.

[2] See Lardner's Works, 8vo. vol. vi. pp. 138, 139; 4to. vol. iii. pp. 203, 204; and other authors, cited in Horne's Introd. vol. i. p. 267.

[3] 2 Phill. on Ev. p. 95 (9th edition).

sary that they should be obtained under a legal commission; it is sufficient if the inquiry is gravely undertaken and pursued, by a person of competent intelligence, sagacity and integrity. The request of a person in authority, or a desire to serve the public, are, to all moral intents, as sufficient a motive as a legal commission.[1] Thus, we know that when complaint is made to the head of a department, of official misconduct or abuse, existing in some remote quarter, nothing is more common than to send some confidential person to the spot, to ascertain the facts and report them to the department; and this report is confidently adopted as the basis of its discretionary action, in the correction of the abuse, or the removal of the offender. Indeed, the result of any grave inquiry is equally certain to receive our confidence, though it may have been voluntarily undertaken, if the party making it had access to the means of complete and satisfactory information upon the subject.[2] If, therefore, Luke's Gospel were to be regarded only as the work of a contemporary historian, it would be entitled to our confidence. But it is more than this. It is the result of careful inquiry and examination, made by a person of science, intelligence and education, concerning

[1] When Abbot, Archbishop of Canterbury, in shooting a deer with a cross-bow, in Bramsil park, accidentally killed the keeper, King James I. by a letter dated Oct. 3, 1621, requested the Lord Keeper, the Lord Chief Justice, and others, to inquire into the circumstances and consider the case and "the scandal that may have risen thereupon," and to certify the King what it may amount to. Could there be any reasonable doubt of their report of the facts, thus ascertained? See Spelman's Posthumous Works, p. 121.

[2] The case of the ill-fated steamer President furnishes an example of this sort of inquiry. This vessel, it is well known, sailed from New York for London in the month of March, 1841, having on board many passengers, some of whom were highly connected. The ship was soon overtaken by a storm, after which she was never heard of. A few months afterwards a solemn inquiry was instituted by three gentlemen of respectability, one of whom was a British admiral, another was agent for the underwriters at Lloyd's, and the other a government packet agent, concerning the time, circumstances and causes of that disaster; the result of which was communicated to the public, under their hands. This document received universal confidence, and no further inquiry was made.

subjects which he was perfectly competent to investigate, and as to many of which he was peculiarly skilled, they being cases of the cure of maladies; subjects, too, of which he already had the perfect knowledge of a contemporary, and perhaps an eye-witness, but beyond doubt, familiar with the parties concerned in the transactions, and belonging to the community in which the events transpired, which were in the mouths of all; and the narrative, moreover, drawn up for the especial use, and probably at the request, of a man of distinction, whom it would not be for the interest nor safety of the writer to deceive or mislead. Such a document certainly possesses all the moral attributes of an inquest of office, or of any other official investigation of facts; and as such is entitled, *in foro conscientiæ*, to be adduced as original, competent and satisfactory evidence of the matters it contains.

§ 23. JOHN, the last of the evangelists, was the son of Zebedee, a fisherman of the town of Bethsaida, on the sea of Galilee. His father appears to have been a respectable man in his calling, owning his vessel and having hired servants.[1] His mother, too, was among those who followed Jesus, and "ministered unto him;"[2] and to John himself, Jesus, when on the cross, confided the care and support of his own mother.[3] This disciple also seems to have been favorably known to the high priest, and to have influence in his family; by means of which he had the privilege of being present in his palace at the examination of his Master, and of introducing also Peter, his friend.[4] He was the youngest of the apostles; was eminently the object of the Lord's regard and confidence; was on various occasions admitted to free and intimate intercourse with him; and is described as "the disciple whom Jesus loved."[5] Hence he

[1] Mark. i. 20. [2] John xix. 26, 27. [3] John xiii. 23.
[4] Matt. xxvii. 55, 56; Mark xv. 40, 41. [5] John xviii. 15, 16.

was present at several scenes, to which most of the others were not admitted. He alone, in company with Peter and James, was present at the resurrection of Jairus's daughter, at the transfiguration on the mount, and at the agony of our Saviour in the garden of Gethsemane.[1] He was the only apostle who followed Jesus to the cross, he was the first of them at the sepulchre, and he was present at the several appearances of our Lord after his resurrection. These circumstances, together with his intimate friendship with the mother of Jesus, especially qualify him to give a circumstantial and authentic account of the life of his Master. After the ascension of Christ, and the effusion of the Holy Spirit on the day of Pentecost, John became one of the chief apostles of the circumcision, exercising his ministry in and near Jerusalem. From ecclesiastical history we learn that, after the death of Mary the mother of Jesus, he proceeded to Asia Minor, where he founded and presided over seven churches, in as many cities, but resided chiefly at Ephesus. Thence he was banished, in Domitian's reign, to the isle of Patmos, where he wrote his Revelation. On the accession of Nerva he was freed from exile, and returned to Ephesus, where he wrote his Gospel and Epistles, and died at the age of one hundred years, about A. D. 100, in the third year of the emperor Trajan.[2]

§ 24. The learned are not agreed as to the time when the Gospel of John was written; some dating it as early as the year 68, others as late as the year 98; but it is generally conceded to have been written after all the others. That it could not have been the work of some Platonic Christian of a subsequent age, as some have without evidence asserted, is manifest from references to it by some of the early fathers, and from the concurring testimony of many other writers of the ancient Christian church.[3]

[1] Luke viii. 51; Matt. xvii. 1, and xxvi. 37.

[2] This account is abridged from Horne's Introd. vol. iv. pp. 286–288.

[3] Horne's Introd. vol. iv. p. 289, and authors there cited.

§ 25. That it was written either with especial reference to the Gentiles, or at a period when very many of them had become converts to Christianity, is inferred from the various explanations it contains, beyond the other Gospels, which could have been necessary only to persons unacquainted with Jewish names and customs.[1] And that it was written after all the others, and to supply their omissions, is concluded, not only from the uniform tradition and belief in the church, but from his studied omission of most of the transactions noticed by the others, and from his care to mention several incidents which they have not recorded. That their narratives were known to him, is too evident to admit of doubt; while his omission to repeat what they had already stated, or, where he does mention the same things, his relating them in a brief and cursory manner, affords incidental but strong testimony that he regarded their accounts as faithful and true.[2]

§ 26. Such are the brief histories of men, whose narratives we are to examine and compare; conducting the examination and weighing the testimony by the same rules and principles which govern our tribunals of justice in similar cases. These tribunals are in such cases governed by the following fundamental rule:—

In trials of fact, by oral testimony, the proper inquiry is not whether it is possible that the testimony may be false, but whether there is sufficient probability that it is true.

It should be observed that the subject of inquiry is a matter of fact, and not of abstract mathematical truth. The latter alone is susceptible of that high degree of proof, usually termed demonstration, which excludes the possibility of error, and which therefore may reasonably be re-

[1] See, among others, John i. 38, 41, and ii. 6, 13, and iv. 9, and xi. 55.

[2] See Horne's Introd. vol. iv. pp. 297, 298.

quired in support of every mathematical deduction. But the proof of matters of fact rests upon moral evidence alone; by which is meant not merely that species of evidence which we do not obtain either from our own senses, from intuition, or from demonstration. In the ordinary affairs of life we do not require nor expect demonstrative evidence, because it is inconsistent with the nature of matters of fact, and to insist on its production would be unreasonable and absurd. And it makes no difference, whether the facts to be proved relate to this life or to the next, the nature of the evidence required being in both cases the same. The error of the sceptic consists in pretending or supposing that there is a difference in the nature of the things to be proved; and in demanding demonstrative evidence concerning things which are not susceptible of any other than moral evidence alone, and of which the utmost that can be said is, that there is no reasonable doubt about their truth.[1]

§ 27. In proceeding to weigh the evidence of any proposition of fact, the previous question to be determined is, *when* may it be said to be proved? The answer to this question is furnished by another rule of municipal law, which may be thus stated:

A proposition of fact is proved, when its truth is established by competent and satisfactory evidence.

By competent evidence, is meant such as the nature of the thing to be proved requires; and by satisfactory evidence, is meant that amount of proof, which ordinarily satisfies an unprejudiced mind, beyond any reasonable doubt. The circumstances which will amount to this degree of proof can never be previously defined; the only legal test to which they can be subjected is, their sufficiency to satisfy the mind and conscience of a man of common

[1] See Gambier's Guide to the Study of Moral Evidence, p. 121.

prudence and discretion, and so to convince him, that he would venture to act upon that conviction in matters of the hightest concern and importance to his own interest.[1] If, therefore, the subject is a problem in mathematics, its truth is to be shown by the certainty of demonstrative evidence. But if it is a question of fact in human affairs, nothing more than moral evidence can be required, for this is the best evidence which, from the nature of the case, is attainable. Now as the facts, stated in Scripture History, are not of the former kind, but are cognizable by the senses, they may be said to be proved when they are established by that kind and degree of evidence which, as we have just observed, would, in the affairs of human life, satisfy the mind and conscience of a common man. When we have this degree of evidence, it is unreasonable to require more. A juror would violate his oath, if he should refuse to acquit or condemn a person charged with an offense, where this measure of proof was adduced.

§ 28. Proceeding further, to inquire whether the facts related by the Four Evangelists are proved by competent and satisfactory evidence, we are led, first, to consider on which side lies the burden of establishing the credibility of the witnesses. On this point the municipal law furnishes a rule, which is of constant application in all trials by jury, and is indeed the dictate of that charity which thinketh no evil.

In the absence of circumstances which generate suspicion, every witness is to be presumed credible, until the contrary is shown; the burden of impeaching his credibility lying on the objector.[2]

This rule serves to show the injustice with which the writers of the Gospels have ever been treated by infidels; an injustice silently acquiesced in even by Christians; in

[1] 1 Stark. on Ev. pp. 514, 577; 1 Greenl. on Ev. §§ 1, 2; Willis on Circumstantial Ev. p. 2; Whately's Logic, b. iv. ch. iii. § 1.

[2] See 1 Stark. on Ev. pp. 16, 480, 521.

requiring the Christian affirmatively, and by positive evidence, *aliunde*, to establish the credibility of his witnesses above all others, before their testimony is entitled to be considered, and in permitting the testimony of a single profane writer, alone and uncorroborated, to outweigh that of any single Christian. This is not the course in courts of chancery, where the testimony of a single witness is never permitted to outweigh the oath even of the defendant himself, interested as he is in the cause; but, on the contrary, if the plaintiff, after having required the oath of his adversary, cannot overthrow it by something more than the oath of one witness, however credible, it must stand as evidence against him. But the Christian writer seems, by the usual course of the argument, to have been deprived of the common presumption of charity in his favor; and reversing the ordinary rule of administering justice in human tribunals, his testimony is unjustly presumed to be false, until it is proved to be true. This treatment, moreover, has been applied to them all in a body; and, without due regard to the fact, that, being independent historians, writing at different periods, they are entitled to the support of each other: they have been treated, in the argument, almost as if the New Testament were the entire production, at once, of a body of men, conspiring by a joint fabrication, to impose a false religion upon the world. It is time that this injustice should cease; that the testimony of the evangelists should be admitted to be true, until it can be disproved by those who would impugn it; that the silence of one sacred writer on any point, should no more detract from his own veracity or that of the other historians, than the like circumstance is permitted to do among profane writers; and that the Four Evangelists should be admitted in corroboration of each other, as readily as Josephus and Tacitus, or Polybius and Livy.[1]

[1] This subject has been treated by Dr. Chalmers, in his Evidences of the

§ 29. But if the burden of establishing the credibility of the evangelists were devolved on those who affirm the truth of their narratives, it is still capable of a ready moral demonstration, when we consider the nature and character of the

Christian Revelation, chapter iii. The following extract from his observations will not be unacceptable to the reader. "In other cases, when we compare the narratives of contemporary historians, it is not expected that all the circumstances alluded to by one will be taken notice of by the rest; and it often happens that an event or a custom is admitted upon the faith of a single historian; and the silence of all other writers is not suffered to attach suspicion or discredit to his testimony. It is an allowed principle, that a scrupulous resemblance betwixt two histories is very far from necessary to their being held consistent with one another. And what is more, it sometimes happens that, with contemporary historians, there may be an apparent contradiction, and the credit of both parties remain as entire and unsuspicious as before. Posterity is, in these cases, disposed to make the most liberal allowances. Instead of calling it a contradiction, they often call it a difficulty. They are sensible that, in many instances a seeming variety of statement has, upon a more extensive knowledge of ancient history, admitted of a perfect reconciliation. Instead, then, of referring the difficulty in question to the inaccuracy or bad faith of any of the parties, they, with more justness and more modesty, refer it to their own ignorance, and to that obscurity which necessarily hangs over the history of every remote age. These principles are suffered to have great influence in every secular investigation; but so soon as, instead of a secular, it becomes a sacred investigation, every ordinary principle is abandoned, and the suspicion annexed to the teachers of religion is carried to the dereliction of all that candor and liberality with which every other document of antiquity is judged of and appreciated. How does it happen that the authority of Josephus should be acquiesced in as a first principle, while every step, in the narrative of the evangelists, must have foreign testimony to confirm and support it? How comes it, that the silence of Josephus should be construed into an impeachment of the testimony of the evangelists, while it is never admitted, for a single moment, that the silence of the evangelists, can impart the slightest blemish to the testimony of Josephus? How comes it, that the supposition of two Philips in one family should throw a damp of scepticism over the Gospel narrative, while the only circumstance which renders that supposition necessary is the single testimony of Josephus; in which very testimony it is necessarily implied that there are two Herods in that same family? How comes it, that the evangelists, with as much internal, and a vast deal more of external evidence in their favor, should be made to stand before Josephus, like so many prisoners at the bar of justice? In any other case, we are convinced that this would be looked upon as *rough handling*. But we are not sorry for it. It has given more triumph and confidence to the argument. And it is no small addition to our

testimony, and the essential marks of difference between true narratives of facts and the creations of falsehoods. It is universally admitted that the credit to be given to witnesses depends chiefly on their ability to discern and comprehend what was before them, their opportunities for observation, the degree of accuracy with which they are accustomed to mark passing events, and their integrity in relating them. The rule of municipal law on this subject embraces all these particulars, and is thus stated by a legal text-writer of the highest repute.

The credit due to the testimony of witnesses depends upon, firstly, their honesty; secondly, their ability; thirdly, their number and the consistency of their testimony; fourthly, the conformity of their testimony with experience; and fifthly, the coincidence of their testimony with collateral circumstances.[1]

Let the evangelists be tried by these tests.

§ 30. And *first*, as to their *honesty*. Here they are entitled to the benefit of the general course of human experience, that men ordinarily speak the truth, when they have no prevailing motive or inducement to the contrary. This presumption, to which we have before alluded, is applied in courts of justice, even to witnesses whose integrity is not wholly free from suspicion; much more is it applicable to the evangelists, whose testimony went against all their worldly interests. The great truths which the apostles declared, where that Christ had risen from the dead, and that only through repentance from sin, and faith in him, could men hope for salvation. This doctrine they asserted with one voice, everywhere, not only under the

faith, that its first teachers have survived an examination, which, in point of rigor and severity, we believe to be quite unexampled in the annals of criticism." See Chalmer's Evidences, pp. 72–74.

[1] See 1 Stark. on Ev. pp. 480, 545.

greatest discouragements, but in the face of the most appalling terrors that can be presented to the mind of man. Their master had recently perished as a malafactor, by the sentence of a public tribunal. His religion sought to overthrow the religions of the whole world. The laws of every country were against the teachings of his disciples. The interests and passions of all the rulers and great men in the world were against them. The fashion of the world was against them. Propagating this new faith, even in the most inoffensive and peaceful manner, they could expect nothing but contempt, opposition, revilings, bitter persecutions, stripes, imprisonments, torments and cruel deaths. Yet this faith they zealously did propagate; and all these miseries they endured undismayed, nay, rejoicing. As one after another was put to a miserable death, the survivors only prosecuted their work with increased vigor and resolution. The annals of military warfare afford scarcely an example of the like heroic constancy, patience and unblenching courage. They had every possible motive to review carefully the grounds of their faith, and the evidences of the great facts and truths which they asserted; and these motives were pressed upon their attention with the most melancholy and terrific frequency. It was therefore impossible that they could have persisted in affirming the truths they have narrated, had not Jesus actually risen from the dead, and had they not known this fact as certainly as they knew any other fact.[1] If it were morally possible for them to have been deceived in this matter, every human

[1] If the witnesses could be supposed to have been biassed, this would not destroy their testimony to matters of fact; it would only detract from the weight of their judgment in matters of opinion. The rule of law on this subject has been thus stated by Dr. Lushington: "When you exanine the testimony of witnesses nearly connected with the parties, and there is nothing very peculiar tending to destroy their credit, when they depose to mere facts, their testimony is to be believed; when they depose as to matter of opinion, it is to be received with suspicion." Dillon *v.* Dillon, 3 Curteis's Eccl. Rep. pp. 96, 102.

motive operated to lead them to discover and avow their error. To have persisted in so gross a falsehood, after it was known to them, was not only to encounter, for life, all the evils which man could inflict, from without, but to endure also the pangs of inward and conscious guilt; with no hope of future peace, no testimony of a good conscience, no expectation of honor or esteem among men, no hope of happiness in this life, or in the world to come.

§ 31. Such conduct in the apostles would moreover have been utterly irreconcilable with the fact, that they possessed the ordinary constitution of our common nature. Yet their lives do show them to have been men like all others of our race; swayed by the same motives, animated by the same hopes, affected by the same joys, subdued by the same sorrows, agitated by the same fears, and subject to the same passions, temptations and infirmities, as ourselves. And their writings show them to have been men of vigorous understandings. If then their testimony was not true, there was no possible motive for this fabrication.

§ 32. It would also have been irreconcilable with the fact that they were good men. But it is impossible to read their writings, and not feel that we are conversing with men eminently holy, and of tender consciences, with men acting under an abiding sense of the presence and omniscience of God, and of their accountability to him, living in his fear, and walking in his ways. Now, though, in a single instance, a good man may fall, when under strong temptations, yet he is not found persisting, for years, in deliberate falsehood, asserted with the most solemn appeals to God, without the slightest temptation or motive, and against all the opposing interests which reign in the human breast. If, on the contrary, they are supposed to have been bad men, it is incredible that such men should have chosen this form of imposture; enjoining, as it does, unfeigned repentance, the utter forsaking and abhorrence of all falsehood and of every other sin, the practice of daily self-denial, self-abasement and self-sacrifice, the crucifixion of the flesh with all its earthly appetites and desires, indifference to the honors, and hearty contempt of the vanities of the world; and inculcating perfect purity of heart and life, and intercourse of the soul with heaven. It is incredible, that bad men should invent falsehoods, to promote the religion of the God of truth. The supposition is suicidal. If they did believe in a future state of retribution, a heaven and a hell hereafter, they took the most certain course, if false witnesses, to secure the latter for their portion. And if, still being bad men, they did not believe in future punishment, how came they to invent falsehoods the direct and certain tendency of which was to destroy all their prospects of worldly honor and happiness, and to insure their misery in this life? From these absurdities there is no escape, but in the perfect conviction and admission that they were good men, testifying to that which they had carefully observed and considered, and well knew to be true.[1]

§ 33. In the *second* place, as to their *ability*. The text writer before cited observes, that the ability of a witness to speak the truth, depends on the opportunities which he has had for observing the fact, the accuracy of his powers of discerning, and the faithfulness of his memory in retaining the facts, once observed and known.[2] Of the latter trait, in these witnesses, we of course know nothing; nor have we any traditionary information in regard to the accuracy of their powers of discerning. But we may well suppose that in these respects they were like the generality of their countrymen, until the contrary is shown by an objector. It is always to be presumed that men are honest, and of sound mind, and of the average and ordinary degree of intelligence. This is not the judgment of mere charity; it is also

[1] This subject has been so fully treated by Dr. Paley, in his view of the Evidences of Christianity, Part I., Prop. I., that it is unnecessary to pursue it farther in this place.

[2] 1 Stark. on Ev. pp. 483, 548.

the uniform presumption of the law of the land; a presumption which is always allowed freely and fully to operate, until the fact is shown to be otherwise, by the party who denies the applicability of this presumption to the particular case in question. Whenever an objection is raised in opposition to ordinary presumptions of law, or to the ordinary experience of mankind, the burden of proof is devolved on the objector, by the common and ordinary rules of evidence, and of practice in courts. No lawyer is permitted to argue in disparagement of the intelligence or integrity of a witness, against whom the case itself afforded no particle of testimony. This is sufficient for our purpose, in regard to these witnesses. But more than this is evident, from the minuteness of their narratives, and from their history. Matthew was trained, by his calling, to habits of severe investigation and suspicious scrutiny; and Luke's profession demanded an exactness of observation equally close and searching. The other two evangelists, it has been well remarked, were as much too unlearned to forge the story of their Master's Life, as these were too learned and acute to be deceived by any imposture.

§ 34. In the *third* place, as to their *number* and the *consistency* of their testimony. The character of their narratives is like that of all other true witnesses, containing, as Dr. Paley observes, substantial truth, under circumstantial variety. There is enough of discrepancy to show that there could have been no previous concert among them; and at the same time such substantial agreement as to show that they all were independent narrators of the same great transaction, as the events actually occurred. That they conspired to impose falsehood upon the world is, moreover, utterly inconsistent with the supposition that they were honest men; a fact, to the proofs of which we have already adverted. But if they were bad men, still the idea of any conspiracy among them is negatived, not only by the discrepancies alluded to, but by many other circumstances which will be mentioned hereafter; from all which, it is manifest that if they concerted a false story, they sought its accomplishment by a mode quite the opposite to that which all others are found to pursue, to attain the same end. On this point the profound remark of an eminent writer is to our purpose; that "in a number of concurrent testimonies, where there has been no previous concert, there is a probability distinct from that which may be termed the sum of the probabilities resulting from the testimonies of the witnesses; a probability which would remain, even though the witnesses were of such a character as to merit no faith at all. This probability arises from the concurrence itself. That such a concurrence should spring from chance, is as one to infinite; that is, in other words, morally impossible. If therefore concert be excluded, there remains no cause but the reality of the fact."[1]

§ 35. The discrepancies between the narratives of the several evangelists, when carefully examined, will not be found sufficient to invalidate their testimony. Many seeming contradictions will prove, upon closer scrutiny, to be in substantial agreement; and it may be confidently asserted that there are none that will not yield, under fair and just criticism. If these different accounts of the same transactions were in strict verbal conformity with each other, the argument against their credibility would be much stronger. All that is asked for these witnesses is, that their testimony may be regarded as we regard the testimony of men in the ordinary affairs of life. This they are justly entitled to; and this no honorable adversary can refuse. We might, indeed, take higher ground than this, and confidently claim for them the severest scrutiny; but our present purpose is merely to try their veracity by the ordinary tests of truth, admitted in human tribunals.

[1] Campbell's Philosophy of Rhetoric, c. v. b. 1. Part 3, p. 125; Whately's Rhetoric, part 1. ch. 2, § 4; 1 Stark. on Ev. p. 487.

§ 36. If the evidence of the evangelists is to be rejected because of a few discrepancies among them, we shall be obliged to discard that of many of the contemporaneous histories on which we are accustomed to rely. Dr. Paley has noticed the contradiction between Lord Clarendon and Burnett and others in regard to Lord Strafford's execution; the former stating that he was condemned to be hanged, which was done on the same day; and the latter all relating that on a Saturday he was sentenced to the block, and was beheaded on the following Monday. Another striking instance of discrepancy has since occurred, in the narratives of the different members of the royal family of France, of their flight from Paris to Varennes, in 1792. These narratives, ten in number, and by eye-witnesses and personal actors in the transactions they relate, contradict each other, some on trivial and some on more essential points, but in every case in a wonderful and inexplicable manner.[1] Yet these contradictions do not, in the general public estimation, detract from the integrity of the narrators, nor from the credibility of their relations. In the points in which they agree, and which constitute the great body of their narratives, their testimony is of course not doubted; where they differ, we reconcile them as well as we may; and where this

[1] See the Quarterly Review, vol. xxviii. p. 465. These narrators were, the Duchess D'Angouleme herself, the two Messrs. De Bouille, the Duc De Choiseul, his servant, James Brissac, Messrs. De Damas and Deslons, two of the officers commanding detachments on the road, Messrs. De Moustier and Valori, the garde du corps who accompanied the king, and finally M. de Fontanges, archbishop of Toulouse, who though not himself a party to the transaction, is supposed to have written from the information of the queen. An earlier instance of similar discrepancy is mentioned by Sully. After the battle of Aumale, in which Henry IV. was wounded, when the officers were around the king's bed, conversing upon the events of the day, there were not two who agreed in the recital of the most particular circumstance of the action. D'Aubigne, a contemporary writer, does not even mention the king's wound, though it was the only one he ever received in his life. See Memoirs of Sully, vol. i. p. 245. If we treated these narratives as sceptics would have us treat those of the sacred writers, what evidence should we have of any battle at Aumale, or of any flight to Varennes?

cannot be done at all, we follow that light which seems to us the clearest. Upon the principles of the sceptic, we should be bound utterly to disbelieve them all. On the contrary, we apply to such cases the rules which, in daily experience, our judges instruct juries to apply, in weighing and reconciling the testimony of different witnesses; and which the courts themselves observe, in comparing and reconciling different and sometimes discordant reports of the same decisions. This remark applies especially to some alleged discrepancies in the reports which the several evangelists have given of the same discourses of our Lord.[1]

[1] Far greater discrepancies can be found in the different reports of the same case, given by the reporters of legal judgments than are shown among the evangelists; and yet we do not consider them as detracting from the credit of the reporters, to whom we still resort with confidence, as to good authority. Some of these discrepancies seem utterly irreconcilable. Thus, in a case, 45 Edw. III. 19, where the question was upon a gift of lands to J. de C. with Joan, the sister of the donor, and to their heirs, Fitzherbert (tit. *Tail*, 14) says it was adjudged fee simple, and not frankmarriage; Statham (tit. *Tail*) says it was adjudged a gift in frankmarriage; while Brook (tit. *Frankmarriage*) says it was not decided. Vid. 10 Co. 118. Others are irreconcilable, until the aid of a third reporter is invoked. Thus, in the case of Cooper *v.* Franklin, Croke says it was not decided, but adjourned (Cro. Jac. 100); Godbolt says it was decided in a certain way, which he mentions (Godb. 269); Moor also reports it as decided, but gives a different account of the question raised (Moor, 848): while Bulstrode gives a still different report of the judgment of the court, which he says was delivered by Croke himself. But by his account it further appears, that the case was previously twice argued; and thus it at length results that the other reporters relate only what fell from the court on each of the previous occasions. Other similar examples may be found in 1 Dougl. 6, n. compared with 5 East, 475, n. in the case of Galbraith *v.* Neville; and in that of Stoughton *v.* Reynolds, reported by Fortescue, Strange, and in Cases temp. Hardwicke. See 3 Barn. & A. 247, 248. Indeed, the books abound in such instances. Other discrepancies are found in the names of the same litigating parties, as differently given by reporters; such as Putt *v.* Roster, 2 Mod. 318; Foot *v.* Rastall, Skin. 49, and Putt *v.* Royston, 2 Show. 211; also, Hosdell *v.* Harris, 2 Keb. 462; Hodson *v.* Harwich, Ib. 533, and Hodsden *v.* Harridge, 2 Saund. 64, and a multitude of others, which are universally admitted to mean the same cases, even when they are not precisely within the rule of *idem sonans*. These diversities, it is well known, have never detracted in the slightest degree from the estimation in which the reporters are all deservedly held, as authors of

§ 37. In the *fourth* place, as to the *conformity of their testimony with experience.* The title of the evangelists to full credit for veracity would be readily conceded by the objector, if the facts they relate were such as ordinarily occur in human expeience, and on this circumstance an argument is founded against their credibility. Miracles, say the objectors, are impossible; and therefore the evangelists were either deceivers or deceived; and in either case their narratives are unworthy of belief. Spinosa's argument against the possibility of miracles, was founded on the broad and bold assumption that all things are governed by immutable laws, or fixed modes of motion and relation, termed the laws of nature, by which God himself is of necessity bound. This erroneous assumption is the tortoise, on which stands the elephant which upholds his system of atheism. He does not inform us who made these immutable laws, nor whence they derive their binding force and irresistible operation. The argument supposes that the creator of all things first made a code of laws, and then put it out of his own power to change them. The scheme of Mr. Hume is but another form of the same error. He deduces the existence of such immutable laws from the uniform course of human experience. This, he affirms, is our only guide in reasoning concerning matters of fact; and whatever is contrary to human experience, he pronounces incredible.[1] Without stopping to examine the correctness of

merit, enjoying, to this day the confidence of the profession. Admitting now, for the sake of argument (what is not conceded in fact), that diversities equally great exist among the sacred writers, how can we consistently, and as lawyers, raise any serious objection against them on that account, or treat them in any manner different from that which we observe towards our reporters?

[1] Mr. Hume's argument is thus refuted by Lord Broughan. "Here are two answers, to which the doctrine proposed by Mr. Hume is exposed, and either appears sufficient to shake it.

"*First*—Our belief in the uniformity of the laws of nature rests not altogether upon an experience. We believe no man ever was raised from the dead,—not merely because we ourselves never saw it, foı

this doctrine, as a fundamental principle in the law of evidence, it is sufficient in this place to remark, that it contains this fallacy ; it excludes all knowledge derived by inference

indeed that would be a very limited ground of deduction; and our belief was fixed on the subject long before we had any considerable experience,—fixed chiefly by authority,—that is, by diference to other men's experience. We found our confident belief in this negative position partly, perhaps chiefly, upon the testimony of others; and at all events, our belief that in times before our own the same position held good, must of necessity be drawn from our trusting the relations of other men—that is, it depends upon the evidence of testimony. If, then, the existence of the law of nature is proved, in great part at least, by such evidence, can we wholly rejeet the like evidence when it comes to prove an exception to the rule—a deviation from the law? The more numerous are the cases of the law being kept—the more rare those of its being broken—the more scrupulous certainly ought we to be in admitting the proofs of the breach. But that testimony is capable of making good the proof there seems no doubt. In truth, the degree of excellence and of strength to which testimony may arise seems almost indefinite. There is hardly any cogency which it is not capable by possible supposition of attaining. The endless multiplication of witnesses,—the unbounded variety of their habits of thinking, their prejudices, their interests,—afford the means of conceiving the force of their testimony, augmented *ad infinitum*, because these circumstances afford the means of diminshing indefinitely the chances of their being all mistaken, all mislead, or all combining to deceive us. Let any man try to calculate the chances of a thousand persons who come from different quarters, and never saw each other before, and who all vary in their habits, stations, opinions, interests,—being mistaken or combining to deceive us, when they give the same account of an event as having happened before their eyes,—these chances are many hundreds of thousands to one. And yet we can conceive them multiplied indefinitely; for one hundred thousand such witnesses may all in like manner bear the same testimony; and they may all tell us their story within twenty-four hours after the transaction, and in the next parish. And yet according to Mr. Hume's argument, we are bound to disbelieve them all, because they speak to a thing contrary to out own experience, and to the accounts which other witnesses had formerly given us of the laws of nature, and which our forefathers had handed down to us as derived from witnesses who lived in the old time before them. It is unnecessary to add that no testimony of the witnesses, whom we are supposing to concur in their relation, contradicts any testimony of our own senses. If it did, the argument would resemble Archbishop Tillotson's upon the Real Presence, and our disbelief would be at once warranted.

"*Secondly*—This leads us to the next objection to which Mr. Hume's argument is liable, and which we have in part anticipated while illustrating the first. He requires us to withhold our belief in circumstances which would force every man of common understanding to lend his assent, and to

or deduction from facts, confining us to what we derive from experience alone, and thus depriving us of any knowledge, or even rational belief, of the existence or character of God.

act upon the supposition of the story told being true. For, suppose either such numbers of various witnesses as we have spoken of; or, what is perhaps stronger, suppose a miracle reported to us, first by a number of relators, and then by three or four of the very soundest judges and most incorruptibly honest men we know,—men noted for their difficult belief of wonders, and, above all, steady unbelievers in miracles, without any bias in favor of religion, but rather accustomed to doubt, if not disbelieve,—most people would lend an easy belief to any miracle thus vouched. But let us add this circumstance, that a friend on his death-bed had been attended by us, and that we had told him a fact known only to ourselves, something that we had secretly done the very moment before we told it to the dying man, and which to no other being we had ever revealed,—and that the credible witnesses we are supposing, informed us that the deceased appeared to them, conversed with them, and remained with them a day or two, accompanying them, and to avouch the fact of his reappearance on this earth, communicated to them the secret of which we had made him the sole depository the moment before his death;—according to Mr. Hume, we are bound rather to believe, not only that those credible witnesses deceived us, or that those sound and unprejudiced men were themselves deceived, and fancied things without real existence, but further, that they all hit by chance upon the discovery of a real secret, known only to ourselves and the dead man. Mr. Hume's argument requires us to believe this as the lesser improbability of the two—as less unlikely than the rising of one from the dead; and yet every one must feel convinced, that were he placed in the situation we have been figuring, he would not only lend his belief to the relation, but if the relators accompanied it with a special warning from the deceased person to avoid a certain contemplated act, he would, acting upon the belief of their story, take the warning, and avoid doing the forbidden deed. Mr. Hume's argument makes no exception. This is its scope; and whether he chooses to push it thus far or no, all miracles are of necessity denied by it, without the least regard to the kind or the quantity of the proof on which they are rested; and the testimony which we have supposed, accompanied by the test or check we have supposed, would fall within the grasp of the argument just as much and as clearly as any other miracle avouched by more ordinary combinations of evidence.

"The use of Mr. Hume's argument is this, and it is an important and a valuable one. It teaches us to sift closely and vigorously the evidence for miraculous events It bids us remember that the probabilities are always, and must always be incomparably greater against, than for, the truth of these relations, because it is always far more likely that the testimony should be mistaken or false, than that the general laws of nature should be suspended. Further than this the doctrine cannot in soundness of reason be carried. It does not go the length of proving that those general

Nay more, it goes to prove that successive generations of men can make no advancement in knowledge, but each must begin *de novo*, and be limited to the results of his own

laws cannot, by the force of human testimony, be shown to have been, in a particular instance, and with a particular purpose, suspended." See his Discourse of Natural Theology, Note 5, p. 210–214, ed. 1835.

Laplace, in his Essai sur les Probabilites, maintains that, the more extraordinary the fact attested, the greater the probability of error or falsehood in the attestor. Simple good sense, he says, suggests this; and the calculation of probabilities confirms its suggestion. There are some things, he adds, so extraordinary, that nothing can balance their improbability. The position here laid down is, that the probability of error, or of the falsehood of testimony, becomes *in proportion* greater, as the fact which is attested is more extraordinary. And hence a fact extraordinary in the highest possible degree, becomes in the highest possible degree improbable; or so much so, that nothing can counterbalance its improbability.

This argument has been made much use of, to discredit the evidence of miracles, and the truth of that divine religion which is attested by them. But however sound it may be, in one sense, this application of it is fallacious. The fallacy lies in the meaning affixed to the term "extraordinary." If Laplace means a fact extraordinary *under* its existing circumstances and relations, that is, a fact remaining extraordinary, notwithstanding all its circumstances, the position needs not here to be controverted. But if the term means extraordinary *in the abstract*, it is far from being universally true, or affording a correct test of truth, or rule of evidence. Thus, it is extraordinary that a man should leap fifteen feet at a bound; but not extraordinary that a strong and active man should do it, under a sudden impulse to save his life. The former is improbable in the abstract; the latter is rendered probable by the circumstances. So, things extraordinary, and therefore improbable under one hypothesis, become the reverse under another. Thus, the occurrence of a violent storm at sea, and the utterance by Jesus of the words, "Peace, be still," succeeded instantly by a perfect calm, are facts which, taken separately from each other, are not in themselves extraordinary. The connection between the command of Jesus and the ensuing calm, as cause and effect, would be extraordinary and improbable if he were a mere man; but it becomes perfectly natural and probable, when his divine power is considered. Each of those facts is in its nature so simple and obvious, that the most ignorant person is capable of observing it. There is nothing extraordinary in the facts themselves; and the extraordinary coincidence, in which the miracle consists, becomes both intelligible and probable upon the hypothesis of the Christian. See the *Christsan Observer* for Oct. 1838, p. 617. The theory of Laplace may, with the same propriety, be applied to the creation of the world. That matter was created out of nothing is extremely improbable, in the abstract, that is, if there is no God; and therefore it is not to be believed. But if the existence of a Supreme Being is conceded, the fact is perfectl credible.

experience. But if we may infer, from what we see and know, that there is a Supreme Being, by whom this world was created, we may certainly, and with equal reason, believe him capable of works which *we* have never yet known him to perform. We may fairly conclude that the power which was originally put forth to create the world is still constantly and without ceasing exerted to sustain it; and that the experienced connection between cause and effect is but the uniform and constantly active operation of the finger of God. Whether this uniformity of operation extends to things beyond the limits of our observation, is a point we cannot certainly know. Its existence in all things that ordinarily concern us may be supposed to be ordained as conducive to our happiness; and if the belief in a revelation of peace and mercy from God is conducive to the happiness of man, it is not irrational to suppose that he would depart from his ordinary course of action, in order to give it such attestations as should tend to secure that belief. "A miracle is improbable, when we can perceive no suffi-

Laplace was so fascinated with his theory, that he thought the calculus of probabilities might be usefully employed in discovering the value of the different methods resorted to, in those sciences which are in a great measure conjectural, as medicine, agriculture, and political economy. And he proposed that there should be kept, in every branch of the administration, an exact register of the trials made of different measures, and of the results, whether good or bad, to which they have led. See the *Edinburgh Review*, vol. xxiii. pp. 335, 336. Napoleon, who appointed him Minister of the Interior, has thus described him: "A geometrician of the first class, he did not reach mediocrity as a statesman. He never viewed any subject in its true light; he was always occupied with subtleties; his notions were all problematic; and he carried into the administration the spirit of the *infinitely small.*" See the *Encyclopedia Britannica*, art. Laplace, vol. xiii. p. 101; Memoires Ecrits â Ste. Helena, i. 3. The injurious effect of deductive reasoning, upon the minds of those who addict themselves to this method alone, to the exclusion of all other modes of arriving at the knowledge of truth in fact, is shown with great clearness and success, by Mr. Whewel, in the ninth of the Bridgwater Treatises, book 3, ch. 6. The calculus of probabilities has been applied by some writers to judicial evidence; but its very slight value as a test, is clearly shown in an able article on Presumptive Evidence, in the *Law Magazine*, vol. i. pp. 28–32 (New Series).

cient cause, in reference to his creatures, why the Deity should not vary his modes of operation; it ceases to be so, when such cause is assigned.[1]

§ 38. But the full discussion of the subject of miracles forms no part of the present design. Their credibility has been fully established, and the objections of sceptics most satisfactorily met and overthrown. by the ablest writers of our own day, whose works are easily accessible.[2] Thus much, however, may here be remarked; that in almost every miracle related by the evangelists, the facts, separately taken, were plain, intelligible, transpiring in public, and about which no person of ordinary observation would be likely to mistake. Persons blind or crippled, who applied to Jesus for relief, were known to have been crippled or blind for many years; they came to be cured; he spake to them; they went away whole. Lazarus had been dead and buried four days; Jesus called him to come forth from the grave; he immediately came forth, and was seen alive for a long time afterwards. In every case of healing, the previous condition of the sufferer was known to all; all saw his instantaneous restoration; and all witnessed the act of

[1] See Mr. Norton's "Discourse on the latest form of Infidelity," p. 18.

[2] The arguments on this subject are stated in a condensed form, by Mr. Horne, in his Introduction to the Study of the Holy Scriptures, vol. i. ch. 4, sec. 2; in which he refers, among others, to Dr. Gregory's Letters on the Evidences of the Christian Revelation; Dr. Campbell's Dissertation on Miracles; Vince's Sermons on the Credibility of Miracles; Bishop Marsh's Lectures, part 6, lect. 30; Dr. Adams's Treatise in reply to Mr. Heum; Bishop Gleig's Dissertation on Miracles, (in the third volume of his edition of Stackhouse's History of the Bible, p. 240, &c.); Dr. Key's Norissian Lectures, vol. i. See also Dr. Howell's Lowell Lectures, lect. I. and II. delivered in Boston in 1844, where this topic is treated with great perspicuity and cogency.

Among the more popular treaties on miracles, are Bogue's Essay on the Divine Authority of the New Testament, ch. 5; Bishop Wilson's Evidences of Christianity, vol. i. lect. 7; Bishop Sumner's Evidences, ch. 10; Gambier's Guide to the Study of Moral Evidence, ch. 5; Mr. Norton's Discourse on the latest form of Infidelity, and Dr. Dewey's Dudleian Lecture, delivered before Harvard University, in May, 1836.

Jesus in touching him, and heard his words.[1] All these, separately considered, were facts, plain and simple in their nature, easily seen and fully comprehended by persons of common capacity and observation. If they were separately testified to, by different witnesses of ordinary intelligence and integrity, in any court of justice, the jury would be bound to believe them ; and a verdict, rendered contrary to the uncontrrdicted testimony of credible witnesses to any of these plain facts, separately taken, would be liable to be set aside, as a verdict against evidence. If one credible witness testified to the fact, that Bartimeus was blind, according to the uniform course of administering justice, this fact would be taken as satisfactorily proved. So also, if his subsequent restoration to sight were the sole fact in question, this also would be deemed established, by the like evidence. Nor would the rule of evidence be at all different, if the fact to be proved were the declaration of Jesus, immediately preceding his restoration to sight, that his faith had made him whole. In each of these cases, each isolated fact was capable of being accurately observed, and certainly known ; and the evidence demands our assent, precisely as the like evidence upon any other indifferent subject. The connection of the word or the act of Jesus with the restoration of the blind, lame and dead, to sight, and health, and life, as cause and effect, is a conclusion which our reason is compelled to admit, from the uniformity of their concurrence, in such a multitude of instances, as well as from the universal conviction of all, whether friends or foes, who beheld the miracles which he wrought. Indeed, if the truth of one of the miracles is satisfactorily established, our belief cannot reasonably be withheld from them all. This is the issue proposed by Dr. Paley; in regard to the evidence of the death of Jesus upon the cross, and his subsequent resurrection, the truth of which he has established in an argument, incapable of refutation.

[1] See Bishop Wilson's Evidences, lect. 7, p. 130.

§ 39. In the *fifth* place, as to *the coincidence of their testimony with collateral and contemporaneous facts and circumstances.* After a witness is dead, and his moral character is forgotten, we can ascertain it only by a close inspection of his narrative, comparing its details with each other, and with contemporary accounts and collateral facts. This test is much more accurate than may at first be supposed. Every event which actually transpires, has its appropriate relation and place in the vast complication of circumstances, of which the affairs of men consist; it owes its origin to the events which have preceded it, is intimately connected with all others which occur at the same time and place, and often with those of remote regions, and in its turn gives birth to numberless others which succeed. In all this almost inconceivable contexture, and seeming discord, there is perfect harmony; and while the fact, which really happened, tallies exactly with every other contemporaneous incident, related to it in the remotest degree, it is not possible for the wit of man to invent a story, which, if closely compared with the actual occurrences of the same time and place, may not be shown to be false.[1] Hence it is, that a false witness will not willingly detail any circumstances, in which his testimony will be open to contradiction, nor multiply them where there is danger of his being detected by a comparison of them with other accounts, equally circumstantial. He will rather deal in general statements and broad assertions; and if he finds it necessary for his purpose to employ names and particular circumstances in his story, he will endeavor to invent such as shall be out of the reach of all opposing proof; and he will be the most forward and minute in details, where he knows that any danger of contradiction is least to be apprehended.[2] Therefore it is, that variety and minuteness of detail are usually regarded as certain tests of sincerity, if the story, in the circumstances related, is of a nature capable of easy refutation if it were false.

[1] 1 Stark. on Ev. p. 496–499. [2] 1 Stark. on Ev. p. 523.

§ 40. The difference, in the detail of circumstances, between artful or false witnesses and those who testify the truth, is worthy of especial observation. The former are often copious and even profuse in their statements, as far as these may have been previously fabricated, and in relation to the principal matter; but beyond this, all will be reserved and meagre, from the fear of detection. Every lawyer knows how lightly the evidence of a *non-mi-recordo* witness is esteemed. The testimony of false witnesses will not be uniform in its texture, but will be unequal, unnatural, and inconsistent. On the contrary, in the testimony of true witnesses there is a visible and striking naturalness of manner, and an unaffected readiness and copiousness in the detail of circumstances, as well in one part of the narative as another, and evidently without the least regard either to the facility or difficulty of verification or detection.[1] It is easier, therefore, to make out the proof of any fact, if proof it may be called, by suborning one or more false witnesses, to testify directly to the matter in question, than to procure an equal number to testify falsely to such collateral and separate circumstances as will, without greater danger of detection, lead to the same false result. The increased number of witnesses to circumstances, and the increased number of the circumstances themselves, all tend to increase the probability of detection if the witnesses are false, because thereby the points are multiplied in which their statements may be compared with each other, as well as with the truth itself, and in the same proportion is increased the danger of variance and inconsistency.[2] Thus the force of circumstantial evidence is found to depend on the number of particulars involved in the narative; the diffculty of fabricating them all, if false, and the great facility of detec-

[1] 1 Stark. on Ev. 487. The Gospels abound in instances of this. See, for example, Mark, xv. 21; John, xviii. 10; Luke, xxiii. 6; Matt. xxvii. 58–60; John xi. 1.

[2] 1 Stark. on Ev. 522, 585.

tion; the nature of the circumstances to be compared, and from which the dates and other facts are to be collected; the intricacy of the comparison; the number of the intermediate steps in the process of deduction; and the circuity of the investigation. The more largely the narative partakes of these characters, the further it will be found removed from all suspicion of contrivance or design, and the more profoundly the mind will repose on the conviction of its truth.

§ 41. The narratives of the sacred writers, both Jewish and Christian, abound in examples of this kind of evidence, the value of which is hardly capable of being properly estimated. It does not, as has been already remarked, amount to mathematical demonstration; nor is this degree of proof justly demandable in any question of moral conduct. In all human transactions, the highest degree of assurance to which we can arrive, short of the evidence of our own senses, is that of probability. The most that can be asserted is, that the narrative is more likely to be true than false; and it may be in the highest degree more likely, but still be short of absolute mathematical certainty. Yet this very probability may be so great as to satisfy the mind of the most cautious, and enforce the assent of the most reluctant and unbelieving. If it is such as usually satisfies reasonable men, in matters of ordinary transaction, it is all which the greatest sceptic has a right to require; for it is by such evidence alone that our rights are determined, in the civil tribunals; and on no other evidence do they proceed, even in capital cases. Thus where a house had been feloniously broken open with a knife, the blade of which was broken and left in the window, and the mutilated knife itself, the parts perfectly agreeing, was found in the pocket of the accused, who gave no satisfactory explanation of the fact, no reasonable doubt remained of his participation in the crime. And where a murder had been committed by shooting with a pistol, and the prisoner was connected with the transaction by proof that the wadding of the pistol was part of a letter addressed to him, the remainder of which was found upon his person, no juror's conscience could have reproached him for assenting to the verdict of condemnation.[1] Yet the evidence, in both cases, is but the evidence of circumstances; amounting, it is true, to the highest degree of probability, but yet not utterly inconsistent with the innocence of the accused. The evidence which we have of the great facts of the Bible history belongs to this class, that is, it is moral evidence ; sufficient to satisfy any rational mind, by carrying it to the highest degree of moral certainty. If such evidence will justify the taking away of human life or liberty, in the one case, surely it ought to be deemed sufficient to determine our faith in the other.

§ 42. All that Christianity asks of men on this subject, is, that they would be consistent with themselves ; that they would treat its evidences as they treat the evidence of other things ; and that they would try and judge its actors and witnesses, as they deal with their fellow men, when testifying to human affairs and actions, in human tribunals. Let the witnesses be compared with themselves, with each other, and with surrounding facts and circumstances ; and let their testimony be sifted, as if it were given in a court of justice, on the side of the adverse party, the witness being subjected to a rigorous cross-examination. The result, it is confidently believed, will be an undoubting conviction of their integrity, ability, and truth. In the course of such an examination, the undesigned coincidences will multiply upon us at every step in our progress ; the probability of the veracity of the witnesses and of the reality of the occurrences which they relate will increase, until it acquires, for all practical purposes, the value and force of demonstration.

[1] See 1 Stark. on Ev. 498. Wills on Circumstantial Evidence, pp. 128, 129.

§ 43. It should be remembered, that very little of the literature of their times and country has come down to us; and that the collateral sources and means of corroborating and explaining their writings are proportionally limited. The contemporary writings and works of art which have reached us, have invariably been found to confirm their accounts, to reconcile what was apparently contradictory, and supply what seemed defective or imperfect. We ought therefore to conclude, that if we had more of the same light, all other similar difficulties and imperfections would vanish. Indeed they have been gradually vanishing, and rapidly too, before the light of modern research, conducted by men of science in our own times. And it is worthy of remark, that of all the investigations and discoveries of travelers and men of letters, since the overthrow of the Roman empire, not a vestige of antiquity has been found, impeaching, in the slightest degree, the credibility of the sacred writers; but, on the contrary, every result has tended to confirm it.

§ 44. The essential marks of difference between true narratives of facts and the creations of fiction, have already been adverted to. It may here be added that these attributes of truth are strikingly apparent throughout the gospel histories, and that the absence of all the others is equally remarkable. The writers allude, for example, to the existing manners and customs, and to the circumstances of the times and of their country, with the utmost minuteness of reference. And these references are never formally made, nor with preface and explanation, never multiplied and heaped on each other, nor brought together, as though introduced by design; but they are scattered broad-cast and singly over every part of the story, and so connect themselves with every incident related, as to render the detection of falsehood inevitable. This minuteness, too, is not peculiar to any one of the historians, but is common to them all. Though they wrote at different periods and without mutual concert, they all alike refer incidentally to the same state of affairs, and to the same contemporary and collateral circumstances. Their testimony, in this view, stands on the same ground with that of four witnesses, separately examined before different commissioners, upon the same interrogatories, and all adverting incidentally to the same circumstances as surrounding and accompanying the principal transaction, to which alone their attention is directed. And it is worthy of observation that these circumstances were at that time of a peculiar character. Hardly a state or kingdom in the world ever experienced so many vicissitudes in its government and political relations, as did Judea, during the period of the gospel history. It was successively under the government of Herod the Great, of Archelaus, and of a Roman magistrate; it was a kingdom, a tetrarchate, and a province; and its affairs, its laws, and the administration of jnstice, were all involved in the confusion and uncertainty naturally to be expected from recent conquest. It would be difficult to select any place or period in the history of nations, for the time and scene of a fictitious history or an imposture, which would combine so many difficulties for the fabricator to surmount, so many contemporary writers to confront with him, and so many facilities for the detection of falsehood.[1]

§ 45. "Had the evangelists been false historians," says Dr. Chalmers, "they would not have committed themselves upon so many particulars. They would not have furnished the vigilant inquirers of that period with such an effectual instrument for bringing them into discredit with the people; nor foolishly supplied, in every page of their narrative, so many materials for a cross-examination, which would infallibly have disgraced them. Now, we of this age can institute the same cross-examination. We can compare the evangelical writers with contemporary authors, and verify

[1] See Chalmers' Evidence, chap. iii.

a number of circumstances in the history, and government, and peculiar economy of the Jewish people. We therefore have it in our power to institute a cross-examination upon the writers of the New Testament; and the freedom and frequency of their allusions to these circumstances supply us with ample materials for it. The fact, that they are borne out in their minute and incidental allusions by the testimony of other historians, gives a strong weight of what has been called circumstantial evidence in their favor. As a specimen of the argument, let us confine our observations to the history of our Saviour's trial, and execution, and burial. They brought him to Pontius Pilate. We know both from Tacitus and Josephus, that he was at that time governor of Judea. A sentence from him was necessary before they could proceed to the execution of Jesus; and we know that the power of life and death was usually vested in the Roman governor. Our Saviour was treated with derision; and this we know to have been a customary practice at that time, previous to the execution of criminals, and during the time of it. Pilate scourged Jesus before he gave him up to be crucified. We know from ancient authors, that this was a very usual practice among Romans. The accounts of an execution generally run in this form: ne was stripped, whipped, and beheaded or executed. According to the evangelists, his accusation was written on the top of the cross; and we learn from Suetonius and others, that the crime of the person to be executed was affixed to the instrument of his punishment. According to the evangelists, this accusation was written in three different languages; and we know from Josephus that it was quite common in Jerusalem to have all public advertisements written in this manner. According to the evangelists, Jesus had to bear his cross; and we know from other sources of information, that this was the constant practice of these times. According to the evangelists, the body of Jesus was given up to be buried at the request of friends. We know that, unless the criminal was infamous, this was the law or the custom with all Roman governors."[1]

§ 46. There is also a striking naturalness in the characters exhibited in the sacred historians, rarely if ever found in works of fiction, and probably nowhere else to be collected in a similar manner from fragmentary and incidental allusions and expressions, in the writings of different persons. Take, for example, that of Peter, as it may be gathered from the evangelists, and it will be hardly possible to conceive that four persons, writing at different times, could have concurred in the delineation of such a character, if it were not real; a character too, we must observe, which is nowhere expressly drawn, but is shown only here and there, casually, in the subordinate parts of the main narrative. Thus disclosed, it is that of a confident, sanguine, and zealous man; sudden and impulsive, yet humble and ready to retract; honest and direct in his purposes; ardently loving his master, yet deficient in fortitude and firmness in his cause.[2] When Jesus put any question to the apostles, it was Peter who was foremost to reply;[3] and if they would inquire of Jesus, it was Peter who was readiest to speak.[4] He had the impetuous courage to cut off the ear of the High Priest's servant, who came to arrest his master; and the weakness to dissemble before the Jews, in the matter of eating with Gentile converts.[5] It was he who ran with John to the sepulchre, on the first intelligence of the resurrection of Jesus, and with characteristic zeal rushed in, while John paused without the door.[6] He had

[1] See Chalmer's Evidence, pp. 76–78, Amer. ed. Proofs of this kind are copiously referred to by Mr. Horne, in his Introduction, &c. vol. i., ch. 3, sect. II. 2.

[2] See Mark viii. 32; ix. 5; and xiv. 29; Matt. xvi. 22; and xvii. 5; Luke ix. 33; and xviii. 18; John xiii. 8; and xviii. 15.

[3] Mark viii. 29; Matt. xvi. 16; Luke ix. 20.

[4] Matt. xviii. 21; and xix. 27; John xiii. 36.

[5] Gal. ii. 11.

[6] John xx. 3–6.

the ardor to desire and the faith to attempt to walk on the water, at the command of his Lord; but as soon as he saw the wind boisterous, he was afraid.[1] He was the first to propose the election of another apostle in the place of Judas;[2] and he it was who courageously defended them all, on the day of Pentecost, when the multitude charged them with being filled with new wine.[3] He was forward to acknowledge Jesus to be the Messiah;[4] yet having afterwards endangered his own life by wounding the servant of the High Priest, he suddenly consulted his own safety by denying the same Master, for whom, but a few hours before, he had declared himself ready to die.[5] We may safely affirm that the annals of fiction afford no example of a similar but not uncommon character, thus incidentally delineated.

§ 47. There are other internal marks of truth in the narratives of the evangelists, which, however, need here be only alluded to, as they have been treated with great fullness and force by able writers, whose works are familiar to all.[6] Among these may be mentioned the nakedness of the narratives; the absence of all parade by the writers about their own integrity, of all anxiety to be believed, or to impress others with a good opinion of themselves or their cause, of all marks of wonder, or of desire to excite astonishment at the greatness of the events they record, and of all appearance of design to exalt their Master. On the contrary, there is apparently the most pefect indifference on their part, whether they are believed or not; or rather, the

[1] Matt. xiv. 30. [2] Acts i. 15. [3] Acts ii. 14.

[4] Matt. xvi. 16; Mark viii. 29; Luke ix. 20; John vi. 69.

[5] Matt. xxvi. 33, 35; Mark xiv. 29.

[6] See Paley's view of the Evidences of Christianity, part ii. chapters iii. iv. v. vi. vii.; Ib. part iii. ch. i.; Chalmers on the Evidence and Authority of the Christian Revelation, ch. iii. iv. viii.; Wilson's Evidences of Christianity, lect. vi.; Bogue's Essay on the Divine Authority of the New Testament, chap. iii. iv.

evident consciousness that they are recording events well known to all, in their own country and times, and undoubtedly to be believed, like any other matter of public history, by readers in all other countries and ages. It is worthy, too, of especial observation, that though the evangelists record the unparalleled sufferings and cruel death of their beloved Lord, and this too, by hands and with the consenting voices of those on whom he had conferred the greatest benefits, and their own persecutions and dangers, yet they have bestowed no epithets of harshness or even of just censure on the authors of all this wickedness, but have everywhere left the plain and unincumbered narrative to speak for itself, and the reader to pronounce his own sentence of condemnation; like true witnesses, who have nothing to gain or to lose by the event of the cause, they state the facts, and leave them to their fate. Their simplicity and artlessness, also, should not pass unnoticed, in readily stating even those things most disparaging to themselves. Their want of faith in their master, their dullness of apprehension of his teachings, their strifes for pre-eminence, their inclination to call fire from heaven upon their enemies, their desertion of their Lord in his hour of extreme peril; these and many other incidents tending directly to their own dishonor, are nevertheless set down with all the directness and sincerity of truth, as by men writing under the deepest sense of responsibility to God. Some of the more prominent instances of this class of proofs will be noticed hereafter, in their proper places, in the narratives themselves.

§ 48. Lastly, the great character they have portrayed is perfect. It is the character of a sinless Being; of one supremely wise and supremely good. It exhibits no error, no sinister intention, no imprudence, no ignorance, no evil passion, no impatience; in a word, no fault; but all is perfect uprightness, innocence, wisdom, goodness and truth. The mind of man has never conceived the idea of such a character, even for his gods; nor has history or poetry shadowed it forth. The doctrines and precepts of Jesus are in strict accordance with the attributes of God, agreeably to the most exalted idea which we can form of them, either from reason or from revelation. They are strikingly adapted to the capacity of mankind, and yet are delivered with a simplicity and majesty wholly divine. He spake as never man spake. He spake with authority; yet addressed himself to the reason and the understanding of men; and he spake with wisdom, which men could neither gainsay nor resist. In his private life, he exhibits a character not merely of strict justice, but of overflowing benignity. He is temperate, without austerity; his meekness and humility are signal; his patience is invincible; truth and sincerity illustrate his whole conduct; every one of his virtues is regulated by consummate prudence; and he both wins the love of his friends, and extorts the wonder and admiration of his enemies.[1] He is represented in every variety of situation in life, from the height of worldly grandeur, amid the acclamations of an admiring multitude, to the deepest abyss of human degradation and woe, apparently deserted of God and man. Yet everywhere he is the same; displaying a character of unearthly perfection, symmetrical in all its proportions, and encircled with splendor more than human. Either the men of Galilee were men of superlative wisdom, and extensive knowledge and experience, and of deeper skill in the arts of deception, than any and all others, before or after them, or they have truly stated the astonishing things which they saw and heard.

The narratives of the evangelists are now submitted to the reader's perusal and examination, upon the principles and by the rules already stated. For this purpose, and for the sake of more ready and close comparison, they are arranged in juxtaposition, after the general order of the

[1] See Bogue's Essay, ch. i. sec. 2; Newcome's Obs. part ii. ch. i. sec. 14.

latest and most approved harmonies. The question is not upon the strict propriety of the arrangement, but upon the veracity of the witnesses and the credibility of their narratives. With the relative merits of modern harmonists, and with points of controversy among theologians, the writer has no concern. His business is that of a lawyer, examining the testimony of witnesses by the rules of his profession, in order to ascertain whether, if they had thus testified on oath, in a court of justice, they would be entitled to credit; and whether their narratives, as we now have them, would be received as ancient documents, coming from the proper custody. If so, then it is believed that every honest and impartial man will act consistently with that result, by receiving their testimony in all the extent of its import. To write out a full commentary or argument upon the text, would be a useless addition to the bulk of the volume; but a few notes have been added for illustration of the narratives, and for the clearing up of apparent discrepancies, as being all that members of the legal profession would desire.

HARMONY OF THE GOSPELS.

PART I.

EVENTS

CONNECTED WITH THE

BIRTH AND CHILDHOOD OF JESUS.

TIME. *About thirteen and a half years.*

§ 1. **Preface to**

MATTHEW.[1] *	MARK.[1] †

§ 2. **An angel appears**

* Appendix, "Notes to Matthew."

† Appendix, "Notes to Mark."

Luke's Gospel.

LUKE.[1] *

CHAPTER I. 1–4.

FORASMUCH as many have taken in
hand to set forth in order a declaration of those things which are most
surely believed among us,
2 Even as they delivered them unto
us, which from the beginning were
eye-witnesses, and ministers of the
word;
3 It seemed good to me also, having had perfect understanding of all
things from the very first, to write
unto thee in order, most excellent
Theophilus,
4 That thou mightest know the
certainty of those things wherein thou
hast been instructed.

JOHN.[1] †

to Zacharias. *Jerusalem.*

CHAPTER I. 5–25.

5 THERE was in the days of Herod
the king of Judea, a certain priest
named Zacharias, of the course of
Abia: and his wife *was* of the daughters of Aaron, and her name *was*
Elisabeth.
6 And they were both righteous
before God, walking in all the commandments and ordinances of the
Lord blameless.
7 And they had no child, because
that Elisabeth was barren; and they
both were *now* well stricken in years.
8 And it came to pass, that, while
he executed the priest's office before
God in the order of his course,
9 According to the custom of the
priest's office, his lot was to burn incense when he went into the temple
of the Lord.
10 And the whole multitude of the
people were praying without, at the
time of incense.
11 And there appeared unto him an
angel of the Lord, standing on the
right side of the altar of incense.
12 And when Zacharias saw *him*, he
was troubled, and fear fell upon him.
13 But the angel said unto him,
Fear not, Zacharias: for thy prayer is
heard; and thy wife Elisabeth shall
bear thee a son, and thou shalt call
his name John.
14 And thou shalt have joy and

* Appendix, "Notes to Luke."

† Appendix, "Notes to John."

§ 2. An angel appears

MATTHEW.	MARK.

to Zacharias. *Jerusalem.*

LUKE.

CHAPTER I. 5–25.

gladness, and many shall rejoice at
his birth.
15 For he shall be great in the
sight of the Lord, and shall drink
neither wine nor strong drink; and
he shall be filled with the Holy Ghost,
even from his mother's womb.
16 And many of the children of
Israel shall he turn to the Lord their
God.
17 And he shall go before him in
the spirit and power of Elias,* to
turn the hearts of the fathers to the
children, and the disobedient to the
wisdom of the just; to make ready a
people prepared for the Lord.
18 And Zacharias said unto the
angel, Whereby shall I know this?
for I am an old man, and my wife
well stricken in years.
19. And the angel, answering, said
unto him, I am Gabriel, that stand in
the presence of God; and am sent[2]
to speak unto thee, and to shew thee
these glad tidings.
20 And behold, thou shalt be dumb,
and not able to speak, until the day
that these things shall be performed,
because thou believest not my words,
which shall be fulfilled in their season.
21 And the people waited for
Zacharias, and marvelled that he
tarried so long in the temple.
22 And when he came out, he
could not speak unto them: and they
perceived that he had seen a vision
in the temple; for he beckoned unto
them, and remained speechless.
23 And it came to pass, that as
soon as the days of his ministration
were accomplished, he departed to
his own house.
24 And after those days his wife
Elisabeth conceived, and hid herself
five months, saying,
25 Thus hath the Lord dealt with
me in the days wherein he looked on
me, to take away my reproach among
men.

JOHN.

* Mal. iv. 5, 6.

§ 3. An Angel appears

MATTHEW.	MARK.

§ 4. Mary vis ts

to **Mary.** *Nazareth.*

LUKE.

CHAPTER I. 26–38.

26 And in the sixth month the
angel Gabriel was sent from God unto
a city of Galilee, named Nazareth,
27 To a virgin espoused to a man
whose name was Joseph, of the house
of David;[3] and the virgin's name *was*
Mary.
28 And the angel came in unto her,
and said, Hail, *thou that art* highly
favoured, the Lord *is* with thee:
blessed *art* thou among women.[4]
29 And when she saw *him*, she
was troubled at his saying, and cast
in her mind what manner of salutation this should be.[5]
30 And the angel said unto her,
Fear not, Mary: for thou hast found
favour with God.
31 And behold, thou shalt conceive
in thy womb, and bring forth a son,
and shalt call his name JESUS.
32 He shall be great, and shall be
called the son of the Highest; and
the Lord God shall give unto him
the throne of his father David.
33 And * he shall reign over the
house of Jacob for ever; and of his
kingdom there shall be no end.
34 Then said Mary unto the angel,
How shall this be, seeing I know not
a man?
35 And the angel answered and said
unto her, The Holy Ghost shall come
upon thee, and the power of the Highest shall overshadow thee; therefore
also that holy thing which shall be born
of thee, shall be called the Son of God.
36 And behold, thy cousin Elisabeth, she hath also conceived a son in
her old age; and this is the sixth month
with her who was called barren:
37 For with God nothing shall be
impossible.
38 And Mary said, Behold the
handmaid of the Lord, be it unto me
according to thy word. And the angel
departed from her.

JOHN.

Elisabeth. *Juttah.*

CHAPTER I. 39–56.

39 And Mary arose in those days,
and went into the hill-country with
haste, into a city of Juda,

* Mic. iv. 7.

§ 4. **Mary visits**

MATTHEW.	MARK.

LUKE.

CHAPTER I. 39–56.

40 And entered into the house of
Zacharias, and saluted Elisabeth.
41 And it came to pass, that when
Elisabeth heard the salutation of
Mary, the babe leaped in her womb:[6]
and Elisabeth was filled with the
Holy Ghost.
42 And she spake out with a loud
voice and said, Blessed *art* thou
among women, and blessed *is* the
fruit of thy womb.
43 And whence *is* this to me, that
the mother of my lord should come to
me?
44 For lo, as soon as the voice of
thy salutation sounded in mine ears,
the babe leaped in my womb for joy.
45 And blessed *is* she that believed:
for there shall be a performance of
those things which were told her from
the Lord.
46 And Mary said, My soul doth
magnify the Lord,
47 And my spirit hath rejoiced in
God my Saviour.
48 For he hath regarded the low
estate of his handmaiden: for behold,
from henceforth all generations shall
call me blessed.
49 For he that is mighty hath done
to me great things; and holy *is* his
name.
50 And his mercy *is* on them that
fear him, from generation to generation.
51 He hath shewed strength with
his arm; he hath scattered the proud
in the imagination of their hearts.
52 He hath put down the mighty
from *their* seats, and exalted them of
low degree.
53 He hath filled the hungry with
good things, and the rich he hath sent
empty away.
54 He hath holpen his servant Israel, in remembrance of *his* mercy;
55 As* he spake to our fathers, to
Abraham, and to his seed, for ever.
56 And Mary abode with her about
three months, and returned to her own
house.

JOHN.

* Is. xli. 8, 9 Gen. xxii. 16, seq.

§ 5. **The** birth of

MATTHEW.	MARK.

John the Baptist. *Juttah.*

LUKE.

CHAPTER I. 57–80.

57 Now Elisabeth's full time came that she should be delivered; and she brought forth a son.

58 And her neighbours and her cousins heard how the Lord had shewed great mercy upon her; and they rejoiced with her.

59 And it came to pass, that on the eighth day they came to circumcise the child; and they called him [7] Zacharias, after the name of his father.

60 And his mother answered and said, not *so;* but he shall be called John.

61 And they said unto her, There is none of thy kindred that is called by this name.

62 And they made signs to his father, how he would have him called.

63 And he asked for a writing-table, and wrote, saying, His name is John. And they marvelled all.

64 And his mouth was opened immediately, and his tongue loosed, and he spake, and praised God.

65 And fear came on all that dwelt round about them: [8] and all these sayings were noised abroad throughout all the hill-country of Judea.

66 And all they that heard *them*, laid *them* up in their hearts, saying, What manner of child shall this be! And the hand [9] of the Lord was with him.

67 And his father Zacharias was filled with the Holy Ghost, and prophesied, saying,

68 Blessed *be* the Lord God of Israel; for he hath visited and redeemed his people,

69 And hath raised up a horn of salvation for us, in the house of his servant David:

70 As he spake by the mouth of his holy prophets, which have been since the world began:

71 That we should be saved from our enemies, and from the hand of all that hate us;

72 To perform the mercy *promised* to our fathers, and to remember his holy covenant;

5

JOHN.

§ 5. The birth of

MATTHEW.

§ 6. An Angel appears

CHAPTER I. 18–25.

18 Now the birth of Jesus Christ
was on this wise: When as his mother Mary was espoused to Joseph,
before they came together, she was
found with child of the Holy Ghost.
19 Then Joseph her husband, being
a just *man*, and not willing to make
her a public example, was minded to
put her away privily.
20 But while he thought on these
things, Behold, the angel of the Lord
appeared unto him in a dream, saying,
Joseph, thou son of David, fear not to
take unto thee Mary thy wife; for that
which is conceived in her is of the
Holy Ghost.
21 And she shall bring forth a son,
and thou shalt call his name JESUS:
for he shall save his people from their
sins.
22 Now all this was done, that it

Matt. i. 19. *husband.*] There was commonly an interval of ten or twelve months, between the making of the contract of marriage and the time of its celebration. *Gen.* xxiv. 55; *Judg.* xiv. 8. During this period, though there was no intercourse between the bride and bridegroom, not even so much as an interchange of conversation, yet they were considered and spoken of as husband and wife. If, at the end of this probationary period, the bride-

John the Baptist. *Juttah.*

LUKE.

CHAPTER I. 57–80.

73 The oath which he sware to our
father Abraham,*
74 That he would grant unto us,
that we, being delivered out of the
hand of our enemies,[10] might serve
him without fear,
75 In holiness and righteousness
before him, all the days of our life.[11]
76 And thou, child, shalt be called
the Prophet of the Highest, for thou
shalt go before the face of the Lord to
prepare his ways;
77 To give knowledge of salvation
unto his people, by the remission of
their sins,[12]
78 Through the tender mercy of our
God; whereby the day-spring from on
high hath visited us,[13]
79 To give light to them that sit in
darkness and *in* the shadow of death,
to guide our feet into the way of peace.
80 And the child grew, and waxed
strong in spirit, and was in the deserts
till the day of his shewing unto Israel.

JOHN.

to Joseph. *Nazareth.*

* Gen. xxii. 16, seq.

groom was unwilling to solemnize his engagements by the marriage of the bride, he was bound to give her a bill of divorce, as if she had been his wife. And if she, during the same period, had illicit intercourse with another man, she was liable to punishment, as an adulteress. JAHN's Archæol. § 154.

§ 6. **An Angel appears**

MATTHEW.

CHAPTER I. 18–25.

might be fulfilled which was spoken
of the Lord by the prophet, saying,
23 Behold,* a virgin shall be with
child, and shall bring forth a son, and
they shall call his name Emmanuel,
which being interpreted is, God with
us.
24 Then Joseph, being raised from
sleep, did as the angel of the Lord had
bidden him, and took unto him his
wife:
25 And knew her not till she had
brought forth her first-born son:[10]
and he called his name JESUS.

MARK.

§ 7. **The birth**

§ 8. **An Angel appears**

* Is. vii. 14.

Luke ii. 1. *a decree.*] This decree was issued eleven years before it was carried into effect, the delay having been procured by Herod. This fact reconciles the evangelist with

to Joseph. *Nazareth.*

LUKE.	JOHN.

of Jesus. *Bethlehem.*

CHAPTER II. 1–7.

AND it came [14] to pass in those days,
that there went out a decree from
Cesar Augustus, that all the world
should be taxed.
2 (And this taxing was first made
when Cyrenius was governor of Syria.)
3 And all went to be taxed,[15] every
one into his own city.
4 And Joseph also went up from
Galilee, out of the city of Nazareth,
into Judea, unto the city of David,
which is called Bethlehem, (because he
was of the house and lineage of David,)
5 To be taxed with Mary his espoused [16] wife, being great with child.
6 And so it was, that while they
were there, the days were accomplished that she should be delivered.
7 And she brought forth her first-
born son, and wrapped him in swad-
dling clothes, and laid him in a man-
ger; because there was no room for
them in the inn.

to the Shepherds. *Near Bethlehem.*

CHAPTER II. 8–20.

8 And there were in the same country shepherds abiding in the field, keeping watch over their flock by night.
9 And lo,[17] the angel of the Lord
came upon them, and the glory of the

---

the Roman historians, from whom it appears that Cyrenius was not governor when the decree was issued, though he held that office when the census was taken and the tax assessed. See TOWNSEND, *in loc.*

§ 8. **An Angel appears**

MATTHEW.	MARK.

§ **9. The circumcision of Jesus and**

to the Shepherds. *Near Bethlehem.*

LUKE.	JOHN.
CHAPTER II. 8–20.	
Lord shone round about them; and they were sore afraid.	
10 And the angel said unto them, Fear not: for behold, I bring you good tidings of great joy, which shall be to all people.[18]	
11 For unto you is born this day, in the city of David, a Saviour, which is Christ the Lord.	
12 And this *shall be* a sign unto you; Ye shall find the babe wrapped in swaddling-clothes, lying[19] in a manger.	
13 And suddenly there was with the angel a multitude of the heavenly host praising God, and saying,	
14 Glory to God in the highest, and on earth peace, good will toward men.[20]	
15 And it came to pass, as the angels were gone away from them into heaven, the shepherds said one to another,[21] Let us now go even unto Bethlehem, and see this thing which is come to pass, which the Lord hath made known unto us.	
16 And they came with haste, and found Mary and Joseph, and the babe lying in a manger.	
17 And when they had seen *it*, they made known abroad the saying which was told them concerning this child.	
18 And all they that heard *it*, wondered at those things which were told them by the shepherds.	
19 But Mary kept all these things, and pondered *them* in her heart.	
20 And the shepherds returned, glorifying and praising God for all the things that they had heard and seen, as it was told unto them.	

his presentation in the temple. *Bethlehem. Jerusalem.*

LUKE.	JOHN.
CHAPTER II. 21–38.	
21 And when eight days were accomplished for the circumcising of the child,*[22] his name was called JESUS, which was so named of the angel before he was conceived in the womb.	
22 And when the days of her purification[23] according to the law of Moses were accomplished, they brought him to Jerusalem, to present *him* to the Lord;	

* Gen. xvii. 12; Lev. xii. 3

§ 9. The circumcision of Jesus and

MATTHEW.	MARK.

his presentation in the Temple. *Bethlehem. Jerusalem.*

LUKE.

CHAPTER II. 21–38.

23 (As it is written in the law of the
Lord,* Every male that openeth the
womb shall be called holy to the Lord;)
24 And to offer a sacrifice according
to that which is said in the law of the
Lord,† A pair of turtle-doves, or two
young pigeons.
25 And behold, there was a man in
Jerusalem, whose name *was* Simeon;
and the same man *was* just and devout,
waiting for the consolation of Israel:
and the Holy Ghost was upon him.
26 And it was revealed unto him
by the Holy Ghost, that he should not
see death, before he had seen the
Lord's Christ.
27 And he came by the Spirit into
the temple; and when the parents
brought in the child Jesus,[24] to do
for him after the custom of the law,
28 Then took he him up in his
arms, and blessed God, and said,
29 Lord, now lettest thou thy servant depart in peace, according to thy
word:
30 For mine eyes have seen thy salvation,
31 Which thou hast prepared before the face of all people;
32 A light to lighten the Gentiles,
and the glory of thy people Israel.
33 And Joseph and his mother
marvelled[25] at those things which
were spoken of him.
34 And Simeon blessed them, and
said unto Mary his mother, Behold,
this child is ‡ set for the fall and rising again of many in Israel: and for
a sign which shall be spoken against,
35 (Yea, a sword shall pierce through
thy own soul also;) that the thoughts
of many hearts[26] may be revealed.
36 And there was one Anna, a pro-
phetess, the daughter of Phanuel, of
the tribe of Aser: she was of a great
age, and had lived with a husband
seven years from her virginity.
37 And she *was* a widow of about
fourscore[27] and four years, which departed not from the temple, but served
God with fastings and prayers night
and day.

JOHN.

* Ex. xiii. 2; Numb. viii. 16, 17. † Lev. xii. 6, 8. ‡ Is. viii.

§ 9. The circumcision of Jesus and

MATTHEW.	MARK.

§ 10. The Magi.

CHAPTER II. 1–12.

Now when Jesus was born in Bethlehem of Judea in the days of Herod the king, behold, there came wise men from the East to Jerusalem,

2 Saying, Where is he that is born king of the Jews? for we have seen his star in the east, and are come to worship him.

3 When Herod the King[11] had heard *these things*, he was troubled, and all Jerusalem with him.

4 And when he had gathered all the chief priests and scribes of the people together, he demanded of them where Christ should be born.

5 And they said unto him, in Bethlehem of Judea: for thus it is written by the prophet,

6 And * thou Bethlehem, *in* the land of Juda, art not the least among the princes of Juda: for[12] out of thee shall come a governor, that shall rule my people Israel.

7 Then Herod, when he had privily called the wise men, inquired of them diligently what time the star appeared.

8 And he sent them to Bethlehem, and said Go, and search diligently for the young child; and when ye have found *him*, bring me word again, that I may come and worship him also.

9 When they had heard the king, they departed; and lo, the star, which they saw in the east, went before them, till it came and stood over where the young child was.

10 When they saw the star, they rejoiced with exceeding great joy.

11 And when they were come into the house, they saw the young child with Mary his mother, and fell

* Mic. v. 2.

Matth. ii, 3, *he was troubled.*] According to Josephus, Herod was always in fear for the stability of his throne, and anxious to pry into futurity to discover whether it was

his presentation in the Temple. *Bethlehem. Jerusalem.*

LUKE.	JOHN.
CHAPTER II. 21–38.	
38 And she coming in that instant, gave thanks likewise unto the Lord,[28] and spake of him to all them that looked for redemption in Jerusalem.	

Jerusalem. Bethlehem.

likely to endure. Thus, when advanced to regal power, he sent for Manahem, an Essene, who had predicted of him when a boy that he would be a king, to inquire of him how long he should reign. JOSEPH. Ant. xv. § 5. BLUNT, Veracity, &c. § ii. 2.

§ 10. The Magi.

MATTHEW.

CHAPTER II. 1–12.

down, and worshipped him: and when
they had opened their treasures, they
presented unto him gifts; gold, and
frankincense, and myrrh.
12 And being warned of God in
a dream that they should not return
to Herod, they departed into their
own country another way.

MARK.

§ 11. The flight into Egypt. Herod's

CHAPTER II. 13–23.

13 And when they were departed,
behold, the angel of the Lord appeareth to Joseph in a dream, saying,
Arise, and take the young child and
his mother, and flee into Egypt, and
be thou there until I bring thee word:
for Herod will seek the young child to
destroy him.
14 When he arose, he took the
young child and his mother by night,
and departed into Egypt:
15 And was there until the death
of Herod: that it might be fulfilled
which was spoken of the Lord by the
prophet, saying,* Out of Egypt have
I called my Son.
16 Then Herod, when he saw
that he was mocked of the wise men,
was exceeding wroth, and sent forth,
and slew all the children that were in
Bethlehem, and in all the coasts thereof, from two years old and under, according to the time which he had
diligently inquired of the wise men.
17 Then was fulfilled that which
was spoken by Jeremy the prophet,
saying,
18 In † Rama was there a voice
heard, lamentation, and[13.] weeping,
and great mourning, Rachel weeping
for her children, and would not be
comforted, because they are not.
19 But, when Herod was dead, behold, an angel of the Lord appeareth
in a dream to Joseph in Egypt,
20 Saying, Arise, and take the
young child and his mother, and go
into the land of Israel: for they are
dead which sought the young child's
life.
21 And he arose, and took the young

* Hos. xi. 1

† Jer. xxxi. 15, and xl. 1.

Jerusalem. Bethlehem.

LUKE.	JOHN.

cruelty. The return. *Bethlehem. Nazareth.*

CHAPTER II. 39, 40.	

§ 11. **The flight into Egypt. Herod's**

MATTHEW.	MARK.
CHAPTER II. 13–23.	
child and his mother, and came into 14 the land of Israel. 22 But when he heard that Arche- laus did reign in Judea in the room of his father Herod, he was afraid to go thither: notwithstanding, being warned of God in a dream, he turned aside into the parts of Galilee: 23 And he came and dwelt in a city called Nazareth: that it might be ful- filled which was spoken by the pro- phets, He shall be called a Nazarene.*	

§ 12. **At twelve years of age, Jesus**

* Is. xi. 1, and liii. 2; Zech. vi. 12; Rev. v. 5.

Matth. ii. 22, *he was afraid.*] The naked statement of this fact, without explanation, is a mark of the sincerity of the Evangelist, for the value of which we are indebted to Josephus, who relates, (Ant. b. 17, ch. 9, § 3,) an instance of savage cruelty in Archelaus, immediately on his coming to the throne, in causing three thousand persons to be butchered in cold blood, at the first passover after Herod's death. Such an act, committed under such circumstances, must have been rapidly made known abroad, and inspired al persons with horror. Well, therefore, might Joseph fear to return. But Matthew's incidental allusion to the cause, is characteristic of a man intent only upon the statement of the main facts, and regardless of appearances or explanations. BLUNT, Veracity, &c. § ii. 3.

Luke ii. 42; *twelve years old.*] Jewish children were not obliged to the observances of the ceremonial law, until they attained to years of discretion, which, in males, was fixed by common consent at twelve years. On arriving at this age they were taken to

cruelty. The return. *Bethlehem. Nazareth.*

LUKE.
CHAPTER II. 39, 40.

39 And when they had performed [29]
all things according to the law of the
Lord, they returned into Galilee, to
their own city Nazareth.
40 And the child grew, and waxed
strong in spirit,[30] filled with wisdom;
and the grace of God was upon him.

JOHN.

goes to the Passover. *Jerusalem.*

CHAPTER II. 41-52.
41 Now his parents went to Jerusalem every year [31] at the feast of the
passover.
42 And when he was twelve years
old, they went up [32] to Jerusalem after
the custom of the feast.
43 And when they had fulfilled the
days, as they returned, the child Jesus
tarried behind in Jerusalem; and
Joseph and his mother knew not *of it.*[33]
44 But they, supposing him to have
been in the company, went a day's
journey; and they sought him among
their kinsfolk and acquaintance.[34]
45 And when they found him not,[35]
they turned back again to Jerusalem,
seeking him.
46 And it came to pass, that after
three days they found him in the temple, sitting in the midst of the doctors,
both hearing them, and asking them
questions.
47 And all that heard him were

Jerusalem at the passover, of which they thenceforth participated, as "sons of commandment," being fully initiated into the doctrines and ceremonies of the Jewish Church, probably after examination by the doctors. This accounts for the circumstance of his being found among them, both hearing, and asking them questions. STACKHOUSE, Hist. N. T. ch. i.; BLOOMFIELD, *in loc.*

Luke ii. 44; *in the company.*] All who came, not only from the same city, but from the same canton or district, made one company. They carried necessaries along with them, and tents for their lodgings at night. Such companies they now call *caravans*, and in several places have houses fitted up for their reception, called *caravanseries.* This account of their manner of travelling furnishes a ready answer to the question, How could Joseph and Mary make a day's journey, without discovering, before night, that Jesus was not in the company? In the day-time, we may reasonably presume, the travellers would mingle with different parties of their friends and acquaintance; but in the evening, when they were about to encamp, every one would join the family to which he belonged. CAMPBELL, *in loc.*

§ 12. **At twelve years of age, Jesus**

MATTHEW.	MARK.

§ 13. **The**

CHAPTER I. 1–17.

THE book of the generation of Jesus Christ, the son of David, the son of Abraham.
2 Abraham begat Isaac; and Isaac begat Jacob; and Jacob begat Judas and his brethren;
3 And Judas begat Phares and Zara[2] of Thamar; and Phares begat Esrom; and Esrom begat Aram;
4 And Aram begat Aminadab; and Aminadab begat Naasson; and Naasson begat Salmon;
5 And Salmon begat Booz of Rachab; and Booz begat Obed of Ruth; and Obed begat Jesse;[3]
6 And Jesse begat David the King; and David the King[4] begat Solomon of her *that had been the wife* of Urias;
7 And Solomon begat Roboam; and Roboam begat Abia; and Abia begat Asa;

goes to the **Passover.** *Jerusalem.*

LUKE.

CHAPTER II. 41–52.

astonished [36] at his understanding and
answers.
48 And when they saw him, they
were amazed: and his mother said
unto him, Son, why hast thou thus
dealt with us? Behold, thy father
and I have sought thee [37] sorrowing.
49 And he said unto them, How is
it that ye sought me? [38] wist ye not that
I must be about my Father's business?
50 And they understood not the
saying which he spake unto them.
51 And he went down with them,
and came to Nazareth, and was subject
unto them: but his mother kept all
these sayings [39] in her heart.
52 And Jesus increased in wisdom
and stature, and in favor with God
and man.

JOHN.

Genealogies.

CHAPTER III. 23–38, INVERTED.

38 *The son* of God, *the son* of
Adam, *the son* of Seth, *the son* of
Enos,
37 *The son* of Cainan, *the son* of
Maleleel, *the son* of Jared, *the son* of
Enoch, *the son* of Mathusala,[60]
36 *The son* of Lamech, *the son* of
Noe, *the son* of Sem, *the son* of Ar-
phaxad, *the son* of Cainan,[59]
35 *The son* of Sala, *the son* of
Heber, *the son* of Phalec, *the son* of
Ragau, *the son* of Saruch,[58]
34 *The son* of Nachor, *the son* of
Thara, *the son* of Abraham, *the son* of
Isaac,[57] *the son* of Jacob,

33 *The son* of Juda, *the son* of
Phares, *the son* of Esrom, *the son* of
Aram, *the son* of Aminadab,[56]
32 *The son* of Naasson, *the son* of
Salmon, *the son* of Booz, *the son* of
Obed, *the son* of Jesse,[55]

31 *The son* of David, *the son* of
Nathan, *the son* of Mattatha, *the son*
of Menan, *the son* of Melea,[54]

§ 13. The

MATTHEW.

CHAPTER I. 1–17.

8 And Asa[6] begat Josaphat; and
Josaphat begat Joram; and Joram
begat Ozias;
9 And Ozias begat Joatham; and
Joatham begat Achaz; and Achaz
begat Ezekias;
10 And Ezekias begat Manasses;
and Manasses begat Amon;[7] and
Amon begat Josias;
11 And Josias begat Jechonias and
his brethren, about the time they were
carried away to Babylon:
12 And after they were brought to
Babylon, Jechonias begat Salathiel;[8]
and Salathiel begat Zorobabel;
13 And Zorobabel begat Abiud;
and Abiud begat Eliakim; and Eliakim begat Azor;
14 And Azor begat Sadoc;[9] and
Sadoc begat Achim; and Achim begat Eliud;
15 And Eliud begat Eleazar; and
Eleazar begat Matthan; and Matthan
begat Jacob;

16 And Jacob begat Joseph the
husband of Mary, of whom was born
Jesus, who is called Christ.
17 So all the generations from
Abraham to David *are* fourteen generations; and from David until the
carrying away into Babylon *are* fourteen generations; and from the carrying away in Babylon unto Christ
are fourteen generations.

MARK.

Note.—The Genealogy of Jesus, as given by Luke, is here inverted for the sake of more convenient comparison with that given by Matthew.

The apparent discrepancies in these accounts are reconciled by Dr. Robinson, in the following manner:

"I. In the genealogy given by Matthew, considered by itself, some difficulties present themselves.

"1. There is some diversity among commentators in making out the three divisions

Genealogies.

LUKE. CHAPTER III. 23–38, INVERTED.	JOHN.

30 *The son* of Eliakim, *the son* of
Jonan,[53] *the son* of Joseph, *the son* of
Juda, *the son* of Simeon,
29 *The son* of Levi, *the son* of
Matthat, *the son* of Joram, *the son* of
Eliezer, *the son* of Jose,[52]
28 *The son* of Er, *the son* of Elmodam,
the son of Cosam, *the son* of Addi,
the son of Melchi,[51]
27 *The son* of Neri, *the son* of Salathiel,
the son of Zorobabel, *the son* of
Rhesa, *the son* of Joanna,[50]
26 *The son* of Juda, *the son* of
Joseph, *the son* of Semei, *the son* of
Mattathias, *the son* of Maath,[49]
25 *The son* of Nagge, *the son* of
Esli, *the son* of Naum, *the son* of
Amos, *the son* of Mattathias,
24 *The son* of Joseph, *the son* of
Janna,[48] *the son* of Melchi, *the son* of
Levi, *the son* of Matthat,
23 *The son* of Heli, the son of
Joseph,—And Jesus himself . . . being[47]
(as was supposed)—

---

each of fourteen generations, v. 17. It is, however, obvious, that the first division begins with Abraham and ends with David. But does the second begin with David, or with Solomon? Assuredly with the former; because, just as the first begins *apo Abraham*, so the second also is said to begin *apo David*. The first extends *heos David*, and includes him; the second extends to an epoch and not to a person; and therefore the persons who are mentioned as coeval with this epoch are not reckoned before it. After the epoch the enumeration begins again with Jechoniah, and ends with Jesus. In this way the three divisions are made out thus:—

§ 13. The

1. Abraham.	1. David.	1. Jechoniah.
2. Isaac.	2. Solomon.	2. Salathiel.
3. Jacob.	3. Roboam.	3. Zorobabel.
4. Judah.	4. Abiah.	4. Abiud.
5. Phares.	5. Asa.	5. Eliakim.
6. Esrom.	6. Josaphat.	6. Azor.
7. Aram.	7. Joram.	7. Sadoc.
8. Aminadab.	8. Uzziah (Ozias)	8. Achim.
9. Naasson.	9. Jotham.	9. Eliud.
10. Salmon.	10. Ahaz.	10 Eleazar.
11. Boaz.	11. Hezekiah.	11. Matthan.
12. Obed.	12. Manasseh.	12. Jacob.
13. Jesse.	13. Amon.	13. Joseph.
14. David.	14. Jos iah.	14. Jesus.

"2. Another difficulty arises from the fact, that between Joram and Ozias, in v. 8. three names of Jewish kings are omitted, viz. Ahaziah, Joash, and Amaziah ; see 2 K. 8, 25 and Chr. 22, 1. 2 K. 11, 2. 21 and 2 Chr. 22, 11. 2 K. 12, 21. 14, 1 and 3 Chr. 24, 27. Further, between Josiah and Jechoniah in v. 11, the name of Jehoiakim is also omitted; 2 K. 23, 34, 2 Chr. 36, 4. comp. 1 Chr. 3, 15, 16. If these four names are to be reckoned, then the second division, instead of fourteen generations, will contain eighteen, in contradiction to v. 17. To avoid this difficulty, Newcome and some others have regarded v. 17 as a mere gloss, 'a marginal note taken into the text.' This indeed is in itself possible ; yet all the external testimony of manuscripts and versions is in favor of the genuineness of that verse. It is better therefore to regard these names as having been customarily omitted in the current genealogical tables, from which Matthew copied. Such omissions of particular generations did sometimes actually occur, 'propterea quod malæ essent et impiæ,' according to R. Sal. Jarchi; Lightfoot, Hor. Heb. in Matth. 1, 8. A striking example of an omission of this kind, apparently without any such reason, is found in Ezra 7, 1–5, compared with 1 Chr. 6, 3–15. This latter passage contains the lineal descent of the high-priests from Aaron to the captivity; while Ezra, in the place cited, in tracing back his own genealogy through the very same line of descent, omits at least six generations. A similar omission is necessarily implied in the genealogy of David, as given Ruth 4, 20–22. 1 Chr. 2, 10–12. Matth. 1, 5, 6. Salmon was contemporary with the capture of Jericho by Joshua, and married Rahab. But from that time until David, an interval of at least four hundred and fifty years (Acts 13. 20,) there intervened, according to the list, only four generations, averaging of course more than one hundred years to each. But the highest average in point of fact is *three* generations to a century ; and if reckoned by the eldest sons they are usually shorter, or three generations for every seventy-five or eighty years. See Sir I. Newton's Chronol. p. 53. Lond. 1728.

"We may therefore rest in the necessary conclusion, that as our Lord's regular descent from David was always asserted, and was never denied even by the Jews; so Matthew, in tracing this admitted descent, appealed to genealogical tables, which were public and acknowledged in the family and tribe from which Christ sprang. He could not indeed do otherwise. How much stress was laid by the Jews upon lineage in general, and how much care and attention were bestowed upon such tables, is well known. See Lightfoot, Hor. Heb. in Matth. 1, 1. Comp. Phil. 3, 4, 5.

"II. Other questions of some difficulty present themselves, when we compare together the two genealogies.

"1. Both tables at first view purport to give the lineage of our Lord through Joseph. But Joseph cannot have been the son by natural descent of both Joseph and Heli (Eli), Matth. 1, 16. Luke 3, 23. Only one of the tables therefore can give his true lineage by generation. This is done apparently in that of Matthew because, beginning at Abraham, it proceeds by natural descent, as we know from history, until after the exile; and then continues on in the same mode of expression until Joseph. Here the phrase is changed; and it is no longer Joseph who 'begat' Jesus, but Joseph 'the husband of Mary, of whom was born Jesus who is called the Christ.' See Augustine de Consensu Evangel. II. 5.

"2. To whom then does the genealogy in Luke chiefly relate? If in any way to Joseph, as the language purports, then it must be because he in some way bore the legal relation of son to Heli, either by adoption or by marriage. If the former simply, it is difficult to comprehend why, along with his true personal lineage as traced by Matthew up through the royal line of Jewish kings to David, there should be given also another subordinate genealogy, not personally his own, and running back through different and

Genealogies.

inferior line to the same great ancestor. If, on the other hand, as is most probable, this relation to Heli came by marriage with his daughter, so that Joseph was truly his *son-in-law* (comp. Ruth 1, 8. 11. 12); then it follows, that the genealogy in Luke is in fact that of Mary the mother of Jesus. This being so, we can perceive a sufficient reason why this genealogy should be thus given, viz. in order to show definitely, that Jesus was in the most full and perfect sense a descendant of David: not only by law in the royal line of kings, through his reputed father, but also in fact by direct personal descent through his mother.

"That Mary, like Joseph, was a descendant of David, is not indeed elsewhere expressly said in the New Testament. Yet a very strong presumption to that effect is to be drawn from the address of the angel in Luke 1, 32; as also from the language of Luke 2, 5, where Joseph, as one of the posterity of David, is said to have gone up to Bethlehem, to *enroll himself with Mary his espoused wife*. The ground and circumstances of Mary's enrollment must obviously have been the same as in the case of Joseph himself. Whether all this arose from her having been an only child and heiress, as some suppose, so that she was espoused to Joseph in accordance with Num. 36, 8, 9, it is not necessary here to inquire. See Michaelis 'Commentaries on the Laws of Moses,' Part II. § 78.

"It is indeed objected, that it was not customary among the Jews to trace back descent through the female line, that is, on the mother's side. There are, however, examples to show that this was sometimes done; and in the case of Jesus, as we have seen, there was a sufficient reason for it. Thus in 1 Chr. 2, 22, Jair is enumerated among the posterity of Judah by regular descent. But the grandfather of Jair had married the daughter of Machir, one of the heads of Manasseh, 1 Chr. 2, 21. 7, 14; and therefore in Num. 32, 40, 41, Jair is called the son (descendant) of Manasseh. In like manner, in Ezra, 2, 61, and Neh 7, 63, a certain family is spoken of as 'the children of Barzillai;' because their ancestor 'took a wife of the daughters of Barzillai the Gileadite, and was called after their name.'

"3. A question is raised as to the identity, in the two genealogies, of the Salathiel and Zorobabel named as father and son, Matt. 1. 12. Luke 3, 27. The Zorobabel of Matthew is no doubt the chief, who led back the first band of captives from Babylon, and rebuilt the temple, Ezra c. 2–6. He is also called the son of Salathiel in Ezra 3, 2. Neh. 12, 1. Hagg. 1, 1. 2, 2. 23. Were then the Salathiel and Zorobabel of Luke the same persons? Those who assume this, must rest solely on the identity of the names; for there is no other possible evidence to prove, either that they were contemporary, or that they were not different persons. On the other hand, there are one or two considerations, of some force, which go to show that they were probably not the same persons.

"First, if Salathiel and Zorobabel are indeed the same in both genealogies, then Salathiel, who according to Matthew, was the son of Jechoniah by natural descent, must have been called the son of Neri in Luke either from adoption or marriage. In that case, his connection with David through Nathan, as given by Luke, was not his own personal genealogy. It is difficult, therefore, to see, why Luke, after tracing back the descent of Jesus to Salathiel, should abandon the true personal lineage in the royal line of kings, and turn aside again to a merely collateral and humbler line. If the mother of Jesus was in fact descended from the Zorobabel and Salathiel of Matthew, she, like them, was descended also from David through the royal line. Why rob her of this dignity, and ascribe to her only a descent through an inferior lineage? See Spanheim Dubia Evangel. I. p. 108, sq.

"Again, the mere identity of names under these circumstances, affords no proof; for nothing is more common even among contemporaries. Thus we have two Ezras; one in Neh. 12, 1. 13, 33; from who Ezra the scribe is expressly distinguished in v. 36. We have likewise two Nehemiahs: one who went up with Zorobabel, Ezra 2, 2; and the other the governor who went later to Jerusalem, Neh. 2, 9, sq. So too, as contemporaries, Joram son of Ahab, king of Israel, and Joram (Jehoram,) son of Jehoshaphat, king of Judah; 2 K. 8, 16, coll. v. 23, 24. Also Joash king of Judah, and Joash king of Israel; 2 K. 13, 9, 10. Further, we find in succession among the descendants of Cain the following names: Enoch, Irad, Mehujael, Methusael, Lamech, Gen. 4, 17, 18; and later among the descendants of Seth these similar ones: Enoch, Methusalah, Lamech, Gen. 5, 21–25. See Dr. Robinson's Greek Harmony of the Gospels, pp. 183–187.

PART II.

ANNOUNCEMENT AND INTRODUCTION

OF

OUR LORD'S PUBLIC MINISTRY.

TIME. *About one year.*

§ **14. The Ministry of**

MATTHEW.
CHAPTER III. 1–12.

IN those days came John the Baptist, preaching in the wilderness of Judea.

2 And [15] saying, Repent ye; for the kingdom of heaven is at hand.

3 For this is he that was spoken of by the prophet Esaias, saying, The voice of one crying in the wilderness, Prepare ye the way of the Lord, make his paths straight.

4 And the same John had his raiment of camel's hair, and a leathern girdle about his loins; and his meat was locusts and wild honey.

5 Then went out to him Jerusalem, and all Judea, and all the region round about Jordan,

6 And were baptized of him [16] in Jordan, confessing their sins.

7 But when he saw many of the Pharisees and Sadducees come to his baptism,[17] he said unto them, O generation of vipers, who hath warned you to flee from the wrath to come?

8 Bring forth therefore fruits [18] meet for repentance:

9 And think not to say within yourselves, We have Abraham to *our* father: for I say unto you, that God is able of these stones to raise up children unto Abraham.

10 And now also [19] the axe is laid unto the root of the trees: therefore every tree which bringeth not forth good fruit is hewn down, and cast into the fire.

MARK.
CHAPTER I. 1–8.

THE beginning of the gospel of Jesus Christ the Son of God;[2]

2 As it is written in the prophets,* Behold, I send my messenger before thy face, which shall prepare thy way before thee;[3]

3 The voice of one crying in the wilderness, Prepare ye the way of the Lord, make his paths straight.

4 John did baptize in the wilderness, and preach the baptism of repentance, for the remission of sins.[4]

5 And there went out unto him all the land of Judea, and they of Jerusalem, and were all baptized [5] of him in the river of Jordan, confessing their sins.

6 And John was clothed with camel's hair, and with a girdle of a skin about his loins; and he did eat locusts and wild honey;

* Mal. iii. 1; Is. xl. 3.

Luke iii. 2, *high priests.*] In the New Testament, the same word is used for *the high priests*, and *the chief priests*, who were the heads of the twenty-four courses. So that the two persons whom the Roman governor considered as the chief of the priests, and whose names stood as such in those public registers which seem here referred to,

John the Baptist. *The desert.* *The Jordan.*

LUKE.

CHAPTER III. 1–18.

Now in the fifteenth year of the reign of Tiberius Cesar, Pontius Pilate being governor of Judea, and Herod being tetrarch of Galilee, and his brother Philip tetrarch of Iturea and of the region of Trachonitis, and Lysanias the tetrarch of Abilene,

2 Annas and Caiaphas being the high priests, the word of God came unto John the son of Zacharias in the wilderness.

3 And he came into all the country about Jordan, preaching the baptism of repentance, for the remission of sins;

4 As it is written in the book of the words of Esaias the prophet, saying,* [40] The voice of one crying in the wilderness, Prepare ye the way of the Lord, make his paths straight.

5 Every valley shall be filled, and every mountain and hill shall be brought low; and the crooked shall be made straight, and the rough ways *shall be* made smooth;

6 And all flesh shall see the salvation of God.

7 Then said he to the multitude that came forth to be baptized of him, O generation of vipers, who hath warned you to flee from the wrath to come?

8 Bring forth therefore fruits worthy of repentance, and begin not to say within yourselves, We have Abraham to *our* father: for I say unto you, That God is able of these stones to raise up children unto Abraham.

9 And now also the axe is laid unto the root of the trees: every tree therefore which bringeth not forth good fruit, is hewn down, and cast into the fire.

10 And the people asked him, saying, What shall we do then?

JOHN.

* Is xl. 3, seq.

---

may be intended. An irregularity had arisen out of the confusion of the times: and the ruler or prince under the Romans, though a *chief* priest, was a distinct person from the *high* priest: Annas being the one, and Caiaphas the other. SCOTT, *in loc.* See also CAMPBELL, *in loc.*

§ 14. The Ministry of

MATTHEW.
CHAPTER III. 1–12.

11 I indeed[20] baptize you with water unto repentance: but he that cometh after me is mightier than I, whose shoes I am not worthy to bear: he shall baptize you with the Holy Ghost, and *with* fire:

12 Whose fan *is* in his hand, and he will thoroughly purge his floor, and gather his wheat into the garner; but he will burn up the chaff with unquenchable fire.

MARK.
CHAPTER I. 1–8.

7 And preached, saying, There cometh one mightier than I after me, the latchet of whose shoes I am not worthy to stoop down and unloose.

8 I indeed have baptized you with water: but he shall baptize[6] you with the Holy Ghost.

§ 15. The Baptism

CHAPTER III. 13–17.

13 Then cometh Jesus from Galilee to Jordan unto John, to be baptized of him.

14 But John[21] forbade him, saying, I have need to be baptized of thee, and comest thou to me?

15 And Jesus answering said unto him, Suffer *it to be so* now: for thus it becometh us to fulfill all righteousness. Then he suffered him.

16 And Jesus, when he was baptized, went up straightway out of the water: and lo, the heavens were opened unto him,[22] and he saw the Spirit of God descending like a dove, and[23] lighting upon him:

CHAPTER I. 9–11.

9 And it came to pass in those days, that Jesus came from Nazareth of Galilee, and was baptized of John in Jordan.[7]

10 And straightway coming up out of the water, he saw the heavens opened, and the Spirit like a dove descending upon him.[8]

11 And there came[9] a voice from heaven *saying*, Thou art my be-

John the Baptist. *The Desert.* *The Jordan.*

LUKE.

CHAPTER III. 1–18.

11 He answereth and saith[41] unto
them, He that hath two coats, let
him impart to him that hath none;
and he that hath meat, let him do
likewise.
12 Then came also publicans to be
baptized, and said unto him, Master,
what shall we do?
13 And he said unto them, Exact
no more[42] than that which is appointed you.
14 And the soldiers likewise demanded of him, saying, And what
shall we do? And he said unto them,
Do violence to no man, neither accuse *any* falsely;[43] and be content
with your wages.
15 And as the people were in expectation, and all men mused in their
hearts of John, whether he were the
Christ, or not;
16 John answered, saying unto *them*
all, I indeed baptize you with water;
but one mightier than I cometh, the
latchet of whose shoes I am not worthy to unloose: he shall baptize you
with the Holy Ghost, and with fire:
17 Whose fan *is* in his hand, and
he will thoroughly purge his floor,
and will gather the wheat into his
garner;[44] but the chaff he will burn
with fire unqenchable.
18 And many other things in his
exhortation preached he unto the
people.

JOHN.

of Jesus. *The Jordan.*

CHAPTER III. 21–23.

21 Now, when all the people were
baptized, it came to pass, that Jesus
also being baptized,

and praying, the
heaven was opened,
22 And the Holy Ghost descended
in a bodily shape like a dove upon him,

§ 15. The Baptism

MATTHEW. CHAPTER III. 13–17.	MARK. CHAPTER I. 9–11.
17 And lo, a voice from heaven, saying, This is my beloved Son, in whom I am well pleased.	loved Son, in whom I am well pleased.

§ 16. The Temptation.

CHAPTER IV. 1–11.	CHAPTER I. 12–13.
THEN was Jesus led up of the Spirit into the wilderness[24] to be tempted of the devil. 2 And when he had fasted forty days and forty nights, he was afterwards an hungered. 3 And when the tempter came to him,[25] he said, If thou be the Son of God, command that these stones be made bread. 4 But he answered and said, It is written * man shall not live by bread alone, but by every word that proceedeth out of the mouth of God. 5 Then the devil taketh him up into the holy city, and setteth him on a pinnacle of the temple, 6 And saith unto him, If thou be the Son of God cast thyself down, for it is written † He shall give his angels charge concerning thee: and in *their* hands they shall bear thee up, lest at any time thou dash thy foot against a stone. 7 Jesus said unto him, It is written again,‡ Thou shalt not tempt the Lord thy God. 8 Again, the devil taketh him up into an exceeding high mountain and sheweth him all the kingdoms of the world, and the glory of them: 9 And saith unto him, All these things will I give thee, if thou wilt fall down and worship me. 10 Then saith Jesus unto him, Get thee hence, Satan: for it is written, §	12 And immediately the Spirit driveth him into the wilderness. 13 And he was there in the wilderness forty days tempted of Satan; and was with the wild beasts; and the angels ministered unto him.

* Deut. viii. 3. † Deut. vi. 16. ‡ Ps. xci. 11. § Deut. vi. 13.

Note.]—There is a seeming discrepancy between Matthew and Luke, in the order of the

of Jesus. *The Jordan.*

LUKE.	JOHN.
CHAPTER III. 21–23. and a voice came from heaven, which said,[46] Thou art my beloved Son; in thee I am well pleased. 23 And Jesus himself began to be about thirty years of age,[47]	

Desert of Judea.

CHAPTER IV. 1–13.

AND Jesus, being full of the Holy Ghost, returned from Jordan, and was led by the Spirit into the wilderness,

2 Being forty days tempted of the devil. And in those days he did eat nothing: and when they were ended, he afterward[61] hungered.

3 And[62] the devil said unto him, If thou be the Son of God, command this stone that it be made bread.

4 And Jesus answered him, saying,[63] It is written, That man shall not live by bread alone, but by every word of God.

9 And[68] he brought him to Jerusalem, and set him on a pinnacle of the temple, and said unto him, If thou be the Son of God, cast thyself down from hence:

10 For[69] it is written, He shall give his angels charge over thee, to keep thee:

11 And in *their* hands they shall bear thee up, lest at any time thou dash thy foot against a stone.

12 And Jesus answering, said unto him, It is said, Thou shalt not tempt the Lord thy God.

5 And the devil, taking him[64] up into a high mountain, shewed unto him, all the kingdoms of the world in a moment of time.

6 And the devil said unto him, All this power will I give thee, and the glory of them: for that is delivered unto me, and to whomsoever I will, I give it.[65]

7 If thou therefore wilt worship me, all[66] shall be thine.

8 And Jesus answered and said

---

temptations; but Luke does not affirm the order; whereas Matthew uses particles, in v. 2 and 8, which seem to fix it as he has written. NEWCOME.

§ 16. The Temptation.

MATTHEW.	MARK.
CHAPTER IV. 1–11. Thou shalt worship the Lord thy God, and him only shalt thou serve. 11 Then the devil leaveth him, and behold, angels came and ministered unto him.	

§ 17. Preface to

Desert of Judea.

LUKE.

CHAPTER IV. 1–13.

unto him, Get thee behind me, Satan:[67] for it is written, Thou shalt worship the Lord thy God, and him only shalt thou serve.

13 And when the devil had ended all the temptation, he departed from him for a season.

JOHN.

John's Gospel.

CHAPTER I. 1–18.

IN the beginning was the Word, and the Word was with God, and the Word was God.

2 The same was in the beginning with God.

3 All things were made by him; and without him was not anything made that was made.

4 In him was[2] life; and the life was the light of men.

5 And the light shineth in darkness; and the darkness comprehended it not.

6 There was a man sent from God, whose name *was* John.

7 The same came for a witness, to bear witness of the Light, that all *men* through him might believe.

8 He was not that Light, but *was sent* to bear witness of that Light.

9 *That* was the true Light, which lighteth every man that cometh into the world.

10 He was in the world, and the world was made by[3] him, and the world knew him not.

11 He came unto his own, and his own received him not.

12 But as many as received him, to them gave he power to become the sons of God, *even* to them that believe on his name:

13 Which were born,[4] not of blood, nor of the will of the flesh, nor of the will of man, but of God.

14 And the Word was made flesh, and dwelt among us, (and we beheld his glory, the glory as of the only begotten of the Father,) full of grace and truth.

15 John bear witness of him, and cried, saying,[5] This was he of whom I spake, He that cometh after me, is

§ 17. Preface to

MATTHEW.	MARK.

§ 18. Testimony of John the Baptist

John i. 21.] John means that he was not really Elias risen from the dead. But when Jesus says, (Matth. xvii. 12, and xi. 14,) that Elias was come already, he means that John had appeared *in the spirit and power of Elias.* Luke i. 17. Thus likewise, John here denies

John's Gospel.

LUKE.	JOHN.
	CHAPTER I. 1–18.
	preferred before me; for he was before me.
	16 And[6] of his fulness have all we received, and grace for grace.
	17 For the law was given by Moses, *but* grace and truth came by Jesus Christ.[7]
	18 No man hath seen God at any time; the only begotten Son,[8] which is in the bosom of the Father, he hath declared *him*.

to Jesus. *Bethany beyond Jordan.*

LUKE.	JOHN.
	CHAPTER I. 19–34.
	19 And this is the record of John, when the Jews sent priests and Levites from Jerusalem,[9] to ask him, Who art thou ?
	20 And he confessed, and denied not; but confessed,[10] I am not the Christ.
	21 And they asked him, What then ? Art thou Elias ?[11] And he saith, I am not. Art thou that prophet ? And he answered, No.
	22 Then said they unto him, Who art thou ? that we may give an answer to them that sent us. What sayest thou of thyself ?
	23 He said,* I *am* the voice of one crying in the wilderness, Make straight the way of the Lord, as said the prophet Esaias.
	24 And they which[12] were sent were of the Pharisees.
	25 And they asked him, and[13] said unto him, Why baptizest thou then, if thou be not that Christ, nor Elias, neither that prophet ?
	26 John answered them, saying, I baptize with water: but there standeth one among you, whom ye know not.
	27 He it is,[14] who coming after me, is preferred before me, whose shoe's latchet I am not worthy to unloose.

* Is. xl. 3.

---

that he is one of the ancient prophets again appearing on earth : see Luke ix. 19; with which our Lord's assertion that he was an eminent prophet, Luke vii. 28, seems perfectly consistent. NEWCOME.

§ 18. Testimony of John the Baptist

MATTHEW.	MARK.

§ 19. Jesus gains

to Jesus. *Bethany beyond Jordan.*

LUKE.

JOHN.

CHAPTER I. 19–34.

28 These things were done in Bethabara,[15] beyond Jordan, where John was baptizing.

29 The next day John [16] seeth Jesus coming unto him, and saith, Behold the Lamb of God, which taketh away the sin of the world!

30 This is he of whom I said, After me cometh a man which is preferred before me; for he was before me.

31 And I know him not: but that he should be made manifest to Israel, therefore am I come baptizing with water.

32 And John bear record, saying,[17] I saw the Spirit descending from heaven like a dove, and it abode upon him.

33 And I knew him not: but he that sent me to baptize with water, the same said unto me, Upon whom thou shalt see the Spirit descending and remaining on him, the same is he which baptizeth with the Holy Ghost.

34 And I saw and bare record, that this is [18] the Son of God.

disciples. *The Jordan. Galilee.*

CHAPTER I. 35–51.

35 Again the next day after, John stood, and two of his disciples;

36 And looking upon Jesus as he walked, he saith, Behold the Lamb of God!

37 And [19] the two disciples heard him speak, and they followed Jesus.

38 Then Jesus turned, and saw them following, and saith unto them,[20] What seek ye? They said unto him, Rabbi, (which is to say, being interpreted, Master,) where dwellest thou?

39 He said unto them, Come and see.[21] They came and saw where he dwelt, and abode with him that day: for it was about the tenth hour.

40 [22] One of the two which heard John *speak*, and followed him, was Andrew, Simon Peter's brother.

41 He first findeth his own brother Simon, and saith unto him, We have found the Messias; which is, being interpreted, the [23] Christ.

§ 19. **Jesus gains**

MATTHEW.	MARK.

John i. 42.] Kings and princes very often changed the name of those who held offices under them, particularly when they first attracted their notice and were taken into their employ; and when subsequently they were elevated to some new station, and crowned with additional honours. Gen. xli. 45; and xvii. 5; and xxxii, 28; and xxxv. 10; 2 Kin. xxiii. 34, 35; and xxiv. 17; Dan. i. 6. Hence a name (*a new name*) occurs tropically, as a token of honour, in Phil. ii. 9; Heb. i. 4; Rev. ii. 17. See also Mark iii. 17. JAHN'S Archæol. § 164.

disciples. *The Jordan. Galilee.*

LUKE.

JOHN.

CHAPTER I. 35–51.

42 And [24] he brought him to Jesus.
And when Jesus beheld him, he said,
Thou art Simon the son of Jona: thou
shalt be called Cephas; which is, by
interpretation, a stone.
43 The day following Jesus [25]
would go forth into Galilee, and findeth Philip, and saith unto him, Follow me.
44 Now [26] Philip was of Bethsaida,
the city of Andrew and Peter.
45 Philip findeth Nathanael, and
saith unto him, We have found him
of whom Moses in the law, and the
prophets, did write, Jesus of Nazareth the son of Joseph.
46 And [27] Nathanael said unto him,
Can there any good thing come out
of Nazareth? Philip saith unto him,
Come and see.
47 Jesus saw Nathanael coming to
him, and saith of him, [28] Behold an
Israelite indeed, in whom is no
guile!
48 Nathanael saith unto him,
Whence knowest thou me? Jesus
answered and said unto him, Before that Philip called thee, when
thou wast under the fig-tree, I saw
thee.
49 Nathanael answered and saith
unto him, Rabbi, [29] thou art the Son
of God; thou art the King of Israel.
50 Jesus answered and said unto
him, Because I said unto thee, I saw
thee under the fig-tree, believest thou?
thou shalt see greater things than
these.
51 And he said unto him, Verily,
verily, I say unto you, Hereafter [30]
ye shall see heaven open, and the
angels of God ascending and descending upon the * Son of man.

* Gen. xxviii 12.

John i. 45, *Nathanael.*] This apostle is supposed to be the same with *Bartholomew*, of whom John says nothing; and the others make no mention of *Nathanael*. This seems to have been his proper name; since the name of *Bartholomew* is not a proper name, but only signifies *the son of Ptolomy*. *Nathanael* is also ranked among the Apostles to whom Jesus showed himself. *John* xxi. 2–4. A. CLARKE, *in loc.*

§ 20. The Marriage

MATTHEW.	MARK.

at Cana of Galilee.

LUKE.

JOHN.

CHAPTER II. 1–12.

AND the third day there was a marriage in Cana of Galilee; and the
mother of Jesus was there.
2 And both Jesus was called, and
his disciples, to the marriage.
3 And when they wanted wine,
the mother of Jesus saith unto him,
They have no wine.[31]
4 Jesus saith unto her,[32] Woman,
what have I to do with thee? mine
hour is not yet come.
5 His mother saith unto the servants, Whatsoever he saith unto you,
do *it*.
6 And there were set[33] there six
water-pots of stone, after the manner
of the purifying of the Jews, containing two or three firkins a piece.
7 [34] Jesus saith unto them, Fill the
water-pots with water. And they
filled them up to the brim.
8 And he saith unto them, Draw
out now, and bear unto the governor
of the feast. And they bare *it*.
9 When the ruler of the feast had
tasted the water that was made wine,
and knew not whence it was, (but
the servants which drew the water
knew,) the governor of the feast
called the bridegroom,
10 And saith unto him,[35] Every
man at the beginning doth set forth
good wine; and when men have well
drunk, then that which is worse; *but*
thou hast kept the good wine until
now.
11 This beginning of miracles did
Jesus in Cana of Galilee, and manifested forth his[36] glory; and his disciples believed on him.
12 After this he went down to
Capernaum,[37] he, and his mother, and
his brethren, and his disciples; and
they continued there not many days.

PART III.

OUR LORD'S FIRST PASSOVER,

AND THE

SUBSEQUENT TRANSACTIONS

UNTIL THE SECOND.

TIME. *One year.*

§ 21. At the Passover Jesus drives

MATTHEW.	MARK.

§ 22. Our Lord's discourse

the traders out of the Temple. *Jerusalem.*

LUKE.	JOHN.
	CHAPTER II. 13–25.
	13 And the Jews' passover was at hand, and Jesus went up to Jerusalem.
	14 And found in the temple those that sold oxen, and sheep, and doves,[38] and the changers of money, sitting:
	15 And when he had made a scourge of small cords, he drove them [39] all out of the temple, and the sheep, and the oxen; and poured out the changers' money, and overthrew the tables;
	16 And said unto them that sold doves, Take these things hence: make not [40] my Father's house an house of merchandise.
	17 [41] And his disciples remembered that it was written,* The zeal of thine house hath eaten me up.
	18 Then answered the Jews, and said unto him, What sign shewest thou unto us, seeing that thou doest these things?
	19 Jesus answered and said unto them, Destroy this temple, and in three days I will raise it up.
	20 Then said the Jews, Forty and six years was this temple in building, and wilt thou rear it up in three days?
	21 But he spake of the temple of his [42] body.
	22 When therefore he was risen from the dead, his disciples remembered that he had said this unto them:[43] and they believed the scripture, and the word which Jesus had said.
	23 Now, when he was in Jerusalem at the passover, in the feast-*day*, many believed in his name, when they saw the miracles which he did.
	24 But Jesus did not commit himself unto them, because he knew all *men*.
	25 And needed not that any should testify of man: for he knew what was in man.

with Nicodemus. *Jerusalem.*

	CHAPTER III. 1–21.
	THERE was a man of the Pharisees named Nicodemus, a ruler of the Jews:
	2 The same came to Jesus [44] by night,

* Ps. lxix. 9.

§ 22. Our Lord's discourse

MATTHEW.	MARK.

with Nicodemus. *Jerusalem.*

LUKE.

JOHN.

CHAPTER III. 1–21.

and said unto him, Rabbi, we know
that thou art a teacher come from
God: for no man can do these miracles that thou doest, except God be
with him.
3 Jesus answered and said unto
him,[45] Verily, verily, I say unto thee,
Except a man be born again, he cannot see the kingdom of God.
4 Nicodemus saith unto him, How
can a man be born when he is old?
can he enter a second time into his
mother's womb, and be born?
5 Jesus answered, Verily, verily, I
say unto thee, Except a man be born
of water, and *of* the Spirit, he cannot
enter into the kingdom of God.[46]
6 That which is born of the flesh,
is flesh; and that which is born of
the Spirit, is spirit.
7 Marvel not that I said unto thee,
Ye must be born again.
8 The wind bloweth where it list-
eth, and thou hearest the sound thereof, but canst not tell whence it cometh, and whither it goeth: so is every
one that is born of the Spirit.[47]
9 Nicodemus answered and said
unto him, How can these things be?
10 Jesus answered and said unto
him, Art thou a[48] master of Israel,
and knowest not these things?
11 Verily, verily, I say unto thee,
We speak that we do know, and testify that we have seen; and ye receive not our witness.
12 If I have told you earthly things,
and ye believe not, how shall ye believe if I tell you *of* heavenly things?
13 And no man hath ascended up
to heaven, but he that came down
from heaven, *even* the Son of man
which is in heaven.[49]
14 And as* Moses lifted up the
serpent in the wilderness, even so
must the Son of man be lifted up:
15 That whosoever believeth in
him should not perish, but have
eternal life.[50]
16 For God so loved the world, that
he gave his only begotten Son,[51] that

* Numb. xxi. 8, seq.

§ 22. Our Lord's discourse

MATTHEW.	MARK.

§ 23. Jesus remains in Judea and baptizes.

with Nicodemus. *Jerusalem.*

LUKE.

JOHN.

CHAPTER III. 1-21.

whosoever believeth in him, should not perish, but have everlasting life.
17 For God sent not his Son [52] into the world to condemn the world, but that the world through him might be saved.
18 He that believeth on him, is not condemned: but [53] he that believeth not, is condemned already, because he hath not believed in the name of the only begotten son of God.
19 And this is the condemnation, that light is come into the world, and men loved darkness rather than light, because their deeds were evil.
20 For every one that doeth evil hateth the light, neither cometh to the light, lest his deeds should be reproved.
21 But he that doeth truth, cometh to the light, that his deeds may be made manifest, that they are wrought in God.

Further testimony of John the Baptist.

CHAPTER III. 22-36.

22 After these things came Jesus and his disciples into the land of Judea; and there he tarried with them, and baptized.
23 And John also was baptizing in Ænon, near to Salim, because there was much water there: and they came, and were baptized.
24 For John was not yet cast into prison.
25 Then there arose a question between *some* of John's disciples and the Jews, [54] about purifying.
26 And they came unto John and said unto him, Rabbi, he that was with thee beyond Jordan, to whom thou bearest witness, behold, the same baptizeth, and all *men* come to him.
27 John answered and said, A man can receive nothing, except it be given him from heaven.
28 Ye yourselves bear me [55] witness, that I said, I am not the Christ, but that I am sent before him.
29 He that hath the bride is the bridegroom: but the friend of the bridegroom, which standeth and hear-

§ 23. Jesus remains in Judea and baptizes.

MATTHEW.	MARK.

§ 24. Jesus departs into Galilee

CHAPTER IV. 12.

12 Now, when Jesus had heard [27] that John was cast into prison, he departed into Galilee.

CHAPTER XIV. 3–5.

3 For Herod had [192] laid hold on John, and bound him, and put *him* in prison for Herodias' sake, his brother Philip's wife.

4 For John said unto him, [193] It is not lawful for thee to have her.

5 And when he would have put him to death, he feared the multitude, because they counted him as a prophet.

CHAPTER I. 14.

14 Now, after that John was put in prison, Jesus came into Galilee.

CHAPTER VI. 17–20.

17 For Herod himself had sent forth and laid hold upon John, and bound him in prison for Herodias' sake,[134] his brother Philip's wife: for he had married her.

18 For John had said unto Herod, It is not lawful for thee to have thy brother's wife.

19 Therefore Herodias had a quarrel against him, and would have killed him; but she could not:

20 For Herod feared John, knowing that he was a just man and an holy, and observed him:[135] and when he heard him, he did many things, and heard him gladly.

Further testimony of John the Baptist.

LUKE.

JOHN.

CHAPTER III. 22–36.

eth him, rejoiceth greatly, because of the bridegroom's voice: this my joy therefore is fulfilled.

30 He must increase, but I *must* decrease.

31 He that cometh from above, is above all: He that is of the earth [56] is earthly, and speaketh of the earth: he that cometh from heaven is above all.

32 And what he hath seen, and heard, that he testifieth; and no man receiveth his testimony.[57]

33 He that hath received his testimony, hath set to his seal that God is true.

34 For he whom God hath sent, speaketh the words of God: for God giveth not [58] the Spirit by measure *unto him.*

35 The Father loveth the Son, and hath given all things into his hand.

36 He that believeth on the Son hath everlasting life: and [59] he that believeth not the Son, shall not see life; but the wrath of God abideth on him.

after John's imprisonment.

LUKE.

CHAPTER IV. 14.

14 And Jesus returned in the power of the Spirit into Galilee:

CHAPTER III. 19–20.

19 But Herod the tetrarch, being reproved by him for Herodias his brother Philip's wife, [45] and for all the evils which Herod had done,

20 Added yet this above all, that he shut up John in prison.

JOHN.

CHAPTER IV. 1–3.

WHEN therefore the Lord [60] knew how the Pharisees had heard that Jesus made and baptized more disciples than John,

2 (Though Jesus himself baptized not, but his disciples,)

3 He left Judea, and departed again [61] into Galilee.

§ 25. Our Lord's discourse with the Samaritan woman.

MATTHEW.	MARK.

Many Samaritans believe on him. *Shechem* or *Neapolis.*

LUKE.

JOHN.

CHAPTER IV. 4–42.

4 And he must needs go through Samaria.

5 Then cometh he to a city of Samaria, which is called Sychar, near to the parcel of ground that Jacob gave to his son Joseph.

6 Now Jacob's well was there. Jesus therefore being wearied with *his* journey, sat thus on the well:[62] *and* it was about the sixth hour.

7 There cometh a woman of Samaria[63] to draw water; Jesus saith unto her, Give me to drink.

8 (For his disciples were gone away unto the city to buy meat.)

9 Then saith the woman of Samaria unto him, How is it that thou, being a Jew, askest drink of me, which am a woman of Samaria? for the Jews have no dealings with the Samaritans.[64]

10 Jesus answered and said unto her, If thou knewest the gift of God, and who it is that saith to thee, Give me to drink; thou wouldest have asked of him, and he would have given thee living water.

11 The woman saith unto him, Sir, thou hast nothing to draw with, and the well is deep: from whence then hast thou that living water?[65]

12 Art thou greater than our father Jacob, which gave us the well, and drank thereof himself,[66] and his children and his cattle?

13 Jesus answered and said unto her, Whosoever drinketh of this water, shall thirst again:

14 But whosoever drinketh of the water that I shall give him, shall never thirst; but the water that I shall give him,[67] shall be in him a well of water springing up into everlasting life.

15 The woman saith unto him, Sir, give me this water, that I thirst not, neither come hither to draw.

16 Jesus saith unto her, [68] Go call thy husband, and come hither.

17 The woman answered and said,[69] I have no husband. Jesus said unto her, Thou hast well said, I have no husband:

18 For thou hast had five hus-

§ 25. Our Lord's discourse with the Samaritan woman.

MATTHEW.	MARK.

Many Samaritans believe on him. *Shechem* or *Neapolis.*

LUKE.

JOHN.

CHAPTER IV. 4–42.

bands, and he whom thou now hast,
is not thy husband: in that saidst
thou truly.
19 The woman saith unto him, Sir,[70]
I perceive that thou art a prophet.
20 Our fathers worshipped in this
mountain; and ye say, that in Jerusalem is the place where [71] men ought
to worship.
21 Jesus saith unto her, Woman,
believe me, the hour cometh, when ye
shall neither in this mountain, nor yet
at Jerusalem, worship the Father.[72]
22 Ye worship ye know not what:
we know what we worship, for salvation is of the Jews.
23 But the hour cometh, and now
is, when the true worshippers shall
worship the Father in spirit and in
truth: for the Father seeketh such
to worship him.
24 God *is* a Spirit: and they that
worship him, must worship *him* [73] in
spirit and in truth.
25 The woman saith unto him, I
know that Messias cometh, which is
called Christ; when he is come, he
will tell us [74] all things.
26 Jesus saith unto her, I that
speak unto thee am *he.*
27 And upon this came his disciples, and marvelled that he talked [75]
with the woman: yet no man said,
What seekest thou? or, Why talkest
thou with her?
28 The woman then left her water-
pot, and went her way into the city,
and saith to the men,
29 Come, see a man which told me
all things that ever I did: is not this
the Christ?
30 Then [76] they went out of the
city, and came unto him.
31 In the meanwhile his disciples
prayed him, saying, Master, eat.
32 But he said unto them, I have
meat to eat that ye know not of.
33 Therefore said the disciples one
to another,[77] Hath any man brought
him *aught* to eat?
34 Jesus saith unto them, My meat
is to do the will of him that sent me,
and to finish his work.

§ 25. Our Lord's discourse with the Samaritan woman.

MATTHEW.	MARK.

§ 26. Jesus teaches

CHAPTER IV. 17. 17 From that time Jesus began to preach, and to say, Repent: for the kingdom of heaven is at hand.	CHAPTER I. 14, 15. preaching the gospel of the kingdom of God,[11] 15 And saying,[12] The time is fulfilled, and the kingdom of God is at hand; repent ye, and believe the gospel.

§ 27. Jesus, again at Cana, heals the son

Many Samaritans believe on him. *Shechem* or *Neapolis.*

LUKE.

JOHN.

CHAPTER IV. 4–42.

35 [78] Say not ye, There are yet four
months, and *then* cometh harvest?
behold, I say unto you, Lift up your
eyes, and look on the fields; for they
are white already to harvest.
36 And he that reapeth receiveth
wages, and gathereth fruit unto life
eternal: that both [79] he that soweth,
and he that reapeth, may rejoice together.
37 And herein is that saying true,
One soweth, and another reapeth.
38 I sent you to reap that whereon
ye bestowed no labour: other men
laboured, and ye are entered into
their labours.
39 And many of the Samaritans of
that city believed on him [80] for the
saying of the woman, which testified,
He told me all that ever I did.
40 So when the Samaritans were
come unto him, they besought him
that he would tarry with them: and
he abode there two days.[81]
41 And many more believed, because of his own word;
42 And said unto the woman, Now
we believe, not because of thy saying:
for we have heard *him* ourselves, and
know that this is indeed the Christ,
the Saviour of the world.[82]

publicly in Galilee.

CHAPTER IV. 14, 15.

and there went out a fame of him
through all the region round about.[70]
15 And he taught in their synagogues, being glorified of all.

CHAPTER IV. 43–45.

43 Now, after two days he departed
thence, and went into Galilee.[83]
44 For Jesus himself testified, that
a prophet hath no honour in his own
country.
45 Then when he was come into
Galilee, the Galileans received him,
having seen all the things that he
did at Jerusalem at the feast: for they
also went unto the feast.

of a nobleman lying ill at Capernaum. *Cana of Galilee.*

CHAPTER IV. 46–54.

46 So Jesus came again into Cana
of Galilee, where he made the water
wine. And there was a certain nobleman, whose son was sick at Capernaum.[84]
47 [85] When he heard that Jesus was

§ 27. **Jesus, again at Cana, heals the son**

MATTHEW.	MARK.

§ 28. **Jesus is rejected at Nazareth,**

of a nobleman lying ill at Capernaum. *Cana of Galilee.*

LUKE.

JOHN.

CHAPTER IV. 46–54.

come out of Judea into Galilee, he went unto him, and besought him[86] that he would come down, and heal his son: for he was at the point of death.

48 Then said Jesus unto him, Except ye see signs and wonders, ye will not believe.

49 The nobleman saith unto him, Sir, come down ere my child[87] die.

50 Jesus saith unto him, Go thy way; thy son liveth. And the man believed the word that Jesus had spoken unto him, and he went his way.[88]

51 And as he was now going down, his servants met him, and told *him*, saying, Thy son liveth.[89]

52 Then inquired he of them the hour when he began to amend. And they said unto him, Yesterday at the seventh hour the fever left him.[90]

53 So the father knew that *it was* at the same hour, in the which Jesus said unto him,[91] Thy son liveth: and himself believed, and his whole house.

54 This *is* again the second miracle *that* Jesus did, when he was come out of Judea into Galilee.

and fixes his abode at Capernaum.

CHAPTER IV. 16–31.

16 And he came to Nazareth, where he had been brought up: and, as his custom was, he went into the synagogue on the sabbath-day, and stood up for to read.

17 And there was delivered unto him the book of the prophet Esaias. And when he had opened the book, he found the place where it was written,*

18 The Spirit of the Lord *is* upon me, because he hath anointed me to preach the gospel to the poor; he hath sent me to heal the broken-hearted,[71] to preach deliverance to the captives, and recovering of sight to the blind, to set at liberty them that are bruised,

* Is. lxi. 1, and lviii. 6.

§ 28. Jesus is rejected at Nazareth,

MATTHEW. CHAPTER IV. 13–16.	MARK.

Luke iv. 20, *sat down.*] The service of the synagogue consisted of reading the scriptures prayer, and preaching. The posture in which the latter was performed, whether in the synagogue or elsewhere, (see *Matth.* v. 1; *Luke* v. 3,) was sitting. Accordingly when our Saviour had read the portion of scripture, in the synagogue at Nazareth, of which he was a member, having been brought up in that city, and then, instead of retiring to his place, *sat down* in the desk or pulpit, it is said "the eyes of all that were present were fastened upon him," because they perceived, by his posture, that he was about to preach to them. See also Acts xiii. 14, 15. JENNINGS, Ant. 375.

and fixes his abode at Capernaum.

LUKE.

CHAPTER IV. 16–31.

19 To preach the acceptable year of the Lord.

20 And he closed the book, and he gave *it* again to the minister, and sat down. And the eyes of all them that were in the synagogue were fastened on him.

21 And he began to say unto them, This day is the scripture fulfilled in your ears.

22 And all bear him witness, and wondered at the gracious words which proceeded out of his mouth. And they said, Is not this Joseph's son?

23 And he said unto them, Ye will surely say unto me this proverb, Physician, heal thyself: whatsoever we have heard done in Capernaum,[72] do also here in thy country.

24 And he said, Verily, I say unto you, No prophet is accepted in his own country.

25 But I tell you of a truth, many widows were in Israel in the days of Elias, when the heaven was shut up three years and six months, when great famine was throughout all the land:

26 But unto none of them was Elias sent, save unto Sarepta, *a city* of Sidon, unto a woman *that was* a widow.*

27 And many lepers were in Israel in the time of Eliseus the prophet; and none of them was cleansed, saving Naaman[73] the Syrian.†

28 And all they in the synagogue, when they heard these things, were filled with wrath,

29 And rose up, and thrust him out of the city, and led him unto the brow of the hill, (whereon their city was built,) that they might cast him down headlong.

JOHN.

* 1 Kings xvii. 1, 9. † 2 Kings v. 14.

Luke iv. 20, *to the minister.*] This word denotes only a subordinate officer, who attended the minister and obeyed his orders in what concerned the more servile part of the work. Among other things he had charge of the sacred books, and delivered them to those to whom he was commanded by his superiors to deliver them. After the reading was over, he deposited them in their proper place. CAMPBELL, *in loc.*

Luke iv. 29, *the brow of the hill.*] The accuracy of this description is attested by travellers, to this day. See ROBINSON'S Travels in Palestine, vol. iii., pp. 186, 187.

§ 28. Jesus is rejected at Nazareth,

MATTHEW.	MARK.
CHAPTER IV. 13–16.	
13 And leaving Nazareth, he came and dwelt in Capernaum,[28] which is upon the sea-coast, in the borders of Zabulon and Napthalim; 14 That it might be fulfilled which was spoken by Esaias the prophet, saying,* 15 The land of Zabulon, and the land of Napthalim, *by* the way of the sea, beyond Jordan, Galilee of the Gentiles: 16 The people which sat in darkness, saw great light; and to them which sat in the region and shadow of death, light is sprung up.	

§ 29. The call of Simon Peter and Andrew, and of James

MATTHEW.	MARK.
CHAPTER IV. 18–22.	CHAPTER I. 16–20.
18 [29] And Jesus, walking by the sea of Galilee, saw two brethren, Simon called Peter, and Andrew his brother,	16 Now as he walked by the sea [13] of Galilee, he saw Simon, and Andrew his brother,

* Is. ix.

Matth. iv. 18, *walking.*] Matthew says that the disciples were called by Christ while walking by the sea, because that calling followed the walk by the sea. "We say that a thing was done by one walking in this or that place, because he took such a walk, whether he who did the act was then walking, or sitting or standing." Spanh. dub. lxxii. v. 2. This remark reconciles "*walking*," Matth. iv. 18 with "*stood*," Luke v. 1. A like remark may be made with respect to the passages placed parallel to Luke v. 6. Jesus is concisely represented as if he had at first seen Peter and Andrew casting a net into the sea, because they were employed thus in consequence of the interview.

Luke does not deny that more than Simon were seen, nor does he affirm that Simon

and fixes his abode at Capernaum

LUKE.

CHAPTER IV. 16-31.

30 But he, passing through the
midst of them, went his way,
31 And came down to Capernaum,
a city of Galilee,

JOHN.

and John, with the miraculous draught of fishes. *Near Capernaum.*

CHAPTER V. 1-11.

[80] AND it came to pass, that as the
people pressed upon him to hear the
word of God, he stood by the lake
of Gennesaret,
2 And saw two [81] ships standing by
the lake: but the fishermen were gone
out of them, and were washing *their*
nets.
3 And he entered into one of the
ships, which was Simon's, and prayed
him that he would thrust out a little
from the land. And he sat down, and
taught the people out of the ship.[82]
4 Now, when he had left speaking,
he said unto Simon, Launch out into
the deep, and let down your nets for
a draught.
5 And Simon, answering, said unto
him,[83] Master, we have toiled all the
night, and have taken nothing; nevertheless, at thy word I will let down
the net.

---

alone was seen. Indeed our Lord is said to have seen *two* ships by the lake. The calling of others beside Simon not only is not denied by Luke, but is sufficiently indicated in v. 11. The words of Matthew (*v.* 21) "going on from thence," are not to be understood as implying a great distance, but as relating to the neighbouring shore. Matthew relates the principal fact, the calling and the following; Luke has the accompanying circumstances. And there is a remarkable harmony between them. Matthew records the repairing of their nets by the fishermen; Luke shows how they became broken,—by the great draught they had taken. What is related by Luke, is not denied by Matthew, but omitted only. Nothing, indeed, is more common than to find the omission of some supplied by the other Evangelists. NEWCOME.

§ 29. The call of Simon Peter and Andrew, and of James

MATTHEW.
CHAPTER IV. 18-22.

casting a net into the sea; for they were fishers.

19 And he saith unto them, Follow me, and I will make you fishers of men.

20 And they straightway left *their* nets, and followed him.

21 And going on from thence, he saw other two brethren, James *the son* of Zebedee, and John his brother, in a ship with Zebedee their father, mending their nets: and he called them.

22 And they immediately left the[30] ship, and their father, and followed him.

MARK.
CHAPTER I. 16-20.

casting a net into the sea: for they were fishers.

17 And Jesus said unto them, Come ye after me, and I will make you to become fishers of men.

18 And straightway they forsook their[14] nets, and followed him.

19 And when he had gone a little[15] farther thence, he saw James the *son* of Zebedee, and John his brother, who also were in the ship mending their nets.

20 And straightway he called them: and they left their father Zebedee in the ship with the hired servants, and went after him.

§ 30. The healing of a demoniac

CHAPTER I. 21-28.

21 And they went into Capernaum; and straightway on the sabbath-day he entered into the synagogue and taught.[16]

22 And they were astonished at his doctrine: for he taught them as one that had authority, and not as the scribes

23 And there was[17] in their synagogue a man with an unclean spirit; and he cried out,

24 Saying, Let *us* alone; what have we to do with thee,[18] thou Jesus of Nazareth? art thou come to de-

---

Matt. iv. 21. *with Zebedee their father.*] The death of Zebedee is nowhere mentioned in the gospels; yet an undesigned coincidence, and proof of the veracity of the Evangelists, is evident by comparing this place with others, in which his death is tacitly alluded to. Thus in Chap. viii. 21, it is related that "another of his *disciples* said.

and John, with the miraculous draught of fishes. *Near Capernaum.*

LUKE.

CHAPTER V. 1–11.

6 And when they had this done, they enclosed a great multitude of fishes: and their net brake.[84]

7 And they beckoned [85] unto *their* partners, which were in the other ship, that they should come and help them. And they came, and filled both the ships, so that they began to sink.

8 When Simon Peter saw *it*, he fell down at Jesus' knees, saying, Depart from me; for I am a sinful man, O Lord.[86]

9 For he was astonished,[87] and all that were with him, at the draught of the fishes which they had taken:

10 And so *was* also James and John the sons of Zebedee, which were partners with Simon. And Jesus said unto Simon, Fear not: from henceforth thou shalt catch men.

11 And when they had brought their ships to land, they forsook all, and followed him.

JOHN.

in the Synagogue. *Capernaum.*

CHAPTER IV. 31–37.

and taught them on the Sabbath-days.

32 And they were astonished at his doctrine: for his word was with power.

33 And in the synagogue there was a man which had a spirit of an unclean devil; and he cried out with a loud voice,

34 Saying,[74] Let *us* alone; what have we to do with thee, *thou* Jesus

unto him, Lord, suffer me first to go and *bury my father;*" and in Chap. xx. 20, it is said, "Then came to him the *mother of Zebedee's children*, with her sons, worshipping him," &c. See also Chap. xxvii. 55. BLUNT, Veracity of the Gospels, Sec. I. 2. See note on Mark vi. 3; Post. § 55.

§ 30. The healing of a demoniac.

MATTHEW.

MARK.

CHAPTER I. 21–28.

stroy us ? I know thee who thou art,
the Holy One of God.
25 And Jesus rebuked him, saying,[19]
Hold thy peace, and come out of him.
26 And when the unclean spirit
had torn him, and cried with a loud
voice, he came out of him.
27 And they were all amazed, insomuch that they questioned among
themselves, saying, What thing is
this ? what new doctrine *is* this ? for
with authority commandeth he even
the unclean spirits, and they do obey
him.[20]
28 And immediately his fame
spread abroad throughout all the
region round about Galilee.[21]

§ 31. The healing of Peter's wife's mother

MATTHEW.

CHAPTER VIII. 14–17.

14 And when Jesus was come into
Peter's house, he saw his wife's
mother laid, and sick of a fever.
15 And he touched her hand, and
the fever left her: and she arose, and
ministered unto them.[90]
16 When the even was come, they
brought unto him many that were
possessed with devils: and he cast
out the spirits with *his* word,[91] and
healed all that were sick;
17 That it might be fulfilled which
was spoken by Esaias the prophet,
saying,* himself took our infirmities,
and bare *our* sicknesses.

MARK.

CHAPTER I. 29–34.

29 And forthwith, when they were
come out of the synagogue, they entered [22] into the house of Simon and
Andrew, with James and John.
30 But Simon's wife's mother lay
sick of a fever: and anon they tell
him of her.
31 And he came and took her by
the hand, and lifted her up; and immediately [23] the fever left her, and
she ministered unto them.
32 And at even when the sun did
set, they brought unto him all that
were diseased, and them that were
possessed with devils.
33 And all the city was gathered
together at the door.
34 And he healed many that were
sick of divers diseases, and cast out
many devils; and suffered not the
devils to speak, because they knew
him.[24]

§ 32. Jesus with his disciples.

MATTHEW.

CHAPTER IV. 23–25.

MARK.

CHAPTER I. 35–39.

35 And in the morning, rising up
a great while before day, he went out

* Is. liii. 4.

Mark i. 26, *torn him.*] There is no inconsistency between this place and the last clause of Luke iv. 35. The word translated *torn*, signifies to move, agitate, convulse. It occurs only twice in the Septuagint. In 2. Sam. xxii. 8, the Hebrew signifies to be shaken, *ut in terræ motu*. In Jer. iv. 19, it is applied to commotion of mind. Here,

in the Synagogue. *Capernaum.*

LUKE.	JOHN.
CHAPTER IV. 31-37. of Nazareth? art thou come to destroy us? I know thee who thou art, the Holy One of God. 35 And Jesus rebuked him, saying, Hold thy peace, and come out of him. And when the devil had thrown him in the midst, he came out of him, and hurt him not. 36 And they were all amazed, and spake among themselves, saying, What a word *is* this! for with authority and power he commandeth the unclean spirits, and they come out. 37 And the fame of him went out into every place of the country round about.	

and many others. *Capernaum.*

CHAPTER IV. 38–41. 38 And he arose [75] out of the synagogue, and entered into Simon's house. And Simon's wife's mother was taken with a great fever; and they besought him for her. 39 And he stood over her, and rebuked the fever; and it left her:[76] and immediately she arose and ministered unto them. 40 Now, when the sun was setting, all they that had any sick with divers diseases, brought them unto him: and he laid his hands on every one of them, and healed them. 41 And devils also came out of many, crying out, and saying, Thou art Christ [77] the Son of God. And he, rebuking *them*, suffered them not to speak: for they knew that he was Christ.	

goes from Capernaum throughout Galilee.

CHAPTER IV. 42–44. 42 And when it was day, he departed, and went into a desert place;	

the demoniac was violently agitated; but the agitation left no lasting bad effect; he was restored to perfect health and soundness. NEWCOME.

Luke iv. 42, *when it was day.*] This clause may be rendered "when the day was coming on," and thus be reconciled with the words of Mark, who says it was a great while before day, namely, before broad day-light. SCOTT, *in loc.*

§ 32. Jesus with his disciples

MATTHEW.

CHAPTER IV. 23–25.

23 And Jesus went [31] about all Galilee, teaching in their synagogues, and preaching the gospel of the kingdom, and healing all manner of sickness, and all manner of disease among the people.

24 And his fame went throughout all Syria: and they brought unto him all sick people that were taken with divers diseases and torments, and [32] those which were possessed with devils, and those which were lunatic, and those which had the palsy; and he healed them.

25 And there followed him great multitudes of people from Galilee, and *from* Decapolis, and *from* Jerusalem, and *from* Judea, and *from* beyond Jordan.

MARK.

CHAPTER I. 35–39.

and departed [25] into a solitary place, and there prayed.

36 And Simon, and they that were with him, followed after him.

37 And when they had found him, they said [26] unto him, All *men* seek for thee.

38 And he said unto them, Let us go into the next towns,[27] that I may preach there also: for therefore came I forth.

39 And he preached [28] in their synagogues throughout all Galilee, and cast out devils.

§ 33. The healing

CHAPTER VIII. 2–4.

2 And behold, there came a leper and worshipped him, saying, Lord, if thou wilt, thou canst make me clean.

3 And Jesus put forth *his* hand, and touched him, saying, I will; be thou clean. And immediately his leprosy was cleansed.[80]

4 And Jesus saith [81] unto him, See thou tell no man: but go thy way,

CHAPTER I. 40–45.

40 And there came a leper to him, beseeching him, and kneeling down to him, and saying unto him, If thou wilt, thou canst make me clean.[29]

41 And Jesus, moved with compassion, put forth *his* hand, and touched him, and saith unto him, I will; be thou clean.[30]

42 And as soon as he had spoken,[31] immediately the leprosy departed from him, and he was cleansed.

43 And he straitly charged him, and forthwith sent him away;

Matth. viii. 4, *tell no man.*] "The miraculous cure of the leprosy was thought by the Jews to be characteristic of the Messiah; and therefore there was peculiar reason for enjoining this man silence." *Benson's Life of Christ*, p. 340. NEWCOME. For the consequence of a premature full manifestation of himself as the Messiah, by awakening the jealousy of the Roman government, might, humanly speaking, have impeded his ministry. Yet there was great propriety in the private exhibition, to the priesthood, of full proof that he was the Messiah; after which, their obstinacy in rejecting him was inexcusable. In this, and divers other instances, our Lord mani-

goes from Capernaum throughout Galilee.

LUKE.

CHAPTER IV. 42–44.

and the people sought him, and came unto him, and stayed him, that he should not depart from them.

43 And he said unto them, I must preach the kingdom of God to other cities also, for therefore am I sent.[78]
44 And he preached in the synagogues of Galilee.[79]

JOHN.

of a leper. *Galilee.*

CHAPTER V. 12–16.

12 And it came to pass, when he was in a certain city, behold, a man full of leprosy: who, seeing Jesus, fell on *his* face, and besought him, saying, Lord, if thou wilt, thou canst make me clean.
13 And he put forth *his* hand[88] and touched him, saying, I will: Be thou clean. And immediately the leprosy departed from him.
14 And he charged him to tell no man: but go, and shew thyself to the

fested his intent not to be generally known to the Jews as their Messiah, till the consummation of his ministry. A general announcement of his divine character at the outset would have been productive of no good; on the contrary it would have excited the malice of the Scribes, Pharisees, and Herodians against him; would have favoured the conceit of the Jews that he was to be their temporal king; would have awakened the jealousy of the Roman government; and in the natural course of things, would have prevented him from giving the many miraculous proofs which he gave of his ministry, and thus laying solid foundations for faith in his divine mission; would have

§ 33. The healing

MATTHEW.

CHAPTER VIII. 2–4.

shew thyself to the priest, and offer the gift that Moses commanded, for a testimony unto them.*

MARK.

CHAPTER I. 40–45.

44 And saith unto him, See thou say nothing [32] to any man; but go thy way, shew thyself to the priest, and offer for thy cleansing those things which Moses commanded, for a testimony unto them.

45 But he went out, and began to publish *it* much, and to blaze abroad the matter, insomuch that Jesus could no more openly enter into the city, but was without in desert places: and they came to him from every quarter.

§ 34. The healing

MATTHEW.

CHAPTER IX. 2–8.

2 And behold, they brought to him a man sick of the palsy, lying on a bed: and Jesus, seeing their faith, said unto the sick of the palsy, Son, be of good cheer; thy sins be forgiven thee.[102]

3 And behold, certain of the scribes said within themselves, this *man* blasphemeth.

4 And Jesus knowing their thoughts, said, Wherefore think ye evil in your hearts?

MARK.

CHAPTER II. 1–12.

AND again he entered into Capernaum, after *some* days; and it was noised that he was in the house.[33]

2 And straightway [34] many were gathered together, insomuch that there was no room to receive *them*, no, not so much as about the door: and he preached the word unto them.

3 And they come unto him, bringing one sick [35] of the palsy, which was borne of four.

4 And when they could not come nigh upon him [36] for the press, they uncovered the roof where he was: and when they had broken *it* up, they let down the bed wherein the sick of the palsy lay.

5 When Jesus saw their faith, he said unto the sick of the palsy, Son, thy sins be forgiven thee.[37]

6 But there were certain of the scribes sitting there, and reasoning in their hearts,

7 Why doth this *man* thus speak blasphemies? [38] who can forgive sins but God only?

8 And immediately, when Jesus perceived in his spirit, that they so reasoned within themselves, he said [39] unto them, Why reason ye these things in your hearts?

* Lev. xiv. 2, seq.

---

exposed him and his religion to the charge of ostentation, vanity, and love of power and display; and would have deprived the world of that example which he gave, of meekness, humility and patient suffering and self-denial. According to human experience, an early assumption of regal splendour, supported by the miracles he wrought, would have been suc-

of a leper. *Galilee.*

LUKE.

CHAPTER V. 12-16.

priest,[89] and offer for thy cleansing.
according as Moses commanded, for
a testimony unto them.
15 But so much the more went
there a fame abroad of him: [90] and
great multitudes came together to
hear and to be healed by him [91] of
their infirmities.
16 And he withdrew himself into
the wilderness, and prayed.

JOHN.

of a paralytic. *Capernaum.*

CHAPTER V. 17-26.

17 And it came to pass on a certain
day, as he was teaching, that there
were Pharisees and doctors of the
law sitting by, which were come out
of every town of Galilee, and Judea,
and Jerusalem: and the power of the
Lord was *present* to heal them.[92]
18 And behold, men brought in a
bed [93] a man which was taken with a
palsy: and they sought *means* to
bring him in, and to lay *him* before
him.
19 And when they could not find
by what *way* they might bring him
in, because of the multitude, they
went upon the house-top, and let
him down through the tiling with *his*
couch, into the midst before Jesus.[94]
20 And when he saw their faith,
he said unto him, Man, thy sins are
forgiven thee.[95]
21 And the scribes and the Pharisees began to reason, saying, Who is
this which speaketh blasphemies?
Who can forgive sins but God alone?
22 But when Jesus perceived their
thoughts, he, answering, said unto
them, What reason ye in your hearts?

cessful, and carried him to the throne instead of the cross; but it would have deprived the world of the great object of his mission. A sufficient number were enlightened to attest his miracles and proclaim his religion, and enough were left in their ignorance, to condemn and crucify him. See A. CLARKE, and SCOTT, *in loc.*

§ 34. **The healing**

MATTHEW.

CHAPTER IX. 1–8.

5 For whether is easier to say, *Thy* sins be forgiven thee;[103] or to say, Arise, and walk?

6 But that ye may know that the Son of man hath power on earth to forgive sins, (then saith he to the sick of the palsy,) Arise, take up thy bed, and go unto thy house.

7 And he arose, and departed to his house.

8 But when the multitude saw *it*, they marvelled,[104] and glorified God, which had given such power unto men.

MARK.

CHAPTER II. 1–12.

9 Whether is it easier to say to the sick of the palsy, *Thy* sins be forgiven thee;[40] or to say, Arise, and take up thy bed, and walk?

10 But that ye may know that the Son of man hath power on earth to forgive sins, (he saith to the sick of the palsy,)

11 I say unto thee, Arise, and take up thy bed,[41] and go thy way into thy house.

12 [42] And immediately he arose, took up the bed, and went forth before them all; insomuch that they were all amazed, and glorified God, saying, We never saw it on this fashion.

§ 35. **The call**

CHAPTER IX. 9.

9 And as Jesus passed forth from thence, he saw a man named Matthew, sitting at the receipt of custom: and he saith unto him, Follow me. And he arose and followed him.[105]

CHAPTER II. 13, 14.

13 And he went forth again by the sea-side; and all the multitude resorted unto him,[43] and he taught them.

14 And as he passed by, he saw Levi the *son* of Alpheus, sitting at the receipt of custom, and said unto him, Follow me. And he arose, and followed him.

Mark ii. 14. *Levi.*] When a Jew became a Roman citizen, he usually assumed a Roman name. It is therefore supposed that Levi was the original Hebrew, and Matthew the assumed

of a paralytic. *Capernaum.*

LUKE.

CHAPTER V. 17–26.

23 Whether is easier, to say, Thy sins be forgiven thee; or to say, Rise up and walk?

24 But that ye may know that the Son of man hath power upon earth to forgive sins (he said unto the sick of the palsy), I say unto thee, Arise, and take up thy couch, and go unto thine house.

25 And immediately he rose up before them,[96] and took up that whereon he lay, and departed to his own house, glorifying God.

26 And they were all amazed, and they glorified God, and were filled with fear saying,[97] We have seen strange things to-day.

JOHN.

of Matthew. *Capernaum.*

CHAPTER V. 27, 28.

27 And after these things he went forth, and saw a publican named Levi, sitting at the receipt of custom: and he said [98] unto him, Follow me.

28 And he left all, rose up, and followed him.

---

assumed Roman name of this evangelist. STOWE's Introd. 120. See also, HARMER's Obs. vol. iv. p. 330; Obs. 94.

PART IV.

OUR LORD'S SECOND PASSOVER,

AND THE

SUBSEQUENT TRANSACTIONS

UNTIL THE THIRD.

TIME. *One year.*

§ 36. **The pool of Bethesda; the healing of the infirm man;**

MATTHEW.	MARK.

John v. 2. *Bethesda.*] It is observable that though John speaks of this pool or bath as existing at the time he wrote, which was upwards of sixty years after the crucifixion, yet he speaks of the efficacy of its waters in the past tense, as something which had long ceased.

JOHN.

CHAPTER V. 1–47.

AFTER this there was a feast[92] of the
Jews: and Jesus went up to Jerusalem.
2 Now there is at Jerusalem, by
the sheep *market*, a pool, wh ch is
called in the Hebrew tongue, Bethesda,[93] having five porches.
3 [94] In these lay a great multitude of
impotent folk, of blind, halt, withered,
waiting for the moving of the water.
4 [95] For an angel went down at a
certain season into the pool, and
troubled the water: whosoever then
first after the troubling of the water
stepped in, was made whole of whatsoever disease he had.
5 And a certain man was there,
which had[96] an infirmity thirty and
eight years.
6 When Jesus saw him lie, and
knew that he had been now[97] a long
time *in that case*, he saith unto him,
Wilt thou be made whole?
7 The impotent man answered
him,[98] Sir. I have no man, when the
water is troubled, to put me into the
pool: but while I am coming, another
steppeth down before me.
8 Jesus said unto him, Rise, take
up[99] thy bed and walk.
9 [100] And immediately the man was
made whole, and took up his bed,
and walked: and on the same day
was the sabbath.
10 The Jews therefore said unto
him that was cured, It is the sabbath-
day; it is not lawful[101] for thee to
carry *thy* bed.
11 He answered them, He that
made me whole, the same said unto
me, Take up thy bed, and walk.[102]
12 [103] Then asked they him, What
man is that which said unto thee,
Take up thy bed, and walk?
13 And he that was healed wist
not who it was: for Jesus had conveyed himself away, a multitude
being in *that* place.
14 Afterward Jesus findeth him in
the temple, and said[104] unto him, Behold, thou art made whole; sin no more,
lest a worse thing come unto thee.

This may account for the silence of Josephus concerning it; whether we suppose it to have been really a miraculous virtue, existing only in the time of our Saviour; or merely a groundless belief of the populace.

§ 36. The pool of Bethesda; the healing of the infirm man;

MATTHEW.	MARK.

and our Lord's s bs quent dis o rs.. *Jerusalem.*

LUKE.

JOHN.

CHAPTER V. 1–47.

15 [105] The man departed, and told the Jews that it was Jesus which had made him whole.

16 And therefore did the Jews persecute Jesus, and sought to slay him, because he had done [106] these things on the sabbath-day.

17 But Jesus answered [107] them, My Father worketh hitherto, and I work.

18 Therefore the Jews sought the more to kill him, because he not only had broken the sabbath, but said also, that God was his Father,[108] making himself equal with God.

19 Then answered Jesus, and said unto them,[109] Verily, verily, I say unto you, The Son can do nothing of himself, but what he seeth the Father do: for what things soever he doeth, these also doeth the Son likewise.

20 For the Father loveth the Son, and sheweth him all things that himself doeth: and he will shew him greater works than these, that ye may marvel.

21 For as the Father raiseth up the dead, and quickeneth *them;* even so the Son quickeneth whom he will.

22 For the Father judgeth no man but hath committed all judgment unto the Son:

23 That all *men* should honour the Son, even as they honour the Father. He that honoureth not the Son, honoureth not the Father which hath sent him.

24 Verily, verily, I say unto you, He that heareth my word, and believeth on him that sent me, hath everlasting life, and shall not come into condemnation; but is passed from death unto life.

25 Verily, verily, I say unto you, The hour is coming, and now is, when the dead shall hear the voice of the Son of God: and they that hear shall live.[110]

26 For as the Father hath life in himself, so hath he given to the Son to have life in himself;

27 And hath given him authority to execute judgment also,[111] because he is the Son of man.

28 Marvel not at this: for the hour is coming, in the which all that are in the graves shall hear his voice,

§ 36. The pool of Bethesda; the healing of the infirm man;

MATTHEW.	MARK.

John v. 37, *heard his voice.*] Spanheim, dub. evang. ii. 185, doubts how the latter part of this verse is reconcilable with Matthew iii. 17, and the parallel verses. But the voice from heaven was not God's *immediate* voice; but uttered at his command, and in

and our Lord's subsequent discourse. *Jerusalem.*

LUKE.

JOHN.

CHAPTER V. 1–47.

29 And shall come forth; they that
have done good, unto the resurrection
of life; and they that have done evil,
unto the resurrection of damnation.
30 I can of mine own self do
nothing: as I hear, I judge: and my
judgment is just: because I seek not
mine own will, but the will of the
Father which hath sent me.[112]
31 If I bear witness of myself, my
witness is not true.
32 There is another that beareth
witness of me, and I know [113] that the
witness which he witnesseth of me is
true.
33 Ye sent unto John, and he bare
witness unto the truth.
34 But I receive not testimony
from man: but these things I say,
that ye might be saved.
35 He was a burning and a shining
light: and [114] ye were willing for a
season to rejoice in his light.
36 But I have greater witness than
that of John: for the works which
the Father hath given me to finish,
the same works that I do, bear witness
of me, that the Father hath sent me.
37 And the Father himself which
hath sent me,[115] hath borne witness
of me. Ye have neither heard his
voice at any time, nor seen his shape.
38 And ye have not his word abiding in you: for whom he hath sent,
him ye believe not.
39 Search the scriptures; for in
them ye think ye have eternal life:
And they are they which testify of me.
40 And ye will not come to me,
that ye might have life.
41 I receive not honour from men.[116]
42 But I know you, that ye have
not the love of God in you.
43 I am come in my Father's name,
and ye receive me not: if another
shall come in his own name, him ye
will receive.
44 How can ye believe, which receive honour one of another, and seek
not the honour that *cometh* from God
only? [117]

---

his person. See Deut. iv. 33; Ex. xx. 1, 2; Comp. Hebr. ii. 2; Gal. iii. 19; Acts vii. 53. NEX
COME.

§ 36. The pool of Bethesda; the healing of the infirm man;

MATTHEW.

MARK.

§ 37. The disciples pluck ears of grain

MATTHEW.

CHAPTER XII. 1–8.

AT that time Jesus went on the sabbath-day through the corn, and his disciples were a hungered, and began to pluck the ears of corn, and to eat.*

2 But when the Pharisees saw *it*, they said unto him, Behold, thy disciples do that which is not lawful to do upon the sabbath-day.

3 But he said unto them, Have ye not read what David did when he was a hungered, and they that were with him;

4 How he entered into the house of God, and did eat the shew-bread, which was not lawful for him to eat, neither for them which were with him, but only for the priests? [149]

5 Or have ye not read in the law how that on the sabbath-days the priests in the temple profane the sabbath, and are blameless? †

6 But I say unto you, that in this place is *one* greater than the temple.[150]

7 But if ye had known what *this* meaneth,‡ I will have mercy, and not sacrifice, ye would not have condemned the guiltless.

8 For the Son of man is Lord even [151] of the sabbath-day.

MARK.

CHAPTER II. 23–28.

23 And it came to pass, that he went through the corn fields on the sabbath-day; and his disciples began, as they went, to pluck the ears of corn.

24 And the Pharisees said unto him, Behold, why do they on the sabbath-day that which is not lawful? [51]

25 And he said [52] unto them, Have ye never read what David did,§ when he had need, and was a hungered, he and they that were with him?

26 How [53] he went into the house of God, in the days of Abiathar the high priest, and did eat the shew-bread, which is not lawful to eat, but for the priests, and gave also to them which were with him?

27 And he said unto them, The sabbath was made for man, and not man [54] for the sabbath:

28 Therefore the Son of man is Lord also of the sabbath.

* Deut. xxiii. 25.
† Numb. xxviii. 9, 10; xviii. 19.
‡ 1 Sam. xxi. 1–7.
§ Hos. vi. 7.

Matth. xii. 2, *to do upon the Sabbath-day.*] The act of plucking the ears of corn by the hand in another's field, was expressly permitted, by the law of Moses, Deut. xxiii. 23; but it was considered so far a species of reaping as to be servile work, and therefore not lawful to be done on the Sabbath. CAMPBELL, *in loc.* See ROBINSON'S Biblical Researches in Palestine, Vol. 2, pp. 192, 201, that this custom is still in use.

and our Lord's subsequent discourse. *Jerusalem.*

LUKE.

JOHN.

CHAPTER V. 1–47.

45 Do not think that I will accuse
you to the Father: there is *one* that
accuseth you,[118] *even* Moses, in whom
ye trust.
46 For had ye believed Moses, ye
would have believed me: for he
wrote of me.
47 But if ye believe not his
writings, how shall ye believe my
words?[119]

on the sabbath. *On the way to Galilee.*

LUKE.

CHAPTER VI. 1–5.

AND it came to pass on the second
sabbath after the first, that he went
through the corn-fields; and his disciples plucked the ears of corn,[108] and
did eat, rubbing *them* in *their* hands.
2 And certain of the Pharisees said
unto them,[109] Why do ye that which is
not lawful to do on the sabbath-days?
3 And Jesus, answering them, said,
Have ye not read so much as this,
what David did, when himself was a
hungered, and they which were with
him;
4 [110] How he went into the house
of God, and did take and eat the
shew-bread, and gave also to them that
were with him, which it is not lawful
to eat but for the priests alone?
5 And he said unto them, That the
Son of man is also Lord of the sabbath.[111]

Mark ii. 26, *Abiathar.*] It appears from 1 Sam. xxi. 1, that Ahimelech was the high priest at the time referred to; but Abiathar his son was the *chief* priest under him, and probably superintended the tabernacle and its stated concerns. Ahimelech was soon after slain; and Abiathar succeeded him in that office, and continued in it about forty years, until after the death of David. This circumstance, and his great eminence, above his father, may account for the use of his name rather than his father's, as illustrating the times of David and Saul. See SCOTT *in loc*

§ 38. The healing of the withered hand

MATTHEW.

CHAPTER XII. 9–14.

9 And when he was departed thence, he went into their synagogue.

10 And behold, there was a man which had *his* hand withered. And they asked him, saying, Is it lawful to heal on the sabbath days? that they might accuse him.

11 And he said unto them, What man shall there be among you, that shall have one sheep, and if it fall into a pit on the sabbath-day, will he not lay hold on it, and lift *it* out?

12 How much then is a man better than a sheep? wherefore it is lawful to do well on the sabbath-days.

13 Then saith he to the man, Stretch forth thy hand. And he stretched *it* forth; and *it* was restored whole, like as the other.[152]

14 Then the Pharisees went out, and held a council[153] against him, how they might destroy him.

MARK.

CHAPTER III. 1–6.

AND he entered again into the synagogue;[55] and there was a man there which had a withered hand.

2 And they watched him, whether he would heal him[56] on the sabbath-day; that they might accuse him.

3 And he saith unto the man which had the withered hand, Stand forth.

4 And he saith unto them, Is it lawful to do good on the sabbath-days, or to do evil? to save life, or to kill? but they held their peace.

5 And when he had looked round about on them with anger, being grieved for the hardness of their hearts, he saith unto the man, Stretch forth thy hand. And he stretched *it* out: and his hand was restored whole as the other.[57]

6 And the Pharisees went forth, and straightway took counsel with the Herodians against him, how they might destroy him.

§ 39. Jesus arrives at the sea of Tiberias,

CHAPTER XII. 15–21.

15 But when Jesus knew *it*, he withdrew himself from thence: and great multitudes followed him,[154] and he healed them all.

16 And charged them that they should not make him known:

17 That it might be fulfilled which was spoken by Esaias the prophet,* saying,

18 Behold my servant, whom I have chosen; my beloved, in whom my soul is well pleased: I will put my Spirit upon him, and he shall shew judgment to the Gentiles.

19 He shall not strive, nor cry; neither shall any man hear his voice in the streets.

20 A bruised reed shall he not break, and smoking flax, shall he not

CHAPTER III. 7–12.

7 But Jesus withdrew himself with his disciples to the sea: and a great multitude from Galilee followed him, and from Judea.[58]

8 And from Jerusalem, and from Idumea, and *from* beyond Jordan; and they about Tyre and Sidon, a great multitude, when they had heard what great things he did, came unto him[59]

9 And he spake to his disciples, that a small ship should wait on him, because of the multitude, lest they should throng him.

10 For he had healed many; insomuch that they pressed upon him for to touch him, as many as had plagues.[60]

11 And unclean spirits, when they saw him, fell down before him, and cried, saying, Thou art the son of God.

* Is. xlii. 1, seq.; Is. xi. 10.

Matth. xii. 20, ***smoking flax.***] There may be an allusion, in these words of the prophet, to an Eastern custom, for those who were grievously afflicted to come to the sovereign for

on the Sabbath. *Galilee.*

LUKE.

CHAPTER VI. 6–11.

6 And it came to pass also[112] on another sabbath, that he entered into the synagogue, and taught: and there was a man whose right hand was withered:

7 And the scribes and Pharisees watched him, whether he would heal[113] on the sabbath-day; that they might find an accusation against him.

8 But he knew their thoughts, and said to the man which had the withered hand, Rise up, and stand forth in the midst. And he arose, and stood forth.

9 [114]Then said Jesus unto them, I will ask you one thing; Is it lawful on the sabbath-days to do good, or to do evil? to save life, or to destroy *it?*

10 And looking round about upon them all, he said unto the man, Stretch forth thy hand. And he did so: and his hand was restored whole as the other.

11 And they were filled with madness; and communed one with another what they might do to Jesus.

JOHN.

and is followed by multitudes. *Lake of Galilee.*

relief or redress, having pots of fire, or of burning straw, or other combustible on their heads, in token of their extreme trouble. Not one of these, the prophet seems to intimate, should go away without redress; he will certainly remove the cause of their complaints, and render truth and justice victorious over falsehood and oppression. 3 CALM. 394.

§ 39. Jesus arrives at the sea of Tiberias,

MATTHEW.

CHAPTER XII. 15–21.

quench, till he send forth judgment unto victory.

21 And in his name shall the Gentiles trust.

MARK.

CHAPTER III. 7–12.

12 And he straightly charged them, that they should not make him known.

§ 40. Jesus withdraws to the Mountain and chooses the Twelve;

CHAPTER X. 2–4.

2 Now the names of the twelve apostles are these; The first, Simon, who is called Peter, and Andrew his brother; James[122] *the son* of Zebedee, and John his brother;

3 Philip and Bartholomew; Thomas, and Matthew the publican; James *the son* of Alpheus, and Lebbeus, whose surname was[123] Thaddeus.

4 Simon the Canaanite,[124] and Judas Iscariot, who also betrayed him.

CHAPTER III. 13–19.

13 And he goeth up into a mountain, and calleth *unto him* whom he would: and they came unto him.[61]

14 And he ordained twelve,[62] that they should be with him, and that he might send them forth to preach.

15 And to have power to heal sicknesses, and [63] to cast out devils.

16 [64] And Simon he surnamed Peter.

17 And James the *son* of Zebedee, and John the brother of James, (and he surnamed them Boanerges, which is, The sons of thunder,)

18 And Andrew, and Philip, and Bartholomew, and Matthew, and Thomas, and James the *son* of Alpheus, and Thaddeus, and Simon the Canaanite.[65]

19 And Judas Iscariot, which also betrayed him: and they went[66] into a house.

Matth. x. 3, *Thomas and Matthew.*] It appears from Mark vi. 7, that the apostles were sent forth by *two and two* to preach; and this accounts for their being here and in the parallel places named in couples. Luke mentions Matthew first, as being regarded as the senior of Thomas his companion; but Matthew modestly places his own name last. Mark is less observant of the order of the names, but he alone states that they were thus associated. The others give the names in couples, but state no reason for it. This is not the method of false witnesses; such incidental corroborations belong only to the narratives of truth.

Matth. x. 3, *Lebbeus.*] Thaddeus, Theudas and Judas (or Jude) are probably names of the same signification, the Greek termination being added to different forms of a Hebrew verb. "The Canaanite," Matth. x. 4, is the same with "Zelotes" in Luke. "Cognomen erat Chald. quod Lucas redditdit Zelotem." Wetstein. Thus, Thomas is rendered Didymus, or, the twin; Cephas, Peter; and Silas, Tertius. Some suppose that this name had been given to Simon on account of his religious zeal; or because he had been of a Jewish sect called Zealots, who were addicted to the Pharisees, and justified themselves by the example of Phinehas, for punishing offenders without waiting for the sentence of the magistrate. NEWCOME.

"Between Matthew (x. 2,) and Mark (iii. 16,) we observe a strict correspondence but the catalogue in St. Luke (vi. 14,) differs from both the first-mentioned writers in two particulars. 1, 'Simon, the Canaanite,' of Matthew and Mark is introduced as 'Simon called Zelotes.' Now if any difference was admitted in this place, we might expect it to extend no farther than to the order of the names, or the addition of a surname; as, for instance, Matthew calls the 'Thaddeus' of Mark also 'Lebbeus;' but here we have one surname changed for another. It is indeed easy to conceive, that Simon might have been commonly distinguished by either appellative, but this we can only conjecture; neither

and is followed by multitudes. *Lake of Galilee.*

LUKE.	JOHN.

multitudes follow him. *Near Capernaum.*

CHAPTER VI. 12–19.
12 And it came to pass in those
days, that he went out into a mountain to pray, and continued all night
in prayer to God.
13 And when it was day, he called
unto him his disciples: and of them
he chose twelve, whom also he named
Apostles;
14 Simon (whom he also named
Peter) and Andrew his brother, James
and John, Philip [116] and Bartholomew,
15 Matthew [117] and Thomas, James
the *son* of Alpheus, and Simon called
Zelotes,
16 And Judas *the brother* of James,
and Judas Iscariot, which also [118] was
the traitor.
17 [119] And he came down with them,
and stood in the plain; and the
company of his disciples, and a great
multitude of people out of all Judea
and Jerusalem, and from the sea-coast
of Tyre and Sidon, which came to

Evangelist adds a word to explain the point. 2, The other discrepancy, however, appears more serious. The Lebbeus or Thaddeus of St. Matthew and Mark, is entirely omitted in the list of St. Luke, who substitutes 'Judas, the brother of James.' Here is certainly a marked difference, for it would not seem very probable, that the Apostle in question passed by three distinct names. Nor could this be a mere oversight in St. Luke, for, in Acts i. 13, where a catalogue of the eleven is inserted, he mentions this individual in exactly the same manner. Are we to suppose then that the Evangelist commits a deliberate error in this particular? We have distinct and satisfactory witnesses to prove that there really was an Apostle besides Iscariot, who bore the name of Judas. Both Matthew (xiii. 55,) and Mark (vi. 3,) concur in speaking of James and Jude as the near relations of Christ, and part of this statement is incidentally confirmed by St. Paul, who calls James 'the Lord's brother.' (Gal. i. 19.) But farther, St. John (xiv. 22,) presents us with a remark made by 'Judas not Iscariot;' evidently one of the Apostles; and St. Jude himself, in the first verse of his Epistle, styles himself 'the brother of James.' There is thus amply sufficient evidence, that all the Gospel writers acknowledge an Apostle of this name, though St. Matthew, with his usual simplicity, familiarly mentions him by two of his appellations, omitting that of Judas, and St. Mark sees no occasion to depart from his language, in a matter of such general notoriety. Luke, on the other hand, usually studious of accuracy, distinguishes this Apostle by the name generally current in the Church, when his Gospel was written. This variation then may, upon the whole, convince us how undesignedly the writers of Scripture confirm each other's statements; yet can this only be the result of a minute examination upon our part, and upon the probability of this, a cautious writer would hardly stake his reputation for truth o exactness." See ROBERTS's "Light shining out of Darkness," pp. 91—93.

§ 40. Jesus withdraws to the Mountain and chooses the Twelve;

MATTHEW.	MARK.

§ 41. The Sermon

CHAPTERS V. VI. VII. VIII. 1.
AND seeing the multitudes, he went
up into a mountain: and when he was
set, his disciples came unto him.[33]
2 And he opened his mouth, and
taught them, saying,
3 Blessed *are* the poor in spirit:
for theirs is the kingdom of heaven.
4 Blessed *are* they that mourn:[34]
for they shall be comforted.
5 Blessed *are* the meek: for they
shall inherit the earth.
6 Blessed *are* they which do hunger
and thirst after righteousness: for
they shall be filled.
7 Blessed *are* the merciful: for
they shall obtain mercy.
8 Blessed *are* the pure in heart: for
they shall see God.
9 Blessed *are* the peace-makers: for
they shall be called the children of God.
10 Blessed *are* they which are
persecuted for righteousness' sake: for
theirs is the kingdom of heaven.
11 Blessed *are* ye when *men* shall
revile you, and persecute *you*, and
shall say all manner of evil against
you falsely, for my sake.
12 Rejoice, and be exceeding glad;
for great *is* your reward in heaven:
for so persecuted they the prophets
which were before you.

Matth. v. 1, *into a mountain.*] It may be objected that Matthew, in saying that this discourse was delivered sitting on a mountain, is contradicted by Luke, who says that Jesus was standing on a plain. Luke vi. 17. But Dr. Clarke, on this latter place, has suggested that Jesus "being pressed with great multitudes of people, might retire from them again to the top of the hill." And Dr. Priestley observes that "Matthew's saying that Jesus was *sat down* after he had gone up the mountain, and Luke's saying that he *stood* on the plain, when he healed the sick before the discourse, are no inconsistencies." Harm. p. 83.

The whole picture is striking. Jesus ascends a mountain, employs the night in prayer, and having thus solemnly invoked the divine blessing, authoritatively separates the twelve apostles from the mass of his disciples. He descends, and heals, in the plain, all among a great multitude, collected from various parts by the fame of his miraculous power. Having

multitudes follow him. *Near Capernaum.*

LUKE.

CHAPTER VI. 12-19.

hear him, and to be healed of their
diseases;
18 And they that were vexed with
unclean spirits: and they were
healed.[120]
19 And the whole multitude sought
to touch him; for there went virtue
out of him, and healed *them* all.

JOHN.

on the Mount. *Near Capernaum.*

CHAPTER VI. 20-49.

20 And he lifted up his eyes on his
disciples, and said, Blessed *be ye* poor;
for yours is the kingdom of God.
21 Blessed *are ye* that hunger now:
for ye shall be filled.[121] Blessed *are ye*
that weep now: for ye shall laugh.
22 Blessed are ye when men shall
hate you, and when they shall separate you *from their company*, and
shall reproach *you*, and cast out your
name as evil, for the Son of man's
sake.
23 Rejoice ye in that day, and leap
for joy: for behold, your reward *is*
great in heaven: for in the like manner[122] did their fathers unto the
prophets.
24 But wo unto you that are rich!
for ye have received your consolation.
25 Wo unto you that are full![123]
for ye shall hunger. Wo unto you
that laugh now! for ye shall mourn
and weep.
25 Wo unto you, when all men
shall speak well of you! for so did
their fathers to the false prophets.[124]

thus created attention, he satisfies the desire of the people to hear his doctrine; and retiring first to the mountain whence he came, that his attentive hearers might follow him, and might better arrange themselves before him. Sacro digna silentio Mirantur *omnes* dicere. *Hor.* NEWCOME.

The different accounts of the Sermon on the Mount may be reconciled, by considering that Matthew wrote chiefly for the Hebrew Christians; and it was therefore important for him to bring out, in full, the manner in which our Lord enforced the spiritual nature of his dispensation and doctrine, in opposition to the mere letter of the Jewish law, and the teaching and practice of Scribes and Pharisees; which he does particularly and with many examples; while Luke, on the contrary, wrote chiefly for Gentile Christians, to whom the contrast with the Jewish law was of less interest; and therefore he omits those parts of the discourse, and dwells only upon those which were of practical importance to all. ROBINSON. NEWCOME.

§ 41. The Sermon

MATTHEW.

CHAPTERS V. VI. VII. VIII. 1.

13 Ye are the salt of the earth: but if the salt has lost his savour, wherewith shall it be salted? it is thenceforth good for nothing, but to be cast out, and to be trodden under foot of men.

14 Ye are the light of the world, A city that is set on a hill cannot be hid.

15 Neither do men light a candle, and put it under a bushel, but on a candlestick: and it giveth light unto all that are in the house.

16 Let your light so shine before men, that they may see your good works,[35] and glorify your Father which is in heaven.

17 Think not that I am come to destroy the law, or the prophets: I am not come to destroy, but to fulfil.

18 For verily, I say unto you, Till heaven and earth pass, one jot or one tittle shall in no wise pass from the law, till all be fulfilled.

19 Whosoever therefore shall break one of these least commandments, and shall teach men so, he shall be called the least in the kingdom of heaven: but whosoever shall do, and teach *them*, the same shall be called great in the kingdom of heaven.

20 For I say unto you, That except your righteousness shall exceed *the righteousness* of the scribes and Pharisees, ye shall in no case enter into the kingdom of heaven.

21 Ye have heard that it was said by them of old time, Thou shalt not kill; and whosoever shall kill, shall be in danger of the judgment:

22 But I say unto you, That whosoever is angry with his brother, without a cause,[36] shall be in danger of the judgment: and whosoever shall say to his brother, Raca, shall be in danger of the council: but whosoever shall say, Thou fool, shall be in danger of hell-fire.

23 Therefore, if thou bring thy gift to the altar, and there rememberest that thy brother hath aught against thee,

24 Leave there thy gift before the altar, and go thy way; first be recon-

MARK.

on the **Mount**. *Near Capernaum*.

LUKE.	JOHN.

§ 41. The Sermon

MATTHEW.

CHAPTERS V. VI. VII. VIII. 1.

ciled to thy brother, and then come and offer thy gift.

25 Agree with thine adversary quickly, while thou art in the way with him; lest at any time the adversary deliver thee to the judge, and the judge deliver thee to the officer, and thou be cast into prison.[37]

26 Verily, I say unto thee, Thou shalt by no means come out thence, till thou hast paid the uttermost farthing.

27 Ye have heard that it was said by them of old time,[38] Thou shalt not commit adultery:

28 But I say unto you, That whosoever looketh on a woman to lust after her,[39] hath committed adultery with her already in his heart.

29 And if thy right eye offend thee, pluck it out, and cast *it* from thee: for it is profitable for thee that one of thy members should perish, and not *that* thy whole body should be cast into hell.

30 And if thy right hand offend thee, cut it off, and cast *it* from thee: for it is profitable for thee that one of thy members should perish, and not[40] *that* thy whole body should be cast into hell.

31 It hath been said, Whosoever shall put away his wife, let him give her a writing of divorcement:

32 But I say unto you, that Whosoever shall put away his wife, saving for the cause of fornication, causeth her to commit adultery: and whosoever shall marry her that is divorced, committeth adultery.[41]

33 Again, ye have heard that it hath been said by them of old time, Thou shalt not forswear thyself, but shalt perform unto the Lord thine oaths:

34 But I say unto you, Swear not at all: neither by heaven; for it is God's throne:

35 Nor by the earth; for it is his footstool: neither by Jerusalem; for it is the city of the great King:

36 Neither shalt thou swear by thy head; because thou canst not make one hair white or black.

37 But let your communication be,

MARK.

on the **Mount.** *Near Capernaum.*

LUKE.	JOHN.

§ 41. The Sermon

MATTHEW.

CHAPTERS V. VI. VII. VIII. 1.

Yea, yea; Nay, nay: for whatsoever
is more than these cometh of evil.
38 Ye have heard that it hath been
said, An eye for an eye, and a tooth
for a tooth.
39 But I say unto you, That ye
resist not evil: but whosoever shall
smite thee on thy right cheek,[42] turn
to him the other also.
40 And if any man will sue thee
at the law, and take away thy coat,
let him have *thy* cloak also.
41 And whosoever shall compel
thee to go a mile, go with him twain.
42 Give to him that asketh thee,
and from him that would borrow of
thee, turn not thou away.
43 Ye have heard that it hath been
said, Thou shalt love thy neighbour,
and hate thine enemy:
44 But I say unto you, Love your
enemies, bless them that curse you,
do good to them that hate you, and
pray for them which despitefully use
you, and persecute you;[43]
45 That ye may be the children
of your Father which is in heaven:
for he maketh his sun to rise on the
evil and on the good, and sendeth
rain on the just and on the unjust.[44]
46 For if ye love them which love
you, what reward have ye? do not
even the publicans the same?[45]
47 And if ye salute your brethren
only, what do ye more *than others?*
do not even the publicans so?[46]
48 Be ye therefore perfect, even as
your Father which is in heaven is
perfect.[47]

CHAPTER VI.

TAKE heed[48] that ye do not your
alms before men, to be seen of them:
otherwise ye have no reward of your
Father which is in heaven.
2 Therefore, when thou doest *thine*
alms, do not sound a trumpet before
thee, as the hypocrites do, in the synagogues, and in the streets, that they

MARK.

Matt. v. 41, *shall compel thee.*] The Greek word here employed is said to be derived from the Persians, among whom the king's messengers or posts were called *Angari.* These had the royal authority for pressing horses, ships, and even men, to assist them in the business on which they were sent. The word therefore signifies, to be compelled by

on the Mount. *Near Capernaum.*

LUKE.
CHAPTER VI. 20–41.

27 But I say unto you which hear,
Love your enemies, do good to them
which hate you,
28 Bless them that curse you,
and [125] pray for them which despitefully use you.
29 And unto him that smiteth thee
on the *one* cheek,[126] offer also the
other; and him that taketh away thy
cloak, forbid not *to take thy* coat also.
30 Give to every man that asketh
of thee: and of him that taketh away
thy goods ask *them* not again.
31 And as ye would that men
should do to you, do ye also [127] to
them likewise.
32 For if ye love them which love
you, what thank have ye? for sinners
also love those that love them.
33 [128] And if ye do good to them
which do good to you, what thank
have ye, for sinners also do even the
same.
34 And if ye lend *to them* of whom
ye hope to receive, what thank have
ye? for sinners also [129] lend to sinners,
to receive as much again.
35 But love ye your enemies, and
do good, and lend, hoping for nothing
again;[130] and your reward shall be
great, and ye shall be the children
of the Highest: for he is kind unto
the unthankful and *to* the evil.
36 Be ye therefore [131] merciful, as
your Father also is merciful.

JOHN.

violence to do any particular service, especially of the public kind, by the king's authority. And the sentiment is a lesson of patience and gentleness under severe exactions from man. *Lightfoot, apud* A. CLARKE, *in loc.* SIR J. CHARDIN'S Travels, Vol. i. p. 238, 257.

§ 41. The Sermon

MATTHEW.

CHAPTERS V. VI. VII. VIII. 1.

may have glory of men. Verily,[49] I say unto you, They have their reward.

3 But when thou doest alms, let not thy left hand know what thy right hand doeth;

4 That thine alms may be in secret, and thy Father which seeth in secret himself shall reward thee openly.[50]

5 And when thou prayest, thou shalt not be[51] as the hypocrites *are;* for they love to pray standing in the synagogues, and in the corners of the streets that they may be seen of men. Verily, I say unto you, They have their reward.

6 But thou, when thou prayest, enter into thy closet, and when thou hast shut thy door, pray to thy Father which is in secret; and thy Father, which seeth in secret, shall reward thee openly.[52]

7 But when ye pray, use not vain repetitions, as the heathen *do:*[53] for they think that they shall be heard for their much speaking.

8 Be not ye therefore like unto them: for your Father[54] knoweth what things ye have need of before ye ask him.

9 After this manner therefore pray ye: Our Father which art in heaven, Hallowed be thy name.

10 Thy kingdom come. Thy will be done in earth as *it is* in heaven.

11 Give us this day our daily bread.

12 And forgive us our debts, as we forgive our debtors.[55]

13 And lead us not into temptation, but deliver us from evil. For thine is the kingdom, and the power, and the glory, for ever. Amen.[56]

14 For if ye forgive men their trespasses, your heavenly Father will also forgive you:

15 But if ye forgive not men their trespasses,[57] neither will your Father forgive your trespasses.

16 Moreover, when ye fast, be not as the hypocrites, of a sad countenance: for they disfigure their faces, that they may appear unto men to fast. Verily, I say unto you, They have their reward.[58]

17 But thou, when thou fastest, anoint thy head, and wash thy face;

18 That thou appear not unto men

MARK.

on the **Mount**. *Near Capernaum.*

LUKE.	JOHN.

§ 41. The Sermon

MATTHEW.

CHAPTERS V. VI. VII. VIII. 1.

to fast, but unto thy Father, which is in secret: and thy Father, which seeth in secret, shall reward thee openly.

19 Lay not up for yourselves treasures upon earth, where moth and rust doth corrupt, and where thieves break through and steal:[60]

20 But lay up for yourselves treasures in heaven, where neither moth nor rust doth corrupt, and where thieves do not break through nor steal.

21 For where your treasure is, there will your heart be also.[61]

22 The light of the body is the eye:[62] if therefore thine eye be single, thy whole body shall be full of light.

23 But if thine eye be evil, thy whole body shall be full of darkness. If therefore the light that is in thee be darkness, how great *is* that darkness!

24 No man can serve two masters: for either he will hate the one, and love the other; or else he will hold to the one, and despise the other. Ye cannot serve God and mammon.

25 Therefore I say unto you, Take no thought for your life, what ye shall eat, or what ye shall drink;[63] nor yet for your body, what ye shall put on. Is not the life more than meat, and the body than raiment?

26 Behold the fowls of the air: for they sow not, neither do they reap, nor gather into barns; yet your heavenly Father feedeth them. Are ye not much better than they?

27 Which of you by taking thought can add one cubit[64] unto his stature?

28 And why take ye thought for raiment? Consider the lilies of the field how they grow; they toil not, neither do they spin;

29 And yet I say unto you, That even Solomon, in all his glory, was not arrayed like one of these.

30 Wherefore, if God so clothe the grass of the field, which to day is, and to-morrow is cast into the oven, *shall he* not much more *clothe* you, O ye of little faith?

31 Therefore take no thought, saying, What shall we eat? or, what shall

MARK.

on the **Mount.** *Near Capernaum.*

LUKE.	JOHN.

§ 41. The Sermon

MATTHEW.

CHAPTERS V. VI. VII. VIII. 1.

we drink? or, wherewithal shall we
be clothed?
32 (For after all these things do
the Gentiles seek) for your heavenly
Father,[65] knoweth that ye have need
of all these things.
33 But seek ye first the kingdom of
God, and his righteousness,[66] and all
these things shall be added unto you.
34 Take therefore no thought for
the morrow: for the morrow shall
take thought for the things of itself.[67]
Sufficient unto the day *is* the evil
thereof.

CHAPTER VII.

JUDGE not, that ye be not judged.
2 For with what judgment ye
judge, ye shall be judged: and with
what measure ye mete, it shall be
measured to you again.[68]
3 And why beholdest thou the mote
that is in thy brother's eye, but con-
siderest not the beam that is in thine
own eye?
4 Or how wilt thou say to thy
brother, Let[69] me pull out the mote
out of thine eye; and behold a beam
is in thine own eye?
5 Thou hypocrite, first cast out the
beam out of thine own eye;[70] and then
shalt thou see clearly to cast out the
mote of thy brother's eye.
6 Give not that which is holy unto
the dogs, neither cast ye your pearls
before swine, lest they trample them
under their feet, and turn again and
rend you.
7 Ask, and it shall be given you;
seek, and ye shall find; knock, and
it shall be opened unto you:
8 For every one that asketh, receiveth; and he that seeketh, findeth;
and to him that knocketh, it shall be
opened.[71]
9 Or what man is there of you,
whom if his son ask[72] bread, will he
give him a stone?
10 Or if he ask[73] a fish, will he give
him a serpent?
11 If ye then being evil know how
to give good gifts unto your children,
how much more shall your Father
which is in heaven give good things
to them that ask him?

MARK.

LUKE.
CHAPTER VI. 20–49.

37 Judge not, and ye shall not be
judged: condemn not, and ye shall
not be condemned:[132] forgive, and ye
shall be forgiven:
38 [133] Give, and it shall be given
unto you; good measure, pressed
down, and shaken together, and running over, shall men give into your
bosom. For with the same measure
that ye mete withal, it shall be measured to you again.
39 And he spake a parable [134] unto
them; Can the blind lead the blind?
shall they not both fall into the ditch?
40 The disciple is not above his
master: but every one that is perfect,
shall be as his master.[135]
41 And why beholdest thou the
mote that is in thy brother's eye, but
perceivest not the beam that is in
thine own eye?
42 Either how [136] canst thou say to
thy brother, Brother, let me pull out
the mote that is in thine eye, when
thou thyself beholdest not the beam
that is in thine own eye? Thou
hypocrite, cast out first the beam out
of thine own eye, and then shalt thou
see clearly to pull out the mote that
is in thy brother's eye.
43 For a good tree bringeth not
forth corrupt fruit; neither [137] doth a
corrupt tree bring forth good fruit.
44 For every tree is known by his
own fruit; for of thorns men do not
gather figs, nor of a bramble-bush
gather they grapes.
45 A good man out of the good
treasure of his heart, bringeth forth

JOHN.

§ 41. The Sermon

MATTHEW.

CHAPTERS V. VI. VII. VIII. 1.

12 Therefore[74] all things whatsoever ye would that men should do to you, do ye even so to them: for this is the law and the prophets.

13 Enter ye in at the strait gate; for wide *is* the gate, and broad *is* the way,[75] that leadeth to destruction, and many there be which go in thereat:

14 Because, strait[76] *is* the gate, and narrow *is* the way, which leadeth unto life, and few there be that find it.

15 Beware of false prophets, which come to you in sheep's clothing, but inwardly they are ravening wolves.

16 Ye shall know them by their fruits: Do men gather grapes of thorns, or figs of thistles?

17 Even so every good tree bringeth forth good fruit; but a corrupt tree bringeth forth evil fruit.

18 A good tree cannot bring forth evil fruit, neither *can* a corrupt tree bring forth good fruit.

19 Every tree that bringeth not forth good fruit is hewn down, and cast into the fire.

20 Wherefore, by their fruits ye shall know them.

21 Not every one that saith unto me Lord, Lord, shall enter into the kingdom of heaven; but he that doeth the will of my father which is in heaven.

22 Many will say to me in that day, Lord, Lord, have we not prophesied in thy name? and in thy name have cast out devils?[77] and in thy name done many wonderful works?

23 And then will I profess unto them, I never knew you, depart from me, ye that work iniquity.

24 Therefore, whosoever heareth these sayings of mine, and doeth them, I will liken[78] him unto a wise man, which built his house upon a rock:

25 And the rain descended, and the floods came, and the winds blew, and beat upon that house; and it fell not: for it was founded upon a rock:

26 And every one that heareth these sayings of mine, and doeth them not, shall be likened unto a foolish man, which built his house upon the sand:

MARK.

on the **Mount**. *Near Capernaum.*

LUKE.

CHAPTER V. 20–49.

that which is good; and an evil man, out of the evil treasure of his heart, bringeth forth that which is evil;[138] for of the abundance of the heart his mouth speaketh.

46 And why call ye me Lord, Lord, and do not the things which I say?

47 Whosoever cometh to me, and heareth my sayings, and doeth them, I will shew you to whom he is like.

48 He is like a man which built a house, and digged deep, and laid the foundation on a rock: and when the flood arose, the stream beat vehemently upon that house, and could not shake it: for it was founded upon a rock.[130]

49 But he that heareth and doeth not, is like a man that without a foundation built a house upon the earth,

JOHN.

§ 41. The Sermon

MATTHEW.

CHAPTERS V. VI. VII. VIII. 1.

27 And the rain descended, and the floods came, and the winds blew, and beat upon that house; and it fell: and great was the fall of it.

28 And it came to pass when Jesus had ended these sayings, the people were astonished at his doctrine.

29 For he taught them as *one* having authority, and not as the [79] scribes.

CHAPTER VIII.

WHEN he was come down from the mountain, great multitudes followed him.

MARK.

§ 42. The healing

CHAPTER VIII. 5-13.

5 [82] And when Jesus was entered into Capernaum, there came unto him a centurion, beseeching him,

6 And saying, Lord,[83] my servant lieth at home sick of the palsy, grievously tormented.

7 [84] And Jesus saith unto him, I will come and heal him.

8 [85] The centurion answered and said, Lord, I am not worthy that thou shouldest come under my roof: but speak the word only, and my servant shall be healed.

9 For I am a man under [86] authority, having soldiers under me; and I say to this *man*, Go, and he goeth; and to another, Come, and he cometh; and to my servant, Do this, and he doeth *it*.

10 When Jesus heard *it*, he marvelled, and said to them that followed, Verily I say unto you, I have not found so great faith, no, not in Israel.[87]

11 And I say unto you, That many shall come from the east and west, and shall sit down with Abraham, and Isaac, and Jacob, in the kingdom of heaven:

12 But the children of the kingdom shall be cast out into [88] outer darkness:

Matt. viii. 5, *came unto him.*] Calvin says that Matthew, being more brief, introduces the centurion himself as speaking; and that Luke expresses more at large his sending by his friends; but that the sense of both is the same. *Harm.* p. 124.

(Toinard quotes Exod. xviii. 6, were the words related as *spoken* by Jethro, were evidently a message *sent* by him to Moses. *Harm.* 147.)

on the Mount. *Near Capernaum.*

LUKE.

CHAPTER VI. 20–49.

against which the stream did beat vehemently, and immediately it fell, and the ruin of that house was great.

JOHN.

of the centurion's servant. *Capernaum.*

CHAPTER VII. 1–10.

Now, when he had ended all his sayings in the audience of the people, he entered into Capernaum.[140]

2 And a certain centurion's servant, who was dear unto him, was sick, and ready to die.[141]

3 And when he heard of Jesus, he sent unto him the elders of the Jews, beseeching him that he would come and heal his servant.

4 And when they came to Jesus, they besought him instantly, saying,[142] That he was worthy for whom he should do this:

5 For he loveth our nation, and he hath built us a synagogue.

6 Then Jesus went with them. And when he was now not far from the house, the centurion sent friends to him, saying unto him, Lord,[143] trouble not thyself: for I am not worthy that thou shouldest enter under my roof;

7 Wherefore neither thought I myself worthy to come unto thee; but say in a word, and my servant shall be healed.

8 For I also am a man set under authority, having under me soldiers, and I say unto one, Go, and he goeth; and to another, Come, and he cometh; and to my servant, Do this, and he doeth *it.*

Considering then the sameness of the scene, of the person, of the words, and of the transaction, I cannot but conclude with Grotius, that the miracle is one and the same, related in general by Matthew, and with greater accuracy by Luke. NEWCOME.

§ 42. The healing

MATTHEW.	MARK.
CHAPTER VIII. 5-13. there shall be weeping and gnashing of teeth. 13 And Jesus said unto the centurion, Go thy way; and as thou hast believed, *so* be it done unto thee. And his servant was healed in the self-same hour.[89]	

§ 43. The raising

§ 44. John the Baptist, in prison,

CHAPTER XI. 2-19. 2 Now when John had heard in the prison the works of Christ, he sent two of his disciples, 3 And said unto him, Art thou he that should come, or do we look for another?	

Matt, xi. 3, *he that should come.*] The nature of our Lord's ministry, as it now appeared, so unlike what John as a Jew expected, may have surprised and perplexed him. And his own misfortune, coming upon this disappointment and perplexity, would increase his doubt and embarrasment. His faith was shaken;—the question implies no more;—and he sent that his

of the centurion's servant. *Capernaum.*

LUKE.

CHAPTER VII. 1–10.

9 When Jesus heard these things,
he marvelled at him, and turned him
about and said unto the people that
followed him, I say unto you, I have
not found so great faith, no, not in
Israel.
10 And they that were sent, returning to the house, found the servant whole that had been sick.[144]

JOHN.

of the widow's son. *Nain.*

CHAPTER VII. 11–17.

11 And it came to pass the day
after, that he went into a city called
Nain: and many of his disciples[145]
went with him, and much people.
12 Now, when he came nigh to the
gate of the city, behold, there was a
dead man carried out,[146] the only son
of his mother, and she was a widow:
and much people of the city was with
her.
13 And when the Lord saw her,
he had compassion on her, and said
unto her, Weep not.
14 And he came and touched the
bier: and they that bare *him* stood
still. And he said, Young man, I say
unto thee, Arise.
15 And he that was dead sat up,
and began to speak: and he delivered
him to his mother.
16 And there came a fear on all:
and they glorified God, saying, That
a great prophet is risen up among us;
and, That God hath visited his people.
17 And this rumour of him[147] went
forth throughout all Judea, and
throughout all the region round about.

sends disciples to Jesus. *Galilee. Capernaum.*

CHAPTER VII. 18–35.

18 And the disciples of John
shewed him of all these things.
19 And John calling *unto him* two
of his disciples, sent *them* to Jesus,[148]
saying, Art thou he that should come?
or look we for another?

---

doubts might be removed, and his faith confirmed. Jesus therefore merely referred John to the miracles which he was doing, and the prophecies which spake of him, and which were fulfilled by those miracles. Bp. SUMNER, *in loc.*

§ 44. John the Baptist, in prison,

MATTHEW.
CHAPTER XI. 2–19.

4 Jesus answered and said unto them, Go and show John again those things which ye do hear and see:
5 The blind receive their sight, and the lame walk, the lepers are cleansed, and the deaf hear, the dead [137] are raised up, and the poor have the gospel preached to them.*
6 And blessed is *he* whosoever shall not be offended in me.
7 And as they departed, Jesus began to say unto the multitudes concerning John, What went ye out into the wilderness to see? A reed shaken with the wind?
8 [138] But what went ye out for to see? A man clothed in soft raiment? Behold, they that wear soft *clothing* are in kings' houses.
9 [139] But what went ye out for to see? A prophet? yea, I say unto you, and more than a prophet.
10 For [140] this is *he* of whom it is written,† Behold, I send my messenger before thy face, which shall prepare thy way before thee.
11 Verily, I say unto you, Among them that are born of women, there hath not risen a greater than John the Baptist: notwithstanding, he that is least in the kingdom of heaven, is greater than he.
12 And from the days of John the Baptist, until now, the kingdom of heaven suffereth violence, and the violent take it by force.
13 For all the prophets and the law prophesied until John.
14 And if ye will receive *it*, this is Elias which was for to come.‡
15 He that hath ears to hear,[141] let him hear.
16 But whereunto shall I liken this generation? It is like unto children sitting in the markets, and calling unto their fellows.[142]

MARK.

* Is. xxxv. 5. seq. † Mal. iii. 1. ‡ Mal. iv. 5.

LUKE.

CHAPTER VII. 18-35.

20 When the men were come[149]
unto him, they said, John Baptist
hath sent us unto thee, saying, Art
thou he that should come? or look
we for another?
21 And in that same hour he cured
many of *their* infirmities, and plagues,
and of evil spirits;[150] and unto many
that were blind he gave sight.
22 Then Jesus answering, said unto
them, Go your way, and tell John
what things ye have seen and heard;
how that the blind see, the lame
walk, the lepers are cleansed, the
deaf hear, the dead are raised, to the
poor the gospel is preached.[151]
23 And blessed is *he*, whosoever
shall not be offended in me.
24 And when the messengers of
John were departed, he began to speak
unto the people concerning John,
What went ye out into the wilderness for to see? A reed shaken with
the wind?
25 But what went ye out for to
see? A man clothed in soft raiment?
Behold, they which are gorgeously
apparelled, and live delicately, are in
kings' courts.
26 But what went ye out for to
see? A prophet? Yea, I say unto you,
and much more than a prophet.
27 This is *he*, of whom it is written,
Behold I send my messenger before
thy face, which shall prepare thy way
before thee.
28 For I say unto you, Among
those that are born of women, there
is not a greater prophet than John the
Baptist:[152] but he that is least in the
kingdom of God, is greater than he.
29 And all the people that heard
him, and the publicans, justified God,
being baptized with the baptism of
John.
30 But the Pharisees and lawyers
rejected the council of God against[153]
themselves, being not baptized of him.
31 And the Lord said,[154] Whereunto
then shall I liken the men of this generation? and to what are they like?
32 They are like unto children sitting in the market-place, and calling
one to another, and saying, We have

JOHN.

§ 44. **John the Baptist, in prison,**

MATTHEW.

CHAPTER XI. 2–19.

17 And saying, we have piped unto you, and ye have not danced; we have mourned unto you,[143] and ye have not lamented.

18 For John came neither eating nor drinking, and they say, He hath a devil.

19 The Son of man came eating and drinking, and they say, Behold a man gluttonous, and a wine bibber, a friend of publicans and sinners. But Wisdom is justified of her children.[144]

MARK.

§ 45. **Reflections of Jesus**

CHAPTER XI. 20–30.

20 Then began he to upbraid the cities wherein most of his mighty works were done, because they repented not.

21 Wo unto thee, Chorazin! wo unto thee, Bethsaida! for if the mighty works which were done in you had been done in Tyre and Sidon, they would have repented long ago in sackcloth and ashes.[145]

22 But I say unto you, It shall be more tolerable for Tyre and Sidon at the day of judgment, than for you.

23 And thou, Capernaum, which art exalted unto heaven, shalt be brought down to hell:[146] for if the mighty works which have been done in thee, had been done in Sodom, it would have remained until this day.

24 But I say unto you, That it shall be more tolerable for the land of Sodom, in the day of judgment, than for thee.

25 At that time Jesus answered and said, I thank thee, O Father, Lord of heaven and earth, because thou hast hid these things from the wise and prudent, and hast revealed them unto babes.

26 Even so, Father, for so it seemed good in thy sight.

27 All things are delivered unto me of my Father;[147] and no man knoweth the Son, but the Father; neither knoweth any man the Father, save the Son, and *he* to whomsoever the Son will reveal *him*.

28 Come unto me, all *ye* that labour,

sends disciples to Jesus. *Galilee. Capernaum.*

LUKE.

CHAPTER VII. 18–35.

piped unto you,[155] and ye have not
danced; we have mourned to you,
and ye have not wept.
33 For John the Baptist came neither eating bread,[156] nor drinking
wine; and ye say, He hath a devil.
34 The Son of man is come eating
and drinking; and ye say, Behold a
gluttonous man, and a wine-bibber, a
friend of publicans and sinners!
35 But Wisdom is justified of all
her children.[157]

JOHN.

on appealing to his mighty works. *Capernaum.*

§ 45. Reflections of Jesus

MATTHEW.	MARK.
CHAPTER XI. 20–30. and are heavy laden, and I will give you rest. 29 Take my yoke upon you, and learn of me: [148] for I am meek and lowly in heart; and ye shall find rest unto your souls. 30 For my yoke *is* easy, and my burden is light.	

§ 46. While sitting at meat with a Pharisee,

on appealing to his mighty works. *Capernaum.*

LUKE.	JOHN.

Jesus is anointed by a woman who had been a sinner. *Capernaum?*

LUKE.

CHAPTER VII. 36–50.

36 And one of the Pharisees desired him that he would eat with him. And he went into the Pharisee's house, and sat down to meat.

37 And behold, a woman in the city, which was a sinner, when she knew [158] that *Jesus* sat at meat in the Pharisee's house, brought an alabaster-box of ointment,

38 And stood at his feet behind [159] *him* weeping, and began to wash his feet with tears, and did wipe *them* with the hairs of her head, and kissed his feet, and anointed *them* with the ointment.

39 Now, when the Pharisee which had bidden him, saw *it*, he spake within himself, saying, This man, if he were a prophet,[160] would have known who, and what manner of woman *this is* that toucheth him: for she is a sinner.

40 And, Jesus answering, said unto him, Simon, I have somewhat to say unto thee. And he saith, Master, say on.

41 There was a certain creditor, which had two debtors: the one owed five hundred pence, and the other fifty.

42 And when they had nothing to pay, he frankly forgave them both. Tell me, therefore, which of them [161] will love him most?

43 Simon answered and said, I suppose that *he*, to whom he forgave most. And he said unto him, Thou has rightly judged.

44 And he turned to the woman, and said unto Simon, Seest thou this woman? I entered into thine house, thou gavest me no water for my feet: but she hath washed my feet with tears, and wiped *them* with the hairs [162] of her head.

§ 46. While sitting at meat with a Pharisee,

MATTHEW.	MARK.

§ 47. Jesus, with the Twelve,

§ 48. The healing of a demoniac.

CHAPTER XII. 22–37.	CHAPTER III. 19–30.
	19 —— and they went[66] into a house. 20 And the multitude cometh together again, so that they could not so much as eat bread. 21 And when his friends heard *of it*, they went out to lay hold on him: for they said, He is beside himself.
22 [155] Then was brought unto him one possessed with a devil, blind and dumb; and he healed him, insomuch that the blind and dumb, both spake and saw.	

Matt. xii. 22.] We here learn that the demoniac was both blind and dumb. St. Luke

Jesus is anointed by a woman who had been a sinner. *Capernaum?*

LUKE.

CHAPTER VII. 36–50.

45 Thou gavest me no kiss: but
this woman, since the time I came in,
has not ceased to kiss my feet.
46 My head with oil thou didst not
anoint: but this woman hath anointed
my feet with ointment.
47 Wherefore I say unto thee, Her
sins which are many, are forgiven;
for she loved much: but to whom
little is forgiven, *the same* loveth
little.[163]
48 And he said unto her, Thy sins
are forgiven.
49 And they that sat at meat with
him, began to say within themselves,
Who is this that forgiveth sins also?
50 And he said to the woman, Thy
faith hath saved thee; go in peace.

JOHN.

makes a second circuit in Galilee.

CHAPTER VIII. 1–3.

AND it came to pass afterward, that
he went throughout every city and
village, preaching and shewing the
glad tidings of the kingdom of God:
and the twelve *were* with him.
2 And certain women, which had
been healed of evil spirits and infirmities, Mary called Magdalene, out of
whom went seven devils,
3 And Joanna the wife of Chuza,
Herod's steward, and Susanna, and
many others, which ministered unto
him of their substance.

The Scribes and Pharisees blaspheme. *Galilee.*

CHAPTER XI. 14, 15, 17–23.

14 And he was casting out a devil,
and it was dumb.[251] And it came to
pass when the devil was gone out,
the dumb spake; and the people wondered.

omits the former circumstance, but does not contradict it. NEWCOME.

§ 48. The healing of a demoniac.

MATTHEW.

CHAPTER XII. 22–37.

23 And all the people were amazed, and said, Is not this the son of David?

24 But when the Pharisees heard *it* they said, This *fellow* doth not cast out devils, but by Beelzebub [156] the prince of the devils.

25 And Jesus knew [157] their thoughts and said unto them, Every kingdom divided against itself, is brought to desolation; and every city or house divided against itself, shall not stand.

26 And if Satan cast out Satan, he is divided against himself; how shall then his kingdom stand?

27 And if I by Beelzebub [158] cast out devils, by whom do your children cast *them* out? therefore they shall be your judges.

28 But if I cast out devils by the Spirit of God, then the kingdom of God is come unto you.

29 Or else, how can one enter into a strong man's house, and spoil his goods, except he first bind the strong man? and then he will spoil his house.

30 He that is not with me is against me; and he that gathereth not with me, scattereth abroad.[159]

31 Wherefore I say unto you, All manner of sin and blasphemy shall be forgiven unto men: but the blasphemy *against* the *Holy* Ghost shall not be forgiven unto men.[160]

32 And whosoever speaketh a word against the Son of man, it shall be forgiven him: but whosoever speaketh against the Holy Ghost, it shall not be forgiven him, neither in this world, neither in the *world* to come.

33 Either make the tree good, and his fruit good; or else make the tree corrupt, and his fruit corrupt: for the tree is known by *his* fruit.

34 O generation of vipers, how can ye, being evil, speak good things? for out of the abundance of the heart the mouth speaketh.

MARK.

CHAPTER III. 19–30.

22 And the scribes which came down from Jerusalem, said, He hath Beelzebub,[67] and by the prince of the devils casteth he out devils.

23 And he called them *unto him*, and said unto them in parables, How can Satan cast out Satan?

24 And if a kingdom be divided against itself, that kingdom cannot stand.

25 And if a house be divided against itself, that house cannot stand.[68]

26 And if Satan rise up against himself and be divided, he cannot stand,[69] but hath an end.

27 [70] No man can enter into a strong man's house, and spoil his goods, except he will first bind the strong man; and then he will spoil his house.

28 Verily, I say unto you, All sins shall be forgiven unto the sons of men, and blasphemies [71] wherewith soever they shall blaspheme:

29 But he that shall blaspheme against the Holy Ghost hath never forgiveness, but is in danger of eternal damnation:[72]

30 Because they said, he hath an unclean spirit.

Matt. xii. 22, *the people were amazed.*] An accurate reader will observe that Matt. xii. 22, and Luke xi. 14, show the general occasion of the blasphemy against Jesus; and that Matt, xii. 24, shews the particular occasion of it, the multitude alarming the Jewish rulers by their question whether Jesus were the Christ. No cause for the absurd and impious insinuation of the Scribes and Pharisees is assigned by St. Mark: however, he suggests an important cir-

The Scribes and Pharisees blaspheme. *Galilee.*

LUKE.
CHAPTER XI. 14, 15, 17–23.

15 But some of them said, He
casteth out devils through Beelzebub,[252] the chief of the devils.
17 But he, knowing their thoughts,
said unto them, Every kingdom divided against itself, is brought to desolation; and a house *divided* against a
house, falleth.
18 If Satan also be divided against
himself, how shall his kingdom stand?
because ye say that I cast out devils
through Beelzebub.[253]
19 And if I by Beelzebub cast out
devils, by whom do your sons cast
them out? therefore shall they be
your judges.
20 But if I with the finger of God
cast out devils, no doubt the kingdom of God is come upon you.
21 When a strong man armed keepeth his palace, his goods are in peace:
22 But when a stronger than he
shall come upon him, and overcome
him, he taketh from him all his ar-
mour, wherein he trusted, and divideth
his spoils.
23 He that is not with me, is against
me: and he that gathereth not with
me scattereth.[254]

JOHN.

cumstance, that they came from Jerusalem to watch the conduct of Jesus. The latter part of Luke viii. 19, shows that his relations were not able to enter the house on account of the press. Thus one Evangelist is wonderfully supplemental to another by notations of time, place, and other circumstances: and the strictest propriety and agreement result from diligently comparing them. NEWCOME.

§ 48. The healing of a demoniac.

MATTHEW.

CHAPTER XII. 22–37.

35 A good man, out of the good treasure of the heart,[161] bringeth forth good things: and an evil man, out of the evil treasure, bringeth forth evil things.

36 But I say unto you, That every idle word that men shall speak, they shall give account thereof in the day of judgment.

37 For by thy words thou shalt be justified, and by thy words[162] thou shalt be condemned.

MARK.

§ 49. The Scribes and Pharisees seek a sign.

CHAPTER XII. 38–45.

38 Then certain of the scribes and of the Pharisees answered,[163] saying, Master, we would see a sign from thee.

39 But he answered and said to them, An evil and adulterous generation seeketh after a sign, and there shall no sign be given to it, but the sign of the prophet Jonas.

40 For as Jonas was three days and three nights in the whale's belly,* so shall the Son of man be three days and three nights in the heart of the earth.

41 The men of Nineveh shall rise in judgment with this generation, and shall condemn it: because they repented at the preaching of Jonas;† and behold, a greater than Jonas *is* here.

42 The queen of the south shall rise up in the judgment with this generation, and shall condemn it: for she came from the uttermost parts of the earth to hear the wisdom of Solomon;‡ and behold, a greater than Solomon *is* here.

* Jonah i. 17. † Jonah iii. 4, 5. ‡ 1 Kings x. 1 seq.

Matt. xii. 39, *shall no sign be given.*] The writer of a false narrative would either have omitted to mention the request for a sign, or would have related that it was complied with.

The Scribes and Pharisees blaspheme. *Galilee.*

LUKE.	JOHN.

Our Lord's reflections. *Galilee.*

CHAPTER XI. 16, 24–36.

16 And others tempting *him*, sought
of him a sign from heaven.
29 And when the people had gathered thick together, he began to
say, This is an evil generation: they
seek a sign, and there shall no sign be
given it, but the sign of Jonas the
prophet.[259]
30 For[260] as Jonas was a sign unto
the Ninevites, so shall also the Son of
man be to this generation.
31 The queen of the south shall
rise up in the judgment with the men of
this generation, and condemn them:
for she came from the utmost parts
of the earth, to hear the wisdom of
Solomon; and behold, a greater than
Solomon *is* here.
32 The men of Nineveh shall rise
up in the judgment with this genera
tion, and shall condemn it: for they
repented at the preaching of Jonas;
and behold a greater than Jonas *is*
here.
33 No man when he hath lighted
a candle, putteth *it* in a secret place,
neither under a bushel, but on a candlestick, that they which come in may
see the light.
34 The light of the body is the eye;
therefore when thine eye is single,[261]
thy whole body also is full of light;
but when *thine eye* is evil, thy body
also *is* full of darkness.
35 Take heed therefore, that the
light which is in thee be not darkness.

He would never have exposed his Master to the suspicion of a want of power. See also, Matt. xvi. 1.

§ 49. The Scribes and Pharisees seek a sign.

MATTHEW.

Chapter XII. 38–45.

43 When the unclean spirit is gone out of a man, he walketh through dry places, seeking rest, and findeth none.

44 Then he saith, I will return into my house from whence I came out; and when he is come, he findeth *it* empty, swept,[164] and garnished.

45 Then goeth he, and taketh with himself seven other spirits more wicked than himself, and they enter in and dwell there: and the last *state* of that man is worse than the first. Even so shall it be also unto this wicked generation.

MARK.

§ 50. The true disciples of Christ

Chapter XII 46–50.

46 While he yet talked to the people, behold, *his* mother and his brethren stood without, desiring to speak with him.[165]

47 Then one said unto him, Behold,[166] thy mother and thy brethren stand without, desiring to speak with thee.

48 But he answered and said unto him that told him, Who is my mother? and who are my brethren?

49 And he stretched forth his[167] hand toward his disciples, and said, Behold my mother and my brethren!

50 For whosoever shall do the will of my Father which is in heaven, the same is my brother, and sister, and mother.

Chapter III. 31–35.

31 There came then his brethren and his mother, and standing without, sent unto him, calling him.[73]

32 And the multitude sat about him; and they said unto him, Behold, thy mother and thy brethren[74] without seek for thee.

33 And he answered him, saying, Who is my mother, or my brethren?[75]

34 And[76] he looked round about on them which sat about him, and said, Behold, my mother and my brethren!

35 For whosoever shall do the will of God, the same is my brother, and my sister,[77] and mother.

§ 51. At a Pharisee's table,

Our Lord's reflections. *Galilee.*

LUKE.

CHAPTER XI. 16, 24-36.

36 If thy whole body therefore be full of light, having no part dark, the whole shall be full of light; as when the bright shining of a candle doth give the light.

24 When the unclean spirit is gone out of a man, he walketh through dry places seeking rest: and finding none, he saith,[255] I will return unto my house whence I came out.

25 And when he cometh, he findeth *it* swept and garnished.

26 Then goeth he, and taketh *to him* seven other spirits[257] more wicked than himself; and they enter in, and dwell there: and the last *state* of that man is worse than the first.

27 And it came to pass, as he spake these things, a certain woman of the company lifted up her voice, and said unto him, Blessed *is* the womb that bare thee, and the paps which thou hast sucked.

28 But he said, Yea, rather blessed *are* they that hear the word of God, and keep it.[258]

JOHN.

his nearest relatives. *Galilee.*

CHAPTER VIII. 19-21.

19 Then came to him *his* mother and his brethren, and could not come at him for the press.

20 And it was told him *by certain*, which said, Thy mother[172] and thy brethren stand without, desiring to see thee.

21 And he answered and said unto them, My mother and my brethren are these which hear the word of God,[173] and do it.

Jesus denounces woes against the Pharisees and others. *Galilee.*

CHAPTER XI. 37-54.

37 And as he spake, a certain Pharisee besought him[262] to dine with him: and he went in and sat down to meat.

§ 51. At a Pharisee's table,

MATTHEW.	MARK.

Luke xi. 38, *had not first washed.*] This omission may seem inconsistent with the character of Jesus, who appears to have generally complied with all the innocent usages of his countrymen; and of course it may be adduced as an objection against the veracity of the Evangelist. Luke simply records the fact, however in may seem to make against the character of his Master, or his own veracity. But Mark, vii. 3-9, in a manner equally

Jesus denounces woes against the **Pharisees and others.** *Galilee.*

LUKE.

CHAPTER XI. 37–54.

38 And when the Pharisee saw *it*,
he marvelled that he had not first
washed before dinner.
39 And the Lord said unto him,
Now do ye Pharisees make clean the
outside of the cup and the platter;
but your inward part is full of ravening and wickedness.
40 *Ye* fools, did not he that made
that which is without, make that
which is within also?
41 But rather give alms of such
things as ye have; and behold, all
things are clean unto you.
42 But wo unto you, Pharisees;
for ye tithe mint, and rue, and all
manner of herbs, and pass over judgment and the love of God:[263] these
ought ye to have done, and not to
leave the other undone.
43 Wo unto you, Pharisees! for ye
love the uppermost seats in the synagogues, and greetings in the markets.
44 Wo unto you, scribes and Pharisees, hypocrites![264] for ye are as graves
which appear not, and the men that
walk over *them* are not aware *of them.*
45 Then answered one of the lawyers, and said unto him, Master, thus
saying, thou reproachest us also.
45 And he said, Wo unto you also,
ye lawyers! for ye lade men with
burdens grievous to be borne, and
ye yourselves touch not the burdens
with one of your fingers.
47 Wo unto you! for ye build the
sepulchres of the prophets, and your
fathers killed them.
48 Truly ye bear witness, that ye
allow the deeds of you fathers: for
they indeed killed them, and ye build
their sepulchres.[265]
49 Therefore also said the wisdom
of God, I will send them prophets
and apostles, and [266] *some* of them they
shall slay and persecute:
50. That the blood of all the pro-

JOHN.

---

incidental and without design, discloses the truth that this washing was superstitious, and connected with the dangerous error of placing the traditions of the elders on equal footing with the commands of God. Where there was danger of his practice being misinterpreted, our Lord withheld his compliance, even in things indifferent. See Bp. SUMNER on Luke, Lect. 41.

§ 51. **At a Pharisee's table,**

MATTHEW.	MARK.

§ 52. **Jesus discourses to his disciples**

Jesus denounces woes against the Pharisees and others. *Galilee.*

LUKE.

CHAPTER XI. 37–54.

phets, which was shed from the foundation of the world, may be required of this generation;

51 From the blood of Abel * unto the blood of Zacharias, which perished between the altar and the temple: verily, I say unto you, It shall be required of this generation.

52 Wo unto you, lawyers! for ye have taken away the key of knowledge: ye entered not in yourselves, and them that were entering in ye hindered.

53 And as he said these things unto them, the scribes [267] and the Pharisees began to urge *him* vehemently, and to provoke him to speak of many things;

54 [268] Laying wait for him, and seeking to catch something out of his mouth, that they might accuse him.

JOHN.

and the multitude. *Galilee.*

CHAPTER XII. 1–59.

IN the mean time, when there were gathered together an innumerable multitude of people, insomuch that they trod one upon another, he began to say unto his disciples first of all, Beware ye of the leaven of the Pharisees, which is hypocrisy.

2 [269] For there is nothing covered, that shall not be revealed; neither hid, that shall not be known.

3 Therefore, whatsoever ye have spoken in darkness, shall be heard in the light; and that which ye have spoken in the ear in closets, shall be proclaimed upon the house-tops.

4 And I say unto you, my friends, be not afraid of them that kill the body, and after that, have no more that they can do.

5 But [270] I will forewarn you whom ye shall fear; Fear him, which, after he hath killed, hath power to cast into hell; yea, I say unto you, Fear him.

6 Are not five sparrows sold for two farthings, and not one of them is forgotten before God?

7 But even the very hairs of your head are all numbered. Fear not therefore: [271] ye are of more value than many sparrows.

* Gen. iv. 8; 2 Chron. xxiv. 20, seq.

§ 52. **Jesus discourses to his disciples**

MATTHEW.	MARK.

and the multitude. *Galilee.*

LUKE.

CHAPTER XII. 1–59.

8 Also I say unto you, Whosoever
shall confess me before men, him shall
the Son of man also confess before
the angels of God.[272]
9 But he that denieth me before
men, shall be denied before the angels
of God.
10 And whosoever shall speak a
word against the Son of man, it shall
be forgiven him: but unto him that
blasphemeth against the Holy Ghost,
it shall not be forgiven.
11 And when they bring you unto
the synagogues, and *unto* magistrates,
and powers, take ye no thought how
or what thing ye shall answer, or
what ye shall say:
12 For the Holy Ghost shall teach
you in the same hour what ye ought
to say.
13 And one of the company said unto
him, Master, speak to my brother, that
he divide the inheritance with me
14 And he said unto him, Man,
who made me a judge, or a divider
over you?
15 And he said unto them, Take
heed, and beware of covetousness:[273]
for a man's life consisteth not in the
abundance of the things which he
possesseth.
16 And he spake a parable unto
them, saying, The ground of a certain
rich man brought forth plentifully:
17 And he thought within himself,
saying, What shall I do, because I
have no room where to bestow my
fruits?
18 And he said, This will I do: I
will pull down my barns, and build
greater; and there will I bestow all
my fruits and my goods.[274]
19 And I will say to my soul, Soul,
thou hast much goods laid up for
many years; take thine ease, eat,
drink, *and* be merry.
20 But God said [275] unto him, *Thou*
fool, this night thy soul shall be required of thee: then whose shall those
things be, which thou hast provided?
21 So *is* he that layeth up treasure
for himself, and is not rich toward God.
22 And he said unto his disciples,
Therefore I say unto you, Take no

JOHN.

§ 52. Jesus discourses to his disc.ples

MATTHEW.	MARK.

LUKE.

CHAPTER XII. 1-59.

thought for your life,[276] what ye shall eat; neither for the body, what ye shall put on.
23 The life is more than meat, and the body *is more* than raiment.
24 Consider the ravens: for they neither sow or reap: which neither have store-house, nor barn; and God feedeth them. How much more are ye better than the fowls?
25 And which of you with taking thought can add to his stature one cubit?[277]
26 If ye then be not able to do that thing which is least, why take ye thought for the rest?
27 Consider the lilies how they grow: they toil not, they spin not; and yet I say unto you, that Solomon in all his glory was not arrayed like one of these.
28 If then God so clothe the grass, which is to-day in the field, and to-morrow is cast into the oven; how much more *will he clothe* you, O ye of little faith?
29 And seek not ye what ye shall eat, or what ye shall drink,[278] neither be ye of doubtful mind.
30 For all these things do the nations of the world seek after: and your father knoweth that ye have need of these things.
31 But rather seek ye the kingdom of God,[279] and all these things shall be added unto you.
32 Fear not, little flock; for it is your Father's good pleasure to give you the kingdom.
33 Sell that ye have, and give alms: provide yourselves bags which wax not old, a treasure in the heavens that faileth not, where no thief approacheth, neither moth corrupteth.
34 For where your treasure is, there will your heart be also.
35 Let your loins be girded about, and *your* lights burning;
36 And ye yourselves like unto men that wait for their lord, when he will return from the wedding; that, when he cometh and knocketh, they may open unto him immediately.
37 Blessed *are* those servants, whom

JOHN

§ 52. **Jesus discourses to his disciples**

MATTHEW.	MARK.

and the multitude. *Galilee.*

LUKE.

CHAPTER XII. 1–59.

the Lord when he cometh shall find watching: verily, I say unto you, that he shall gird himself, and make them to sit down to meat, and will come forth and serve them.

38 And if ye shall come in the second watch, or come in the third watch, and find *them* so, blessed are those servants.[280]

39 And this know, that if the good man of the house had known what hour the thief would come, he would have watched, and not have suffered[281] his house to be broken through.

40 Be ye therefore[282] ready also: for the Son of man cometh at an hour when ye think not.

41 Then Peter said unto him, Lord, speakest thou this parable unto us, or even to all?

42 And the Lord said, Who then is that faithful and wise steward, whom *his* lord shall make[283] ruler over his household, to give *them their* portion of meat in due season?

43 Blessed *is* that servant, whom his lord when he cometh shall find so doing.

44 Of a truth I say unto you, That he will make him ruler over all that he hath.

45 But and if that servant say in his heart, My lord delayeth his coming; and shall begin to beat the menservants, and maidens, and to eat and drink, and to be drunken;

46 The lord of that servant will come in a day when he looketh not for *him*, and at an hour when he is not aware, and will cut him in sunder, and will appoint him his portion with the unbelievers.

47 And that servant which knew his lord's will, and prepared not *himself*, neither[284] did according to his will, shall be beaten with many *stripes*.

48 But he that knew not, and did commit things worthy of stripes, shall be beaten with few *stripes*. For unto whomsoever much is given, of him shall much be required; and to whom men have committed much, of him they will ask the more.

49 I am come to send fire on the

JOHN.

§ 52. Jesus discourses to his disciples

MATTHEW.	MARK.

§ 53. The slaughter of certain Galileans.

Luke xii. 54, *out of the West.*] The autumnal rains in Palestine come mostly from the west or south-west. ROBINSON'S Biblical Researches, vol. ii. p. 97. The

and the multitude. *Galilee.*

LUKE.

CHAPTER XII. 1–50.

earth, and what will I, if it be already kindled?

50 But I have a baptism to be baptized with; and how am I straitened till it be accomplished!

51 Suppose ye that I am come to give peace on earth? I tell you, Nay; but rather division:

52 For from henceforth there shall be five in one house divided, three against two, and two against three.

53 The father shall be divided against the son, and the son against the father; the mother against the daughter, and the daughter against the mother; the mother-in-law against her daughter-in-law, and the daughter-in-law against her mother-in-law.[285]

54 And he said also to the people, When ye see a cloud rise out of the west,[286] straightway ye say, There cometh a shower; and so it is.

55 And when *ye see* the south wind blow, ye say, There will be heat;[287] and it cometh to pass.

56 *Ye* hypocrites, ye can discern the face of the sky and of the earth; but how is it, that ye do not discern this time?[288]

57 Yea, and why even of yourselves judge ye not what is right?

58 When thou goest with thine adversary to the magistrate, *as thou art* in the way, give diligence that thou mayest be delivered from him; lest he hale thee to the judge, and the judge deliver thee to the officer, and the officer cast thee into prison.

59 I tell thee, thou shalt not depart thence, till thou hast paid the very last mite.

JOHN.

Parable of the barren fig-tree. *Galilee.*

CHAPTER XIII. 1–9.

THERE were present at that season some that told him of the Galileans, whose blood Pilate had mingled with their sacrifices.

2 And Jesus answering, said unto them,[289] Suppose ye that these Galileans

incidental allusion here made to that fact, would hardly have been made by a writer of fiction.

§ 53. The slaughter of certain Galileans.

MATTHEW.

MARK.

§ 54. The parable

MATTHEW.

CHAPTER XIII. 1–23.

THE same day went Jesus out of the house, and sat by the sea-side.

2 And great multitues were gathered together unto him, so that he went into a ship, and sat; and the whole multitude stood on the shore.

3 And he spake many things unto them in parables, saying, Behold a sower went forth to sow;

4 And when he sowed, some *seeds* fell by the way-side, and the fowls came and devoured them up:

5 Some fell upon stony places, where they had not much earth: and forthwith they sprung up, because they had no deepness of earth:

6 And when the sun was up, they were scorched; and because they had no root, they withered away.

7 And some fell among thorns; and the thorns sprung up, and choked them:

8 But other fell into good ground,

MARK.

CHAPTER IV. 1–25.

AND he began again to teach by the sea-side: and there was gathered unto him a great multitude,[78] so that he entered into a ship, and sat in the sea; and the whole multitude was by the sea, on the land.

2 And he taught them many things by parables, and said unto them in his doctrine,

3 Hearken: Behold, there went out a sower to sow.

4 And it came to pass as he sowed, some fell by the way-side, and the fowls of the air[79] came and devoured it up.

5 And some fell on stony ground, where it had not much earth; and immediately it sprang up, because it had no depth of earth:

6 But when the sun was up it was scorched; and because it had no root, it withered away.

7 And some fell among thorns, and the thorns grew up, and choked it, and it yielded no fruit.

8 And other fell on good ground,

Parable of the barren fig-tree. *Galilee.*

LUKE.	JOHN.
CHAPTER XIII. 1–9.	

were sinners above all the Galileans,
because they suffered such things ? [290]
3 I tell you, Nay; but, except ye
repent, ye shall all likewise perish.
4 Or those eighteen, upon whom the
tower in Siloam fell, and slew them,
think ye that they were sinners above
all men that dwelt in Jerusalem ?
5 I tell you, Nay; but, except ye
repent, ye shall all likewise perish.
6 He spake also this parable: A
certain *man* had a fig-tree planted in
his vineyard; and he came and sought
fruit thereon, and found none.
7 Then said he unto the dresser of
his vineyard, Behold, these three
years I come seeking fruit on this fig-
tree, and find none: cut it down; why
cumbereth it the ground ? [291]
8 And he answering, said unto
him, Lord, let it alone this year also,
till I shall dig about it, and dung *it*:
9 And if it bear fruit, *well*: [292] and
if not, *then* after that thou shalt cut
it down.

of the sower. *Lake of Galilee.* *Near Capernaum ?*

CHAPTER VIII. 4–18.

4 And when much people were
gathered together, and were come to
him out of every city, he spake by a
parable:
5 A sower went out to sow his
seed: and as he sowed, some fell by
the way-side; and it was trodden
down, and the fowls of the air devoured it.
6 And some fell upon a rock; and
as soon as it was sprung up, it withered
away, because it lacked moisture.
7 And some fell among thorns;
and the thorns sprang up with it, and
choked it.
8 And other fell on [166] good ground,

§ 54. The parable.

MATTHEW.

CHAPTER XIII. 1–23.

and brought forth fruit, some a hundred-fold, some sixty-fold, some thirty-fold.

9 Who hath ears to hear,[168] let him hear.

10 And the disciples came, and said unto him, Why speakest thou unto them in parables?

11 He answered and said unto them,[169] Because it is given unto you to know the mysteries of the kingdom of heaven, but to them it is not given.

12 For whosoever hath, to him shall be given, and he shall have more abundance: but whosoever hath not, from him shall be taken away even that he hath.

13 Therefore speak I to them in parables: because they seeing, see not; and hearing, they hear not; neither do they understand.

14 And in them is fulfilled the prophecy of Esaias,*[170] which saith, By hearing ye shall hear, and shall not understand; and seeing ye shall see, and shall not perceive:

15 For this people's heart is waxed gross, and *their* ears are dull of hearing, and their eyes they have closed; lest at any time they should see with *their* eyes, and hear with *their* ears, and should understand with *their* heart, and should be converted, and I should heal them.

16 But blessed *are* your eyes, for they see: and your ears, for they hear.

17 For,[171] verily I say unto you, That many prophets and righteous *men* have desired to see *those things* which ye see, and have not seen *them;* and to hear *those things* which ye hear, and have not heard *them.*

18 Hear ye therefore the parable of the sower.

19 When any one heareth the word of the kingdom, and understandeth *it* not, then cometh the wicked *one*, and catcheth away that which was sown in his heart. This is he which received seed by the way-side.

MARK.

CHAPTER IV. 1–25.

and did yield fruit that sprang up, and increased,[80] and brought forth some thirty, and some sixty, and some a hundred.

9 And he said unto them,[81] He that hath ears to hear, let him hear.

10 And when he was alone, they that were about him, with the twelve, asked of him the parable.[82]

11 And he said unto them, Unto you it is given to know the mystery[83] of the kingdom of God: but unto them that are without, all *these* things are done in parables:

12 That seeing they may see, and not perceive; and hearing they may hear, and not understand; lest at any time they should be converted, and *their* sins should be forgiven them.[84]

13 And he said unto them, Know ye not this parable? and how then will ye know all parables?

14 The sower soweth the word.

15 And these are they by the way-side, where the word is sown; but when they have heard, Satan cometh immediately, and taketh away the word that was sown in their hearts.[85]

* Is. vi. 9, 10.

of the sower. *Lake of Galilee. Near Capernaum?*

LUKE.

CHAPTER VIII. 4–18.

and sprang up, and bare fruit a hundred-fold. And when he had said these things, he cried, He that hath ears to hear, let him hear.

9 And his disciples asked him, saying, What might this parable be? [167]

10 And he said, Unto you it is given to know the mysteries of the kingdom of God: but to others in parables; that seeing they might not see, and hearing they might not understand.[168]

11 Now the parable is this: The seed is the word of God.

12 Those by the way-side, are they that hear: [169] then cometh the devil, and taketh away the word out of their hearts, lest they should believe and be saved.

13 They on the rock *are they*, which, when they hear, receive the word with joy; and these have no

JOHN.

§ 54. The parable

MATTHEW.

CHAPTER XIII. 1–23.

20 But he that received the seed into stony places, the same is he that heareth the word, and anon with joy receiveth it;

21 Yet hath he not root in himself, but dureth for a while: for when tribulation or persecution ariseth because of the word, by and by he is offended.

22 He also that received seed among the thorns is he that heareth the word; and the care of this world,[172] and the deceitfulness of riches, choke the word, and he becometh unfruitful.

23 But he that received seed into the good ground is he that heareth the word, and understandeth *it;* which also beareth fruit, and bringeth forth, some a hundred-fold, some sixty, some thirty.

MARK.

CHAPTER IV. 1–25.

16 And these are they likewise which are sown on stony ground; who, when they have heard the word, immediately receive it with gladness;

17 And have no root in themselves, and so endure but for a time: afterward, when affliction or persecution ariseth for the word's sake, immediately they are offended.

18 And these are they which are sown among thorns; such as hear the word,[86]

19 And the cares of this world, and the deceitfulness of riches, and the lusts of other things entering in, choke the word, and it becometh unfruitful.[87]

20 And these are they which are sown on good ground; such as hear the word, and receive *it*, and bring forth fruit, some thirty-fold, some sixty, and some a hundred.

21 And he said unto them, Is a candle brought to be put under a bushel, or under a bed? and not to be set on a candlestick?

22 For there is nothing hid, which shall not be manifested; neither was any thing kept secret, but that it should come abroad.

23 If any man have ears to hear, let him hear.

24 And he said unto them, Take heed what ye hear: With what measure ye mete, it shall be measured to you: and unto you that hear shall more be given:[88]

25 For he that hath, to him shall be given: and he that hath not, from him shall be taken even that which he hath.

§ 55. Parable of the tares.

CHAPTER XIII. 24–53.

24 Another parable put he forth unto them, saying, The kingdom of heaven is likened unto a man which sowed good seed in his field:

25 But while men slept, his enemy came and sowed tares among the wheat, and went his way.

26 But when the blade was sprung up, and brought forth fruit, then appeared the tares also.

CHAPTER IV. 26–34.

of the sower. *Lake of Galilee. Near Capernaum?*

LUKE.

CHAPTER VIII. 4–18.

root,[170] which for a while believe, and in time of temptation fall away.

14 And that which fell among thorns, are they, which, when they have heard, go forth, and are choked with cares, and riches, and pleasures of *this* life, and bring no fruit to perfection.

15 But that on the good ground are they, which, in an honest and good heart, having heard the word, keep *it*, and bring forth fruit with patience.

16 No man, when he hath lighted a candle, covereth it with a vessel, or putteth *it* under a bed; but setteth *it* on a candlestick, that they which enter in may see the light.[171]

17 For nothing is secret, that shall not be made manifest; neither *anything* hid, that shall not be known, and come abroad.

18 Take heed therefore how ye hear: for whosoever hath, to him shall be given: and whosoever hath not, from him shall be taken even that which he seemeth to have.

JOHN.

Other parables. *Near Capernaum?*

§ 55. Parable of the tares.

MATTHEW.

CHAPTER XIII. 24–53.

27 So the servants of the householder came and said unto him, Sir, didst not thou sow good seed in thy field? from whence then hath it tares?[173]

28 He said unto them, An enemy hath done this. The servant said unto him,[174] Wilt thou then that we go and gather them up?

29 But he said, [175] Nay; lest while ye gather up the tares, ye root up also the wheat with them.

30 Let both grow together until the harvest: and in the time of harvest I will say to the reapers, Gather ye together first the tares, and bind them in bundles to burn them: but gather the wheat into my barn.

31 Another parable put he forth unto them, saying, The kingdom of heaven is like to a grain of mustard-seed, which a man took, and sowed in his field:

32 Which indeed is the least of all seeds: but when it is grown, it is the greatest among herbs, and becometh a tree, so that the birds of the air come and lodge in the branches thereof.

33 Another parable spake he unto them;[176] The kingdom of heaven is like unto leaven, which a woman took, and hid in three measures of meal, till the whole was leavened.

34 All these things spake Jesus unto the multitude in parables; and without a parable spake he not [177] unto them:

35 That it might be fulfilled which was spoken by the prophet,* saying, I will open my mouth in parables; I will utter things which have been kept secret from the foundation of the world.[178]

36 Then Jesus sent the multitude away, and went into the house:[179] and his disciples came unto him, saying, Declare unto us the parable of the tares of the field.

37 He answered and said unto them,[180] He that soweth the good seed is the Son of man;

38 The field is the world; the good seed are the children of the kingdom;

MARK.

CHAPTER IV. 26–34.

26 And he said, So is the kingdom of God, as if a man should cast seed into the ground;

27 And should sleep, and rise night and day, and the seed should spring and grow up, he knoweth not how.

28 For [89] the earth bringeth forth fruit of herself; first the blade, then the ear, after that the full corn in the ear.

29 But when the fruit is brought forth, immediately he putteth in the sickle, because the harvest is come.

30 And he said, Whereunto shall we liken the kingdom of God? or with what comparison shall we compare it?

31 *It is* like a grain of mustard-seed, which when it is sown in the earth, is less than all the seeds that be in the earth:

32 But when it [90] is sown, it groweth up, and becometh greater than all herbs, and shooteth out great branches; so that the fowls of the air may lodge under the shadow of it.

33 And with many such parables spake he the word unto them, as they were able to hear *it*.

34 But without [91] a parable spake he not unto them: and when they were alone, he expounded all things to his disciples.

* Ps. lxxviii. 2.

Other parables. *Near Capernaum?*

LUKE	JOHN.

§ 55. **Parable of the tares.**

MATTHEW.

CHAPTER XIII. 24–53.

but the tares are the children of the wicked *one;*

39 The enemy that sowed them is the devil; the harvest is the end of the world; and the reapers are the angels.

40 As therefore the tares are gathered and burned in the fire; so shall it be in the end of this world.[181]

41 The Son of man shall send forth his angels,[182] and they shall gather out of his kingdom all things that offend, and them which do iniquity;

42 And shall cast them[183] into a furnace of fire: there shall be wailing and gnashing of teeth.

43 Then shall the righteous shine forth as the sun in the kingdom of their Father. Who hath ears to hear,[184] let him hear.

44 Again,[185] The kingdom of heaven is like unto treasure hid in a field; the which when a man hath found, he hideth, and for joy thereof goeth and selleth all that he hath, and buyeth that field.

45 Again, the kingdom of heaven is like unto a merchant man[186] seeking goodly pearls:

46 Who, when he[187] had found one pearl of great price, went and sold all that he had, and bought it.

47 Again, The kingdom of heaven is like unto a net, that was cast into the sea, and gathered of every kind:

48 Which, when it was full, they drew to shore, and sat down, and gathered the good into vessels, but cast the bad away.

49 So shall it be at the end of the world: the angels shall come forth, and sever the wicked from among the just,

50 And shall cast them[188] into the furnace of fire: there shall be wailing and gnashing of teeth.

51 Jesus saith unto them, Have ye understood all these things? They say unto him, Yea, Lord.[189]

52 Then said he unto them, Therefore every scribe *which is* instructed unto the kingdom of heaven, is like unto a man *that is* a household,

MARK.

Other parables. *Near Capernaum?*

LUKE.	JOHN.

§ 55. Parable of the tares.

MATTHEW.

CHAPTER XIII. 24–53.

which bringeth forth out of his treasure *things* new and old.

53 And it came to pass, *that* when Jesus had finished these parables, he departed thence.

MARK.

§ 56. Jesus directs to cross the lake. Incidents.

MATTHEW.

CHAPTER VIII. 18–27.

18 Now when Jesus saw great multitudes,[92] about him, he gave commandment to depart unto the other side.

19 And a certain scribe came, and said unto him, Master, I will follow thee whithersoever thou goest.

20 And Jesus saith unto him, The foxes have holes, and the birds of the air *have* nests; but the Son of man hath not where to lay *his* head.

21 And another of his disciples,[93] said unto him, Lord, suffer me first to go and bury my father.

22 But Jesus said [94] unto him, Follow me; and let the dead bury their dead.

23 And when he was entered into a ship,[95] his disciples followed him.

24 And behold, there arose a great tempest in the sea, insomuch that the ship was covered with the waves: but he was asleep.

25 And his disciples came to *him*, and awoke him, saying, Lord, save us: we perish.[96]

26 And he saith unto them, Why are ye fearful, O ye of little faith? Then he arose, and rebuked the winds[97] and the sea; and there was a great calm.

MARK.

CHAPTER IV. 35–41.

35 And the same day, when the even was come, he saith unto them, Let us pass over unto the other side.

36 And when they had sent away the multitude, they took him even as he was in the ship. And there were also with him other little ships.[92]

37 And there arose a great storm of wind, and the waves beat into the ship, so that it was now full.[93]

38 And he was in the hinder part of the ship, asleep on a pillow: and they awake him, and say unto him, Master, carest thou not that we perish?

39 And he arose and rebuked the wind, and said unto the sea, Peace, be still: and the wind ceased, and there was a great calm.

40 And he said unto them, Why are ye so fearful? how is it that ye have no faith?[94]

Other parables. *Near Capernaum?*

LUKE.	JOHN.

The tempest stilled. *Lake of Galilee.*

LUKE.	JOHN.
CHAPTER VIII. 22–25. CHAPTER IX. 57–62. 22 Now it came to pass on a certain day, that he went into a ship with his disciples: and he said unto them, Let us go over unto the other side of the lake. CHAPTER IX. 57 And it came to pass, that as they went in the way, a certain *man* said unto him, Lord,[221] I will follow thee whithersoever thou goest. 58 And Jesus said [222] unto him, Foxes have holes, and birds of the air *have* nests; but the Son of man hath not where to lay *his* head. 59 And he said unto another, Follow me. But he said, Lord, suffer me first to go and bury my father. 60 Jesus said unto him, Let the dead bury their dead: but go thou and preach the kingdom of God. 61 And another also said, Lord, I will follow thee; but let me first go bid them farewell which are at home at my house. 62 And Jesus said unto him,[223] No man having put his hand to the plough, and looking back, is fit for the kingdom of God. CHAPTER VIII. 22 And they launched forth. 23 But as they sailed, he fell asleep: and there came down a storm of wind on the lake; and they were filled *with water*, and were in jeopardy. 24 And they came to him, and awoke him, saying, Master, Master, we perish. Then he arose, and rebuked the wind, and the raging of the water: and they ceased,[174] and there was a calm. 25 And he said unto them, Where is your faith? And they being afraid,	

§ 56. Jesus directs to cross the lake. Incidents.

MATTHEW.
CHAPTER VIII 18–27.

27 But the men marvelled, saying, What manner of man is this, that even the winds and the sea obey him!

MARK.
CHAPTER IV. 35–41.

41 And they feared exceedingly, and said one to another, What manner of man is this, that even the wind and the sea obey him?

§ 57. The two demoniacs

CHAPTER VIII. 28–34.
CHAPTER IX. 1.

28 And when he was come to the other side, into the country of the Gergesenes,[98] there met him two possessed with devils, coming out of the tombs, exceeding fierce, so that no man might pass by that way.

29 And behold, they cried out,

CHAPTER V. 1–21.

AND they came over unto the other side of the sea, into the country of the Gadarenes.[95]

2 And when he was come out of the ship, immediately [96] there met him out of the tombs a man with an unclean spirit,

3 Who had *his* dwelling among the tombs; and no man could bind him, no, not with his chains:[97]

4 Because that he had been often bound with fetters and chains, and the chains had been plucked asunder by him, and the fetters broken in pieces: neither could any *man* tame him.[98]

5 And always, night and day, he was in the mountains, and in the tombs,[99] crying, and cutting himself with stones.

6 But when he [100] saw Jesus afar off, he ran and worshipped him,

7 And cried with a loud voice, and said, What have I to do with thee, Jesus, *thou* Son of the most high God? [101] I adjure thee by God, that thou torment me not.

8 (For he said [102] unto him, Come out of the man, *thou* unclean spirit.)

9 And he asked him, What *is* thy

Matth. viii. 28, *Gergesenes.*] This is made consistent with the other Evangelists, by reading "Gadarenes." If Gergasa was subordinate to Gadara, the metropolis of Perea, as Cellarius and Reland judge, and St. Mark did not write in Judea, what wonder that he chose the more general name, which was best known in the world? But Cellarius from Eusebius takes notice that some esteemed Gergasi, so Eusebius writes it, and Gadara two names of the same city; and this he thinks was the sentiment of the Syriac translator. To this Sir Richard Ellis most inclines, in his "Fortuita Sacra." TOWNSON, p. 72.

The tempest stilled. *Lake of Galilee.*

LUKE.	JOHN.
CHAPTER VIII. 22–25. CHAPTER IX. 57–62. wondered, saying one to another,[175] What manner of man is this! for he commandeth even the winds and water, and they obey him.	

of Gadara. *S. E. coast of the Lake of Galilee.*

LUKE.	JOHN.
CHAPTER VIII. 26–40. 26 And they arrived at the country of the Gadarenes,[176] which is over against Galilee. 27 And when he went forth to land, there met him out of the city a certain man, which had devils long time, and ware no clothes,[177] neither abode in *any* house, but in the tombs. 28 When he saw Jesus, he cried out, and fell down before him, and with a loud voice said, What have I to do with thee, Jesus, *thou* Son of God most high? I beseech thee torment me not. 29 (For he had commanded the unclean spirit to come out of the man. For oftentimes it had caught him: and he was kept bound with chains, and in fetters; and[178] he brake the bands, and was driven of the devil into the wilderness.) 30 And Jesus[179] asked him, saying,	

In Matthew mention is made of two demoniacs: in Mark and Luke of one only. Here Le Clerc's maxim is undoubtedly true: Qui plura narrat, pauciora complectitur: qui pauciora memorat, plura non negat. *Harm.* p. 524.

We may collect a reason from the Gospels themselves, why Mark and Luke mention only one demoniac; because one only being grateful for the miracle, his cure only was recorded by the two Evangelists, who mention this gratitude, and who are more intent on inculcating the moral, than on magnifying our Lord's power. NEWCOME.

§ 57. The two demoniacs

MATTHEW.
CHAPTER VIII. 28-34.
CHAPTER IX. 1.

saying, What have we to do with thee, Jesus,[99] thou Son of God? art thou come hither to torment us before the time?

30 And there was a good way off from them a herd of many swine, feeding.

31 So the devils besought him, saying, If thou cast us out, suffer us to go away into the herd [100] of swine.

32 And he said unto them, Go. And when they were come out, they went into the herd of swine: [101] and behold, the whole herd of swine ran violently down a steep place into the sea, and perished in the waters.

33 And they that kept them, fled, and went their ways into the city, and told everything; and what was befallen to the possessed of the devils.

34 And behold, the whole city came out to meet Jesus: and when they saw him, they besought him that he would depart out of their coasts.

CHAPTER IX.

AND he entered into a ship, and passed over, and came into his own city.

MARK.
CHAPTER V. 1-21.

name? And he answered, saying,[103] My name *is* Legion: for we are many.

10 And he besought [104] him much that he would not send them away out of the country.

11 Now there was there nigh unto the mountains[105] a great herd of swine feeding.

12 And all the devils besought him,[106] saying, Send us into the swine, that we may enter into them.

13 And forthwith Jesus gave them leave. And the unclean spirits went out, and entered into the swine: and the herd ran violently down a steep place into the sea, (they were about two thousand) and were choked in the sea.[107]

14 [108] And they that fed the swine fled, and told *it* in the city, and in the country. And they went out to see what it was that was done.

15 And they come to Jesus, and see him that was possessed with the devil, and had the legion, sitting, and clothed,[109] and in his right mind: and they were afraid.

16 And they that saw *it* told them how it befell to him that was possessed with the devil, and *also* concerning the swine.

17 And they began to pray him to depart out of their coasts.

18 And when he was come [110] into the ship, he that had been possessed with the devil prayed him that he might be with him.

19 Howbeit Jesus suffered him not,[111] but said unto him, Go home to thy

---

Matth. viii. 30, *a good way off.*] There is no contradiction here between Matthew and Mark. The demoniacs met Jesus on the shore, as he came out of the ship. Luke viii. 27. The swine were within sight, on the ascending ground, Luke viii. 32, at the side of the mountain, Mark v. 11, which was at some distance from the shore where they stood. Matth. viii. 30.

Mark v. 11. *herd of swine.*] Since swine were held in abhorrence by the Jews, how happened a herd of them to be feeding by the sea of Tiberias? The answer shows the accuracy of the Evangelist and his intimate knowledge of the local circumstances of Judea; for it appears from Josephus, Antiq. xvii. 11, 4, that *Gadara* was a *Grecian city*, the inhabitants of which, therefore were not Jews. BLUNT, Veracity, &c. sect. ii. 6.

of Gadara. *S. E. coast of the Lake of Galilee.*

LUKE.
CHAPTER VIII. 26-40.

What is thy name? And he said, Legion: because many devils were entered into him.
31 And they besought him, that he would not command them to go out into the deep.
32 And there was there a herd of many swine feeding on the mountain: and they besought him that he would suffer them to enter into them. And he suffered them.[180]
33 Then went the devils out of the man, and entered into the swine: and the herd ran violently down a steep place into the lake,[181] and were choked.

34 When they that fed *them* saw what was done, they fled, and went [182] and told *it* in the city and in the country.
35 Then they went out to see what was done; and came to Jesus, and found the man out of whom the devils were departed, sitting at the feet of Jesus, clothed, and in his right mind: and they were afraid.
36 They also [183] which saw *it*, told them by what means he that was possessed of the devils was healed.

37 Then the whole multitude of the country of the Gadarenes round about, besought them to depart from them; for they were taken with great fear. And he went up into the ship,[184] and returned back again.
38 Now the man out of whom the devils were departed, besought him that he might be with him. But Jesus sent him away,[185] saying,

JOHN.

Luke viii. 35, *sitting at the feet of Jesus.*] Here is a reference to an Eastern custom, which affords internal evidence of the truth of the narrative. The master sat on a higher seat, and the scholars sat at his feet. Sitting at the feet, was the posture of a learner; and indicated the reverence and submission due to the teacher. Thus Moses says of the people, to whom God gave the law from Mount Sinai,—"they sat down at thy feet." Deut. xxxiii. 3. Isaiah, speaking of Abraham, who was taught of God, says "he called him to his foot." Is. xli. 2. Mary "sat at Jesus's feet and heard his words." Luke x. 39. Paul was brought up "at the feet of Gamaliel;" Acts xxii. 3; studied law with him. And the restored maniac sat down at Jesus's feet, in the posture of a humble learner, desiring no other wisdom than to be taught of him.

§ 57. The two demoniacs

MATTHEW.

MARK.

CHAPTER V. 1–21.

friends, and tell them how great things the Lord hath done for thee, and hath had compassion on thee.

20 And he departed, and began to publish in Decapolis how great things Jesus had done for him. And all *men* did marvel.

21 And when Jesus was passed over again by ship unto the other side, much people gathered unto him: and he was nigh unto the sea.

§ 58. Levi's feast.

MATTHEW.

CHAPTER IX. 10–17.

10 And it came to pass, as Jesus sat at meat[106] in the house, behold, many publicans and sinners came and sat down with him and his disciples.

11 And when the Pharisees saw *it*, they said unto his disciples, Why eateth your Master with publicans and sinners?

12 But when Jesus heard *that*, he said unto them,[107] They that be whole need not a physician, but they that are sick.

13 But go ye and learn what *that* meaneth,* I will have mercy, and not sacrifice: for I am not come to call the righteous, but sinners to repentance.[108]

14 Then came to him the disciples of John, saying, Why do we and the Pharisees fast oft,[109] but thy disciples fast not?

15 And Jesus said unto them, Can the children of the bride-chamber mourn, as long as the bridegroom is with them? but the days will come, when the bridegroom shall be taken from them, and then shall they fast.

16 No man putteth a piece of new cloth unto an old garment: for that

MARK.

CHAPTER II. 15–22.

15 [44] And it came to pass, that as Jesus sat at meat in his house, many publicans and sinners sat also together with Jesus and his disciples; for there were many, and they followed him.[45]

16 [46] And when the scribes and Pharisees saw him eat with publicans and sinners, they said unto his disciples, How is it that he eateth and drinketh with publicans and sinners?

17 When Jesus heard *it*, he saith unto them, They that are whole, have no need of the physician, but they that are sick: I came not to call the righteous, but sinners to repentance.[47]

18 And the disciples of John, and of the Pharisees, used to fast:[48] and they come, and say unto him, Why do the disciples of John, and of the Pharisees fast, but thy disciples fast not?

19 And Jesus said unto them, Can the children of the bride-chamber fast, while the bridegroom is with them? As long as they have the bridegroom with them, they cannot fast.

20 But the days will come, when the bridegroom shall be taken away from them, and then shall they fast in those days.[49]

21 No man also seweth a piece of new cloth on an old garment: else

* Hos. vi. 6; 1 Sam. xv. 22.

Matth. ix. 10, *in the house.*] Both Mark and Luke state that this was in Matthew's own house; and Luke calls it a great feast, made in honour of Jesus. The omission of this fact

of Gadara. *S. E. coast of the Lake of Galilee.*

LUKE.	JOHN.
CHAPTER VIII. 26–40. 39 Return to thine own house, and shew how great things God hath done unto thee. And he went his way and published throughout the whole city, how great things Jesus had done unto him. 40 And it came to pass, that, when Jesus was returned, the people *gladly* received him: for they were all waiting for him.[186]	

Capernaum.

LUKE.	JOHN.
CHAPTER V. 29–39. 29 And Levi made him a great feast in his own house; and there was a great company of publicans, and of others that sat down with them. 30 [100] But their scribes and Pharisees murmured against his disciples, saying, why do ye eat and drink with publicans and sinners? 31 And Jesus answering, said unto them, They that are whole need not a physician; but they that are sick. 32 I came not to call the righteous, but sinners to repentance.[101] 33 And they said unto him, Why do the disciples of John fast often,[102] and make prayers, and likewise *the disciples* of the Pharisees; but thine eat and drink? 34 [103] And he said unto them, Can ye make the children of the bridechamber fast while the bridegroom is with them? 35 [104] But the days will come, when the bridegroom shall be taken away from them, and then shall they fast in those days. 36 And he spake also a parable unto them: No man putteth a piece of a new garment upon an old: if other-	

---

by Matthew, not only shows his modesty and humility, but adds much to the weight of evidence in his favour, both as a man, and as a witness. See BLUNT'S Veracity of the Gospels. Sect. i. 4.

§ 58. Levi's feast.

MATTHEW.

CHAPTER IX. 10–17.

which is put in to fill it up, taketh from the garment, and the rent is made worse.

17 Neither do men put new wine into old bottles: else the bottles break, and the wine runneth out, and the bottles perish: but they put [110] new wine into new bottles, and both are preserved.

MARK.

CHAPTER II. 15–22.

the new piece that filled it up, taketh away from the old, and the rent is made worse.

22 And no man putteth new wine into old bottles: else the new wine doth burst the bottles, and the wine is spilled, and the bottles will be marred: but new wine must be put into new bottles.[50]

§ 59. The raising of Jarius's daughter.

CHAPTER IX. 18–26.

18 While he spake these things unto them, behold, there came a certain ruler, and worshipped him, saying, My daughter is even now dead: but come and lay thy hand upon her, and she shall live.

19 And Jesus arose and followed him, and *so did* his disciples.

20 (And behold a woman which was diseased with an issue of blood twelve years, came behind *him*, and touched the hem of his garment.

21 For she said within herself, If I may but [111] touch his garment, I shall be whole.

22 But Jesus turned [112] him about, and when he saw her, he said, Daughter, be of good comfort: thy faith hath made thee whole. And the woman was made whole from that hour.)

CHAPTER V. 22–43.

22 And behold, there cometh one of the rulers of the synagogue, Jairus by name; and when he saw him, he fell [112] at his feet.

23 And besought him [113] greatly, saying, My little daughter lieth at the point of death: *I pray thee*, come and lay thy hands on her, that she may be healed; and she shall live.

24 And *Jesus* went with him; and much people followed him, and thronged him.

25 And a certain woman [114] which had an issue of blood twelve years,

26 And had suffered many things of many physicians, and had spent all that she had, and was nothing bettered, but rather grew worse,

27 When she had heard of Jesus,[115] came in the press behind, and touched his garment:

28 For she said, If I may touch but [116] his clothes, I shall be whole.

29 And straightway the fountain of her blood was dried up; and she felt in *her* body that she was healed of that plague.

30 And Jesus, immediately knowing in himself that virtue had gone out of him, turned him about in the press, and said, Who touched my clothes?

31 And his disciples said unto him, Thou seest the multitude thronging thee, and sayest thou, Who touched me?

32 And he looked round about to see her that had done this thing.

Capernaum.

LUKE.

CHAPTER V. 29–39.

wise, when both the new maketh a rent,
and the piece that was *taken* out of the
new, agreeth not with the old.[105]
37 And no man putteth new wine
into old bottles; else the new wine
will burst the bottles, and be spilled,
and the bottles shall perish.
38 But new wine must be put into
new bottles, and both are preserved.[106]
39 No man also having drunk old
wine, straightway desireth new: for
he saith, the old is better.[107]

JOHN.

The woman with a bloody flux. *Capernaum.*

CHAPTER VIII. 41–56.

41 And behold there came a man
named Jarius, and he was a ruler of
the synagogue: and he fell down at
Jesus' feet, and besought him that
he would come into his house:
42 For he had one only daughter,
about twelve years of age, and she lay
a-dying. But as he went, the people
thronged him.
43 And a woman having an issue
of blood twelve years, which had
spent all her living upon physicians,[187]
neither could be healed of any,
44 Came behind *him* and touched
the border of his garment: and immediately her issue of blood stanched.
45 And Jesus said, Who touched
me? When all denied, Peter, and
they that were with him, said, Master,
the multitude throng thee, and press
thee, and sayest thou, Who touched
me?[188]
46 And Jesus said, Somebody hath
touched me: for I perceive that virtue
is gone out of me.

§ 59. The raising of Jairus's daughter.

MATTHEW.

CHAPTER IX. 18–26.

23 And when Jesus came into the ruler's house, and saw the minstrels and the people making a noise,

24 He said unto them, [113] Give place: for the maid is not dead but sleepeth. And they laughed him to scorn.

25 But when the people were put forth, he went in, and took her by the hand, and the maid arose.

26 And the fame hereof [114] went abroad into all that land.

MARK.

CHAPTER V. 22–43.

33 But the woman, fearing and trembling, knowing [117] what was done in her, came and fell down before him, and told him all the truth.

34 And he said unto her, Daughter, thy faith hath made the whole; go in peace, and be whole of thy plague.

35 While he yet spake, there came from the ruler of the synagogue's *house certain* which said, Thy daughter is dead: why troublest thou the Master any further?

36 As soon as Jesus heard the word [118] that was spoken, he saith unto the ruler of the synagogue, Be not afraid, only believe.

37 And he suffered no man to follow him, save Peter and James, and John the brother of James.

38 And he cometh to the house of the ruler of the synagogue, and seeth [119] the tumult, and them that wept and wailed greatly.

39 And when he was come in, he saith unto them, Why make ye this ado, and weep? the damsel is not dead, but sleepeth.

40 And they laughed him to scorn. But, when he had put them all out, he taketh the father and the mother of the damsel, and them that were with him, and entereth in where the damsel was lying.[120]

41 And he took the damsel by the hand, and said unto her, Talitha-cumi: which is, being interpreted, Damsel, (I say unto thee) arise.

42 And straightway the damsel arose, and walked; for she was *of the age* of twelve years. And they were astonished with a great astonishment.[121]

43 And he charged them straitly that no man should know it; and commanded that something should be given her to eat.

§ 60. Two blind men healed,

CHAPTER IX. 27–34.

27 And when Jesus departed thence, two blind men followed him,[115] crying, and saying, *Thou* son of David, have mercy on us.

The woman with a bloody flux. *Capernaum.*

LUKE.

CHAPTER VIII. 41–56.

47 And when the woman saw that
she was not hid, she came trembling,
and falling down before him, she declared unto him[189] before all the
people for what cause she had touched
him, and how she was healed immediately.
48 And he said unto her,[190] Daughter, be of good comfort: thy faith
hath made thee whole; go in peace.
49 While he yet spake, there cometh one from the ruler of the synagogue's *house*, saying to him,[191] Thy
daughter is dead: trouble not the
Master.
50 But when Jesus heard *it*, he
answered him, saying, Fear not:[192]
believe only, and she shall be made
whole.
51 And when he came into the
house, he suffered no man to go in,
save Peter, and James, and John, and
the father and the mother of the
maiden.
52 And all wept and bewailed her:
but he said, Weep not: she is not
dead,[193] but sleepeth.
53 And they laughed him to scorn,
knowing that she was dead.
54 And he put them all out,[194] and
took her by the hand, and called,
saying, Maid, arise.
55 And her spirit came again, and
she arose straightway:[195] and he commanded to give her meat.
56 And her parents were astonished: but he charged them that they
should tell no man what was done.

JOHN.

and a dumb spirit cast out. *Capernaum.*

§ 60. Two blind men healed,

MATTHEW.

CHAPTER IX. 27–34.

28 And when he was come [116] into the house, the blind men came to him: and Jesus saith unto them, Believe ye that I am able to do this?[117] They said unto him, Yea, Lord.

29 Then touched he their eyes, saying, According to your faith, be it unto you.

30 And their eyes were opened; and Jesus straitly charged them, saying, See *that* no man know *it*.

31 But they, when they were departed, spread abroad his fame in all [118] that country.

32 As they went out, behold, they brought to him a dumb man [119] possessed with a devil.

33 And when the devil was cast out, the dumb spake: and the multitudes marvelled, saying, It was never so seen in Israel.

34 But the Pharisees said, He casteth out devils, through the prince of the devils.

MARK.

§ 51. Jesus again at Nazareth,

MATTHEW. CHAPTER XIII. 54–58.

54 And when he was come into his own country, he taught them in their synagogue, insomuch that they were astonished, and said, Whence has this *man* his wisdom, and *these* mighty works?

55 Is not this the carpenter's son? is not his mother called Mary? and his brethren, James and Joses,[190] and Simon, and Judas?

56 And his sisters, are not they all with us? Whence then hath this *man* all these things?

57 And they were offended in him. But Jesus said unto them, A prophet is not without honour, save in his own country,[191] and in his own house.

58 And he did not many mighty works there, because of their unbelief.

MARK. CHAPTER VI. 1–6.

AND he went out from thence, and came [122] into his own country; and his disciples follow him.

2 And when the sabbath-day was come, he began to teach in the synagogue: and many hearing *him* were astonished, saying, From whence hath this *man* these things? and what wisdom *is* this which is given unto him, that even such mighty works are wrought by his hands?[123]

3 Is not this the carpenter, the son of Mary, the brother of James, and Joses,[124] and of Juda, and Simon? and are not his sisters here with us? And they were offended at him.

4 But Jesus said unto them, A prophet is not without honour, but in his own country, and among his own kin,[125] and in his own house.

5 And he could there do no mighty work, save that he laid his hands upon a few sick folk, and healed *them*.

6 And he marvelled because of their unbelief.

Mark vi. 3, *son of Mary*.] Neither of the Evangelists expressly mentions the death of Joseph; yet from all four of them it may indirectly be inferred to have happened

and a dumb spirit cast out. *Capernaum.*

LUKE.	JOHN.

and again rejected.

while Jesus was yet alive. Comp. Luke viii. 19, John ii. 12, and xix. 25-27. Such harmony as this could not have been the effect of concert. See BLUNT's Veracity, &c. Sect. i 7.

§ 62. A third circuit in Galilee.

MATTHEW.
CH. IX. 35–38. CH. X. 1, 5–42.
CHAPTER XI. 1.

35 And Jesus went about all the cities and villages, teaching in their synagogues, and preaching the gospel of the kingdom, and healing every sickness, and every disease among the people.[120]

36 But when he saw the multitudes, he was moved with compassion on them, because they fainted,[121] and were scattered abroad as sheep having no shepherd.

37 Then saith he unto his disciples, the harvest truly *is* plenteous, but the labourers *are* few.

38 Pray ye therefore the Lord of the harvest, that he will send forth labourers into his harvest.

CHAPTER X.

AND when he had called unto *him* his twelve disciples, he gave them power *against* unclean spirits, to cast them out, and to heal all manner of sickness, and all manner of disease.

5 These twelve Jesus sent forth, and commanded them, saying,[125] Go not into the way of the Gentiles, and into *any* city of the Samaritans, enter ye not.

6 But go rather to the lost sheep of the house of Israel.

7 And as ye go, preach, saying, The kingdom of heaven is at hand.

8 Heal the sick, cleanse the lepers, raise the dead, cast out devils:[126] freely ye have received, freely give.

9 Provide neither gold, nor silver, nor brass in your purses;

10 Nor scrip for *your* journey, neither two coats, neither shoes, nor yet staves:[127] (for the workman is worthy of his meat.)

11 And into whatever city or town ye shall enter, inquire who in it is[128] worthy; and there abide till ye go thence.

12 And when ye come into a house, salute it.[129]

MARK.
CHAPTER VI. 6–13.

7 And he called *unto him* the twelve, and began to send them forth by two and two, and gave them power over unclean spirits;

8 And commanded them that they should take nothing for *their* journey, save a staff only; no scrip, no bread,[127] no money in *their* purse:

9 But *be* shod with sandals; and not put on two coats.

10 And he said[128] unto them, In what place soever ye enter into a house, there abide till ye depart from that place.

Matth. x. 10, *shoes.*] Commentators have noted two inconsistent circumstances in this section. In Matthew, *shoes* are forbidden; in Mark the Apostles are commanded to be shod with *sandals.* But the true solution appears to be this, that the Apostles

The Twelve instructed and sent forth. *Galilee.*

LUKE.
CHAPTER IX. 1–6.

THEN he called his twelve disciples together,[196] and gave them power
and authority over all devils, and to
cure diseases.
2 And he sent them to preach the
kingdom of God, and to heal the
sick.[197]
3 And he said unto them, Take
nothing for *your* journey, neither
staves,[198] nor scrip, neither bread,
neither money; neither have two
coats apiece.
4 And whatsoever house ye enter
into, there abide, and thence depart.
5 And whosoever will not receive
you,[199] when ye go out of that city,
shake off the very dust from your
feet for a testimony against them.

JOH[N].

should not furnish themselves with *spare* garments, and should wear the simplest covering for their feet. "Non vult ullis rebus studiose comparatis onerari." BEZA. See NEWCOME. *in loc.*

§ 62. A third circuit in Galilee.

MATTHEW.
Ch. IX. 35–38. Ch. X. 1, 5–42.
Chapter XI. 1.

13 And if the house be worthy, let your peace come upon it: but if it be not worthy, let your peace return to you.[130]

14 And whosoever shall not receive you, nor hear your words, when ye depart out of that house, or city,[131] shake off the dust of your feet.

15 Verily, I say unto you, It shall be more tolerable for the land of Sodom and Gomorrah,[132] in the day of judgment, than for that city.

16 Behold, I send you forth as sheep in the midst of wolves: be ye therefore wise as serpents,[133] and harmless as doves.

17 But beware of men: for they will deliver you up to the councils, and they will scourge you in their synagogues.

18 And ye shall be brought before governors and kings for my sake, for a testimony against them and the Gentiles.

19 But when they deliver you up, take no thought how or what ye shall speak, for it shall be given you in that same hour what ye shall speak.

20 For it is not ye that speak, but the Spirit of your Father which speaketh in you.

21 And the brother shall deliver up the brother to death, and the father the child: and the children shall rise up against *their* parents, and cause them to be put to death.

22 And ye shall be hated of all *men* for my name's sake: but he that endureth to the end shall be saved.

23 But when they persecute you in this city, flee ye into another: for verily I say unto you, Ye shall not have gone over the cities of Israel till the Son of man be come.

24 The disciple is not above *his* master, nor the servant above his lord.

MARK.
Chapter VI. 6–13.

11 And whosoever shall not receive you, nor hear you, when ye depart thence, shake off the dust under your feet, for a testimony against them. Verily, I say unto you, it shall be more tolerable for Sodom and Gomorrah in the day of judgment, than for that city.[129]

✎ Matth. x 17, *in their synagogues.*] The synagogues were used, not only for divine service, but for holding courts of Justice, especially for ecclesiastical affairs; and the lesser punishments, such as whipping, were inflicted in the synagogue, immediately after sentence, as the burning in the hand was formerly inflicted in England, upon praying the benefit of clergy. Jennings, Ant. p. 376. Such an allusion as this would not be likely to have been found in a work of fiction.

The Twelve instructed and sent forth. *Galilee.*

LUKE.	JOHN.

§ 62. A third circuit in Galilee.

MATTHEW.

CH. IX. 35–38. CH. X. 1, 5–42.
CHAPTER XI. 1.

25 It is enough for the disciple that he be as his master, and the servant as his lord: if they have called the master of the house Beelzebub,[134] how much more *shall they call* them of his household?

26 Fear them not therefore: for there is nothing covered, that shall not be revealed; and hid, that shall not be known.

27 What I tell you in darkness, *that* speak ye in light: and what ye hear in the ear, *that* preach ye upon the house-tops.

28 And fear not them which kill the body, but are not able to kill the soul: but rather fear him which is able to destroy both soul and body in hell.

29 Are not two sparrows sold for a farthing? and one of them shall not fall on the ground without your Father.

30 But the very hairs of your head are all numbered.

31 Fear ye not therefore, ye are of more value than many sparrows.

32 Whosoever therefore shall confess me before men, him will I confess also before my Father which is in heaven.

33 But whosoever shall deny me before men, him will I also deny before my Father which is in heaven.

34 Think not that I am come to send peace on earth; I came not to send peace, but a sword.

35 For I am come to set a man at variance against his father, and the daughter against her mother, and the daughter-in-law against her mother-in-law.

36 And a man's foes *shall be* they of his own household.*

37 He that loveth father or mother more than me, is not worthy of me: and he that loveth son or daughter more than me, is not worthy of me.

38 And he that taketh not his cross and followeth after me, is not worthy of me.

39 He that findeth his life shall

MARK.

* Mic. vii. 6.

The Twelve instructed and sent forth. *Galilee.*

LUKE.	JOHN.

§ 62. A third circuit in Galilee.

MATTHEW.
CH. IX. 35–38. CH. X. 1, 5–42.
CHAPTER XI. 1.

lose it: and he that loseth his life for my sake, shall find it.

40 He that receiveth you, receiveth me; and he [135] that receiveth me, receiveth him that sent me.

41 He that receiveth a prophet in the name of a prophet, shall receive a prophet's reward; and he that receiveth a righteous man in the name of a righteous man, shall receive a righteous man's reward.

42 And whosoever shall give to drink unto one of these little ones, a cup of cold *water* only, in the name of a disciple, verily, I say unto you, he shall in no wise lose his reward.

CHAPTER XI.

AND it came to pass when Jesus had made an end of commanding his twelve disciples, he departed thence to teach and to preach in their cities.

MARK.
CHAPTER VI. 6–13.

6 And he went [126] round about the villages teaching.

12 And they went out, and preached that men should repent. [130]

13 And they cast out many devils, and anointed with oil many that were sick, and healed *them*.

§ 63. Herod holds Jesus to be John the Baptist,

CHAPTER XIV. 1, 2, 6–12.

AT that time Herod the tetrarch heard of the fame of Jesus,

2 And said unto his servants, This is John the Baptist; he is risen from the dead; and therefore mighty works do shew forth themselves in him.

6 But when Herod's birth-day was kept, the daughter of Herodias danced before them, and pleased Herod.

7 Whereupon he promised with an oath to give her whatsoever she would ask.

CHAPTER VI. 14–16, 21–29.

14 And king Herod heard *of him*, (for his name was spread abroad,) and he said, [131] That John the Baptist was risen from the dead, and therefore mighty works do shew forth themselves in him.

15 [132] Others said, that it is Elias. And others said, That it is a prophet, or as one of the prophets.

16 But when Herod heard *thereof*, he said, It is John, whom I beheaded: he is risen from the dead. [133]

21 And when a convenient day was come, that Herod on his birth-day made a supper to his lords, high captains, and chief *estates* of Galilee:

22 And when the daughter of the said Herodias came in, and danced, and pleased Herod, and them that sat with him, [136] the king said unto the damsel, Ask of me whatsoever thou wilt, and I will give *it* thee.

23 And he sware unto her, What-

Matth. xiv. 2, *unto his servants.*] Matthew alone mentions, and without any apparent reason for such minuteness, that Herod addressed his remark to his *servants.* Luke, in the parallel passage, says he *heard of all that was done by him*: but by referring to Luke viii. 3, and to Acts xiii. 1, we find that Christ had followers from among the household of this very Prince, with whom Herod was likely to converse on

The Twelve instructed and sent forth.

LUKE.	JOHN.
6 And they departed, and went through the towns, preaching the gospel, and healing everywhere.	

whom he had just before beheaded. *Galilee? Perea.*

CHAPTER IX. 7–9. 7 Now Herod the tetrarch heard of all that was done by him:[200] and he was perplexed, because that it was said of some, that John was risen from the dead; 8 And of some, that Elias had appeared; and of others, that one of the old prophets was risen again. 9 And Herod said,[201] John have I beheaded; but who is this of whom I hear such things? And he desired to see him.	

a subject in which they were better informed than himself. BLUNT, Veracity, &c., sec. i. 8.

Matth. xiv. 6, *birth-day was kept.*] Here is a very natural passing allusion to what we learn from Josephus was a settled custom in the family of Herod; namely, the making of a feast on his birth-day, at which the officers of his government were guests. JOSEPHUS, Ant. xix. vii. § 1.

§ 63. Herod holds Jesus to be John the Baptist,

MATTHEW. CHAPTER XIV. 1, 2, 6–12.	MARK. CHAPTER VI. 14–16, 21–29.
	soever thou shalt ask of me,[137] I will give *it* thee, unto the half of my kingdom.
	24 And she went forth, and said unto her mother, What shall I ask? And she said, The head of John the Baptist.
8 And she, being before instructed of her mother, said, Give me here John Baptist's head in a charger.	25 And she came in [138] straightway with haste unto the king, and asked, saying, I will that thou give me, by and by, in a charger, the head of John the Baptist.
9 And the king was sorry: nevertheless for the oath's sake, and them which sat with him at meat, he commanded *it* to be given *her*. 10 And he sent, and beheaded John in the prison.	26 And the king was exceeding sorry; *yet* for his oath's sake, and for their sakes which sat with him, he would not reject her. 27 And immediately the king sent an executioner, and commanded his head to be brought: [139] and he went and beheaded him in the prison;
11 And his head was brought in a charger, and given to the damsel: and she brought *it* to her mother.	28 And brought his head in a charger, and gave it to the damsel; and the damsel gave it to her mother.
12 And his disciples came, and took up the body, and buried it,[194] and went and told Jesus.	29 And when his disciples heard *of it*, they came and took up his corpse, and laid it in a tomb.[140]

§ 64. The Twelve return. Jesus retires with them across the lake.

CHAPTER XIV. 13–21.	CHAPTER VI. 30–44.
13 When Jesus heard *of it*, he departed thence by ship into a desert place apart: and when the people had heard *thereof*, they followed him on foot out of the cities.	30 And the apostles gathered themselves together unto Jesus, and told him all things, both what they had done, and what they had taught.[141]
14 And Jesus [195] went forth, and saw a great multitude, and was moved with compassion toward them, and he healed their sick.	31 And he said unto them, Come ye yourselves apart into a desert place, and rest awhile: for there were many coming and going, and they had no leisure so much as to eat.
	32 And they departed into a desert place by ship privately.
	33 And the people saw them departing, and many knew him, and ran afoot thither out of all cities, and

---

Mark vi. 31, *many coming and going.*] Mark incidently mentions the great multitude coming and going, and the purpose of Jesus to withdraw *awhile.* The occasion of this great multitude of *travellers* is stated in the like incidental manner by John, [vi. 4,] that the *passover* was nigh at hand; and hence, if Jesus withdrew awhile, the throng would be drawn off towards Jerusalem. These undesigned coincidences tend to verify both the narratives. BLUNT. Veracity, &c. sect. i. 13.

John vi. 5, *saith unto Philip.*] Why Jesus addressed this question to Philip, and why John mentioned so unimportant a fact, is not here explained. Nor does Luke indicate any reason for his own statement of the place where this miracle was wrought, namely,

whom he had just before beheaded. *Galilee? Perea.*

LUKE.

JOHN.

Five thousand are fed. *Capernaum. N. E. coast of the lake.*

CHAPTER IX. 10–17.

10 And the apostles, when they were returned, told him all that they had done. And he took them, and went aside privately into a desert place, belonging to the city called Bethsaida.[202]

11 And the people, when they knew *it*, followed him: and he received them, and spake unto them of the kingdom of God, and healed them that had need of healing.

CHAPTER VI. 1–14.

AFTER these things Jesus went over the sea of Galilee, which is *the sea* of Tiberias.

2 And a great multitude followed him, because they saw his miracles[120] which he did on them that were diseased.

3 [121] And Jesus went up into a mountain, and there he sat with his disciples.

4 And the passover, a feast of the Jews, was nigh.

near Bethsaida. But John, in another place, (ch. i. 44,) with apparently as little reason, gratuitously states that Philip was of Bethsaida; and this fact renders both the others intelligible and significant. Jesus, intending to furnish bread for the multitude by a miracle, first asked Philip, who belonged to the city and was perfectly acquainted with the neighbourhood, whether bread could be procured there. His answer amounts to saying that it was not possible. These slight circumstances, thus collected together, constitute very cogent evidence of the veracity of the narrative, and evince the reality of the miracle itself. See BLUNT, Veracity &c. sect. i. 13.

§ 64. The Twelve return. Jesus retires with them across the lake.

MATTHEW.
CHAPTER XIV. 13–21.

15 And when it was evening his disciples came to him, saying, This is a desert place, and the time is now past; send the [196] multitude away, that they may go into the villages, and buy themselves victuals.

16 But Jesus said [197] unto them, They need not depart; give ye them to eat.

17 And they said unto him, We have here but five loaves, and two fishes.

18 He said, Bring them hither to me.

19 And he commanded the multitude to sit down on the grass, and took the five loaves, and the two fishes, and looking up to heaven, he blessed, and brake, and gave the loaves to *his* disciples, and the disciples to the multitude.

20 And they did all eat, and were filled: and they took up of the fragments that remained twelve baskets full.

21 And they that had eaten were about five thousand men, besides women and children.

MARK.
CHAPTER VI. 30–44.

outwent them, and came together unto him.[142]

34 And Jesus, when he came out, saw [143] much people, and was moved with compassion toward them, because they were as sheep not having a shepherd: and he began to teach them many things.

35 And when the day was now far spent, his disciples came unto him, and said,[144] This is a desert place, and now the time *is* far passed:

36 Send them away, that they may go into the country round about, and into the villages, and buy themselves bread: for they have nothing to eat.[145]

37 He answered and said unto them, Give ye them to eat. And they say unto him, Shall we go and buy two hundred pennyworth of bread, and give them to eat?

38 He saith unto them, How many loaves have ye? go and see. And when they knew, they say,[146] Five, and two fishes.

39 And he commanded them to make all sit down by companies upon the green grass.

40 And they sat down in ranks, by hundreds, and by fifties.

41 And when he had taken the five loaves, and the two fishes, he looked up to heaven, and blessed, and brake the loaves, and gave *them* to his disciples [147] to set before them; and the two fishes divided he among them all.

42 And they did all eat, and were filled.

43 And they took up twelve baskets full of the fragments, and of the fishes.[148]

44 And they that did eat of the loaves, were about five thousand men.[142]

§ 65. Jesus walks upon the water.

CHAPTER XIV. 22–36.

22 [198] And straightway Jesus constrained his disciples to get into a ship, and to go before him unto the

CHAPTER VI. 45–56.

45 And straightway he constrained his disciples to get into the ship, [150] and to go to the other side before unto

Luke ix. 14, *by fifties.*] In Luke, Jesus commands that the people should be made to sit down by *fifties.* In Mark it is said that they sat down by *hundreds and by fifties.*

Five thousand are fed. *Capernaum. N. E. coast of the lake.*

LUKE.
CHAPTER IX. 10–17.

12 And when the day began to wear away,[203] then came the twelve, and said unto him, Send the multitude away, that they may go into the towns and country round about, and lodge, and get victuals: for we are here in a desert place.

13 But he said unto them, Give ye them to eat. And they said, We have no more but five loaves and two fishes; except we should go and buy meat for all this people.

14 (For they were about five thousand men.) And he said to his disciples, Make them sit down by fifties[204] in a company.

15 And they did so, and made them all sit down.

16 Then he took the five loaves, and the two fishes, and looking up to heaven, he blessed them, and brake, and gave to the disciples to set before the multitude.

17 And they did eat, and were all filled: and there was taken up of fragments that remained to them[205] twelve baskets.

JOHN.
CHAPTER VI. 1–14.

5 When Jesus then lifted up *his* eyes and saw a great company come unto him, he saith unto Philip, Whence shall we buy bread that these may eat?

6 (And this he said to prove him: for he himself[122] knew what he would do.)

7 Philip answered him, Two hundred pennyworth of bread is not sufficient for them, that every one of them may take a little.[123]

8 One of his disciples, Andrew, Simon Peter's brother, saith unto him,

9 There is a lad here, which hath five barley loaves, and two small fishes: but what are they among so many?

10 And[124] Jesus saith, Make the men sit down. (Now there was much grass in the place.) So the men sat down in number about five thousand.

11 And Jesus took the loaves; and when he had given thanks, he distributed to the disciples, and the disciples to them that were set down; and likewise of the fishes, as much as they would.[125]

12 When they were filled, he said unto his disciples, Gather up the fragments that remain, that nothing be lost.

13 Therefore they gathered *them* together, and filled twelve baskets with the fragments of the five barley loaves which remained over and above unto them that had eaten.

14 Then those men, when they had seen the miracle that Jesus did,[126] said, This is of a truth that Prophet that should come into the world.

Lake of Galilee. Gennesaret.

CHAPTER VI. 15–21.

15 When Jesus therefore perceived that they would come and take him by force, to make him a king, he de-

Piscator, and Pearce, in a dissertation at the end of his comment on St. Paul's Epistles, say that they sat an hundred in front, and fifty deep; which very satisfactorily solves the seeming variation. NEWCOME.

§ 65. Jesus walks upon the water.

MATTHEW.

CHAPTER XIV. 22–36.

other side, while he sent the multitudes away.

23 And when he had sent the multitudes away,[199] he went up into a mountain apart to pray: and when the evening was come, he was there alone.

24 But the ship was now in the midst of the sea,[200] tossed with waves: for the wind was contrary.

25 And in the fourth watch of the night Jesus went [201] unto them, walking on the sea.

26 And when the disciples saw him [202] walking on the sea, they were troubled, saying, it is a spirit; and they cried out with fear.

27 But straightway Jesus spake [204] unto them, saying, Be of good cheer; it is I; be not afraid.

28 And Peter answered him and said, Lord, if it be thou,[204] bid me come unto thee on the water.

29 And he said, Come. And when Peter was come down out of the ship, he walked on the water, to go to Jesus.[205]

30 But when he saw the wind boisterous,[206] he was afraid; and beginning to sink, he cried, saying, Lord, save me.

31 And immediately Jesus stretched forth *his* hand, and caught him, and said unto him, O thou of little faith, wherefore didst thou doubt?

32 And when they were come into the ship, the wind ceased.

33 Then they that were in the ship came and [207] worshipped him, saying, Of a truth thou art the Son of God.

34 And when they were gone over, they came into the land of Gennesaret.[208]

35 And when the men of that place [209] had knowledge of him, they sent out into all that country round about, and brought unto him all that were diseased;

36 And besought him that they might only touch the hem of his garment: and as many as touched were made perfectly whole.

MARK.

CHAPTER VI. 45–56.

Bethsaida, while he sent away the people.

46 And when he had sent them away, he departed into a mountain to pray.

47 And when even was come, the ship was in the midst of the sea, and he alone on the land.

48 And he saw them toiling in rowing; for the wind was contrary unto them: and about the fourth watch of the night he cometh unto them, walking upon the sea, and would have passed by them.

49 But when they saw him walking upon the sea, they supposed it had been a spirit, and cried out.

50 (For they all saw him, and were troubled.) And immediately he talked with them, and saith unto them, Be of good cheer: It is I; be not afraid.

51 And he went up unto them into the ship; and the wind ceased; and they were sore amazed in themselves beyond measure, and wondered.[151]

52 For they considered not *the miracle* of the loaves; for their heart was hardened.

53 And when they had passed over, they came into the land of Gennesaret, and drew to the shore.

54 And when they were come out of the ship, straightway they knew him.[152]

55 And ran through that whole region round about, and began to carry about in beds those that were sick, where they heard he was.

56 And whithersoever he entered, into villages, or cities, or country,[153] they laid the sick in the streets, and besought him that they might touch, if it were but the border of his garment: and as many as touched him were made whole.

Lake of Galilee. Gennesaret.

LUKE.

JOHN.

CHAPTER VI. 15–21.

parted again [127] into a mountain himself alone.
16 And when even was *now* come,
his disciples went down unto the sea,
17 And entered into a ship, and
went over the sea toward Capernaum.
And it was now dark, and Jesus was
not come to them.[128]
18 And the sea arose by reason of
a great wind that blew.
19 So when they had rowed about
five and twenty or thirty furlongs,
they see Jesus walking on the sea,
and drawing nigh unto the ship: and
they were afraid.
20 But he saith [129] unto them, It is
I; be not afraid.
21 Then they willingly received
him into the ship: and immediately
the ship was at the land whither they
went.[130]

§ 66. **Our Lord's discourse in the Synagogue at Capernaum.**

MATTHEW.	MARK.

John vi. 25, *Rabbi, when camest thou hither?*] This seemingly idle inquiry becomes important as a note of veracity in the narrator, when compared with the account of Matthew. John indeed tells us, v. 18, that the wind blew a gale, but he does not state from what quarter. He also says that there were boats from Tiberias, near the place where the miracle of bread was wrought, v. 23, but this does not at all explain the inquiry of the people how Jesus came to Capernaum. But Matthew states that "the wind was contrary," that is west, Matth. xiv. 22. This fact, and the geographical position of the places, explains the whole. The miracle was wrought near Bethsaida, on the east side of the lake. The

LUKE.

JOHN.

CHAPTER VI. 22–71. CHAPTER VII. 1.

22 [131] The day following, when the people which stood on the other side of the sea saw that there was none other boat there, save that one whereinto his disciples were entered,[132] and that Jesus went not with his disciples into the boat, but *that* his disciples were gone away alone;

23 [133] (Howbeit [134] there came other boats from Tiberias nigh unto the place where they did eat bread, after that the Lord had given thanks:)

24 When the people therefore saw that Jesus was not there, neither his disciples, they also took shipping, and came to Capernaum, seeking for Jesus.[135]

25 And when they had found him on the other side of the sea, they said unto him, Rabbi, when camest thou hither?

26 Jesus answered them and said, Verily, verily, I say unto you, Ye seek me, not because ye saw the miracles, but because ye did eat of the loaves, and were filled.

27 Labour not for the meat which perisheth, but for that meat which endureth unto everlasting life, which the Son of man shall give unto you: for him hath God the Father sealed.[136]

28 Then said they unto him,[137] What shall we do, that we might work the works of God?

29 Jesus answered and said unto them, This is the work of God, that ye believe on him whom he hath sent.

30 They said therefore unto him, what sign shewest thou then,[138] that we may see, and believe thee? what dost thou work?

31 Our fathers did eat manna in the

---

people saw the disciples take the only boat which was there, and depart for Capernaum, which was on the west side of the lake, and saw that Jesus was not with them. In the night it blew a tempest from the west. In the morning, the storm being over, the people crossed over to Capernaum and found Jesus already there. Well might they ask him, with astonishment, how he came thither. For though there were boats over from Tiberias which was also on the west side of the lake, yet he could not have returned in one of them, for the wind would not have permitted them to cross the lake. BLUNT, Veracity of the Gospels, sect. i. 17.

§ 66. **Our Lord's discourse in the Synagogue at Capernaum.**

MATTHEW.	MARK.

Many disciples turn back. Peter's profession of faith. *Capernaum.*

LUKE.

JOHN.

CHAPTER VI. 22–72. CHAPTER VII. 1.

desert; as it is written.* He gave
them bread from heaven to eat.
32 Then Jesus said unto them,
Verily, verily, I say unto you, Moses
gave you not that bread from heaven;
but my Father giveth you the true
bread from heaven.
33 For the bread of God is he
which cometh down from heaven, and
giveth life unto the world.
34 Then said they unto him, Lord,
ever more give us this bread.
35 [139] And Jesus said unto them, I
am the bread of life: He that cometh
to me, shall never hunger; and he that
believeth on me, shall never thirst.
36 But I said unto you, That ye
also have seen me,[140] and believe not.
37 All that the Father giveth me,
shall come to me; and him that cometh to me, I will in no wise cast out.
38 For I came down from heaven,
not to do [141] mine own will, but the
will of him that sent me.
39 And this is the Father's will
which hath [142] sent me, that of all
which he hath given me, I should
lose nothing, but should raise it up
again at the last day.
40 And this is the will of him that
sent me,[143] that every one which seeth
the Son, and believeth on him, may
have everlasting life: and I will raise
him up at the last day.
41 The Jews then murmured at
him, because he said, I am the bread
which came down from heaven.
42 And they said, Is not this Jesus
the son of Joseph, whose father and
mother we know? how is it then that
he saith,[144] I came down from heaven?
43 Jesus therefore answered and
said [145] unto them, Murmur not
among yourselves.
44 No man can come to me, except
the Father [146] which hath sent me
draw him; and I will raise him up
at the last day.
45 It is written in the prophets,†
And they shall be all taught of God.
Every man therefore that hath heard,

* Ps. lxxviii. 24. Ex. xvi. 15.

† Isa. liv. 13. Jer. xxxi. 33, seq.

§ 66. Our Lord's discourse in the Synagogue at Capernaum.

MATTHEW.	MARK.

Many disciples turn back. Peter's profession of faith. *Capernaum.*

LUKE.

JOHN.

CHAPTER VI. 22–71. CHAPTER VII. 1.

and hath learned of the Father, cometh unto me.[147]

46 Not that any man hath seen the Father, save he which is of God, he hath seen the Father.[148]

47 Verily, verily, I say unto you, He that believeth on me[149] hath everlasting life.

48 I am that bread of life.*

49 Your fathers did eat manna in the wilderness, and are dead.

50 This is the bread which cometh down from heaven, that a man may eat thereof, and not die.

51 I am the living bread which came down from heaven: if any man eat of this bread, he shall live for ever: and the bread that I will give is my flesh, which I will give for the life of the world.[150]

52 The Jews therefore strove among themselves, saying, How[151] can this man give us *his* flesh to eat?

53 Then Jesus said unto them, Verily, verily, I say unto you, Except ye eat the flesh of the Son of man, and drink his blood, ye have no life in you.[152]

54 Whoso eateth my flesh, and drinketh my blood, hath eternal life; and I will raise him up at the last day.

55 For my flesh is meat indeed, and my blood is drink indeed.[153]

56 He that eateth my flesh, and drinketh my blood, dwelleth in me, and I in him.

57 As the living Father hath sent me, and I live by the Father: so he that eateth me, even he shall live by me.

58 This is that bread which came down from heaven: not as your fathers did eat manna, and are dead:[154] he that eateth of this bread shall live for ever.

59 These things said he in the synagogue, as he taught in Capernaum.[155]

60 Many therefore of his disciples, when they had heard *this*, said, This is a hard saying; who can hear it?

* Ex. xvi. 15.

§ 66. Our Lord's discourse in the Synagogue at Capernaum.

MATTHEW.	MARK

John vi. 66, *went back.*] The truth of the Gospels has been argued from the *confessions* they contain. On this verse Paley asks, "Was it the part of a writer, who dealt in suppression and disguise, to put down *this* anecdote?" *Evid.* 255.

John vi. 70, *a devil.*] The admission of *Judas Iscariot* into the domestic and confidential circle of our Lord, was the result of profound and even of divine wisdom. It showed that Jesus was willing to throw open his most secret actions, discourses, and

Many disciples turn back. Peter's profession of faith. *Capernaum.*

LUKE.

JOHN.

CHAPTER VI. 22–71. CHAPTER VII. 1.

61 When Jesus knew in himself that his disciples murmured at it, he said unto them,[156] Doth this offend you?

62 *What* and [157] if ye shall see the Son of man ascend up where he was before?

63 It is the Spirit that quickeneth; the flesh profiteth nothing: the words that I speak unto you, *they* are spirit, and *they* are life.[158]

64 But there are some of you that believe not. For Jesus knew from the beginning who they were that believed not, and who should betray him.[159]

65 And he said, Therefore said I unto you, that no man can come unto me, except it were given unto him of my Father.[160]

66 From that *time* many of his disciples [161] went back, and walked no more with him.

67 Then said Jesus unto the twelve, will ye also go away?

68 Then [162] Simon Peter answered him, Lord, to whom shall we go? thou hast the words of eternal life.

69 And we believe, and are sure that thou art that Christ, the Son of the living God.[163]

70 Jesus answered them, Have not I chosen you twelve, and one of you is a devil? [164]

71 He spake of Judas Iscariot, *the son* of Simon: for he it was that should betray him,[165] being one of the twelve.

CHAPTER VII.

AFTER these things Jesus walked in Galilee: for he would not walk in Jewry, because the Jews sought to kill him.

---

views, not merely to his devoted friends, but to a sagacious and hardened enemy. If Judas had ever discovered the least fault in the character or conduct of Jesus, he certainly would have disclosed it; he would not have publicly confessed that he had betrayed innocent blood, and have sunk down in insupportable anguish and despair. See TAPPIN'S Lect. on Eccl. Hist. ii.

PART V.

FROM OUR LORD'S THIRD PASSOVER,

UNTIL HIS

FINAL DEPARTURE FROM GALILEE,

AT THE

FESTIVAL OF TABERNACLES.

TIME. *Six months.*

§ 67. Our Lord justifies his Disciples for eating with

MATTHEW.
CHAPTER XV. 1–20.

THEN came to Jesus scribes and Pharisees,[210] which were of Jerusalem, saying,
2 Why do thy disciples transgress the tradition of the elders? for they wash not their hands[211] when they eat bread.

MARK.
CHAPTER VII. 1–23.

THEN came together unto him the Pharisees, and certain of the scribes, which came from Jerusalem.
2 And when they saw some of his disciples eat bread with defiled (that is to say, with unwashen) hands, they found fault.[154]

Matth. xv. 2, *the tradition of the elders.*] The traditions of the elders were unwritten ordinances of indefinite antiquity, the principal of which, as the Pharisees alleged, were delivered to Moses in the mount, and all of which were transmitted through the High Priests and Prophets, down to the members of the great Sanhedrim in their own times; and from these as the Jews say, they were handed down to Gamaliel, and ultimately to Rabbi Jehudah, by whom they were digested and committed to writing, toward the close of the second century. This collection is termed the Mishna; and in many cases it is esteemed among the Jews as of higher authority than the law itself. In like manner there are said to be many Christians, at the present day, who receive ancient traditionary usages and opinions as authoritative exponents of Christian doctrine. They say that the preached gospel was before the written gospel; and that the testimony of those who heard it is entitled to equal credit with the written evidence of the Evangelists; especially as the latter is but a brief record, while the oral preaching was a more full and copious announcement of the glad tidings.

These traditions both of the Jewish and the Christian Church, seem to stand *in pari ratione*, the arguments in favor of the admissibility and effect of the one, applying with the same force, in favor of the other. All these arguments may be resolved into two grounds, namely, contemporaneous practice subsequently and uniformly continued; and contemporaneous declarations, as part of the *res gestæ*, faithfully transmitted to succeeding times. It is alleged that those to whom the law of God was first announced, best knew its precise import and meaning, and that therefore their interpretation and practice, coming down concurrently with the law itself, is equally obligatory.

But this argument assumes what cannot be admitted; for it still remains to be shown that those who first heard the law, when orally announced, had any better means of understanding it than those to whom the same words were afterwards read. The Ten Commandments were spoken in the hearing of Aaron and all the congregation of Israel; immediately after which they made and worshipped a golden calf. Surely this will not be adduced as a valid contemporaneous exposition of the second commandment. The error of the argument lies in the nature of the subject. The human doctrine of contemporaneous exposition is applicable only to human laws and the transactions of men, as equals, and not to the laws of God. Among men, when *their own* language is doubtful and ambiguous, *their own* practice is admissible, to expound it; because both the language and the practice are but the outward and visible signs of the meaning and intention of one and the same mind and will, which inward meaning and intention is the thing sought after. It is on the same ground, that, where a statute, capable of divers interpretation, has uniformly been acted upon in a certain way, this is held a sufficient exposition of its true intent. In both cases it is the conduct of *the parties* themselves which is admitted to interpret their own language; expressed, in cases of contract, by themselves in person, and in statutes, through the medium of the legislators who were their agents and representatives, and in both cases, it is merely the interpretation of what a man says, by what he does. But this rule has never been applied, in the law, to the language of any other person than the party himself; never, to the command or direction of his superior or employer. And even the language of the *parties*, when it is contained in a sealed instrument, is at this day held incapable of being expounded by their actions, on account of the greater solemnity of the instrument. See Baynham *v.*

LUKE.	JOHN.

Guy's Hospital, 3 Vesey's Rep. 295. Eaton *v.* Lyon, Ibid. 690, 694. The practice of men, therefore, can be no just exponent of the law of God. If they have mistaken the meaning of his command from the beginning, the act of contravention remains a sin in the last transgressor, as well as the first; for the word of God cannot be changed or affected by the gloss of human interpretation.

The other ground, namely, that the testimony of those who heard Jesus and his apostles preach, is of equal authority with the Scriptures, being contemporaneous declarations, and parts of the *res gestæ*, and therefore admissible in aid of the exposition of the written word, is equally inconsistent with the sound and settled rules of law respecting writings. When a party has deliberately committed his intention and meaning to writing, the law regards the writing as the sole repository of his mind and intention, and does not admit any oral testimony to alter, add to, or otherwise affect it. The reasons for this rule are two; first, because the writing is the more solemn act, by the party himself, designed to prevent mistake, and to remain as the perpetual memorial of his intention; and, secondly, because of the great uncertainty and weakness of any secondary evidence. For no one can tell whether the by-standers heard precisely what was said, nor whether they heard it all, nor whether they continued to remember it with accuracy until the time when they wrote it down, or communicated it to those who wrote it; to say nothing of the danger of their mixing up the language of the speaker with what was said by others, or with their own favorite theories. And where the witnesses were not the original auditors of what was said, no one knows how much the truth may have suffered from the many channels through which it has passed, in coming from the first speaker to the last writer or witness. On all these accounts, the law rejects oral testimony of what the parties said, in regard to anything that has already been solemnly committed to writing by the parties themselves, and rejects the secondary evidence of hearsay, when evidence of a higher degree, as, for example, a written declaration of the party, can be obtained.

Now, inasmuch as the writings of the Evangelists and Apostles were penned under the inspiration of the Holy Spirit, why should not the documentary evidence of the Gospel, thus drawn up by them, be treated with at least as much respect as other written documents? If they were inspired to write down those great truths for a perpetual memorial to after ages, then this record is the primary evidence of those truths. It is the word of God, penned by his own dictation, and sealed, as it were, with his own seal. If it were a man's word and will, thus solemnly written, no verbal or secondary evidence could be admitted, by the common law, to explain, add to, or vary it, nothing could be engrafted upon it; nor could any person be admitted to testify what he heard the party say, in regard to what was written. The courts would at once reject all such attempts, and confine themselves strictly to the writing before them, the only inquiry being as to the meaning of the language contained in that document, and not as to what the party may elsewhere have spoken. The law presumes that the writing alone is the source to which he intended that resort should be had, in order to ascertain his meaning. But by calling in the fathers, with their traditions, to prove what Christ and his Apostles taught, beyond what is solemnly recorded in the Scriptures, the principle of this plain and sound rule of law is violated; resort is had to secondary evidence of the truths of our religion, when the primary evidence is already at hand; and the pure fountain is deserted for the muddy stream.

§ 67. Our Lord justifies his Disciples for eating with

MATTHEW.
CHAPTER XV. 1–20.

3 But he answered and said unto them, Why do ye also [212] transgress the commandment of God by your tradition?

4 For God commanded,* [213] saying, Honour thy father and mother: and, He that curseth father or mother, let him die the death.

5 But ye say, Whosoever shall say to *his* father or *his* mother, *It is* a gift, by whatsoever thou mightest be profited by me; [214]

6 And honour not his father or his mother *he shall be free.* Thus have ye made the commandment of God of none effect by your tradition.[215]

7 *Ye* hypocrites, well did Esaias prophesy of you,† saying,

8 This people draweth nigh unto me with their mouth, and [216] honoureth me with *their* lips; but their heart is far from me.

9 But in vain they do worship me, teaching *for* doctrines the commandments of men.

MARK.
CHAPTER VII. 1–23.

3 For the Pharisees, and all the Jews, except they wash *their* hands oft, eat not, holding the tradition of the elders.

4 And *when they come* from the market, except they wash, they eat not. And many other things there be, which they have received to hold, *as* the washing of cups, and pots, and brazen vessels, and tables.[155]

5 Then the Pharisees and scribes asked him, Why walk not thy disciples according to the tradition of the elders, but eat bread with unwashen hands? [156]

6 He answered and [157] said unto them, Well hath Esaias prophesied of you hypocrites, as it is written, This people honoureth me with *their* lips, but their heart is far from me.

7 Howbeit, in vain do they worship me, teaching *for* doctrines the commandments of men.

8 For, laying aside the commandment of God, ye hold the tradition of men, *as* the washing of pots and cups: and many other such like things ye do.[158]

9 And he said unto them, Full well ye reject the commandment of God, that ye may keep your own tradition.

10 For Moses said, Honour thy father and thy mother; and, Whoso curseth father or mother, let him die the death:

11 But ye say, If a man shall say to his father or mother, *It is* Corban, that is to say, a gift, by whatsoever thou mightest be profited by me; *he shall be free.*

12 And [159] ye suffer him no more to do aught for his father or his mother;

* Ex. xxii. 12. Ex. xxi. 17. Deut v. 16. † Is. xxix. 13.

Mark vii. 3, 4.] Matthew was not only a Jew himself, but it is evident, from the whole structure of his Gospel, especially from his numerous references to the Old Testament, that he

unwashen hands. Pharisaic traditions. *Capernaum.*

LUKE.	JOHN.

wrote for Jewish readers.—*Paley.* But the explanation here given by Mark is an additional evidence of the fact asserted by Jerome and Clement of Alexandria, that he wrote at Rome, for the benefit chiefly of the converts of that nation.

§ 67. Our Lord justifies his Disciples for eating with

MATTHEW.
CHAPTER XV. 1–20.

10 And he called the multitude, and said unto them, Hear, and understand:

11 Not that which goeth into the mouth defileth a man; but that which cometh out of the mouth, this defileth a man.

12 Then came his disciples, and said [217] unto him, Knowest thou that the Pharisees were offended after they heard this saying?

13 But he answered and said, Every plant, which my heavenly Father hath not planted, shall be rooted up.

14 Let them alone: they be blind leaders of the blind.[218] And if the blind lead the blind, both shall fall into the ditch.

15 Then answered Peter and said unto him, Declare unto us this parable.[219]

16 And Jesus said,[220] Are ye also yet without understanding?

17 Do not ye yet [221] understand, that whatsoever entereth in at the mouth goeth into the belly, and is cast out into the draught?

18 But those things which proceed out of the mouth come forth from the heart; and they defile the man.

19 For out of the heart proceed evil thoughts, murders, adulteries, fornications, thefts, false witness, blasphemies:

20 These are *the things* which defile a man: but to eat with unwashen hands defileth not a man.

MARK.
CHAPTER VII. 1–23.

13 Making the word of God of none effect through your tradition, which ye have delivered: and many such like things do ye.

14 And when he had called all the people *unto him*, he said unto them, Hearken unto me every one *of you*,[160] and understand.

15 There is nothing from without a man, that entereth into him, can defile him: but the things which come out of him,[161] those are they that defile the man.

16 [162] If any man has ears to hear, let him hear.

17 And when he was entered into the house from the people, his disciples asked him concerning the parable.[163]

18 And he saith unto them, Are ye so without understanding also? Do ye not perceive, that whatsoever thing from without entereth into the man, *it* cannot defile him:[164]

19 Because it entereth not into his heart, but into the belly, and goeth out into the draught, purging all meats?

20 And he said, That which cometh out of the man, that defileth the man.

21 For from within, out of the heart of men, proceed evil thoughts, adulteries, fornications, murders,[165]

22 Thefts,[166] covetousness, wickedness, deceit, lasciviousness, an evil eye, blasphemy, pride, foolishness;

23 All these evil things come from within, and defile the man.[167]

§ 68. The daughter of a Syrophenician woman

MATTHEW.
CHAPTER XV. 21-28.

21 Then Jesus went thence, and departed into the coasts of Tyre and Sidon.

MARK.
CHAPTER VII. 24–30.

24 And from thence he arose, and went into the borders of [168] Tyre and Sidon, and entered into a house, and

unwashen hands. Pharisaic traditions. *Capernaum.*

LUKE.	JOHN.

is healed. *Region of Tyre and Sidon.*

§ 68. The daughter of a Syrophenician woman

MATTHEW.

CHAPTER XV. 21–28.

22 And behold, a woman of Canaan came out of the same coasts, and cried unto him,[222] saying, Have mercy on me, O Lord, *thou* son of David; my daughter is grievously vexed with a devil.

23 But he answered her not a word. And his disciples came and besought him, saying, Send her away; for she crieth after us.

24 But he answered and said, I am not sent but unto the lost sheep of the house of Israel.

25 Then came she and worshipped him, saying, Lord, help me.

26 But he answered and said, It is not meet to take the children's bread and to cast *it* to dogs.

27 And she said, Truth, Lord: yet the dogs eat of the crumbs which fall from their master's table.

28 Then Jesus answered and said unto her, O woman, great *is* thy faith: be it unto thee even as thou wilt. And her daughter was made whole from that very hour.

MARK.

CHAPTER VII. 24–30.

would have no man know *it:* but he could not be hid.

25 [169] For a *certain* woman, whose young daughter had an unclean spirit, heard of him, and came and fell at his feet:

26 (The woman was a Greek, a Syrophenician by nation,) and she besought him that he would cast forth the devil out of her daughter.

27 But Jesus said unto her,[170] Let the children first be filled: for it is not meet to take the children's bread, and to cast it unto the dogs.

28 And she answered and said unto him, Yes, Lord: yet the dogs under the table eat[171] of the children's crumbs.

29 And he said unto her, For this saying, go thy way; the devil is gone out of thy daughter.

30 And when she was come to her house, she found the devil gone out, and her daughter laid upon the bed.[172]

§ 69. A deaf and dumb man healed; also many others.

CHAPTER XV. 10–17.

29 And Jesus departed from thence, and came nigh unto the sea of Galilee; and went up into a mountain, and sat down there.

30 And great multitudes came unto him, having with them *those that were* lame, blind, dumb, maimed, and many others, and cast them down at Jesus' feet; and he healed them:[223]

CH. VII. 31–37. CH. VIII. 1–9.

31 And again departing from the coasts of Tyre and Sidon, he came unto the sea of Galilee, through the midst of the coasts of Decapolis.[173]

32 And they bring unto him one that was deaf, and had an impediment in his speech; and they beseech him to put his hand [174] upon him.

33 And he took him aside from the multitude, and put his fingers into his ears, and he spit and touched his tongue:

34 And looking up to heaven, he sighed, and saith unto him, Ephphatha, that is, Be opened.

35 And straightway [175] his ears were

Mark vii. 26, *Syrophenician.*] Mark designates the woman by the country where she dwelt; Matthew calls her a woman of Canaan, because of the people to whom she belonged. Thus they do not contradict each other. The treatment of this woman by our Lord has been the subject of remark, as evasive and insincere. But it was far otherwise. He had a twofold object; to call the attention of his disciples to the fact of her being a foreigner, in order to show them that his ministry, though primarily and chiefly to the Jews, was in truth designed for the benefit of the Gentiles also; and to

is healed. *Region of Tyre and Sidon.*

LUKE.	JOHN.

Four thousand are fed. *The Decapolis.*

draw out, as it were, the great faith of the woman, in order to teach them the effect of faithful and persevering supplication. To attain these objects, he took the direct and most obvious method. In this instance also, as in those of the centurion, (Matth. viii. 5-13,) and of the Samaritan leper, (Luke xvii. 16-18,) he indicated that the gospel would be more readily received by the Gentiles than by the Jews. See A. CLARKE, *in loc.* NEWCOME, Obs. on our Lord, p. 165. Bp. Horsley's Sermons on this subject, Serm. xxxvii. and xxxviii. p. 444–464.

§ 69. A deaf and dumb man healed; also many others.

MATTHEW.

CHAPTER XV. 29–38.

31 Insomuch that the multitude wondered, when they saw the dumb to speak, the maimed to be whole, the lame to walk, and the blind to see: and they glorified the God of Israel.[224]

32 Then Jesus called his disciples *unto him*, and said, I have compassion on the multitude, because they continue with me now three days, and have nothing to eat: and I will not send them away fasting, lest they faint in the way.[225]

33 And his disciples[226] say unto him, Whence should we have so much bread in the wilderness, as to fill so great a multitude?

34 And Jesus saith unto them, How many loaves have ye? And they said, Seven, and a few little fishes.

35 And he commanded the multitude to sit down on the ground.

36 And he took the seven loaves and the fishes, and gave thanks, and brake *them*, and gave to his disciples,[227] and the disciples to the multitude.

37 And they did all eat, and were filled: and they took up of the broken *meat* that was left seven baskets full.

38 And they that did eat were four thousand men, besides women and children.[228]

MARK.

CH. VII. 24–37. CH. VIII. 1–9.

opened, and the string of his tongue was loosed, and he spake plain.

36 And he charged them that they should tell no man: but the more he charged them, so much the more a great deal they published *it;*

37 And were beyond measure astonished, saying, He hath done all things well; he maketh[176] both the deaf to hear, and the dumb to speak.

CHAPTER VIII.

IN those days the multitude being very great, and having nothing to eat, Jesus called his disciples *unto him*, and saith unto them,[177]

2 I have compassion on the multitude, because they have now been with me three days, and have nothing to eat:

3 And if I send them away fasting to their own houses, they will faint by the way: for divers of them came from far.[178]

4 And his disciples answered him,[179] From whence can a man satisfy these *men* with bread here in the wilderness?

5 And he asked them, How many loaves have ye? And they said, Seven.

6 And he commanded[180] the people to sit down on the ground: and he took the seven loaves, and gave thanks, and brake, and gave to his disciples to set before *them;* and they did set *them* before the people.

7 And they had a few small fishes: and he blessed,[181] and commanded to set them also before *them.*

8 So they did eat,[182] and were filled: and they took up of the broken *meat* that was left, seven baskets.

9 And they that had eaten were about four thousand:[183] and he sent them away.

§ 70. The Pharisees and Sadducees again

CH. XV. 39. CH. XVI. 1–4.

39 And he sent away the multitude, and took ship, and came into the coasts of Magdala.[229]

CHAPTER VIII. 10–12.

10 And straightway he entered into a ship with his disciples, and came into the parts of Dalmanutha.[184]

Matth. xv. 39, *Magdala.*] Cellarius and Lightfoot think that Dalmanutha and Magdala were neighbouring towns. See Calmet, voc. Dalmanutha. It is probable that Dalmanutha

Four thousand are fed. *The Decapolis.*

LUKE.	JOHN.

require a sign. *Near Magdala.*

and Magdala were in Gaulanitis, towards the south-east part part of the lake. See Matth. xv 21.; Mark vii. 24. NEWCOME.

§ 70. The Pharisees and Sadducees again

MATTHEW.

CHAPTER XVI. 1–4.

THE Pharisees also with the Sadducees came, and, tempting, desired him that he would show them a sign from heaven.

2 [230] He answered and said unto them, When it is evening, ye say, *It will be* fair weather: for the sky is red.

3 And in the morning, *It will be* foul weather to-day: for the sky is red and lowering. O *ye* hypocrites, ye can discern the face of the sky; but can ye not *discern* the signs of the times?

4 A wicked and adulterous generation seeketh after a sign; and there shall be no sign be given unto it, but the sign of the prophet Jonas.[231]

MARK.

CHAPTER VIII. 10–12.

11 And the Pharisees came forth, and began to question with him, seeking of him a sign from heaven,[185] tempting him.

12 And he sighed deeply in his spirit, and saith, Why doth this generation seek after a sign? Verily I say unto you,[186] There shall no sign be given unto this generation.

§ 71. The disciples cautioned against the leaven

MATTHEW.

CHAPTER XVI. 4–12.

4 And he left them and departed.

5 And when his disciples [232] were come to the other side, they had forgotten to take bread.

6 Then Jesus said unto them,[233] Take heed and beware of the leaven of the Pharisees and of the Sadducees.

7 And they reasoned among themselves, saying, *It is* because we have taken no bread.

8 *Which* when Jesus perceived, he said unto them, O ye of little faith, why reason ye among yourselves, because ye have brought no bread?[234]

9 Do ye not yet understand, neither remember the five loaves of the five thousand, and how many baskets ye took up?

10 Neither the seven loaves of the four thousand, and how many baskets ye took up?

MARK.

CHAPTER VIII. 13–21.

13 And he left them, and entering into the ship [187] again, departed to the other side.

14 Now *the disciples* had forgotten to take bread, neither had they in the ship with them more than one loaf.

15 And he charged them, saying, Take heed, beware of the leaven of the Pharisees, and *of* the leaven of Herod.

16 And they reasoned among themselves, saying, *It is* because we have no bread.[188]

17 And when Jesus knew *it*, he saith unto them, Why reason ye, because ye have no bread? perceive ye not yet, neither understand? have ye your heart yet hardened?[189]

18 Having eyes, see ye not? and [190] having ears, hear ye not? and do ye not remember?

19 When I brake the five loaves among five thousand, how many [191] baskets full of fragments took ye up? They say unto him, Twelve.

20 [192] And when the seven among four thousand, how many baskets full of fragments took ye up? And they said, Seven.

Matth. xvi. 9, 10.] Our Lord's words, Matth. xvi. 8, 10, and Mark viii. 17, 20, are the same in substance, though differently modified. The evangelists are not scrupulous in adhering to the precise words used by Christ. They often record them in a general manner, non numer-

require a sign. *Near Magdala.*

LUKE.	JOHN.

of the Pharisees, &c. *N. E. coast of the lake of Galilee.*

antes, sed tanquem appendentes; regarding their purport, and not superstitiously detailing them. However, in this place, after uttering what Matthew relates, Jesus *may* have asked the questions recorded by Mark. NEWCOME.

§ 71. The disciples cautioned against the leaven

MATTHEW.

CHAPTER XVI. 4–12.

11 How is it that ye do not understand that I spake *it* not to you concerning bread, that he should beware of[235] the leaven of the Pharisees and of the Sadducees?

12 Then understood they how that he bade *them* not beware of the leaven of bread, but of the doctrine of the Pharisees and of the Sadducees.[236]

MARK.

CHAPTER VIII. 13–21.

21 And he said unto them, How is it that ye do not understand?[193]

§ 72. A blind man healed.

CHAPTER VIII. 22–26.

22 And he cometh[194] to Bethsaida; and they bring a blind man unto him, and besought him to touch him.

23 And he took the blind man by the hand, and led him out of the town; and when he had spit on his eyes, and put his hands upon him, he asked him if he saw aught.[195]

24 And he looked up, and said, I see men as trees walking.[196]

25 After that, he put *his* hands again upon his eyes, and made him look up: and he was restored, and saw every man clearly.[197]

26 And he sent him away to his house, saying,[198] Neither go into the town, nor tell *it* to any in the town.

§ 73. Peter and the others again profess their

CHAPTER XVI. 13–20.

13 When Jesus came into the coasts of Cesarea Philippi, he asked his disciples, saying, Whom do men say that I, the Son of man, am?[237]

14 And they said, Some *say that thou art* John the Baptist: some, Elias; and others, Jeremias, or one of the prophets.

15 He saith unto them, But whom say ye that I am?

16 And Simon Peter answered and said, Thou art the Christ, the Son of the living God.

17 And Jesus answered[238] and said unto him, Blessed art thou, Simon

CHAPTER VIII. 27–30.

27 And Jesus went out, and his disciples, into the towns of Cesarea Philippi: and by the way he asked his disciples,[199] saying unto them, Whom do men say that I am?

28 And they answered,[200] John the Baptist: but some *say*, Elias; and others, One of the prophets.

29 And he saith unto them, But whom say ye that I am? And Peter answereth and saith unto him, Thou art the Christ.

Mark viii. 23, *out of the town.*] The notice of this circumstance affords a proof of the veracity of the evangelist; for he barely states a fact having no apparent connexion with any other in his narrative. The reason of it is found in facts stated by the other evangelists. The

of the **Pharisees, &c.** *N. E. coast of the lake of Galileo.*

LUKE	JOHN.

Bethsaida. (Julias.)

faith in Christ. *Region of Cesarea Philippi.*

CHAPTER IX. 18–21.

18 And it came to pass, as he was
alone praying, his disciples were with
him; and he asked them, saying,
Whom say the people that I am?[206]

19 They, answering, said, John the
Baptist; but some *say*, Elias; and
others *say*, that one of the old prophets is risen again.
30 He said unto them, But whom
say ye that I am? Peter, answering,
said, The Christ of God.

people of Bethsaida had already witnessed the miracles of our Lord, but these only served to increase their rage against him; and they were therefore abandoned to the consequences of their unbelief. Matth. xi. 21.

§ 73. Peter and the others again profess their

MATTHEW.

CHAPTER XVI. 13–20.

Bar-jona: for flesh and blood hath not revealed *it* unto thee, but my Father which is in heaven.

18 And I say also unto thee, That thou art Peter, and upon this rock I will build my church: and the gates of hell shall not prevail against it.

19 [239] And I will give unto thee the keys of the kingdom of heaven: and whatsoever thou shalt bind on earth, shall be bound in heaven; and whatsoever thou shalt loose on earth, shall be loosed in heaven.

20 Then charged he his disciples that they should tell no man that he was Jesus the Christ.[240]

MARK.

CHAPTER VIII. 27–30.

30 And he charged them that they should tell no man of him.

§ 74. Our Lord foretells his own death and resurrection,

CHAPTER XVI. 21–28.

21 From that time forth began Jesus [241] to show unto his disciples, how that he must go unto Jerusalem, and suffer many things of the elders, and chief priests, and scribes, and be killed, and be raised again the third day.

22 Then Peter took him, and began to rebuke him, saying,[242] Be it far from thee, Lord: this shall not be unto thee.

23 But he turned, and said unto Peter, Get thee behind me, Satan; thou art an offence unto me: for thou savourest not the things that be of God, but those that be of men.

24 Then said Jesus unto his disciples, If any *man* will come after me, let him deny himself, and take up his cross and follow me.

CH. VIII. 31–38. CH. IX. 1.

31 And he began to teach them, that the Son of man must suffer many things, and be rejected of the elders, and *of* the chief priests, and scribes, and be killed, and after three days rise again.

32 And he spake that saying openly. And Peter took him, and began to rebuke him.

33 [202] But when he had turned about and looked on his disciples, he rebuked Peter, saying, Get thee behind me Satan: for thou savourest not the things that be of God, but the things that be of men.

34 And when he had called the people *unto him*, with his disciples also, he said unto them, Whosoever will come after me, let him deny himself, and take up his cross, and follow me.

Matth. xvi. 21, *the third day.*] The phrase *three days and three nights* is equivalent to *three days*, three natural days of twenty-four hours. Gen. i. 5; Dan. viii. 14. Comp. Gen. vii. 4, 17.

(It is a received rule among the Jews, *that a part of a day is put for the whole;* so that whatsoever is done in any part of the day, is properly said to be done that day. 1 Kings, xx. 29; Esth. iv. 16. "When eight days were accomplished for the circumcision of the child," &c. Yet the day of his birth and of his circumcision were two of these eight days. *Whitby* quoted by SCOTT, on Matth. xii. 40.)

Grotius establishes this way of reckoning the *parts* of the first and third days for *two* days, by Aben Ezra on Lev. xii. 3.

faith in Christ. *Region of Cesarea Philippi.*

LUKE. CHAPTER IX. 18–21.	JOH
21 And he strictly charged them, and he commanded *them* to tell no man that thing.	

and the trials of his followers. *Region of Cesarea Philippi.*

CHAPTER IX. 22–27.	
22 Saying, the Son of man must suffer many things, and be rejected of the elders, and chief priests, and scribes, and be slain, and be raised [207] the third day.	
23 And he said to *them* all, If any *man* will come after me, let him deny himself, and take up his cross daily, and follow me.	

(In proof that the phrase "*after three days*," is sometimes equivalent to "*on the third day*,' compare Deut. xiv. 23 with xxvi. 12; 1 Sam. xx. 12 with v. 19; 2 Chron. x. 5 with v. 12; Matth. xxvi. 2 with xxvii. 63, 64; Luke ii. 21 with i. 59.)

St. Luke omits our Lord's sharp reproof of Peter, and the occasion of it; though he records the discourse in consequence of it. Le Clerc's 12th canon is "Qui pauciora habet, non negat plura dicta aut facta; modo ne ulla sit exclusionis nota." Perhaps the disciple and companion of that apostle who had withstood Peter to his face, Gal. ii. 11, willingly made this omission, as he omits some aggravating circumstances in Peter's denial of Christ, Luke xxii. 60, though he carefully records the greatness of his sorrow, v. 62. NEWCOME.

§ 74. Our Lord foretells his own death and resurrection,

MATTHEW.

CHAPTER XVI. 21–28.

25 For whosoever will save his life, shall lose it: and whosoever will lose his life for my sake, shall find it.

26 For what is a man profited,[243] if he shall gain the whole world, and lose his own soul? or what shall a man give in exchange for his soul?

27 For the Son of man shall come in the glory of his Father, with his angels; and then he shall reward every man according to his works.

28 Verily I say unto you, There be[244] some standing here, which shall not taste of death, till they see the Son of man coming in his kingdom.

MARK.

CH. VIII. 31–38. CH. IX. 1.

35 For whosoever will save his life, shall lose it; but whosoever shall lose his life for my sake and the gospel's, the same[203] shall save it.

36 For what shall it profit a man,[204] if he shall gain the whole world, and lose his own soul?

37 Or what shall a man give[205] in exchange for his soul?

38 Whosoever therefore shall be ashamed of me, and of my words, in this adulterous and sinful generation, of him also shall the Son of man be ashamed, when he cometh in the glory of his Father with the holy angels.

CHAPTER IX.

AND he said unto them, Verily, I say unto you, That there be some of them that stand here which shall not taste of death, till they have seen the kingdom of God come with power.

§ 75. The transfiguration. Our Lord's subsequent discourse

MATTHEW.

CHAPTER XVII. 1–13.

AND after six days, Jesus taketh Peter, James, and John his brother, and bringeth them up into a high mountain apart,

2 And was transfigured before them: and his face did shine as the sun, and his raiment was white as the light.

3 And behold, there appeared unto them Moses and Elias talking with him.

4 Then answered Peter, and said unto Jesus, Lord, it is good for us to be here: if thou wilt, let us make[245] here three tabernacles; one for thee, and one for Moses, and one for Elias.

MARK.

CHAPTER IX. 2–13.

2 And after six days, Jesus taketh *with him* Peter, and James, and John, and leadeth them up into a high mountain[206] apart by themselves; and he was transfigured before them.

3 And his raiment became shining, exceeding white as snow;[207] so as no fuller on earth can white them.

4 And there appeared unto them Elias, with Moses: and they were talking with Jesus.

5 And Peter answered and said to Jesus, Master, it is good for us to be here: and let us make three tabernacles; one for thee, and one for Moses, and one for Elias.

6 For he wist not what to say:[208] for they were sore afraid.

Matth. xvii. 1, *after six days.*] It has been shown, §74, that "*after six days*" *may* signify on the sixth day. But we are not hence to conclude that the phrase has *always* such a signification. Here it means six days complete, after the discourse recorded in § 74. The eight day mentioned by St. Luke include that of Peter's reproof, and of the transfiguration; which two days Matthew and Mark exclude. Macknight furnishes us with the following apposite reference tc Tacitus; Hist. i. 29. Piso says, *Sextus dies* agitur--ex quo

and the trials of his followers. *Region of Cesarea Phillippi.*

LUKE.	JOHN.
CHAPTER IX. 22–27. 24 For whosoever shall save his life, shall lose it: but whosoever will lose his life for my sake, the same shall save it. 25 For what is a man advantaged, if he gain the whole world, and lose himself, or be cast away? 26 For whosoever shall be ashamed of me, and of my words, of him shall the Son of man be ashamed, when he shall come in his own glory, and *in his* Father's, and of the holy angels. 27 But I tell you of a truth, there be some standing here which shall not taste of death till they see the kingdom of God.	

with the three disciples. *Region of Cesarea Philippi.*

CHAPTER IX. 28–36. 28 And it came to pass, about an eight days after these sayings, he took Peter, and John, and James, and went up into a mountain to pray. 29 And as he prayed, the fashion of his countenance was altered, and his raiment *was* white *and* glistering. 30 And behold, there talked with him two men, which were Moses and Elias: 31 Who appeared in glory, and spake of his decease which he should accomplish at Jerusalem. 32 But Peter and they that were with him were heavy with sleep: and when they were awake, they saw his glory, and the two men that stood with him. 33 And it came to pass, as they departed from him, Peter said unto	

—Cæsar adscitus sum; and yet, § 48 of the same book, Tacitus speaks of Piso as *quatriduo* Cæsar.

Grotius on Matth. xvii. 1, has another solution; Quod Lucas dicit, tale est quale cum vulgo dicimus *post septimanam circiter*. Nam Judæos *octo dies* appellasse id quod ab uno sabbato est ad alterum apparet, Joan. 20, 26, &c. NEWCOME.

§ 75. **The transfiguration. Our Lord's subsequent discourse**

MATTHEW. CHAPTER XVII. 1–13.	MARK. CHAPTER IX. 2–13.
5 While he yet spake, behold, a bright cloud overshadowed them: and behold a voice out of the cloud, which said, This is my beloved Son, in whom I am well pleased: hear ye him.	7 And there was a cloud that overshadowed them: and a voice came out of the cloud,[209] saying, This is my beloved Son: hear him.
6 And when the disciples heard it, they fell on their face, and were sore afraid.	
7 And Jesus came and touched them, and said, Arise and be not afraid.	
8 And when they had lifted up their eyes, they saw no man, save Jesus only.[246]	8 And suddenly, when they had looked round about, they saw no man any more, save Jesus only with themselves.
9 And as they came down from the mountain, Jesus charged them, saying, Tell the vision to no man, until the Son of man be risen again from the dead.	9 And as they came down from the mountain, he charged them that they should tell no man what things they had seen, till the Son of man were risen from the dead.
	10 And they kept that saying with themselves, questioning one with another what the rising from the dead should mean.
10 And his disciples[247] asked him, saying, Why then say the scribes, that Elias must first come?	11 And they asked him, saying, Why say the scribes[210] that Elias must first come?
11 And Jesus answered and said unto them, Elias truly shall first come, and restore all things:[248]	12 And he answered and[211] told them, Elias verily cometh first, and restoreth all things; and how it is written of the Son of man, that he must suffer many things; and be set at naught.
12 But I say unto you, That Elias is come already, and they knew him not, but have done unto him whatsoever they listed: likewise shall also the Son of man suffer of them.	13 But I say unto you, That Elias is indeed come, and they have done unto him whatsoever they listed, as it is written of him.
13 Then the disciples understood that he spake unto them of John the Baptist.	

§ 76. **The healing of a demoniac, whom the disciples**

CHAPTER XVII. 14–21.	CHAPTER IX. 14–29.
14 And when they were come to the multitude, there came to him a	14 And when he came to *his* disciples he saw a great multitude about

Luke ix. 36, *told no man.*] It is remarkable that Luke assigns no reason for this extraordinary silence; leaving the narrative in this place imperfect and obscure, which an

with the three disciples *Region of Cesarea Philippi.*

LUKE.

CHAPTER IX. 28–36.

Jesus, Master, it is good for us to be here: and let us make three tabernacles; one for thee, and one for Moses, and one for Elias: not knowing what he said.
34 While he thus spake, there came a cloud, and overshadowed them:[208] and they feared as they entered into the cloud.
35 And there came a voice out of the cloud, saying, This is my beloved Son:[209] hear him.

36 And when the voice was past, Jesus was found alone. And they kept *it* close, and told no man in those days any of those things which they had seen.

JOHN.

could not heal. *Region of Cesarea Philippi.*

CHAPTER IX. 37–43.

37 And it came to pass, that on the next day, when they were come

impostor would not have done. It is explained by the command of Jesus, related only by Matthew and Mark.

§ 76. The healing of a demoniac, whom the disciples

MATTHEW.

CHAPTER XVII. 14–21.

certain man kneeling down to him, and saying,

15 Lord have mercy on my son; for he is lunatic, and sore vexed, for oft-times he falleth into the fire, and oft into the water.[249]

16 And I brought him to thy disciples, and they could not cure him.

17 Then Jesus answered and said,[250] O faithless and perverse generation, how long shall I be with you? how long shall I suffer you? Bring him hither to me.

18 And Jesus rebuked the devil, and he departed out of him: and the child was cured[251] from that very hour.

MARK.

CH. IX. 14–29.

them, and the scribes questioning with them.[212]

15 And straightway all the people, when they beheld him, were greatly amazed, and, running to *him*, saluted him.

16 And he asked the scribes, What question ye with them?[213]

17 And one of the multitude answered and said,[214] Master, I have brought unto thee my son, which hath a dumb spirit;

18 And wheresoever he taketh him, he teareth him; and he foameth and gnasheth with his teeth, and pineth away; and I spake to thy disciples that they should cast him out, and they could not.

19 He answereth him,[215] and saith, O faithless generation, how long shall I be with you? how long shall I suffer you? Bring him unto me.

20 And they brought him unto him: and when he saw him, straightway the spirit tare him; and he fell on the ground, and wallowed, foaming.

21 And he asked his father, How long is it ago since this came unto him? And he said, Of a child.

22 And oft-times it hath cast him into the fire, and into the waters to destroy him: but if thou canst do any thing, have compassion on us, and help us.

23 Jesus said unto him, If thou canst believe,[216] all things *are* possible to him that believeth.

24 [217] And straightway the father of the child cried out, and said with tears, Lord, I believe: help thou mine unbelief.

25 When Jesus saw that the people came running together, he rebuked the foul spirit, saying unto him, *Thou* dumb and deaf spirit, I charge thee, come out of him, and enter no more into him.

26 And *the spirit* cried, and rent him sore, and came out of him: and he was as one dead; insomuch that many said, He is dead.

27 But Jesus took him by the hand, and lifted him up; and he arose.

could not heal. *Region of Cesarea Philippi.*

LUKE.

CHAPTER IX. 37–43.

down from the hill, much people met
him.
38 And behold a man of the company cried out, saying, Master, I beseech thee look upon my son: for he is mine only child.
39 And lo, a spirit taketh him, and he suddenly crieth out; and it teareth him[210] that he foameth again, and, bruising him, hardly departeth from him.
40 And I besought thy disciples to cast him out, and they could not.

41 And Jesus, answering, said, O faithless and perverse generation, how long shall I be with you, and suffer you? Bring thy son hither.

42 And as he was yet a coming, the devil threw him down, and tare *him*. And Jesus rebuked the unclean spirit and healed the child, and delivered him again to his father.
43 And they were all amazed at the mighty power of God.

JOHN.

§ 76. The healing of a demoniac, whom the disciples

MATTHEW.	MARK.
CHAPTER XVII. 14–21.	CHAPTER IX. 14–29.
19 Then came the disciples to Jesus apart and said, Why could not we cast him out ?	28 And when he was come into the house, his disciples asked him privately, Why could we not cast him out ?
20 And Jesus said unto them,[252] Because of your unbelief: [253] for verily I say unto you, if ye have faith as a grain of mustard-seed, ye shall say unto this mountain, Remove hence to yonder place; and it shall remove; and nothing shall be impossible unto you.	29 And he said unto them, This kind can come forth by nothing, but by prayer and fasting.[218]
21 [254] Howbeit, this kind goeth not out, but by prayer and fasting.	

§ 77. Jesus again foretells his own death and resurrection.

CHAPTER XVII. 22, 23.	CHAPTER IX. 30–32.
	30 And they departed thence, and passed through Galilee; and he would not that any man should know *it*.
22 And while they abode in Galilee, Jesus said unto them, the Son of man shall be betrayed into the hands of men:	31 For he taught his disciples, and said unto them,[219] The Son of man is delivered into the hands of men, and they shall kill him; and after that he is killed, he shall rise the third day.
23 And they shall kill him, and the third day he shall be raised again. And they were exceeding sorry.	32 But they understood not that saying, and were afraid to ask him.

§ 78. The tribute-money

CHAPTER XVII. 24–27.	CHAPTER IX. 33.
24 And when they were come to Capernaum,[255] they that received tribute-*money*, came to Peter, and said, Doth not your Master pay tribute ?	33 And he came to Capernaum:
25 He said, Yes. And when he was come [256] into the house, Jesus prevented him, saying, What thinkest thou, Simon? of whom do the kings of the earth take custom or tribute ? of their own children, or of strangers ?	
26 [257] Peter saith unto him, Of strangers. Jesus saith unto him, Then are the children free.	
27 Notwithstanding, lest we should offend them, go thou to the sea, and cast a hook, and take up the fish that first cometh up: and when thou hast opened his mouth, thou shalt find a piece of money: [258] that take, and give unto them for me and thee.	

Matth. xvii. 24, *tribute*.] The original word is *didrachma*, denoting, not tribute or tax in general, but a specific and particular offering which every Jew paid to God. See Josephus,

could not heal. *Region of Cesarea Philippi.*

LUKE.	JOHN.

[See § 74.] *Galilee.*

CHAPTER IX. 43–45.
43 But while they
wondered every one at all things which
Jesus did,[211] he said unto his disciples,
44 Let these sayings sink down into
your ears: for the Son of man shall
be delivered into the hands of men.

45 But they understood not this
saying, and it was hid from them,
that they perceived it not: and they
feared to ask him of that saying.

miraculously provided. *Capernaum.*

Ant. xviii. x. § 1. This minute accuracy of the evangelist is worthy of note, as an indication of veracity.

§ 79. The disciples contend who should be the greatest. Jesus

MATTHEW.

CHAPTER XVIII. 1–35.

[259] AT the same time came the disciples unto Jesus, saying, Who is the greatest in the kingdom of heaven?

2 And Jesus called [260] a little child unto him, and set him in the midst of them,

3 And said, Verily, I say unto you, Except ye be converted, and become as little children, ye shall not enter into the kingdom of heaven.

4 Whosoever therefore shall humble himself as this little child, the same is greatest in the kingdom of heaven.

5 And whoso shall receive one such little child in my name, receiveth me.

6 But whoso shall offend one of these little ones which believe in me, it were better for him that a millstone were hanged about his neck, and *that* he were drowned in the depth of the sea.

7 Wo unto the world because of offences! for it must needs be that offences come; but wo to that man by whom the offence cometh:

8 Wherefore, if thy hand or thy foot offend thee, cut them off, and cast *them* from thee; it is better for thee to enter into life halt or maimed,[261] rather than having two hands or two feet, to be cast into everlasting fire.

9 And if thine eye offend thee, pluck it out, and cast *it* from thee: it is better for thee to enter into life with one eye, rather than having two eyes, to be cast into hell-fire.

10 Take heed that ye despise not one of these little ones: for I say

MARK.

CHAPTER IX. 33–50.

33 And being in the house, he asked them, What was it that ye disputed among yourselves [220] by the way?

34 But they held their peace: for by the way[221] they had disputed among themselves who *should be* the greatest.

35 And he sat down, and called the twelve, and saith unto them, If any man desire to be first, *the same* shall be last of all, and servant of all.

36 And he took a child, and set him in the midst of them: and when he had taken him in his arms, he said unto them,

37 Whosoever shall receive one of such children in my name, receiveth me:[222] and whosoever shall receive me, receiveth not me, but him that sent me.

38 And John answered him, saying, Master, we saw one casting out devils in thy name, and he followeth not us; and we forbade him, because he followeth not us.[223]

39 But Jesus said, Forbid him not: for there is no man which shall do a miracle in my name, that can lightly speak evil of me.

40 For he that is not against us, is on our part.[224]

41 For whosoever shall give you a cup of water to drink in my name, because ye belong to Christ,[225] verily I say unto you, he shall not lose his reward.

42 And whosoever shall offend one of *these* little ones that believe in me,[226] it is better for him that a millstone were hanged about his neck, and he were cast into the sea.

43 And if thy hand offend thee, cut it off: It is better for thee to enter into life maimed, than having two hands to go [227] into hell, into the fire that never shall be quenched:

44 [228] Where their worm dieth not, and the fire is not quenched.

Luke ix. 49, *one casting out devils.*] The twelve apostles and the seventy disciples were commissioned and sent forth *at different times.* Hence the person here alluded to may, for aught that appears, have been one of the seventy, not personally known to John and to those who were with him. *Letters on Evil Spirits*, p. 39.

Mark ix. 40. Luke ix. 50.] Here Jesus says, He that is not against us is for us

exhorts to humility, forbearance, and brotherly love. *Capernaum.*

LUKE.
CHAPTER IX. 46–50.

46 Then there arose a reasoning among them, which of them should be the greatest.

47 And Jesus perceiving[212] the thought of their heart, took a child, and set him by him,
48 And said unto them, Whosoever shall receive this child in my name, receiveth me; and whosoever shall receive me, receiveth him that sent me:[213] for he that is least among you all, the same shall be great.
49 And John answered and said, Master, we saw one casting out devils in thy name; and we forbade him, because he followeth not with us.
50 And Jesus said unto him, Forbid *him* not: for he that is not against us, is for us.

JOHN.

but in Matth. xii. 30, he says, He that is not with me is against me. Grotius regards both as proverbial sayings;—Proverbia in utramque partem usurpata, veritatem suam habent pro materia cui aptantur:—and alludes to similar forms in Prov. xxvi. 4, 5. NEWCOME.

§ 79. **The disciples contend who should be the greatest. Jesus**

MATTHEW.

CHAPTER XVIII. 1–35.

unto you, that in heaven their angels do always behold the face of my Father which is in heaven.

11 [262] For the Son of man is come to save that which was lost.

12 How think ye? If a man have a hundred sheep, and one of them be gone astray, doth he not leave the ninety and nine, and goeth into the mountains,[263] and seeketh that which is gone astray?

13 And if so be that he find it, verily I say unto you, he rejoiceth more of that *sheep*, than of the ninety and nine which went not astray.

14 Even so it is not the will of your Father which is in heaven, that one of these little ones should perish.

15 Moreover, if thy brother shall trespass against thee,[264] go and tell him his fault between thee and him alone: if he shall hear thee, thou hast gained thy brother.

16 But if he will not hear *thee, then* take with thee one or two more, that in the mouth of two or three witnesses every word may be established.

17 And if he shall neglect to hear them, tell *it* unto the church: but if he neglect to hear the church, let him be unto thee as a heathen man and a publican.

18 Verily, I say unto you, Whatsoever ye shall bind on earth, shall be bound in heaven: and whatsoever ye shall loose on earth, shall be loosed in heaven.

19 Again I say [265] unto you, That if two of you shall agree on earth, as touching anything that they shall ask, it shall be done for them of my Father which is in heaven.

20 For where two or three are gathered together in my name, there am I in the midst of them.

21 Then came Peter to him, and said,[266] Lord, how oft shall my brother sin against me, and I forgive him? till seven times?

22 Jesus saith unto him, I say not unto thee, Until seven times: but, Until seventy times seven.

23 Therefore is the kingdom of heaven likened unto a certain king

MARK.

CHAPTER IX. 33–50.

45 And if thy foot offend thee, cut it off: it is better for thee to enter halt into life, than having two feet to be cast into hell, into the fire that never shall be quenched:[229]

46 [230] Where their worm dieth not, and the fire is not quenched.

47 And if thine eye offend thee, pluck it out: it is better for thee to enter into the kingdom of God with one eye, than having two eyes, to be cast into hell fire: [231]

48 Where their worm dieth not, and the fire is not quenched.

49 For every one shall be salted with fire, and every sacrifice shall be salted with salt.[232]

50 Salt *is* good: but if the salt have lost his saltness, wherewith will ye season it? Have salt in yourselves, and have peace one with another.

exhorts to humility, forbearance, and brotherly love. *Capernaum.*

LUKE.	JOHN.

§ 79. The disciples contend who should be the greatest. Jesus

MATTHEW.

CHAPTER XVIII. 1–35.

which would take account of his servants.

24 And when he had begun to reckon, one was brought unto him which owed him ten thousand talents.[267]

25 But forasmuch as he had not to pay, his lord commanded him to be sold, and his wife and children, and all that he had, and payment to be made.[268]

26 The servant therefore fell down, and worshipped him, saying, Lord,[269] have patience with me, and I will pay thee all.

27 Then the lord of that servant[270] was moved with compassion, and loosed him, and forgave him the debt.

28 But the same servant went out, and found one of his fellow-servants, which owed him a hundred pence: and he laid hands on him, and took *him* by the throat, saying, Pay me that thou owest.[271]

29 And his fellow servant fell down at his feet, and besought him, saying, Have patience with me, and I will pay thee all.[272]

30 And he would not: but went[273] and cast him into prison, till he should pay the debt.

31 So when his fellow-servants saw what was done, they were very sorry, and came,[264] and told unto their lord all that was done.

32 Then his lord, after that he had called him, said unto him, O thou wicked servant, I forgave thee all that debt, because thou desiredst me:

33 Shouldest not thou also have had compassion on thy fellow-servant, even as I had pity on thee?

34 And his lord was wroth, and delivered him to the tormentors, till he should pay all that was due unto him.

35 So likewise shall my heavenly Father do also unto you, if ye from your hearts forgive not every one his brother their trespasses.[275]

MARK.

§ 80. The Seventy instructed, and sent out.

exhorts to humility, forbearance, and brotherly love. *Capernaum.*

LUKE.	JOHN.

Capernaum.

CHAPTER X. 1–16.

AFTER these things, the Lord appointed other seventy also,[222] and sent

§ 80. The Seventy instructed, and sent out.

MATTHEW.

MARK.

Capernaum.

LUKE.

CHAPTER X. 1–16.

them two and two before his face
into every city, and place, whither
he himself would come.
2 Therefore said he[223] unto them,
The harvest truly *is* great, but the
labourers *are* few: pray ye therefore
the Lord of the harvest, that he would
send forth labourers into his harvest.
3 Go your ways: behold, I send
you forth as lambs[224] among wolves.
4 Carry neither purse, nor scrip,
nor shoes: and[225] salute no man by
the way.*
5 And into whatsoever house ye
enter, first say, Peace *be* to this house.
6 And if the son of peace[226] be
there, your peace shall rest upon it:
if not, it shall turn to you again.
7 And in the same house remain,
eating and drinking such things as
they give: for the labourer *is* worthy of
his hire. Go not from house to house.
8 And into whatsoever city ye enter, and they receive you, eat such
things as are set before you.
9 And heal the sick that are therein, and say unto them, The kingdom
of God is come nigh unto you.
10 But into whatsoever city ye
enter, and they receive you not, go
your ways out into the streets of the
same, and say,
11 Even the very dust of your city
which cleaveth on us, we do wipe off
against you: notwithstanding, be ye
sure of this, that the kingdom of God
is come nigh unto you.[227]
12 But[228] I say unto you, That it
shall be more tolerable in that day
for Sodom than for that city.
13 Wo unto thee, Chorazin! wo
unto thee, Bethsaida! for if the mighty
works had been done in Tyre and
Sidon, which have been done in you,
they had a great while ago repented,
sitting in sackcloth and ashes.
14 But it shall be more tolerable
for Tyre and Sidon at the judgment,
than for you.
15 And thou, Capernaum,[229] which

JOHN.

* 2 Kings iv. 29.

§ 80. The Seventy instructed, and sent out.

MATTHEW.	MARK.

§ 81. Jesus goes up to the feast of tabernacles. His final

§ 82. Ten lepers cleansed.

Luke ix. 53, *did not receive him.*] This was near the passover; when Jesus, going to celebrate it at Jerusalem, plainly indicated that men ought to worship *there;* contrary to the practice of the Samaritans, who, in opposition to the Holy City, had set up a temple at Gerazim. Hence the cause of their hostility to him as well as to all others travelling in that direction *at that season.* This account perfectly harmonizes with the respectful

Capernaum.

LUKE.	JOHN.
CHAPTER X. 1-16. art exalted to heaven, shall be thrust down to hell. 16 He that heareth you, heareth me; and he that despiseth you, despiseth me; and he that despiseth me, despiseth him that sent me.	

departure from Galilee. Incidents in Samaria.

CHAPTER IX. 51-56. 51 And it came to pass, when the time was come that he should be received up, he steadfastly set his face to go to Jerusalem, 52 And sent messengers before his face: and they went and entered into a village [215] of the Samaritans, to make ready for him. 53 And they did not receive him, because his face was as though he would go to Jerusalem. 54 And when his disciples James and John saw *this*, they said, Lord, wilt thou that we command fire to come down from heaven, and consume them, even as Elias did? [216] 55 But he turned, and rebuked them, and said,[217] Ye know not what manner of spirit ye are of. 56 For the Son of man is not come to destroy men's lives, but to save *them*.[218] And they went to another village.	CHAPTER VII. 2-10. 2 Now the Jews' feast of tabernacles was at hand. 3 His brethren therefore said unto him, Depart hence, and go into Judea, that thy disciples also may see the works that thou doest. 4 For *there is* no man *that* doeth any thing in secret, and he himself seeketh to be known openly. If thou do these things, show thyself to the world. 5 (For neither did his brethren believe in him.) 6 Then Jesus said unto them, My time is not yet come:[166] but your time is always ready. 7 The world cannot hate you; but me it hateth, because I testify of it,[167] that the works thereof are evil. 8 Go ye up unto this feast: I go not up yet unto this feast;[168] for my time is not yet full come. 9 When he had said these words unto them, he abode *still* in Galilee.[169] 10 But when his brethren were gone up, then went he also up unto the feast, not openly, but as it were [170] in secret.

Samaria.

CHAPTER XVII. 11-19. 11 And it came to pass, as he went to Jerusalem, that he passed through the midst of Samaria and Galilee. 12 And as he entered into a certain village, there met him ten men that were lepers, which stood afar off: [344] 13 And they lifted up *their* voices,	

deportment of the Samaritans towards him at the time of his interview with the woman at Jacob's well, John iv. 1-42; for he was then coming *from* Judea, and it was not the season of resorting thither for any purposes of devotion. John iv. 35. BLUNT, Veracity, &c., sect. i. 16.

§ 82. **Ten lepers cleansed.**

MATTHEW.	MARK.

Samaria.

LUKE.

CHAPTER XVII. 11-19.

and said, Jesus, Master, have mercy
on us.
14 And when he saw *them*, he said
unto them, Go shew yourselves unto
the priests. And it came to pass, that,
as they went, they were cleansed.
15 And one of them, when he saw
that he was healed, turned back, and
with a loud voice glorified God,
16 And fell down on *his* face at his
feet, giving him thanks: and he was
a Samaritan.
17 And Jesus answering, said,
Were there not ten cleansed? but
where *are* the nine?
18 There are not found that returned to give glory to God, save this
stranger.
19 And he said unto him, Arise, go
thy way: thy faith hath made thee
whole.[346]

JOHN.

PART VI.

THE FESTIVAL OF TABERNACLES

AND THE

SUBSEQUENT TRANSACTIONS,

UNTIL

OUR LORD'S ARRIVAL AT BETHANY,

SIX DAYS BEFORE THE FOURTH PASSOVER.

TIME. *Six months, less one week.*

§ 83. Jesus at the festival of Tabernacles.

MATTHEW.	MARK.

His public teaching. *Jerusalem.*

LUKE.

JOHN.

CH. VII. 11–53. CH. VIII. 1.

11 Then the Jews sought him at
the feast, and said, Where is he?
12 And there was much murmuring
among the people concerning him:
for some said, He is a good man:
others said, Nay; but he deceiveth
the people.
13 Howbeit, no man spoke openly
of him, for fear of the Jews.
14 Now, about the midst of the
feast, Jesus went up into the temple
and taught.
15 And the Jews [171] marvelled, saying, How knoweth this man letters,
having never learned?
16 Jesus [172] answered them, and
said, My doctrine is not mine, but his
that sent me.
17 If any man will do his will, he
shall know of the doctrine, whether
it be of God, or *whether* I speak of
myself.
18 He that speaketh of himself,
seeketh his own glory: but he that
seeketh [173] his glory that sent him, the
same is true, and no unrighteousness
is in him.
19 Did not Moses give you the law,
and *yet* none of you keepeth the law?
Why go ye about to kill me?
20 The people answered and said,[174]
Thou hast a devil: who goeth about
to kill thee?
21 Jesus answered and said unto
them, I have done one work, and ye
all marvel.
22 Moses therefore gave unto you
circumcision, (not because it is of
Moses, but of the fathers;) [175] and ye
on the sabbath-day circumcise a man.*
23 If a man on the sabbath-day
receive circumcision, that the law of
Moses should not be broken; are ye
angry at me, because I have made a
man every whit whole on the sabbath-
day?
24 Judge not according to the appearance, but judge righteous judg
ment.
25 Then said some of them of Jerusalem, Is not this he whom they
seek to kill?

* Lev. xii. 3.

§ 83. **Jesus at the festival of Tabernacles.**

MATTHEW.	MARK.

John vii. 37, *great day of the feast.*] On this day, which was one of great joy and festivity, it was the custom of the Jews to fetch water from the pool of Siloam, some of which they drank with loud acclamations of joy and thanksgiving; and some they brought to the altar, in commemoration of the miraculous relief of their forefathers, when

His public teaching. *Jerusalem.*

LUKE.

JOHN.

CH. VII. 11–35. CH. VIII. 1.

26 But lo, he speaketh boldly, and
they say nothing unto him. Do the
rulers know indeed that this is the
very Christ?[176]

27 Howbeit, we know this man,
whence he is: but[177] when Christ cometh, no man knoweth whence he is.

28 Then cried Jesus in the temple,
as he taught, saying, Ye both know
me, and ye know whence I am: and
I am not come of myself, but he that
sent me is true, whom ye know not.

29 But I know him; for I am from
him,[178] and he hath sent me.

30 Then they sought to take him:
but no man laid hands on him, because his hour was not yet come.

31 And many of the people believed
on him, and said, When Christ cometh, will he do more miracles than
these which this *man* hath done?[179]

32 The Pharisees[180] heard that the
people murmured such things concerning him: and the Pharisees and the
chief priests sent officers to take him.

33 Then said Jesus unto them,[181]
Yet a little while am I with you, and
then I go unto him that sent me.

34 Ye shall seek me, and shall not
find *me*: and where I am, *thither* ye
cannot come.

35 Then said the Jews among
themselves,[182] Whither will he go, that
we shall not find him? will he go
unto the dispersed among the Gentiles, and teach the Gentiles?

36 What *manner* of saying is this
that he said, Ye shall seek me, and
shall not find *me*: and where I am,
thither ye cannot come?

37 In the last day, that great *day*
of the feast, Jesus stood and cried,
saying, If any man thirst, let him
come unto me, and drink.[183]

38 He that believeth on me, as the
scripture hath said,* out of his belly
shall flow rivers of living water.

* Isa. lv. 1, and lviii. 11, and xliv. 3. Zech. xiii. 1, and xiv. 8.

---

thirsting in the wilderness; and some they brought as a drink-offering to God, to pray for rain against the following seed-time. See BENSON's Life of Christ, p. 412. JENNINGS, Ant. p. 495. The existence of this custom, thus remotely alluded to, gives great truthfulness to the narrative.

§ 83. Jesus at the festival of Tabernacles.

MATTHEW.	MARK.

John viii. 1, *to the Mount of Olives.*] It is apparent, from various incidental allusions in the Evangelists, that it was the habit of our Lord at this period to spend his days in Jerusalem, in teaching the people and healing the sick, and his nights in the Mount of Olives, in prayer. Yet it is nowhere directly asserted ; and the manner in which it is

His public teaching. *Jerusalem.*

LUKE.

JOHN.

CH. VII. 11–53. CH. VIII. 1.

39 (But this spake he of the Spirit, which they that believe on him should receive, for the Holy Ghost was not *given*,[184] because that Jesus was not yet glorified.)

40 Many of the people therefore, when they heard this saying,[185] said, Of a truth this is the Prophet.

41 Others said, This is the Christ. But some said,[186] Shall Christ come out of Galilee?

42 Hath not the scripture said,* That Christ cometh of the seed of David, and out of the town of Bethlehem, where David was?

43 So there was a division among the people because of him.

44 And some of them would have taken him;[187] but no man laid hands on him.

45 Then came the officers to the chief priests and Pharisees; and they said[188] unto them, Why have ye not brought him?

46 The officers answered, Never man spake like this man.[189]

47 Then answered them the Pharisees,[190] Are ye also deceived?

48 Have any of the rulers, or of the Pharisees believed on him?[191]

49 But this people who knoweth not the law are cursed.

50 Nicodemus saith unto them, (he that came to Jesus by night, being one of them,)[192]

51 Doth our law judge *any* man before it hear him, and know what he doeth?[193]

52 They answered and said unto him, Art thou also of Galilee: Search, and look: for out of Galilee ariseth no prophet.

53 [194] And every man went unto his own house.

CHAPTER VIII.

[195] JESUS went unto the mount of Olives:

* Ps. lxxxix. 4, and cxxxii. 11. Mic. v. 2.

slightly mentioned or alluded to by the sacred writers, is worthy of particular notice, as a proof of their veracity, never met with, in works of fiction. Compare Matth. xxiv. 3, and xxvi. 30; Mark xiii. 3, and xiv. 26; Luke vi. 12. and xxi. 37, 38, and xxii. 39; John viii. 1, 2, and xvii. 1.

§ 84. The woman taken in

MATTHEW.	MARK.

§ 85. **Further public teaching of Our Lord. He reproves the**

John viii. 5, *should be stoned.*] The Romans, in settling the provincial government of Judea, which they had conquered, deprived the Jewish tribunals of the power of inflicting capital punishments. John xviii. 31. The law of Moses, however, condemned adulterers to be stoned to death. "This woman had been caught in the very fact. Jesus must therefore determine against the law, which inflicted death; or against the Romans, who suffered them not to put any body to death, and who would still less have permitted it for such a crime as adultery, which was not capital among them.—If *he* condemned not the adulteress *to death* when he was alone with her, he hereby teaches us

adultery. *Jerusalem.*

LUKE.	JOHN.
	CHAPTER VIII. 2–11.
	2 And early in the morning he came again into the temple, and all the people came unto him; and he sat down and taught them.
	3 And the scribes and Pharisees brought unto him a woman taken in adultery: and when they had set her in the midst,
	4 They say unto him, Master, this woman was taken in adultery, in the very act.
	5 Now Moses in the law * commanded us, that such should be stoned: but what sayest thou?
	6 This they said, tempting him, that they might have to accuse him. But Jesus stooped down, and with *his* finger wrote on the ground, *as though he heard them not.*
	7 So when they continued asking him, he lifted up himself, and said unto them, He that is without sin among you, let him first cast a stone at her.
	8 And again he stooped down, and wrote on the ground.
	9 And they which heard *it*, being convicted by their own conscience, went out one by one, beginning at the eldest, *even* unto the last: and Jesus was left alone, and the woman standing in the midst.
	10 When Jesus had lifted up himself, and saw none but the woman, he said unto her, Woman, where are those thine accusers? hath no man condemned thee?
	11 She said, No man, Lord. And Jesus said unto her, Neither do I condemn thee: go, and sin no more.

unbelieving Jews, and escapes from their hands. *Jerusalem.*

	CHAPTER VIII. 12–59.
	12 Then spake Jesus again unto them, saying, I am the light of the

* Lev. xx. 10. Deut. xxii. 21.

to submit to the civil laws of the places where we live." BASNAGE, *Hist. Jud.* lib. v. c. xx. § 2.

John viii. 7, *let him first cast a stone.*] When one was condemned to death, those witnesses, whose evidence decided the sentence, inflicted the first blows, in order to add the last degree of certainty to their evidence. DUPIN, Trial of Jesus, p. 7. SALVADOR, Histoire des Institutions de Moise, &c. Liv. iv. ch. ii. p. 76.

19

§ 85. **Further public teaching of Our Lord. He reproves the**

MATTHEW.	MARK.

John viii. 14, *ye cannot tell.*] John vii. 18, is consistent with John viii. 14. "Ye both know my transactions among you, and whence, as a man, I derive my descent: (ch. vi. 42,) and yet there is a sense in which ye know not whence I am, as I came not," &c. *Kai* is used in the same manner, Matth. ix. 19. *And yet wisdom*, &c. See also

unbelieving **Jews**, and escapes from their hands. *Jerusalem.*

LUKE.

JOHN.

CHAPTER VIII. 12–59.

world: he that followeth me shall
not walk in darkness, but shall have [196]
the light of life.
13 The Pharisees therefore said
unto him, Thou bearest record of thyself; thy record is not true.
14 Jesus answered and said unto
them, Though I bear record of myself, *yet* my record is true: for I know
whence I came, and whither I go:
but ye cannot tell whence I come,
and whither I go.[197]
16 Ye judge after the flesh, I judge
no man.
16 And yet if I judge, my judgment is true: for I am not alone, but
I and the Father that sent me.[198]
17 It is also written in your law,
that the testimony of two men is true.*
18 I am one that bear witness of
myself; and the Father that sent me,
beareth witness of me.
19 Then said they unto him, Where
is thy Father? Jesus answered, Ye
neither know me, nor my Father:[199]
if ye had known me, ye should have
known my Father also.
20 These words spake Jesus in the
treasury, as he taught in the temple:[200]
and no man laid hands on him, for
his hour was not yet come.
21 Then said Jesus again unto
them, I [201] go my way, and ye shall
seek me, and shall die in your sins:
whither I go, ye cannot come.
22 Then said the Jews, Will he
kill himself? because he saith,
Whither I go, ye cannot come.
23 And he said unto them,[202] Ye
are from beneath; I am from above:
ye are of this world; I am not of this
world.
24 I said therefore unto you, that
ye shall die in your sins: for if ye believe not that I am *he*,[203] ye shall die
in your sins.
25 Then said they unto him, Who
art thou? And Jesus saith unto them,[204]

* Deut. xvii. 6, and xix. 15.

John ix. 30. In this latter sense (ch. viii. 14,) the Jews knew not whence Jesus came, knew not his divine mission, and that he would return to the Father at his ascension, NEWCOME.

§ 85. **Further public teaching of Our Lord. He reproves the**

MATTHEW.	MARK.

John viii. 30, *many believed on him.*] The Jews who are said to have believed on Jesus (John viii. 30) are not the same with those whom our Lord accuses of seeking to kill him, ver. 40, nor with those who insulted him, ver. 48, &c., although these are not distinguished from

unbelieving Jews, and escapes from their hands. *Jerusalem.*

LUKE.	JOHN.
	CHAPTER VIII. 12–59.
	Even *the same* that I said unto you from the beginning.
	26 I have many things to say, and to judge of you: but he that sent me, is true; and I speak to the world those things which I have heard of him.[205]
	27 They understood not that he spake to them of the Father.[206]
	28 Then said Jesus unto them, When ye have lifted up the Son of man, then shall ye know that I am *he*, and *that* I do nothing of myself; but as my Father hath taught me, I speak these things.[207]
	29 And he that sent me is with me: the Father hath not left me alone; for I do always those things that please him.[208]
	30 As he spake these words, many believed on him.
	31 Then said Jesus to those Jews which believed on him, If ye continue in my word, *then* are ye my disciples indeed;[209]
	32 And ye shall know the truth, and the truth shall make you free.
	33 They answered him, We be Abraham's seed, and were never in bondage to any man: how sayest thou, Ye shall be made free?
	34 Jesus answered them, Verily, verily, I say unto you, Whosoever committeth sin, is the servant of sin.
	35 And the servant abideth not in the house for ever, *but* the Son abideth for ever.[210]
	36 If the Son therefore shall make you free, ye shall be free indeed.
	37 I know that ye are Abraham's seed; but ye seek to kill me, because my word hath no place in you.
	38 I speak that which I have seen with my Father: and ye do that which ye have seen with your father.[211]
	39 They answered and said unto him, Abraham is our father. Jesus saith unto them,[212] If ye were Abraham's children, ye would do the works of Abraham.

the others in the narrative of John, who always mentions the Jews indiscriminately as speaking with Jesus. Cler. Harm. 528. NEWCOME.

§ 85. **Further public teaching of Our Lord. He reproves the**

MATTHEW.	MARK.

LUKE.

JOHN.

CHAPTER VIII. 12–59.

40 But now ye seek to kill me, a man that hath told you the truth, which I have heard of God: this did not Abraham.

41 Ye do the deeds of your father. Then said they to him,[213] We be not born of fornication; we have one Father, *even* God.

42 Jesus said unto them, If God were your Father, ye would love me: for I proceeded forth and came from God; neither came I of myself, but he sent me.

43 Why do ye not understand my speech? *even* because ye cannot hear my word.

44 Ye are of *your* father the devil, and the lusts of your father ye will do: he was a murderer from the beginning, and abode not in the truth; because there is no truth in him. When he speaketh a lie, he speaketh of his own: for he is a liar, and the father of it.

45 And because I tell you the truth, ye believe me not.

46 Which of you convinceth me of sin? And[214] if I say the truth, why do ye not believe me?

47 He that is of God, heareth God's words: ye therefore hear *them* not, because ye are not of God.

48 Then answered the Jews,[215] and said unto him, Say we not well that thou art a Samaritan, and hast a devil?

49 Jesus answered,[216] I have not a devil; but I honour my Father, and ye do dishonour me.

50 And I seek not mine own glory: there is one that seeketh and judgeth.

51 Verily, verily, I say unto you, If a man keep my saying, he shall never see death.

52 Then said the Jews unto him, Now we know that thou hast a devil. Abraham is dead, and the prophets; and thou sayest, If a man keep my saying, he shall never taste of death.[217]

53 Art thou greater than our father Abraham, which is dead? and the prophets are dead: whom makest thou thyself?

54 Jesus answered, If I honour

§ 85. **Further public teaching of Our Lord. He reproves the**

MATTHEW.	MARK.

§ 86. **A lawyer instructed. Love to our neighbour defined.**

Luke x. 28, *this do, and thou shalt live.*] The professional reader will not fail to observe the wisdom of this reply. The lawyer sought to learn from Jesus the terms of the condition on which eternal life could be attained; and was made to answer for himself, that, by the law, it was attainable by nothing short of the highest degree of love, to God and to his neighbour. The lawyer thus was reminded, out of his own code, that this being a condition precedent, he could have no title to that which was promised, unless he fully performed every part of the condition; and that in this sense, whosoever offended

unbelieving Jews, and escapes from their hands. *Jerusalem.*

LUKE.	JOHN.
	CHAPTER VIII. 12-59. myself, my honour is nothing: it is my Father that honoureth me, of whom ye say, that he is your God.[218] 55 Yet ye have not known him; but I know him: and if I should say, I know him not, I should be a liar like unto you: but I know him, and keep his saying. 56 Your father Abraham rejoiced to see my day: and he saw *it*, and was glad. 57 Then said the Jews unto him, Thou art not yet fifty years old, and hast thou seen Abraham ?[219] 58 Jesus said unto them, Verily, verily, I say unto you, Before Abra- ham was, I am.[220] 59 Then took they up stones to cast at him: but Jesus hid himself, and went out of the temple, going through the midst of them, and so passed by.[221]

Parable of the Good Samaritan. *Near Jerusalem.*

LUKE.	JOHN.
CHAPTER X. 25–37. 25 And behold, a certain lawyer stood up, and tempted him, saying, Master, what shall I do to inherit eternal life ? 26 He said unto him, What is written in the law ? how readest thou ? 27 And he answering said, Thou shalt love the Lord thy God with all thy heart, and with all thy soul, and with all thy strength, and with all thy mind; and thy neighbour as thyself.* 28 And he said unto him, Thou hast answered right: this do, and thou shalt live. 29 But he, willing to justify him- self, said unto Jesus, And who is my neighbour ?	

* Deut. vi. 5. Lev. xix. 18, and xviii. 5.

in one point, or was deficient in performing any part of the condition, was guilty of all—lost the benefit of all. If he murmured at the hardship of losing the reward of all the good deeds he had done, merely for the omission to do a little more; the well known rule of law and of reason would teach him that nothing is to be allowed for acts of past performance of a condition precedent unless they are beneficial to the party for whom they are performed.

§ 86. A lawyer instructed. Love to our neighbour defined.

MATTHEW.	MARK.

§ 87. Jesus in the house of Martha

Luke x. 30, *down.*] A note of minute accuracy in the historian, Jericho being situ-

Parable of the good Samaritan. *Near Jerusalem.*

LUKE.

CHAPTER X. 25–37.

30 And [236] Jesus answering, said, A certain *man* went down from Jerusalem to Jericho, and fell among thieves, which stripped him of his raiment, and wounded *him*, and departed, leaving *him* half dead.

31 And by chance there came down a certain priest that way; and when he saw him, he passed by on the other side.

32 And likewise a Levite, when he was at the place, came and looked *on him*, and passed by [237] on the other side.

33 But a certain Samaritan, as he journeyed, came where he was: and when he saw him, he had compassion *on him*,

34 And went to *him*, and bound up his wounds, pouring in oil and wine, and set him on his own beast, and brought him to an inn, and took care of him.

35 And on the morrow, when he departed,[238] he took out two pence, and gave *them* to the host, and said unto him, Take care of him: and whatsoever thou spendest more, when I come again, I will repay thee.

36 Which now [239] of these three, thinkest thou, was neighbour unto him that fell among the thieves?

37 And he said, He that shewed mercy on him. Then said Jesus unto him,[240] Go, and do thou likewise.

JOHN.

and Mary. *Bethany.*

CHAPTER X. 38–42.

38 Now it came to pass, as they went, that he entered into a certain village: and a certain woman, named Martha, received him into her house.[241]

39 And she had a sister called Mary, which also sat at Jesus' feet,[242] and heard his word.

40 But Martha was cumbered about much serving, and came to him, and said, Lord, dost thou not care that my sister hath left me to serve alone? bid her therefore that she help me.

41 And Jesus [243] answered, and said

---

ated in the plain or valley of Jordan, and Jerusalem being among the mountains of Judea.

§ 87. Jesus in the house of Martha

MATTHEW.	MARK.

§ 88. The disciples again taught

Luke xi. 5, *at midnight.*] An incidental and very natural allusion to the well-known custom in that country. For in those hot regions, men travel in the cool of the evening and night,

and Mary. *Bethany.*

LUKE.

CHAPTER X. 38–42.

unto her, Martha, Martha, thou art
careful, and troubled about many
things:
42 But one thing is needful; and
Mary hath chosen that good part,[244]
which shall not be taken away from
her.

JOHN.

how to pray. *Near Jerusalem.*

CHAPTER XI. 1–13.

AND it came to pass, that as he was
praying in a certain place, when he
ceased, one of his disciples said unto
him, Lord, teach us to pray, as John
also [245] taught his disciples.
2 And he said unto them, When
ye pray, say, Our Father which art
in heaven, Hallowed be thy name.
Thy kingdom come. Thy will be
done, as in heaven, so in earth.[246]
3 Give us day by day our daily
bread.
4 And forgive us our sins; for
we also forgive every one that is indebted to us. And lead us not into
temptation; but deliver us from evil.[247]
5 And he said unto them, Which of
you shall have a friend, and shall go
unto him at midnight, and say unto
him, Friend, lend me three loaves:
6 For a friend of mine in his journey is come to me, and I have nothing
to set before him?
7 And he from within shall answer
and say, Trouble me not: the door
is now shut, and my children are
with me in bed; I cannot [248] rise and
give thee.
8 I say unto you, Though he will
not rise and give him, because he is
his friend, yet because of his importu-
nity he will rise and give him as many
as he needeth.
9 And I say unto you, Ask, and it
shall be given you; seek, and ye
shall find; knock, and it shall be
opened unto you.
10 For every one that asketh receiveth; and he that seeketh findeth;

---

and rest in the day time; looking for refreshment, if they are not among total strangers, to the hospitality of friends.

§ 88. **The disciples again taught**

MATTHEW.	MARK.

§ 89. **The Seventy return.**

how to pray. *Near Jerusalem.*

LUKE.

CHAPTER IX. 1–13.

and to him that knocketh, it shall be
opened.[219]
11 If a son shall ask bread of any
of you that is a father, will ye give
him a stone? or if *he ask* a fish, will
he for a fish give him a serpent?
12 Or if he shall ask an egg, will
he offer him a scorpion?
13 If ye then, being evil, know how
to give good gifts unto your children,
how much more shall *your* heavenly
Father give the Holy Spirit to them
that ask him?

JOHN.

Jerusalem?

CHAPTER X. 17–24.

17 And the seventy[230] returned again
with joy, saying, Lord, even the devils
are subject unto us through thy name.
18 And he said unto them, I beheld Satan as lightning fall from
heaven.
19 Behold, I give [231] unto you power
to tread on serpents and scorpions,
and over all the power of the enemy:
and nothing shall by any means hurt
you.
20 Notwithstanding, in this rejoice
not, that the spirits are subject unto
you; but rather [232] rejoice, because
your names are written in heaven.
21 In that hour Jesus rejoiced in
spirit, and said, [233] I thank thee, O
Father, Lord of heaven and earth, that
thou hast hid these things from the
wise and prudent, and hast revealed
them unto babes: even so, Father;
for so it seemed good in thy sight.
22 [234] All things are delivered to me
of my Father: and no man knoweth
who the Son is, but the Father; and
who the Father is, but the Son, and
he to whom the Son will reveal *him*.
23 And he turned him unto *his*
disciples, and said privately, Blessed
are the eyes which see the things that
ye see.
24 For I tell you, That many
prophets and kings have desired to
see those things which ye see, and
have not seen *them;* and to hear [235]
those things which ye hear, and have
not heard *them*.

§ 90. A man born blind is healed on the Sabbath.

MATTHEW.	MARK.

Our Lord's subsequent discourses. *Jerusalem.*

LUKE.

JOHN.

CH. IX. 1–41. CH. X. 1–21.

AND as *Jesus* passed by, he saw a man which was blind from *his* birth.

2 And his disciples asked him, saying, Master, who did sin, this man, or his parents, that he was born blind?

3 Jesus answered, Neither hath this man sinned, nor his parents: but that the works of God should be made manifest in him.

4 I must work the works of him that sent me,[222] while it is day: the night cometh, when no man can work.

5 As long as I am in the world, I am the light of the world.

6 When he had thus spoken, he spat on the ground, and made clay of the spittle, and he anointed the eyes of the blind man with the clay,[223]

7 And said unto him, Go, wash in the pool of Siloam,[224] (which is by interpretation, Sent.) He went his way therefore, and washed, and came seeing.

8 The neighbours therefore, and they which before had seen him that he was blind,[225] said, Is not this he that sat and begged?

9 Some said, This is he: others *said*, He is like him:[226] *but* he said, I am *he*.

10 Therefore said they unto him, How were[227] thine eyes opened?

11 He answered and said, A man that is called Jesus, made clay, and anointed mine eyes, and said unto me, Go to the pool of Siloam, and wash: and I went and washed,[228] and I received sight.

12 Then said[229] they unto him, Where is he? He said, I know not.

13 They brought to the Pharisees him that aforetime was blind.

14 And it was the sabbath-day when Jesus made the clay, and opened his eyes.

15 Then again the Pharisees also asked him how he had received his sight. He said unto them,[230] He put clay upon mine eyes, and I washed, and do see.

16 Therefore said some of the Pharisees, This man is not of God, because he keepeth not the sabbath

§ 90. A man born blind is healed on the Sabbath.

MATTHEW.	MARK.

LUKE.

JOHN.

CH. IX. 1–41. CH. X. 1–21.

day. Others[231] said, How can a man that is a sinner do such miracles? And there was a division among them.

17 They say unto the blind man again,[232] What sayest thou of him, that he hath opened thine eyes? He said, He is a prophet.

18 But the Jews did not believe concerning him, that he had been blind, and received his sight, until they called the parents of him that had received his sight.

19 And they asked them, saying,[233] Is this your son, who ye say was born blind? How then doth he now see?

20 His parents[234] answered them and said, We know that this is our son, and that he was born blind:

21 But by what means he now seeth, we know not; or who hath opened his eyes, we know not: he is of age;[235] ask him: he shall speak for himself.

22 These *words* spake his parents, because they feared the Jews: for the Jews had agreed already, that if any man did confess that he was Christ, he should be put out of the synagogue.

23 Therefore said his parents, He is of age; ask him.[236]

24 Then again called they the man that was blind, and said[237] unto him, Give God the praise: we know that this man is a sinner.

25 He answered and said, Whether he be a sinner *or no*, I knew not: one thing I know, that, whereas I was blind, now I see.

26 Then said they to him again,[238] What did he to thee? how opened he thine eyes?

27 He answered them, I have told you already, and ye did not hear: wherefore would ye hear *it* again? will ye also be his disciples?

28 Then[239] they reviled him, and said, Thou art his disciple; but we are Moses' disciples.

29 We know that God spake unto Moses; *as for* this *fellow*, we know not from whence he is.

§ 90. **A man born blind is healed on the Sabbath.**

MATTHEW.	MARK.

Our Lord's subsequent discourses. *Jerusalem.*

LUKE.

JOHN.

CH. IX. 1–41. CH. X. 1–21.

30 The man answered and said unto them, Why, herein is a marvellous thing, that ye know not from whence he is, and *yet* he hath opened mine eyes.

31 Now we know that God heareth not sinners: but if any man be a worshipper of God, and doeth his will,[240] him he heareth.

32 Since the world began was it not heard that any man opened the eyes of one that was born blind.

33 If this man were not of God, he could do nothing.

34 They answered and said unto him, Thou wast altogether born in sins, and dost thou teach us? And they cast him out.

35 Jesus heard that they had cast him out: and when he had found him, he said unto him, Dost thou believe on the Son of God? [241]

36 He answered and said, Who is he, Lord,[242] that I might believe on him?

37 And [243] Jesus said unto him, Thou hast both seen him, and it is he that talketh with thee.

38 [244] And he said, Lord, I believe. And he worshipped him.

39 And Jesus said,[245] For judgment I am come into this world; that they which see not might see; and that they which see might be made blind.

40 And *some* of the Pharisees which were with him heard these words, and said unto him,[246] Are we blind also?

41 Jesus said unto them, If ye were blind, ye should have no sin: but now ye say, We see; therefore [247] your sin remaineth.

CHAPTER X.

VERILY, verily, I say unto you, He that entereth not by the door into the sheepfold, but climbeth up some other way, the same is a thief and a robber.

2 But he that entereth in by the door is the shepherd of the sheep.

3 To him the porter openeth; and the sheep hear his voice: and he calleth his own sheep by name, and leadeth them out.

§ 90. A man born blind is healed on the Sabbath.

MATTHEW.	MARK.

Our Lord's subsequent discourses. *Jerusalem.*

LUKE.

JOHN.

CH. IX. 1–41. CH. X. 1–21.

4 And when he putteth forth his
own sheep,[248] he goeth before them,
and the sheep follow him: for they
know his voice.
5 And a stranger will they not follow, but will flee from him: for they
know not the voice of strangers.
6 This parable spake Jesus unto
them: but[249] they understood not
what things they were which he spake
unto them.
7 Then said Jesus unto them again,[250]
Verily, verily, I say unto you, I am
the door of the sheep.
8 All that ever came before me[251]
are thieves and robbers: but the sheep
did not hear them.
9 I am the door: by me if any man
enter in, he shall be saved, and shall
go in and out, and find pasture.
10 The thief cometh not, but for
to steal, and to kill, and to destroy:
I am come that they might have life,[252]
and that they might have *it* more
abundantly.
11 I am the good shepherd: the
good shepherd giveth his life for the
sheep.
12 But he that is a hireling, and
not the shepherd, whose own the sheep
are not, seeth the wolf coming, and
leaveth the sheep, and fleeth; and the
wolf catcheth them, and scattereth the
sheep.[253]
13 The hireling fleeth,[254] because he
is a hireling, and careth not for the
sheep.
14 I am the good shepherd, and I
know my *sheep*, and am known of
mine.[255]
15 As the Father knoweth me,
even so know I the Father: and I lay
down my life for the sheep.
16 And other sheep I have, which
are not of this fold: them also I must
bring, and they shall hear my voice;
and there shall be one fold,[256] *and* one
shepherd.
17 Therefore doth my Father love
me, because I lay down my life, that
I might take it again.
18 No man taketh[257] it from me, but
I lay it down of myself. I have power

§ 90. A man born blind is healed on the Sabbath.

MATTHEW.	MARK.

§ 91. Jesus at Jerusalem at the feast of dedication.

Our Lord's subsequent discourses. *Jerusalem.*

LUKE.	JOHN.
	CH. IX. 1–41. CH. X. 1–21. to lay it down, and I have power to take it again. This commandment have I received of my Father. 19 There was a division therefore [258] again among the Jews for these sayings. 20 And [259] many of them said, He hath a devil, and is mad; why hear ye him? 21 [260] Others said, These are not the words of him that hath a devil. Can the devil open the eyes of the blind?

He retires beyond Jordan. *Jerusalem. Bethany beyond Jordan.*

LUKE.	JOHN.
	CHAPTER X. 22–42. 22 And it was at Jerusalem the feast of the dedication, and it was winter.[261] 23 And Jesus walked in the temple in Solomon's porch. 24 Then came the Jews round about him, and said unto him, How long dost thou make us to doubt? If thou be the Christ, tell us plainly. 25 Jesus answered them,[262] I told you, and ye believed not: the works that I do in my Father's name, they bear witness of me. 26 But ye believe not, because ye are not of my sheep, as I said unto you.[263] 27 My sheep hear my voice, and I know them, and they follow me: 28 And I give unto them eternal life; and they shall never perish, neither shall any pluck them out of my hand. 29 My Father, which gave *them* me, is greater than all; and none is able to pluck *them* out of my Father's hand.[264] 30 I and *my* Father are one. 31 Then [265] the Jews took up stones again to stone him. 32 Jesus answered them, Many good works have I shewed you from my Father;[266] for which of those works do ye stone me? 33 The Jews answered him, saying, For a good work we stone thee not; but for blasphemy, and because that thou, being a man, makest thyself God.[267]

§ 91. Jesus at Jerusalem at the feast of dedication.

MATTHEW.	MARK.

§ 92. The raising of Lazarus.

He retires beyond Jordan. *Jerusalem.* *Bethany beyond Jordan.*

LUKE.

JOHN.

CHAPTER X. 22–42.

34 Jesus answered them, Is it not
written in your law,[268] I said, Ye are
gods? *
35 If he called them gods, unto
whom the word of God came, and the
scripture cannot be broken;
36 Say ye of him whom the Father
hath sanctified, and sent into the
world, Thou blasphemest; because I
said, I am the Son of God?
37 If I do not the works of my
Father, believe me not.
38 But if I do, though ye believe
not me, believe the works: that ye
may know and believe that the
Father *is* in me, and I in him.[269]
39 Therefore they sought again [270]
to take him; but he escaped out of
their hand,
40 And went away again beyond
Jordan, into the place where John at
first baptized; and there he abode.[271]
41 And many resorted unto him,
and said, John did no miracle; but
all things that John spake of this
man were true.
42 And many believed on him
there.

Bethany.

CHAPTER XI. 1–46.

Now a certain *man* was sick,
named Lazarus, of Bethany, the town
of Mary and her sister [272] Martha.
2 (It was *that* Mary which anointed
the Lord with ointment, and wiped
his feet with her hair, whose brother
Lazarus was sick.)
3 Therefore his sisters sent unto
him, saying, Lord, behold, he whom
thou lovest is sick.
4 When Jesus heard *that*, he said,
This sickness is not unto death, but
for the glory of God, that the Son of
God might be glorified thereby.
5 Now Jesus loved Martha, and
her sister, and Lazarus.
6 When he had heard therefore
that he was sick, he abode two days
still in the same place where he was.
7 Then after that saith he to *his*
disciples, Let us go into Judea again.[273]

* Ps. lxxxii. 6. Ex. xxii. 7. seq

§ 92. The raising of Lazarus.

MATTHEW.	MARK.

Bethany.

LUKE.

JOH .

CHAPTER XI. 1-46.

8 *His* disciples say unto him, Master, the Jews of late sought to stone thee; and goest thou thither again?

9 Jesus answered, Are there not twelve hours in the day? If any man walk in the day, he stumbleth not, because he seeth the light of this world.

10 But if a man walk in the night, he stumbleth, because there is no light in him.

11 These things said he: and after that he saith unto them, Our friend Lazarus sleepeth; but I go that I may awake him out of sleep.

12 Then said his disciples,[274] Lord, if he sleep, he shall do well.

13 Howbeit Jesus spake of his death:[275] but they thought that he had spoken of taking of rest in sleep.

14 Then said Jesus unto them plainly, Lazarus is dead.

15 And I am glad for your sakes that I was not there, to the intent ye may believe; nevertheless, let us go unto him.

16 Then said Thomas, which is called Didymus, unto his fellow-disciples, Let us also go, that we may die with him.

17 Then when Jesus came,[276] he found that he had *lain* in the grave four days already.

18 (Now Bethany was nigh unto Jerusalem, about fifteen furlongs off:)

19 And many of the Jews came to Martha and Mary, to comfort them concerning their brother.

20 Then Martha, as soon as she heard that Jesus was coming, went and met him: but Mary sat *still* in the house.

21 Then said Martha unto Jesus, Lord, if thou hadst been here, my brother had not died.

22 But I know that even now,[277] whatsoever thou wilt ask of God, God will give *it* thee.

23 Jesus saith unto her, Thy brother shall rise again.

24 Martha said unto him, I know that he shall rise again in the resurrection at the last day.

25 Jesus said[278] unto her, I am the

§ 92. The raising of Lazarus.

MATTHEW.	MARK.

Bethany.

LUKE.

JOHN.

CHAPTER XI. 1–46.

resurrection, and the life: he that believeth in me, though he were dead, yet shall he live:

26 And whosoever liveth, and believeth in me, shall never die. Believest thou this?

27 She saith unto him, Yea, Lord: I believe that thou art the Christ, the Son of God, which should come into the world.

28 And when she had so said, she went her way, and called Mary her sister secretly, saying, The master is come, and calleth for thee.

29 As soon as [279] she heard *that*, she arose quickly, and came unto him.

30 Now Jesus was not yet come into the town, but was [280] in that place where Martha met him.

31 The Jews then which were with her in the house, and comforted her, when they saw Mary that she rose up hastily, and went out, followed her, saying,[281] She goeth unto the grave to weep there.

32 Then when Mary was come where Jesus was, and saw him, she fell down at his feet, saying unto him, Lord, if thou hadst been here, my brother had not died.

33 When Jesus therefore saw her weeping, and the Jews also weeping which came with her, he groaned in the spirit and was troubled,

34 And said, Where have ye laid him? They say unto him, Lord, come and see.

35 [282] Jesus wept.

36 Then said the Jews, Behold how he loved him!

37 And some of them said, Could not this man, which opened the eyes of the blind, have caused that even this man should not have died?

38 Jesus therefore again groaning in himself, cometh to the grave. It was a cave, and a stone lay upon it.

39 Jesus said, Take ye away the stone. Martha, the sister of him that was dead, saith unto him, Lord, by this time he stinketh: for he hath been *dead* four days.

40 Jesus saith unto her, Said I not

§ 92. The raising of Lazarus.

MATTHEW.	MARK.

§ 93. The counsel of Caiaphas against Jesus. He

Bethany.

LUKE.

JOHN.

CHAPTER XI. 1–46.

unto thee, that if thou wouldest believe, thou shouldest see the glory of God?

41 Then they took away the stone *from the place* where the dead was laid.[283] And Jesus lifted up *his* eyes, and said, Father, I thank thee that thou hast heard me:

42 And I knew that thou hearest me always: but because of the people which stand by, I said *it*, that they may believe that thou hast sent me.

43 And when he thus had spoken, he cried with a loud voice, Lazarus, come forth.

44 And he that was dead came forth, bound hand and foot with graveclothes: and his face was bound about with a napkin. Jesus saith unto them, Loose him, and let him go.

45 Then many of the Jews which came to Mary, and had seen the things which Jesus did,[284] believed on him.

46 But some of them went their ways to the Pharisees, and told them what things Jesus had done.

retires from Jerusalem. *Jerusalem. Ephraim.*

CHAPTER XI. 47–54.

47 Then gathered the chief priests and the Pharisees a council, and said, What do we? for this man doeth many miracles.

48 If we let him thus alone, all *men* will believe on him:[285] and the Romans shall come, and take away both our place and nation.

49 And one of them, *named* Caiaphas, being the high priest that same year, said unto them, Ye know nothing at all,

50 Nor consider that it is expedient for us,[286] that one man should die for the people, and that the whole nation perish not.

51 And this spake he not of himself: but being high priest that year, he prophesied that Jesus should die for that nation;

52 And not for that nation only, but that he should also gather together

§ 93. **The counsel of Caiaphas against Jesus. He**

MATTHEW.	MARK.

§ 94. **Jesus, beyond Jordan, is followed by multitudes. The healing**

CHAPTER XIX. 1, 2. AND it came to pass, *that* when Jesus had finished these sayings, he departed from Galilee, and came into the coasts of Judea, beyond Jordan: 2 And great multitudes followed him, and he healed them there.	CHAPTER X. 1. And he arose from thence, and cometh into the coasts of Judea, by the farther side [233] of Jordan: and the people resort unto him again; and, as he was wont, he taught them again.

retires from Jerusalem. *Jerusalem.* *Ephraim.*

LUKE.

JOHN.

CHAPTER XI. 47–54.

in one of the children of God that were scattered abroad.

53 Then from that day forth they took counsel together for to put him to death.

54 Jesus therefore walked no more openly among the Jews; but went thence unto a country near to the wilderness, into a city called Ephraim, and there continued with his disciples.[287]

of the infirm woman on the Sabbath. *Valley of Jordan.* *Perea.*

CHAPTER XIII. 10–21.

10 And he was teaching in one of the synagogues on the sabbath.

11 And behold, there was a woman which had a spirit of infirmity eighteen years, and was bowed together, and could in no wise lift up *herself*.

12 And when Jesus saw her, he called *her to him*, and said unto her, Woman, thou art loosed from thine infirmity.

13 And he laid *his* hands on her: and immediately she was made straight, and glorified God.

14 And the ruler of the synagogue answered with indignation, because that Jesus had healed on the sabbath-day, and said unto the people, There are six days in which men ought to work: in them therefore come and be healed, and not on the sabbath-day.

15 The Lord then answered him,[292] and said, *Thou* hypocrite, doth not each one of you on the sabbath loose his ox or *his* ass from the stall, and lead *him* away to watering?

16 And ought not this woman, being a daughter of Abraham, whom Satan hath bound, lo, these eighteen years, be loosed from this bond on the sabbath-day?

17 And when he had said these things, all his adversaries were ashamed: and all the people rejoiced for all the glorious things that were done by him.

18 Then said he, Unto what is the kingdom of God like? and whereunto shall I resemble it?

19 It is like a grain of mustard-

§ 94. Jesus beyond Jordan, is followed by multitudes. The healing

MATTHEW.	MARK.

§ 95. Our Lord goes teaching and journeying towards Jerusalem.

of the infirm woman on the Sabbath. *Valley of Jordan. Perea.*

LUKE.

CHAPTER XIII. 10–21.

seed, which a man took, and cast into
his garden, and it grew, and waxed a
great [293] tree; and the fowls of the
air lodged in the branches of it.
20 And again he said, Where unto
shall I liken the kingdom of God ?
21 It is like leaven, which a woman
took and hid in three measures of
meal, till the whole was leavened.

JOHN.

He is warned against Herod. *Perea.*

CHAPTER XIII. 22–35.

22 And he went through the cities
and villages, teaching, and journeying
toward Jerusalem.
23 Then said one unto him, Lord,
are there few that be saved? And he
said unto them,
24 Strive to enter in at the strait
gate: [294] for many, I say unto you,
will seek to enter in, and shall not be
able.
25 When once the Master of the
house is risen up, and hath shut to
the door, and ye begin to stand without, and to knock at the door, saying,
Lord, Lord, open unto us; [295] and he
shall answer and say unto you, I know
you not whence ye are:
26 Then shall ye begin to say,
We have eaten and drunk in thy
presence, and thou hast taught in our
streets.
27 But he shall say, I tell you, I
know you not whence ye are; [296] depart
from me, all *ye* workers of iniquity.
28 There shall be weeping and
gnashing of teeth, when ye shall see
Abraham, and Isaac, and Jacob, and
all the prophets, in the kingdom of
God, [297] and *yourselves* thrust out.
29 And they shall come from the
east, and *from* the west, and from the
north, and *from* the south, and shall
sit down in the kingdom of God.
30 And behold, there are last,
which shall be first; and there are
first, which shall be last.
31 The same day [298] there came
certain of the Pharisees, saying unto
him, Get thee out, and depart hence;
for Herod will kill thee.
42 And he said unto them, Go ye

§ 95. Our Lord goes teaching and journeying towards Jerusalem.

MATTHEW.	MARK.

§ 96. Our Lord dines with a chief Pharisee

He is warned against Herod. *Perea.*

LUKE.

CHAPTER XIII. 22–35.

and tell that fox, Behold, I cast out devils, and I do cures to-day and to-morrow, and the third *day* I shall be perfected.

33 Nevertheless, I must work to-day and to-morrow, and the *day* following: for it cannot be that a prophet perish out of Jerusalem.

34 O Jerusalem, Jerusalem, which killest the prophets, and stonest them that are sent unto thee; how often would I have gathered thy children together, as a hen *doth gather* her brood under *her* wings, and ye would not!

35 Behold, your house is left unto you desolate.* And verily, I say unto you, Ye shall not see me, until *the time* come when ye shall say, Blessed *is* he that cometh in the name of the Lord.[299]

JOHN.

on the Sabbath. Incidents. *Perea.*

CHAPTER XIV. 1–24.

AND it came to pass, as he went into the house of one of the chief Pharisees to eat bread on the sabbath-day, that they watched him.

2 And behold, there was a certain man before him which had the dropsy.

3 And Jesus answering, spake unto the lawyers and Pharisees, saying, Is it lawful to heal on the sabbath-day?[300]

4 And they held their peace. And he took *him*, and healed him, and let him go:

5 And answered them saying,[301] Which of you shall have an ass or an ox fallen into a pit, and will not straightway pull him out on the sabbath-day?

6 And they could not answer him again to these things.

7 And he put forth a parable to those which were bidden, when he marked how they chose out[302] the chief rooms; saying unto them,

8 When thou art bidden of any *man* to a wedding, sit not down in the highest room, lest a more honourable man than thou be bidden of him;

* Ps. lxix. 25. Jer. [illegible] 7, and xxii. 5,

§ 96. Our Lord dines with a chief Pharisee

MATTHEW.	MARK.

on the Sabbath. Incidents. *Perea.*

LUKE.

CHAPTER XIV. 1–24.

9 And he that bade thee and him come and say to thee, Give this man place; and thou begin with shame to take the lowest room.

10 But when thou art bidden, go and sit down in the lowest room; that when he that bade thee cometh, he may say unto thee, Friend, go up higher: then shalt thou have worship in the presence of them that sit [303] at meat with thee.

11 For whosoever exalteth himself shall be abased, and he that humbleth himself shall be exalted.

12 Then said he also to him that bade him, When thou makest a dinner or a supper, call not thy friends, nor thy brethren, neither thy kinsmen, nor *thy* rich neighbours: lest they also bid thee again, and a recompense be made thee.

13 But when thou makest a feast, call the poor, the maimed, the lame, the blind;

14 And [304] thou shalt be blessed: for they cannot recompense thee: for thou shalt be recompensed at the resurrection of the just.

15 And when one of them that sat at meat with him heard these things, he said unto him,[305] Blessed *is* he that shall eat bread in the kingdom of God.

16 Then said he unto him, A certain man made a great supper, and bade many:

17 And sent his servant at suppertime, to say to them that were bidden, Come, for all things are now ready.[306]

18 And they all with one *consent* began to make excuse. The first said unto him, I have bought a piece of ground, and I must needs go and see it: I pray thee have me excused.

19 And another said, I have bought five yoke of oxen, and I go to prove them: I pray thee have me excused.

20 And another said, I have married a wife: and therefore I cannot come.

21 So that servant came, and shewed his lord these things. Then

JOHN.

MATTHEW.

§ 96. Our Lord dines with a chief Pharisee

MATTHEW.	MARK.

§ 97. What is required of true

on the Sabbath. **Incidents.** *Perea.*

LUKE.	JOHN.
CHAPTER XIV. 1–24.	
the master of the house being angry, said to his servant, Go out quickly into the streets and lanes of the city, and bring in hither the poor, and the maimed, and the halt, and the blind.[307]	
22 And the servant said, Lord, it is done as thou hast commanded,[308] and yet there is room.	
23 And the lord said unto the servant, Go out into the highways and hedges, and compel *them* to come in, that my house may be filled.	
24 For I say unto you, that none of those men which were bidden, shall taste of my supper.	

disciples. *Perea.*

CHAPTER XIV. 25–35.

25 And there were great multitudes with him: and he turned and said unto them,

26 If any *man* come to me and hate not his father, and mother, and wife, and children, and brethren, and sisters, yea, and his own life also, he cannot be my disciple.

27 And [309] whosoever doth not bear his cross, and come after me, cannot be my disciple.

28 For which of you, intending to build a tower, sitteth not down first and counteth the cost, whether he hath *sufficient* to finish *it?*

29 Lest haply after he hath laid the foundation, and is not able to finish *it*, all that behold *it* begin to mock him,

30 Saying, This man began to build, and was not able to finish.

31 Or what king going, to make war against another king, sitteth not down first, and consulteth [310] whether he be able with ten thousand to meet him that cometh against him with twenty thousand?

32 Or else, while the other is yet a great way off, he sendeth an ambassage, and desireth conditions of peace.

33 So likewise, whosoever he be of you that forsaketh not all that he hath, he cannot be my disciple.

§ 97. **What is required of true**

MATTHEW.	MARK.

§ 98. **Parables of the lost Sheep, &c.**

disciples. *Perea.*

LUKE.

CHAPTER XIV. 25-35.

34 Salt *is* good: but if the salt [311]
have lost his flavour, wherewith shall
it be seasoned?
35 It is neither fit for the land, nor
yet for the dunghill; *but* men cast it
out. He that hath ears to hear, let
him hear.

JOHN.

and of the **Prodigal Son.** *Perea.*

CHAPTER XV. 1-32.

THEN drew near unto him all the
publicans and sinners for to hear him.
2 And the Pharisees and scribes
murmured, saying, This man receiveth [312] sinners and eateth with them.
3 And he spake this parable unto
them, saying,
4 What man of you having a hundred sheep, if he lose one of them,
doth not leave the ninety and nine in
the wilderness, and go after that
which is lost, until he find it?
5 And when he hath found it, he
layeth *it* on his shoulders rejoicing.
6 And when he cometh home, he
calleth together *his* friends and neighbours, saying unto them, Rejoice with
me; for I have found my sheep which
was lost.
7 I say unto you, that likewise joy
shall be in heaven over one sinner
that repenteth, more than over ninety
and nine just persons which need no
repentance.
8 Either what woman having ten
pieces of silver, if she lose one piece,
doth not light a candle, and sweep
the house, and seek diligently till she
find *it*?
9 And when she hath found *it*, she
calleth *her* friends and *her* neighbours
together, saying, Rejoice with me;
for I have found the piece which I
had lost.
10 Likewise I say unto you, There
is joy in the presence of the angels of
God over one sinner that repenteth.
11 And he said, A certain man had
two sons:
12 And the younger of them said
to *his* father, Father,[313] give me the
portion of goods that falleth *to me*.
And he divided unto them *his* living.

§ 98. Parables of the lost Sheep, &c.

MATTHEW.	MARK.

and of the **Prodigal** Son. *Perea.*

LUKE.

CHAPTER XV. 1-32.

13 And not many days after, the
younger son gathered all together,
and took his journey into a far
country, and there wasted his substance with riotous living.
14 And when he had sent all, there
arose a mighty famine in that land;
and he began to be in want.
15 And he went and joined himself
to a citizen of that country; and he
sent him into his fields to feed swine.
16 And he would fain have filled
his belly [314] with the husks that the
swine did eat; and no man gave unto
him.
17 And when he came to himself,
he said, How many hired servants of
my father's have bread enough and to
spare, and I perish with hunger! [315]
18 I will arise [316] and go to my
father, and will say unto him, Father,
I have sinned against heaven, and
before thee,
19 And [317] am no more worthy to be
called thy son: make me as one of
thy hired servants.
20 And he arose, and came to his
father. But when he was yet a great
way off, his father saw him, and had
compassion, and ran, and fell on his
neck, and kissed him.
21 And the son said unto him,
Father, I have sinned against heaven,
and in thy sight, and am no more
worthy to be called thy son. [318]
22 But the father said to his servants, Bring forth [319] the best robe,
and put *it* on him; and put a ring on
his hand, and shoes on *his* feet:
23 And bring hither the fatted
calf, and kill *it;* and let us eat, and
be merry:
24 For this my son was dead, and
is alive again; [320] he was lost, and is
found. And they began to be merry.
25 Now his elder son was in the
field: and as he came and drew nigh
to the house, he heard music and
dancing.
26 And he called one of the servants, and asked what these things
meant.
27 And he said unto him, Thy

JOHN.

§ 98. Parables of the lost Sheep, &c.

MATTHEW.	MARK.

§ 99. Parable of the Unjust

and of the **Prodigal Son.**

LUKE.

CHAPTER XV. 1–32.

brother is come; and thy father hath
killed the fatted calf, because he hath
received him safe and sound.
28 And he was angry, and would
not go in; therefore came his father
out,[321] and entreated him.
29 And he, answering, said to *his*
father, Lo, these many years do I
serve thee, neither transgressed I at
any time thy commandment; and yet
thou never gavest me a kid, that I
might make merry with my friends:
30 But as soon as this thy son was
come, which hath devoured thy
living with harlots, thou hast killed
for him the fatted calf.
31 And he said unto him, Son,
thou art ever with me; and all that
I have is thine.
32 It was meet that we should
make merry, and be glad: for this thy
brother was dead, and is alive again;
and was lost, and is found.[322]

JOHN.

Steward. *Perea.*

CHAPTER XVI. 1–13.

AND he said also unto his disciples,
There was a certain rich man which
had a steward; and the same was accused
unto him that he had wasted
his goods.[323]
2 And he called him, and said unto
him, How is it that I hear this of
thee? give an account of thy stewardship:[324]
for thou mayest be no longer
steward.
3 Then the steward said within
himself, What shall I do? for my
lord taketh away from me the stewardship:
I cannot dig; to beg I am
ashamed.[325]
4 I am resolved what to do, that
when I am put out of the stewardship,
they may receive me into their
houses.
5 So he called every one of his
lord's debtors *unto him*, and said unto
the first, How much owest thou unto
my lord?
6 And he said, A[326] hundred measures
of oil. And he said unto him,
Take thy bill, and sit down quickly,
and write fifty.
7 Then said he to another, And

§ 99. **Parable of the Urjust**

MATTHEW.	MARK.

§ 1C0. **The Pharisees reproved. Parable of**

Steward. *Perea.*

LUKE.

CHAPTER XVI. 1–13.

how much owest thou? And he said,
A hundred measure of wheat.[327] And
he said unto him, Take thy bill, and
write four-score.
8 And the lord commended the
unjust steward, because he had done
wisely: for the children of this world
are in their generation wiser than the
children of light.
9 And I say unto you, Make to
yourselves friends of the mammon of
unrighteousness: that when ye fail,[328]
they may receive you into everlasting
habitations.
10 He that is faithful in that which
is least, is faithful also in much; and
he that is unjust in the least, is unjust also in much.
11 If therefore ye have not been
faithful in the unrighteous mammon,
who will commit to your trust the
true *riches?*
12 And if ye have not been faithful
in that which is another man's who
shall give you that which is your own?
13 No servant can serve two masters: for either he will hate the one,
and love the other: or else he will
hold to the one, and despise the other.
Ye cannot serve God and mammon.

JOHN.

the Rich Man and Lazarus. *Perea.*

CHAPTER XVI. 14–31.

14 And the Pharisees also,[329] who
were covetous, heard all these things,
and they derided him.
15 And he said unto them, Ye are
they which justify yourselves before
men; but God knoweth your hearts:
for that which is highly esteemed
among men, is abomination in the
sight of God.
16 The law and the prophets *were*
until John: since that time the kingdom of God is preached, and every
man presseth into it.[330]
17 And it is easier for heaven and
earth to pass, that one tittle of the
law to fail.
18 Whosoever putteth away his
wife, and marrieth another, committeth adultery; and whosoever marrieth [331] her that is put away from her
husband, committeth adultery.

§ 100. The Pharisees reproved. Parable of

MATTHEW.	MARK.

The Rich Man and Lazarus. *Perea.*

LUKE.

CHAPTER XVI. 14-31.

19 There was a certain rich man, which was clothed in purple and fine linen, and fared sumptuously every day:
20 And there was a certain beggar named Lazarus, which was laid [332] at his gate full of sores,
21 And desiring to be fed with the crumbs which fell [333] from the rich man's table: moreover, the dogs came and licked his sores.
22 And it came to pass, that the beggar died, and was carried by the angels into Abraham's bosom. The rich man also died, and was buried.
23 And [334] in hell he lifted up his eyes, being in torments, and seeth Abraham afar off, and Lazarus in his bosom.
24 And he cried, and said, Father Abraham, have mercy on me, and send Lazarus, that he may dip the tip of his finger in water, and cool my tongue: for I am tormented in this flame.
25 But Abraham said, Son, remember that thou in thy lifetime receivedst thy good things, and likewise Lazarus evil things: but now he is comforted, [335] and thou art tormented.
26 And besides all this, between us and you there is a great gulf fixed: so that they which would pass from hence to you, cannot; neither can they pass to us, that *would come* from thence.
27 Then he said, I pray thee therefore, father, that thou wouldest send him to my father's house:
28 For I have five brethren; that he may testify unto them, lest they also come into this place of torment.
19 Abraham saith unto him, [336] They have Moses and the prophets, let them hear them.
30 And he said, Nay, father Abraham: but if one went unto them from the dead, [337] they will repent.
31 And he said unto him, If they hear not Moses and the prophets, neither will they be persuaded, though one rose from the dead.

JOHN.

§ 101. Jesus inculcates forbearance,

MATTHEW.	MARK.

§ 102. Christ's coming will be

faith, humility. *Perea.*

LUKE.

Chapter XVII. 1–10.

Then said he unto his disciples,[338]
It is impossible but that offences will
come; but wo *unto him* through whom
they come!
2 It were better for him that a
millstone were hanged about his neck,
and he cast into the sea, than that he
should offend one of these little ones.
3 Take heed to yourselves: If thy
brother trespass against thee,[339] rebuke
him; and if he repent, forgive him.
4 And if he trespass against thee
seven times in a day, and seven times
in a day [340] turn again to thee, saying,
I repent; thou shalt forgive him.
5 And the apostles said unto the
Lord, Increase our faith.
6 And the Lord said, If ye had
faith as a grain of mustard-seed, ye
might say unto this [341] sycamine-tree,
Be thou plucked up by the root, and
be thou planted in the sea; and it
should obey you.
7 But which of you having a servant ploughing, or feeding cattle,
will say unto him by and by, when
he is come from the field, Go and sit
down to meat?
8 And will not rather say unto him,
Make ready wherewith [342] I may sup,
and gird thyself, and serve me, till I
have eaten and drunk; and afterward thou shalt eat and drink?
9 Doth he thank that servant, because he did the things that were
commanded him? [343] I trow not.
10 So likewise ye, when ye shall
have done all those things [344] which
are commanded you, say, We are unprofitable servants: we have done
that which was our duty to do.

JOHN.

sudden. *Perea.*

Chapter XVII. 20–37.

20 And when he was demanded of
the Pharisees, when the kingdom of
God should come, he answered them
and said, The kingdom of God cometh
not with observation.
21 Neither shall they say, Lo here!
or, Lo there! for behold, the kingdom of God is within you.[347]
22 And he said unto the disciples [348]

§ 102. Christ's coming will be

MATTHEW.	MARK.

LUKE.

CHAPTER XVII. 20–37.

The days will come, when ye shall
desire to see one of the days of the
Son of man, and ye shall not see *it.*
23 And they shall say to you, See
here! or, See there! go not after
them, nor follow *them.*[349]
24 For as the lightning that light-
eneth out of the one *part* under
heaven, shineth unto the other *part*
under heaven; so shall also the Son
of man be in his day.[350]
25 But first must he suffer many
things, and be rejected of this generation.
26 And as it was in the days of
Noe, so shall it be also in the days of
the Son of man.
27 They did eat, they drank, they
married wives, they were given in
marriage, until the day that Noe entered into the ark, and the flood
came, and destroyed them all.* [351]
28 Likewise also [352] as it was in the
days of Lot: they did eat, they drank,
they bought, they sold, they planted,
they builded;
29 But the same day that Lot went
out of Sodom, it rained fire and brimstone [353] from heaven, and destroyed
them all: †
30 Even thus shall it be in the day
when the Son of man is revealed.
31 In that day, he which shall be
upon the house-top, and his stuff in
the house,[354] let him not come down
to take it away: and he that is in the
field, let him likewise not return back.
32 Remember Lot's wife.‡
33 Whosoever shall seek to save
his life, shall lose it; and whosoever
shall lose his life, shall preserve it.
34 I tell you, in that night there
shall be two *men* in one bed: the one
shall be taken, and the other shall be
left.
35 Two *women* shall be grinding
together; the one shall be taken, and
the other left.
36 [355] Two *men* shall be in the field;
the one shall be taken, and the other
left.

JOHN.

* Gen. vii. 4, 7. † Gen. xix. 15, seq. ‡ Gen. xix. 26.

§ 102. Christ's coming will be

MATTHEW.	MARK.

§ 103. Parables. The importunate Widow.

sudden. *Perea.*

LUKE.	JOHN.
CHAPTER XVII. 20-37. 37 And they answered and said unto him, Where, Lord? And he said unto them, Wheresoever the body *is*, thither will [356] the eagles be gathered together.	

The Pharisee and Publican. *Perea.*

CHAPTER XVIII. 1-14.

AND he spake a parable unto them
to this end, that men ought always [357]
to pray, and not to faint;
2 Saying, There was in a city a
judge, which feared not God, neither
regarded man.
3 And there was a widow in that
city; and she came unto him, saying,
Avenge me of mine adversary.
4 And he would not for a while:
but afterward he said within himself,
Though I fear not God, nor regard
man;
5 Yet, because this widow troubleth
me, I will avenge her, lest by her con-
tinual coming she weary me.
6 And the Lord said, Hear what
the unjust judge saith.
7 And shall not God avenge his
own elect, which cry day and night
unto him, though he bear long with
them?
8 I tell you that he will avenge
them speedily. Nevertheless, when
the Son of man cometh, shall he find
faith on the earth?
9 And he spake this parable unto
certain which trusted in themselves
that they were righteous, and despised
others:
10 Two men went up into the
temple to pray; the one a Pharisee,
and the other a publican.
11 The Pharisee stood and prayed
thus with himself,[358] God, I thank
thee, that I am not as other men *are*,
extortioners, unjust, adulterers, or
even as this publican.
12 I fast twice in the week, I give
tithes of all that I possess.[359]
13 And the publican, standing afar
off, would not lift up so much as *his*
eyes unto heaven, but smote upon his
breast, saying,[360] God be merciful to
me a sinner.

§ 103. Parables. The importunate Widow.

MATTHEW.	MARK.

§ 104. Precepts respecting divorce.

MATTHEW.

CHAPTER XIX. 3–12.

3 [276]The Pharisees also came unto him, tempting him, and saying unto him, Is it lawful for a man to put away his wife for every cause?

4 And he answered and said unto them,[277] Have ye not read,* that he which made *them* at the beginning, made them male and female,

5 And said,† For this cause shall a man leave father and mother, and shall cleave to his wife: and they twain shall be one flesh?

6 Wherefore they are no more twain, but one flesh. What therefore God hath joined together, let not man put asunder.

7 They[278] say unto him, Why did Moses then command to give a writing of divorcement, and to put her away?‡

8 He saith unto them, Moses, because of the hardness of your hearts, suffered you to put away your wives: but from the beginning it was not so.

9 And I say unto you, Whosoever shall put away his wife, except *it be* for fornication, and shall marry another, committeth adultery: and whoso marrieth her which is put away, doth commit adultery.[279]

10 His disciples say unto him,[280] If the case of the man be so with *his* wife, it is not good to marry.

11 But he said unto them, All *men* cannot receive this saying, save *they* to whom it is given.

MARK.

CHAPTER X. 2–12.

2 And the Pharisees[234] came to him, and asked him, Is it lawful for a man to put away *his* wife? tempting him.

3 And he answered and said unto them, What did Moses command you?

4 And they said, Moses suffered to write a bill of divorcement, and to put *her* away.

5 And Jesus answered and said[235] unto them, For the hardness of your heart, he wrote you this precept:

6 But from the beginning of the creation, God made[236] them male and female.

7 For this cause shall a man leave his father and mother, and cleave to his wife;[237]

8 And they twain shall be one flesh: so then they are no more twain, but one flesh.

9 What, therefore, God hath joined together, let no man put asunder.

10 And in the house his disciples asked him again of the same *matter*.[238]

11 And he saith unto them, Whosoever shall put away his wife, and marry another, committeth adultery against her.

12 And if a woman shall put away her husband, and be married to another, she committeth adultery.[239]

* Gen. i. 27. † Gen. ii. 24. ‡ Deut. xxiv. 1.

Matt. xix. 1-12.] The two Evangelists go on to relate our Lord's observations about divorce and marriage: they agree in substance, which is sufficient; though they differ in the form of the dialogue, neither adhering scrupulously to the exact manner in which the words passed, though we may learn it, by comparing both. Thus Matt. v. 9, reduces to a plain assertion, what Mark informs us was a reply to an inquiry made by the disciples apart. Or, we may suppose with Le Clerc, that this assertion was first advanced to the Pharisees, and then repeated to the disciples. NEWCOME.

The Pharisee and Publican. *Perea.*

LUKE.	JOHN.
CHAPTER XVIII. 1–14. 14 I tell you, this man went down to his house justified *rather* than the other: for every one that exalteth himself shall be abased; and he that humbleth himself shall be exalted.	

Perea.

Mark x. 12, *put away her husband.*] The practice of divorcing the husband, unwarranted by the law, had been introduced, as Josephus informs us (Antiq. XV. vii. 10), by Salome, sister of Herod the Great, who sent a bill of divorce to her husband Costobarus; which bad example was afterwards followed by Herodias and others. CAMPBELL. This natural allusion to an existing illegal custom is in perfect harmony with the whole history, it being true; but it seldom if ever has a parallel in the annals of forgery.

§ 104. **Precepts respecting divorce.**

MATTHEW.	MARK.
CHAPTER XIX. 3–12. 12 For[281] there are some eunuchs, which were so born from *their* mother's womb: and there are some eunuchs, which were made eunuchs of men: and there be eunuchs, which have made themselves eunuchs for the kingdom of heaven's sake. He that is able to receive *it*, let him receive *it*.	

§ 105. **Jesus receives and blesses little**

CHAPTER XIX. 13–15.	CHAPTER X. 13–16.
13 Then there were brought unto him little children, that he should put *his* hands on them, and pray: and the disciples rebuked them.	13 And they brought young children to him, that he should touch them; and *his* disciples rebuked those that brought *them*.[240]
	14 But when Jesus saw *it*, he was much displeased, and said unto them,
14 But Jesus said,[262] Suffer little children, and forbid them not, to come unto me: for of such is the kingdom of heaven.	Suffer the little children to come unto me, and[241] forbid them not: for of such is the kingdom of God.
	15 Verily I say unto you, Whosoever shall not receive the kingdom of God as a little child, he shall not enter therein.
15 And he laid *his* hands on them, and departed thence.	16 And he took them up in his arms; put *his* hands upon them, and blessed them.[242]

§ 106. **The rich young man. Parable of the**

CH. XIX. 16–30. CH. XX. 1–16.	CHAPTER X. 17–31.
16 And behold, one came and said unto him, Good Master, what good thing shall I do that I may have eternal life.[283]	17 And when he was gone forth into the way, there came one running,[243] and kneeled to him, and asked him, Good Master, what shall I do that I may inherit eternal life?
17 And he said unto him, Why callest thou me good? *there is* none good but one, *that is*, God:[284] but if thou wilt enter into life, keep the commandments.	18 And Jesus said unto him, Why callest thou me good? *there is* none good, but one, *that is* God.
18 He saith unto him,[285] Which? Jesus said, Thou shalt do no murder, Thou shalt not commit adultery, Thou shalt not steal, Thou shalt not bear false witness,	19 Thou knowest the commandments, Do not commit adultery, Do not kill, Do not steal, Do not bear false witness, Defraud not, Honour thy father and mother.[244]
19 Honour thy father and *thy* mother:[286] and, Thou shalt love thy neighbour as thyself.*	
20 The young man saith unto him, All these things have I kept from my youth up:[287] what lack I yet?	20 And he answered and said unto him,[245] Master, all these have I observed from my youth.

* Ex. xx. 12, seq. Lev. xix. 18.

Perea.

LUKE.	JOHN.

children. *Perea.*

LUKE	JOHN
CHAPTER XVIII. 15–17. 15 And they brought unto him also infants, that he would touch them: but when *his* disciples saw *it*, they rebuked them. 16 But Jesus called them *unto him*, and said, Suffer little children to come unto me, and forbid them not: for of such is the kingdom of God. 17 Verily, I say unto you, Whosoever shall not receive the kingdom of God as a little child, shall in no wise enter therein.	

Labourers in the Vineyard. *Perea.*

LUKE	JOHN
CHAPTER XVIII. 18–30. 18 And a certain ruler asked him, saying, good Master, what shall I do to inherit eternal life? 19 And Jesus said unto him, Why callest thou me good? none *is* good, save one, *that is* God. 20 Thou knowest the commandments, Do not commit adultery, Do not kill, Do not steal, Do not bear false witness, Honor thy father and thy mother.[361] 21 And he said, All these have I kept from my youth up.	

§ 106. The rich young man. Parable of the

MATTHEW.

Ch. XIX. 16–30. Ch. XX. 1–16.

21 Jesus said[288] unto him, If thou wilt be perfect, go *and* sell that thou hast, and give to the poor, and thou shalt have treasure in heaven: and come *and* follow me.

22 But when the young man heard that saying, he went away sorrowful: for he had great possessions.[289]

23 Then said Jesus unto his disciples, Verily, I say unto you, That a rich man shall hardly enter into the kingdom of heaven.

24 And again I say unto you,[290] It is easier for a camel to go through the eye of a needle, than for a rich man to enter into the kingdom of God.

25 When his[291] disciples heard *it*, they were exceedingly amazed, saying, Who then can be saved ?

26 But Jesus beheld *them*, and said unto them, With men this is impossible, but with God all things are possible.

27 Then answered Peter, and said unto him, Behold, we have forsaken all, and followed thee; what shall we have therefore ?

28 And Jesus said unto them, Verily, I say unto you, That ye which have followed me in the regeneration, when the Son of man shall sit in the throne of his glory, ye also shall sit upon twelve thrones, judging the twelve tribes of Israel.

29 And every one that hath forsaken houses, or brethren, or sisters, or father, or mother, or wife, or children, or lands, for my name's sake, shall receive a hundred-fold, and shall inherit everlasting life.[292]

30 But many *that are* first shall be last, and the last *shall be* first.[293]

Chapter XX.

For the kingdom of heaven is like unto a man *that is* a householder,

MARK.

Chapter X. 17–31.

21 Then Jesus beholding him, loved him, and said unto him, One thing thou lackest: go thy way, sell whatsoever thou hast, and give to the poor, and thou shalt have treasure in heaven; and come, take up the cross, and follow me.[246]

22 And he was sad at that saying, and went away grieved: for he had great possessions.

23 And Jesus looked round about, and saith[247] unto his disciples, How hardly shall they that have riches enter into the kingdom of God!

24 And the disciples were astonished at his words. But Jesus answereth again, and saith unto them, Children, how hard is it for them that trust in riches[248] to enter into the kingdom of God!

25 It is easier for a camel to go[249] through the eye of a needle, than for a rich man to enter into the kingdom of God.

26 And they were astonished out of measure, saying among themselves, Who[250] then can be saved ?

27 And Jesus, looking upon them, saith,[251] With men *it is* impossible, but not with God: for with God all things are possible.

28 Then Peter began to say unto him, Lo, we have left all, and have followed thee.[252]

29 And Jesus answered and said, Verily I say unto you, There is no man that hath left house, or brethren, or sisters, or father, or mother, or wife, or children, or lands, for my sake, and the gospel's,[253]

30 But he shall receive a hundred-fold now in this time, houses, and brethren, and sisters, and mothers, and children, and lands, with persecutions;[254] and in the world to come, eternal life.

31 But many *that are* first shall be last; and the last first.

Labourers in the Vineyard. *Perea.*

LUKE.

CHAPTER XVIII. 18–30.

22 Now, when Jesus heard these
things, he said unto him, Yet lackest
thou one thing: [362] sell all that thou
hast, and distribute unto the poor,
and thou shalt have treasure in
heaven: and come, follow me.

23 And when he heard this, [363] he
was very sorrowful: for he was very
rich.
24 And when Jesus saw that he
was very sorrowful, he said, How
hardly shall they that have riches
enter [364] into the kingdom of God!

25 For it is easier for a camel to
go through a needle's eye, than for a
rich man to enter into the kingdom
of God.
26 And they that heard *it*, said,
Who then can be saved?

27 And he said, The things which
are impossible with men, are possible
with God.

28 Then Peter said, Lo, we have
left all, and followed thee.

29 And he said unto them, Verily,
I say unto you, there is no man that
hath left house, or parents, or brethren, or wife, or children, [365] for the
kingdom of God's sake,

30 Who shall not receive manifold
more in this present time, and in the
world to come life everlasting.

JOHN.

§ 106. **The rich young man. Parable of the**

MATTHEW.

CH. XIX. 16–30. CH. XX. 1–16.

which went out early in the morning to hire labourers into his vineyard.

2 And when he had agreed with the labourers for a penny a day, he sent them into his vineyard.

3 And he went out about the third hour, and saw others standing idle in the market place,

4 And said unto them, Go ye also into the vineyard;[294] and whatsoever is right, I will give you. And they went their way.

5 Again he went out about the sixth and ninth hour, and did likewise.

6 And about the eleventh hour he went out, and found others standing idle, and saith unto them, Why stand ye here all the day idle?[295]

7 They say unto him, Because no man hath hired us. He saith unto them, Go ye also into the vineyard; and whatsoever is right, *that* shall ye receive.[296]

8 So when evening was come, the lord of the vineyard saith unto his steward, Call the labourers, and give them *their* hire,[297] beginning from the last unto the first.

9 And when[298] they came that *were hired* about the eleventh hour, they received every man a penny.

10 But when[299] the first came, they supposed that they should have received more; and they likewise received every man a penny.

11 And when they had received *it*, they murmured against the good man of the house,

12 Saying, These last have wrought *but* one hour, and thou hast made them equal unto us, which have borne the burden and heat of the day.

13 But he answered one of them, and said, Friend, I do thee no wrong: didst not thou agree with me for a penny?

14 Take *that* thine *is*, and go thy way: I will give unto this last, even as unto thee.

15 Is it not lawful for me to do what I will with mine own? is thine eye evil because I am good?

16 So the last shall be first, and the first last: for many be called, but few chosen.[300]

MARK.

Labourers in the Vineyard. *Perea.*

LUKE.	JOHN.

§ 107. Jesus a third time foretells his Death

MATTHEW.

CHAPTER XX. 17–19.

17 And Jesus, going up to Jerusalem, took the twelve disciples apart in the way, and said unto them,[301]

18 Behold, we go up to Jerusalem; and the Son of man shall be betrayed unto the chief priests, and unto the scribes, and they shall condemn him to death,[302]

19 And shall deliver him to the Gentiles to mock, and to scourge, and to crucify *him:* and the third day he shall rise again.

MARK.

CHAPTER X. 32–34.

32 And they were in the way, going up to Jerusalem; and Jesus went before them: and they were amazed; and as they followed, they were afraid. And he took again the twelve, and began to tell them what things should happen unto him,

33 *Saying*, Behold, we go up to Jerusalem; and the Son of man shall be delivered unto the chief priests, and unto the scribes;[255] and they shall condemn him to death, and shall deliver him to the Gentiles;

34 And they shall mock him, and shall scourge him, and shall spit upon him,[256] and shall kill him: and the third day he shall rise again.

§ 108. James and John prefer their ambitious

CHAPTER XX. 20–28.

20 Then came to him the mother of Zebedee's children, with her sons, worshipping *him*, and desiring a certain thing of him.

21 And he said unto her, What wilt thou? She saith unto him,[303] Grant that these my two sons may sit, one on thy right hand, and the other on the left, in thy kingdom.

22 But Jesus answered and said, Ye know not what ye ask. Are ye able to drink of the cup that I shall drink of, and to be baptized with the baptism that I am baptized with?[304] They say unto him, we are able.

23 And he saith unto them, Ye shall drink indeed of my cup, and be baptized with the baptism that I am baptized with: but, to sit on my right hand, and on my left,[305] is not mine to give, but *it shall be given to them* for whom it is prepared of my Father.

24 And when the ten heard *it*, they were moved with indignation against the two brethren.[306]

CHAPTER X. 35–45.

35 And James and John, the sons of Zebedee, come unto him,[257] saying, [258] Master, we would that thou shouldest do for us whatsoever we shall desire.

36 And he said unto them, What would ye that I should do for you?

37 They said unto him, Grant unto us that we may sit, one on thy right hand, and the other on thy left hand, in thy glory.

38 But Jesus said unto them, Ye know not what ye ask: can ye drink of the cup that I drink of? and be baptized[259] with the baptism that I am baptized with?

39 And they said unto him, We can. And Jesus said unto them, Ye shall indeed[260] drink of the cup that I drink of; and with the baptism that I am baptized withal shall ye be baptized:

40 But to sit on my right hand and on my left hand, is not mine to give; but *it shall be given to them* for whom it is prepared.[261]

41 And when the ten heard *it*, they began to be much displeased with James and John.[262]

Matt. xx. 21, *she saith.*] As all three came to Jesus, the *action* of the sons expressed, that they joined in the petition uttered by the mother. They are therefore represented as saying

and Resurrection. [See § 74, § 77.] *Perea.*

LUKE.

CHAPTER XVIII. 31-34.

31 Then he took *unto him* the
twelve, and said unto them, Behold,
we go up to Jerusalem, and all things
that are written by the prophets concerning the Son of man shall be accomplished.
32 For he shall be delivered unto
the Gentiles, and shall be mocked,
and spitefully entreated, and spitted
on;
33 And they shall scourge *him*, and
put him to death: and the third day
he shall rise again.
34 And they understood none of
these things: and this saying was
hid from them, neither knew they
the things which were spoken.

JOHN.

request. *Perea.*

what was said with their consent, and probably by their suggestion. Luke XIX. 11, will show how suitable this request was to the time, according to the ideas of our Lord's disciples. NEWCOME.

§ 108. James and John prefer their ambitious

MATTHEW.

CHAPTER XX. 20–28.

25 But Jesus called them *unto him*, and said, Ye know that the princes of the Gentiles exercise dominion over them, and they that are great exercise authority upon them.

26 But it shall not be so among you:[307] but whosoever shall be great among you, let him be your minister;

27 And whosoever will be chief among you, let him be your servant:

28 Even as the Son of man came not to be ministered unto, but to minister, and to give his life a ransom for many.

MARK.

CHAPTER X. 35–45.

42 But Jesus called them *to him*, and saith unto them, Ye know that they which are accounted to rule over the Gentiles, exercise lordship over them; and their great ones exercise authority upon them.[263]

43 But so shall it not be[264] among you: but whosoever will be great among you, shall be your minister:

44 And whosoever of you[265] will be the chiefest, shall be servant of all.

45 For even the Son of man came not to be ministered unto, but to minister, and to give his life a ransom for many.

§ 109. The healing of two

CHAPTER XX. 29–34.

29 And as they departed from Jericho, a great multitude followed him.[308]

30 And behold, two blind men sitting by the wayside, when they heard that Jesus passed by, cried out, saying, Have mercy upon us, O Lord, *thou* son of David.[309]

31 And the multitude rebuked them, because they should hold their peace: but they cried the more, saying, Have mercy upon us, O Lord, *thou* son of David.[310]

32 And Jesus stood still, and called them,

and said, what will ye that I shall do unto you?

CHAPTER X. 46–52.

46 And they came to Jericho: and as he went out of Jericho with his disciples, and a great number of people, blind Bartimeus, the son of Timeus, sat by the highway side, begging.[266]

47 And when he heard that it was Jesus of Nasareth, he began to cry out and say, Jesus, *thou* son of David, have mercy on me.

48 And many charged him that he should hold his peace: but he cried the more a great deal, *Thou* son of David, have mercy on me.

49 And Jesus stood still, and commanded him to be called:[267] and they call the blind man, saying unto him, Be of good comfort, rise; he calleth thee.

50 And he, casting away his garment, rose,[268] and came to Jesus.

51 And Jesus answered and said unto him, What wilt thou that I should do unto thee? The blind man

---

Luke xviii. 35, *come nigh.*] According to St. Mark, Jesus comes to Jericho; by which may be meant that he is a temporary inhabitant of that city. See Mark vi. 1. and viii. 22. Jesus therefore may be represented (Matt. xx. 29; Mark x. 46), not as *finally leaving* Jericho for Jerusalem, but as *occasionally going out* of Jericho; in which city he had made some abode, it matters not for how few days. See Mark xi. 19. Jericho was a very considerable city; and we do not read that it was visited by our Lord at any other time. We may therefore suppose that Jesus, accompanied by his disciples and the multitude, and intent on his great work of propagating the gospel, went out of this city, knowing that a fit occasion of working a miracle would present itself; and that on his return, as

request. *Perea.*

LUKE.	JOHN.

blind men near Jericho.

LUKE.	JOHN.
CH. XVIII. 35–43. CH. XIX. 1. 35 And it came to pass, that as he was come nigh unto Jericho, a cer- tain blind man sat by the wayside begging; 36 And hearing the multitude pass by, he asked what it meant. 37 And they told him,[366] that Jesus of Nazareth passeth by. 38 And he cried, saying, Jesus,[367] *thou* son of David, have mercy on me. 39 And they which went before rebuked him, that he should hold his peace: but he cried so much the more, *Thou* son of David,[368] have mercy on me. 40 And Jesus stood[369] and com- manded him to be brought unto him: and when he was come near, he asked him, 41 Saying,[370] What wilt thou that I	

he drew nigh unto Jericho (Luke xviii. 35), he restored the blind men to sight. It is likewise probable that Jesus, having given this proof of his divine mission, or foreseeing that so great a miracle would create too much attention in the people, prudently and humbly passed through Jericho on his return to it (Luke xix. 1), and continued his journey to Jerusalem.

As to the remaining difficulty, that Matthew mentions two blind men, and the other Evangelists only one, I must refer to Le Clerc's maxim, before quoted; (see § 57, note); adding that Bartimeus may have been the more remarkable of the two, and the more eminent for his faith in Jesus. NEWCOME.

§ 109. The healing of two

MATTHEW.

CHAPTER XX. 29–34.

33 They say unto him, Lord, that our eyes may be opened.
34 So Jesus had compassion *on them*, and touched their eyes: and immediately their eyes received sight,[311] and they followed him.

MARK.

CHAPTER X. 46–52.

said unto him, Lord, that I might receive my sight.
52 And Jesus said unto him, Go thy way; thy faith hath made thee whole. And immediately he received his sight, and followed Jesus in the way.[269]

§ 110. The visit to Zaccheus. Parable of

blind men near Jericho.

LUKE.	JOHN.
CH. XVIII. 35–43. CH. XIX. 1. shall do unto thee? And he said, Lord, that I may receive my sight. 42 And Jesus said unto him, Re- ceive thy sight: thy faith hath saved thee. 43 And immediately he received his sight, and followed him, glorify- ing God: and all the people, when they saw *it*, gave praise unto God. CHAPTER XIX. AND *Jesus* entered and passed through Jericho.	

the ten Minæ. *Jericho.*

CHAPTER XIX. 2–28.

2 And behold *there was* a man
named Zaccheus, which was the
chief among the publicans, and he
was rich.[371]

3 And he sought to see Jesus who
he was; and could not for the press,
because he was little of stature.

4 And he ran before, and climbed
up into a sycamore-tree to see him;
for he was to pass that *way*.

5 And when Jesus came to the
place, he looked up, and saw him,[372]
and said unto him, Zaccheus, make
haste, and come down: for to-day I
must abide at thy house.

6 And he made haste, and came
down, and received him joyfully.

7 And when they saw *it*, they all
murmured, saying, That he was gone
to be guest with a man that is a
sinner.

8 And Zaccheus stood, and said
unto the Lord; Behold, Lord, the
half of my goods I give to the poor;
and if I have taken any thing from
any man, by false accusation, I restore
him four-fold.

9 And Jesus said unto him, This
day is salvation come to this[373]
house, forasmuch as he also is a son
of Abraham.

10 For the Son of man is come to
seek and to save that which was lost.

11 And as they heard these things,
he added and spake a parable, because he was nigh to Jerusalem, and
because they thought that the kingdom
of God should immediately appear.

§ 110. The visit to Zaccheus. Parable of

MATTHEW.

MARK.

Luke xix. 12.] Here is a fine allusion to historical facts, first observed by Le Clerc. "Thus Herod the Great solicited the kingdom of Judea at Rome (Jos. Antiq. Jud. XIV. xiv. 4, 5 ; XV. vi. 6, 7), and was appointed king by the interest of Anthony with the senate; and afterwards he sailed to Rhodes, divested himself of his diadem, and received it again from Augustus. In like manner his sons Archelaus and Antipas

the ten Minæ. *Jericho.*

LUKE.

CHAPTER XIX. 2–28.

12 He said therefore, a certain nobleman went into a far country to receive for himself a kingdom, and to return.

13 And he called his ten servants, and delivered them ten pounds, and said unto them, Occupy till I come.

14 But his citizens hated him, and sent a message after him, saying, We will not have this *man* to reign over us.

15 And it came to pass, that when he was returned, having received the kingdom, then he commanded these servants to be called unto him, to whom he had given the money, that he might know how much every man had gained by trading.[374]

16 Then came the first, saying, Lord, thy pound hath gained ten pounds.

17 And he said unto him, Well, thou good servant: because thou hast been faithful in a very little, have thou authority over ten cities.

18 And the second came, saying, Lord, thy pound hath gained five pounds.

19 And he said likewise to him, Be thou also over five cities.

20 And another came, saying, Lord, behold *here is* thy pound, which I have kept laid up in a napkin:

21 For I feared thee, because thou art an austere man: thou takest up that thou layedst not down, and reapest that thou didst not sow.

22 And [375] he saith unto him, Out of thine own mouth will I judge thee, *thou* wicked servant. Thou knewest that I was an austere man, taking up that I laid not down, and reaping that I did not sow:

23 Wherefore then gavest not thou my money into the bank, that at my coming I might have required mine own with usury?

JOHN.

---

repaired to the imperial city, that they might obtain the kingdom on their father's death; and we read (Jos. Antiq. Jud. XIV. xi. 1, and xiii. 2), that the Jews sent an embassy thither, with accusations against Archelaus. NEWCOME, Obs. on our Lord, p. 83.

§ 110. The visit to Zaccheus. The Parable of

MATTHEW.	MARK.

§ 111. Jesus arrives at Bethany six days

the ten **Minæ.** *Jericho.*

LUKE.

CHAPTER XIX. 2–28.

24 And he said unto them that stood by, Take from him the pound, and give *it* to him that hath ten pounds.

25 (And they said unto him, Lord, he hath ten pounds.)

26 For I say unto you, That unto every one which hath, shall be given; and from him that hath not, even that he hath shall be taken away from him.[374]

27 But those mine enemies, which would not that I should reign over them, bring hither, and slay *them* before me.

28 And when he had thus spoken, he went before, ascending up to Jerusalem.

JOHN.

before the **Passover.** *Bethany.*

JOHN.

CH. XI. 55–57. CH. XII. 1, 9–11.

55 And the Jews' passover was nigh at hand: and many went out of the country up to Jerusalem before the passover, to purify themselves.

56 Then sought they for Jesus, and spake among themselves, as they stood in the temple, What think ye, that he will not come to the feast?

57 Now both the chief priests and the Pharisees had given a commandment,[288] that, if any man knew where he were, he should shew *it*, that they might take him.

CHAPTER XII.

THEN Jesus, six days before the passover, came to Bethany, where Lazarus was which had been dead, whom he raised from the dead.[289]

9 Much people of the Jews therefore knew that he was there: and they came, not for Jesus' sake only, but that they might see Lazarus also, whom he had raised from the dead.[293]

10 But the chief priests consulted that they might put Lazarus also to death;

11 Because that by reason of him many of the Jews went away, and believed on Jesus.

PART VII.

OUR LORD'S PUBLIC ENTRY INTO JERUSALEM,

AND THE

SUBSEQUENT TRANSACTIONS

BEFORE

THE FOURTH PASSOVER.

TIME. *Five days.*

§ 112. Our Lord's public entry into Jerusalem.

MATTHEW.

CHAPTER XXI. 1–11, 14–17.

AND when they drew nigh unto Jerusalem, and were come to Bethphage, unto the mount of Olives, then sent Jesus two disciples,

2 Saying unto them, Go into the village over against you, and straightway ye shall find an ass tied, and a colt with her: loose *them*, and bring *them* unto me.

3 And if any *man* say aught unto you, ye shall say, The Lord hath need of them;[312] and straightway he will send them.

4 All[313] this was done, that it might be fulfilled which was spoken by the prophet, saying,*

5 Tell ye the daughter of Sion, Behold, thy King cometh unto thee, meek, and sitting upon an ass, and a colt the foal of an ass.

6 And the disciples went, and did as Jesus commanded them,

7 And brought the ass and the colt, and put on them their clothes, and they set *him* thereon.[314]

8 And a very great multitude spread their garments in the way: others cut down branches from the trees, and strewed *them* in the way.

MARK.

CHAPTER XI. 1–11.

AND when they came nigh to Jerusalem, unto Bethphage,[270] and Bethany, at the mount of Olives, he sendeth forth two of his disciples,

2 And saith unto them, Go your way into the village over against you: and as soon as ye be entered into it, ye shall find a colt tied, whereon never man sat;[271] loose him, and bring *him*.

3 And if any man say unto you, Why do ye this? say ye that the Lord hath need of him; and straightway he will send him hither.[272]

4 And they went their way and found the colt tied by the door without, in a place where two ways met;[273] and they loose him.

5 And certain of them that stood there said unto them, What do ye, loosing the colt?

6 And they said unto them even as Jesus had commanded:[274] and they let them go.

7 And they brought the colt to Jesus, and cast their garments on him; and he sat upon him.[275]

8 And many spread their garments in the way: and others cut down branches off the trees,[276] and strewed *them* in the way.

* Zech. ix. 9.

Matth. xxi. 7, *and put on them their clothes.*] Thus acknowledging him to be their *king;* for this was a custom observed by the people when they found that God had appointed a man to the kingdom. When Jehu was anointed King by Elisha the prophet, at the command of God, and his captains knew what was done, *every man took his garment and spread it under him on the top of the steps, and blew the trumpets, saying Jehu is king.* 2 King ix. 13. A. CLARKE. See JENNINGS, Ant. vol. ii. p. 245. "*Thereon,*" that is, on the garments. The princes of Israel were forbidden to multiply *horses* to themselves. Deut. xvii. 16, and xx. 1. This law was imposed as a standing mark of distinction between them and other nations; and a trial of prince and people, whether they had confidence in God their deliverer, who wanted neither horses nor footmen to fight his battles. It was observed for near four hundred

(FIRST DAY OF THE WEEK.) *Bethany.* *Jerusalem.*

LUKE.

CHAPTER XIX. 29–44.

29 And it came to pass, when he was come nigh to Bethphage and Bethany, at the mount called *the mount* of Olives, he sent two of his[377] disciples,

30 Saying, Go ye into the village over against *you;* in the which at your entering ye shall find a colt tied, whereon yet never man sat: loose him, and bring *him thither.*

31 And if any man ask you, Why do ye loose *him?* thus shall ye say unto him,[418] Because the Lord hath need of him.

32 And they that were sent went their way, and found even as he had said unto them.

33 And as they were loosing the colt, the owners thereof said unto them, Why loose ye the colt?

34 And they said, The Lord hath need of him.

35 And they brought him to Jesus: and they cast their garments upon the colt and they set Jesus thereon.

36 And as he went, they spread their clothes in the way.

JOHN.

CHAPTER XII. 12–19.

12 On the next day, much people that were come to the feast, when they heard that Jesus was coming to Jerusalem,

---

years, until some time in the reign of Solomon; for David himself rode on a mule: as did Solomon also on the day of his coronation. 1 Kings i. 33, 34. See Judges x. 4, and xii. 14; 1 Saml. xxv. 20. Subsequently the kings of Israel and Judah violated this command, by copying the example of the neighboring princes in the establishment of their cavalry. The displeasure of God for this offence is indicated by several of the prophets; Isaiah ii. 6, 7. and xxi. 1; Hosea xiv. 3, and i. 7; Micah v. 10, 11.—In opposition to the character of these warlike and disobedient princes, it was predicted that Messiah would come as a just king, having salvation;—a deliverer—riding upon an ass, after the manner of the ancient deliverers of Israel, who came only in the strength and power of the Lord. Zech. ix. 9. See Bishop SHERLOCK's Dissert. IV. MICHAELIS, vol. ii. pp. 439–449.

§ 112. Our Lord's public entry into Jerusalem.

MATTHEW.

CHAPTER XXI. 1–11, 14–17.

9 And the multitudes that went before,[315] and that followed, cried, saying, Hosanna to the Son of David: Blessed *is* he that cometh in the name of the Lord: Hosanna in the highest.

10 And when he was come into Jerusalem, all the city was moved, saying, Who is this?

11 And the multitude said, This is Jesus the prophet[316] of Nazareth of Galilee.

14 And the blind and the lame came to him in the temple; and he healed them.

15 And when the chief priests and scribes saw the wonderful things that he did, and the children crying in the temple, and saying, Hosanna to the son of David; they were sore displeased,

16 And said unto him, Hearest thou what these say? And Jesus saith unto them, Yea: have ye never read, Out of the mouth of babes and sucklings thou hast perfected praise?*

17 And he left them, aud went out of the city[319] into Bethany, and he lodged there.

MARK.

CHAPTER XI. 1–11.

9 And they that went before, and they that followed, cried, saying,[277] Hosanna: Blessed *is* he that cometh in the name of the Lord.

10 Blessed *be* the kingdom of our father David, that cometh in the name of the Lord:[278] Hosanna in the highest.

11 And Jesus entered into Jerusalem, and into the temple:[279] and when he had looked round about upon all things, and now the eventide was come, he went out unto Bethany, with the twelve.

* Ps. viii. 3.

(FIRST DAY OF THE WEEK.) *Bethany. Jerusalem.*

LUKE.

CHAPTER XIX. 29-44.

37 And when he was come nigh, even now at the descent at the mount of Olives, the whole multitude of the disciples began to rejoice and praise God with a loud voice for all the mighty works that they had seen;

38 Saying, Blessed *be* the King that cometh in the name[379] of the Lord: Peace in heaven, and glory in the highest.

39 And some of the Pharisees from among the multitude said unto him, Master, rebuke thy disciples.

40 And he answered and said unto them,[380] I tell you, that if these should hold their peace, the stones would immediately cry out.

41 And when he was come near, he beheld the city, and wept over it.

42 Saying, If thou hadst known, even thou, at least in this thy day,[382] the things *which belong* unto thy peace! but now they are hid from thine eyes.

43 For the days shall come upon thee, that thine enemies shall cast a trench about thee, and compass thee round, and keep thee in on every side,

44 And shall lay thee even with the ground, and thy children within thee: and they shall not leave in thee one stone upon another; because thou knewest not the time of thy visitation.

JOHN.

CHAPTER XII. 12–19.

13 Took branches of palm-trees, and went forth to meet him, and cried, Hosanna; Blessed *is* the King of Israel that cometh in the name of the Lord.*[294]

14 And Jesus, when he had found a young ass, sat thereon; as it is written,

15 Fear not, daughter of Sion, behold, thy King cometh,[295] sitting on an ass's colt.

16 These things understood not his disciples at the first: but when Jesus was glorified, then remembered they that these things were written of him, and *that* they had done these things unto him.

17 The people therefore that was with him when he called Lazarus out of his grave, and raised him from the dead, bare record.

18 For this cause the[296] people also met him, for that they heard that he had done this miracle.

19 The Pharisees therefore said among themselves, Perceive ye how ye prevail nothing? behold, the world is gone after him.

* Ps. cxviii. 26.

§ 113. The barren Fig-tree. The cleansing of the

MATTHEW.

CHAPTER XXI. 12, 13, 18, 19.

18 Now in the morning, as he returned into the city, he hungered.

19 And when he saw a fig-tree in the way, he came to it, and found nothing thereon,[320] but leaves only, and said unto it, Let no fruit grow on thee henceforward for ever. And presently the fig-tree withered away.

12 And Jesus went into the temple of God,[317] and cast out all them that sold and bought in the temple, and overthrew the tables of the money-changers, and the seats of them that sold doves,

13 And said unto them, It is written,* My house shall be called the house of prayer, but ye have made it [318] a den of thieves.

MARK.

CHAPTER XI. 12–19.

12 And on the morrow, when they were come from Bethany, he was hungry.

13 And seeing a fig-tree afar off, having leaves, he came, if haply he might find any thing thereon: and when he came to it, he found nothing but leaves: for the time of figs was not *yet*.

14 And Jesus answered [280] and said unto it, No man eat fruit of thee hereafter for ever. And his disciples heard *it*.

15 And they come to Jerusalem: and Jesus went into the temple, and began to cast out them that sold and bought in the temple,[281] and overthrew the tables of the money-changers, and the seats of them that sold doves;

16 And would not suffer that any man should carry *any* vessel through the temple.

17 And he taught, saying unto them, Is it not written, My house shall be called, of all nations, the house of prayer ?[282] but ye have made it a den of thieves.

18 And the scribes and chief priests[283] heard *it*, and sought how they might destroy him: for they feared him, because all the people was astonished at his doctrine.

19 And when even was come, he went out [284] of the city.

§ 114. The barren Fig-tree withers away.

CHAPTER XXI. 20–22.

20 And when the disciples saw *it*, they marvelled, saying, How soon is the fig-tree withered away!

21 Jesus answered and said unto them, Verily, I say unto you, If ye have faith, and doubt not, ye shall not only do this *which is done* to the fig-tree, but also, if ye shall say unto

CHAPTER XI. 20–26.

20 And in the morning, as they passed by, they saw the fig-tree dried up from the roots.

21 And Peter calling to remembrance, saith unto him, Master, behold, the fig-tree which thou cursedst is withered away.

22 [285] And Jesus answering, saith unto them, Have faith in God.

23 For verily I say unto you, That whosoever shall say unto this mountain, Be thou removed, and be thou

* Isa. lvi. 7. Jer. vii. 11.

Matth. xxi. 20, *the disciples*. Mark xi. 21. *Peter*.] These may be thus reconciled. Peter addresses himself to Jesus : the disciples turn their attention to the object ;

Temple. (SECOND DAY OF THE WEEK.) *Bethany. Jerusalem.*

LUKE.
CH. XIX. 45–48. CH. XXI. 37, 38.

45 And he went into the temple,
and began to cast out them that sold
therein, and them that bought,[382]
46 Saying unto them, It is written,
My house is the house of prayer,[383]
but ye have made it a den of thieves.
47 And he taught daily in the
temple. But the chief priests, and
the scribes, and the chief of the people
sought to destroy him,
48 And could not find what they
might do: for all the people were
very attentive to hear him.

CHAPTER XXI.

37 And in the day-time he was
teaching in the temple; and at night
he went out, and abode in the mount
that is called *the mount* of Olives.
38 And all the people came early
in the morning to him in the temple,
for to hear him.

JOHN.

(THIRD DAY OF THE WEEK.) *Between Bethany and Jerusalem.*

Jesus addresses all. Or, Peter's remark may be attributed to all the disciples. See § 141. NEWCOME.

§ 114. The barren Fig-tree withers away.

MATTHEW.

CHAPTER XXI. 20–22.

this mountain, Be thou removed, and be thou cast into the sea; it shall be done.

22 And all things whatsoever ye shall ask in prayer, believing, ye shall receive.

MARK.

CHAPTER XXI. 20–26.

cast into the sea; and shall not doubt in his heart, but shall believe that those things which he saith shall come to pass; he shall have whatsoever he saith.

24 Therefore I say unto you, What things soever ye desire when ye pray,[287] believe that ye receive *them*, and ye shall have *them*.

25 And when ye stand praying, forgive, if ye have aught against any: that your Father also which is in heaven may forgive you your trespasses.

26 [288] But if ye do not forgive, neither will your Father which is in heaven forgive your trespasses.

§ 115. Christ's authority questioned. Parable of the

CHAPTER XXI. 23–32.

23 And when he was come into the temple, the chief priests and the elders of the people came unto him as he was teaching, and said, By what authority doest thou these things? and who gave thee this authority?

24 And Jesus answered and said unto them, I also will ask you one thing, which if ye tell me, I in like wise will tell you by what authority I do these things.

25 The baptism of John, whence was it? from heaven, or of men? And they reasoned with themselves, saying, If we shall say, from heaven; he will say unto us, Why did ye not then believe him?

26 But if we shall say, Of men; we fear the people: for all hold John as a prophet.

27 And they answered Jesus, and said, We cannot tell. And he [321] said unto them, Neither tell I you by what authority I do these things.

28 But what think ye? A *certain* man had two sons; And he came to the first, and said, Son, go work to-day in my vineyard.[322]

CHAPTER XXI. 27–33.

27 And they come again to Jerusalem: and as he was walking in the temple, there come to him the chief priests, and the scribes, and the elders,

28 And say [289] unto him, By what authority doest thou these things? and who gave thee this authority to do these things?

29 And Jesus answered and said unto them,[290] I will also ask of you one question, and answer me, and I will tell you by what authority I do these things.

30 The baptism of John, was *it* from heaven, or of men? [291] answer me.

31 And they reasoned with themselves, saying, If we shall say, From heaven; he will say, Why then did ye not believe him?

32 But if we shall say, Of men; they feared the people: for all *men* counted John, that he was a prophet indeed.[292]

33 And they answered and said unto Jesus, We cannot tell. And Jesus answering [293] saith unto them, Neither do I tell you by what authority I do these things.

(THIRD DAY OF THE WEEK.) *Between Bethany and Jerusalem.*

LUKE. | JOHN.

two Sons. (THIRD DAY OF THE WEEK.) *Jerusalem.*

CHAPTER XX. 1-18.

AND it came to pass, *that* on one of those days, as he taught the people in the temple, and preached the gospel, the chief priests [384] and the scribes came upon *him*, with the elders,

2 And spake unto him, saying, Tell us,[385] By what authority doest thou these things? or who is he that gave thee this authority?

3 And he answered and said unto them, I will also ask you one thing; and answer me:

4 The baptism of John, was it from heaven or of men?

5 And they reasoned with themselves, saying, If we shall say, From heaven; he will say, Why then [386] believed ye him not?

6 But and if we say, Of men; all the people will stone us: for they be persuaded that John was a prophet.

7 And they answered, That they could not tell whence *it was*.

8 And Jesus said unto them,[387] Neither tell I you by what authority I do these things.

§ 115. Christ's authority questioned. Parable of the

MATTHEW.

CHAPTER XXI. 23–32.

29 He answered and said, I will not; but afterward he repented, and went.[323]

30 And he came to the second, and said likewise. And he answered and said, I *go*, sir: and went not.[324]

31 Whether of them twain did the will of *his* father? They say unto him, The first.[325] Jesus saith unto them, Verily I say unto you, That the publicans and the harlots go into the kingdom of God before you.

32 For John came unto you in the way of righteousness, and ye believed him not: but the publicans and the harlots believed him: and ye, when ye had seen *it*, repented not afterward,[326] that ye might believe him.

MARK.

§ 116. Parable of the wicked husbandmen.

MATTHEW.

CHAPTER XXI. 33-46.

33 Hear another parable; There was a certain householder,[327] which planted a vineyard, and hedged it round about, and digged a wine-press in it, and built a tower, and let it out to husbandmen, and went into a far country:

34 And when the time of the fruit drew near, he sent the servants to the husbandmen, that they might receive the fruits of it.

35 And the husbandmen took his servants, and beat one, and killed another, and stoned another.

36 Again he sent [328] other servants more than the first: and they did unto them likewise.

37 But last of all he sent unto them his son, saying, They will reverence my son.

MARK.

CHAPTER XII. 1–12.

AND he began to speak unto them by parables. A *certain* man planted a vineyard, and set an hedge about *it*, and digged *a place for* the winefat, and built a tower, and let it out to husbandmen, and went into a far country.

2 And at the season he sent to the husbandmen a servant, that he might receive from the husbandmen of the fruit [294] of the vineyard.

3 And they caught *him*, and beat him, and sent *him* away empty.

4 And again, he sent unto them another servant: and at him they cast stones, and wounded *him* in the head, and sent *him* away shamefully handled.[295]

5 And again [296] he sent another; and him they killed, and many others; beating some, and killing some.

6 Having yet therefore one son, his well-beloved, he sent him also last unto them,[297] saying, they will reverence my son.

Matth. xxi. 34, 35, *servants.*] Many servants are sent; some of whom are beaten, some slain, some stoned. Here St. Matthew is more circumstantial than the other two Evangelists, who mention only one servant as sent, and one of the three injurious modes of treatment. Some suppose that this servant was chief among the rest.

Matth. xxi. 36. Here Mark mentions one servant among the others, as stoned,

two Sons. (THIRD DAY OF THE WEEK.) *Jerusalem.*

LUKE.	JOHN.

(THIRD DAY OF THE WEEK.) *Jerusalem.*

CHAPTER XX. 9–19.

9 Then began he to speak to the
people this parable: A certain man
planted a vineyard, and let it forth
to husbandmen, and went into a far
country for a long time.[388]

10 And at the season he sent a
servant to the husbandmen, that they
should give him of the fruit of the
vineyard: but the husbandmen beat
him, and sent *him* away empty.

11 And again he sent another servant: and they beat him also, and
entreated *him* shamefully, and sent
him away empty.

12 And again he sent a third: and
they wounded him also, and cast *him*
out.

13 Then said the Lord of the vineyard, What shall I do? I will send
my beloved son: It may be they will
reverence *him* when they see him.[389]

---

wounded in the head, and sent away dishonoured; and Luke selects the circumstance that that one was beaten. Then Mark and Luke mention a third passage, about which Matthew is silent. But, "qui pauciora memorat, plura non negat." St. Luke may be understood as saying that a mortal wound was inflicted on the third messenger. NEWCOME.

§ 116. Parable of the wicked husbandmen.

MATTHEW.

CHAPTER XXI. 33–46.

38 But when the husbandmen saw the son, they said among themselves, This is the heir; come, let us kill him, and let us seize on his inheritance.

39 And they caught him, and cast *him* out of the vineyard, and slew *him*.

40 When the lord therefore of the vineyard cometh, what will he do unto those husbandmen?

41 They say unto him, He will miserably destroy those wicked men, and will let out *his* vineyard unto other husbandmen, which shall render him the fruits in their seasons.

42 Jesus saith unto them, Did ye never read in the scriptures, The stone which the builders rejected, the same is become the head of the corner: this is the Lord's doing, and it is marvellous in our eyes?*

43 Therefore say I unto you, The kingdom of God shall be taken from you, and given to a nation bringing forth the fruits thereof.

44 And whosoever shall fall on this stone, shall be broken: but on whomsoever it shall fall, it will grind him to powder. †

45 And [329] when the chief priests and Pharisees had heard his parables, they perceived that he spake of them.

46 But when they sought to lay hands on him, they feared the multitude, because they took him for a prophet.

MARK.

CHAPTER XII. 1-12.

7 But those husbandmen said among themselves, This is the heir; come, let us kill him, and the inheritance shall be ours.

8 And they took him, and killed *him*, and cast *him* out of the vineyard.

9 What shall therefore [298] the lord of the vineyard do? He will come and destroy the husbandmen, and will give the vineyard unto others.

10 And have ye not read this scripture; The stone which the builders rejected is become the head of the corner:

11 This was the Lord's doing, and it is marvellous in our eyes?

12 And they sought to lay hold on him, but feared the people; for they knew that he had spoken the parable against them: and they left him, and went their way.

§ 117. Parable of the marriage of the King's Son.

CHAPTER XXII. 1–14.

AND Jesus answered and spake unto them again by parables, and said,

2 The kingdom of heaven is like unto a certain king, which made a marriage for his son,

3 And sent forth his servants to call them that were bidden to the wedding: and they would not come.

4 Again he sent forth other servants, saying, Tell them which are bidden, Behold, I have prepared my dinner: my oxen and *my* fatlings *are* killed, and all things *are* ready: come unto the marriage.

* Ps. cxviii. 22. † Isa. viii. 14, seq. Zech. xii. 3. Dan. ii. 34, seq., 44, seq.

(THIRD DAY OF THE WEEK.) *Jerusalem.*

LUKE.

CHAPTER XX. 9-19.

14 But when the husbandmen saw him, they reasoned among themselves, saying, This is the heir: come,[390] let us kill him, that the inheritance may be ours.

15 So they cast him out of the vineyard, and killed *him*. What therefore shall the lord of the vineyard do unto them?

16 He shall come and destroy these husbandmen, and shall give the vineyard to others. And when they heard *it*, they said, God forbid.

17 And he beheld them, and said, What is this then that is written, The stone which the builders rejected, the same is become the head of the corner?

18 Whosoever shall fall upon that stone, shall be broken: but on whomsoever it shall fall, it will grind him to powder.

19 And the chief priests and the scribes the same hour sought to lay hands on him; and they feared the people: for they perceived that he had spoken this parable against them.[391]

JOHN.

(THIRD DAY OF THE WEEK.) *Jerusalem.*

§ 117. Parable of the marriage of the King's Son.

MATTHEW.

CHAPTER XXII. 1–14.

5 But they made light of *it*, and went their ways, one to his farm, another to his merchandise.

6 And the remnant took his servants, and entreated *them* spitefully, and slew *them*.

7 But when the king heard *thereof*, he was wroth:[330] and he sent forth his armies, and destroyed those murderers, and burned up their city.

8 Then saith he to his servants, The wedding is ready, but they which were bidden were not worthy.

9 Go ye therefore into the highways, and as many as ye shall find, bid to the marriage.

10 So those servants went out into the highways, gathered together all as many as they found, both bad and good: and the wedding[331] was furnished with guests.

11 And when the king came in to see the guests, he saw there [332] a man which had not on a wedding-garment:

12 And he saith unto him, Friend, how camest thou in hither, not having a wedding-garment? And he was speechless.

13 Then said the king to the servants, Bind him hand and foot, and take him away,[333] and cast *him* into outer darkness: there shall be weeping and gnashing of teeth.

14 For many are called, but few *are* chosen.

MARK.

§ 118. Insidious question of the Pharisees. Tribute

CHAPTER XXII. 15–22.

15 Then went the Pharisees, and took counsel how they might entangle him in *his* talk.[334]

CHAPTER XII. 13–17.

13 And they sent unto him certain of the Pharisees, and of the Herodians, to catch him in *his* words.

Matth. xxii. 11-13.] In the East, where the fashions of dress rarely, if ever change, much of their riches consists in the number and splendour of their robes, or *caffetans*. Presents of garments are frequently alluded to in Scripture. Gen. xlv. 22. 2 Chron. ix. 24. Judges xiv. 12. 2 Kings v. 5. Ezra ii. 69. Neh. vii. 70, where "the Tirshatha gave five hundred and thirty priests' garments."

Presents were considered as tokens of honour;—not meant as offers of payment or enrichment (1 Sam. ix. 7); and especially presents of dresses. 1 Sam. xviii. 4. Luke xv. 22. *Tavernier*, p. 42, mentions a *nazar*, whose virtue so pleased a king of Persia, that he caused himself to be disappareled, and gave his own habit to the *nazar*, which is *the greatest honour a king of Persia can bestow on a subject.*

(THIRD DAY OF THE WEEK.) *Jerusalem.*

LUKE.	JOHN.

to Cesar. (THIRD DAY OF THE WEEK.) *Jerusalem.*

CHAPTER XX. 20–26.
20 And they watched *him*, and sent
forth spies, which should feign themselves just men, that they might take

---

Such presents are given by kings on great occasions, especially at the marriages of their children. The Sultan Achmet, at the marriage of his eldest daughter, "gave presents to above 20,000 persons." Knolle's Hist. of the Turks, p. 1311. So Ahasuerus "gave gifts *according to the state of the king*." Esth. ii. 18.

The king gives his garment of honour *before* the wearer is admitted into his presence;—De La Mottraye's Trav. p. 199; (Does this illustrate Zech. iii. 3, 4?)—and would resent it if any, having received robes of him, should appear in his presence without wearing these marks of his liberality. And to refuse such favours, when offered, is considered as one of the greatest indignities. Sir John Chardin relates an instance where such a refusal cost a vizier his life. See 4 CALM. DICT. pp. 64, 126, 514.

§ 118. Insidious question of the Pharisees. Tribute

MATTHEW.
CHAPTER XXII. 15–22.

16 And they sent out unto him their disciples, with the Herodians, saying, Master, we know that thou art true, and teachest the way of God in truth, neither carest thou for any *man*: for thou regardest not the person of men.
17 Tell us therefore, What thinkest thou? Is it lawful to give tribute unto Cesar, or not?
18 But Jesus perceived their wickedness, and said, Why tempt ye me, *ye* hypocrites?
19 Shew me the tribute-money. And they brought unto him a penny.
20 And he saith unto them, Whose *is* this image, and superscription?
21 They say unto him,[335] Cesar's. Then saith he unto them, Render therefore unto Cesar, the things which are Cesar's; and unto God, the things that are God's.
22 When they had heard *these words*, they marvelled, and left him, and went their way.

MARK.
CHAPTER XII. 13–17.

14 And when they were come, they say unto him, Master, we know that thou art true, and carest for no man: for thou regardest not the person of men, but teachest the way of God in truth: Is it lawful to give tribute to Cesar, or not?
15 Shall we give, or shall we not give? But he, knowing their hypocrisy, said unto them, Why tempt ye me? bring me a penny, that I may see *it*.[299]
16 And they brought *it*. And he saith unto them, Whose *is* this image and superscription? And they said[300] unto him, Cesar's.
17 And Jesus answering, said unto them,[301] Render to Cesar the things that are Cesar's, and to God the things that are God's. And they marvelled at him.

§ 119. Insidious question of the Sadducees. The

CHAPTER XXII. 23–33.

23 The same day came to him the Sadducees,[336] which say that there is no resurrection, and asked him,
24 Saying, Master, Moses said, If a man die, having no children, his brother shall marry his wife, and raise up seed unto his brother.*
25 Now, there were with us seven brethren: and the first, when he had married a wife, deceased: and having no issue, left his wife unto his brother.
26 Likewise the second also, and the third, unto the seventh.
27 And last of all the woman died also.[337]

CHAPTER XII. 18–27.

18 Then come unto him the Sadducees, which say there is no resurrection; and they asked him, saying,
19 Master, Moses wrote unto us, If a man's brother die, and leave *his* wife *behind him*, and leave no children, that his brother should take his wife,[302] and raise up seed unto his brother.
20 Now,[303] there were seven brethren: and the first took a wife, and dying left no seed.
21 And the second took her, and died, neither left he any seed:[304] and the third likewise.
22 And the seven had her, and left no seed:[305] last of all the woman died also.

* Deut. xxv. 5.

to **Cesar.** (THIRD DAY OF THE WEEK.) *Jerusalem.*

LUKE.

CHAPTER XX. 20-26.

hold of his words, that so they might
deliver him unto the power and authority of the governor.
21 And they asked him, saying,
Master, we know that thou sayest
and teachest rightly, neither acceptest
thou the person *of any*, but teachest
the way of God truly:
22 Is it lawful for us to give tribute
unto Cesar, or no?
23 But he perceived their craftiness, and said unto them, Why tempt
ye me? [392]

24 Shew me a penny. Whose image
and superscription hath it? They
answered and said, Cesar's. [393]

25 And he said unto them, Render
therefore unto Cesar the things which
be Cesar's, and unto God the things
which be God's.
26 And they could not take hold
of his words before the people: and
they marvelled at his answer, and held
their peace.

JOHN.

Resurrection. (THIRD DAY OF THE WEEK.) *Jerusalem.*

CHAPTER XX. 27-40.

27 Then came to *him* certain of
the Sadducees (which deny that there
is any resurrection) [394] and they asked
him,
28 Saying, Master, Moses wrote
unto us, if any man's brother die,
having a wife, and he die [395] without
children, that his brother should take
his wife, and raise up seed unto his
brother.
29 There were therefore seven
brethren: and the first took a wife,
and died without children.

30 [396] And the second took her to
wife, and he died childless.
31 And the third took her; [397] and
in like manner the seven also: and
they left no children, and died.
32 Last of all [398] the woman died also.

§ 119. Insidious question of the Sadducees. The

MATTHEW.

CHAPTER XXII. 23–33.

28 Therefore, in the resurrection, whose wife shall she be of the seven? for they all had her.

29 [338] Jesus answered and said unto them, Ye do err, not knowing the scriptures, nor the power of God.

30 For in the resurrection they neither marry, nor are given in marriage, but are as the angels of God [339] in heaven.

31 But, as touching the resurrection of the dead, have ye not read that which was spoken unto you by God, saying,

32 I am the God of Abraham, and the God of Isaac, and the God of Jacob?* God [340] is not the God of the dead, but of the living.

33 And when the multitude heard *this*, they were astonished at his doctrine.

MARK.

CHAPTER XII. 18–27.

23 In the resurrection therefore, when they shall rise,[306] whose wife shall she be of them? for the seven had her to wife.

24 And Jesus answering, said unto them,[307] Do ye not therefore err, because ye know not the scriptures, neither the power of God?

25 For when they shall rise from the dead, they neither marry, nor are given in marriage; but are as the angels which are in heaven.[308]

26 And as touching the dead, that they rise; have ye not read in the book of Moses, how in the bush God [309] spake unto him, saying, I *am* the God of Abraham, and the God of Isaac, and the God of Jacob?

27 He is not the God of the dead, but the God of the living: ye therefore do greatly err.[310]

§ 120. A lawyer questions Jesus. The two great

CHAPTER XXII. 34–40.

34 But when the Pharisees had heard that he had put the Sadducees to silence, they were gathered together.

35 Then one of them *which was* a lawyer, asked *him a question*, tempting him, and saying,[341]

36 Master, which *is* the great commandment in the law?

37 Jesus said [342] unto him, Thou shalt love the Lord thy God with all thy heart, and with all thy soul, and with all thy mind.†

CHAPTER XII. 28–34.

28 And one of the scribes came, and having heard them reasoning together, and perceiving [311] that he had answered them well, asked him, Which is the first commandment of all?

29 And Jesus answered him, The first of all the commandments *is*, Hear, O Israel; [312] The Lord our God is one Lord:

30 And thou shalt love the Lord thy God with all thy heart, and with all thy soul, and with all thy mind,

* Ex. iii. 6.

† Deut. vi. 4, 5.

Luke xx. 36, *Neither can they die any more.*] Here is a minute indication of St. Luke's veracity, derived from his medical profession. No other Evangelist records

Resurrection. (THIRD DAY OF THE WEEK.) *Jerusalem.*

LUKE.

CHAPTER XX. 27–40.

33 Therefore in the resurrection,
whose wife of them is she? [399] for
seven had her to wife.

34 And Jesus answering,[400] said
unto them, The children of this world
marry, and are given in marriage:
35 But they which shall be accounted worthy to obtain that world,
and the resurrection from the dead,
neither marry, nor are given in marriage:
36 Neither can they die any more:
for they are equal unto the angels;
and are the children of God, being
the children of the resurrection.
37 Now that the dead are raised,
even Moses shewed at the bush, when
he calleth the Lord the God of Abraham, and the God of Isaac, and the
God of Jacob.

38 For he is not a God of the dead,
but of the living: for all live unto him.
39 Then certain of the scribes answering, said, Master, thou hast well
said.
40 And [401] after that, they durst not
ask him any *question at all.*

JOHN.

Commandments. (THIRD DAY OF THE WEEK.) *Jerusalem.*

this remark; but it would not be likely to escape the notice of a physician. See on Luke xxii. 44.

§ 120. A lawyer questions Jesus. The two great

MATTHEW.

CHAPTER XXII. 34–40.

38 This is the first and great[343] commandment.

39 [344] And the second *is* like unto it, Thou shalt love thy neighbour as thyself.*

40 On these two commandments hang all[345] the law and the prophets.

MARK.

CHAPTER XII. 28-34.

and with all thy strength: this *is* the first commandment.[313]

31 And the second *is* like, *namely* this, Thou shalt love thy neighbour as thyself: there is none other commandment greater than these.[314]

32 And the scribe said unto him, Well, Master, thou hast said the truth: for there is one God;[315] and there is none other but he:

33 And to love him with all the heart, and with all the understanding, and with all the soul, and with all the strength, and to love *his* neighbour as himself,[316] is more than all whole burnt offerings and sacrifices.

34 And when Jesus saw that he answered discreetly, he said unto him, Thou art not far from the kingdom of God. And no man after that durst ask him *any question*.

§ 121. How is Christ the Son of David?

CHAPTER XXII. 41–46.

41 While the Pharisees were gathered together, Jesus asked them,

42 Saying, What think ye of Christ? Whose son is he? They say unto him, *The son* of David.

43 He saith unto them, How then doth David in spirit call him Lord, saying,

44 The LORD said unto my Lord, Sit thou on my right hand, till I make thine enemies thy footstool?[346]†

45 If David then call him Lord, how is he his son?

46 And no man was able to answer him a word, neither durst any *man*, from that day forth, ask him any more *questions*.

CHAPTER XII. 35–37.

35 And Jesus answered and said, while he taught in the Temple, How say the scribes that Christ is the son of David?

36 For David himself said by the Holy Ghost, The LORD said unto my Lord, Sit thou on my right hand, till I make thine enemies thy footstool.[317]

37 David therefore himself calleth him Lord, and whence is he[318] *then* his son? And the common people heard him gladly.

§ 122. Warnings against the evil example of the Scribes

CHAPTER XXIII. 1-12.

THEN spake Jesus to the multitude, and to his disciples,

2 Saying, The scribes and the Pharisees sit in Moses' seat:

CHAPTER XII. 38, 39.

38 And he said unto them[319] in his doctrine, Beware of the scribes, which love to go in long clothing, and *love* salutations in the market-places,

39 And the chief seats in the synagogues, and the uppermost rooms at feasts:

* Lev. xix. 18.

† Ps. cx. 1.

Commandments. (THIRD DAY OF THE WEEK.) *Jerusalem.*

LUKE.	JOHN.

(THIRD DAY OF THE WEEK.) *Jerusalem.*

CHAPTER XX. 41–44.

41 And he said unto them, How
say they [402] that Christ is David's son?
42 And [403] David himself saith in
the book of Psalms, The LORD saith
unto my Lord, Sit thou on my right
hand,
43 Till I make thine enemies thy
footstool.
44 David therefore calleth him
Lord, how is he then his son?

and Pharisees. (THIRD DAY OF THE WEEK.) *Jerusalem.*

CHAPTER XX. 45–46.

45 Then in the audience of all the
people, he said unto his disciples.[404]
46 Beware of the scribes, which
desire to walk in long robes, and love
greetings in the markets, and the
highest seats in the synagogues, and
the chief rooms at feasts;

§ 122. Warnings against the evil example of the Scribes

MATTHEW.

CHAPTER XXIII. 1–12.

3 All therefore whatsoever they bid you observe, *that* observe and do:[347] but do not ye after their works: for they say, and do not.

4 For they bind heavy burdens, and grievous to be borne, and lay *them* on men's shoulders; but they *themselves* will not move them with one of their fingers.[348]

5 But all their works they do for to be seen of men: they make broad their phylacteries, and enlarge the borders of their garments,[349]

6 And love the uppermost rooms at feasts, and the chief seats in the synagogues,

7 And greetings in the markets, and to be called of men, Rabbi, Rabbi.[350]

8 But be ye not called Rabbi: for one is your Master, *even* Christ;[351] and all ye are brethren.

9 And call no *man* your father upon the earth: for one is your Father[352] which is in heaven.

10 Neither be ye called masters: for one is your Master,[353] *even* Christ.

11 But he that is greatest among you, shall be your servant.

12 And whosoever shall exalt himself, shall be abased; and he that shall humble himself, shall be exalted.

MARK.

§ 123. Woes against the Scribes and Pharisees. Lamentation

MATTHEW.

CHAPTER XXIII. 13–39.

13 But[354] wo unto you, scribes and Pharisees, hypocrites! for ye shut up the kingdom of heaven against men: for ye neither go in *yourselves*, neither suffer ye them that are entering, to go in.

14 [355] Wo unto you, scribes and Pharisees, hypocrites! for ye devour widows' houses, and for a pretence make long prayer: therefore ye shall receive the greater damnation.

15 Wo unto you, scribes and Pharisees, hypocrites! for ye compass sea and land to make one proselyte; and when he is made, ye make him two-fold more the child of hell than yourselves.

16 Wo unto you, *ye* blind guides,

MARK.

CHAPTER XII. 40.

40 Which devour widows' houses, and for a pretence make long prayers: these shall receive greater damnation.

and Pharisees. (THIRD DAY OF THE WEEK.) *Jerusalem.*

LUKE.	JOHN.

over Jerusalem. (THIRD DAY OF THE WEEK.) *Jerusalem.*

CHAPTER XX. 47.

47 Which devour widows' houses, and for a shew make long prayers: the same shall receive greater damnation.

§ 123. **Woes against the Scribes and Pharisees. Lamentation**

MATTHEW.

CHAPTER XXIII. 13–39.

which say, Whosoever shall swear by the temple, it is nothing; but whosoever shall swear by the gold of the temple, he is a debtor.

17 *Ye* fools, and blind! for whether is greater, the gold, or the temple that sanctifieth the gold?

18 And whosoever shall swear by the altar, it is nothing; but whosoever sweareth by the gift that is upon it, he is guilty.

19 *Ye* fools, and blind![356] for whether *is* greater, the gift, or the altar that sanctifieth the gift?

20 Whoso therefore shall swear by the altar, sweareth by it, and by all things thereon.

21 And whoso shall swear by the temple, sweareth by it, and by him that dwelleth therein.

22 And he that shall swear by heaven, sweareth by the throne of God, and by him that sitteth thereon.

23 Wo unto you, scribes and Pharisees, hypocrites! for ye pay tithe of mint, and anise, and cummin, and have omitted the weightier *matters* of the law, judgment, mercy, and faith: these ought ye[357] to have done, and not to leave the other undone.

24 *Ye* blind guides, which strain at a gnat, and swallow a camel.

25 Wo unto you, scribes and Pharisees, hypocrites! for ye make clean the outside of the cup and of the platter, but within they are full of extortion and excess.

26 *Thou* blind Pharisee, cleanse first that *which is* within the cup and platter, that the outside of them[358] may be clean also.

27 Wo unto you, scribes and Pharisees, hypocrites! for ye are like unto whited sepulchres, which indeed appear[359] beautiful outward, but are within full of dead *men's* bones, and of all uncleanness.

28 Even so ye also outwardly appear righteous unto men, but within ye are full of hypocrisy and iniquity.

29 Wo unto you, scribes and Pharisees, hypocrites! because ye build the tombs of the prophets, and garnish the sepulchres of the righteous,

MARK.

LUKE.	JOHN.

§ 123. **Woes against the Scribes and Pharisees. Lamentation**

MATTHEW.

CHAPTER XXIII. 13-39.

30 And say, if we had been in the
days of our fathers, we would not
have been partakers with them in
the blood of the prophets.
31 Wherefore ye be witnesses unto
yourselves, that ye are the children
of them which killed the prophets.
32 Fill ye up then the measure [360]
of your fathers.
33 *Ye* serpents, *ye* generation of
vipers, how can ye escape the damnation of hell?
34 Wherefore, behold, I send unto
you prophets, and wise men, and
scribes; and *some* [361] of them ye shall
kill and crucify, and *some* of them
shall ye scourge in your synagogues,
and persecute *them* from city to city:
35 That upon you may come all
the righteous blood shed upon the
earth, from the blood of righteous
Abel, unto the blood of Zacharias, [362]
son of Barachias, whom ye slew between the temple and the altar.*
36 Verily, I say unto you, All
these things shall come upon this
generation.
37 O Jerusalem, Jerusalem, *thou*
that killest the prophets, and stonest
them which are sent unto thee, how
often would I have gathered thy
children together, even as a hen
gathereth her chickens under *her*
wings, and ye would not!
38 Behold, your house is left unto
you desolate.[363] †
39 For I say unto you, Ye shall not
see me henceforth, till ye shall say,
Blessed *is* he that cometh in the
name of the Lord. ‡

MARK.

§ 124. **The Widow's Mite.** (THIRD DAY OF

CHAPTER XII 41-44.

41 And Jesus sat [320] over against
the treasury, and beheld how the
people cast money into the treasury:
and many that were rich cast in much.
32 And there came a certain poor
widow, and she threw in two mites,
which make a farthing.

* Gen. iv. 8. 2 Chron. xxiv. 20-22.

† Ps. lxix. 26. Jer. xii. 7, and xxii. 5.

‡ Ps. cxviii. 26.

over Jerusalem. (THIRD DAY OF THE WEEK.) *Jerusalem.*

LUKE.	JOHN.

THE WEEK.) *Jerusalem.*

CHAPTER XXI. 1–4.

AND he looked up and saw the rich men casting their gifts into the treasury.

2 And he saw also [405] a certain poor widow, casting in thither two mites.

§ **124. The Widow's Mite.** (THIRD DAY OF

MATTHEW.	MARK.
	CHAPTER XII. 41–44.
	43 And he called *unto him* his disciples, and saith [321] unto them, Verily, I say unto you, That this poor widow hath cast more in, than all they which have cast into the treasury.
	44 For all *they* did cast in of their abundance: but she of her want did cast in all that she had, *even* all her living.

§ **125. Certain Greeks desire to see Jesus.**

THE WEEK.) *Jerusalem.*

LUKE.	JOHN.
CHAPTER XXI. 1–4. 3 And he said, of a truth I say unto you, That this poor widow hath cast in more than they all. 4 For all these have of their abundance cast in unto the offerings of God:[406] but she of her penury hath cast in all the living that she had.	

(THIRD DAY OF THE WEEK.) *Jerusalem.*

CHAPTER XII. 17–19.

20 And there were certain Greeks among them, that came up to worship at the feast.

21 The same came therefore to Philip, which was of Bethsaida of Galilee, and desired him, saying, Sir, we would see Jesus.

22 Philip cometh and telleth Andrew: and again, Andrew and Philip tell Jesus.[297]

23 And Jesus answered[298] them, saying, The hour is come, that the Son of man should be glorified.

24 Verily, verily, I say unto you, Except a corn of wheat fall into the ground and die, it abideth alone: but if it die, it bringeth forth much fruit.

25 He that loveth his life shall lose it;[299] and he that hateth his life in this world, shall keep it unto life eternal.

26 If any man serve me, let him follow me, and where I am, there shall also my servant be:[300] if any man serve me, him will *my* Father honour.

27 Now is my soul troubled; and what shall I say? Father, save me from this hour: but for this cause came I unto this hour.

28 Father, glorify thy[301] name. Then came there a voice from heaven, *saying*, I have both glorified *it*, and will glorify *it* again.

29 The people therefore that stood by, and heard *it*,[302] said that it thundered. Others said, an angel spake to him.

30 Jesus answered and said,[303] This voice came not because of me, but for your sakes.

31 Now is the judgment of this

§ 125. Certain Greeks desire to see Jesus.

MATTHEW.	MARK.

§ 126. Reflections upon the unbelief of the Jews.

(THIRD DAY OF THE WEEK.) *Jerusalem.*

LUKE.	JOHN.
	CHAPTER XII. 20–36.

world: now shall the prince of this world be cast out.

32 And I, if I be lifted up from the earth, will draw all *men* [304] unto me.

33 (This he said, signifying what death he should die.)

34 The people [305] answered him, we have heard out of the law that Christ abideth for ever:* and how sayest thou, The Son of man must be lifted up? Who is this Son of man?

35 Then Jesus said unto them, Yet a little while is the light with you.[306] Walk while ye have the light, lest darkness come upon you: for he that walketh in darkness knoweth not whither he goeth.

36 While ye have light, believe in the light, that ye may be the children of light. These things spake Jesus, and departed, and did hide himself from them.

(THIRD DAY OF THE WEEK.) *Jerusalem.*

CHAPTER XII. 37–50.

37 But though he had done so many miracles before them, yet they believed not on him.

38 That the saying of Esaias the prophet might be fulfilled, which he spake, Lord, who hath believed our report? and to whom hath the arm of the Lord been revealed?†

39 Therefore they could not believe, because that Esaias said again,

40 He hath blinded their eyes, and hardened their heart; that they should not see with *their* eyes, nor understand with *their* heart, and be converted, and I should heal them.‡

41 These things said Esaias, when he saw [307] his glory, and spake of him.§

42 Nevertheless, among the chief rulers also many believed on him; but because of the Pharisees they did not confess *him*, lest they should be put out of the synagogue:

43 For they loved the praise of men more than the praise of God.

44 Jesus cried, and said, He that

* 2 Sam. vii. 13. Ps. lxxxix. 30, 37; cx. 4.
† Is. liii. 1. ‡ Is. vi. 10. § Is. vi. 1, seq.

§ 126. Reflections upon the unbelief of the Jews.

MATTHEW.	MARK.

§ 127. Jesus, on taking leave of the Temple, foretells its destruction, etc.

MATTHEW.

CHAPTER XXIV. 1–14.

AND Jesus went out, and departed from the temple:[364] and his disciples came to *him* for to shew him the buildings of the temple.

2 And Jesus said unto them,[365] See ye not all these things? verily, I say unto you, There shall not be left here one stone upon another, that shall not be thrown down.

3 And as he sat upon the mount of Olives, the disciples came unto him privately, saying, Tell us, when shall these things be? and what *shall be* the sign of thy coming, and of the end of the world?

4 And Jesus answered and said unto them, Take heed that no man deceive you.

5 For many shall come in my name, saying I am Christ; and shall deceive many.

6 And ye shall hear of wars, and rumours of wars: see that ye be not troubled: for all *these things* must come to pass,[366] but the end is not yet.

MARK.

CHAPTER XIII. 1–13.

AND as he went out of the temple, one of his disciples saith unto him, Master, see what manner of stones, and what buildings *are here!*

2 And Jesus answering,[322] saith unto him, Seest thou these great buildings? there shall not be left one stone upon another, that shall not be thrown down.

3 And as he sat upon the mount of Olives, over against the temple. Peter, and James, and John, and Andrew, asked him privately,

4 Tell us, when shall these things be? and what *shall be* the sign when all these things shall be fulfilled?

5 And Jesus answering them, began to say,[323] Take heed lest any *man* deceive you:

6 For[324] many shall come in my name, saying, I am *Christ;* and shall deceive many.

7 And when ye shall hear of wars, and rumours of wars, be ye not troubled: for *such things* must needs be; but the end *shall* not *be* yet.[325]

(THIRD DAY OF THE WEEK.) *Jerusalem.*

LUKE.	JOHN.
	CHAPTER XII. 37–50. believeth on me, believeth not on me, but on him that sent me. 45 And he that seeth me, seeth him that sent me. 46 I am come a light into the world, that whosoever [308] believeth on me should not abide in darkness. 47 And if any man hear my words, and believe not,[309] I judge him not: for I came not to judge the world, but to save the world. 48 He that rejecteth me, and re- ceiveth not my words, hath one that judgeth him: the word that I have spoken, the same shall judge him in the last day. 49 For I have not spoken of my- self; but the Father which sent me, he gave me a commandment, what I should say, and what I should speak. 50 And I know that his command- ment is life everlasting: whatsoever I speak therefore, even as the Father said unto me, so I speak.

(THIRD DAY OF THE WEEK.) *Jerusalem. Mount of Olives.*

LUKE.	JOHN.
CHAPTER XXI. 5–19. 5 And as some spake of the temple, how it was adorned with goodly stones, and gifts, he said, 6 *As for* these things which ye behold, the days will come, in the which there shall not be left one stone upon another,[407] that shall not be thrown down. 7 And they asked him, saying, Master, but when shall these things be? and what sign *will there be* when these things shall come to pass? 8 And he said, Take heed that ye be not deceived: for many shall come in my name, saying, I am *Christ;* and the time draweth near: go ye not therefore [408] after them. 9 But when ye shall hear of wars, and commotions, be not terrified: for these things must first come to pass; but the end *is* not by and by.	

§ 127. Jesus, on taking leave of the Temple, foretells its destruction, etc.

MATTHEW.

CHAPTER XXIV. 1–14.

7 For nation shall rise against nation, and kingdom against kingdom: and there shall be famines, and pestilence, and earthquakes in [367] divers places.

8 All these *are* the beginning of sorrows.

9 Then shall they deliver you up to be afflicted, and shall kill you: and ye shall be hated of all nations [368] for my name's sake.

10 And then shall many be offended, and shall betray one another, and shall hate one another.[369]

11 And many false prophets shall rise, and shall deceive many.

12 And because iniquity shall abound, the love of many shall wax cold.

13 But he that shall endure unto the end, the same shall be saved.

14 And this gospel of the kingdom shall be preached in all the world, for a witness unto all nations; and then shall the end come.

MARK.

CHAPTER XIII. 1–13.

8 For nation shall rise against nation, and kingdom against kingdom: and there shall be earthquakes in *divers* places, and there shall be famines, and troubles: [326] these *are* the beginnings of sorrows.

9 But take heed to yourselves: [327] for they shall deliver you up to councils; and in the synagogues ye shall be beaten: and ye shall be brought before rulers and kings for my sake, for a testimony against them.

10 And the gospel must first be published among all nations.

11 But when they shall lead *you*, and deliver you up, take no thought beforehand what ye shall speak, neither do ye premeditate: [328] but whatsoever shall be given you in that hour, that speak ye: for it is not ye that speak, but the Holy Ghost.

12 Now, the brother shall [329] betray the brother to death, and the father the son: and children shall rise up against *their* parents, and shall cause them to be put to death.

13 And ye shall be hated of all *men* for my name's sake: but he that shall endure unto the end, the same shall be saved.

§ 128. The signs of Christ's coming to destroy Jerusalem, etc.

MATTHEW.

CHAPTER XXIV. 15–42.

15 When ye, therefore, shall see the abomination of desolation, spoken of by Daniel the prophet,* stand in the holy place, (whoso readeth, let him understand,)

16 Then let them which be in Judea flee into the mountains:

17 Let him which is on the housetop not come down to take any thing out of [370] his house:

MARK.

CHAPTER XIII. 14–37.

14 But when ye shall see the abomination of desolation, spoken of by Daniel the prophet,[330] standing where it ought not, (let him that readeth understand) then let them that be in Judea flee to the mountains:

15 And let him that is on the housetop not go down into the house,[331] neither enter *therein*, to take any thing out of his house:

* Danl. ix. 27.

(THIRD DAY OF THE WEEK.) *Jerusalem. Mount of Olives.*

LUKE.

CHAPTER XXI. 5–19.

10 Then said he unto them, Nation shall rise against nation, and kingdom against kingdom:

11 And great earthquakes shall be in divers places, and famines, and pestilences: [409] and fearful sights, and great signs shall there be from heaven.

12 But before all these they shall lay their hands on you, and persecute *you*, delivering *you* up to the synagogues, and into prisons, being brought before kings and rulers for my name's sake.

13 And [410] it shall turn to you for a testimony.

14 Settle *it* therefore [411] in your hearts, not to meditate before what ye shall answer.

15 For I will give you a mouth and wisdom, which all your adversaries shall not be able to gainsay nor resist. [412]

16 And ye shall be betrayed both by parents, and brethren, and kinsfolks, and friends; and *some* of you shall they cause to be put to death.

17 And ye shall be hated of all *men* for my name's sake.

18 But there shall not an hair of your head perish.

19 In your patience possess [413] ye your souls.

JOHN.

(THIRD DAY OF THE WEEK.) *Mount of Olives.*

CHAPTER XXI. 20–36.

20 And when ye shall see Jerusalem compassed with armies, then know that the desolation thereof is nigh.

21 Then let them which are in Judea flee to the mountains; and let them which are in the midst of it depart out; and let not them that are in the countries enter thereinto.

22 For these be the days of vengeance, that all things which are written may be fulfilled.

Luke xxi. 16, *put to death.*] No impostor would have warned his followers, as Jesus did, of the persecutions they would have to submit to.

§ 128. The signs of Christ's coming to destroy Jerusalem, etc.

MATTHEW.

CHAPTER XXIV. 15-42.

18 Neither let him which is in the field return back to take his clothes.[371]

19 And wo unto them that are with child, and to them that give suck in those days!

20 But pray ye that your flight be not in the winter, neither on the sabbath-day:

21 For then shall be great tribulation, such as was not since the beginning of the world to this time, no, nor ever shall be.

22 And except those days should be shortened,[372] there should no flesh be saved: but for the elect's sake those days shall be shortened.

23 Then if any man shall say unto you, Lo, here *is* Christ, or there; believe *it* not.

24 For there shall arise false Christs, and false prophets, and shall shew great signs and wonders: insomuch that, if *it were* possible, they shall deceive the very elect.[373]

25 Behold, I have told you before.

26 Wherefore,[374] if they shall say unto you, Behold, he is in the desert; go not forth: behold, he *is* in the secret chambers; believe *it* not.

27 For as the lightning cometh out of the east, and shineth even unto the west; so shall also [375] the coming of the Son of man be.

28 For [375] wheresoever the carcass is, there will the eagles be gathered together.

29 Immediately after the tribulation of those days, shall the sun be darkened, and the moon shall not give her light, and the stars shall fall from heaven, and the powers of the heavens shall be shaken:*

30 And then shall appear the sign of the Son of man in heaven: and then shall all the tribes of the earth mourn,[376] and they shall see the Son of man coming in the clouds of heaven with power and great glory.

31 And he shall send his angels with a great sound of a trumpet, and

MARK.

CHAPTER XIII. 14-37.

16 And let him that is in the field not turn back again for to take up his garment.

17 But wo to them that are with child, and to them that give suck in those days!

18 And pray ye that your flight be not [332] in the winter.

19 For *in* those days shall be affliction, such as was not from the beginning of the creation which God created unto this time, neither shall be.

20 And except that the Lord had shortened those days, no flesh should be saved: but for the elect's sake, whom he hath chosen, he hath shortened the days.

21 And then, if any man shall say to you, Lo, here *is* Christ; or lo, *he is* there; believe *him* not.

22 For false Christs, and false prophets shall rise, and shall shew signs and wonders, to seduce, if *it were* possible, even the elect.[333]

23 But take ye heed: behold, I have foretold you all things.

24 But in those days, after that tribulation, the sun shall be darkened and the moon shall not give her light,

25 And the stars of heaven shall fall,[334] and the powers that are in heaven shall be shaken.

26 And then shall they see the Son of man coming in the clouds with great power and glory.

27 And then shall he send his angels, and shall gather together his

* Is xiii. 9, 10. Joel, iii. 15.

LUKE.

CHAPTER XXI. 20-36.

23 But wo unto them that are with child, and to them that give suck in those days! for there shall be great distress in the land, and wrath upon this people.[414]

24 And they shall fall by the edge of the sword, and shall be led away captive into all nations: and Jerusalem shall be trodden down of the Gentiles, until the times of the Gentiles be fulfilled.

25 And there shall be signs in the sun, and in the moon, and in the stars; and upon the earth distress of nation , with perplexity; the sea and the waves roaring;[415]

26 Men's hearts failing them for fear, and for looking after those things which are coming on the earth: for the powers of heaven shall be shaken.

27 And then shall they see the Son of man coming in a cloud, with power and great glory.

28 And when these things begin to come to pass, then look up, and lift up your heads: for your redemption draweth nigh.

JOHN.

§ 128. The signs of Christ's coming to destroy Jerusalem, etc.

MATTHEW.
CHAPTER XXIV. 15–42.

they shall gather together [377] his elect from the four winds, from one end of heaven to the other.

32 Now learn a parable of the fig-tree; When his branch is yet tender, and putteth forth leaves, ye know that summer *is* nigh:
33 So likewise ye, when ye shall see all these things, know that it is near, *even* at the doors.

34 Verily, I say unto you, This generation shall not pass, till all these things be fulfilled.
35 [378] Heaven and earth shall pass away, but my words shall not pass away.
36 But of that day and hour knoweth no *man*, no, not the angels of heaven,[379] but my Father only.
37 But [380] as the days of Noe *were*, so shall also the coming of the Son of man be.

38 For as in the days that were [381] before the flood, they were eating and drinking, marrying and giving in marriage, until the day that Noe entered into the ark,*
39 And knew not until the flood came, and took them all away: so shall also [382] the coming of the Son of man be.
40 Then shall two be in the field; the one shall be taken, and the other left.
41 Two *women shall be* grinding at the mill; the one shall be taken, and the other left.
42 Watch therefore; for ye know not what hour [383] your Lord doth come.

MARK
CHAPTER XIII. 14–37.

elect [335] from the four winds, from the uttermost part of the earth to the uttermost part of heaven.

28 Now learn a parable of the fig-tree: When her branch is yet tender, and putteth forth leaves, ye know that summer is near:
29 So ye in like manner, when ye shall see these things come to pass, know that it is nigh, *even* at the doors.

30 Verily, I say unto you, That this generation shall not pass, till all these things be done.
31 Heaven and earth shall pass away: but my words shall not pass away.
32 But of that day and *that* hour knoweth no man, no, not the angels which are in heaven,[336] neither the Son, but the Father.
33 Take ye heed, watch and pray:[337] for ye know not when the time is.

34 *For the Son of man is* as a man taking a far journey, who left his house, and gave authority to his servants, and [338] to every man his work; and commanded the porter to watch.

35 Watch ye therefore: for ye know not when the master of the house cometh, at even,[339] or at midnight, or at the cock-crowing, or in the morning:
36 Lest coming suddenly, he find you sleeping.
37 And what I say unto you, I say unto all, Watch.

* Gen. vii. 4, seq.

LUKE.
CHAPTER XXI. 20–36.

29 And he spake to them a parable; Behold the fig-tree, and all the
trees;
30 When they now shoot forth, ye
see and know of your ownselves that
summer is now nigh at hand.
31 So likewise ye, when ye see
these things come to pass, know ye
that the kingdom of God is nigh at
hand.
32 Verily, I say unto you, This
generation shall not pass away, till
all be fulfilled.
33 Heaven and earth shall pass
away: but my words shall not pass
away.
34 [416] And take heed to yourselves,
lest at any time your hearts be over-
charged with surfeiting and drunken-
ness, and cares of this life, and *so* that
day come upon you unawares.[417]
35 For as a snare shall it come on
all them that dwell on the face of the
whole earth.

36 Watch ye therefore, and pray
always, that ye may be accounted
worthy to escape[418] all these things
that shall come to pass, and to stand
before the Son of man.

JOHN.

§ **129. Transition to Christ's final coming. Exhortation.**

MATTHEW.

CH. XXIV. 43–51. CH. XXV. 1–30.

43 But know this, that if the good man of the house had known in what watch the thief would come, he would have watched, and would not have suffered his house to be broken up.

44 Therefore be ye also ready: for in such an hour as ye think not, the Son of man cometh.

45 Who then is a faithful and wise servant, whom his lord hath made ruler over his household,[384] to give them meat in due season?

46 Blessed *is* that servant, whom his lord, when he cometh, shall find so doing.

47 Verily I say unto you, That he shall make him ruler over all his goods.

48 But and if that evil servant shall say in his heart, My lord delayeth his coming;[385]

49 And shall begin to smite *his* fellow servants, and to eat and drink with the drunken;

50 The lord of that servant shall come in a day when he looketh not for *him*, and in an hour that he is not aware of,

51 And shall cut him asunder, and appoint *him* his portion with the hypocrites: there shall be weeping and gnashing of teeth.

CHAPTER XXV.

THEN shall the kingdom of heaven be likened unto ten virgins, which took their lamps, and went forth to meet the bridegroom.

2 And five of them were wise, and five *were* foolish.[386]

3 They that *were* foolish took their lamps, and took no oil with them:

4 But the wise took oil in their vessels[387] with their lamps.

5 While the bridegroom tarried, they all slumbered and slept.

6 And at midnight there was a cry made, Behold, the bridegroom cometh: go ye out to meet him.[388]

7 Then all those virgins arose, and trimmed their lamps.

8 And the foolish said unto the wise, Give us of your oil:[389] for our lamps are gone out.

MARK

Parables. (THIRD DAY OF THE WEEK.) *Mount of Olives.*

LUKE.	JOHN.

§ 129. **Transition to Christ's final coming. Exhortation.**

MATTHEW.	MARK.
CH. XXIV. 43–51. CH. XXV. 1–30.	
9 But the wise answered, saying, *Not so*; lest there be not enough for us and you:[390] but go ye rather to them that sell, and buy for yourselves. 10 And while they went to buy, the bridegroom came; and they that were ready, went in with him to the marriage: and the door was shut. 11 Afterward came also the other virgins, saying, Lord, Lord, open to us. 12 But he answered and said, Verily, I say unto you, I know you not. 13 Watch therefore, for ye know neither the day nor the hour wherein the Son of man cometh.[391] 14 For *the kingdom of heaven is* as a man travelling in a far country, *who* called his own servants, and delivered unto them his goods. 15 And unto one he gave five talents, to another two, and to another one; to every man according to his several ability; and straightway took his journey. 16 Then he who had received the five talents, went and traded with the same, and made *them* other five talents.[392] 17 And likewise he that *had received* two, he also gained other two.[393] 18 But he that had received one, went and digged in the earth,[394] and hid his lord's money. 19 After a long time the lord of those servants cometh, and reckoneth with them. 20 So he that had received five talents, came and brought other five talents, saying, Lord, thou deliveredst unto me five talents: behold, I have gained besides them five talents more.[395] 21 His lord said unto him, Well done, *thou* good and faithful servant; thou hast been faithful over a few things, I will make thee ruler over many things: enter thou into the joy of thy lord. 22 He also that had received two talents came, and said, Lord, thou deliveredst unto me two talents: be-	

Parables. (THIRD DAY OF THE WEEK.) *Mount of Olives.*

LUKE.	JOHN.

§ 129. Transition to Christ's final coming. Exhortation.

MATTHEW.

CH. XXIV. 43–51. CH. XXV. 1–30.

hold, I have gained two other talents
besides them.[396]
23 His lord said unto him, Well
done, good and faithful servant; thou
hast been faithful over a few things,
I will make thee ruler over many
things: enter thou into the joy of
thy lord.
24 Then he which had received
the one talent came, and said, Lord,
I knew thee that thou art an hard
man, reaping where thou hast not
sown, and gathering where thou hast
not strewed:
25 And I was afraid, and went and
hid thy talent in the earth: lo, *there*
thou hast *that is* thine.
26 His lord answered and said unto
him, *Thou* wicked and slothful servant, thou knewest that I reap where
I sowed not, and gather where I
have not strewed:
27 Thou oughtest therefore to have
put my money to the exchangers, and
then at my coming I should have received mine own with usury.
28 Take therefore the talent from
him, and give *it* unto him which hath
ten talents.
29 For unto every one that hath
shall be given, and he shall have
abundance: but from him that hath
not, shall be taken away even that
which he hath.
30 And cast ye the unprofitable
servant into outer darkness: there
shall be weeping and gnashing of
teeth.

MARK.

§ 130. Scenes of the Judgment Day.

CHAPTER XXV. 31–46.

31 When the Son of man shall
come in his glory, and all the holy[397]
angels with him, then shall he sit
upon the throne of his glory:
32 And before him shall be gathered all nations: and he shall separate them one from another, as a
shepherd divideth *his* sheep from
the goats:

Matth. xxv. 26, *thou knewest.*] Interrogatively and sarcastically. That is, Was such thy

Parables. (THIRD DAY OF THE WEEK.) *Mount of Olives.*

LUKE.	JOHN.

(THIRD DAY OF THE WEEK.) *Mount of Olives.*

wicked opinion? Then "out of thine own mouth will I judge thee;" thou oughtest to have acted according to that opinion. Bp. SUMNER, *in loc.*

§ 130. Scenes of the Judgment Day.

MATTHEW.

CHAPTER XXV. 31-46.

33 And he shall set the sheep on
his right hand, but the goats on the
left.[398]
34 Then shall the King say unto
them on his right hand, Come, ye
blessed of my Father, inherit the
kingdom prepared for you from the
foundation of the world:
35 For I was an hungered, and ye
gave me meat: I was thirsty, and ye
gave me drink: I was a stranger, and
ye took me in:
36 Naked, and ye clothed me: I
was sick, and ye visited me: I was in
prison, and ye came unto me.
37 Then shall the righteous answer
him, saying, Lord, when saw we thee
an hungered, and fed *thee?* or thirsty,
and gave *thee* drink?
38 When saw we thee a stranger,
and took *thee* in? or naked, and
clothed *thee?*
39 Or when saw we thee sick, or in
prison, and came unto thee?
40 And the King shall answer and
say unto them, Verily I say unto you,
Inasmuch as ye have done *it* unto one
of the least of these my brethren,[399]
ye have done *it* unto me.
41 Then shall he say also unto
them on the left hand, Depart from
me, ye cursed, into everlasting fire,
prepared for the devil and his angels:
42 For I was an hungered, and ye
gave me no meat: I was thirsty,[400]
and ye gave me no drink:
43 I was a stranger, and ye took me
not in; naked, and ye clothed me
not: sick, and in prison, and ye visited
me not.
44 Then shall they also[401] answer
him, saying, Lord, when saw we thee
an hungered, or athirst, or a stranger,
or naked, or sick, or in prison, and
did not minister unto thee?
45 Then shall he answer them,
saying, Verily, I say unto you, Inasmuch as ye did *it* not to one of the
least of these, ye did *it* not to me.
46 And these shall go away into
everlasting punishment: but the righteous into life eternal.

MARK.

(THIRD DAY OF THE WEEK.) *Mount of Olives.*

LUKE.	JOHN.

§ 131. The rulers conspire. The Supper at Bethany. Treachery

MATTHEW.

CHAPTER XXVI. 1–16.

AND it came to pass, when Jesus had finished all these sayings, he said unto his disciples,

2 Ye know that after two days is *the feast of* the passover, and the Son of man is betrayed to be crucified.

3 Then assembled together the chief priests, and the scribes, and the elders of the people,[402] unto the palace of the high priest, who was called Caiaphas.

4 And consulted that they might take Jesus by subtilty, and kill *him*.[403]

5 But they said, Not on the feast-*day*, lest there be an uproar among the people.

6 Now when Jesus was in Bethany, in the house of Simon the leper,

7 There came unto him a woman having an alabaster-box of very precious ointment, and poured *it* on his head as he sat *at meat*.

8 But when his[404] disciples saw *it*, they had indignation, saying, To what purpose *is* this waste?

9 For this ointment might[405] have been sold for much, and given to the poor.

10 When Jesus understood *it*, he said unto them, Why trouble ye the woman? for she hath wrought a good work upon me.

MARK.

CHAPTER XIV. 1, 11.

AFTER two days was *the feast of* the passover, and of unleavened bread: and the chief priests, and the scribes, sought how they might take him by craft, and put *him* to death.

2 But[340] they said, Not on the feast-*day*, lest there be an uproar of the people.

3 And being in Bethany, in the house of Simon the leper, as he sat at meat, there came a woman having an alabaster-box of ointment of spikenard, very precious; and[341] she brake the box, and poured *it* on his head.

4 And there were some that had indignation within themselves, and said,[342] Why was this waste of the ointment made?

5 For it might have been sold[343] for more than three hundred pence, and have been given to the poor. And they murmured against her.

6 And Jesus said, Let her alone: why trouble ye her? she hath[344] wrought a good work on me.

Matth. xxvi. 8, *his disciples.*] In St. John, Judas alone murmurs; in St. Matthew, the disciples have indignation; or, as St. Mark expresses it, some have indignation among themselves. Dr. Lardner says, Serm. v. 2, p. 316, "It is well known to be very common with all writers to use the plural number when one person only is intended. Nor is it impossible that others might have some uneasiness about it, though they were far from being so disgusted at it as Judas was. And their concern for the poor was sincere; his was self-interested and mere pretence." See also Grotius *in loc.* NEWCOME.

John xii. 3, *the feet.*] It is nowhere asserted that the unction was of Jesus's head *only*, or of his feet *only*. Both actions are consistent; and St. John, in his supplemental history, may very well have added the respectful conduct of Mary, that after

of Judas. (FOURTH DAY OF THE WEEK.) *Jerusalem. Bethany.*

LUKE.
CHAPTER XXII. 1–6.

Now the feast of unleavened bread drew nigh, which is called the Passover.

2 And the chief priests and scribes sought how they might kill him: for they feared the people.

JOHN.
CHAPTER XII. 2–8.

2 There they made him a supper; and Martha served: but Lazarus was one of them that sat at the table with him.
3 Then took Mary a pound of ointment of spikenard, very costly, and anointed the feet of Jesus, and wiped his feet with her hair: and the house was filled with the odour of the ointment.
4 Then saith one of his disciples, Judas Iscariot, Simon's *son*, which should betray him,[290]
5 Why was not this ointment sold for three hundred pence, and given to the poor?
6 This he said, not that he cared for the poor; but because he was a thief, and had the bag, and bare what [291] was put therein.
7 Then said Jesus, Let her alone: against the day of my burying hath she kept this.[292]

---

having anointed Jesus's head, she proceeded to anoint his feet, and even to wipe them with her hair. NEWCOME.

John xii. 4, *Judas Iscariot.*] The other Evangelists mention that indignation was caused by the supposed waste of the ointment: John fixes it upon Judas. That Judas went to the High Priest's on the evening or night of our Wednesday, may be collected from Matth. xxvi. 14, 17, and the parallel places; and he seems to have acted partly from disgust at what had passed. The story has a remarkably apt connection with the preceding and subsequent history. The Jewish rulers consult how they may take Jesus by craft, and without raising a tumult among the people. An incident happens, which offends one of Jesus's familiar attendants, who immediately repairs to the enemies of Jesus, and receives from them a bribe to betray him in the absence of the multitude. NEWCOME.

§ 131. **The Rulers conspire. The supper at Bethany. Treachery**

MATTHEW.
CHAPTER XXVI. 1-16.

11 For ye have the poor always with you; but me ye have not always.

12 For in that she hath poured this ointment on my body, she did *it* for my burial.

13 Verily, I say unto you, Wheresoever this gospel shall be preached in the whole world, *there* shall also this, that this woman hath done, be told for a memorial of her.

14 Then one of the twelve, called Judas Iscariot, went unto the chief priests,

15 And said *unto them*, What will ye give me, and I will deliver him unto you? And they covenanted with him for thirty pieces of silver.

16 And from that time he sought opportunity to betray him.

MARK.
CHAPTER XIV. 1-11.

7 For ye have the poor with you always, and whensoever ye will ye may do them good:[345] but me ye have not always.

8 She hath done what she could: she is come aforehand to anoint my body to the burying.

9 Verily, I say unto you, Wheresoever this gospel[346] shall be preached throughout the whole world, *this* also that she hath done shall be spoken of, for a memorial of her.

10 And Judas Iscariot, one of the twelve,[347] went unto the chief priests, to betray him unto them.

11 And when they heard *it*, they were glad, and promised to give him money. And he sought how he might conveniently betray him.

§ 132. **Preparation for the Passover.**

CHAPTER XXVI. 17-19.

17 Now the first *day* of the *feast of* unleavened bread, the disciples came to Jesus, saying unto him,[400] Where wilt thou that we prepare for thee to eat the passover?

18 And he said, Go into the city to such a man, and say unto him, The Master saith, My time is at hand; I will keep the passover at thy house with my disciples.

19 And the disciples did as Jesus had appointed them; and they made ready the passover.

CHAPTER XIV. 12-16.

12 And the first day of unleavened bread, when they killed the passover, his disciples said unto him, Where wilt thou that we go and prepare, that thou mayest eat the passover?

13 And he sendeth forth two of his disciples, and saith unto them, Go ye into the city, and there shall meet you a man bearing a pitcher of water: follow him.

14 And wheresoever he shall go in, say ye to the good man of the house, The Master saith, Where is the[348] guest-chamber, where I shall eat the passover with my disciples?

15 And he will shew you a large upper room furnished *and* prepared: there make ready for us.[349]

16 And his disciples went forth, and came into the city,[350] and found as he had said unto them: and they made ready the passover.

Matt. xxvi. 18, *with my disciples.*] Here is a very natural, yet incidental recognition of a rule, universally respected among the Jews, that this feast was to be celebrated not alone, but

of Judas. (FOURTH DAY OF THE WEEK.) *Jerusalem. Bethany.*

LUKE.
CHAPTER XXII. 1-6.

3 Then entered Satan into Judas, surnamed Iscariot, being of the number of the twelve.
4 And he went his way, and communed with the chief priests and captains, how he might betray him unto them.
5 And they were glad, and covenanted to give him money.
6 And he promised, and sought opportunity [419] to betray him unto them in the absence of the multitude.

JOHN.
CHAPTER XII. 2-8.

8 For the poor always ye have with you; but me ye have not always.

(FIFTH DAY OF THE WEEK.) *Jerusalem. Bethany.*

CHAPTER XXII. 7-13.

7 Then came the day of unleavened bread, when the passover must be killed.
8 And he sent Peter and John, saying, Go and prepare us the passover, that we may eat.
9 And they said unto him, Where wilt thou that we prepare? [420]
10 And he said unto them, Behold, when ye are entered into the city, there shall a man meet you, bearing a pitcher of water; [421] follow him into the house where he entereth in.
11 And ye shall say unto the good man of the house, The Master saith unto thee, Where is the guest-chamber,[422] where I shall eat the passover with my disciples?
12 And he shall shew you a large upper room furnished: there make ready.[423]
13 And they went and found as he had said unto them: and they made ready the passover.

---

by companies of not less than ten persons, See JOSEPHUS, Bell. Jud. vi. ix. § 3. BLUNT, Veracity, &c. Sect. ii. 8.

PART VIII.

THE FOURTH PASSOVER; OUR LORD'S PASSION;

AND THE

ACCOMPANYING EVENTS

UNTIL

THE END OF THE JEWISH SABBATH.

TIME. *Two days.*

§ 133. The Passover Meal. Contention among the Twelve.

MATTHEW.

CHAPTER XXVI. 20.

20 Now when the even was come, he sat down with the twelve.[407]

MARK.

CHAPTER XIV. 17.

17 And in the evening he cometh with the twelve.

§ 134. Jesus washes the feet of his disciples. (EVENING

(EVENING INTRODUCING THE SIXTH DAY OF THE WEEK.) *Jerusalem.*

LUKE.

CHAPTER XXII. 14–18, 24–30.

14 And when the hour was come, he sat down, and the twelve apostles[424] with him.

15 And he said unto them, With desire I have desired to eat this passover with you before I suffer.

16 For I say unto you, I will not any more eat thereof,[425] until it be fulfilled in the kingdom of God.

17 And he took the cup, and gave thanks, and said, Take this, and divide *it* among yourselves.[426]

18 For I say unto you, I will not drink of the fruit of the vine,[427] until the kingdom of God shall come.

24 And there was also[430] a strife among them, which of them should be accounted the greatest.

25 And he said unto them, The kings of the Gentiles exercise lordship over them; and they that exercise authority upon them are called benefactors.[431]

26 But ye *shall* not *be* so: but he that is greatest among you, let him be as the younger; and he that is chief, as he that doth serve.

27 For whether *is* greater, he that sitteth at meat, or he that serveth? *is* not he that sitteth at meat? but I am among you as he that serveth.

28 Ye are they which have continued with me in my temptations.

29 And I appoint unto you a kingdom, as my Father hath appointed unto me;[432]

30 That ye may eat and drink at my table in my kingdom, and sit on thrones, judging the twelve tribes of Israel.

JOHN.

INTRODUCING THE SIXTH DAY OF THE WEEK.) *Jerusalem.*

CHAPTER XIII. 1–20.

Now before the feast of the passover, when Jesus knew that his hour was come that he should depart out of this world unto the Father, having loved his own which were in the world, he loved them unto the end.

2 And supper being ended, (the devil having now put into the heart of Judas Iscariot Simon's *son*, to betray him,)[310]

§ 134. **Jesus washes the feet of his disciples.** (EVENING

MATTHEW.	MARK.

LUKE.

JOHN.

CHAPTER XIII. 1–20.

3 Jesus[311] knowing that the Father
had given all things into his hands,
and that he was come from God, and
went to God;
4 He riseth from supper, and laid
aside his garments; and took a towel,
and girded himself.
5 After that, he poureth water into
a basin, and began to wash the disciples'
feet, and to wipe *them* with
the towel wherewith he was girded.
6 Then cometh he to Simon Peter:
and Peter saith unto him, Lord,[312]
dost thou wash my feet?
7 Jesus answered and said unto
him, What I do thou knowest not
now; but thou shalt know hereafter.
8 Peter saith unto him, Thou shalt
never wash my feet. Jesus answered
him, If I wash thee not, thou hast
no part with me.
9 Simon Peter saith unto him,
Lord,[313] not my feet only, but also *my*
hands and *my* head.
10 Jesus saith to him, He that is
washed needeth not save to wash *his*
feet,[314] but is clean every whit: and
ye are clean, but not all.
11 For he knew who should betray
him: therefore said he, Ye are not
all clean.
12 So after he had washed their
feet, and had taken his garments,
and was set down again,[315] he said
unto them, Know ye what I have
done to you?
13 Ye call me Master, and Lord:
and ye say well; for *so* I am.
14 If I then, *your* Lord and Master,
have washed your feet; ye also ought
to wash one another's feet.
15 For I have given you an example,
that ye should do as I have done
to you.
16 Verily, verily, I say unto you,
The servant is not greater than his
lord; neither he that is sent greater
than he that sent him.
17 If ye know these things, happy
are ye if ye do them.
18 I speak not of you all; I know[316]
whom I have chosen; but that the

§ 134. **Jesus washes the feet of his disciples.** (EVENING

MATTHEW.

MARK.

§ 135. **Jesus points out the traitor. Judas withdraws.**

MATTHEW.

CHAPTER XXVI. 21–25.

21 And as they did eat, he said,[408] Verily I say unto you, That one of you shall betray me.

22 And they were exceedingly sorrowful, and began every one of them[409] to say unto him, Lord, is it I?

23 And he answered and said, He that dippeth *his* hand with me in the dish, the same shall betray me.

24 The Son of man goeth, as it is written of him: but wo unto that man by whom the Son of man is betrayed! it had been good for that man if he had not been born.

25 Then Judas, which betrayed him, answered and said, Master, is it I? He said unto him,[410] Thou hast said.

MARK.

CHAPTER XIV. 18–21.

18 And as they sat, and did eat, Jesus said, Verily I say unto you, One of you which eateth with me,[351] shall betray me.

19 And they began to be sorrowful, and to say unto him one by one, *Is* it I? and another *said*, *Is* it I?[352]

20 And he answered and said unto them, *It is* one of the twelve that dippeth with me in the dish.[353]

21 The Son of man indeed goeth, as it is written of him: but wo to that man by whom the Son of man is betrayed! good were it for that man if he had never been born.

INTRODUCING THE SIXTH DAY OF THE WEEK.) *Jerusalem.*

LUKE.

JOHN.

CHAPTER XIII. 1–20.

scripture may be fulfilled, He that
eateth bread with me, hath lifted up
his heel against me.*
19 Now I tell you before it come,
that when it is come to pass, ye may
believe that I am *he*.
20 Verily, verily, I say unto you,
He that receiveth whomsoever I send,
receiveth me; and he that receiveth
me, receiveth him that sent me.

(EVENING INTRODUCING THE SIXTH DAY OF THE WEEK.) *Jerusalem.*

LUKE.

CHAPTER XXII. 21–23.

21 But behold, the hand of him
that betrayeth me *is* with me on the
table.
22 And truly [420] the Son of man goeth
as it was determined: but wo unto
that man by whom he is betrayed!
23 And they began to inquire
among themselves, which of them it
was that should do this thing.

JOHN.

CHAPTER XIII. 21–35.

21 When Jesus had thus said, he
was troubled in spirit, and testified,
and said, Verily, verily, I say unto
you, that one of you shall betray
me.
22 Then [317] the disciples looked one
on another, doubting of whom he
spake.
23 Now [318] there was leaning on
Jesus' bosom, one of his disciples,
whom Jesus loved.
24 Simon Peter therefore beckoned
to him, that he should ask who it
should be of whom he spake.[319]
25 He then,[320] lying on Jesus'
breast, saith unto him, Lord, who is it?
26 Jesus answered, He it is to
whom I shall give a sop, when I have
dipped *it*. And when he had dipped
the sop, he gave *it* to Judas Iscariot
the son of Simon.[321]
27 And after the sop Satan entered
into him. Then said Jesus unto him,
That thou doest, do quickly.
28 Now [322] no man at the table
knew for what intent he spake this
unto him.
29 For some *of them* thought, because Judas had the bag, that Jesus
had said unto him, Buy *those things*
that we have need of against the
feast; or, that he should give something to the poor.
30 He then, having received the
sop, went immediately out: and it
was night.[323]
31 Therefore, when he was gone
out, Jesus said, Now is the Son of

* Ps. xli. 10.

§ 135. **Jesus points out the traitor. Judas withdraws.**

MATTHEW.	MARK.

§ 136. **Jesus foretells the fall of Peter, and the dispersion of the Twelve.**

MATTHEW.	MARK.
CHAPTER XXVI. 31-35.	CHAPTER XIV. 27-31.
31 Then saith Jesus unto them, All ye shall be offended because of me this night: for it is written, I will smite the Shepherd, and the sheep of the flock shall be scattered abroad.*	27 And Jesus saith unto them, All ye shall be offended because of me this night:[367] for it is written, I will smite the Shepherd, and the sheep shall be scattered.
32 But after I am risen again, I will go before you into Galilee.	28 But after that I am risen, I will go before you into Galilee.
33 Peter answered and said unto him, Though all *men* shall be offended because of thee, *yet* will I never be offended.[413]	29 But Peter said unto him, Although all shall be offended, yet *will* not I.
34 Jesus said unto him, Verily, I say unto thee, That this night, before the cock crow, thou shalt deny me thrice.	30 And Jesus saith unto him, Verily, I say unto thee, That this day, *even* in this night, before the cock crow twice,[368] thou shalt deny me thrice.
35 Peter said unto him, Though I should die with thee, yet will not I deny thee. Likewise also said all the disciples.	31 But he spake the more vehemently, If I should die with thee, I will not deny thee in any wise. Likewise also said they all.

* Zech. xiii. 7.

Mark xiv. 30, *Before the cock crow twice.*] The other Evangelists simply say, Before the cock *crow*.—It is observed, that the cock crows about midnight; and about the fourth watch, or about three in the morning, when that watch began. When *gallicinium* (*cock-crowing*) stands alone, it means this latter time, which is referred to. Aristoph. Eccles. 390. Juv. Sat. ix. 107. The four Evangelists therefore denote the same time,—sc. galliciniis secundis, as Ammianus expresses it, 1, 22; and any part of the period thus marked out may be understood. See BOCHART de anim. pars, 2nd 119, and GROTIUS on Matth. xxvi. 34. NEWCOME.

Luke xxii. 36, *and he that hath no sword let him sell his garment and buy one.*] In the animated language of the prophets, their predictions are often announced under the form of commands. The prophet Isaiah, in the sublime prediction he has given

(EVENING INTRODUCING THE SIXTH DAY OF THE WEEK.) *Jerusalem.*

LUKE.

JOHN.

CHAPTER XIII. 21-35.

man glorified, and God is glorified in him.

32 If God be glorified in him, God shall also glorify him in himself, and shall straightway glorify him.

33 Little children, yet a little while I am with you. Ye shall seek me; and, as I said unto the Jews, Whither I go, ye cannot come, so now I say to you.

34 A new commandment I give unto you, That ye love one another; as I have loved you, that ye also love one another.[325]

35 By this shall all *men* know that ye are my disciples, if ye have love one to another.

(EVENING INTRODUCING THE SIXTH DAY OF THE WEEK.) *Jerusalem.*

LUKE.

CHAPTER XXII. 31-38.

31 And the Lord said,[433] Simon, Simon, behold, Satan hath desired *to have* you, that he may sift *you* as wheat:

32 But I have prayed for thee, that thy faith fail not: and when thou art converted, strengthen thy brethren.

33 And he said unto him, Lord, I am ready to go with thee, both into prison, and to death.

34 And he said, I tell thee, Peter, the cock shall not crow this day, before that thou shalt[434] thrice deny that thou knowest me.

35 And he said unto them, When I sent you without purse, and scrip, and shoes, lacked ye anything? And they said, Nothing.

36 Then said he unto them,[435] But now, he that hath a purse, let him take *it*, and likewise *his* scrip: and he that hath no sword, let him sell his garment, and buy one.

JOHN.

CHAPTER XIII. 36-38.

36 Simon Peter said unto him, Lord, whither goest thou? Jesus answered him, Whither I go, thou canst not follow me now; but thou shalt follow me afterward.[326]

37 Peter saith unto him Lord,[327] why cannot I follow thee now? I will lay down my life for thy sake.

38 Jesus answered him,[328] Wilt thou lay down thy life for my sake? Verily, verily, I say unto thee, The cock shall not crow, till thou hast denied me thrice.

---

us of the fate of the king of Babylon, thus foretells the destruction of his family:—*Prepare slaughter for his children*, &c. Isa. xiv. 21. The prophet Jeremiah in like manner foretells the approaching destruction of the children of Zion: *Call for the mourning women, that they may come: and send for cunning women; and let them make haste, and take up a wailing*, &c. Jer. ix. 17, 18. There, matter of sorrow is predicted, by commanding the common attendants on mourning and lamentation to be gotten in readiness; here, warning is given of the most imminent dangers, by orders to make the customary preparation against violence, and to account a weapon more necessary than a garment. CAMPBELL, *in loc.*

§ 136. Jesus foretells the fall of Peter, and the dispersion of the Twelve.

MATTHEW.	MARK.

§ 137. The Lord's Supper. (EVENING INTRODUCING

MATTHEW.	MARK.
CHAPTER XXVI. 26–29.	CHAPTER XIV. 22–25.
26 And as they were eating, Jesus took bread, and blessed *it*, and brake *it*,[411] and gave *it* to the disciples, and said, Take, eat; this is my body.	22 And as they did eat, Jesus took bread, and blessed, and brake *it*, and gave to them, and said, Take, eat: this is my body.[354]
27 And he took the cup, and gave thanks, and gave *it* to them, saying, Drink ye all of it;	23 And he took the cup, and when he had given thanks, he gave *it* to them: and they all drank of it.
28 For this is my blood of the new [412] testament, which is shed for many for the remission of sins.	24 And he said unto them, This is my blood of the new [355] testament, which is shed for many.

Matt. xxvi. 26-29, &c.] This account of the institution of the Lord's Supper is corroborated by that of Paul, in 1 Cor. xi. 23-25, which is usually inserted by Harmonists in this place as parallel testimony; but as the plan of this work leads me to deal with the four Gospels alone, the insertion of other parts of Scripture in the text, here and elsewhere, is omitted.

Matt. xxvi. 26, *as they were eating.*] The Evangelists have determined, by some general expressions, the order of the following events between the sitting down to the paschal supper, and the going to Gethsemane. Before the eating of the paschal lamb, Jesus rises from supper to wash the disciples' feet. John xiii. 1, 4. While they are eating, a declaration is made of Judas's treachery, and the bread is instituted, Matt. xxvi. 21, 26. See also Mark. After the cup is instituted, Luke xxii. 20; 1 Cor. xi. 25. But as to the particular and precise order of the facts and discourses during this period, Pilkington's words relating to one of them are applicable to all. "It is observable that St. Luke mentions the institution of the communion before the declaration of Judas's treachery; whereas the other Evangelists place these in a different order. But it is a liberty, I think, very allowable in any historian, to neglect taking notice of the exact order of all the facts, when he is only giving a general account of what was done at a certain time. And if so, whichsoever was the true successive order, there can be no just imputation upon any of the Evangelists for neglecting to observe it in the narration." Harm. p. 52. NEWCOME.

Matt. xxvi. 28, *my blood of the new testament.*] The use of the word *testament* (*diatheke*), in a sense involving also the idea of a *covenant*, and in connexion with the circumstances of a compact, has greatly perplexed many English readers of the Bible. The difficulty occurs in Matt. 26, 28, and the parallel places, where our Lord employs the word *testament*, or last will, in connexion with the sacrificial shedding of his own blood; a ceremony which, by means of a suitable animal, usually was adopted among the ancients, upon the making of the most solemn engagements; and instead of which, the mutual partaking of the sacrament of the Lord's Supper, by the contracting parties, was substituted among Christians in later times. The same embarrassment occurs, perhaps in a greater degree, in the exposition of several passages in the eighth and ninth chapters of the Epistle to the Hebrews (manifestly written by a profound lawyer, be he Paul or Apollos), where he uses language applicable indifferently both to a covenant *inter vivos* and a last will. For with us, a testament is simply a declaration

(EVENING INTRODUCING THE SIXTH DAY OF THE WEEK.) *Jerusalem.*

LUKE.	JOHN.
CHAPTER XXII. 31–38. 37 For I say unto you, that this that is written must yet be accomplished in me, And he was reckoned among the transgressors:* for the things concerning me have an end.[436] 38 And they said, Lord,[437] behold, here *are* two swords. And he said unto them, It is enough.	

THE SIXTH DAY OF THE WEEK.) *Jerusalem.*

CHAPTER XXII. 19–20. 19 And he took bread, and gave thanks, and brake *it*, and gave unto them, saying,[438] This is my body which is given for you: this do in remembrance of me. 20 Likewise also the cup after supper, saying, This cup *is* the new testament in my blood, which is shed for you.	

* Isa. liii. 12.

---

of the last will of the testator, in regard to the disposition of his property after his decease, irrespective of any consent, or even knowledge, at the time, on the part of him to whom the estate is given; while a covenant requires the mutual consent of both parties, as essential to its existence. The one is simply the *ultima voluntas* of an individual, the other is the *aggregatio mentium* of both or all.

The solution of this difficulty belongs rather to the theologians, whose province it is by no means intended here to invade; but perhaps a reference to the laws and usages in force in Judea in the times of our Saviour and his Apostles may furnish some aid, which a lawyer might contribute without transgressing the limit of his profession.

It is first to be observed that the municipal laws of Greece and Rome were strikingly similar; those of Greece having been freely imported into the Roman jurisprudence. In like manner the similarity of the Grecian laws and usages with those extant in Asia Minor, indicated a common origin; and thus, what Greece derived from Egypt and the states of Asia Minor, these states, after many ages, received again as the laws of their Roman masters. It should also be remembered that Palestine had been reduced to a Roman province some years before the time of our Saviour; long enough, indeed, to have become familiar with Roman laws and usages, even had they been previously unknown: and that Paul, to whom the Epistle to the Hebrews is generally attributed, was himself a thorough-bred lawyer, well versed in the customs of his country, whether ancient or modern. Among those nations, the civil magistrate often exercised the functions of the priesthood, these dignities being in some respects identical; and thus, whatever was transacted before the magistrate, might naturally seem to partake of the character of an act of religion. Covenants were always made with particular formalities, and to those of graver nature, religious solemnities were often superadded. They were frequently confirmed by an oath, the most solemn form of which was taken standing before the altar; and whosoever swore by the altar, swore by the sacrifice thereon, and was held as firmly bound as though he had passed between the dismembered parts of the victim. Of the latter kind was the oath, by which God confirmed his covenant with Abraham (Gen. xv.) when the visible light of his presence passed between the pieces which the patriarch had divided and laid "each piece one against another."

§ 137. The Lord's Supper. (EVENING INTRODUCING

MATTHEW. CHAPTER XXVI. 26–29.	MARK. CHAPTER XIV. 22–25.
29 But I say unto you, I will not drink henceforth of this fruit of the vine, until that day when I drink it new with you in my Father's kingdom.	25 Verily, I say unto you, I will drink no more of the fruit [356] of the vine, until that day that I drink it new in the kingdom of God.

§ 138. Jesus comforts his disciples. The Holy Spirit promised.

With these things in view, we may now look at some of the modes of transferring property, practised by the nations alluded to.

Among the methods of alienation or sale of property by the owner, in his lifetime was that which in the Roman law was termed *mancipatio ;* a mode by which the vendor conveyed property, to the purchaser, each party being present either in person or by his agent, representative or factor. Five witnesses were requisite, one of whom was called *libripens*, or the balance-holder. This form had its origin in the sale of goods by weight, but was gradually extended to all sales; and the practice was for the buyer to strike the balance with a piece of money called a *sestertius*, which was immediately paid over to the vendor as part of the price ; and hence the expression *per æs et libram vendere.*

Wills and testaments were made with great solemnity. One method among the Romans, probably common in its principal traits, to the other nations before mentioned, was termed the testament *per æs et libram*, it being effected in the form of a sale. This mode seems to have been resorted to whenever the estate was given to a stranger, (*hæres extraneus*,) to the exclusion of the *hæres suus*, or *necessarius*, or, as we should say, the heir at law; and it was founded on a purchase of the estate by the adopted heir, who succeeded to the privileges of the child. The forms of a sale by *mancipatio* were therefore scrupulously observed ; the presence and agreement of the purchaser, either in person or by his representative or negotiator, being necessary to its validity. The reason for requiring this form was because it *involved a covenant* on the part of the adopted heir or legatee, by which he became bound to pay all the debts of the testator. Having entered into this covenant, he had the best possible title in law to the inheritance, namely, that of a purchaser for a valuable consideration. Among the Greeks, and probably among the Romans also, this was transacted in the presence of a magistrate, who sanctioned it by his sentence of approval. This was the

THE SIXTH DAY OF THE WEEK.) *Jerusalem.*

LUKE.	JOHN.

(EVENING INTRODUCING THE SIXTH DAY OF THE WEEK.) *Jerusalem.*

JOHN.

CHAPTER XIV. 1–31.

LET not your heart be troubled: ye
believe in God, believe also in me.
2 In my Father's house are many
mansions: if *it were* not *so*, I would
have told you. I go to prepare,[329] a
place for you.
3 And if I go and prepare[330] a
place for you, I will come again and
receive you unto myself; that where
I am, *there* ye may be also.
4 And whither I go ye know, and
the way ye know.[331]
5 Thomas saith unto him, Lord,
we know not whither thou goest;
and how can we know the way?[332]
6 Jesus saith unto him, I am the
way, and the truth, and the life: no
man cometh unto the Father, but by
me.
7 If ye had known me, ye should
have known my Father also: and
from henceforth ye know him, and
have seen him.[333]

---

most ancient form of a will; and it does not seem to have been abrogated until the time of Constantine.

Now, when our Saviour speaks of the *new testament in his blood*, or of his *blood of the new testament*, and when Paul uses similar forms of expression may not the figure have reference to the custom above stated? And if so may not this custom guide us to the true meaning of the words? Does it intimate to us that the promised inheritance was first given to man, as it were by a testament in this ancient form, upon a covenant of *his own* perfect *obedience* to every part of the law of God; that having broken this covenant, his title became forfeited; that the inheritance was afterwards promised, in the same manner, to every one, Jew or Gentile, upon a new covenant and condition, namely of a true *faith* in Christ; a faith evinced in the fruits of a holy life; that this inheritance by a new testament and covenant was negotiated, as it were, and obtained for man by the mediation of Jesus Christ ("the mediator of the new testament," Heb. 9. 15.) as the representative of all who shall accept it by such faith, and their surety for the performance of its conditions; that it was purchased by *his* obedience and solemnized by the sacrifice of himself as the victim?

This solution is suggested with much diffidence. That it carries these passages clear of all difficulty is not pretended. The very nature of the subject renders it difficult of illustration by any reference to human affairs; and the embarrassment is proportionally increased, whenever the simile is pressed beyond its principal point of resemblance.

See Ayliffe's Pandect, pp. 349, 393, *367-*369, Book iii. tit. xii. xv. Leges Atticæ, De Testamentis, &c. tit. vi. S. Petit. Comm. in Leges Attic. p. 479–481. Justin. Inst. lib. 2. tit. 10, § 1. Ibid. tit. 19, § 5, 6. Cooper's Justinian, p. 486. Cod. lib. 6. tit. 23, 1, 15. Fuss's Roman Antiq. ch. 1. §§ 87, 97, 103, 107, 183. Michaelis, LL. Moses, vol. 4, art. 302. Bp. Patrick, quoted in Bush's Illustrations, p. 254.

§ 138. **Jesus comforts his disciples. The Holy Spirit promised.**

MATTHEW.	MARK.

(EVENING INTRODUCING THE SIXTH DAY OF THE WEEK.) *Jerusalem.*

LUKE.

JOHN.

CHAPTER XIV. 1–31.

8 Philip saith unto him, Lord,
show us the Father, and it sufficeth
us.
9 Jesus saith unto him, Have I
been so long time with you, and yet
hast thou not known me, Philip?
he that hath seen me, hath seen the
Father; and [334] how sayest thou *then*,
Shew us the Father?
10 Believest thou not that I am in
the Father, and the Father in me?
the words that I speak unto you, I
speak not of myself: but the Father,
that dwelleth in me, he doeth the
works.[335]
11 Believe me that I *am* in the
Father, and the Father in me: or else
believe me for the very works' sake.[336]
12 Verily, verily, I say unto you,
He that believeth on me, the works
that I do shall he do also; and greater
works than these shall he do; because
I go unto my Father.[337]
14 And whatsoever ye shall ask in
my name, that will I do, that the
Father may be glorified in the Son.
14 If ye shall ask anything in my
name, I will do *it*.[338]
15 If ye love me, keep [339] my commandments:
16 And I will pray the Father,
and he shall give you another Comforter, that he may abide [340] with you
forever;
17 *Even* the Spirit of truth; whom
the world cannot receive, because it
seeth him not, neither knoweth him:
but ye know him; for he dwelleth
with you, and shall be in you.[341]
18 I will not leave you comfortless:[342] I will come to you.
19 Yet a little while, and the
world seeth me no more: but ye see
me: because I live, ye shall live also.
20 At that day ye shall know that
I *am* in my Father, and ye in me, and
I in you.
21 He that hath my commandments, and keepeth them, he it is
that loveth me: and he that loveth
me, shall be loved of my Father, and
I will love him, and will manifest
myself to him.
22 Judas saith unto him, (not

§ 138. Jesus comforts his disciples. The Holy Spirit promised.

MATTHEW.	MARK.

§ 139 Christ the true Vine. His disciples hated by the world.

(EVENING INTRODUCING THE SIXTH DAY OF THE WEEK.) *Jerusalem.*

LUKE.

JOHN.

CHAPTER XIV. 1–31.

Iscariot) Lord, how is it [343] that thou wilt manifest thyself unto us, and not unto the world?

23 Jesus answered and said unto him, If a man love me, he will keep my words: and my Father will love him, and we will come unto him, and make our abode with him.

24 He that loveth me not, keepeth not my sayings: and the word which ye hear is not mine, but the Father's which sent me.

25 These things have I spoken unto you, being *yet* present with you.

26 But the Comforter, *which is* the Holy Ghost, whom the Father will send in my name, he shall teach you all things, and bring all things to your remembrance, whatsoever I have said unto you.

27 Peace I leave with you, my peace I give unto you: not as the world giveth, give I unto you.[344] Let not your heart be troubled, neither let it be afraid.

28 Ye have heard how I said unto you, I go away, and come *again* unto you. If ye loved me, ye would rejoice, because I said, I go unto the Father: for my Father is greater than I.[345]

29. And now I have told you before it come to pass, that when it is come to pass, ye might believe.

30 Hereafter I will not talk much with you: for the prince of this [346] world cometh, and hath nothing in me.

31 But that the world may know that I love the Father; and as the Father gave me commandment, even so I do. Arise, let us go hence.

(EVENING INTRODUCING THE SIXTH DAY OF THE WEEK.) *Jerusalem.*

CHAPTER XV. 1–27.

I AM the true vine, and my Father is the husbandman.

2 Every branch in me that beareth not fruit, he taketh away: and every *branch* that beareth fruit, he purgeth it, that it may bring forth more fruit.

3 Now ye are clean through the word which I have spoken unto you.

4 Abide in me, and I in you. As

§ 139. Christ the true Vine. His disciples hated by the world.

MATTHEW.	MARK.

LUKE.

JOHN.

CHAPTER XV. 1–27.

the branch cannot bear fruit of itself,
except it abide in the vine: no more
can ye, except ye abide in me.
5 I am the vine, ye *are* the branches:
He that abideth in me, and I in him,
the same bringeth forth much fruit:
for without me ye can do nothing.
6 If a man abide not in me, he is
cast forth as a branch, and is withered; and men gather them, and cast
them[347] into the fire, and they are
burned.
7 If ye abide in me, and my words
abide in you, ye shall ask[348] what ye
will, and it shall be done unto you.
8 Herein is my Father glorified,
that ye bear much fruit: so shall ye
be my disciples.
9 As the Father hath loved me,
so have I loved you: continue ye in
my love.
10 If ye keep my commandments,
ye shall abide in my love: even as I
have kept my[349] Father's commandments, and abide in his love.
11 These things have I spoken unto
you, that my joy might remain in
you,[350] and *that* your joy might be full.
12 This is my commandment, That ye
love one another, as I have loved you.
13. Greater love hath no man than
this, that a man lay down his life for
his friends.
14 Ye are[351] my friends, if ye do
whatsoever I command you.
15 Henceforth I call you not servants: for the servant knoweth not
what his lord doeth; but I have
called you friends; for all things that
I have heard of my Father, I have
made known unto you.
16 Ye have not chosen me, but I
have chosen you, and ordained you,
that ye should go and bring forth
fruit, and *that* your fruit should remain: that whatsoever ye shall ask
of the Father in my name, he may
give it you.[352]
17 These things I command you,
that ye love one another.
18 If the world hate you, ye know
that it hated me before *it hated* you.
19 If ye were of the world, the
world would love his own; but be-

§ 139. Christ the true Vine. His disciples hated by the world.

MATTHEW.	MARK.

§ 140. Persecution foretold. Further promise of the Holy Spirit.

(EVENING INTRODUCING THE SIXTH DAY OF THE WEEK.) *Jerusalem.*

LUKE.	JOHN.

JOHN.

CHAPTER XV. 1–27.

cause ye are not of the world, but I
have chosen you out of the world,
therefore the world hateth you.
20 Remember the word that I said
unto you, The servant is not greater
than his lord. If they have persecuted me, they will also persecute
you: if they have kept my saying,
they will keep yours also.
21 But all these things will they
do unto you for my name's sake, because they know not him that sent me.
22 If I had not come and spoken
unto them, they had not had sin:
but[353] now they have no cloak for
their sin.
23 He that hateth me, hateth my
Father also.
24 If I had not done among them
the works which none other man did,
they had not had sin: but now have
they both seen, and hated both me
and my Father.
25 But *this cometh to pass*, that the
word might be fulfilled that is written
in their law, They hated me without
a cause.*
26 But[354] when the Comforter is
come, whom I will send unto you
from the Father, *even* the Spirit of
truth, which proceedeth from the
Father, he shall testify of me.
27 And ye also shall bear witness,
because ye have been with me from
the beginning.

(EVENING INTRODUCING THE SIXTH DAY OF THE WEEK.) *Jerusalem.*

CHAPTER XVI. 1–33.

THESE things have I spoken unto
you, that ye should not be offended.
2 They shall put you out of the
synagogues: yea, the time cometh,
that whosoever killeth you, will think
that he doeth God service.[355]
3 And these things will they do
unto you,[356] because they have not
known the Father, nor me.
4 But these things have I told you,
that when the time shall come, ye may
remember that I told you of them.[357]
And these things I said not unto you

* Ps. lxix. 5.

§ 140. **Persecution foretold. Further promise of the Holy Spirit.**

MATTHEW.	MARK.

LUKE.

JOHN.

CHAPTER XVI. 1-33.

at the beginning because I was with
you.
5 But now I go my way to him that
sent me, and none of you asketh me,
Whither goest thou?
6 But[358] because I have said these
things unto you, sorrow hath filled
your heart.
7 Nevertheless, I tell you the
truth: It is expedient for you that
I go away: for if I go not away, the
Comforter will not come unto you;
but if I depart, I will send him unto
you.
8 And when he is come, he will
reprove[359] the world of sin, and of
righteousness, and of judgment:
9 Of sin, because they believe not
on me;
10 Of righteousness, because I go
to my[360] Father, and ye see me no
more;
11 Of judgment, because the prince
of this world is judged.
12 I have yet many things to say
unto you, but ye cannot bear them
now.[361]
13 Howbeit, when he, the Spirit
of truth is come, he will guide you
into all truth: for he shall not speak
of himself; but whatsoever he shall
hear, *that* shall he speak: and he will
shew you things to come.
14 He shall glorify me: for he
shall receive of mine, and shall shew
it unto you.[362]
15 All things that the Father hath
are mine: therefore said I, that he
shall take of mine, and shall shew *it*
unto you.[363]
16 A little while, and ye shall not
see me: and again, a little while, and
ye shall see me, because I go to the
Father.[364]
17 Then said *some* of his disciples
among themselves, What is this that
he saith unto us, A little while, and
ye shall not see me: and again, a
little while, and ye shall see me;
and, Because I go to the Father?
18 They said therefore, What is
this that he saith, A little while?
we cannot tell what he saith.[365]
19 Now Jesus knew that they were

§ 140. **Persecution foretold. Further promise of the Holy Spirit.**

MATTHEW.	MARK.

(EVENING INTRODUCING THE SIXTH DAY OF THE WEEK.) *Jerusalem.*

LUKE.

JOHN.

CHAPTER XVI. 1–33.

desirous to ask him, and said unto them,[366] Do ye inquire among yourselves of that I said, A little while, and ye shall not see me: and again, a little while, and ye shall see me?

20 Verily, verily, I say unto you, that ye shall weep and lament, but the world shall rejoice: and[367] ye shall be sorrowful, but your sorrow shall be turned into joy.

21 A woman when she is in travail hath sorrow, because her hour is come: but as soon as she is delivered of the child, she remembereth no more the anguish, for joy that a man is born into the world.

22 And ye now therefore hath sorrow:[368] but I will see you again, and your heart shall rejoice, and your joy no man taketh from you.

23 And in that day ye shall ask me nothing. Verily, verily, I say unto you, Whatsoever ye shall ask the Father in my name, he will give *it* you.[369]

24 Hitherto have ye asked nothing in my name: ask, and ye shall receive, that your joy may be full.

25 These things have I spoken unto you in proverbs: but the time cometh when I shall no more speak unto you in proverbs, but I shall shew you plainly of the Father.

26 At that day ye shall ask in my name:[370] and I say not unto you, that I will pray the Father for you:

27 For the Father himself loveth you, because ye have loved me, and have believed that I came out from God.[371]

28 I came forth from the Father, and am come into the world: again, I leave the world, and go to the Father.

29 His disciples said unto him,[372] Lo, now speakest thou plainly, and speaketh no proverb.

30 Now are we sure that thou knowest all things, and needest not that any man should ask thee: by this we believe that thou camest forth from God.

31 Jesus answered them, Do ye now believe?

§ 140. Persecution foretold. Further promise of the Holy Spirit.

MATTHEW.	MARK.

§ 141. Christ's last prayer with his disciples. (EVENING

(EVENING INTRODUCING THE SIXTH DAY OF THE WEEK.) *Jerusalem.*

LUKE.

JOHN.

CHAPTER XVI. 1–33.

32 Behold, the hour cometh, yea,
is now come,[373] that ye shall be scattered every man to his own, and shall leave me alone: and yet I am not alone, because the Father is with me.

33 These things I have spoken unto
you, that in me ye might have peace. In the world ye shall have [374] tribulation, but be of good cheer: I have overcome the world.

INTRODUCING THE SIXTH DAY OF THE WEEK.) *Jerusalem.*

CHAPTER XVII. 1–26.

THESE words spake Jesus, and lifted up his eyes to heaven, and said, Father, the hour is come; glorify thy Son, that thy Son also may glorify thee:[375]

2 As thou hast given him power
over all flesh, that he should give eternal life to as many as thou hast given him.

3 And this is life eternal, that they
might know thee the only true God, and Jesus Christ whom thou hast sent.

4 I have glorified thee on the earth:
I have finished the work [376] which thou gavest me to do.

5 And now, O Father, glorify thou
me with thine own self, with the glory which I had with thee before the world was.

6 I have manifested thy name unto
the men which thou gavest me out of the world: thine they were, and thou gavest them me; and they have kept thy word.

7 Now they [377] have known that all
things whatsoever thou hast given me are of thee:

8 For I have given unto them the
words which thou gavest me; and they have received *them*, and have known surely that I came out from thee, and they have believed that thou didst send me.

9 I pray for them: I pray not for
the world, but for them which thou hast given me; for they are thine.

10 And all mine are thine, and
thine are mine;[378] and I am glorified in them.

11 And now I am no more in the

§ 141. **Christ's last prayer with his disciples.** (EVENING

MATTHEW.	MARK.

LUKE.

JOHN.

CHAPTER XVII. 1–26.

world, but these are in the world,
and I come to thee. Holy Father,
keep through thine own name those
whom thou has given me, that they
may be one, as we *are.*[379]
12 While I was with them in the
world, I kept them in thy name:
those that thou gavest me I have
kept, and none of them is lost,[380] but
the son of perdition; that the scripture
might be fulfilled.*
13 And now come I to thee, and
these things I speak in the world,
that they might have my joy fulfilled
in themselves.
14 I have given them thy word;
and the world hath hated them, because
they are not of the world, even
as I am not of the world.
15 I pray not that thou shouldest
take them out of the world, but that
thou shouldest keep them from the
evil.
15 They are not of the world, even
as I am not of the world.
17 Sanctify them through thy truth:
thy word is truth.[381]
18 As thou hast sent me into the
world, even so have I also sent them
into the world.
19 And for their sakes I sanctify
myself, that they also might be
sanctified through the truth.
20 Neither pray I for these alone;
but for them also which shall believe
on me[382] through their word:
21 That they all may be one; as
thou, Father, *art* in me, and I in thee,
that they also may be one in us: that
the world may believe that thou hast
sent me.
22 And the glory which thou gavest
me, I have given them; that they may
be one, even as we are one;[383]
23 I in them, and thou in me, that
they may be made perfect in one; and
that the world may know that thou
hast sent me, and hast loved them as
thou hast loved me.[384]
24 Father, I will that they also
whom thou hast given me be with me

* Ps. xli. 9, and cix. 8, 17.

§ 141. Christ's last prayer with his disciples. (EVENING

MATTHEW.

MARK.

§ 142. The agony in Gethsemane. (EVENING

MATTHEW.

CHAPTER XXVI. 30, 36–46.

30 And when they had sung a hymn, they went out into the mount of Olives.

36 Then cometh Jesus with them unto a place called Gethsemane: and saith unto the disciples, Sit ye here, while I go and pray yonder.[414]

37 And he took with him Peter, and the two sons of Zebedee, and began to be sorrowful and very heavy.

38 Then saith he unto them, My soul is exceeding sorrowful, even unto death: tarry ye here, and watch with me.

39 And he went a little further, and fell on his face, and prayed, saying, O my Father, if it be possible, let this cup pass from me: nevertheless, not as I will, but as thou *wilt.*

MARK.

CHAPTER XIV. 26, 32–42.

26 And when they had sung an hymn, they went out into the mount of Olives.

32 And they came to a place which was named Gethsemane: and he saith to his disciples, Sit ye here,[359] while I shall pray.

33 And he taketh with him Peter, and James and John, and began to be sore amazed, and to be very heavy:

34 And saith unto them, My soul is exceeding sorrowful unto death: tarry ye here, and watch.

35 And he went forward a little, and fell on the ground, and prayed that, if it were possible, the hour might pass from him.

36 And he said, Abba, Father, all things *are* possible unto thee; take away this cup from me: nevertheless, not what I will, but what thou wilt.

Luke xxii. 44, *as it were great drops of blood.*] The strangeness of such a profusion of blood has been urged, first, against the probability, and then against the truth, of the narrative. But learned men have related instances of mental agony so great as to force the blood through the pores; and if this has ever occurred, it may well be believed to have occurred in the present case. See *Bloomfield* and *A. Clarke,* in loc. It should be ob-

INTRODUCING THE SIXTH DAY OF THE WEEK.) *Jerusalem.*

LUKE.

JOHN.

CHAPTER XVII. 1-26.

where I am; that they may behold my glory which thou hast given me: for thou lovest me before the foundation of the world.

26 O righteous Father, the world hath not known thee: but I have known thee, and these have known that thou hast sent me.

26 And I have declared unto them thy name, and will declare *it*: that the love wherewith thou hast loved me,[385] may be in them, and I in them.

INTRODUCING THE SIXTH DAY OF THE WEEK.) *Mount of Olives.*

LUKE.

CHAPTER XXII. 39-46.

39 And he came out, and went, as he was wont, to the mount of Olives; and his disciples also followed him.[438]

40 And when he was at the place, he said unto them, Pray that ye enter not into temptation.

41 And he was withdrawn from them about a stone's cast, and kneeled down, and prayed,

42 Saying, Father, if thou be willing, remove this cup from me: nevertheless, not my will, but thine, be done.

43 [439] And there appeared an angel unto him from heaven, strengthening him.

44 And being in an agony, he prayed more earnestly: and his sweat was as it were great drops of blood falling down to the ground.

45 And when he rose up from

JOHN.

CHAPTER XVIII. 1.

WHEN Jesus had spoken these words, he went forth with his disciples over the brook Cedron, where was a garden, into the which he entered, and his disciples.

---

served, however, that Luke does not directly affirm that it was blood. He only *compares* the sweat to that of blood, using a term of similitude (*quasi* grumi sanguinis—*Beza; tanquam* demissiones sanguinis—*Tremellius; sicut* guttæ sanguinis—*Vulg.* and *Molinæus;*) which may signify no more than that the drops of sweat were as large as drops of blood, which, from its viscidity, are very large.

§ 142. The agony in Gethsemane (EVENING

MATTHEW.

CHAPTER XXVI. 30, 36-46.

40 And he cometh unto the disciples, and findeth them asleep, and saith unto Peter, What! could ye not watch with me one hour?

41 Watch and pray, that ye enter not into temptation: the spirit indeed *is* willing, but the flesh *is* weak.

42 He went away again the second time, and prayed, saying, O my Father, if this cup may not pass away from me,[415] except I drink it, thy will be done.

43 And he came and found them asleep again:[416] for their eyes were heavy.

44 And he left them, and went away again, and prayed the third time, saying the same words.[417]

45 Then cometh he to his disciples, and saith unto them, Sleep on now, and take *your* rest:[418] behold the hour is at hand, and the Son of man is betrayed into the hands of sinners.

46 Rise, let us be going: behold, he is at hand that doth betray me.

MARK.

CHAPTER XIV. 26, 32-42.

37 And he cometh, and findeth them sleeping, and saith,[340] unto Peter, Simon, sleepest thou? couldst not thou watch one hour?

38 Watch ye and pray, lest ye enter into temptation.[361] The spirit truly *is* ready, but the flesh *is* weak.

39 And again he went away, and prayed, and spake the same words.

40 And when he returned, he found them asleep again,[362] (for their eyes were heavy;) neither wist they what to answer him.

41 And he cometh the third time, and saith unto them, Sleep on now, and take *your* rest: it is enough, the hour is come; behold, the Son of man is betrayed into the hands of sinners.

42 Rise up, let us go; lo, he that betrayeth me is at hand.

§ 143. Jesus betrayed and made prisoner. (EVENING

MATTHEW.

CHAPTER XXVI. 47-56.

47 And while he yet spake, lo, Judas, one of the twelve, came, and with him a great multitude with swords and staves, from the chief priests and elders of the people.

48 Now, he that betrayed him, gave them a sign, saying, Whomsoever I shall kiss, that same is he; hold him fast.

49 And forthwith he came to Jesus, and said, Hail, Master; and kissed him.

50 And Jesus said unto him,[419] Friend, wherefore art thou come? Then came they, and laid hands on Jesus, and took him.

MARK.

CHAPTER XIV. 43-52.

43 And immediately while he yet spake, cometh Judas,[363] one of the twelve, and with him a great multitude with swords and staves, from the chief priests, and the scribes, and the elders.

44 And he that betrayed him, had given them a token, saying, Whomsoever I shall kiss, that same is he; take him, and lead *him* away safely.

45 And as soon as he was come, he goeth straightway to him, and saith, Master, Master; and kissed him.

46 And they lay their hands on him, and took him.

Luke xxii. 45, *sleeping for sorrow.*] No other Evangelist mentions the cause of their slumber, except Luke, who ascribes it to their sorrow. It is observable, that Luke was a physician (Col. iv. 14), and therefore well knew that deep mental distress frequently induced sleep. To this cause may perhaps be referred the fact, that persons condemned to die are often waked from sound sleep by the executioner. The internal evidence here afforded of

INTRODUCING THE SIXTH DAY OF THE WEEK.) *Mount of Olives.*

LUKE.

CHAPTER XXII. 39-46.

prayer, and was come to his disciples,[440] he found them sleeping for sorrow,

46 And said unto them, Why sleep ye? rise and pray, lest ye enter into temptation.

JOHN.

INTRODUCING THE SIXTH DAY OF THE WEEK.) *Mount of Olives.*

LUKE.

CHAPTER XXII. 47–53.

47 And[441] while he yet spake, behold a multitude, and he that was called Judas, one of the twelve, went before them, and drew near unto Jesus to kiss him.

48 But Jesus said unto him, Judas,[442] betrayest thou the Son of Man with a kiss?

49 When they which were about him, saw what would follow, they said unto him,[443] Lord, shall we smite with the sword?

JOHN.

CHAPTER XVIII. 2–12.

2 And Judas also, which betrayed him, knew the place: for Jesus ofttimes resorted thither with his disciples.

3 Judas then, having received a band *of men* and officers from the chief priests and Pharisees, cometh thither[386] with lanterns, and torches, and weapons.

4 Jesus therefore, knowing all things that should come unto him, went forth, and said unto them,[387] Whom seek ye?

5 They answered him, Jesus of Nazareth. Jesus saith unto them, I am *he.*[388] And Judas also, which betrayed him, stood with them.

6 As soon then as he had said unto

---

the truth of Luke's narrative, is corroborated by his notice of the bloody sweat. ver. 44, and of the miraculous healing of the ear of Malchus, ver. 51; facts which are not related by any other Evangelist, but which would naturally attract the attention of a physician.

John xviii. 5, *I am he.*] In the order of events, Jesus first voluntarily discriminates himself; after which Judas gives the agreed sign to his enemies. NEWCOME.

§ 143. Jesus betrayed and made prisoner. (EVENING

MATTHEW.
CHAPTER XXVI. 47-56.

51 And behold, one of them which
were with Jesus,[420] stretched out *his*
hand, and drew his sword, and struck
a servant of the high priest, and smote
off his ear.
52 Then said Jesus unto him, Put
up again thy sword into his place:
for all they that take the sword, shall
perish with the sword.*
53 Thinkest thou that I cannot
now pray to my Father, and he shall
presently give me more than twelve
legions of angels? [421]
54 But how then shall the scriptures
be fulfilled, that thus it must be?
55 In that same hour said Jesus to
the multitudes, Are ye come out as
against a thief with swords and
staves for to take me? I sat daily
with you [422] teaching in the temple,
and ye laid no hold on me.
56 But all this was done, that the
Scriptures of the prophets might be
fulfilled.
Then all the [423] disciples forsook him, and fled.

MARK.
CHAPTER XIV. 43-52.

47 And one of them that stood by,
drew a sword, and smote a servant of
the high priest, and cut off his ear.

48 And Jesus answered and said
unto them, Are ye come out as against
a thief, with swords and *with* staves
to take me?
49 I was daily with you in the
temple, teaching, and ye took me not:
but the scriptures must be fulfilled.

50 And they all forsook him and
fled.
51 And there followed him a certain young man, having a linen cloth
cast about *his* naked *body;* and the
young men laid hold on him.[364]
52 And he left the linen cloth, and
fled from them [365] naked.

§ 144. Jesus before Caiaphas. Peter thrice denies him. (NIGHT

CHAPTER XXVI. 57, 58, 69-75.
57 And they that had laid hold on
Jesus, led *him* away to Caiaphas th

CHAPTER XIV. 53, 44, 66-72.
53 And they led Jesus away to the
high priest: and with him were as-

* Gen. ix. 6.

John xviii. 10, *Simon Peter.*] Lenfant and Bp. Pearce think that Peter was named by John because he was then dead; and that he was named by the other Evangelists because when they wrote he was living and the action might have subjected him to public justice or at least to reproach. NEWCOME.

INTRODUCING THE SIXTH DAY OF THE WEEK.) *Mount of Olives.*

LUKE.
CHAPTER XXII. 47–53.

50 And one of them smote the servant of the high priest, and cut off his right ear.

51 And Jesus answered and said, Suffer ye thus far. And he touched his ear,[444] and healed him,

52 Then Jesus said unto the chief priests, and captains of the temple, and the elders which were come to him, Be ye come out as against a thief, with swords and staves?
53 When I was daily with you in the temple, ye stretched forth no hands against me: but this is your hour,[445] and the power of darkness.

JOHN.
CHAPTER XVIII. 2–12.
them, I am *he*, they went backward, and fell to the ground.[389]
7 Then asked he them again, Whom seek ye? and they said, Jesus of Nazareth.
8 Jesus answered, I have told you that I am *he*. If therefore ye seek me, let these go their way:
9 That the saying might be fulfilled which he spake, Of them which thou gavest me, have I lost none.
10 Then Simon Peter, having a sword, drew it, and smote the high priest's servant, and cut off his right ear. The servant's name was Malchus.
11 Then said Jesus unto Peter, Put up thy [390] sword into the sheath: the cup which my Father hath given me, shall I not drink it?

12 Then the band and the captain, and officers of the Jews took Jesus, and bound him.

INTRODUCING THE SIXTH DAY OF THE WEEK.) *Jerusalem.*

CHAPTER XXII. 54–62.
54 Then took they him, and led *him*, and brought him into the high

CHAPTER XVIII. 13–18, 25–27.
13 And led him away to Annas first,[391] (for he was father-in-law to

John xviii. 13, *to Annas first.*] Probably by way of compliment to the past high priest, who was also the father-in-law of Caiaphas. If this circumstance never happened, it is difficult to discover how the introduction of it could serve the purposes of fiction. See ROBERTS, Light Shining, &c. pp. 171, 172.

§ 144. **Jesus before Caiaphas. Peter thrice denies him.** (NIGHT

MATTHEW.

CHAPTER XXVI. 57, 58, 69–75.

high priest, where the scribes and the elders were assembled.

58 But Peter followed him afar off, unto the high priest's palace, and went in, and sat with the servants to see the end.

69 Now Peter sat without in the palace: and a damsel came unto him, saying, Thou also wast with Jesus of Galilee.

70 But he denied before *them* all,[429] saying, I know not what thou sayest.

71 And when he was gone out into the porch, another *maid* saw him, and said unto them that were there, This *fellow* was also with Jesus of Nazareth.

72 And again he denied with an oath, I do not know the man.

73 And after a while came unto *him* they that stood by, and said to Peter, Surely thou also art *one* of them: for thy speech bewrayeth thee.

74 Then began he to curse and to swear, *saying*, I know not the man. And immediately the cock crew.

MARK.

CHAPTER XIV. 53, 54, 66–72.

sembled all the chief priests, and the elders and the scribes.[366]

54 And Peter followed him afar off, even into the palace of the high priest: and he sat with the servants, and warmed himself at the fire.

66 And as Peter was beneath in the palace, there cometh one of the maids [372] of the high priest:

67 And when she saw Peter warming himself, she looked upon him, and said, And thou also wast with Jesus of Nazareth.

68 But he denied, saying, I know not, neither understand I what thou sayest. And he went out into the porch; and the cock crew.[373]

69 And a maid saw him again, and began to say to them that stood by, This is *one* of them.[374]

70 And he denied it again. And a little after, they that stood by said again to Peter, Surely thou art *one* of them: for thou art a Galilean, and thy speech agreeth *thereto*.[375]

71 But he began to curse and to swear, *saying*, I know not this man of whom ye speak.[376]

72 And the second time the cock

Matth. xxvi. 71, *into the porch.*] Here is a minute indication of veracity, which would have been lost upon us but for the narrative of John. Matthew only states the fact that the maid in the porch recognized Peter as one of the disciples of Jesus; but John (xviii. 16,) informs us how she knew him to be so; namely, because he was brought in by John, who was a frequent guest at the house of her master the high priest. BLUNT, Veracity &c., Sect. i. 12, 18.

Luke xxii. 60, *Man, I know not.*] The seeming contradiction between Luke, who relates

LUKE.

CHAPTER XXII. 54–62.

priest's house. And Peter followed afar off.

55 And when they had kindled a fire in the midst of the hall, and were set down together, Peter sat down among them.

56 But a certain maid beheld him as he sat by the fire, and earnestly looked upon him, and said, This man was also with him.

57 And he denied him, saying, Woman, I know him not.[446]

58 And after a little while another saw him, and said, Thou art also of them. And Peter said, Man, I am not.

59 And about the space of one hour after, another confidently affirmed, saying, Of a truth this *fellow* also was with him; for he is a Galilean.

60 And Peter said, Man, I know not what thou sayest. And immediately, while he yet spake, the[447] cock crew.

JOHN.

CH. XVIII. 13–18, 25–27.

Caiaphas, which was the high priest that same year.)

14 Now Caiaphas was he which gave counsel to the Jews, that it was expedient that one man should die for the people.

15 And Simon Peter followed Jesus, and *so did* another disciple. That disciple was known unto the high priest, and went in with Jesus, into the palace of the high priest.

16 But Peter stood at the door without. Then went out that other disciple which was known unto the high priest, and spake unto her that kept the door, and brought in Peter.

18 And the servants and officers stood there, who had made a fire of coals; (for it was cold) and they warmed themselves: and Peter stood[392] with them, and warmed himself.

17 Then saith the damsel that kept the door unto Peter, Art not thou also *one* of this man's disciples? He saith, I am not.

25 And Simon Peter stood and warmed himself. They said therefore unto him, Art not thou also *one* of his disciples? He denied *it*, and said,[395] I am not.

26 One of the servants of the high priest (being *his* kinsman whose ear Peter cut off) saith, did not I see thee in the garden with him?

27 Peter then denied again: and immediately the cock crew.

---

that it was a *man* who charged Peter with being a follower of Jesus, and Matthew and Mark, who state that he was accused by a *maid*, is reconciled by attending to the narrative of John (xviii 25), who writes, "*They* said." Whence it appears that there were several who spake on this occasion, and that each Evangelist refers to the accusation which made the deepest impression on his own mind. See MICHAELIS and Bp. MIDDLETON, cited in 4 HORNE'S *Introd.*, p. 258, note 1.

§ **144. Jesus before Caiaphas. Peter thrice denies him.** (NIGHT

MATTHEW.

CHAPTER XXVI. 57, 58, 69–75.

75 And Peter remembered the word
of Jesus, which said unto him,[430] Before the cock crow thou shalt deny
me thrice. And he went out, and
wept bitterly.

MARK.

CHAPTER XIV. 53, 54, 66–72.

crew. And Peter called to mind the
word that Jesus said unto him, Before the cock crow twice thou shalt
deny me thrice. And when he
thought thereon, he wept.[377]

§ **145. Jesus before Caiaphas. He declares himself to be the**

CHAPTER XXVI. 59–68.

59 Now the chief priests and elders,[424] and all the council, sought
false witness against Jesus, to put
him to death;
60 But found none: yea, though
many false witnesses came, *yet* found
they none. At the last came two
false witnesses,[425]

61 And said, This *fellow* said, I am
able to destroy the temple of God,
and to build it in three days.

62 [426] And the high priest arose,
and said unto him, Answereth thou
nothing? what *is it which* these witness against thee?
63 But Jesus held his peace. And
the high priest answered and [427] said

CHAPTER XIV. 55–65.

55 And the chief priests, and all
the council sought for witness[367]
against Jesus to put him to death;
and found none:
56 For many bare false witness
against him, but their witness agreed
not together.
57 And there arose certain, and
bare false witness against him, saying,
58 We heard him say,[368] I will destroy this temple that is made with
hands, and within three days I will
build another made without hands.
59 But neither so did their witness
agree together.
60 And the high priest stood up in
the midst, and asked Jesus, saying,
Answerest thou nothing? what *is it*
which these witness against thee?[369]
61 But he held his peace, and
answered nothing. Again the high

---

§ 144.] Matthew and Mark relate Peter's denials of Christ after his condemnation, and the insults consequent upon it. It is plain that they happened while the High Priest and council were sitting in judgment. But instances of recurring in this manner to what had been omitted in its proper place are common in the Gospels; and in this place the thread of the narration is preserved unbroken.

It having been expressly mentioned by each Evangelist, that Peter would *thrice* deny Jesus, we may conclude that each has related the *three* denials which Jesus foretold.

Peter's first denial. Peter was *without*, or *beneath*, in the hall of Caiaphas's house. Dr. Scott, on Matth. xxvi. 3, observes that *aule* signifies an house (Luke xi. 21), and that emphatically it signifies the king's house, or palace. But in Luke xxii. 55, it seems to signify a spacious apartment, probably the High Priest's judgment-hall. It was the place in which Jesus stood before the High Priest (Luke xxii. 61) and had an *atrium* or *vestibulum* at its entrance. This was an unfit place for the tribunal of the High Priest at such an hour (John xviii. 18). Sir John Chardin says, "In the lower Asia the day is always hot; and in the height of summer the nights are as cold as at Paris in the month of March." It remains therefore that we understand it of a spacious chamber, such as Shaw mentions, Travels, 4to. pp. 207, 8.

Peter was not in the *higher* part, where Jesus stood before the High Priest; but *without* that division of the hall, and in the *lower* part, with the servants and officers. The damsel, who kept the door, had entered into the hall when she charged Peter.

Peter's second denial. Peter, having once denied Jesus, naturally retired from the

INTRODUCING THE SIXTH DAY OF THE WEEK.) *Jerusalem.*

LUKE.	JOHN.
CHAPTER XXII. 54–62.	
61 And the Lord turned, and looked upon Peter. And Peter remembered the word of the Lord, how he had said unto him, Before the cock crow,[448] thou shalt deny me thrice.	
62 And Peter [449] went out and wept bitterly.	

Christ, &c. (MORNING OF THE SIXTH DAY OF THE WEEK.) *Jerusalem.*

CHAPTER XXII. 63–71.	CHAPTER XVIII. 19–24.
66 And as soon as it was day, the elders of the people, and the chief priests, and the scribes, came together, and led him into their council, saying,	
67 Art thou the Christ? tell us. And he said unto them, If I tell you,[452] ye will not believe.	19 The high priest then asked Jesus of his disciples, and of his doctrine.
68 And if I also ask *you*, ye will not answer me, nor let *me* go.[453]	20 [393] Jesus answered him, I spake openly to the world; I ever taught
69 [454] Hereafter shall the Son of man	in the synagogue, and in the temple,

place where his accuser was, to the vestibule of the hall, Matt. xxvi. 71); and it was the time of the first cock-crowing, or soon after midnight. After remaining here a short time, perhaps near an hour, another damsel sees him, and says to those who were standing by in the vestibule, that he was one of them. Peter, to avoid this charge, withdraws into the hall, and stands and warms himself, (John xviii. 25.) The damsel, and those to whom she had spoken, follow him; the communication between the places being immediate. Here *a man* enforces the charge of the damsel, according to Luke; and *others* urge it according to John, (though by him the plural may be used for the singular,) and Peter denies Jesus vehemently.

Peter's third denial. Peter was now in the hall. Observe Matt. xxvi. 75, and Luke xxii. 62. He was also within sight of Jesus, though at such a distance from him that Jesus could know what passed only in a supernatural way. About an hour after his second denial, those who stood by founded a charge against him on his being a Galilean, which, Luke says, one in particular strongly affirmed, (though here Matthew and Mark may use the plural for the singular,) and which according to John, was supported by one of Malchus's relations. This occasioned a more vehement denial than before; and immediately the cock crew the second time. The first denial may have been between our twelve and one; and the second between our two and three. We must further observe, that Matt. xxvi. 57, lays the scene of Peter's denials in the house of Caiaphas; whereas the transactions of John xviii. 15–23 seem to have passed in the house of Annas. But John xviii. 24 is here transposed to its regular place, with Le Clerc. NEWCOME.

§ 145. Jesus before Caiaphas. He declares himself to be the

MATTHEW.

CHAPTER XXVI. 59–68.

unto him, I adjure thee by the living God, that thou tell us whether thou be the Christ, the Son of God.

64 Jesus saith unto him, Thou hast said: nevertheless, I say unto you, Hereafter shall ye see the Son of man sitting on the right hand of power, and coming in the clouds of heaven.

65 Then the high priest rent his clothes, saying, He hath spoken blasphemy; what further need have we of witnesses? behold, now ye have heard his blasphemy.[428]

66 What think ye? They answered and said, He is guilty of death.

67 Then did they spit in his face, and buffeted him; and others smote *him* with the palms of their hands,

68 Saying, Prophesy unto us, thou Christ, who is he that smote thee?

MARK.

CHAPTER XIV. 55–65.

priest asked him, and said unto him, Art thou the Christ, the Son of the Blessed?[370]

62 And Jesus said, I am: and ye shall see the Son of man sitting on the right hand of power, and coming in the clouds of heaven.

63 Then the high priest rent his clothes, and saith, What need we any further witnesses?

64 Ye have heard[371] the blasphemy: what think ye? And they all condemned him to be guilty of death.

65 And some began to spit on him, and to cover his face, and to buffet him, and to say unto him, Prophesy: and the servants did strike him with the palms of their hands.

§ 146. The Sanhedrim lead Jesus away to Pilate.

MATTHEW.

CHAPTER XXVII. 1, 2, 11–14.

WHEN the morning was come, all the chief priests and elders of the people took counsel against Jesus to put him to death.

2 And when they had bound him, they led *him* away, and delivered him[431] to Pontius Pilate the governor.

11 And Jesus stood before the governor: and the governor asked him, saying, Art thou the King of the Jews? And Jesus said unto him,[435] Thou sayest.

MARK.

CHAPTER XV. 1–5.

AND straightway in the morning the chief priests held a consultation with the elders and scribes, and the whole council, and bound Jesus, and carried *him* away, and delivered *him* to Pilate.

2 And Pilate asked him, Art thou the King of the Jews? And he answering, said unto him, Thou sayest *it*.[378]

Matt. xxvi. 68, *Prophesy unto us.*] Matthew alone states this fact: and he states nothing in explanation of it. The other Evangelists add another fact, which shows that the Jews were quite consistent in asking him to designate who struck him, namely, that they had previously "blindfolded him." Now the omissions of particulars are characteristic of one to

Christ. (MORNING OF THE SIXTH DAY OF THE WEEK.) *Jerusalem.*

LUKE.	JOHN.
CHAPTER XXII. 63–71.	CHAPTER XVIII. 19–24.
sit on the right hand of the power of God.	whither the Jews always resort; and in secret have I said nothing.
70 Then said they all, Art thou then the Son of God? and he said unto them, Ye say that I am.	21 Why askest thou me? ask them which heard me, what I have said unto them: behold, they know what I said.
71 And they said, What need we any further witness? for we ourselves have heard of his own mouth.	22 And when he had thus spoken, one of the officers which stood by, struck Jesus with the palm of his hand, saying, Answereth thou the high priest so?
63 And the men that held Jesus,[450] mocked him, and smote *him*.	
64 And when they had blindfolded him, they struck him on the face, and asked him,[451] saying, Prophesy, who is it that smote thee?	23 Jesus answereth him,[394] If I have spoken evil, bear witness of the evil: but if well, why smitest thou me?
65 And many other things blasphemously spake they against him.	24 (Now Annas had sent him bound unto Caiaphas the high priest.)

(SIXTH DAY OF THE WEEK.) *Jerusalem.*

LUKE.	JOHN.
CHAPTER XXIII. 1–5.	CHAPTER XVIII. 28–38.
AND the whole multitude of them arose, and led him unto Pilate.	28 Then led they Jesus from Caiaphas unto the hall of judgment: and it was early; and they themselves went not into the judgment-hall, lest they should be defiled; but that they might eat the passover.
2 And they began to accuse him, saying, We found this *fellow* perverting the nation, and forbidding to give tribute to Cesar, saying, That he himself is Christ, a King.[455]	29 Pilate then went out unto them, and said,[396] What accusation bring ye against this man?
	30 They answered and said unto him, If he were not a malefactor, we would not have delivered him up unto thee.
	31 Then said Pilate unto them, Take ye him, and judge him according[397] to your law. The Jews therefore said unto him, It is not lawful for us to put any man to death:
	32 That the saying of Jesus might be fulfilled, which he spake,[398] signifying what death he should die.
3 And Pilate asked him saying, Art thou the King of the Jews? And he answered him and said, Thou sayest *it*.[456]	33 Then Pilate entered into the judgment-hall again, and called Jesus, and said unto him, Art thou the King of the Jews?

whom it never occurs that they are wanted to make his statement credible, but who, conscious of his own integrity, states his facts and leaves them to their fate; and they cannot fairly be accounted for, upon any other supposition than the truth of the narrative. BLUNT, Veracity, &c., sec. i. 10.

§ 146. The Sanhedrim lead Jesus away to Pilate.

MATTHEW.

CHAPTER XXVII. 1, 2, 11–14.

12 And when he was accused of the chief priests and elders, he answered nothing.

13 Then saith Pilate unto him, Hearest thou not how many things they witness against thee?

14 And he answered him to never a word; insomuch that the governor marvelled greatly.

MARK.

CHAPTER XV. 1–5.

3 And the chief priests accused him of many things: but he answered nothing.

4 And Pilate asked him again, saying,[379] Answerest thou nothing? behold how many things they witness against thee.

5 But Jesus yet answered nothing: so that Pilate marvelled.

§ 147. Jesus before Herod.

John xviii. 36, *then would my servants fight.*] Jesus seems here almost to have challenged inquiry into the assault so lately committed by Peter upon the servant of the high priest. St. Luke, however, states a fact which accounts for their not making such inquiry, ch. xxii. 51. *He touched his ear and healed him.* An inquiry into the truth would have frustrated the malicious purpose of the enemies of Jesus, by proving his own compassionate nature, his submission to the laws, and his miraculous powers. BLUNT, Veracity, &c., sec. i. 19.

Luke xxiii. 7, *was also at Jerusalem at that time.*] Here is an obscure intimation that neither

(SIXTH DAY OF THE WEEK.) *Jerusalem.*

LUKE.
CHAPTER XXIII. 1-5.

4 Then said Pilate to the chief priests, and *to* the people, I find no fault in this man.

5 And they were the more fierce, saying, he stirreth up the people, teaching [457] throughout all Jewry, beginning from Galilee to this place.

JOHN.
CHAPTER XVIII. 28-38.

34 Jesus answered him, Sayest thou this thing [399] of thyself, or did others tell it thee of me?

35 Pilate answered, Am I a Jew? Thine own nation, and the chief priests,[400] have delivered thee unto me. What hast thou done?

36 Jesus answered, My kingdom is not of this world: if my kingdom were of this world, then would my [401] servants fight, that I should not be delivered to the Jews: but now is my kingdom not from hence.

37 Pilate therefore said unto him, Art thou a king then? Jesus answered, Thou sayest that I am a king. To this end [402] was I born, and for this cause came I into the world, that I should bear witness unto the truth. Every one that is of the truth, heareth my voice.

38 Pilate saith unto him, What is truth? And when he had said this, he went out again unto the Jews, and saith unto them, I find in him no fault *at all.*

(SIXTH DAY OF THE WEEK.) *Jerusalem.*

CHAPTER XXIII. 6-12.

6 When Pilate heard of Galilee,[458] he asked whether the man were a Galilean.

7 And as soon as he knew that he belonged unto Herod's jurisdiction, he sent him to Herod, who himself was also at Jerusalem at that time.[459]

8 And when Herod saw Jesus, he was exceeding glad: for he was desirous to see him of a long *season*, because he had heard many things of him; and he hoped to have seen some miracle done by him.[460]

Pilate nor Herod were residents at Jerusalem; and the manner of the insinuation deserves notice, as a mark of conscious veracity in the narrator. Now it appears from Josephus that this Herod was the very opposite of his successor, Herod Agrippa; the former being partial to the Greeks, and a hater of the Jews; while the latter so loved the Jews that he took pleasure in constantly dwelling at Jerusalem. It is therefore evident that Herod's presence at Jerusalem at this time was merely casual; so that of Pilate certainly was, the Roman governors residing at Cæsarea. See Josephus, Ant. xviii. iv. § 1.—xix. vii. § 3.—xx. iv. § 4. BLUNT, Veracity, &c. sect. II. 11.

§ 147. Jesus before Herod.

MATTHEW.	MARK.

§ 148. Pilate seeks to release Jesus. The Jews demand

MATTHEW.

CHAPTER XXVII. 15-26.

15 Now at *that* feast, the governor was wont to release unto the people a prisoner, whom they would.[436]

16 And they had then a notable prisoner, called Barabbas.

17 Therefore, when they were gathered together, Pilate said unto them, Whom will ye that I release unto you? Barabbas, or Jesus, which is called Christ?

18 (For he knew that for envy they had delivered him.)

19 When he was set down on the judgment-seat, his wife sent unto him, saying, Have thou nothing to do with that just man: for I have suffered many things this day in a dream, because of him.

20 But the chief priests and elders persuaded the multitude that they should ask Barabbas, and destroy Jesus.

21 The governor answered and said unto them, Whether of the twain, will ye that I release unto you? They said, Barabbas.

22 Pilate said unto them, What shall I do then with Jesus, which is called Christ? *They* all say unto him,[437] Let him be crucified.

23 And the governor said,[438] Why! what evil hath he done? But they cried out the more, saying, Let him be crucified.

24 When Pilate saw that he could

MARK.

CHAPTER XV. 6-15.

6 Now at *that* feast he released unto them one prisoner, whomsoever they desired.

7 And there was *one* named Barabbas, *which lay* bound with them that had made insurrection with him, who had committed murder in the insurrection.

8 And the multitude crying aloud, began to desire *him to do* as he had ever done unto them.[380]

9 But Pilate answered them, saying, Will ye that I release unto you the King of the Jews?

10 (For he knew[381] that the chief priests had delivered him for envy.)

11 But the chief priests moved the people that he should rather release Barabbas unto them.

12 And Pilate answered, and said again unto them, What will ye then, that I shall do *unto him* whom ye call the King of the Jews?[382]

13 And they cried out again, Crucify him.

14 Then Pilate said unto them, Why, what evil hath he done? And they cried out the more exceedingly,[383] Crucify him.

(SIXTH DAY OF THE WEEK.) *Jerusalem.*

LUKE.

CHAPTER XXIII. 6–12.

9 Then he questioned with him in many words; but he answered him nothing.[461]

10 and the chief priests and scribes stood and vehemently accused him.

11 And Herod with his men of war set him at nought, and mocked *him*, and arrayed him in a gorgeous robe, and sent him again to Pilate.[462]

12 And the same day Pilate and Herod[463] were made friends together; for before they were at enmity between themselves.

JOHN.

Barabbas. (SIXTH DAY OF THE WEEK.) *Jerusalem.*

LUKE.

CHAPTER XXIII. 13–25.

13 And Pilate, when he had called together the chief priests, and the rulers, and the people,

14 Said unto them, Ye have brought this man unto me, as one that perverteth the people: and behold, I, having examined *him* before you, have found no fault in this man, touching those things whereof ye accuse him:

15 No, nor yet Herod: for I sent you to him;[464] and lo, nothing worthy of death is done unto him:

16 I will therefore chastise him, and release *him*.

17 [465] (For of necessity he must release one unto them at the feast.)

18 And they cried out all at once, saying, Away with this *man*, and release unto us Barabbas:

19 (Who, for a certain sedition made in the city, and for murder, was cast into[466] prison.)

20 Pilate therefore,[467] willing to release Jesus, spake again unto them.

21 But they cried, saying, Crucify *him*, crucify him.

22 And he said unto them the third time, Why, what evil hath he done? I have found no cause of death in him; I will therefore chastise him, and let *him* go.

JOHN.

CHAPTER XVIII. 39, 40.

39 But ye have a custom that I should release unto you one at the passover: will ye therefore, that I release unto you the king of the Jews?

40 Then cried they all[403] again, saying, Not this man, but Barabbas. Now Barabbas was a robber.

§ 148. Pilate seeks to release Jesus. The Jews demand

MATTHEW.
CHAPTER XXVII. 15-26.

prevail nothing, but *that* rather a tumult was made, he took water, and washed *his* hands before the multitude saying, I am innocent of the blood of this just person: see ye *to it.*[438]

25 Then answered all the people, and said, His blood *be* on us, and on our children.

26 Then released he Barabbas unto them:

MARK.
CHAPTER XV. 6-15.

15 And *so* Pilate, willing to content the people, released Barabbas unto them,

§ 149. Pilate delivers up Jesus to death. He is scourged

CHAPTER XXVII. 26-30.

26 And when he had scourged Jesus, he delivered *him* to be crucified.

27 Then the soldiers of the governor took Jesus into the common hall, and gathered unto him the whole band *of soldiers.*

28 And they stripped him,[440] and put on him a scarlet robe.

29 And when they had platted a crown of thorns, they put *it* upon his head, and a reed in his right hand: and they bowed the knee before him, and mocked him, saying, Hail, King of the Jews!

30 And they spit upon him, and took the reed, and smote him on the head.

CHAPTER XV. 15-19.

15 And delivered Jesus, when he had scourged *him*, to be crucified.

16 And the soldiers led him away into the hall, called Pretorium; and they call together the whole band;

17 And they clothed him with purple, and platted a crown of thorns, and put it about his *head*,

18 And began to salute him,[384] Hail, King of the Jews!

19 And they smote him on the head with a reed, and did spit upon him, and bowing *their* knees, worshipped him.

§ 150. Pilate again seeks to release Jesus.

Luke xxiii. 24, *gave sentence.*] The accuracy of Luke, as a man of education, is observable

Barabbas. (SIXTH DAY OF THE WEEK.) *Jerusalem.*

LUKE.

CHAPTER XXIII. 13–25.

23 And they were instant with loud voices, requiring that he might be crucified: and the voices of them, and of the chief priests prevailed.[468]

24 And Pilate gave sentence that it should be as they required.

25 And he released unto them[469] him that for sedition and murder was cast into prison, whom they had desired; but he delivered Jesus to their will.

JOHN.

and mocked. *Jerusalem.*

CHAPTER XIX. 1–3.

THEN Pilate therefore took Jesus and scourged *him.*

2 And the soldiers platted a crown of thorns, and put *it* on his head, and they put on him a purple robe,

3 And said,[404] Hail, King of the Jews! and they smote him with their hands.

(SIXTH DAY OF THE WEEK.) *Jerusalem.*

CHAPTER XIX. 4–16.

4 Philip therefore went forth again, and saith unto them, Behold, I bring him forth to you, that ye may know that I find no fault in him.[405]

5 Then came Jesus forth, wearing the crown of thorns, and the purple robe. And *Pilate* saith unto them, Behold the man!

6 When the chief priests therefore and officers saw him, they cried out, saying, Crucify *him*, crucify *him.*[406] Pilate saith unto them, Take ye him, and crucify *him:* for I find no fault in him.

7 The Jews answered him, We

---

in this statement of the formal judgment pronounced by Pilate, which is only implied in the narratives of the other Evangelists.

§ 150. Pilate again seeks to release Jesus.

MATTHEW.	MARK.

§ 151. Judas repents, and hangs himself.

CHAPTER XXVII. 3-10. 3 Then Judas, which had betrayed him, when he saw that he was condemned, repented himself, and brought again the thirty pieces of silver to the chief priests and elders,	

John xix. 14, *sixth hour*] The apparent contradiction between John and Mark, (ch. xv 25,) who mentions the third hour, is reconciled by Dr. Campbell, in a critical note upon the

(SIXTH DAY OF THE WEEK.) *Jerusalem.*

LUKE.

JOHN.

CHAPTER XIX. 4-16.

have a law, and by our law[407] he ought to die, because he made himself the Son of God.

8 When Pilate therefore heard that saying, he was the more afraid;

9 And went again[408] into the judgment-hall, and saith unto Jesus, Whence art thou? But Jesus gave him no answer.

10 Then said Pilate unto him, Speakest thou not unto me? knowest thou not, that I have power to crucify thee, and have power to release thee?[409]

11 Jesus answered, Thou couldest have no power[410] *at all* against me, except it were given thee from above: therefore he that delivered me unto thee hath the greater sin.

12 And from thenceforth Pilate sought to release him: but the Jews cried out, saying,[411] If thou let this man go, thou art not Cesar's friend. Whosoever maketh himself a king, speaketh against Cesar.

13 When Pilate therefore heard that saying, he brought Jesus forth, and sat down in the judgment-seat, in a place that is called the Pavement, but in the Hebrew, Gabbatha.[412]

14 And it was the preparation of the passover, and[413] about the sixth hour: and he saith unto the Jews, Behold your King!

15 But they cried out,[414] Away with *him*, away with *him*, crucify him. Pilate saith unto them, shall I crucify your King? The chief priests answered, We have no king but Cesar.

16 Then delivered he him therefore unto them to be crucified.

(SIXTH DAY OF THE WEEK.) *Jerusalem.*

force of the expressions in the original, which he interprets as equivalent to saying, in the one case, that it was *past three*, and in the other, that it was *towards six*. See CAMPBELL, *in loc.*

§ 151. Judas repents, and hangs himself.

MATTHEW.

CHAPTER XXVII. 3-10.

4 Saying, I have sinned in that I have betrayed the [432] innocent blood. And they said, What *is that* to us? see thou *to that*.

5 And he cast down the pieces of silver in the temple, and departed, and went and hanged himself.

6 And the chief priests took the silver pieces, and said, It is not lawful for to put them into the treasury, because it is the price of blood.

7 And they took counsel, and bought with them the potter's field, to bury strangers in.

8 Wherefore that field was called, The field of blood, unto this day.

9 Then was fulfilled that which [433] was spoken by Jeremy the prophet, saying, And they took the thirty pieces of silver, the price of him that was valued, whom they of the children of Israel did value;

10 And [434] gave them for the potter's field, as the Lord appointed me.*

MARK.

§ 152. Jesus is led away to be crucified.

CHAPTER XXVII. 31–34.

31 And after that they had mocked him, they took the robe off from him, and put his own raiment on him, and led him away to crucify *him*.

32 And as they came out, they found a man of Cyrene, Simon by name: him they compelled to bear his cross.

CHAPTER XV. 20–23.

20 And when they had mocked him, they took off the purple from him, and put his own clothes on him, and led him out crucify him.[385]

21 And they compel one Simon a Cyrenian, who passed by, coming out of the country, the father of Alexander and Rufus, to bear his cross.

* Zech, xi. 12, seq. Jer. xxxii. 6, seq.

Matt. xxvii. 9. *Jeremy.*] The passage here quoted is found in the prophecy of Zechariah, and not in Jeremiah. Dr. Lightfoot says, that anciently among the Jews the Old Testament was divided into three parts. The first, beginning with the law, was called *The Law.* The second, beginning with Psalms, was called *The Psalms.* The third, beginning, with the prophecy of Jeremiah, which anciently stood first, was called *Jeremiah*, under which name all quotations from the prophets were made. See A. CLARKE, *in loc.* JENNINGS, Jewish Antiq., pp. 594, 595. Others account for the apparent error in Matthew's quotation, by supposing that he omitted the name of the prophet, as he frequently did in his citations of scripture, and that the name of Jeremiah was inserted by a subsequent copyist. 1 HORNE'S *Introd.* p. 582.

(SIXTH DAY OF THE WEEK.) *Jerusalem.*

LUKE.	JOHN.

(SIXTH DAY OF THE WEEK.) *Jerusalem.*

CHAPTER XXIII. 26–33.	CHAPTER XIX. 16–17.
26 And as they led him away, they laid hold upon one Simon a Cyrenian, coming out of the country, and on him they laid the cross, that he might bear *it* after Jesus.	16 And they took Jesus, and led *him* away.
27 And there followed him a great company of people, and of women, which also bewailed and lamented him.[470]	17 And he bearing his cross [415]
28 But Jesus turning unto them, said, Daughters of Jerusalem, weep not for me, but weep for yourselves, and for your children.	

Mark xv. 21, *and Rufus.*] Clement, of Alexandria, and Jerome both relate that Mark wrote this Gospel at *Rome*, and we find in Romans xiv. 13, that a disciple named Rufus, of considerable note, resided in that city. Admitting that both Mark and Paul speak of the same person, which is highly probable, as they refer to the same period of time and to a disciple of distinction, there is an evident consciousness of veracity in the Evangelist, in making this reference to Rufus, then living among them, since he could not but have known the particulars of the crucifixion, in which his own father was so intimately concerned. BLUNT'S Veracity, &c., sect. i. 13. See also EUSEBIUS, lib. 2, ch. 15.

§ 152. **Jesus is led away to be crucified.**

MATTHEW.
CHAPTER XXVII. 31–34.

33 And when they were come unto a place called Golgotha,[441] that is to say, A place of a skull,

34 They gave him vinegar[442] to drink, mingled with gall: and when he had tasted *thereof*, he would not drink.

MARK.
CHAPTER XV. 20–23.

22 And they bring him unto the place Golgotha,[386] which is, being interpreted, The place of a skull.

23 And they gave him to drink,[387] wine mingled with myrrh: but he received *it* not.

§ 153. **The Crucifixion.**

CHAPTER XXVII. 35–38.

35 And they crucified him, and parted his garments, casting lots: that it might be fulfilled which was spoken by the prophet; They parted my garments among them, and upon my vesture did they cast lots.[443] *

36 And sitting down, they watched him there:

37 And set up over his head his accusation written, THIS IS JESUS THE KING OF THE JEWS.

CHAPTER XV. 24–28.

24 And when they had crucified him, they parted his garments,[388] casting lots upon them, what every man should take.

25 And it was the third hour, and they crucified him.

26 And the superscription of his accusation was written over, THE KING OF THE JEWS.

* Ps. xxii. 19.

Matt. xxvii. 37, *his accusation.*] As to the title itself, the precise wording may have differed in the different languages; and MSS. represent it differently.

But the same verbal exactness is not necessary in historians, whose aim is religious instruction, as in recorders of public inscriptions. It is enough that the Evangelists agree as to the main article, "*the King of the Jews*," referred to, John xix. 21. That their manner is to regard the sense, rather than the words, appears from many places. Compare Matt. iii. 17, and ix. 11, and xv. 27, and xvi. 6, 9, and xix. 18, and xx. 33, and xxi. 9, and xxvi. 39, 64, 70, and xxviii. 5, 6, with the parallel verses in this Harmony. Compare also John xi. 40, with ver. 23, 25. One of the most solemn and awful of our Lord's discourses is, in some parts, variously expressed. See Matt. xxvi. 28, Mark xiv. 24, Luke xxii. 20, 1 Cor. xi. 25. Now as each of these writers has beyond all doubt, faithfully represented the meaning of Christ, we see that it might be truly done in different words, or in a different form of the same words. His sentences, also, sometimes admitted a difference of arrangement; for the order in which two

(SIXTH DAY OF THE WEEK.) *Jerusalem.*

LUKE.

CHAPTER XXIII. 26–33.

29 For behold, the days are coming, in the which they shall say, Blessed *are* the barren, and the wombs that never bare, and the paps which never gave suck.*
30 Then shall they begin to say to the mountains, Fall on us; and to the hills, Cover us.†
31 For if they do these things in a green tree, what shall be done in the dry?
32 And there were also two others, malefactors, led with him to be put to death.
33 And when they were come to the place which is called Calvary,[471]

JOHN.

CHAPTER XIX. 16, 17.

went forth into a place called *the place* of a skull, which is called in the Hebrew, Golgotha.

(SIXTH DAY OF THE WEEK.) *Jerusalem.*

CHAPTER XXIII. 33, 34, 38.

33 There they crucified him, and the malefactors; one on the right hand, and the other on the left.
34 [472] Then said Jesus, Father, forgive them: for they know not what they do. And they parted his raiment, and cast lots.
38 And a superscription also was written over him, in letters of Greek, and Latin, and Hebrew, THIS IS THE KING OF THE JEWS.[476]

CHAPTER XIX. 18–24.

18 Where they crucified him, and two other with him, on either side one, and Jesus in the midst.
19 And Pilate wrote a title, and put *it* on the cross. And the writing was, JESUS OF NAZARETH, THE KING OF THE JEWS.
20 This title then read many of the Jews: for the place where Jesus was

* Is, liv. 1. † Hos. x. 8.

---

sentences, or the several members of the same sentence, are disposed by St. Matthew, is, in several places, inverted by St. Mark. And with regard to his actions, though the most material parts of whatever they were going to relate, must command their attention, yet there was no such superior attraction in one specific number and order of secondary circumstances, as could turn their thoughts absolutely and exclusively to them. This is plain from instances to the contrary. One Evangelist is sometimes distinct, while another is concise; and describes what the other passes over. TOWNSON, pp. 60-1.

We may reasonably suppose St. Matthew to have cited the Hebrew,—St. John, the Greek,—and St. Mark, the Latin, which was the shortest, and without mixture of foreign words. St. Mark is followed by St. Luke; only that he has brought down "THIS IS" from above, as having a common reference to what stood under it. NEWCOME.

§ 153. The Crucifixion.

MATTHEW. CHAPTER XXVII. 35–38.	MARK. CHAPTER XV. 24–28.
38 Then were there two thieves crucified with him: one on the right hand, and another on the left.	27 And with him they crucify [389] two thieves, the one on his right hand, and the other on his left. 28 [390] And the scripture was fulfilled, which saith, And he was numbered with the transgressors.*

§ 154. The Jews mock at Jesus on the cross. He commends

CHAPTER XXVII. 39–44.	CHAPTER XV. 29–32.
39 And they that passed by, reviled him, wagging their heads, 40 And saying, Thou that destroyest the temple, and buildest *it* in three days, save thyself. If thou be the Son of God, come down from the cross.[444] 41 Likewise also the chief priests mocking *him*, with the scribes and elders, said,[445] 42 He saved others; himself he cannot save. If he be the King [446] of	29 And they that passed by, railed on him, wagging their heads, and saying, Ah, thou that destroyest the temple, and buildest *it* in three days, 30 Save thyself, and come down [391] from the cross. 31 Likewise also the chief priests mocking, said among themselves with the scribes, He saved others; himself he cannot save. 32 Let Christ the King of Israel descend now from the cross, that we

* Is. liii. 12.

John xix. 23, *four parts.*] We have here an incidental allusion to a practice well known at that time. The malefactor about to be crucified, having borne his own cross to the place of execution, was stripped, and made to drink a stupefying potion; the cross was then laid on the ground, the sufferer distended upon it, and *four* soldiers, two on each side, were employed in driving four large nails through his hands and feet. For this service they had a right to his clothes as a perquisite. See Dr. Harwood's Introd., cited in HORNE's *Introd.*, vol. i pp. 94, 95.

Luke xxiii. 36, *vinegar.*] Here the common drink of the Roman soldiers is offered by them to Jesus on the cross, while they are deriding him; which is a different act from that in Matt. xxvii. 34, 48, as appears by the place assigned to it. NEWCOME.

Luke xxiii. 39, *one of the malefactors.*] What was true of only one of the malefactors, is

(SIXTH DAY OF THE WEEK.) *Jerusalem.*

LUKE.

JOHN.

CHAPTER XIX. 18–24.

crucified was nigh to the city: and it
was written in Hebrew, *and* Greek,
and Latin.[416]
21 Then said the chief priests of
the Jews to Pilate, Write not, The
King of the Jews; but that he said,
I am King of the Jews.
22 Pilate answered, What I have
written, I have written.

23 Then the soldiers, when they
had crucified Jesus, took his garments, and made four parts, to every
soldier a part; and also *his* coat:[417]
now the coat was without seam,
woven from the top throughout.
24 They said therefore among
themselves, Let us not rend it, but
cast lots for it whose it shall be:
that the scripture might be fulfilled,
which saith,[418] They parted my raiment among them, and for my vesture
they did cast lots. These things
therefore the soldiers did.

his mother to John. (SIXTH DAY OF THE WEEK.) *Jerusalem.*

CHAPTER XXIII. 35–37, 39–43.

35 And the people stood beholding.
And the rulers also with them[473]
derided *him*, saying, He saved others;
let him save himself, if he be Christ,
the chosen of God.
36 And the soldiers also[474] mocked
him, coming to him, and offering him
vinegar,
37 And saying, If thou be the
King[475] of the Jews, save thyself.
39 And one of the malefactors,
which were hanged, railed on him,

---

attributed to both in the concise relations of Matthew and Mark; the plural being often used in the Gospels for the singular. This the Evangelists themselves show in some instances. Compare Mark vii. 17, and Matt. xv. 15; Mark v. 31, and Luke viii. 45; Matt. xiv. 17, and Mark vi. 38, Luke ix. 13, John vi. 8, 9; Matt. xxvi. 8, and Mark xiv. 4. John xii. 4, Matt. xxiv. 1, and Mark xiii. 1; Matt. xxvii. 37, and John xix. 19; Matt. xxvii. 48, and Mark xv. 36, John xix. 29. See also Luke xxii. 67. In the following places the plural is used, while the sense shows that one is spoken of. John xi. 8, Luke xx. 21, 39, and xxiv. 5, Matt. xv. 1. 12.—The Evangelists, therefore, when from attention to brevity they avoid particularizing, often attribute to many what is said or done by single persons; nor does any striking peculiarity in the case omitted, lead them to deviate from their manner; for instance, the case of Judas, Matth. xxvi. 8, and the parallel places. NEWCOME.

§ 154. **The Jews mock at Jesus on the cross. He commends**

MATTHEW.

CHAPTER XXVII. 39–44.

Israel, let him now come down from the cross, and we will believe him.

43 He trusted in God; let him deliver him now if he will have him: for he said, I am the Son of God.* [447]

44 The thieves also which were crucified with him, cast the same in his teeth.

MARK.

CHAPTER XV. 29–32.

may see and believe. And they that were crucified with him, reviled him.

§ 155. **Darkness prevails. Christ expires on the cross.**

CHAPTER XXVII. 45–50.

45 Now, from the sixth hour there was darkness over all the land [448] unto the ninth hour.

46 And about the ninth hour Jesus cried with a loud voice, saying, Eli, Eli, lama [449] sabachthani? that is to say, My God, my God, why hast thou forsaken me? †

47 Some of them that stood there, when they heard *that*, said, This *man* calleth for Elias.

48 And straightway one of them [450]

CHAPTER XV. 33–37.

33 And when the sixth hour was come, there was darkness over the whole land, until the ninth hour.

34 And at the ninth hour Jesus cried with a loud voice, saying, Eloi, Eloi, lama sabachthani? which is, being interpreted, My God, my God, why hast thou forsaken me? [392]

35 And some of them that stood by,[393] when they heard *it*, said, Behold, he calleth Elias.

36 And one ran and filled [394] a spunge

* Ps. xxii. 7, 8.

† Ps. xxii. 1.

Luke xxiii. 44, *over all the earth.*] The objection urged by infidels, upon this passage, against the veracity of the Evangelists, from the silence of profane writers concerning so remarkable an event, is met and answered by Bp. Watson in his Reply to Gibbon, Let. 5. See also HORNE'S *Introd.* Vol. 1, p. 210–216. The word translated *earth*, in Luke, is

his mother to John. (SIXTH DAY OF THE WEEK.) *Jerusalem.*

LUKE.
CHAPTER XXIII. 35-37, 39-43.

saying, If thou be Christ, save thyself and us.[477]

40 But the other answering, rebuked him, saying,[418] Dost not thou fear God, seeing thou art in the same condemnation?

41 And we indeed justly; for we receive the due reward of our deeds: but this man hath done nothing amiss.

42 And he said unto Jesus, Lord, remember me when thou comest into thy kingdom.[479]

43 And Jesus said[480] unto him, Verily, I say unto thee, To day shalt thou be with me in paradise.

JOHN.
CHAPTER XIX. 25-27.

25 Now there stood by the cross of Jesus, his mother, and his mother's sister, Mary the *wife* of Cleophas, and Mary Magdalene.

26 When Jesus therefore saw[419] his mother, and the disciple standing by whom he loved, he saith unto his mother, Woman, behold thy son!

27 Then saith he to his disciple, Behold thy mother! And from that hour that disciple took her unto his own *home*.

(SIXTH DAY OF THE WEEK.) *Jerusalem.*

CHAPTER XXIII. 44-46.

44 And it was about the sixth hour, and[481] there was a darkness over all the earth until the ninth hour.

45 And the sun was darkened,[482]

CHAPTER XIX. 28-30.

28 After this, Jesus knowing that all things were not accomplished, that the scripture might be fulfilled, saith, I thirst.*

29 Now there was set a vessel full of vinegar: and they filled a spunge

* Ps. lxix. 22.

the same which is rendered *land*, in the others, and applies equally to both. Taken in the latter sense, it may limit the darkness to Judea. But the Evangelists do not mention the degree of darkness; if, therefore, it was slight, though it extended over the whole globe, the objection of its not being recorded by Pliny or Seneca vanishes at once.

§ 155. Darkness prevails. Christ expires on the cross.

MATTHEW. CHAPTER XXVII. 45–50.	MARK. CHAPTER XV. 33–37.
ran, and took a spunge, and filled *it* with vinegar, and put *it* on a reed, and gave him to drink.	full of vinegar, and put *it* on a reed, and gave him to drink, saying, Let alone; let us see whether Elias will come to take him down.
49 The rest said, Let be, let us see whether Elias will come to save him.[451]	
50 Jesus, when he had cried again with a loud voice, yielded up the ghost.	37 And Jesus cried with a loud voice, and gave up the ghost.

§ 156. The vail of the Temple rent. The graves opened.

CHAPTER XXVII. 51–56.	CHAPTER XV. 38–41.
51 And behold, the vail of the temple was rent in twain from the top to the bottom: and the earth did quake, and the rocks rent;	38 And the vail of the temple was rent in twain, from the top to the bottom.
52 And the graves were opened,[452] and many bodies of the saints which slept, arose,	
53 And came out of the graves after his resurrection, and went[453] into the holy city, and appeared unto many.	
54 Now, when the centurion, and they that were with him, watching Jesus, saw the earthquake, and those things that were done, they feared greatly, saying, Truly this was the Son of God.	39 And when the centurion which stood over against him, saw that he so cried out, and gave up the ghost,[395] he said, Truly this man was the Son of God.
55 And many women were there[454] (beholding afar off) which followed Jesus from Galilee, ministering unto him:	40 There were also women looking on afar off, among whom was Mary Magdalene, and Mary the Mother of James the less, and of Joses, and Salome;
56 Among which was Mary Magdalene, and Mary the mother of James and Joses, and the mother of Zebedee's children.[455]	41 Who also,[396] when he was in Galilee, followed him, and ministered unto him; and many other women came up with him unto Jerusalem.

Matth. xxvii. 48, *vinegar.*] *Hil* or *Hila* was the old Syriac for *vinegar*. Hence one of the bystanders, hearing our Saviour's exclamation on the cross, thought he wanted vinegar to alleviate his thirst, and straightway filled a spunge. See BUCHANAN'S *Researches*, p. 153.

Matth. xxvii. 49, *Elias.*] The Jews gave a literal interpretation to Mal. iv. 5, expecting Elijah to appear in person, as the forerunner of the Messiah; and hence they, on this occasion, sneeringly adverted to the want of this testimony to the mission of Christ. JONES, *Lect.* 147. This incidental allusion to the popular opinion, by Matthew and Mark, may be noticed as additional evidence of their veracity.

(SIXTH DAY OF THE WEEK.) *Jerusalem.*

LUKE. CHAPTER XXIII. 44-46.	JOHN. CHAPTER XIX. 28–30.
	with vinegar, and put *it* upon hyssop,[420] and put *it* to his mouth.
46 And when Jesus had cried with a loud voice, he said, Father, into thy hands I commend my spirit: and having said thus, he gave up the ghost.	30 When Jesus therefore had received the vinegar, he said, It is finished: and he bowed his head, and gave up the ghost.

The women at the cross. (SIXTH DAY OF THE WEEK.) *Jerusalem.*

CHAPTER XXIII. 45, 47–49.	
45 And the vail of the temple was rent in the midst.	
47 Now, when the centurion saw what was done, he glorified God, saying, Certainly this was a righteous man.	
48 And all the people that came together to that sight, beholding the things which were done,[483] smote their breasts and returned.	
49 And all his acquaintance, and the women that followed him from Galilee, stood afar off, beholding these things.	

Matt. xxvii. 55, *afar off.*] This and the parallel verses are reconciled with John xix. 25, by the following observation in Wall's critical notes, p. 116. "Mary stood as yet (John xix. 25) so nigh the cross as to hear what Christ said. But at the time of his departure, Matthew, Mark, and Luke say, the women stood afar off." See also Watson's Reply to Gibbon, Let. 5, (Evangelical Family Library, Vol. xiv. pp. 276, 277). It is natural to suppose that our Lord's relations and friends, mentioned in John xix. 25, were too much struck with commiseration and grief to remain long near the cross; and that they would retire from the horror of the concluding scene. NEWCOME.

§ 157. The taking down from the cross.

MATTHEW.
CHAPTER XXVII. 57–61.

57 When the even was come, there came a rich man of Arimathea, named Joseph, who also himself was Jesus' disciple:
58 He went to Pilate, and begged the body of Jesus. Then Pilate commanded the body to be delivered.[456]

59 And when Joseph had taken the body, he wrapped it in a clean linen cloth,
60 And laid it in his own new tomb, which he had hewn out in the rock; and he rolled a great stone to the door of the sepulchre, and departed.

MARK.
CHAPTER XV. 42–47.

42 And now, when the even was come, (because it was the preparation, that is, the day before the sabbath,)
43 Joseph of Arimathea, an honourable counsellor, which also waited[397] for the kingdom of God, came, and went in boldly unto Pilate, and craved the body of Jesus.
44 And Pilate marvelled if he were already dead: and calling *unto him* the centurion, he asked him whether he had been any while dead.
45 And when he knew *it* of the centurion, he gave the body to Joseph.
46 And he bought fine linen, and took him down, and wrapped him in the linen, and laid him in a sepulchre which was hewn out of a rock, and rolled a stone unto the door of the sepulchre.[398]

Matt. xxvii. 58, *begged the body.*] Here is another of those incidental allusions to existing customs, which show the naturalness and veracity of the narrative. Those who were crucified by the Romans are said to have been usually exposed to the birds of prey; and a guard was set to prevent their friends from burying the bodies. The body of Jesus therefore could not be

The burial. *Jerusalem.*

LUKE.
CHAPTER XXIII. 50–56.

50 And behold, *there was* a man
named Joseph, a counsellor: *and he
was* a good man, and a just:[484]
51 (The same had not consented
to the counsel and deed of them :)
he was of Arimathea, a city of the
Jews; who also himself[485] waited for
the kingdom of God.
52 This *man* went unto Pilate, and
begged the body of Jesus.

53 And he took it down, and
wrapped it in linen, and laid it in a
sepulchre[486] that was hewn in stone,
wherein never man before was laid.

JOHN.
CHAPTER XIX. 31–42.
31 The Jews therefore, because it
was the preparation, that the bodies
should not remain upon the cross on
the sabbath-day (for that sabbath-
day was an high day) besought Pilate
that their legs might be broken, and
that they might be taken away.
32 Then came the soldiers, and
brake the legs of the first, and of the
other which was crucified with him.
33 But when they came to Jesus,
and saw that he was dead already,
they[421] brake not his legs.
34 But one of the soldiers with a
spear, pierced his side, and forthwith
came thereout blood and water.
35 And he that saw *it*, bare record,
and his record is true: and he knoweth that he saith true, that ye might
believe.[422]
36 For these things were done,
that the scripture should be fulfilled,
A bone of him shall not be broken.*
37 And again another scripture
saith, They shall look on him whom
they pierced.†
38 And after this Joseph of Arimathea (being a disciple of Jesus, but
secretly for fear of the Jews) besought
Pilate that he might take away the
body of Jesus: and Pilate gave *him*
leave. He came therefore and took
the body of Jesus.[423]
39 And there came also Nicodemus
(which at the first came to Jesus by
night)[424] and brought a mixture of
myrrh and aloes, about an hundred
pounds *weight.*
40 Then took they the body of
Jesus, and wound it in linen clothes
with the spices, as the manner of the
Jews is to bury.[425]
41 Now in the place where he was
crucified, there was a garden; and in
the garden a new sepulchre, wherein
was never man yet laid.

* Ex. xxii. 46. Ps. xxiv. 20. † Zech. xii. 10.

---

obtained for burial, without leave from Pilate; which the Evangelists relate was applied for but without explaining the cause.

§ 157. The taking down from the cross.

MATTHEW. CHAPTER XXVII. 57–61.	MARK. CHAPTER XV. 42–47.
61 And there was Mary Magdalene, and the other Mary, sitting over against the sepulchre.	47 And Mary Magdalene and Mary *the mother* of Joses beheld where he was laid.

§ 158. The watch at the sepulchre. (SEVENTH

CHAPTER XXI. 62-66.	
62 Now, the next day that followed the day of the preparation, the chief priests and Pharisees came together unto Pilate, 63 Saying, Sir, we remember that that deceiver said, while he was yet alive, After three days I will rise again. 64 Command therefore that the sepulchre be made sure until the third day, lest his disciples come by night,[457] and steal him away, and say unto the people, He is risen from the dead: so the last error shall be worse than the first. 65 Pilate said unto them, Ye have a watch: go your way, make *it* as sure as you can. 66 So they went and made the sepulchre sure, sealing the stone, and setting a watch.	

Matt. xxvi. 86, *setting a watch.*] The mention of this circumstance by Matthew, and not by the other Evangelist, is in perfect keeping with his previous occupation; which led him to watch for fraud, in all places where it might be perpetrated.

The burial. *Jerusalem.*

LUKE. CHAPTER XXIII. 50–56.	JOHN. CHAPTER XIX. 31–42.
54 And that day was the preparation, and [487] the sabbath drew on.	42 There laid they Jesus therefore, because of the Jews' preparation-*day;* for the sepulchre was nigh at hand.
55 And the women also,[488] which came with him from Galilee, followed after, and beheld the sepulchre, and how his body was laid.	
56 And they returned, and prepared spices and ointments; and rested the sabbath-day, according to the commandment.	

DAY OF THE WEEK, OR SABBATH.) *Jerusalem.*

Luke xxiii. 54, *drew on.*] We must not understand this word of the morning light. The Jewish sabbath began at six in the evening, before which time our Lord's body was deposited in the tomb. NEWCOME.

PART IX.

OUR LORD'S RESURRECTION,

HIS SUBSEQUENT APPEARANCES,

AND

HIS ASCENSION.

TIME *Forty days.*

§ 159. The morning of the Resurrection.

MATTHEW.	MARK.
CHAPTER XXVIII. 2–4.	CHAPTER XVI. 1.
	AND when the sabbath was past, Mary Magdalene, and Mary the *mother* of James, and Salome, had bought sweet spices, that they might come and anoint him.
2 And behold, there was a great earthquake; for the angel of the Lord descended from heaven, and came and rolled back the stone from the door,[458] and sat upon it. 3 His countenance was like lightning, and his raiment white as snow. 4 And for fear of him the keepers did shake, and became as dead *men*.	

§ 160. Visit of the women to the sepulchre. Mary

MATTHEW.	MARK.
CHAPTER XXVIII. 1.	CHAPTER XVI. 2–4.
IN the end of the sabbath, as it began to dawn toward the first *day* of the week, came Mary Magdalene, and the other Mary to see the sepulchre.	2 And very early in the morning, the first *day* of the week, they came unto the sepulchre at the rising of the sun:[399] 3 And they said among themselves, Who shall roll us away the stone from the door of the sepulchre? (4 And when they looked, they saw that the stone was rolled away,) for it was very great.

§ 161. Vision of angels in the Sepulchre.

MATTHEW.	MARK.
CHAPTER XXVIII. 5–7.	CHAPTER XVI. 5–7.
	5 And entering into the sepulchre, they saw a young man sitting on the right side, clothed in a long white garment; and they were affrighted.
5 And the angel answered and said unto the women,[459] Fear not ye: for I know that ye seek Jesus, which was crucified. 6 He is not here: for he is risen, as he said. Come, see the place where the Lord lay.[460]	6 And he saith unto them, Be not affrighted: ye seek Jesus of Nazareth,[400] which was crucified: he is risen; he is not here: behold the place where they laid him.
7 And go quickly, and tell his disciples, that he is risen from the dead, and behold, he goeth before you into Galilee; there shall ye see him: lo, I have told you.	7 But go your way, tell his disciples and Peter, that he goeth before you into Galilee: there shall ye see him, as he said unto you.

(FIRST DAY OF THE WEEK.) *Jerusalem.*

LUKE.	JOHN.

Magdalene returns. (FIRST DAY OF THE WEEK.) *Jerusalem.*

LUKE.	JOHN.
CHAPTER XXIV. 1–3. Now upon the first *day* of the week, very early in the morning, they came unto the sepulchre, bringing the spices which they had prepared, and certain *others* with them.[489]	CHAPTER XX. 1–2. The first *day* of the week cometh Mary Magdalene early, when it was yet dark, unto the sepulchre, and seeth the stone taken away from the sepulchre.[426]
2 And they found the stone rolled away from the sepulchre.	
3 And they entered in, and found not the body of the Lord Jesus.	
	2 Then she runneth, and cometh to Simon Peter, and to the other disciple whom Jesus loved, and saith unto them, They have taken away the Lord out of the sepulchre, and we know not where they have laid him.

(FIRST DAY OF THE WEEK.) *Jerusalem.*

LUKE.	JOHN.
CHAPTER XXIV. 4–8. 4 And it came to pass, as they were much perplexed thereabout, behold, two men stood by them in shining garments.[490] 5 And as they were afraid, and bowed down *their* faces to the earth, they said unto them, Why seek ye the living among the dead ? 6 He is not here, but is risen. Remember how he spake unto you when he was yet in Galilee, 7 Saying, The Son of man must be delivered into the hands of sinful men, and be crucified, and the third day rise again. 8 And they remembered his words,	

§ 162. The women return to the city. Jesus meets them.

MATTHEW.

CHAPTER XXVIII. 8-10.

8 And they departed quickly from
the sepulchre, with fear and great
joy; and did run to bring his disciples word.
9 And as they went to tell his disciples,[461] behold Jesus met them, saying, All hail. And they came, and
held him by the feet, and worshipped
him.
10 Then said Jesus unto them, Be
not afraid: go tell my brethren,[462]
that they go into Galilee, and there
shall they see me.

MARK.

CHAPTER XVI. 8.

8 And they went out quickly,[401]
and fled from the sepulchre; for they
trembled, and were amazed: neither
said they any thing to any *man;* for
they were afraid.

§ 163. Peter and John run to the Sepulchre.

§ 164. Our Lord is seen by Mary Magdalene at the

(FIRST DAY OF THE WEEK.) *Jerusalem.*

LUKE.

CHAPTER XXIV. 9–11.

9 And returned from the sepulchre, and told all these things unto the eleven, and to all the rest.

10 It was Mary Magdalene, and Joanna, and Mary *the mother* of James, and other *women that were* with them, which told these things unto the apostles.[491]

11 And their[492] words seemed to them as idle tales, and they believed them not.

JOHN.

(FIRST DAY OF THE WEEK.) *Jerusalem.*

CHAPTER XXIV. 12.

12 Then arose Peter, and ran unto the sepulchre, and stooping down, he beheld the linen clothes laid by themselves,[493] and departed, wondering in himself at that which was come to pass.

CHAPTER XX. 3–10.

3 Peter therefore went forth, and that other disciple, and came to the sepulchre.[427]

4 So they ran both together: and the other disciple did outrun Peter,[428] and came first to the sepulchre.

3 And he stooping down, *and looking in,* saw the linen clothes lying; yet went he not in.

6 Then cometh Simon Peter[429] following him, and went into the sepulchre, and seeth the linen clothes lie;

7 And the napkin that was about his head, not lying with the linen clothes, but wrapped together in a place by itself.

8 Then went in also that other disciple which came first to the sepulchre, and he saw, and believed.

9 For as yet they[430] knew not the scripture, that he must rise again from the dead.

10 Then the disciples went away again unto their own home.

Sepulchre. (FIRST DAY OF THE WEEK.) *Jerusalem.*

CHAPTER XX. 11–18.

11 But Mary stood without at the sepulchre[431] weeping: and as she wept she stooped down *and looked* into the sepulchre,

12 And seeth two[432] angels in white, sitting, the one at the head, and the other at the feet, where the body of Jesus had lain.

13 And they say unto her, Woman, why weepest thou? She saith unto

§ 164. **Our Lord is seen by Mary Magdalene at the**

MATTHEW.

MARK.
CHAPTER XVI. 9-11.

9 [402] Now, when *Jesus* was risen
early, the first *day* of the week, he appeared first to Mary Magdalene, out
of whom he had cast seven devils.

10 *And* she went and told them
that had been with him, as they
mourned and wept.
11 And they, when they had heard
that he was alive, and had been seen
of her, believed not.

§ 165. **Report of the watch.**

CHAPTER XXVIII. 11-15.
11 Now, when they were going,
behold, some of the watch came into
the city, and showed unto the chief
priests all the things that were done.
12 And when they were assembled
with the elders, and had taken counsel, they gave large money unto the
soldiers,[403]
13 Saying, Say ye, His disciples
came by night, and stole him *away*
while we slept.
14 And if this come to the governor's ears, we will persuade him,[404]
and secure you.
15 So they took the money, and
did as they were taught: and this
saying is commonly reported among
the Jews until this day.

Sepulchre. (SIXTH DAY OF THE WEEK.) *Jerusalem.*

LUKE.

JOHN.

CHAPTER XX. 11–18.

them,[433] because they have taken
away my Lord, and I know not where
they have laid him.
14 And [434] when she had thus said,
she turned herself back, and saw
Jesus standing, and knew not that it
was Jesus.
15 Jesus saith unto her, Woman,
why weepest thou? whom seekest
thou? She [435] supposing him to be the
gardener, saith unto him, Sir, if thou
have borne him hence, tell me where
thou hast laid him, and I will take
him away.
16 Jesus saith unto her, Mary. She
turned herself, and saith unto him,[436]
Rabboni, which is to say, Master.
17 Jesus saith unto her, Touch me
not: for I am not yet ascended to my
Father: but go to my brethren, and
say unto them, I ascend [437] unto my
Father and your Father, and *to* my
God and your God.
18 Mary Magdalene came and told
the disciples that she had seen the
Lord, and *that* he had spoken these
things unto her.

(FIRST DAY OF THE WEEK.) *Jerusalem.*

§ 166. Our Lord is seen of Peter; then by two disciples on the

MATTHEW.	MARK. CHAPTER XVI. 12, 13.
	12 [402] After that, he appeared in another form unto two of them, as they walked, and went into the country.

LUKE.

CHAPTER XXIV. 13-35.

13 And behold two of them went
that same day to a village called
Emmaus, which was from Jerusalem
about threescore furlongs.[494]
14 And they talked together of all
these things which had happened.
15 And it came to pass, that, while
they communed *together*, and reasoned,
Jesus himself[495] drew near, and went
with them.
15 But their eyes were holden, that
they should not know him.
17 And he said unto them, What
manner of communications *are* these
that ye have one to another, as ye
walk, and are sad?[496]
18 And the one of them, whose
name was Cleopas, answering, said
unto him, Art thou only a stranger
in Jerusalem, and hast not known
the[497] things which are come to pass
there in these days?
19 And he said unto them, What
things? And they said unto him, Concerning
Jesus of Nazareth, which was
a prophet mighty in deed and word[498]
before God, and all the people:
20 And how the chief priests and
our rulers delivered him to be condemned
to death, and have crucified
him.
21 But we trusted that it had been
he which should have redeemed
Israel: and besides all this, to-day is
the third day[499] since these things
were done.
22 Yea, and certain women also of
our company made us astonished,
which were early at the sepulchre.
23 And when they found not his
body, they came, saying, that they
had also seen a vision of angels, which
said that he was alive.
24 And certain of them which were
with us, went to the sepulchre, and
found *it* even so as the women had
said: but him they saw not.
25 Then he said unto them, O fools,
and slow of heart to believe all that
the prophets have spoken!
26 Ought not Christ to have suffered
these things, and to enter into
his glory?

JOHN.

§ **166. Our Lord is seen of Peter; then by two disciples on the**

MATTHEW.	MARK. CHAPTER XV. 12, 13.
	13 [402] And they went and told *it* unto the residue: neither believed they them.

§ **167. Jesus appears in the midst of the Apostles, Thomas being absent.**

	CHAPTER XVI. 14–18.
	14 [402] Afterward he appeared unto the eleven, as they sat at meat, and upbraided them with their unbelief, and hardness of heart, because they believed not them which had seen him after he was risen.[403]

Luke xxiv. 34, *appeared unto Simon.*] This appearance of Jesus is not alluded to by any other Evangelist; but it was a fact well known among the disciples, and is

way to Emmaus. (FIRST DAY OF THE WEEK.) *Emmaus.*

LUKE.

CHAPTER XXIV. 13–35.

27 And beginning at Moses, and
all the prophets, he expounded unto
them in all the scriptures the things [500]
concerning himself.
28 And they drew nigh unto the
village whither they went: and he
made as though he would have gone
further.
29 But they constrained him, saying,
Abide with us: for it is toward
evening, and the day is far [501] spent.
And he went in to tarry with them.
30 And it came to pass, as he sat
at meat with them, he took bread
and blessed *it*, and brake, and gave
to them.
31 And their eyes were opened,
and they knew him: [502] and he vanished
out of their sight.
32 And they said one to another,
Did not our heart burn within us
while he talked with us by the way,
and while he opened to us the scriptures?
[503]
33 And they rose up the same hour,
and returned to Jerusalem, and found
the eleven gathered together, and
them that were with them,
33 Saying, The Lord is risen indeed,
[504] and hath appeared to Simon.
35 And they told what things *were*
done in the way, and how he was
known of them in breaking of bread.

JOHN.

(EVENING FOLLOWING THE FIRST DAY OF THE WEEK.) *Jerusalem.*

CHAPTER XXIV. 36–49.

36 And as they thus spake, Jesus
himself [505] stood in the midst of them,
and saith unto them, Peace *be* unto
you.
37 But they were terrified and affrighted,
and supposed that they had
seen a spirit.
38 And he said unto them, Why are
ye troubled? and why do thoughts
arise in your hearts? [506]

CHAPTER XX. 19–23.

19 Then the same day at evening,
being the first *day* of the week, when
the doors were shut where the disciples
were assembled for fear of the
Jews, came Jesus and stood in the
midst, and saith unto them, [438] Peace
be unto you.

---

expressly stated by Paul, in 1 Cor. xv. 5,—"and that he was seen of Cephas, then of the twelve."

Mark xvi. 14, *unto the eleven.*] This appearance of Jesus is also affirmed by Paul, in 1 Cor. xv. 5.

§ 167. Jesus appears in the midst of the Apostles, Thomas being absent.

MATTHEW.

MARK.
CHAPTER XVI. 14–18.

15 [402] And he saith unto them, Go
ye into all the world, and preach the
gospel to every creature.
16 He that believeth and is baptized, shall be saved; but he that believeth not, shall be damned.
17 And these signs shall follow
them that believe: In my name shall
they cast out devils; they shall speak
with new tongues:
18 They shall take up serpents;
and if they drink any deadly thing,
it shall not hurt them; they shall
lay hands on the sick, and they shall
recover.

§ 168. Jesus appears in the midst of the Apostles, Thomas being present.

(EVENING FOLLOWING THE FIRST DAY OF THE WEEK.) *Jerusalem.*

LUKE.

CHAPTER XIV. 36-49.

39 Behold my hands and my feet,[507]
that it is I myself: handle me, and
see; for a spirit hath not flesh and
bones, as ye see me have.
40 And when he had thus spoken,
he shewed them *his* hands and *his*
feet.
41 And while they yet believed not
for joy, and wondered,[508] he said unto
them, Have ye here any meat?
42 And they gave him a piece of a
broiled fish, and of an honey-comb.[509]
43 And he took *it*, and did eat
before them.[510]
44 And he said unto them, These
are the words[511] which I spake unto
you, while I was yet with you, that
all things must be fulfilled which
were written in the law of Moses,
and[512] *in* the prophets, and *in* the
psalms, concerning me.
45 Then opened he their understanding, that they might understand
the scriptures,
46 And said unto them, Thus it is
written, and thus it behoved Christ
to suffer, and to rise[513] from the dead
the third day:
47 And that repentance and remission[544] of sins should be preached in
his name among all nations, beginning at Jerusalem.
48 And[515] ye are witnesses of these
things.
49 And behold, I send the promise
of my Father unto you: but tarry ye
in the city of Jerusalem,[516] until ye be
endued with power from on high.

JOHN.

CHAPTER XX. 19-23.

20 And when he had so said, he
shewed unto them *his* hands and his
side. Then were his disciples glad
when they saw the Lord.
21 Then said Jesus to them again,
Peace *be* unto you: as *my* Father hath
sent me, even so send I you.[439]
22 And when he had said this, he
breathed on *them*, and saith unto
them, Receive ye the Holy Ghost.
23 Whose soever sins ye remit,
they are remitted unto them;[440] *and*
whose soever *sins* ye retain, they are
retained.

(EVENING FOLLOWING THE FIRST DAY OF THE WEEK.) *Jerusalem.*

CHAPTER XX. 24-29.

24 But Thomas, one of the twelve,
called Didymus, was not with them
when Jesus came.[441]
25 The other disciples therefore
said unto him, We have seen the
Lord. But he said unto them, Except
I shall see in his hands the print of
the nails, and put my finger into the
print of the nails,[442] and thrust my
hand into his side, I will not believe.
26 And after eight days again his
disciples[443] were within, and Thomas

§ 168. **Jesus appears in the midst of the Apostles, Thomas being present.**

MATTHEW.	MARK

§ 169. **The Apostles go away into Galilee. Jesus shows**

CHAPTER XXVIII. 16. 16 Then the eleven disciples went away into Galilee,	

(EVENING FOLLOWING FIRST DAY OF WEEK AFTER RESURRECTION.) *Jerusalem.*

LUKE.

JOHN.

CHAPTER XX. 24–29.

with them: *then* came Jesus, the doors
being shut, and stood in the midst,
and said, Peace *be* unto you.
27 Then said he to Thomas, Reach
hither thy finger, and behold my
hands; and reach hither thy hand,
and thrust *it* into my side; and be
not faithless, but believing.
28 And [444] Thomas answered and
said unto him, My Lord and my God.
29 Jesus saith unto him, Thomas,
because thou hast seen me, thou hast
believed: blessed *are* they that have
not seen,[445] and *yet* have believed.

himself to seven of them at the Sea of Tiberias. *Galilee.*

CHAPTER XXI. 1–24.

AFTER these things Jesus shewed
himself again to the disciples at the
sea of Tiberias: and on this wise
shewed he *himself.*
2 There were together Simon Peter,
and Thomas called Didymus, and
Nathanael of Cana in Galilee, and
the *sons* of [448] Zebedee, and two other
of his disciples.
3 Simon Peter saith unto them, I
go a fishing. They say unto him,
We also go with thee. They went
forth,[449] and entered into a ship immediately; and that night they
caught nothing.
4 But when the morning was now [450]
come, Jesus stood on the shore; but
the disciples knew not that it was
Jesus.
5 Then Jesus saith unto them,
Children, have ye any meat? They
answered him, No.
6 And he said unto them, Cast the
net on the right side of the ship, and
ye shall find. They cast therefore,
and now they were not able [451] to
draw it for the multitude of fishes.
7 Therefore that disciple whom
Jesus loved saith unto Peter, It is the
Lord. Now when Simon Peter heard
that it was the Lord, he girt *his*
fisher's coat *unto him,* (for he was
naked) and did cast himself into the
sea.
8 And the other disciples came in
a little ship (for they were not far

§ 169. The Apostles go away into Galilee. Jesus shows

MATTHEW.	MARK.

himself to seven of them at the Sea of Tiberias. *Galilee.*

LUKE.

JOHN.

CHAPTER XXI. 1–24.

from land, but as it were two hundred
cubits) dragging the net with fishes.
9 As soon then as they were come
to land, they saw a fire of coals there,
And fish laid thereon, and bread.
10 Jesus saith unto them, Bring of
the fish which ye have now caught.
11 Simon Peter[452] went up, and
drew the net to land full of great
fishes, an hundred and fifty and three:
and for all there were so many, yet
was not the net broken.
12 Jesus saith unto them, Come
and dine. And none of the disciples
durst ask him, Who art thou? knowing that it was the Lord.
13 Jesus then[453] cometh, and taketh
bread, and giveth them, and fish
likewise.
14 This is now the third time that
Jesus shewed himself to his disciples,[454]
after that he was risen from the dead.
15 So when they had dined, Jesus
saith to Simon Peter, Simon, *son* of
Jonas,[455] lovest thou me more than
these? He saith unto him, Yea, Lord:
thou knowest that I love thee. He
saith unto him, Feed my lambs.
16 He saith to him again the
second time, Simon, *son* of Jonas,[456]
lovest thou me? He saith unto him,
Yea,[457] Lord: thou knowest that I
love thee. He saith unto him, Feed
my sheep.
17 He saith unto him the third
time, Simon, *son* of Jonas, lovest thou
me? Peter was grieved because he
said unto him the third time, Lovest
thou me? And he said unto him,
Lord, thou knowest all things; thou
knowest that I love thee. Jesus saith
unto him, Feed my sheep.[458]
18 Verily, verily, I say unto thee,
When thou wast young, thou girdest
thyself, and walkedst whither thou
wouldest: but when thou shalt be
old, thou shalt stretch forth thy
hands, and another shall gird thee,
and carry *thee* whither thou wouldest
not.[459]
19 This spake he, signifying by
what death he should glorify God.
And when he had spoken this, he
saith unto him, Follow me.

§ 169. The Apostles go away into Galilee. Jesus shows

MATTHEW.	MARK.

§ 170. Jesus meets the Apostles and above five hundred

CHAPTER XXVIII. 16–20.

16 into a mountain where Jesus had appointed them.

17 And when they saw him,[465] they worshipped him: but some doubted.

18 And Jesus came, and spake unto them,[466] saying, All power is given unto me in heaven and in earth.

19 Go ye therefore [467] and teach all nations, baptizing them in the name of the Father, and of the Son, and of the Holy Ghost;

20 Teaching them to observe all things whatsoever I have commanded you: and lo, I am with you alway, *even* unto the end of the world. Amen.[468]

Matth. xxviii. 17, *they saw him.*] Many and perhaps most Harmonists and Commentators refer 1 Cor. xv. 6, to this place, where it is related that Jesus was seen of above five hundred brethren at once. Such is the opinion of Dr. Robinson and Bishop J. B. Sumner, and such seems to have been the opinion of Abp. Newcome, Dr. Macknight, and Dr. Pilkington. See

himself to seven of them at the Sea of Tiberias. *Galilee.*

LUKE.	JOHN.
	CHAPTER XXI. 1–24.
	20 Then Peter, turning about, seeth the disciple whom Jesus loved, following; (which also leaned on his breast at supper, and said, Lord, which is he that betrayeth thee?)
	21 Peter seeing him, saith to Jesus, Lord, and what *shall* this man *do?*
	22 Jesus saith unto him, If I will that he tarry till I come, what *is that* to thee? Follow thou me.
	23 Then went this saying abroad among the brethren, that that disciple should not die: yet Jesus said not unto him, He shall not die; but, if I will that he tarry till I come, what *is that* to thee?[461]
	24 This is the disciple which[462] testifieth of these things, and wrote these things: and we know that his testimony is true.

brethren on a mountain in Galilee. *Galilee.*

NEWCOME, *in loc.* The fact is deemed by some to have an important bearing upon the extent of the commission then given or repeated by our Lord; but the plan of this work does not require any further notice of the question.

§ 171. Our Lord is seen of James;

MATTHEW.	MARK.

§ 171. The title of this section is inserted, for the sake of preserving the system of arrangement which has been followed in this Harmony; but as the appearances of Jesus which are here referred to, are related only by Luke in Acts i. 3-8, and by Paul in 1 Cor. xv. 7, the par-

§ 172. The Ascension.

	CHAPTER XVI. 19, 20.
	19 So[402] then, after the Lord had spoken unto them, he was received up into heaven, and sat on the right hand of God. 20 And they went forth, and preached every where, the Lord working with *them*, and confirming the word with signs following. Amen.[403]

§ 173. Conclusion of

Luke xxiv. 50, *Bethany.*] This is perfectly consistent with the statement of Luke in Acts i. 12, as Bethany was not only the name of a town, but of a district of Mount Olivet, adjoining

then of all the Apostles. *Jerusalem.*

LUKE.	JOHN.

ticular insertion of those passages is omitted, for the reasons already given. See § 137, note. The subject of this and the eleven preceding sections, respecting the resurrection of Jesus, is discussed in the note on the Resurrection.

Bethany.

CHAPTE XXIV. 50–53.

50 And he led them out as far as
to Bethany:[517] and he lifted up his
hands, and blessed them.

51 And it came to pass, while he
blessed them, he was parted from
them, and carried up into heaven.[518]

52 And they worshipped him, and returned to Jerusalem with great [519] joy:

53 And were continually in the
temple, praising and blessing God.
Amen.[520]

John's Gospel.

CHAPTER XX. 30, 31.

30 And many other signs truly did
Jesus in the presence of his [446]disciples,
which are not written in this book.

31 But these are written that ye
might believe that Jesus is the Christ,
the Son of God: and that believing ye
might have life through his name.[447]

CHAPTER XXI. 25.

25 [463]And there are also many
other things which Jesus did, the
which, if they should be written
every one, I suppose that even the
world itself could not contain the
books that should be written. Amen.

the town. See WATSON's Reply to Gibbon, Letter vi. in Evangelical Family Library, Vol. xiv. p. [278].

APPENDIX.

THE

VARIOUS VERSIONS OF THE BIBLE:

BY

CONSTANTINE TISCHENDORF.

NOT to mention earlier English versions, in the reign of Elizabeth, in the year 1568, the English nation received at the hands of the Bishops with Parker at their head, an authorised translation of the Bible. Fifty years later King James I. ordered a revision to be undertaken by a select body of learned divines, and in this amended form, it has continued until now in the hands of everybody as The Authorized Version. Formed from the original Greek text as it was in use among Protestant theologians in the days of Elizabeth and James the First, and executed with scholarship, conscientiousness, and love, this translation of the New Testament has not only become an object of great reverence, but has deserved to be such. The English Church possesses in it a national treasure. Only the German Church inherits one equal to it, in its New Testament by the hand of Luther. But the Greek text of the Apostolic writings, has, since its origin in the first century, experienced sundry vicissitudes in the hands of faithful men who have studied and made use of it; copies continually departed more and more from the first, and in this way numerous variations obtained currency. The English Authorised Version, equally with the Lutheran translation, is based upon the editions of the Greek text which Erasmus in 1516, and Robert Stephens in 1550, had founded upon manuscripts written after the tenth century. Whether those Greek copies out of which Erasmus and Stephens prepared their editions, were altogether reliable, that is, whether they exhibited as far as possible the Apostolic text, has long been matter of earnest discussion with the learned. Since the sixteenth century, Greek manuscripts have become known far older than those of Erasmus and Robert Stephens, and besides the Greek, also Syriac, Egyptian, Latin, and Gothic, into which languages the original text was translated in the second, third and fourth centuries; moreover, in the works of the Christian Fathers who wrote in the second and following centuries, many citations from texts of the New Testament have been found and compared. What was the result? The learned saw, on the one hand, that the text of Erasmus and

Stephens had been for the most part in use in the Byzantine national Church long before the tenth century; but on the other hand, they learned the existence of thousands of readings which had not been edited by Erasmus and Stephens. Now the problem came to be, what reading in each instance most correctly represented that which the Apostles had written. This problem is by no means an easy one; for variations in the documents are very ancient; Jerome already notices them. Even in the fourth century there were diversities in very many places of the New Testament text. The learned have been and are very much divided in opinion as to which readings represent the word of God most exactly; but one thing has been admitted by most who understand the matter, and it is that the oldest documents must come nearer to the original text than those that are later.

Providence has ordered it so that the New Testament can appeal to a far larger number of all kinds of original sources than the whole of the rest of ancient Greek literature. Before all others which it possesses, Christian scholars have for a long time highly valued two manuscripts, which to great antiquity add the distinction that they contain, not merely more or fewer portions of the Sacred text, but the greater part of the entire New Testament as well as the Old. One of these manuscripts is deposited in the Vatican at Rome, and the other in the British Museum. To these, within these ten years a third has been added, brought from Mount Sinai and now at St. Petersburg. These three hold undoubtedly the first place among the many copies of the New Testament of a thousand years old; and by their authority will have to be judged and rectified, both the earlier Greek editions of the New Testament, and all existing modern translations of it. Indeed it is to be hoped that out of them a Greek text will be prepared for the good of theological science in general; and that it will be taken as the basis of new translations for the use of Christian Churches everywhere. Before this comes to pass, it is for all Christians, who highly value and esteem the Holy Scriptures, of great interest to learn to know the relation wherein the current European and American translations stand to the oldest copies of the original text of so great authority. And therefore it appeared to Baron Tauchnitz and to myself, as at once a work of piety and of learning, on the occasion of the thousandth volume of this collection, to present to English readers of the Bible an edition of the New Testament, in which they would find, along with their authorised text, the readings which vary from it in the three most ancient and important manuscripts.

This comparison of the current English text with the most ancient authorities is fitted to draw attention to the degree in which these last confirm it, as well as to the frequency with which they deviate from it. It should not be forgotten, however, that the three manuscripts of which we speak, differ among themselves both in age and importance, and that not one of them stands so high as to exclude all gainsaying of its bare authority. But it would be either unwarrantable arrogance or blameworthy indolence, to treat these primeval documents with neglect; it would be a misunderstanding of the dispensations of Providence, which have preserved these documents for fourteen or fifteen centuries, amid all the vicissitudes of time, and given them into our hands, if we were not ready most thankfully to give heed to them as instruments worthy of the highest respect for the recovery of the truth.

Is our undertaking by any possibility adverse to religion? May that which by long use for several centuries in churches and schools and houses has won respect and affection, be called in question as uncertain, and distrusted as inexact? He who should recognise irreligion in our testing and even calling into doubt that text of the Bible, respect for which simply results from common use, would greatly err. It seems to us much rather the greatest act of piety, to regard confidently as the Word of God, nothing which is not accredited and established as such by the most ancient, and also most trustworthy evidences which the Lord has placed in our hands. From this point of view and with this conviction, the writer of this introduction has for thirty years past explored the libraries of Europe as well as the recesses of monasteries in the Asiatic and African East, in search of the most ancient copies of Holy Scripture; and he has devoted his whole energy to collect all the most weighty documents of the kind, to labour upon them, to publish them for the benefit of posterity, and to restore on the basis of scientific research the very original text of the Apostles. With the same conviction he has undertaken this popular task, this work upon the English New Testament. No nation has distinguished his labours and their happy results by so extensive a reception as the English, ever since he visited London, Oxford, and Cambridge for the first time, a quarter of a century ago; he may hope then, that the same nation will receive with genuine interest the book which we now place in its hands.

But before we proceed to speak of our indication of the various readings, it is but fitting that we should give a few more specific details about the three famous manuscripts which have been employed for the undertaking.

The *Codex Vaticanus* came first into the possession of learned Europe. From what place it came into the Vatican Library is not known, but it is entered in the very first catalogue of the collection dating from 1475. It contains the Old and New Testaments. Of the New it at present contains the four Gospels, the Acts, the seven General Epistles, nine of St. Paul's Epistles, and that to the Hebrews as far as Chap. 9, 14; but all that followed this place is lost, namely, the last chapters of the Hebrews, the two Epistles to Timothy, the Epistles to Titus and Philemon, and the Revelation. The text is written in three columns to a page. The peculiarity of the handwriting, the arrangement of the manuscript, and the character of the text itself, more especially certain remarkable readings, induce the opinion that the codex is to be referred to the fourth century, and probably to about the middle of that century. During a long period the Roman Court very seldom granted access to the manuscript for any critical use of it; but in the year 1828, by the command of Leo the XIIth, the late Cardinal Angelo Mai undertook an edition of it. His edition first appeared in 1857, three years after his death, and was found to be full of mistakes. The writer of the present introduction corrected Mai's New Testament in several hundreds of passages in his *Novum Testamentum Vaticanum*, published in 1867. Still further corrections are supplied in the fac-simile edition of 1868 by Vercellone and Cozza; inserted also in the *Appendix Novi Testamenti Vaticani*, 1869.

The *Codex Alexandrinus* was, in 1628, sent as a present to King Charles I. of England, from Cyril Lucar, patriarch of Constantinople. Cyril Lucar, who had formerly been patriarch of Alexandria, brought it with him to Constantinople; and this explains why it is called the Alexandrian Codex. It is written in two columns to a page, and contains the Old and New Testaments. It is imperfect in the New Testament, having lost Matt. I, 1 to XXV, 6; John VI, 50 to VIII, 52, and 2 Cor. IV, 13 to XII, 6. It contains, however, the two epistles by Clement of Rome, which in it alone have descended to posterity; also an epistle of Athanasius, and a production by Eusebius on the Psalter. On palæographic and other grounds, it is believed to have been written in the middle of the fifth century. The New Testament was edited in 1786 by C. G. Woide, and republished with corrections by B. Harris Cowper in an octavo edition issued in 1860.

The *Codex Sinaiticus* I was so happy as to discover in 1844 and 1859 in the monastery of St. Katharine on Mount Sinai. In the year last named I was travelling in the East under the patronage of the Emperor Alexander the Second of Russia, and to him it was my good fortune to transfer the manuscript. It contains the Old and New Testaments, and is written with four columns to a page. The New Testament is perfect, not having been deprived of a single leaf. To the twenty-seven books of the New Testament are appended the Epistle of Barnabas complete, and part of the Shepherd of Hermas, which books, even at the beginning of the fourth century, were reckoned for Holy Scripture by a good many. We are led, by all the data upon which we calculate the antiquity of manuscripts, to assign the Codex Sinaiticus to the middle of the fourth century. The evidence in favour of so great an age is more certain in the case of the Sinaitic Codex, than in that of the Vatican manuscript. It is even not impossible that the Sinaitic Codex,—we cannot say as much of the Vatican MS.—formed one of the fifty copies of the Bible which in the year 331 the Emperor Constantina ordered to be executed for Constantinople under the direction of Eusebius, the bishop of Cæsarea, best known as a Church historian. In this case it must be understood that the Emperor Justinian, the founder of the Sinaitic monastery, sent it as a present from Constantinople to the monks at Sinai. The manuscript was edited by the discoverer in 1862 at the cost of the Russian Emperor Alexander II., in a form as literally exact as it was splendid; the New Testament of the same was reproduced for ordinary use in a cheaper form in 1863 and 1865.

From all that has been said it follows, that the first place for antiquity and extent, among the three chief manuscripts, belongs to the Sinaitic Codex, the second place belongs to the Vatican, and the third to the Alexandrian. This arrangement is altogether confirmed by the condition of the text of the manuscripts. That text is not only in accordance with the writing of manuscripts in the fourth and fifth centuries, the same which was read in the East in precisely those centuries; but rather, for the most part of it truly represents the text which was then copied from much earlier documents by Alexandrian scribes who knew very little of Greek, and, therefore, did not intentionally make the least alteration;—that is to say the very text which, in the third and second centuries, was spread over a great part of Christendom. In further confirmation of this idea we may refer to the agreement of our three ancient copies with the oldest translations,—the Latin, made in the second century in proconsular Africa; the Syriac version of the Gospels made at the same time, and recently brought from the Nitrian desert in Egypt to the British Museum; and the Coptic or Egyptian versions of the third century. The same opinion is also further confirmed by the agreements of the text of the three great MSS. with Irenæus, Clement of Alexandria, Origen, and others of the older Fathers of the Church. What we have been saying applies most of all to the Codex Sinaiticus, which, for example, is unapproachable in its close relation to the Latin version of the second century; it applies in a lesser degree to the Vatican MS., and still less to the Alexandrian, which, however, is far preferable in the Acts, Epistles and Revelation, to what it is in the Gospels.

There are two remarkable readings which are very instructive towards determining the age of the manuscripts and their authority, and these we shall forthwith take the liberty to lay before the reader.

1. The ordinary conclusion of the Gospel of S. Mark (chap. XVI, 9—21), is to be found in more than five hundred Greek manuscripts, in all Syriac and Coptic manuscripts, in almost all the Latin, and in the Gothic version. But Eusebius and Jerome say expressly that in nearly all correct copies of their time, S. Mark's Gospel ended with the 8th verse of the last chapter, and was without verses 9—21. With these famous accurate manuscripts of Eusebius (who died A. D. 340), there agree,—among all extant Greek MSS.,—only the Sinaitic and the Vatican.

2. In the beginning of the Epistle to the Ephesians we read, "to the saints which are at Ephesus;" but Marcion (A. D. 130—140), did not find the words "at Ephesus" in his copy. The same is true of Origen (A. D. 185--254); and Basil the Great (who died A. D. 379), affirmed that those words were wanting in *old* copies. And this omission accords very well with the encyclical or general character of the epistle. At the present day, our ancient Greek MSS., and all ancient versions, contain the words "at Ephesus;" yea, even Jerome knew no copy with a different reading. Now, only the Sinaitic and the Vatican correspond with the *old* copies of Basil, and those of Origen and Marcion.

To these examples others might be added: thus Origen says on John I, 4, that in some copies it was written, "in Him *is* life," for "in Him *was* life." This is a reading which we find in sundry quotations before the time of Origen; but now, among all known Greek MSS. it is only in the Sinaitic, and the famous old Codex Beza, a copy of the Gospels at Cambridge; yet it is also found in most of the early Latin versions, in the most ancient Syriac, and in the oldest Coptic. Again, in Matt. XIII, 35, Jerome observes that in the third century Porphyry, the antagonist of Christianity, had found fault with the Evangelist Matthew for having said, "which was spoken by the prophet Esaias." A writing of the second century had already witnessed to the same reading; but Jerome adds further that well-informed men had long ago removed the name of Esaias. Among all our MSS. of a thousand years old and upwards, there is not a solitary example containing the name of Esaias in the text referred to,—except the Sinaitic, to which a few of less than a thousand years old may be added. Once more, Origen quotes John XIII, 10, six times; but only the Sinaitic and several ancient Latin MSS. read it the same as Origen: "He that is washed needeth not to wash, but is clean every whit." In John VI, 51, also, where the reading is very difficult to settle, the Sinaitic is alone among all Greek copies indubitably correct, and Tertullian, at the end of the second century, confirms the Sinaitic reading: "If any man eat of my bread, he shall live for ever. The bread that I will give for the life of the world is my flesh." We omit to indicate further illustrations of this kind, although there are many others like them.

While the text of the English Authorised Version is faithfully represented in this work, such readings as differ from it in the three great authorities are indicated in the notes. The letter S means the Sinaitic MS., V the Vatican, and A the Alexandrian. S*, V*, A* point out any reading of S, V, or A, which has been altered by some later hand; though we give the orginal and not the altered reading in such cases. When we give an altered reading, it is marked S^2, V^2, or A^2; but as a rule, only original readings are noted, and reference is made but seldom to changes introduced by ancient correctors. The abbreviation "*om.*" signifies the omission of the word or words to which it refers; "*adds*" or "*add*," point to the omission of a word or words in one or more of our MSS. If two or more notes belong to the same words of the Text, they are divided by a comma, and not by a semicolon. If words of the Text itself are quoted, they have after them the sign :, and then follow the readings of the Codices. Sundry manifest slips of the pen which occur in the MSS., especially in those of the Alexandrian scribes, have been passed over in silence. Yet there are some which have been noted which are to be regarded as erroneous, even if not pointed out by the words "*an error*," or "*a mere error*." I have no doubt that in the very earliest ages after our Holy Scriptures were written, and before the authority of the Church protected them, wilful alterations, and especially additions, were made in them. Many various readings consist only in the forms of words and their arrangement, and are of small import. Many others did not at all require to be noticed here, because they merely relate to the Greek idiom. In some cases I have allowed myself to indicate an inaccurate or unsuitable rendering of the Greek, prefixing "*translate*," or "*all MS.*" Distinguished scholars, such as Trench, Scrivener, and Alford, whom I have usually followed in these cases, know how to supply still more of these rectifications; but a larger introduction of them was not in accordance with the plan of this work.

For no single book of classic Greek antiquity is it possible to summon three primitive witnesses comparable to the Sinaitic, the Vatican, and the Alexandrian codices, for the confirmation and rectification of its text. That we can manifestly do this in the case of the most holy and influential Book which the world possesses, calls for our profoundest gratitude to the Lord our God.

NOTES TO MATTHEW.

[*For Explanation of Abbreviations, see p.* 512.]

[1] Title : SV After Matthew.

[2] **Chapter I.** 3 V Zare [3] 5 SV Boes; SV Iobed [4] 6 SV and David (*om.* the king) begat [5] 7 SV Asaph [6] 8 SV Asaph [7] 10 SV Amos [8] 12 V Salathiel [9] 14 S* Sadoch [10] 25 SV had brought forth a son.

[11] **II.** 3 SV the king Herod [12] 6 S *om* for [13] 18 SV *om.* lamentation and [14] 21 SV and entered into

[15] **III.** 2 SV *om.* and [16] 6 S* *om.* of him: SV in the river of Jordan [17] 7 S*V to the baptism [18] 8 SV fruit [19] 10 SV *om.* also [20] 11 S for I indeed [21] 14 SV but he forbad him [22] 16 S*V *om.* unto him; [23] SV *om.* and *before* lighting

[24] **IV.** 1 V into the wilderness by the spirit [25] 3 S came , he said unto him [26] 5 S V and set him [27] 12 SV when he had heard [28] 13 SV Capharnaum [29] 18 SV he saw (*om.* Jesus) [30] 22 S* left their ship [31] 23 V And he went; S* about Galilee; S* teaching them [32] 24 V *om.* and *after* torments

[33] **V.** 1 V *om.* unto him [34] S² that mourn now [35] 16 your good works: V* your good things [36] 22 SV *om.* without a cause [37] 25 SV with him in the way; SV and the judge to the (*om.* deliver thee) [38] 27 SV *om.* by them of old time [39] 28 S* *om.* after her [40] 30 and not: S* rather than [41] 32 SV whosoever putteth away; V and whosoever marrieth her [42] 39 S on the right cheek [43] 44 SV *om.* bless them that curse you, do good to them that hate you SV. *om.* despitefully use you and [44] 45 S* *om.* and sendeth rain on the just and on the unjust [45] 46 do not even *etc.:* S* the publicans also do the same [46] 47 SV do not even the heathen the same? [47] 48 SV your heavenly Father is perfect

[48] **VI.** 1. S but take heed; SV your righteousness [49] 2 S* verily, verily, [50] 4 SV in secret, shall reward thee (*om.* openly) [51] 5 SV and when ye pray, ye shall not be [52] 6 SV *om.* openly [53] 7 V as the hypocrites *do* [54] 8 S*V for God your Father [55] 12 S*V as we have forgiven [56] 13 SV *om.* for thine is the kingdom — Amen. [57] 15 S *om.* their trespasses; S the Father forgive you your tresp. [58] 16 S* as hypocrites; S* their face; S* for verily [59] 18 S* and the Father; SV *om.* openly [60] 20 S and steal [61] 21 SV thy treasure; SV thine heart; V *om.* also [62] 22 V of the body is thine eye; S *om.* therefore [63] 25 S *om.* or what ye shall drink; S* for the body [64] 27 *translate* add to his life one span (*literally* one cubic) [65] 32 S* for God your Father [66] 33 his kingdom and righteousness, V his righteousness and kingdom [67] 34 SV shall take thought for itself

[68] **VII.** 2 VS *om.* again [69] 4 S* or how sayest thou; S to thy brother, Brother, let [70] 5 S cast out of thine own eye the beam [71] 8 V it is opened [72] 9 SV of whom his son shall ask [73] 10 SV or shall ask [74] 12 S* *om.* therefore [75] 13 S* for wide and broad is the way [76] 14 S²V² how strait [77] 22 S* cast out many devils [78] 24 SV shall be likened [79] 29 SV as their scribes

[80] **VIII.** 3 SV And he put forth; S* *om.* immediately [81] 4 S* said [82] 5 SV when he was· SV Caphar-

naum [83] 6 S* *om.* Lord [84] 7 V *om.* And; SV he saith; S* follow me, I will come [85] 8 SV but the centurion [86] 9 SV a man set under authority [87] 10 V with no man in Israel [88] 12 S* shall come out into [89] 13 SV way, as thou; SV and the servant; S* in the selfsame hour. And the centurion returning to his house in that same hour found the servant whole. [90] 15 S*V unto him [91] 16 All MSS. with a word [92] 18 S* saw multitudes, V saw a multitude [93] 21 SV of the disciples [94] 22 S but he saith, V but Jesus saith [95] 23 S into the ship [96] 25 SV and they came to him; SV save: we perish [97] 26 S* the wind [98] 28 S* when they were come; S* of the Gazerenes, V of the Gadarenes [99] 29 SV *om.* Jesus; S* to destroy us [100] 31 SV out, send us forth into the herd [101] 32 SV into the swine; SV the whole herd (*om.* of swine) ran

[102] **IX.** 2 SV *om.* thee [103] 5 SV *om.* thee; S* *om.* and [104] 8 SV they were afraid [105] 9 S* *om.* from thence; S* of custom: he saith [106] 10 S* And as they sat at meat; S* *om.* came and [107] 12 S when he heard; SV *om.* unto them; S do not need physicians [108] 13 SV *om.* to repentance [109] 14 S*V *om.* oft [110] 17 S but new wine must be put [111] 21 S* *om.* but [112] 22 S* But he turned [113] 24 SV *om.* unto them; S* to scorn, knowing that she was dead [114] 26 S her fame [115] 27 V *om.* him [116] 28 S* was entered [117] 28 S* the two blind men; S* to do this unto you [118] 31 S* *om.* all [119] 32 S *om.* man. [120] 35 S* *om.* and *before* preaching; V *om.* among the people; S* people, and they followed him [121] 36 SV because they were harassed

[122] **X.** 2 SV and James [123] 3 S *om.* and Lebbaeus, whose surname was, V *om.* Lebbaeus, whose surname was [124] 4 All MSS. the Cananite [125] 5 S* *om.* saying [126] 8 SV raise the dead, cleanse the lepers; S[2] *om.* raise the dead [127] 10 SV nor yet a staff [128] 11 S enquire in it who is [129] 12 S* salute it, saying, Peace to this house. [130] 13 SV return upon you [131] 14 S house or city or town [132] 15 S and the land of Gomorrha [133] 16 S* as the serpent [134] 25 SV Belzebul [135] 40 and he: S* but he

[136] **XI.** 2 SV he sent by his disciples [137] 5 S and the dead [138] 8 S* why went ye out? to see a man; SV *om.* raiment [139] 9 S*V why went ye out? to see a prophet? [140] 10 SV *om.* for [141] 15 V *om.* to hear [142] 16 SV calling to others [143] 17 SV *om.* unto you *after* mourned [144] 19 of her children; SV* of her works [145] 21 S sitting in sackcloth [146] 23 SV Capharnaum, shalt thou be exalted unto heaven? thou shalt be [147] 27 S* unto me of the Father [148] 29 S* *om.* of me

[149] **XII.** 4 SV and they did eat the shewbread; V a thing which it was not [150] 6 SV that something greater than the temple is here [151] 8 SV *om.* even [152] 13 S *om.* like as the other [153] 14 SV and took counsel [154] 15 SV and many followed him [155] 22 V they brought; S that the dumb spake and [156] 24 SV Belzebul [157] 25 SV And he knew [158] 27 SV Belzebul [159] 30 S scattereth me abroad [160] 31 V shall be forgiven unto you men; SV shall not be forgiven (*om.* unto men) [161] 35 SV *om.* of the heart [162] 37 S and by words [163] 38 V *om.* and of the Pharisees; SV answered him [164] 44 S* *om.* when he is come; S and swept [165] 46 S* *om.* desiring to speak with him [166] 47 S*V *om.* *this whole verse;* S[2] then said one of his disciples, Behold, thy mother and thy brethren without seek for thee [167] 49 S* the hand

[168] **XIII.** 9 S*V *om.* to hear [169] 11 S *om.* unto them [170] 14 SV and by them [171] 17 S *om.* for [172] 22 S*V of the world [173] 27 S* hath it the tares [174] 28 the servants: V they; SV say unto him [175] 29 SV saith [176] 33 S spake he unto them, saying [177] 34 not: SV nothing [178] 35 S* Esaias the prophet; S*V *om.* of the world [179] 36 SV then he sent; S and entered into [180] 37 SV *om.* unto them [181] 40 SV of the world [182] 41 S the angels [183] 42 S* and they cast them [184] 43 S*V *om.* to hear [185] 44 SV *om.* again; V *om.* all [186] 45 S*V *om.* man [187] 46 SV but when he [188] 50 S and they cast them [189] 51 SV *om.* Jesus saith unto them; SV *om.* Lord [190] 55 Joses: S John, V Joseph [191] 57 S but he said; V in his country

[192] **XIV.** 3 V For Herod had then

[193] 4 S *om.* unto him [194] 12 S* his body, and buried him [195] 14 SV and he went forth [196] 15 SV the disciples; S send therefore [197] 16 S* but he said [198] 22 S And he constrained the disciples, V And straightw. he constr. his disciples; S into the ship [199] 23 S* *om.* when he had sent the multitudes away [200] 24 V was now many furlongs distant from the land [201] 25 SV he came [202] 26 S* but when they saw him, S²V but when the disciples saw him [203] 27 S* he spake [204] 28 S If it be thou, Lord [205] 29 to go to Jesus: V and came to Jesus S* to come. Therefore he came to Jesus [206] 30 S*V* *om.* boisterous [207] 33 SV *om.* came and [208] 34 SV came to land unto Gennesaret [209] 35 S of the place

[210] **XV.** 1 SV then came to Jesus from Jerusalem Pharisees and scribes [211] 2 SV the hands [212] S* *om.* also [213] 4 V for God said; SV Honour Father [214] 5 S* by me; it is nothing [215] 6 and honour not: SV he shall not at all honour; SV *om.* or his mother; V the word of God [216] 8 SV *om.* draweth nigh unto me with their mouth, and [217] 12 SV the disciples; V and say [218] 14 S*V *om.* of the blind [219] 15 SV the parable [220] 16 SV and he said [221] 17 V *om.* yet [222] 22 SV *om.* unto him [223] 30 S blind, maimed, dumb, V maimed, blind, dumb; SV at his feet [224] 31 V the dumb to hear; S *om.* the maimed to be whole; S and the lame [225] 32 S the disciples; S² said to them V *om.* now [226] 33 SV the disciples; [227] 36 S* and the two fishes; SV and gave to the disciples [228] 38 S beside children and women [229] 39 All MS. took the ship; SV of Magadan

[230] **XVI.** 2, 3 SV *om.* When it is evening — the signs of the times [231] 4 SV the sign of Jonas [232] 5 S V the disciples [233] 6 S *om.* unto them [234] 8 SV *om.* unto them; SV ye have no bread [235] 11 SV concerning bread? but beware of [236] 12 S* not beware of the leaven of the Pharisees and of the Sadducees, but [237] 13 SV that the Son of man is? [238] 17 SV but Jesus answered [239] 19 SV *om.* And *before* I will give [240] 20 SV the disciples; S*V that he was the Christ [241] 21 S*V* Jesus Christ [242] 22 V and saith unto him rebuking [243] 26 SV for what shall a man be profited [244] 28 SV that there be

[245] **XVII.** 4 SV let me make [246] 8 SV save Jesus himself only [247] 10 S the disciples [248] 11 SV and he answered; V *om.* unto them; SV *om.* first [249] 15 S *om.* Lord SV and is sick [250] 17 S* but he answered and said unto them [251] S 18 and he was cured [252] 20 SV and he saith unto them [253] 20 SV of your little faith [254] 21 S*V *om. this verse* [255] 24 SV Capharnaum [256] 25 S he was entering [257] 26 V now when he said, Of strangers, Jesus said unto him, S now he said, Of strangers. Now when he said, Of strangers, Jesus said unto him [258] 27 a piece of money: all MSS. a stater

[259] **XVIII.** 1 V Now at the same [260] 2 SV and he called [261] 8 SV cut it off and cast it; SV maimed or halt [262] 11 SV *om. this verse* [263] 12 S* *om.* into the mountains [264] 15 SV *om.* against thee; SV go, tell him [265] 19 V again verily I say [266] 21 S* came Peter and said, V came Peter and said unto him [267] 24 S* many talents [268] 25 SV the lord; SV and wife and children [269] 26 V *om.* lord; [270] 27 V of the servant [271] 28 V *om.* same; SV *om.* me [272] 29 SV *om.* at his feet; S*V *om.* all [273] 30 S* and went [274] 31 S now they came [275] 35 SV *om.* their trespasses

[276] **XIX.** 3 V *om.* The; SV *om.* unto him; SV *om.* for a man [277] 4 SV *om.* unto them; V he who created *them* [278] 8 S Jesus saith unto them [279] 9 V *om.* and shall marry another; V causeth her to commit adultery; S *om.* and whoso marrieth — adultery [280] 10 SV the disciples say; *om.* unto him [281] 12 S* *om.* for [282] 14 S said unto them [283] 16 SV one came to him and said, Master, what; S may inherit [284] 17 SV why asketh thou me concerning what is good? He who is good is One [285] 18 *om.* unto him [286] 19 SV Honour father and mother [287] 20 S*V *om.* from my youth up [288] 21 V saith; S* become perfect [289] 22 S *om.* that saying; V great riches [290] 24 S that it is [291] 25 SV the disciples [292] 29 S* *om.* houses or.

S^2 *adds* or houses *after* or lands; V *om.* or wife; V receive manifold [293] 30 S last shall be first, and first last

[294] **XX.** 4 S into my vineyard [295] 6 SV. *om.* hour; SV *om.* idle [296] 7 S* *om.* us; SV *om.* and whatsoever — ye receive [297] 8 S and give the hire [298] 9 V but when [299] 10 V and when [300] 16 SV *om.* for many be called, but few chosen [301] 17 V but when Jesus was about to go up to Jerusalem, he took; SV apart, and in the way he said unto them [302] 18 V *om.* to death [303] 21 V but she said, Grant, [304] 22 SV *om.* and to be baptized with the baptism that I am baptized with [305] 23 SV *om.* And; SV *om.* and be baptized with the baptism that I am baptized with; V or on my left [306] 24 S they began to be much displeased with [307] 26 SV *om.* but; V it is not so [308] 29 S* *om.* him [309] 30 S Have mercy on us, Jesus, thou son V O Lord, have mercy on us, thou son [310] 31 SV O Lord, have mercy on us, thou son [311] 34 SV immediately they received

[312] **XXI.** 3 S hath need of it [313] 4 S but this [314] 7 S*V the clothes; V and he sat thereon [315] 9 SV went before him [316] 11 SV is the prophet Jesus of [317] 12 SV *om.* of God [318] 13 SV but ye make it [319] 17 S* *om.* of the city [320] 19 S* and nothing *was* thereon — and he said [321] 27 S Jesus said unto them [322] 28 S* two sons. He came; S in the vineyard [323] 29 V said, I *go* sir, and went not; S* *om.* but [324] 30 S* to the other; V said I will not: afterward he repented, and went [325] 31 SV *om.* unto him; V The last [326] V 32 neither repented afterward [327] 33 SV There was a householder [328] 36 S* And again he sent [329] 45 S but when

[330] **XXII.** 7 SV But the king was wroth [331] 10 SV* the bridechamber [332] 11 S* *om.* there [333] 13 SV *om.* and take him away; SV and cast him [334] 15 S* *om.* in *his* talk [335] 21 SV *om.* unto him [336] 23 S* And the same day came Sadducees [337] SV *om.* also [338] 29 S And Jesus answered [339] 30 V *om.* of God [340] 32 SV He is not the God [341] 35 SV *om.* and saying [342] 37 SV but he said [343] 38 SV the great and first [344] 39 S*V *om.* And; V the second *is* likewise, Thou [345] 40 S* *om.* all [346] 44 SV till I put thine enemies under thy feet

[347] **XXIII.** 3 SV *om.* observe *after* bid you; that observe and do: S* that do, S^2V that do and observe [348] 4 SV But they bind; S great heavy burdens, and lay them; SV but they themselves will not [349] 5 SV for they make; SV *om.* of their garments [350] 7 SV Rabbi *instead of* Rabbi, Rabbi [351] 8 SV *om. even* Christ [352] 9 SV your heavenly Father [353] 10 V because your master is one [354] 13 S* *om.* But [355] 14 SV *om. this verse* [356] 19 S Ye blind (*without* fools and) [357] 23 V but these ought ye [358] 26 V* the outside of it [359] 27 S* indeed they appear [360] 32 V* And ye shall fill up the measure [361] 34 SV scribes; *some* of them [362] 35 S* *om.* son of Barachias [363] 38 V *om.* desolate

[364] **XXIV.** 1 SV went out from the temple and departed [365] 2 SV But he answered and said unto them [366] 6 SV for it must come [367] 7 shall be earthquakes and famines in; V shall be famines and earthquakes in [368] 9 S* of the nations [369] 10 S and shall deliver up one another to tribulation; S *om.* and shall hate one another [370] 17 SV to take the things out of [371] 18 SV his garment [372] 22 S* were shortened *instead of* shall be shortened [373] 24 S that, if it were possible, even the elect would be deceived [374] 26 *om.* wherefore [375] 27 SV *om.* also 28 SV *om.* for [376] 30 S* and all the tribes of the earth shall mourn [377] 31 S with a great trumpet; S and he shall gather together [378] 35 S* *om. this verse* [379] 36 SV *add* nor the Son *after* not the angels of heaven [380] 37 V For as the days [381] 38 in those days that were [382] 39 V *om.* also [383] 42 SV what day [384] 45 SV the lord; S shall make ruler [385] 48 S if the evil servant; SV *om.* his coming; SV and eateth and drinketh

[386] **XXV.** 2 SV were foolish, and five *were* wise [387] 4 SV in the vessels [388] 6 SV *om.* cometh; SV *om.* him [389] 8 A oil of your oil [390] 9 S* for you and us; SV *om.* but *before* go ye [391] 13 SVA *om.* wherein the Son of man cometh [392] 16 VA^2 and gained

other; V *om.* talents [393] 17 SV *om.* And; SV *om.* he also [394] 18 A one talent; SV digged the earth [395] 20 A but he that; S received the five, came; SV *om.* besides them 22 [396] A the two came and; S *om.* Lord; SV. *om.* beside them [397] 31 SV *om.* holy [398] 33 SA on the right hand; S on his left [399] 40 V* unto one of these least, ye [400] 42 V* and I am thirsty [401] 44 S* *om.* also; SVA *om.* him

[402] **XXVI.** 3 SVA *om.* and the scribes; V* *om.* of the people [40] 4 V* *om.* and kill him [404] 8 S the disciples [405] 9 SVA for this might [406] 17 SV *om.* unto him [407] 20 SA with the twelve disciples [408] 21 S he saith [409] 22 SV *om.* of them [410] 25 S Jesus saith unto him [411] 26 A the bread, and gave thanks and brake *it* [412] 28 SV *om.* new [413] 33 SVA unto him, If (S* *om.* If) all; SVA because of thee, I will never [414] 36 SVA Gethsemani; SA unto his disciples; S *om.* here [415] 42 V *om.* saying; SVA *om.* cup; SV *om.* from me [416] 43 SV and he came again and found them asleep [417] 44 A *om.* the third time; S the same words again [418] 45 SVA to the disciples; V for behold the hour [419] 50 S but he said unto him [420] 51 V which were with him [421] 53 SV *om.* now; S* presently give me here [422] 55 SV *om.* with you [423] 56 V all his disciples [424] 59 SV *om.* and elders [425] 60 SV but found none, though many false witnesses came. At the; SV *om.* false witnesses *after* came two, A **om.* false [426] 62-63 S* *om.* Answerest thou — and said unto him [427] 63 S^2V *om.* answered and [428] 65 S* saying, Behold, he hath spoken; S heard the blasphemy [429] 70 A before them all [430] 75 SV *om.* unto him

[431] **XXVII.** 2 SV *om.* him *after* delivered; SV *om.* Pontius [432] 4 All MSS. *om.* the; V^2 betrayed just blood [433] 9 S* And that was fulfilled which; S And I took [434] 10 S and I gave [435] 11 SV *om.* unto him [436] 15 S* they asked [437] 22 SVA *om.* unto him [438] 23 SV And he said [439] 24 V *om.* just; S* but you will see [440] 28 VS^2 And they clothed him [441] 33 S unto the place Golgotha [442] 34 SV wine to drink [443] 35 SVA *om.* that it might be — did they cast lots [444] 40 SA save thyself if thou be the Son of God, and come down [445] 41 SA *om.* also; S with the elders and scribes [446] 42 SV save. He is the King [447] 43 A *om.* now; SV let him now, if he will, deliver him [448] 45 S* *om.* over all the land [449] 46 SV Eloi, Eloi; SV lema, A lima [450] 48 S *om.* of them [451] 49 SV *after* to save him *add* but another took a spear and pierced his side, and there came out water and blood [452] 52 S* *om.* And the graves were opened [453] 53 SV *om.* and went [454] 55 S were also there [455] 56 S* Among whom was Mary the *mother* of James and the Mary of Joseph and the Mary of the sons of Zebedee; Joses: S^2 Joseph [456] 58 SV commanded *it* to be delivered [457] 64 SVA *om.* by night

[458] **XXVIII.** 2 SV *om.* from the door [459] 5 S* *om.* unto the women [460] 6 SV where he lay [461] 9 SV *om.* as they went to tell his disciples [462] 10 S* go tell the brethren [463] 12 S* with the elders, they took counsel and took large money and gave it unto [464] 14 SV *om.* him [465] 17 SV *om.* him [466] 18 S* *om.* unto them [467] 19 SA *om.* therefore [468] 20 SVA* *om.* Amen

NOTES TO MARK.

[1] Title: SV After Mark; A The Gospel after *or* according to Mark.

[2] **Chapter I.** 1 S* *om.* the Son of God [3] 2 SV in Esaias the prophet; S I will send; SV *om.* before thee [4] 4 S* And John; SV John the Baptist was in the wilderness; V preaching *instead of* and preach [5] 5 S* and they of Jerusalem were all baptized [6] 8 SV *om.* indeed; S* *om.* you *after* shall baptize [7] 9 V *om.* And *before* it came to pass; SV in Jordan of John [8] 10 S descending and remaining on him [9] 11 S* a voice (*om.* came); SV in thee I am well pleased [10] 13 SVA *om.* there; A and angels [11] 14 V And after; SV the Gospel of God [12] 15 S* *om.* and saying, S^2A *om.* *only* and [13] 16 SV And as he passed along by the sea; SV and Andrew the brother of Simon; SV casting *nets* here and there into the sea, A casting a net here and there into the sea [14] 18 SV the nets [15] 19 S* *om.* a little V *om.* thence [16] 21 SV Capharnaum; S on the sabb. day he taught in the synagogue [17] 23 SV And straightway there was [18] 24 S*V *om.* Let us alone; S we know thee [19] 25 S*A* *om.* saying [20] 27 S *om.* among themselves; SV What is this? A new doctrine with authority! He commandeth even the unclean spirits [21] 28 S* *om.* immediately; S^2V spread abroad everywhere throughout; S* Judæa *instead of* Galilee [22] 29 V when he was come out of the synagogue, he entered [23] 31 SV *om.* immediately [24] 34 S* *om.* of divers diseases; S^2V because they knew that he was Christ [25] 35 V *om.* and departed [26] 37 SV And they found him, and say [27] 38 SV Let us go elsewhere into the next towns [28] 39 S* And he came to preach, S^2V And he came preaching [29] 40 V *om.* and kneeling down to him and, S *om.* to him; V Lord if thou wilt [30] 41 SV And he moved; S *om.* unto him [31] 42 SV *om.* as soon as he had spoken [32] 44 SA *om.* nothing

[33] **II.** 1 SV And when he entered again into Capharnaum after some days, it was noised [34] 2 SV *om.* straightway [35] 3 SV they come bringing unto him one sick [36] 4 SV not bring *him* unto him [37] 5 S* My son; SV *om.* thee [38] 7 SV Why doth this *man* thus speak? He blasphemeth [39] 8 V *om.* so; SV he saith; V *om.* unto them [40] 9 SV *om.* thee [41] 11 SV Arise, I say unto thee, take up [42] 12 SV And he arose, and immediately took up; V *om.* saying; S* saying, It was never so seen in Israel [43] 13 S* And they went forth again to the sea; S* resorted unto them [44] 15 SV And it cometh to pass, that he sitteth at meat in his house, and many; A came also and sat together [45] 15–16 S and there followed him also scribes of the Pharisees, and when they saw that he was eating [46] 16 V And when the scribes of the Pharisees saw that he eateth with sinners and publicans; S that your master eateth; SV *om.* and drinketh [47] 17 SVA *om.* to repentance [48] 18 SVA and the Pharisees; used to fast: *translate* were fasting; SV and the disciples of the Pharisees, A *om.* and of the Pharisees [49] 20 SVA shall they fast in that day [50] 22 SV else the wine shall burst *them;* and the wine is spilled, and the bottles will be marred: V and the wine perisheth and the bottles; S*V but new wine *must be put* into new bottles [51] 24 A why do that which is not lawful on the sabbath day [52] 25 S saith [53] 26 V *om.* How [54] 27 A for man, not man

[55] **III.** 1 SV into a synagogue [56] 2 S whether he healeth him [57] 5 SVA *om.* whole as the other [58] 7 SV Jesus with his disciples withdrew to the sea; S from Galilee and from Judæa followed him [59] 8 S* *om.* and from Idumæa; S* from beyond Jordan,

they about Tyre; SV hearing [60] 10 A also as many as had plagues [61] 13 S but they came [62] 14 SV twelve, whom also he named apostles [63] 15 SV *om.* to heal sicknesses and [64] 16 SV And he ordained the twelve, and Simon he surnamed [65] 18 All MSS. the Cananite [66] 19 S* And he went [67] 22 S Beelzebul, V Beezebul [68] 25 S that house will not be able to stand [69] 26 S* rise up against himself, he is divided and cannot stand [70] 27 SV But no man [71] 28 SVA and the blasphemies [72] 29 S but shall be in danger; SV of eternal sin [73] 31 S and his mother cometh, and his brethren, V and his mother and his brethren come; calling him: A seeking for him [74] 32 SV and they say unto him; A and thy brethren and thy sisters [75] 33 SV and my brethren [76] 34 V *om.* And *before* he looked [77] 35 V *om.* For; SVA my brother and sister

[78] **IV.** 1 SV and there gathereth unto him a very great multitude [79] 4 SVA *om.* of the air [80] 8 SV and did yield fruit, in that it sprang up and increased (*literally* springing up and increasing) [81] 9 SVA *om.* unto them [82] 10 SV the parables [83] 11 SVA Unto you is given the mystery [84] 12 SV and it should be forgiven them (*om.* their sins) [85] 15 SV that was sown in them, A that was sown out of their hearts [86] 18 SV And there are others who are; SV these are such as have heard [87] 19 SV of the world; S* and the dec. of riches choke the word, and the lusts of other things entering in, and it [88] 24 SV and more shall be given unto you (*om.* that hear) [89] 28 SVA *om.* For [90] 32 SV And when it [91] 34 V And without [92] 36 SVA other ships [93] 37 S^2V so that the ship was now full, S* *om.* so that it was now full [94] 40 SV Why are ye fearful? have ye not yet faith?

[95] **V.** 1 S*V of the Gerasenes, S^2 of the Gergesenes [96] 2 V *om.* immediately [97] 3 S and no man could any more bind him even with chains, V and no man could any more bind him even with a chain [98] 4 tame him: A bind him [99] 5 SVA he was in the tombs and in the mountains [100] 6 SV and when he [101] 7 SVA and saith; A Son of the living God? [102] 8 S And he said [103] 9 SVA And he saith unto him, My name [104] 10 A And they besought; S send him away [105] 11 SVA unto the mountain [106] 12 SV And they besought him [107] 13 SV And he gave them leave; A* *om.* unclean; SV into the sea, about two thousand, and [108] 14 SV they that fed them fled; S^2VA And they went to see [109] 15 S And they came; SV sitting, clothed [110] 18 SVA And when he cometh [111] 19 SVA And he suffered him not [112] 22 SV *om.* behold; SVA he falleth [113] 23 S and beseecheth him [114] 25 SVA And a woman [115] 27 SV had heard the things concerning Jesus [116] 28 V *om.* but; S but his garment [117] 33 S* and knowing [118] 36 SV But Jesus having casually heard the word [119] 38 SVA And they come — and he seeth [120] 40 SV in where the damsel was (*om.* lying) [121] 42 S for she was about twelve years old; and they were straightway astonished

[122] **VI.** 1 SV and cometh [123] 2 S all these things; that even etc.: SV and such mighty works which are wrought [124] 3 S of James and Joseph [125] 4 S* *om.* and among his own kin [126] 6 S And Jesus went [127] 8 SV no bread, no scrip [128] 10 A And he saith [129] 11 And whatsoever place shall not receive you; SV *om.* verily I say unto you — than for that city [130] 12 S and preached unto them [131] 14 V and they said [132] 15 SVA But others said; S And others, That it is; SVA *om.* or [133] 16 V he said, John, whom I beheaded, he is risen, S he said, He whom I beheaded, this John is risen [134] 17 A had sent forth and put John into prison, and bound him for Herodias' sake [135] 20 V knowing that he was a just man and an holy, he kept him; observed: *translate* kept; SV and when he heard him, he hesitated much [136] 22 SV came and danced, she pleased Herod, and them that sat with him. Now the king said [137] 23 S *om.* of me [138] 25 came in: S came [139] 27 SV and commanded *him* to bring his head [140] 29 S and laid him in a tomb [141] 30 S* all things, what they

had done and taught [142] 33 SVA And they saw them departing; S and many knew them; SV *om.* and came together unto him [143] 34 SV And when he came out, he saw [144] 35 S* came and said [145] 36 V and buy themselves something to eat (*om.* for they *etc.*), S and buy themselves victuals, something to eat (*om.* for they *etc.*) [146] 38 And when they knew, they say: S And they come and say, A they say unto him [147] 41 SV gave *them* to the disciples [148] 43 S and of the two fishes [149] 44 S *om.* of the loaves; VA *om.* about [150] 45 S into a ship [151] 51 SV *om.* beyond measure and wondered [152] 54 A straightway the men of that place knew him [153] 56 SV or into cities or into country

[154] **VII.** 2 SVA *om.* they found fault [155] 4 SV *om.* and of tables (*translate* of beds *or* couches) [156] 5 Then: SV And; SV with defiled hands [157] 6 SV *om.* answered and [158] 8 SV *om.* For; SV *om.* as the washing of pots and cups: and many other (A *om.* other) such like things ye do [159] 12 SV *om.* And [160] 14 SV And when he had called the people again unto him; V he saith; S Hearken and understand (*om.* unto me every one of you) [161] 15 SV which come out of the man [162] 16 SV *om. this verse* [163] 17 SV asked of him the parable [164] 18 S Do ye not yet perceive; S from without entereth, it defileth not the man [165] 21 SV proceed evil thoughts, fornications, thefts, murders [166] 22 thefts: SV adulteries [167] 23 S and they defile the man [168] 24 SV into the coasts of [169] 25 SV But straightway a woman; S and came in and [170] 27 SV And he said unto her [171] 28 S yet the dogs eat under the table of the [172] 30 SV she found her daughter laid upon the bed and the devil gone out [173] 31 SV from the coasts of Tyre he came through Sidon unto the sea [174] 32 S* his hands [175] 35 SV *om.* straightway; S and straightway the skin of his tongue [176] 37 V as he maketh

[177] **VIII.** 1 SV being again great 1 SVA he called his (S the) disciples unto him [178] 3 SV and divers of them; V are from far [179] 4 S And his disciples answered and said, From [180] 6 SV And he commandeth [181] 7 A and he blessed them; S* and he blessed and set them before *them* [182] 8 S And all did eat, V and they did eat [183] 9 S And they were four thousand, V And they were about four thousand [184] 10 S* And straightway Jesus entered; SV into the ship; V Dalmanuntha [185] 11 S seeking of him to see a sign [186] 12 V *om.* unto you [187] 13 S *om.* into the ship, A into a ship [188] 16 SV *om.* saying; V they have no bread [189] 17 V And when he knew *it;* SV have ye your heart hardened? [190] 18 S* *om.* and *before* having ears [191] 19 S and how many [192] 20 S And when the seven loaves; V *om.* and *before* when; S And they say, V And they say unto him [193] 21 S unto them, Do ye not yet understand? A unto them, How is it that ye do not yet understand? [194] 22 S^2V And they come [195] 23 A and put his hands upon *him;* V he asked him, Seest thou ought? [196] 24 SVA I see men, because I see *them* as trees, walking [197] 25 SV upon his eyes, and he saw and was restored, and saw everything clearly [198] 26 S* saying, Go not into the town, S^2V saying, Go not even into the town; SV *om.* nor tell it to any in the town [199] 27 A he asked the disciples [200] 28 SV And they told him saying [201] 29 SV And he asked them, V *om.* And *before* Peter; S the Christ, the Son of God [202] 33 A But when Jesus had turned about; SV and saith *instead of* saying [203] 35 SVA *om.* the same [204] 36 A For what shall it profit the man, SV For what profiteth it a man [205] SV For what giveth a man in exchange

[206] **IX.** 2 S into an exceeding high mountain [207] 3 SV *om.* as snow [208] 6 SV what to answer [209] 7 SV and there was a voice out of the cloud, This is [210] 11 S Why say the Pharisees and the scribes [211] 12 SV And he told them (*om.* answered and); A as it is written *instead of* and how it is wr. [212] 14 SV And when they came to the disciples, they saw; S*(VA) questioning among themselves [213] 16 SV And he asked them;

SA(V) What question ye among yourselves [214] 17 SV *om.* and said [215] 19 SVA He answereth unto them [216] 23 SV If thou canst (*om.* believe) [217] 24 And straightway: S* *om.* straightway, S²V *om.* And; SVA* *om.* with tears; SVA *om.* Lord [218] 29 S*V *om.* and fasting [219] 31 V *om.* unto them [220] 33 SV And they came to Capharnaum; SV *om.* among yourselves [221] 34 A *om.* by the way [222] 37 S one of these children; S and whosoever receiveth me [223] 38 And John answ. him saying: SV John said unto him; SV *om.* and he followeth not us; SV because he followed not us [224] 40 A against you, is on your part [225] 41 S²V in the name, that ye belong to Christ [226] 42 SV *om.* in me [227] 43 to go: S* to enter [228] 44 SV *om.* this verse [229] 45 S to enter maimed or halt into life; SV *om.* into the fire that never shall be quenched [230] 46 SV *om.* *this verse* [231] 47 SV into hell (*om.* fire) [232] 49 SV *om.* and every sacrifice shall be salted with salt

[233] **X.** 1 by the farther side: SV and the farther side [234] 2 VA And Pharisees [235] 5 SV And Jesus said [236] 6 God made: SV he made [237] 7 S and his mother; SV *om.* and cleave to his wife [238] 10 SV the disciples; SVA of this matter [239] 12 SV And if she shall put away her husband and marry another [240] 13 SVA and the disciples; SV rebuked them *instead of* rebuked those that brought them [241] 14 V *om.* and *before* forbid [242] 16 SV in his arms, and blessed them, and put his hands upon them [243] 17 A into the way, behold, a certain rich man came running [244] 19 S* *om.* Do not commit adultery, S² *reads* Do not kill, Do not commit adultery; V* *om.* Defraud not; S* and thy mother [245] 20 S And he said unto him [246] 21 A Then he beholding him; S Yet one thing; SV *om.* take up the cross [247] 23 S and said [248] 24 A But he answereth and; SV *om.* for them that trust in riches [249] 25 to go: SVA to enter [250] 26 SV saying unto him, Who [251] 27 SV *om.* And *before* Jesus; S* said [252] 28 SVA *om.* Then; S and have followed thee, what shall we have therefore? [253] 29 And Jesus *etc.*: S Jesus said unto him, Verily, V Jesus said, Verily; V or mother, or father; SV *om.* or wife; S* for the gospel (*om.* my sake and) [254] 30 S* *om.* houses and brethren and sisters and mothers (S²A *read* mother) and children and lands with persecutions [255] 33 S* *om.* and unto the scribes [256] 34 SV and shall spit upon him, and shall scourge him [257] 35 V the two sons; S saying unto him; S²V whatsoever we shall ask of thee [258] 35-37 S* Master, we would that we may sit one on thy right (*om.* That thou shouldest — Grant unto us) [259] 38 and be baptized: SV or be baptized [260] 39 SV *om.* indeed [261] 40 SV or on my left hand; S is prepared of my Father [262] 41 A they were much displeased with the two brethren [263] 42 But Jesus: SV And Jesus; and their great ones: S and the kings [264] 43 S But so is it not among you [265] 44 of you: SV among you [266] 46 SV Bartimæus, the Son of Timæus, blind and a beggar (V a blind beggar) sat by the highway side [267] 49 SV and commanded, Call him [268] 50 rose: SV sprang up [269] 52 SVA and followed him in the way

[270] **XI.** 1 A to Jerusalem and to Bethphage [271] 2 S* *om.* over against you; SVA whereon never man yet sat [272] 3 SVA he sendeth him again (A *om.* again) hither [273] 4 V a colt tied by a door without; in a place where two ways met: *translate* in a cross road [274] 6 SV as Jesus had said [275] 7 SV And they bring; S and they set *him* upon him [276] 8 SV and others *spread* branches, which they had cut out of the fields [277] 9 SV *om.* saying [278] 10 A And blessed *be;* SV *om.* in the name of the Lord [279] 11 SV And he entered into Jerusalem into the temple [280] 14 SVA And he answered [281] 15 SV and he went; A that sold and bought therein, and [282] 17 SV And he taught and said unto them (V *om.* unto them) shall be called of all nations the house of prayer: *translate* shall be called the house of prayer unto all nations [283] 18 SVA the chief priests and the scribes [284] 19 VA they went out [285] 20 S* And in the morning he passed by, and they saw

[286] 22, 23 S If you have faith in God, verily I say unto you; V *om.* For; SV he shall have it (*om.* whatsoever he saith) [287] 24 SV What things soever ye pray and desire [288] 26 SV *om. this verse* [289] 28 SV and said unto him; SV or who gave thee [290] 29 SV And Jesus said unto them [291] 30 S The baptism of John whence was it? from heaven or of men? [292] 32 SV But should we say, Of men; they feared; S* *om.* indeed [293] 33 SVA and say unto Jesus; SV. *om.* answering

[294] **XII.** 2 SV of the fruits [295] 4 S* *om.* servant; SV *om.* and at him they cast stones; SV and they wounded him in the head and entreated him shamefully [296] 5 SV *om.* again [297] 6 SV He had yet one well-beloved son, he sent him last unto them [298] 9 V *om.* therefore [299] 15 knowing: S* seeing; S* bring me a penny hither [300] 16 And they said: A they say [301] 17 SV *om.* answering; V *om.* unto them [302] 19 V and leave no child; SV should take the wife [303] 20 SVA *om.* Now [304] 21 neither left he any seed: SV and left not any seed [305] 22 A And the seven had her likewise, and left no seed, SV And the seven left no seed [306] 23 SV *om.* therefore; SV *om.* when they shall rise [307] 24 And Jesus *etc.*: SV Jesus said unto them [308] 25 S but are as angels in heaven [309] 26 *translate* in the book of Moses, at the bush, how God [310] 27 SVA but of the llving (*om.* the God); SV *om.* therefore [311] 28 perceiving: S* seeing [312] 29 And Jesus *etc.*: SV Jesus answered, The first is, Hear, O Israel [313] 30 A and with all thy mind, and with all thy soul; SV. *om.* this is the first commandment [314] 31 And the second *etc.*: SV The second is this; S but there is none [315] 32 V *om.* And *before* the scribe; SVA for he is one, (*om.* God) and there [316] 33 S with all thy heart; SV *om.* and with all the soul; S* and to love thy neighbour [317] 36 SV *om.* for; thy footstool: V under thy feet [318] 37 *om.* therefore; S* and how is he [319] 38 SV *om.* unto them [320] 41 SV and he sat [321] 43 SVA and said

[322] **XIII.** 2 SV *om.* answering [323] 5 SV And Jesus began to say unto them [324] 6 SV *om.* For [325] 7 S see that ye be not troubled; S*V *om.* for [326] 8 SV *om.* and *after* kingdom *and after* places; SV *om.* and troubles; SV the beginning [327] 9 S* *om.* to yourselves; V *om.* for *before* they [328] 11 SV And when they; SV *om.* neither do ye premeditate [329] 12 SV And the brother shall [330] 14 SV *om.* spoken of by Daniel the prophet [331] 15 SV *om.* into the house [332] 18 S*V that *it* be not [333] 22 S But false Christs; SV *om.* even [334] 25 SVA And the stars shall fall from heaven [335] 27 S And then he sendeth; V the angels [336] 32 VA of that day or hour; V no not an angel in heaven [337] 33 V *om.* and pray [338] 34 V *om.* and *before* to every man [339] 35 SV whether at even

[340] **XIV.** 2 SV For they said [341] 3 SV *om.* and *before* she brake [342] 4 SV *om.* and said [343] 5 S For the ointment might have been sold, V For this ointment *etc.* [344] 6 S For she hath [345] 7 S^2V ye may always do them good, S* ye may do good [346] 9 SV But verily I say; SV the gospel [347] 10 A *om.* one of the twelve [348] 14 SV Where is my guest-chamber [349] 15 A *om.* and prepared; SV and there make [350] 16 SV And the disciples; S* went forth into the city [351] 18 V which eat with me [352] 19 SV *om.* And *before* they began; A one by one, Is it I, Master; SV *om.* and another *said*, Is it I? [353] 20 SV And he said (*om.* answered and); A that dippeth his hand with me [354] 22 S^2V he took bread; SVA *om.* eat *after* Take [355] 24 V *om.* unto them; SV *om.* new [356] 25 S I will not drink of the fruit [357] 27 SV *om.* because of me this night [358] 30 S *om.* twice [359] 32 SVA Gethsemani; A to the disciples; V* *om.* here [360] 37 and saith: A he saith [361] 38 SV lest ye come into temptation [362] 40 SV And again he came and found them asleep, for [363] 43 A Judas Iscariot; SV *om.* great [364] 51 SV a young man (*om.* certain); SV and they laid hold on him [365] 52 SV *om.* from them [366] 53 S and *here* were assembled; A and the scribes and the elders [367] 55 A for false witness [368] 58 We heard him say: S he said; A I destroy [369] 60 V Answerest thou nothing that these

[370] 61 SA But Jesus held his peace; of the Blessed: S* of God, A of God the Blessed [371] 64 S Behold, now ye have heard [372] 66 S a maid [373] 68 SV I neither know, nor understand; SV *om.* and the cock crew [374] 69 *translate:* And the maid seeing him again began to say; V and said to them [375] 70 S* *om.* And *before* a little after; SV *om.* and thy speech agr. thereto [376] 71 S* *om.* of whom ye speak [377] 72 S *om.* the second time; S. *om.* twice

[378] **XV.** 2 SV saith [379] 4 S* *om.* saying [380] 8 crying aloud: SV coming up; SV as he was wont to do [381] 10 S* he had known; V that they had delivered him [382] 12 V What shall I do, say, to the King; A that I shall do to the King [383] 14 S* *om.* unto them; S *adds* saying *after* exceedingly [384] 18 S to salute him and to say [385] 20 S *om.* him *after* to crucify [386] 22 S* unto the Golgotha [387] 23 SV *om.* to drink [388] 24 V And they crucify him and part his garments; SA they part [389] 27 V they crucified [390] 28 SVA *om. this verse* [391] 30 SV save thyself *by* coming down [392] 34 SV *om.* saying; S lema, A lima; S* sabactani, A sibacthani, V zabaphthani; A being interpreted, God, my God, why, V being interpreted, My God, why [393] 35 A that stood there [394] 36 V And one ran, filled [395] 39 SV that he so gave up the ghost [396] 41 SV *om.* also [397] 43 which also waited: S* and himself waited [398] 46 SV *om.* and *before* took him down; S a great stone

[399] **XVI.** 2 at the rising of the sun: All MSS. when the sun was risen [400] 6 S* *om.* of Nazareth [401] 8 SVA *om.* quickly [402] 9–20 Now when *Jesus* was risen early — and confirming the word with signs following. Amen: SV *om. all these verses* [403] 14 A But afterward; A after he was risen from the dead [404] 20 A *om.* Amen.

NOTES TO LUKE.

[1] Title: SV After Luke, A The Gospel after *or* according to Luke

[2] **Chapter I.** 19 *translate* and I was sent [3] 27 S of the house and lineage of David [4] 28 V And he came in; A came unto her; SV *om.* blessed art thou among women [5] 29 SV *om.* when she saw him; SV at the saying [6] 41 S* the babe leaped in her womb for joy [7] 59 *translate* and they were calling him [8] 65 S* on all that dwelt round about them and in all the hill country of Judæa because of these sayings [9] 66 And the hand: S For the hand [10] 74 SV of enemies [11] 75 all the days of our life: SVA all our days [12] 77 A our sins [13] 78 SV shall visit us

[14] **II.** A *om.* and *before* it came [15] 3 S* And they went [16] 5 SV his espoused (*om.* wife), being [17] 9 SV *om.* lo; S* shone over them [18] 10 S* which is to all people [19] 12 V and lying, S *om.* lying [20] 14 S*V*A and on earth peace among men of good pleasure [21] 15 S the shepherds spake one to another, saying [22] 21 SVA for the circumcising of him [23] 22 SVA of their purification [24] 27 S* *om.* Jesus [25] 33 SV And his father and his mother [26] 35 S* that the bad thoughts [27] 37 S* of about seventy-four years [28] 38 SV gave thanks likewise unto God; SV for the redemption of Jerusalem [29] 39 S* And when he had performed — he returned [30] 40 SV *om.* in spirit [31] 41 every year: S* according to custom [32] 42 S* and they went up [33] 43 S* *om.* Jesus; SV and his parents knew

not *of it* [34] 44 S* *om.* and acquaintance [35] 45 SV And when they found *him* not [36] 47 V And all were astonished [37] 48 S* thy father and I seek thee [38] 49 S* that ye seek me; *translate* that I must be in my Father's house [39] 51 S*V all the sayings

[40] **III.** 4 SV *om.* saying [41] 11 S Now he answered and said [42] 13 S* And he *said*, Exact no more [43] 14 S* accuse not any falsely [44] 17 S*V Whose fan is in his hand to purge throughly his floor and to gather the wheat [45] 19 SV his brother's wife; S* *om.* and [46] 22 SV *om.* which said [47] 23 SV And Jesus himself was, when he began, about thirty years of age [48] 24 SV of Janne [49] 26 SV of Semein; SV of Josech; SV of Joda [50] 27 S* of Jonan, S²VA of Joanan; A Zorombabel [51] 28 S* of Cosa; SV of Elmadam [52] 29 SV of Jesu; S* of Eliazer; [53] 30 SV of Jonam, A of Joanan [54] 31 SV of Menna, A *om.* which was *the son* of Menan; V Mettatha; S*V of Natham [55] 32 SV of Jobel, A of Jobed; of Booz: S* of Balls, S²VA of Boos; of Salmon: S*V of Sala [56] 33 of Aminadab: S* of Adam, V *om.* which was *the son* of Aminadab; which was *the son* of Aram: SV which was *the son* of Admin, which was *the son* of Arni; V of Esron; A *om.* which was *the son* of Phares [57] 34 S* of Isac [58] 35 SVA of Seruch [59] 36 SV of Cainam [60] 37 SV of Jaret, A of Jareth; S* of Meleleel; S of Cainam

[61] **IV.** 2 SV *om.* afterward [62] 3 And: SV Now [63] 4 SV *om.* saying; SV *om.* but by every word of God [64] 5 SV And he taking him up, shewed unto him [65] 6 I give it: S* I will give it [66] 7 A it all shall [67] 8 SV *om.* Get thee behind me, Satan; SVA *om.* for [68] 9 SV Now he brought him [69] 10 S* *om.* For [70] 14 S *om.* round about [71] 18 SV *om.* to heal the brokenhearted [72] 23 SV in Capharnaum [73] 27 SVA Naiman [74] 34 SV *om.* Saying [75] 38 A Jesus arose [76] 39 S and the fever left her [77] 41 SV *om.* Christ [78] 43 S* preach the Gospel of God; SV was I sent [79] 44 of Galilee: SV of Judæa

[80] **V.** 1 S* as the people was gathered together and heard the word of God; to hear: VA and heard [81] 2 S* *om.* two [82] 3 S And he sat down in the ship and taught the people [83] 5 SV *om.* unto him [84] 6 SV their nets; brake: *translate* were breaking [85] 7 S* And he beckoned [86] 8 S* *om.* O Lord [87] 9 S* For they were astonished [88] 13 S* his hands [89] 14 S* *om.* and shew thyself to the priest [90] 15 a fame abroad of him: S* his fame [91] 15 SV *om.* by him [92] 17 SV *om.* them *after* to heal [93] 18 S men brought a man lying on a bed [94] 19 before Jesus: V before all [95] 20 SV *om.* unto him; S *om.* thee [96] 25 S before him [97] 26 A and were filled with fear, and glorified God, saying [98] 27 S and he saith [99] 29 S *om.* him; S* *om.* and of others [100] 30 SV But the Pharisees and the (V their) scribes [101] 32 S* but ungodly to repentance [102] 33 V unto him, The disciples of of John fast often [103] 34 SV And Jesus said; S* Can the children of the br. fast [104] 35-36 S and then shall they fast. In those days he spake a parable unto them [105] 36 SV No man rendeth a piece of a new garment and putteth it upon an old; A *om.* the piece; SV will make a rent; SVA will not agree with the old [106] 38 S* But they put new wine; SV *om.* and both are preserved [107] 39 SV *om.* straightway; SV The old is good

[108] **VI.** 1 SV on the sabbath, that he went through corn fields; S plucked ears of corn [109] 2 SV *om.* unto them; V *om.* to do [110] 4 How he went: V He went; S *om.* and did take [111] 5 SV unto them, The Son of man is Lord of the sabbath [112] 6 SV *om.* also [113] 7 A *om.* him *after* watched; SA whether he healeth [114] 9 SV Now Jesus said; SV I ask you whether it is lawful; A to kill *for* to destroy 10 A he said to him; S And he stretched *it* forth *for* And he did so; A *om.* whole, SV *om.* whole as the other [115] 11 A *adds* saying *after* one another [116] **14** SV and James and John and Philip [117] 15 SV And Matthew; S and James [118] 16 SV *om.* also [119] 17 SV and a great company of his disciples; S* *om.* of people; S* *adds* and Peræa *after* and Jerusalem [120] 18 SVA And

they that were vexed with unclean spirits were healed [121] 21 S Blessed *are* they which hunger now: for they shall be filled [122] 23 S* for in this manner [123] 25 SV that are full now [124] 26 SVA Woe when all; V for likewise they did to the false prophets [125] 28 SVA *om.* and *before* pray [126] 29 S* on the right cheek [127] 31 V *om.* also [128] 33 S*V For if ye do good; SV sinners also [129] 34 SV sinners also [130] 35 hoping for nothing again: S causing no one to despair; S²A shall be great in heaven [131] 36 SV *om.* also [132] 37 SV and condemn not; A that ye be not judged [133] 38 SV pressed down, shaken together, running over; SV For with what measure ye mete, it shall be; V* *om.* again [134] 39 SV Now he spake also a parable [135] 40 SV above the master; VA but every one shall be perfected as his master, S but let him be perfected as his master [136] 42 Either how: S And how, V How [137] 43 SV neither again [138] 45 SV and the evil out of the evil bringeth forth [139] 48 SV and could not shake it, because it was well built

[140] **VII.** 1 S* *om.* all; SV into Capharnaum [141] 2 S* was ready to die (*om.* sick and) [142] 4 A saying unto him [143] 6 SV sent friends, saying (V unto him) Lord [144] 10 SV *om.* that had been sick [145] 11 S* into the city of Nain; SV and his disciples [146] 12 A there was *a man* carried out [147] 17 S* *om.* of him [148] 19 V sent *them* to the Lord [149] 20 S* When they were come [150] 21 And in that same hour: S²V in that hour, S* in that day; S* and of unclean spirits [151] 22 SV Then he answering; SV seen and heard: the blind see; SV and the deaf hear; S and to the poor [152] 28 SV *om.* For: S Verily I say; SV there is none greater than John: but [153] 30 S *om.* against themselves [154] 31 SVA *om.* And the Lord said; S Now whereunto shall I [155] 32 SV *om.* to you [156] 33 SV not eating bread [157] 35 S of all her works [158] 37 SV a woman which was in the city a sinner, and knowing [159] 38 A at the feet of Jesus, behind [160] 39 V* if he were the prophet [161] 42 Tell me therefore, which of them: SVA Which of them therefore [162] 44 SVA wiped them with her hairs [163] 47 S I said unto thee; V *the samo* also

[164] **VIII.** 2 S of unclean spirits [165] 3 V unto them [166] 8 SVA into *for* on [167] 9 SV asked him, what this parable might be [168] 10 S and hearing, they might hear and not understand [169] 12 SVA are they that have heard [170] 13 S* the word of God with joy; these have no root [171] 16 V *om.* that they which enter in, may see the light [172] 20 SV And it was told him, Thy mother [173] 21 S *om.* of God [174] 24 S and it ceased [175] 25 SV Where *is* your faith? S *om.* one to another [176] 26 S of the Gergesenes, V of the Gerasenes [177] 27 SV which had devils, and long time ware no clothes [178] 29 S* *om.* and *before* he brake [179] 30 S And he asked him [180] 32 S* and he suffered (*om.* them) [181] 33 S into the sea [182] 34 SVA *om.* and went [183] 36 SV *om.* also; S told them saying [184] 37 S of the Gergesenes, V of the Gerasenes; SV into a ship [185] 38 SV but he sent him away [186] 40 waiting for him: S* waiting for God [187] 43 V which could not be healed of any (*om.* had spent all her living upon physicians [188] 45 V *om.* and they that were with him; SV *om.* and sayest thou, Who touched me [189] 47 SVA *om.* unto him [190] 48 *om.* unto her [191] 49 SV *om.* to him; SV trouble no more [192] 50 S he said to him, Fear not, S²V he answered him, Fear not [193] 52 SV for she is not dead [194] 54 SV And he took her (*om.* put them all out, and) [195] 55 S* *om.* and she arose straightway

[196] **IX.** 1 VA he called the twelve together, S he called the twelve apostles together [197] 2 V *om.* the sick [198] 3 SV neither staff [199] 5 SV whoever receive you not [200] 7 S* *om.* the tetrarch; SV *om.* by him [201] 9 SV But Herod said [202] 10 S *om.* all; A *adds* and that they had taught *after* done, S²V privately into the city called Bethsaida, S* *om.* belonging to a city called Bethsaida [203] 12 V And when the day already began to wear away [204] 14 S Now they were; SV by about fifties [205] 17 S *om.* to them [206] 18 S and Jesus asked them: the people: A the men [207] 22 A and

rise again [208] 34 SV and it was overshadowing them [209] 35 SV my chosen Son [210] 39 S *om.* lo; S and it dasheth and teareth him [211] 43 SVA which he (A Jesus) was doing [212] 47 SV And Jesus knowing the thought [213] 48 S and whosoever receiveth me; SV the same is great [214] 50 SV But Jesus said; SVA against you; V is for you [215] 52 S* into a city [216] 54 SV And when the disciples; SV *om.* even as Elias did [217] 55 SV *om.* and said, Ye know not what manner spirit ye are of [218] 56 SVA *om.* For the Son of man — but to save them [219] 57 SV And as they went in the way; SV* *om.* Lord [220] 60 SV He said [221] 62 *om.* unto him

[222] **X.** 1 V seventy-two; V *om.* also [223] SV And he said [224] 3 A as sheep [225] 4 S* *om.* and *before* salute [226] 6 VA a son of peace [227] 11 SVA on us on our feet; SV *om.* unto you [228] 12 VA *om.* But [229] 15 SV Capharnaum; SV shalt thou be exalted to heaven? thou shalt be thrust (V come *instead of* be thrust) down to hell [230] 17 V the seventy-two [231] 19 SV I have given [232] 20 SVA *om.* rather [233] 21 SV he rejoiced in the Holy Spirit, and said [234] 22 A And he turned him unto his disciples and said, All things are [235] 24 V and to hear of me those things [236] 30 S*V *om.* And *before* Jesus [237] 32 SV when he came to the place and looked on him, passed by [238] 35 SV *om.* when he departed [239] 36 SV *om.* now [240] 37 SV Now Jesus said unto him [241] 38 SV Now as they went, he entered; V *om.* into her house [242] 39 SV^2 at the Lord's feet [243] 41 SV* And the Lord answered [244] 42 SV but there is need of few things or of one; SV for Mary hath chosen

[245] **XI.** 1 S* *om.* also [246] SV say, Father, Hallowed be thy name; V *om.* Thy will be done as in heaven, so in earth [247] 4 SV *om.* but deliver us from evil [248] 7 S and I cannot [249] 10 V it is opened [250] 14 SV he was casting out a dumb devil [251] 15 SV Beezebul, A Beelzebul; A *adds* (*after* of the devils) He answered and said, How can Satan cast out Satan [252] 18 S* Why say ye that I cast out devils through Beezebul? SV Beezebul, A Beelzebul [253] 23 S scattereth me [254] 24 S^{2}V and finding none, then he saith [255] 25 S^{2}V he findeth it empty, swept and [256] 26 S and taketh with himself seven other sp. [257] 28 S* that hear the word of God, and keep the word of God [258] 29 SA this generation is an evil generation; SV *om.* the prophet [259] 30 S. *om.* for [260] 34 SVA The light of the body is thine eye; SV when thine eye is single [261] 37 SV beseecheth him [262] 42 V* *om.* of God [263] 44 SV *om.* scribes and Pharisees, hypocrites [264] 48 SV *om.* their sepulchres [265] 49 A *om.* and *after* apostles [266] 53 SV And as he went thence, the scribes [267] 54 SV laying wait for him (S *om.* for him), to catch; A *om.* and *before* seeking; SV *om.* that they might accuse him

[268] **XII.** 2 For: VA But, S *om.* [269] 5 S *om.* But [270] 7 V *om.* therefore [271] 8 before the angels of God: S* before God [272] 15 SVA of all covetousness [273] 18 all my fruits: V all my wheat; S *om.* and my goods [274] 20 A the Lord said [275] 23 SV For the life [276] 25 *translate* can add to his life one span (*literally* one cubit) [277] 29 SV and what ye shall drink [278] 31 the kingdom of God: SV his kingdom [279] 38 SV And if he shall come in the second or (*literally* and if) in the third watch; SV blessed are they [280] 39 S* he would not have suffered [281] 40 SV *om:* therefore [282] 42 steward: S* servant; S* whom his lord made [283] 47 neither: SV or [284] 53 S and the mother against; S* against the daughter-in-law; SV against the mother-in-law [285] 54 S in the west [286] 55 S* There cometh heat [287] 56 SV that ye cannot discern this time

[288] **XIII.** 2 S And he answered and said unto them [289] 2 *translate* because they have suffered; SV these things [290] 7 V* why cumbereth it the place? [291] 9 SV And if it bear fruit after that, *well;* but if not, thou shalt [292] 15 SV But the Lord answered him; SVA Ye hypocrites [293] 19 SV *om.* great [294] 24 SV at the rstait door [295] 25 SV saying, Lord, open unto us [296] 27 S And he shall say to you, I know you not, V And he shall

speak saying unto you, I know you not [297] 28 A in his kingdom [298] 31 SVA The same hour [299] 35 SVA *om.* desolate; SVA And (S *om.*) I say unto you; SV ye shall not see me, till ye shall say

[300] **XIV.** 3 SV *add* or not *after* on the sabbath day [301] 5 V and he said unto them; VA a son or an ox [302] 7 *translate* how they were choosing out [303] 10 SVA in the presence of all that sit [304] 14 S* but thou shalt be [305] 15 S And when one of them that sat at meat with him heard it, he said, Blessed [306] 17 S for it is now ready (*literally* for things are now ready) [307] 21 SVA So the servant came; SV and the blind and the halt, A *om.* and the halt [308] 22 SV what thou hast commanded is done [309] 27 S *om.* And *before* whosoever; V Whosoever therefore [310] 31 S shall not sit down first and consult [311] 34 SV Therefore salt is good: but if even the salt

[312] **XV.** 2 A the scribes and Pharisees; S saying, He receiveth [313] 12 S* *om.* Father *before* give me [314] 16 SV And he was desiring to be fed with the husks [315] 17 SV and I perish here with hunger [316] 18 S But I will arise [317] 19 SVA I am no more (*om.* And) [318] 21 SVA in thy sight, I am no more; SV *add* make me as one of thy hired servants *after* thy son [319] 22 SV Bring forth quickly [320] 24 V *om.* again; S* *om.* And *before* they began [321] 28 SVA but his father came out [322] 32 S*V *om.* again; S he was lost (*instead of* and was lost)

[323] **XVI.** 1 SV unto the disciples; *translate* that he wasted [324] 2 S *om.* unto him; A of the stewardship [325] 3 V and to beg I am ashamed [326] 6 S said unto him, An [327] 7 S of wheat. But he said, V of wheat. He said [328] 9 V²A when it faileth [329] 14 S *om.* also [330] 16 S* *om.* and every man presseth into it [331] 18 V and he who marrieth [332] 20 SV And a certain beggar named Lazarus, was laid [333] 21 SV with that which falleth [334] 23 S* *om.* And *before* in hell [335] 25 SVA but now here he is comforted [336] 29 SVA But Abraham saith; SV *om.* unto him [337] 30 S but if one rose from the dead *and went* unto them

[338] **XVII.** 1 SVA unto his disciples [339] 3 SVA *om.* against thee [340] 4 SV *om.* in a day *before* turn; A and if seven times in a day he shall turn (SV *also* he shall turn *for* turn) [341] 6 S unto the sycamine tree [342] 8 S Make ready for me wherewith [343] 9 S²VA the servant, S* *om.* that servant; SVA *om.* him [344] 10 S* *om.* all, A all these things [345] 12 S* *om.* which stood afar off [346] 19 V *om.* thy faith hath made thee whole [347] 21 SV Lo here, or there; *translate* is among you [348] 22 A unto his disciples [349] 23 SV See there and (V or) see here; V *om.* go not after *them*, V do not follow *them* [350] 24 SVA *om.* also; V *om.* in his day [351] 27 S and took them all away [352] 28 SV *om.* also [353] 29 A brimstone and fire [354] 31 S and his stuff in his house [355] 36 SVA *om. this verse* [356] 37 SV thither also will

[357] **XVIII.** 1 SVA that they ought always [358] 11 S* *om.* with himself [359] 12 *translate* of all that I acquire [360] 13 SV But the publican; S* *om.* God [361] 20 VA and mother [362] 22 SV Now when Jesus heard; S* Thou lackest one thing (*om.* Yet) [363] 23 S when he heard all these things [364] 24 SV And when Jesus saw him (*om.* that he was very sorrowful); V How hardly do they that have riches enter [365] 29 SV house, wife, or brethren, or parents, or children [366] 37 S* *om.* him [367] 38 A *om.* Jesus [368] 39 A which went by; S Jesus thou son of David [369] 40 A And he stood [370] 41 SV *om.* Saying

[371] **XIX.** 2 S and was rich [372] 5 SV *om.* and saw him [373] 9 A in this house [374] 15 SV how much they had gained [375] 22 SV *om.* And *before* he saith [376] 26 SV *om.* For; S* *om.* unto you, S*V *om.* from him *after* away [377] 29 SV two of the disciples [378] 31 SV *om.* unto him [379] 38 S* Blessed *be* the King in the name, V Blessed *be* he who cometh King in the name [380] 40 SV *om.* unto them [381] 42 SV even thou in this day the things *which belong* unto peace; A in this day [382] 45 SV them that sold (*om.* therein, and them that bought) [383] 46 V It is written, And my house shall be; *translate* a house of prayer

[384] **XX.** 1 SV on one of the days; A the priests [385] 2 SV and spake saying unto him; S* *om.* Tell us [386] 5 SV *om.* then [387] 8 S* And he answered and said [388] 9 SV A man (*om.* certain); V* for a time [389] 13 V* *om.* What shall I do; SV *om.* when they see him [390] 14 A *om.* come [391] 19 VA And the scribes and the chief priests; S* the people, bceause he had spoken [392] 23 SV *om.* Why tempt ye me [393] 24 S Shew me a penny. And they shewed unto him *a penny.* And he said: Whose image; SV And they said [394] 27 SV which say that there is no resurrection [395] 28 SV and he be without children [396] 30–31 SV And the second and the third took her, and in like manner also the seven left no children and died [397] 31 A and the third took her in like manner, and in like manner [398] 32 S At last the woman died also [399] 33 S* (*om.* Therefore) In the resurrection whose wife (S^2 *adds* of them) shall be? [400] 34 SV *om.* answering [401] 40 SV For after that [402] 41 A how say some [403] 42 SV For David himself [404] 45 V unto the disciples

[405] **XXI.** 2 SV *om.* also [406] 4 SV *om.* of God [407] 6 SV *add* here *after* upon another [408] 8 SV *om.* therefore [409] 11 SV shall be, and in divers places famines and pestilences (V pestilences and famines) [410] 13 S*V *om.* And *before* it shall [411] 14 S* *om.* therefore [412] 15 SV to resist nor gainsay [413] 19 *translate* acquire ye *instead of* possess ye, V ye shall acquire [414] 23 V *om.* But; S* in those days, for there shall be in those days great distress [416] 25 S *adds* and *after* nations; SVA with perplexity on account of the noise of the sea and the waves [416] 34 S *om.* And *before* take heed [417] 34–35 SV come upon you unawares as a snare; for it shall come on all [418] 36 SV But watch ye and pray always, that ye may be able to escape

[419] **XXII.** 6 S* And he sought opportunity (*om.* promised and) [420] 9 V that we prepare for thee to eat the passover [421] 10 S* *om.* of water [422] 11 S saying, The Master saith; S where is my guestchamber [423] 12 S and there make ready [424] 14 S*V and the apostles [426] 16 SVA I will not eat it (A thereof) [426] 17 S* Take and divide *it* among you [427] 18 SV I will not drink henceforth [428] 19 A saying, Take, this is [429] 22 SV For truly (S* *om.* truly) the Son of man [430] 24 S *om.* also [431] 25 S* and their rulers exercise authority over them and are called [432] 29 A And I appoint unto you a covenant, as my Father hath appointed unto me a kingdom [433] 31 V *om.* And the Lord said; S said, Simon, behold [434] 34 SV until thou shalt [435] 36 SV But he said unto them [436] 37 SVA *om.* yet; SV for that which concerneth me hath an end [437] 38 S* *om.* Lord [438] 39 V* *om.* also *before* followed; SVA and the disciples [439] 43–44 S^2VA *om.* *these two verses* [440] 45 SVA to the disciples [441] 47 SVA *om.* And *before* while [442] 48 S* *om.* Judas [443] 49 SV *om.* unto him [444] 51 A *om.* And *before* Jesus; SV the ear [445] 53 S* but this is the hour and [446] 57 SV And he denied, saying; SV I know him not, woman [447] 60 SVA a cock crew [448] 61 SV *add* to-day *after* crow [449] 62 SV And he went out [450] 63 SV that held him [451] 64 SV they asked him (*om.* struck him on the face, and) [452] 67 S* *om.* you *after* I tell [453] 68 SV *om.* also; SV you will not answer (*om.* me, nor let me go) [454] 69 SVA But hereafter

[455] **XXIII.** 2 SV perverting our nation; SV and saying, that he himself [456] 3 S and saith [457] 5 S* *om.* teaching; S and beginning [458] 6 SV When Pilate heard *it* (*om.* of Galilee) [459] 7 S* at the same time [460] 8 S* When Herod (*om.* And); SV *om.* many things [461] 9 S *om.* Then; S not *for* nothing [462] 11 S And Herod also; S* *om.* again [463] 12 SV Herod and Pilate [464] 15 SV for he sent him to us [465] 17 VA *om.* this verse [466] 19 S* was in prison [467] 20 SVA But Pilate willing [468] 23 SV and their voices prevailed [469] 25 SVA *om.* unto them [470] 27 VA *om.* also; S and of women: they bewailed and lamented him [471] 33 *translate* which is called A Skull [472] 34 S^2V *om.* Then said Jesus — what they do; A *om.* Father [473] 35 S *om.* also; SV *om.* with them [474] 36 SA *om.* also [475] 37 A and say-

ing, Thou art the King [476] 38 SV was over him (*om.* written); S* of Greek, of Latin, of Hebrew, S²V *om.* in letters of Greek and Latin and Hebrew; SV The king of the Jews is this [477] 39 V *om.* saying; SV Art thou not the Christ? Save thyself [478] 40 SV answering *and* rebuking him said [479] 42 S*V and he said, Jesus, remember me; SA when thou comest in thy kingdom [480] 43 SV And he said [481] 44 S* *om.* and *before* there was [482] 45 And the sun was darkened: SV the sun being eclipesd [483] 48 SV having beheld the things, A *om.* beholding the things which were done [484] 50 V a counsellor, a good man *and* just [485] 51 SV who waited (*om.* also himself) [486] 53 S and laid him in a sepulchre [487] 54 A *om.* and *before* the sabbath [488] 55 SVA *om.* also

[489] **XXIV.** 1 SV *om.* and certain others with them [490] 4 SV in shining raiment [491] 10 A *om.* It was; S*VA *om.* which [492] 11 SV And these words [493] 12 S *om.* laid by themselves, V *om.* laid, A *om.* by themselves [494] 13 A that same hour; S about a hundred and threescore [495] 15 V* *om.* himself [496] 17 SVA* as ye walk? And they stood sad [497] 18 S these things [498] 19 S mighty in word and deed [499] 21 S we trust that it is he which shall redeem; SV and beside all this it is the third day [500] 27 S unto them, what in all the scriptures were the things [501] 29 SV is already far spent [502] 31 S* *om.* and they knew him [503] 32 V *om.* within us; SV *om.* and *before* while he opened [504] 34 SV Indeed the Lord is risen [505] 36 SV he himself [506] 38 V in your heart [507] 39 S my feet and my hands [508] 41 A believed him not and wondered for joy [509] 42 SVA *om.* and of an honeycomb [510] 43 A before all [511] 44 VA These are my words [512] 44 S. *om.* and *after* Moses [513] 46 SV Thus it is written, that the Christ would suffer and rise [514] 47 SV repentance for the remission [515] 48 SV *om.* And [516] 49 S *om.* behold; SV *om.* of Jerusalem [517] 50 SV And he led them out unto Bethany [518] 51 S* *om.* and carried up into heaven [519] 52 V* *om.* great [520] 53 A* *om.* in the temple; SV *om.* praising and; S. *om.* Amen.

NOTES TO JOHN.

[1] Title: SV After John, A The Gospel after *or* according to John.

[2] **Chapter I.** 4 S In him is life [3] 10 S* was made because of him [4] 13 V*A which were made [5] 15 S *om.* saying; S* This was he who cometh after me, who is preferred before me [6] 16 SV Because of his fulness [7] 17 S *om.* Christ [8] 18 SV the only begotten God which is (S *om.* which is) in the [9] 19 VA unto him from Jerusalem [10] 20 S *om.* but confessed [11] 21 S And they asked again; S *om.* And *after* Elias; S Art thou a prophet? [12] 24 SVA* And they were sent of the Pharisees [13] 25 S And they said unto him (*om.* asked him and) [14] 27 SV who cometh (*om.* he it is); SV *om.* is preferred before me [15] 28 SVA in Bethany; S beyond the river of Jordan [16] 29 SVA The next day he seeth [17] 32 S *om.* saying; S and abiding [18] 34 A that he is; S that this is the chosen of God [19] 37 S *om.* And *before* the two [20] 38 S *om.* Then; S *om.* unto them [21] 39 V Come and ye shall see; SVA They came therefore; SVA *om.* for; A the sixth hour [22] 40 A Now one of the two [23] 41 All MSS. *om.* the *before* Christ [24] 42 SV *om.* And *before* he brought; SVA *om.* And *before* when; SV the son of John [25] 43 SVA he would go; SVA and Jesus saith unto

him [26] 44 S *om.* Now [27] 46 S *om.* And *before* Nathanael [28] 47 S and saith of Nathanael [29] 49 S and said, Rabbi; V *om.* and saith unto him; A thou art king [30] 51 SV *om.* Hereafter

[31] **II.** 3 S* And they had no wine, because the wine of the marriage was finished. Then saith the mother of Jesus unto him, There is no wine [32] 4 VA And Jesus saith [33] 6 S *om.* set [34] 7 S And Jesus [35] 10 S *om.* unto him; SV *om.* then; S but [36] 11 S *his* glory [37] 12 SV Capharnaum; S *om.* and his disciples; A and he continued [38] 14 S that sold sheep and oxen [39] 15 S He made a scourge of small cords and drove them [40] 16 A and make not [41] 17 SV *om.* And *before* his disciples; SVA of thine house eateth me up [42] 21 S of the temple of the body [43] 22 SVA *om.* unto them

[44] **III.** 2 SVA the same came to him; S and no man [45] 3 S *om.* and said unto him [46] 5 S he cannot see the kingdom of heaven [47] 8 A or whither it goeth; S that is born of the water and of the Spirit [48] 10 *translate* the master of Israel [49] 13 SV *om.* which is in heaven [50] 15 A on him; SV should have eternal life (*om.* not perish but) [51] 16 SV the only begotten Son [52] 17 SV the Son [53] 18 SV *om.* but [54] 25 S^2VA and a Jew [55] 28 S *om.* me [56] 31 S but he that is on the earth [57] 31–32 S he that cometh from heaven, testifieth what (S* whom) he hath seen and heard [58] 34 SV for he giveth not; V* *om.* the Spirit [59] 36 S *om.* and *before* he that believeth not

[60] **IV.** 1 S When therefore Jesus knew [61] 3 AV* *om.* again [62] 6 *translate* by the well [63] 7 S a certain woman [64] 9 S The woman of Sam. saith unto him; S *om.* for the Jews have no dealings with the Samaritans. [65] 11 SV She saith unto him; S *om.* then [66] 12 he drank also thereof himself [67] 14 S *om.* him *before* shall be [68] 16 V He saith unto her [69] 17 V answered and said unto him, S *om.* and said [70] 19 S *om.* Sir [71] 20 S that it is in Jerusalem where [72] 21 SV Believe me, woman; A the hour cometh that ye shall [73] 24 S *om.* him *after* worship; S in the spirit of truth [74] 25 S he telleth us [75] 27 S said unto him [76] 30 VA *om.* Then [77] 33 S The disciples say one to another (*om.* Therefore) [78] 35–36 SVA for they are white to harvest. Already (A *adds* also) he that reapeth [79] 36 V *om.* both [80] 39 S *om.* on him; SV *om.* ever [81] 40 V were come together unto him; S and he abode with them two days [82] 42 S of thy testimony; S we have heard him ourselves; SV *om.* the Christ [83] 43 SV he departed thence into Galilee [84] 46 S So they came again, V So he came again; S* where they made [85] 46–47 S Now there was a certain nobleman, whose son was sick at Capharnaum (Capharnaum *also* V): he hearing that Jesus was come out of Jud. into Galilee, went therefore unto him [86] 47 SV *om.* him *after* besought [87] 49 A ere my son die [88] 50 SV *om.* And *before* the man; S the word of Jesus and went his way [89] 51 S the servants met him and told that his son liveth, V *om.* and told *him*, VA that his son liveth [90] 52 V the very hour wherein [91] 53 S in the which he said unto him

[92] **V.** 1 S was the feast [93] 2 by (S^2A in) the sheep *market* a pool: S a sheep pool; S Bethzatha, V Bethsaida [94] 3 SV *om.* great; SVA* *om.* waiting for the moving of the water [95] 4 SV *om.* this verse; A an angel of the Lord washed at a certain season [96] 5 S And there was a certain man which had [97] 6 S *om.* now [98] 7 A saith unto him [99] 8 A Rise and take up [100] 9 S *om.* And immediately; S whole, and rose, and took up [101] 10 SVA and it is not lawful [102] 11 SVA But he answered; S told me to take up the bed and walk [103] 12 SV They asked him *for* Then *etc.;* S told thee to take up *the bed* and walk 13 S being present [104] 14 S findeth him that had been healed in the temple, and saith [105] 15 A And the man; S departed, and said unto the Jews [106] 16 SV *om.* and sought to slay him; *translate* because he did [107] 17 SV But he answered [108] 18 S *om.* Therefore; *translate* that God was his own Father [109] 19 S Then Jesus said unto them, Verily I say [110] 25 S* *om.* and

now is; S* and when they hear, they shall live [111] 27 SA *om.* also [112] 30 S* *om.* and; SVA But the will of him that hath sent me [113] 32 S and ye know [114] 35 S *om.* and *before* ye [115] 37 SV And the Father, he which hath sent me [116] 41 A from man [117] 44 V that cometh from the only (*om.* God) [118] 45 V there is one that accuseth you to the Father [119] 47 V how believe ye my words

[120] **VI.** 2 SVA they saw the miracles [121] 3 S And Jesus went into; S* *om.* there [122] 6 S For this he said to prove him, but he himself [123] 7 S Then Philip answereth, Two; S *om.* for them; SVA *om.* of them [124] 10 S *om.* And; S* about three thousand [125] 11 VA Therefore Jesus; S and gave thanks and gave to them that were set down; VA. *om.* to the disciples, and the disciples [126] 14 S the miracle that he did, V the miracles which he did [127] 15 S and take him by force and appoint him king, he fleeth again [128] 17 S and come over the sea; SV Capharnaum; S and the darkness overtook them, and Jesus was not yet come to them [129] 20 S And he saith [130] 21 S Then they came to receive him; S whither it went [131] 22 The day following the people which stood on the other side of the sea saw that there was none other boat there, save that, whereinto the disciples of Jesus were entered, and that Jesus went not with them into the boat, but his disciples alone; A *om.* when [132] 22 VA save one (*om.* whereinto *etc.*), and that [133] 23–24 S when therefore the boats came from Tiberias, which was nigh *unto* where they did also eat bread, after that the Lord had given thanks, and when they saw that — they took shipping and came to Capharnaum [134] 23 V *om.* howbeit [135] 24 VA *om.* also; V to Capharnaum [136] 27 S but for that which; S which the Son of man giveth unto you [137] 28 A They said unto him [138] 30 S *om.* then [139] 35 V *om.* And *before* Jesus, S Then Jesus [140] 36 SA *om.* me [141] 38 S For I came not down from heaven to do [142] 39 SVA And this is the will of him which hath [143] 40 SVA For this is; SV the will of my Father, that [144] 42 S* whose father also we know; V how now saith he [145] 43 V *om.* therefore; S answered them and said [146] 44 A except he which [147] 45 SV *om.* therefore: A and hath learned the truth of the Father [148] 46 S save he which is of the Father, he hath seen God [149] 47 SV *om.* on me [150] 51 S eat of my bread; S *om.* and *after* for ever; S the bread that I will give for the life of the world, is my flesh; V *om.* which I will give *before* for the life [151] 52 S How therefore can this man [152] 53 S not everlasting life [153] 55 V is true meat; V is true drink [154] 58 S The bread which cometh down from heaven is not; SV not as the fathers did eat, and are dead [155] 59 SV in Capharnaum [156] 61 S Jesus therefore knew in himself — and he said [157] 62 S *om.* and [158] 63 S they are spirit and life [159] 64 S For the Saviour knew; S that believed, and who it was which should betray him [160] 65 S *om.* unto him; SV of the Father [161] 66 S From that *time* therefore many of the disciples [162] 68 SV *om.* Then [163] 69 SV that thou art the holy one of God [164] 70 S Jesus answered and said unto them; S and among you is a devil [165] 71 S of Judas *the son* of Simon, who was of Cariotus; S that should also betray him

[166] **VII.** 6 S *om.* Then; S is not come [167] 7 S *om.* of it [168] 8 V unto the feast; S I go not up unto this feast [169] 9 S said these words, he himself abode [170] 10 S *om.* as it were [171] 15 SV Therefore the Jews [172] 16 SV Therefore Jesus [173] 18 S and he that seeketh [174] 20 SV *om.* and said [175] 22 S *om.* therefore; S but because *it is* of the fathers [176] 26 S Do the chief priests know; SV is the Christ (*om.* very) [177] 27 S *om.* but [178] 29 S I am with him [179] 31 S than *those* which this *man* doeth [180] 32 S Now the Pharisees [181] 33 SV *om.* unto them [182] 35 S *om.* among themselves [183] 37 S let him come and drink [184] 39 S *om.* Holy; V was not yet given [185] 40 S Some of the people; S these his sayings, V these sayings [186] 41 But some said: S Others said [187] 44 S Some of them said they should take him [188] 45 S and they say [189] 46

S But the officers; S Never man spake thus as this man speaketh, V Never man spake thus [190] 47 S The Pharisees answered them [191] 48 Doth any of the rulers or of the Phar. believe on him? [192] 50 S But Nicodemus said unto them, being one of them [193] 51 S before it hear and know [194] 53 SV *om. this verse*

[195] **VIII.** 1–11 SV *om. all these verses* [196] 12 S but he hath [197] 14 S Jesus said unto them; S *om.* but; V whence I come or whither [198] 16 S but I and he who sent me [199] 19 S Jesus answered and said; S the Father also [200] 20 SV spake he in the; S *om.* as he taught in the temple [201] 21 S Then said he unto them [202] 23 S He said therefore [203] 24 S *om.* therefore; S if ye believe me not that [204] 25 S They said; S Then Jesus said unto them [205] 26 S but the Father that sent me; S heard with him [206] 27 S of the Father God [207] 28 S Then said Jesus again; V *om.* unto them; S as the Father; S so I speak [208] 29 S And he that sent me hath not left me alone: he is with me, for I do [209] 31 S *then* are ye disciples indeed [210] 35 S *om.* but the Son abideth ever [211] 38 V with the Father; S which ye have seen from your father, V which ye have heard from *your* father [212] 39 S Jesus answered them [213] 41 SV They said to him [214] 46 SV *om.* And [215] 48 SV The Jews answered [216] 49 S Jesus answered and said [217] 52 SV The Jews said; V he shall never see death [218] 54 A of whom ye say, He is our God [219] 57 S and hath Abraham seen thee? [220] 58 *translate* Before Abraham was born, I am [221] 59 V *om.* but; SV *om.* going through the midst of them, and so passed by

[222] **IX.** 4 SV We must work; S that sent us [223] 6 S and he anointed *his* eyes with his clay, V and he put his clay upon *his* eyes, A with his clay [224] 7 A Go to the pool of Siloam and wash [225] 8 blind: SVA beggar [226] 9 SV others said, No, but he is like him [227] 10 S How therefore were [228] 11 SV *om.* and said; SV Go to Siloam; SV I went therefore [229] 12 SV And they said, A They said [230] 15 A He said also unto them [231] 16 SV But others [232] 17 SVA They say therefore; S unto the formerly blind man [233] 19 S *om.* saying [234] 20 SV His parents therefore, A But his parents [235] 21 V ask him, he is of age, S *om.* ask him [236] 23 A and ask him [237] 25 SVA *om.* and said; S but one thing [238] 26 V Therefore they said to him, What, S They said to him, What [239] 28 A *om.* Then; SV And they reviled him [240] 31 SV *om.* Now; *translate* and do his will [241] 35 S And Jesus heard; SV *om.* unto him; SV on the Son of man? [242] 36 V *om.* answered and; A *om.* and said; S Lord, and who is he, V And who is he, Lord [243] 37 SV *om.* And *before* Jesus [244] 38 S* *om. this verse* [245] 39 S* *om.* And Jesus said [246] 40 SV *om.* And *before* some; S heard *it*, and said [247] 41 SV *om.* therefore

[248] **X.** 4 S his own (*om.* sheep), V all his own (*om.* sheep) [249] 6 S and they understood not [250] 7 S *om.* unto them again [251] 8 S *om.* before me [252] 10 S might have everlasting life [253] 12 V *om.* But; SV *om.* the sheep *after* scattereth [254] 13 SVA* *om.* The hireling fleeth [255] 14 SV and mine know me [256] 16 *translate* and there shall be one flock [257] 18 SV No man hath taken it [258] 19 SV *om.* therefore [259] 20 SV Therefore many [260] 21 S But others [261] 22 V It was then; SV *om.* and *before* it was winter [262] 25 S *om.* them [263] 26 SV *om.* as I said unto you [264] 29 S The Father; SV of the Father's hand [265] 31 SV *om.* Then [266] 32 SV from the Father [267] 33 SVA *om.* saying; S *om.* and *before* because [268] 34 S in the law [269] 38 V that ye may know and understand; SV and I in the Father [270] 39 S *om.* again [271] 40 S *om.* into the place; A He went away therefore again

[272] **XI.** 1 A his sister [273] 7 A to his disciples; S *om.* again [274] 12 SV Then said the disciples unto him, A Then said they unto him [275] 13 S of death [276] 17 A came to Bethany [277] 22 SV Even now I know [278] 25 S But Jesus said [279] 29 SV And as soon as [280] 30 SV but was still in that place [281] 31 SV thinking, She goeth [282] 35 S And Jesus [283] 41 A the stone where he was; SV *om.* from the place where the dead was laid [284] 45 S

And many; VA what he had done [285] 48 S all men believe on him [286] 50 S *om.* for us, V for you [287] 54 SV with the disciples [288] 57 SVA *om.* both; SV had given commandments

[289] **XII.** 1 SV *om.* which had been dead; SVA whom Jesus raised [290] 4 SV But saith; SV *om.* Simon's son [291] 6 SV and having the bag bare what [292] 7 SV Let her alone, that she may keep this against the day of my burying [293] 9 A whom Jesus had raised [294] 13 SA and cried saying; SV Blessed *is* he who cometh in the name of the Lord, and the King of Israel [295] 15 A the King cometh [296] 18 S For this cause much people [297] 22 SVA and again (VA *om.* and again) Andrew and Philip come and tell Jesus [298] 23 SV answereth [299] 25 shall lose: SV loseth [300] 26 A and if (*after* be) [301] 28 V glorify my name [302] 29 V *om.* therefore; S when they heard *it* [303] 30 S *om.* and said [304] 32 all *men:* S all *things* [305] 34 SV Therefore the people [306] 35 SV among you [307] 41 SVA because he saw [308] 46 V that he who believeth [309] 47 SVA and keep *them* not

[310] **XIII.** 2 SV And during supper; SV into *his* heart that Judas Isc. Simon's son should betray him [311] 3 SV *om.* Jesus [312] 6 SV and (V *om.*) he saith unto him; S *om.* Lord [313] 9 V Peter Simon; S *om.* Lord [314] 10 S needeth not to wash, but [315] 12 SA their feet, he took his garments and sat down again. He said [316] 18 SA for I know [317] 22 V *om.* Then [318] 23 V *om.* Now [319] 24 that he should ask *etc.:* V and saith unto him, Say who it is of whom he speaketh; he spake: S *adds* and saith unto him, Say who it is of whom he speaketh [320] 25 S he therefore lying, V he lying thus [321] 26 V Jesus therefore answereth, S Jesus answereth and saith — All MSS. give the sop; V he taketh and giveth *it* [322] 28 V *om.* Now [323] 30–31 A and it was night when he went out. Jesus [324] 32 SV And God shall glorify him in himself (*om.* If God be glorified in him) [325] 34 S as I have loved you, love ye also [326] 36 V *om.* him; SVA but thou shalt follow afterwards [327] 37 S *om.* Lord [328] 38 SVA Jesus answereth, Wilt thou

[329] **XIV.** 2 SVA for I go to prepare [330] 3 A And if I go, I will prepare [331] 4 SV And wh. I go, ye know the way [332] 5 V *om.* and; V how know we the way? [333] 7 A *om.* me; S If ye have known me, ye shall know; V *om.* and *before* from [334] 9 SV *om.* and *before* how sayest [335] 10 V but the Father dwelling in me, doeth his works; S in me, doeth his works [336] 11 A *om.* and the Father in me; S or else believe the very works [337] 12 SVA unto the Father [338] 14 VA that will I do [339] 15 S *om.* me; V ye shall keep [340] 16 SV that he may be [341] 17 SV *om.* but; V and is in you [342] 18 *translate* orphans *for* comfortless [343] 22 S Lord, and how is [344] 27 S not as the world giveth unto you give I unto you [345] 28 SVA rejoice, because I go; VA for the Father [346] 30 SVA of the world

[347] **XV.** 6 S and men gather it and cast *it* [348] 7 ye shall ask: VA ask [349] 10 V the Father's commandments [350] 11 VA my joy might be in you [351] 14 S For ye are [352] 16 A bring forth much fruit; S *om.* that *before* whatsoever; S he shall give [353] 22 S *om.* but [354] 26 S *om.* But

[355] **XVI.** 2 S For they may; A doeth service to the Lord [356] 3 S they may do unto you; VA *om.* unto you [357] 4 V when their time shall come; S that I spake of them [358] 6 A *om.* But [359] 8 *translate* he will convince the world [360] 10 SV to the Father [361] 12 S *om.* now [362] 14 S and sheweth *it* unto you [363] 15 S said I unto you that he; SV that he taketh of mine and shall shew [364] 16 SV no longer see me; SV *om.* because I go to the Father [365] 18 S What is this little while; V what is this little while that he saith? we cannot tell [366] 19 SV *om.* Now; S that they were going to ask him; A *om.* unto them [367] 20 SV *om.* and *after* rejoice [368] 22 A shall have sorrow [369] 23 SV ask the Father, he will give *it* you in my name [370] 26 S At that day ask ye [371] 27 V From the Father [372] 29 S The disciples; V *om.* unto him [373] 32 SVA *om.* now; S yea the hour is come [374] 33 SVA in the world ye have

[375] **XVII.** 1 SV that the Son may

glorify thee; A *om.* also [376] 4 SVA on the earth, having finished the work [377] 7 S Now I have known [378] 10 S And thou hast given them to me *instead of* And all mine are thine, and thine are mine [379] 11 SV but they are in the world; SVA keep them through thine own name wherein thou hast given *them* to me; V as we *are* also [380] 12 SV *om.* in the world; V in thy name, wherein thou gavest *them* to me, and guarded *them*, S in thy name and guarded *them* [381] 17 SVA through the truth; V thy word is the truth [382] 20 SVA which believe on me [383] 22 V even as we *are* one. S even as we: [384] 23 and that the world: S *om.* that, V *om.* and [385] 26 wherewith thou hast loved them

[386] **XVIII.** 3 S and from the Pharisees: S *om.* thither [387] 4 S But Jesus knowing; V and saith [388] 5 V He saith unto them, I am Jesus [389] 6 A *om.* then; S *om.* unto them [390] 11 SVA Put up the sword [391] 13 SV and led *him* to Annas first [392] 18 S also stood there; SV and Peter also stood [393] 20 S And Jesus; SVA whither all the Jews resort [394] 23 S But Jesus said unto him [395] 25 A He denied *it*, and saith [396] 29 SV and saith [397] 31 A But Pilate said; S and judge according [398] 32 S *om.* which he spake [399] 34 VA *om.* him; S hast thou said this thing [400] 35 S and the chief priest [401] 36 S then would also my [402] 37 A To this end also [403] 40 SV *om.* all

[404] **XIX.** 3 SV and came to him and said [405] 4 S Pilate went forth, VA And Pilate went forth; S *om.* in him [406] 6 S *om.* saying; SA Crucify, crucify him; S And Pilate [407] 7 S *om.* him; SV and by the law [408] 9 S *om.* again [409] 10 SA Pilate saith unto him (*om.* Then): SVA that I have power to release thee, and have power to crucify thee [410] 11 SV answered him; SA Thou hast no power [411] 12 S but the Jews said, If [412] 13 SVA these things; SA *om.* but [413] 14 SVA *om.* and *before* about [414] 15 S But they said, Therefore they cried out [415] 17 SV And he bearing the cross by himself [416] 20 SV in Hebrew *and* Latin *and* Greek [417] 23 S which had crucified Jesus; S *om.* and also his coat [418] 24 SV *om.* which saith [419] 26 Now when Jesus saw [420] 29 VA *om.* Now; S therefore they put a spunge full of vinegar upon hyssop [421] 33 S But when they came to Jesus, they found that he was dead already, and brake not [422] 35 SA that ye also might believe [423] 38 S they came therefore and took him; V took his body [424] 39 VA which at the first came to him by night [425] 40 A the body of God; S was to bury

[426] **XX.** 1 S from the door of the sepulchre [427] 3 S *om.* and came to the sepulchre [428] 4 S And they ran both together, but *the other* did outrun Peter; A but the other [429] 6 SV Then cometh also Simon Peter [430] 9 S For as yet he knew not [431] 11 S But Mary stood in the sepulchre; A *om.* without [432] 12 S *om.* two [433] 13 S *om.* and *before* they say; V And she saith [434] 14 SVA *om.* And *before* when [435] 15 S Now she supposing [436] 16 S But she turned herself; SV and saith unto him in Hebrew [437] 17 SV to the Father; S but (A *om.*) go to the brethren; S Behold, I ascend [438] 19 SVA *om.* assembled; S *om.* unto them [439] 21 S Then said he; even so will I send you [440] 23 S it shall be remitted unto them [441] 24 S was not with them. When therefore Jesus came, the other disciples said unto him [442] 25 S and put my finger into his hand, A and put my finger into the place of the nails [443] 26 S the disciples [444] 28 SV *om.* And *before* Thomas [445] 29 S But Jesus said; SVA *om.* Thomas; S thou hast also believed; S that have not seen me; A *om.* and *before* yet [446] 30 VA of the disciples [447] 31 S *om.* and *after* God; S everlasting life

[448] **XXI.** 2 S and the sons of [449] 3 S Therefore they went forth, A And they went forth; SV *om.* immediately [450] 4 S *om.* now [451] 6 S He (*om.* And) saith unto them; S And they cast, and were no longer able [452] 11 SV Therefore Simon Peter [453] 13 SV *om.* then [454] 14 S And this is now; SVA to the disciples [455] 15 V son of John, S *om.* son of Jonas [456] 16 S *om.* the second time· SV son

of John [457] 16 S *om.* Yea [458] 17 SV son of John; S Now Peter was grieved; S And lovest thou me? And he saith unto him; A He (*om.* And) saith unto him; V *om.* unto him; S that I love thee. And he saith [459] 18 S thy hand, and others shall gird thee and do to thee what thou willest not [460] 20 VA *om.* Then; S *om.* following; S and saith unto him [461] 23 S *om.* what is that to thee [462] 24 V which also testifieth [463] 25 S* *om. this verse;* VA *om.* Amen.

NOTE ON THE RESURRECTION.

§ 1. *The Time of the Resurrection.*

Matt. 26: 1, 2. Mark 16: 1, 2, 9. Luke 24: 1. John 20: 1.

That the resurrection of our Lord took place before full daylight, on the first day of the week, follows from the unanimous testimony of the Evangelists respecting the visit of the women to the sepulchre. But the exact time at which he rose is nowhere specified. According to the Jewish mode of reckoning, the Sabbath ended and the next day began at sunset; so that had the resurrection occurred even before midnight, it would still have been upon the first day of the week, and the third day after our Lord's burial. The earthquake had taken place and the stone had been rolled away before the arrival of the women; and so far as the immediate narrative is concerned, there is nothing to show that all this might not have happened some hours earlier. Yet the words of Mark in another place render it certain, that there could have been no great interval between these events and the arrival of the women; since he affirms in v. 9, that Jesus "had risen *early*, the first day of the week;" while in v. 2, he states that the women went out "*very early.*" A like inference may be drawn from the fact, that the affrighted guards first went to inform the chief priests of these events, when the women returned to the city (Matt. 28: 11); for it is hardly to be supposed, that after having been thus terrified by the earthquake and the appearance of an angel, they would have waited any very long time before sending information to their employers.—The body of Jesus had therefore probably lain in the tomb not less than about thirty-six hours.

§ 2. *The Visit of the Women to the Sepulchre.*

Matt. 26: 1–8. Mark 16: 1–8. Luke 24: 1–11. John 20: 1, 2.

The first notices we have of our Lord's resurrection, are connected with the visit of the women to the sepulchre, on the morning of the first day of the week. According to Luke, the women who had stood by the cross, went home and rested during the sabbath (23: 56); and Mark adds that after the sabbath was ended, that is, after sunset, and during the evening, they prepared spices in order to go and embalm our Lord's body. They were either not aware of the previous embalming by Joseph and Nicodemus; or else they also wished to testify their respect and affection to their Lord, by completing, more perfectly, what before had been done in haste; John 19: 40–42.

It is in just this portion of the history, which relates to the visit of the women to the tomb and the appearance of Jesus to them, that most of the alleged difficulties and discrepancies in this part of the Gospel narratives are found. We will therefore take up the chief of them in their order.

I. *The Time.* All the Evangelists agree in saying that the women went out *very early* to the sepulchre. Matthew's expression is, *as the day was dawning.* Mark's words are, *very early:* which indeed are less definite, but are appropriate to denote the same point of time. Luke has the more poetic term : *deep morning,* i. e. early dawn. John's language is likewise definite: *early, while it was yet dark.* All these expressions go to fix the time at what we call *early dawn,* or *early twilight;* after the break of day, but while the light is yet struggling with darkness.

Thus far there is no difficulty; and none would ever arise, had not Mark added the phrase, *the sun being risen;* or, as the English version has it, *at the rising of the sun.* These words seem, at first, to be at direct variance both with the *very early* of Mark himself, and with the language of the other Evangelists. To harmonize this apparent discrepancy, we may premise, that since Mark himself first specifies the point of time by a phrase sufficiently definite in itself, and supported by all the other Evangelists, we must conclude that when he adds, *at the rising of the sun,* he did not mean to contradict himself, but used this latter phrase in a broader and less definite sense. As the sun is the source of light and of the day, and as his earliest rays produce the contrast between darkness and light, between night and dawn, so the term *sunrising* might easily come in popular language, by a metonymy of cause for effect, to be put for all that earlier interval, when his rays, still struggling with darkness, do nevertheless usher in the day.

Accordingly, we find such a popular usage prevailing among the Hebrews; and several instances of it occur in the Old Testament. Thus in Judg. 9: 33, the message of Zebul to Abimelech, after directing him to lie in wait with his people in the field during the night, goes on as follows: "and it shall be, in the morning, as soon as the sun is up thou shalt rise early and set upon the city;" yet we cannot for a moment suppose that Abimilech with his ambuscade was to wait until the sun actually appeared above the horizon, before he made his onset. So the Psalmist (104: 22), speaking of the young lions that by night roar after their prey, goes on to say: "The sun ariseth, they gather themselves together, and lay them down in their dens." But wild animals do not wait for the actual appearance of the sun ere they shrink away to their lairs; the break of day, the dawning light, is the signal for their retreat. See also Sept. 2 K. 3: 22. 2 Sam. 23: 4. In all these passages the language is entirely parallel to that of Mark; and they serve fully to illustrate the principle, that the rising of the sun is here used in a popular sense as equivalent to the *rising of the day* or early dawn.

II. *The Number of the Women.* Matthew mentions Mary Magdalene and the other Mary; v. 1. Mark enumerates Mary Magdalene, Mary the mother of James, and Salome; v. 1. Luke has Mary Magdalene, Joanna, Mary the mother of James, and others with them; v. 10. John speaks of Mary Magdalene alone, and says nothing of any other. The first three Evangelists accord then in respect to the two Marys, but no further; while John differs from them all. Is there here a real discrepancy?

We may at once answer, No; because, according to the sound canon of Le Clerc: * "*Qui plura narrat, pauciora complectitur; qui pauciora memorat, plura non negat.*" Because John, in narrating circumstances with which he was personally connected, sees fit to mention only Mary Magdalene, it does not at all follow that others were not present. Because Matthew, perhaps for like reasons, speaks only of the two Marys, he by no means excludes the presence of others. Indeed, the very words which John puts into the mouth of Mary Magdalene, (v. 2), presupposes the fact, that others had gone with her to the sepulchre. That there was something in respect to Mary Magdalene, which gave her a peculiar prominence in these transactions, may be inferred from the fact, that not only John mentions her alone, but likewise all the other Evangelists name her first, as if holding the most conspicuous place.

The instance here under consideration is parallel to that of the demoniacs of Gadara, and the blind men at Jericho; where, in both cases, Matthew speaks of two persons, while Mark and Luke mention only one.† Something peculiar in the station or character of one of the persons, rendered him in each case more prominent, and led the two latter Evangelists to speak of him particularly. But there, as here, their language is not exclusive; nor is there in it anything that contradicts the statements of Matthew.

III. *The Arrival at the Sepulchre.* According to Mark, Luke, and John, the women on reaching the sepulchre found the great stone, with which it had been closed, already rolled away. Matthew, on the other hand, after narrating that the women went out to see the sepulchre, proceeds to mention the earthquake, the descent of the angel, his rolling away the stone and sitting upon it, and the terror of the watch, as if all these things took place in the presence of the women. The angel too (in v. 5) addresses the women, as if still sitting upon the stone he had rolled away.

The apparent discrepancy, if any, here arises simply from Matthew's brevity in omitting to state in full what his narrative presupposes. According to v. 6, Christ was already risen; and therefore the earthquake and its accompaniments must have taken place at an earlier point of time, to which the sacred writer returns back in his narration. And although Matthew does not represent the women as entering the sepulchre, yet in v. 8, he speaks of them as going out of it; so that of course their interview with the angel took place, not outside of the sepulchre, but in it, as narrated by the other Evangelists. When therefore the angel says to them in v. 6, "Come, see the place where the Lord lay," this is not said without the tomb to induce them to enter, as Strauss avers; but within the sepulchre, just as in Mark v. 6.

* Harm. p. 525. Can. XII. fin.

† Matt. 8: 28. Mark 5: 2. Luke 8: 27.—Matt. 20: 30. Mark 10: 46. Luke 18: 35.

IV. *The Vision of Angels in the Sepulchre.* Of this John says nothing. Matthew and Mark speak of one angel; Luke of two. Mark says he was sitting; Luke speaks of them as standing. This difference in respect to numbers is parallel to the case of the women, which we have just considered; and requires therefore no further illustration.

There is likewise some diversity in the language addressed to the women by the angels. In Matthew and Mark, the prominent object is the charge to the disciples to depart into Galilee. In Luke this is not referred to; but the women are reminded of our Lord's own previous declaration; that he would rise again on the third day. Neither of the Evangelists here professes to report *all* that was said by the angels; and of course there is no room for contradiction.

§ 3. *The return of the Women to the city, and the first appearance of our Lord.*

Matt. 28: 7—10. Mark 16: 8. Luke 24: 9—11. John 20: 1, 2.

John, speaking of Mary Magdalene alone, says that having seen that the stone was taken away from the sepulchre, she went in haste (ran) to tell Peter and John. He says nothing of her having seen the angels, nor of her having entered the sepulchre at all. The other Evangelists, speaking of the women generally, relate that they entered the tomb, saw the angels and then entered into the city. On their way Jesus meets them. They recognize him; fall at and embrace his feet; and receive his charge to the disciples. Was Mary Magdalene now with the other women? Or did she enter the city by another way? Or had she left the sepulchre before the rest?

It is evident that Mary Magdalene was not with the other women when Jesus thus met them. Her language to Peter and John forbids the supposition, that she had already seen the Lord: "They have taken away the Lord out of the sepulchre, and we know not where they have laid him." She therefore must have entered the city by another path and gate; or else have left the sepulchre before the rest; or possibly both these positions may be true. She bore her tidings expressly to Peter and John, who would seem to have lodged by themselves in a different quarter of the city; while the other women went apparently to the rest of the disciples. But this supposition of a different route is essential, only in connection with the view, that she left the tomb with the other women. That, however, she actually departed from the sepulchre before her companions, would seem most probable; inasmuch as she speaks to Peter and John only of the absence of the Lord's body; says nothing in this connection of a vision of angels; and when, after returning again to the tomb, she sees the angels, it is evidently for the first time; and she repeats to them as the cause of her grief her complaint as to the disappearance of the body; John 20: 12,13. She may have turned back from the tomb without entering it at all, so soon as she saw that it was open; inferring from the removal of the stone, that the sepulchre had been rifled. Or, she may first have entered with the rest, when, according to Luke, "they found not the body of the Lord Jesus," and "were much perplexed thereabout," before the angels became visible to them. The latter supposition seems best to meet the exigences of the case.

"As the other women went to tell his disciples, behold Jesus met them, saying, All hail. And they came, and held him by the feet, and worshipped him. Then Jesus said unto them, Be not afraid; go, tell my brethren, that they go into Galilee, and there shall they see me." The women had left the sepulchre "with fear and great joy" after the declaration of the angels that Christ was risen; or, as Mark has it, "they trembled and were amazed." Jesus meets them with words of gentleness to quiet their terrors; "Be not afraid." He permits them to approach, and embrace his feet, and testify their joy and homage. He reiterates to them the message of the angels to his "brethren," the eleven disciples; see v. 16.

This appearance and interview is narrated only by Matthew; none of the other Evangelists give any hint of it. Matthew here stops short. Mark simply relates that the women fled from the tomb; "neither said they anything to any one, for they were afraid." This of course can only mean, that they spoke of what they had thus seen to no one while on their way to the city; for the very charge of the angels, which they went to fulfil, was, that they should "go their way and tell his disciples;" v. 7. Luke narrates more fully, that "they returned from the sepulchre, and told all these things unto the eleven, and to all the rest.—And their words seemed to them as idle tales, and they believed them not." We may perhaps see in this language one reason why the other Evangelists have omitted to mention this appearance of our Lord. The disciples *disbelieved the report of the women*, that they had seen Jesus. In like manner they afterwards disbelieved the report of Mary Magdalene to the same effect; Mark 16: 11. They were ready, it would seem, to admit the testimony of the women to the absense of the body, and to the vision of angels; but not to the resurrection of Jesus and his appearance to them; Luke 24: 21—24. And afterwards, when the eleven had become convinced by the testimony of their own senses, those first two appearances to the women became of less importance and were less regarded. Hence the silence of three Evangelists as to the one; of two as to the other; and of Paul as to both; 1 Cor. 15: 5, 6.

§ 4. *Peter and John visit the Sepulchre. Jesus appears to Mary Magdalene.*

John 20: 3—18. Luke 24: 12. Mark 16: 9—11.

The full account of these two events is given solely by John. Matthew has not a word of either; Luke merely mentions, in general, that Peter, on the report of the women, went to the sepulchre; while Mark speaks only of our Lord's appearance to Mary Magdalene, which he seems to represent as his *first* appearance.

According to John's account, Peter and the beloved disciple, excited by the tidings of Mary Magdalene that the Lord's body had been taken away, hasten to the sepulchre. They run; John outruns Peter, comes first to the tomb, and stooping down, sees the grave-clothes lying, but he does not enter. The other women are no longer at the tomb; nor have the disciples met them on the way. Peter now comes up; he enters the tomb, and sees the grave-clothes lying, and the napkin that was about his head not lying with the rest, but wrapped together in a place by itself. John too now enters the sepulchre; "and he saw and believed."

What was it that John thus believed? The mere report of Mary Magdalene, that the body had been removed? So much he must have believed when he stooped down and looked into the sepulchre. For this, there was no need that he should enter the tomb. His belief must have been of something more and greater. The grave-clothes lying orderly in their place, and the napkin folded together by itself, made it evident that the sepulchre had not been rifled nor the body stolen by violent hands; for these garments and spices would have been of more value to thieves, than merely a naked corpse; at least, they would not have taken the trouble thus to fold them together. The same circumstances showed also that the body had not been removed by friends; for they would not thus have left the grave-clothes behind. All these considerations produce in the mind of John the germ of a belief that Jesus was risen from the dead. He believed *because* he saw; "*for* as yet they knew not the Scripture;" (v. 9). He now began more fully to recall and understand our Lord's repeated declaration, that he was to rise again on the third day; * a declaration on which the Jews had already acted in setting a watch.† In this way, the difficulty which is sometimes urged of an apparent want of connection between verses 8 and 9, disappears.

The two disciples went their way, "wondering in themselves at what was come to pass." Mary Magdalene, who had followed them back to the sepulchre, remained before it weeping. While she thus wept, she too, like John, stooped down and looked in, "and seeth two angels, in white, sitting, the one at the head and the other at the feet, where the body of Jesus had lain." To their inquiry why she wept, her reply was the same report which she had before borne to the two disciples: "Because they have taken away my Lord, and I know not where they have laid him," v. 13. Of the angels we learn nothing further. The whole character of this representation seems to show clearly, that Mary had not before seen the angels; and also that she had not before been told, that Jesus was risen. We must otherwise regard her as having been in a most unaccountably obtuse and unbelieving frame of mind; the very contrary of which seems to have been the fact. If also she had before informed the two disciples of a vision of angels and of Christ's resurrection, it is difficult to see, why John should omit to mention this circumstance, so important and so personal to himself.

After replying to the angels, Mary turns herself about, and sees a person standing near, whom, from his being present there, she takes to be the keeper of the garden. He too inquires, why she weeps. Her reply is the same as before; except that she, not unnaturally, supposes him to have been engaged in removing the body, which she desires to recover. He simply utters in reply, in well-known tones, the name Mary! and the whole truth flashes upon her soul; doubt is dispelled, and faith triumphs. She exclaims: "Rabboni!" as much as to say, "My dearest Master!" and apparently,

* Matt. 16: 21. 17: 23. Luke 9: 22. 24: 6, 7. al.

† Matt. 28: 63 sq.

like the other women,* falls at his feet in order to embrace and worship him. This Jesus forbids her to do, in these remarkable words: "Touch me not; for I am not yet ascended to my Father. But go to my brethren, and say unto them, I ascend unto my Father and your Father, and to my God and your God;" v. 17.

There remains to be considered the circumstance, that Mark, in v. 9, seems to represent this appearance of Jesus at the sepulchre to Mary Magdalene, as his first appearance: "Now, being risen early the first of the week, he appeared *first* to Mary Magdalene." In attempting to harmonize this with Matthew's account of our Lord's appearance to the other women on their return from the sepulchre, several methods have been adopted; but the most to the purpose is the view which regards the word *first*, Mark v. 9, as put not absolutely, but relatively. That is to say, Mark narrates three, and only three, appearances of our Lord; *of these three*, that to Mary Magdalene takes place *first*, and that to the assembled disciples the same evening occurs *last*, v. 14. A similar example occurs in 1 Cor. 15: 5–8, where Paul enumerates those to whom the Lord showed himself after his resurrection, viz. to Peter, to the twelve, to five hundred brethren, to James, to all the appostles, and *last of all* to Paul also. Now had Paul written here, as with strict propriety he might have done, "he was seen *first* of Cephas," assuredly no one would ever have understood him as intending to assert that the appearance to Peter was the first absolutely; that is, as implying that Jesus was seen of Peter before he appeared to Mary Magdalene and the other women. In like manner when John declares (21: 14) that Jesus showed himself to his disciples by the lake of Galilee for the *third* time after he was risen from the dead; this is said relatively to the two previous appearances to the assembled apostles; and does by no means exclude the four still earlier appearances, viz. to Peter, to the two at Emmaus, to Mary Magdalene, and to the other women,—one of which John himself relates in full.

In this way the old difficulty in the case before us disappears; and the complex and cumbrous machinery of earlier commentators becomes superfluous.

After her interview with Jesus, Mary Magdalene returns to the city, and tells the disciples that she had seen the Lord and that he had spoken these things unto her. According to Mark (vs. 10, 11), the disciples were "mourning and weeping;" and when they heard that Jesus was alive and had been seen of her, they believed not.

§ 5. *Jesus appears to two disciples on the way to Emmaus. Also to Peter.*

Luke 24: 13–35. Mark 16: 12, 13. 1 Cor. 15: 5.

This appearance on the way to Emmaus is related in full only by Luke. Mark merely notes the fact; while the other two Evangelists and Paul (1 Cor. 15: 5) make no mention of it.

On the afternoon of the same day on which our Lord arose, two of his disciples, one of them named Cleopas, were on their way on foot to a village

* Matt. 28: 9.

called Emmaus, sixty stadia or seven and a half Roman miles distant from Jerusalem,—a walk of some two or two and a half hours. They had heard and credited the tidings brought by the women, and also by Peter and John, that the sepulchre was open and empty; and that the women had also seen a vision of angels, who said that Jesus was alive. They had most probably likewise heard the reports of Mary Magalene and the other women, that Jesus himself had appeared to them: but these they did not regard, and do not mention them (v. 24); because they, like the other disciples, had looked upon them "as idle tales, and they believed them not;" v. 11. As they went they were sad, and talked together of all these things which had happened. After some time Jesus himself drew near and went with them. But they knew him not. Mark says he was in another form; Luke affirms that "their eyes were holden, that they should not know him;" v. 16. Was there in this anything miraculous? The "another form" of Mark, Doddridge explains by "a different habit from what he ordinarily wore." His garments, of course, were not his former ones; and this was probably one reason why Mary Magdalene had before taken him for the keeper of the garden.* It may be, too, that these two disciples had not been intimately acquainted with the Lord. He had arrived at Jerusalem only six days before his crucifixion; and these might possibly have been recent converts, who had not before seen him. To such, the change of garments, and the unexpectedness of the meeting, would render a recognition more difficult; nor could it be regarded as surprising, that under such circumstances they should not know him. Still, all this is hypothesis; and the averment of Luke, that "their eyes were holden," and the manner of our Lord's parting from them afterwards, seem more naturally to imply that the idea of a supernatural agency, affecting not Jesus himself, but the eyes or minds of the two disciples, was in the mind of the sacred writer.

Jesus inquires the cause of their sadness; chides them for their slowness of heart to believe what the prophets had spoken; and then proceeds to expound unto them "in all the Scriptures the things concerning himself." They feel the power of his words; and their hearts burn within them. By this time they drew nigh to the village whither they went; it was toward evening, and the day was far spent. Their journey was ended; and Jesus was about to depart from them. In accordance with oriental hospitality they constrained him to remain with them. He consents; and as he sat at meat with them, he took bread, and blessed, and brake, and gave unto them. At this time, and in connection with this act, their eyes were opened; they knew him; and he vanished away from them. Here too the question is raised, whether the language necessarily implies anything miraculous? Our English translators have rendered this passage in the margin, "he ceased to be seen of them;" and have referred to Luke 4: 30, and John 8: 59, as illustrating this idea. They might also have referred to Acts 8: 39. Still, the language is doubtless such as the sacred writers would most naturally have employed in order directly to express the idea of supernatural agency.

Full of wonder and joy, the two disciples set off the same hour to return

* See also John 21: 4.

to Jerusalem. They find the eleven and other disciples assembled; and as they enter, they are met with the joyful exclamation: "The Lord is risen indeed, and hath appeared unto Simon;" v. 34. They then rehearse what had happened to themselves: but, according to Mark, the rest believed them not. As in the case of the women, so here, there would seem to have been something in the position or character of these two disciples, which led the others to give less credit to their testimony, than to that of Peter, one of the leading apostles.

This appearance to Peter is mentioned by no other Evangelist; and we know nothing of the particular time, nor of the attending circumstances. It would seem to have taken place either not long before, or else shortly after, that to the two disciples. It had not happened when they left Jerusalem for Emmaus; or, at least, they had not heard of it. It had occurred when they returned; and that long enough before to have been fully reported to all the desciples and believed by them. It may perhaps have happened about the time when the two disciples set off, or shortly afterwards.

Paul, in enumerating those by whom the Lord was seen after his resurrection (1 Cor. 15: 5), mentions Peter first; passing over the appearances to the women, and also that to the two disciples; probably because they did not belong among the apostles.

§ 6. *Jesus appears to the Apostles in the absence of Thomas; and afterwards when Thomas is present.*

Mark 16: 14–18. Luke 24: 36–48. John 20: 19–29. 1 Cor. 15: 5.

The narrative of our Lord's first appearaece to the apostles is most fully given by Luke: John adds a few circumstances; and Mark, as well as Luke, has preserved the first charge thus privately given to the apostles, to preach the Gospel in all the world,--a charge afterwards repeated in a more public and solemn manner on the mountain in Galilee. When Paul says the Lord appeared to *the twelve*, he obviously employs this number as being the usual designation of the apostles; and very probably includes both the occasions narrated in this section. Mark and Luke speak in like manner of *the eleven;* and yet we know from John, that Thomas was not at first among them; so that of course only *ten* were actually present.

According to Mark, the disciples were at their evening meal; which implies a not very late hour. John says the doors were shut for fear of the Jews. While the two who had returned from Emmaus were still recounting what had happened unto them, Jesus himself "came and stood in the midst of them, and saith unto them, Peace be unto you!" The question here again is raised, whether this entrance of our Lord was miraculous? That it might have been so, there is no reason to doubt. He who in the days of his flesh walked upon the waters, and before whose angel the iron gate of the prison opened of its own accord so that Peter might pass out;* he who was himself just risen from the dead; might well in some miraculous way present himself to his followers in spite of bolts and bars. But does the language here necessarily imply a miracle? The doors indeed were

* Acts 12: 10.

35

shut; but the word used does not of itself signify that they were bolted or fastened. The object no doubt was, to prevent access to spies from the Jews; or also to guard themselves from the danger of being arrested; and both these objects might perhaps have been as effectually accomplished by a watch at or before the door. Nor do the words used of our Lord strictly indicate anything miraculous. We do not find here a form of the word commonly employed to express the sudden appearance of angels; but, "he *came* and stood in the midst of them;" implying *per se* nothing more than the ordinary mode of approach. There is, in fact, nothing in the whole account to suggest a miracle, except the remark of John respecting the doors; and as this circumstance is not mentioned either by Mark or Luke, it may be doubtful whether we are necessarily compelled by the language to regard the mode of our Lord's entrance as miraculous.

At this interview Thomas was not present. On his return the other disciples relate to him the circumstances. But Thomas now disbelieved the others; as they before had disbelieved the women. His reply was, "except I shall see in his hands the print of the nails, and put my finger into the print of the nails, and thrust my hand into his side, I will not believe." Our Lord had compassion upon his perverseness. Eight days afterwards, when the disciples were again assembled and Thomas with them, our Lord came as before, and stood in the midst, and said, Peace be unto you! He permits to Thomas the test he had demanded; and charges him to be not faithless, but believing. Thomas, convinced and abashed, exclaims in the fulness of faith and joy, My Lord and my God! recognizing and acknowledging thereby the divine nature thus manifested in the flesh. The reply of our Lord to Thomas is strikingly impressive and condemnatory of his want of faith: "Thomas, because thou hast seen me, thou hast believed; blessed are they that have not seen, and yet have believed!" He and the other disciples, who were to be the heralds of the Lord's resurrection to the world as the foundation of the hope of the Gospel, refused to believe except upon the evidence of their own senses; while all who after them have borne the Christian Name, have believed this great fact of the Gospel solely upon their testimony. God has overruled their unbelief for good, in making it a powerful argument for the truth of their testimony in behalf of this great fact, which they themselves were so slow to believe. Blessed, indeed, are they who have received their testimony.

§ 7. *Our Lord's appearance in Galilee.*

John 21: 1–24. Matt. 28: 16–20. 1 Cor. 15 : 6.

It appears from the narrative of Matthew, that while the disciples were yet in Jerusalem, our Lord had appointed a time, when he would meet them in Galilee, upon a certain mountain.* They therefore left Jerusalem after the passover, probably soon after the interview at which Thomas was present, and returned to Galilee, their home. While waiting for the appointed time, they engaged in their usual occupation of fishermen. On a certain day, as John relates, towards the evening, seven of them being

* See Matt. 26: 32.

together, including Peter, Thomas, and the sons of Zebedee, they put out upon the lake with their nets in a fishing boat; but during the whole night they caught nothing. At early dawn Jesus stood upon the shore, from which they were not far off, and directed them to cast the net upon the right side of the boat. "They cast therefore, and now they were not able to draw it for the multitude of the fishes." Recognizing in this miracle their risen Lord, they pressed around him. Peter, with his characteristic ardour, threw himself into the water in order to reach him the sooner. At their Lord's command they prepared a meal from the fish they had thus taken. "Jesus then cometh and taketh bread, and giveth them, and fish likewise." This was his third appearance to the eleven; or rather to a large number of them together. It was on this occasion, and after their meal, that our Lord put to Peter the touching and thrice repeated question, "Lovest thou me?"

At length the set time arrived; and the eleven disciples went away into the mountain "where Jesus had appointed them." It would seem most probable, that this time and place had been appointed of our Lord for a solemn and more public interview, not only with the eleven, whom he had already met, but with all his disciples in Galilee; and that therefore it was on this same occasion, when, according to Paul, "He was seen of above five hundred brethren at once."* That the interview was not confined to the eleven alone, would seem evident from the fact that "some doubted;" for this could hardly be supposed true of any of the eleven, after what had already happened to them in Jerusalem and Galilee, and after having been appointed to meet their risen Lord at this very time and place. The appearance of the five hundred must at any rate be referred to Galilee; for even after our Lord's ascension, the number of the names in Jerusalem were together only about an hundred and twenty.† I do not hesitate, therefore, to hold with Flatt, Olshausen, Hengstenberg, and others, that the appearances thus described by Matthew and Paul, were identical. It was a great and solemn occasion. Our Lord had directed that the eleven and all his disciples in Galilee should thus be convened upon the mountain. It was the closing scene of his ministry in Galilee. Here his life had been spent. Here most of his mighty works had been done and his discourses held. Here his followers were as yet most numerous. He therefore here takes leave on earth of those among whom he had lived and laboured longest; and repeats to all his disciples in public the solemn charge, which he had already given in private to the apostles: "Go ye therefore and teach all nations:—and lo, I am with you alway, even unto the end of the world." It was doubtless his last interview with his disciples in that region,—his last great act in Galilee.

§ 8. *Our Lord's further Appearances at Jerusalem, and his Ascension.*

1 Cor. 15: 7. Acts 1: 3–12. Luke 24: 49–53. Mark 16: 19, 20.

Luke relates, in Acts 1: 3, that Jesus showed himself alive to his apostles, "after his passion, by many infallible proofs, being seen of them forty days, and speaking of the things pertaining to the kingdom of God."

* 1 Cor. 15: 6. † Acts 1: 15.

This would seem to imply interviews and communications, as to which we have little more than this very general notice. One of these may have been the appearance to James, mentioned by Paul alone (1 Cor. 15: 7), as subsequent to that to the five hundred brethren. It may be referred with most probability to Jerusalem, after the return of the Apostles from Galilee. That this return took place by the Lord's direction, there can be no doubt; although none of the Evangelists have given us the slightest hint as to any such direction. Indeed, it is this very brevity,—this omission to place on record the minor details which might serve to connect the great facts and events of our Lord's last forty days on earth, that has occasioned all the doubt and difficulty with which this portion of the written history of these events has been encompassed.—The James here intended was probably our Lord's brother; who was of high consideration in the church, and is often, in the latter books, simply so named without any special designation.* At the time when Paul wrote, the other James, "the brother of John," as he is called, was already dead.†

After thus appearing to James, our Lord, according to Paul, was seen "of all the apostles." This, too, was apparently an appointed meeting; and was doubtless the same of which Luke speaks, as occurring in Jerusalem immediately preceding the ascension. It was, of course, the Lord's last interview with his apostles. He repeats to them the promise of the baptism with the Holy Spirit as soon to take place; and charges them not to depart from Jerusalem until this should be accomplished.‡ Strange as it may appear, the twelve, in this last solemn moment, put to him the question, "Lord, wilt thou at this time restore the kingdom to Israel?" How, indeed, were they to believe! Their gross and darkened minds, not yet enlightened by the baptism of the Spirit, clung still to the idea of a temporal Prince and Saviour, who should deliver his people, not from their sins, but from the galling yoke of Roman dominion. Our Lord deals gently with their ignorance and want of faith: "It is not for you to know the times and seasons;—but ye shall receive the power of the Holy Ghost coming upon you; and ye shall be witnesses unto me—unto the uttermost part of the earth."

During this discourse, or in immediate connection with it, our Lord leads them out *as far as to* Bethany, and lifting up his hands he blessed them; Luke 24: 50. This act of blessing must be understood, by all the laws of language, as having taken place at or near Bethany. "And it came to pass, *while* he blessed them, he was parted from them, and carried up into heaven." Our Lord's ascension, then, took place at or near Bethany. Indeed, the sacred writer could hardly have found words to express this fact more definitely and fully; and a doubt on this point could never have suggested itself to the mind of any reader, but for the language of the same writer, in Acts 1: 12, where he relates that after the ascension the disciples "returned unto Jerusalem by the mount called Olivet." Luke obviously did not mean to contradict himself; and the most that his expression can be made to imply, is, that from Bethany, where their Lord had ascended, which lies on the eastern

* See Acts 12: 17. 15: 13. 21: 18. Gal. 2: 9, 12 al. † Acts 12: 1
‡ To this interview belongs also Luke 24: 44.

slope of the Mount of Olives, a mile or more below the summit of the ridge, the disciples returned to Jerusalem by a path across the mount.

As these disciples stood gazing and wondering, while a cloud received their Lord out of their sight, two angels stood by them in white apparel, announcing unto them, that this same Jesus, who was thus taken up from them into heaven, shall again so come, in like manner as they had seen him go into heaven. With this annunciation closes the written history of our Lord's resurrection and ascension.

AN ACCOUNT OF THE TRIAL OF JESUS.

THE death of Jesus is universally regarded among Christians as a cruel murder, perpetrated under the pretence of a legal sentence, after a trial, in which the forms of law were essentially and grossly violated. The Jews to this day maintain, that, whatever were the merits of the case, the trial was at least regular, and the sentence legally just; that he was accused of blasphemy, and convicted of that offence by legal evidence. The question between them involves two distinct points of inquiry, namely, first, whether he was guilty of blasphemy; and, secondly, whether the arraignment and trial were conducted in the ordinary forms of law. But there will still remain a third question, namely, whether, admitting that, as a mere man, he had violated the law against blasphemy, he could legally be put to death for that cause; and if not, then whether he was justly condemned upon the new and supplemental accusation of treason or of sedition, which was vehemently urged against him. The first and last of these inquiries it is proposed briefly to pursue; but it will be necessary previously to understand the light in which he was regarded by the Jewish rulers and people, the state of their criminal jurisprudence and course of proceeding, and especially the nature and extent of the law concerning blasphemy, upon which he was indicted.

In the early period of the ministry of Jesus, he does not appear to have excited among the Pharisees any emotion but wonder and astonishment, and an intense interest respecting the nature of his mission. But the people heard him with increasing avidity, and followed him in countless throngs. He taught a purer religion than the Scribes and Pharisees, whose pride and corruption he boldly denounced. He preached charity and humility, and perfect holiness of heart and life, as essential to the favor of God, whose laws he expounded in all the depth of their spirituality, in opposition to the traditions of the elders, and the false glosses of the Scribes and Pharisees. These sects he boldly charged with making void and rejecting the law of God, and enslaving men by their traditions; he accused them of hypocrisy, covetousness, oppression, and lust of power and popularity; and denounced them as hinderers of the salvation of others, as a generation of serpents and vipers, doomed to final perdition. It was natural that these terrific denunciations, from such a personage, supported by his growing power and the increasing acclamations of the people, should alarm the partisans of the ancient theocracy, and lead them to desire his destruction. This alarm evidently increased with the progress of his ministry; and was greatly heightened by the raising of Lazarus from the dead, on which occasion the death of Jesus was definitely resolved on;* but no active measures against him seem to have been attempted, until the time when, under the parable of the wicked husbandmen who cast the heir out of the vineyard and slew him, he declared that the kingdom of God should be taken from them, and given to others more worthy. Perceiving that he spake this parable against them, from that hour they sought to lay hands on him, and were restrained only by fear of the popular indignation.†

Having thus determined to destroy Jesus at all events, as a person whose very existence was fatal to their own power, and perhaps, in their view, to the safety of their nation, the first step was to render him odious to the people; without which the design would undoubtedly recoil on the heads of its contrivers, his popularity being unbounded. Countless numbers had received the benefit of his miraculous gifts; and it was therefore deemed a vain attempt to found an accusation, at that time, on any past transaction of his life. A new occasion was accordingly sought, by

* See John xi. 47–54.

† Matt. xxi. 33–46. Mark xxii. 1–12. Luke xx. 9–19.

endeavoring to "entangle him in his talk;" a measure, planned and conducted with consummate cunning and skill. The Jews were divided into two political parties. One of these consisted of the Pharisees, who held it unlawful to acknowledge or pay tribute to the Roman emperor, because they were forbidden, by the law of Moses,* to set a king over them who was a stranger, and not one of their own countrymen. The other party was composed of the partisans of Herod, who understood this law to forbid only the voluntary election of a stranger, and therefore esteemed it not unlawful to submit and pay tribute to a conqueror. These two parties, though bitterly opposed to each other, united in the attempt to entrap Jesus, by the question,—"Is it lawful to give tribute to Cæsar, or not?"† If he answered in the negative, the Herodians were to accuse him to Pilate, for treason; if in the affirmative, the Pharisees would denounce him to the people, as an enemy to their liberties.‡ This insidious design was signally frustrated by the wisdom of his reply, when, referring to Cæsar's image and legend, on the coins which they all received as legally current, he showed the inconsistency of withholding the honor due to one thus implicitly acknowledged by both parties to be their lawful sovereign.

Defeated in this attempt to commit him politically, their next endeavor was to render him obnoxious to one or the other of the two great religious sects, which were divided upon the doctrine of the resurrection, the Pharisees affirming, and the Sadducees denying, that the dead would rise again. The latter he easily silenced, by a striking exposition of their own law. They asked him which, of several husbands, would be entitled in the next world to the wife whom they successively had married in this; and in reply, he showed them that in heaven the relation of husband and wife was unknown.§

Their last trial was made by a lawyer, who sought to entrap him into an assertion that one commandment in the

* Deut. xvii. 15.

† Matt. xxii. 15–22. Mark xii. 13–17. Luke xx. 20–26.

‡ Tappan's Jewish Ant. p. 239.

§ Matt. xxii. 23–33. Mark xii. 18–27. Luke xx. 27–39.

law was greater than another; a design rendered abortive by his reply that they were all of equal obligation.*

It being apparent, from these successive defeats, that any farther attempt to find new matter of accusation would result only in disgrace to themselves, the enemies of Jesus seem to have come to the determination to secure his person secretly, and afterwards to put him to death, in any manner that would not render them odious to the people. In execution of this design, they first bribed Judas to betray him by night into their hands. This object being attained, the next step was to destroy his reputation, and if possible to render him so vile in the public estimation, as that his destruction would be regarded with complacency. Now no charge could so surely produce this effect, and none could so plausibly be preferred against him, as that of blasphemy; a crime which the Jews regarded with peculiar horror. Even their veneration of Jesus, and the awe which his presence inspired, had not been sufficient to restrain their rising indignation on several occasions, when they regarded his language as the blasphemous arrogation of a divine character and power to himself; and could they now be brought to believe him a blasphemer, and see him legally convicted of this atrocious crime, his destruction might easily be brought about, without any very scrupulous regard to the form, and even with honor to those by whom it might be accomplished.

It will now be necessary to consider more particularly the nature of the crime of blasphemy, in its larger signification, as it may be deduced from the law of God. That the spirit of this law requires from all men, everywhere, and at all times, the profoundest veneration of the Supreme Being, and the most submissive acknowledgment of Him as their rightful Sovereign, is too plain to require argument. If proof were wanted, it is abundantly furnished in the Decalogue,† which is admitted among Christians to be of

* Matt. xxii. 25–40, 46. Mark xii. 28–34.

† Exodus xx. 1–7. And God spake all these words, saying, I *am* the Lord thy God, which have brought thee out of the land of Egypt, out of the house of bondage. Thou shalt have no other gods before me. Thou shalt not make unto thee any graven image, or any likeness of *anything* that *is* in heaven above, or that *is* in the earth beneath, or that *is* in the water

universal obligation. At the time when the Jewish Theocracy was established, idolatry had become generally prevalent, and men had nearly lost all just notions of the nature and attributes of their Creator. It is therefore supposed that the design of Jehovah, in forming the Jewish constitution and code of laws, was to preserve the knowledge of himself as the true God, and to retain that people in the strictest possible allegiance to him alone; totally excluding every acknowledgment of any other being, either as an object of worship or a source of power. Hence the severity with which he required that sorceries, divinations, witchcrafts and false prophecies, as well as open idolatries, should be punished, they being alike acts of treason, or, as we might say, of *præmunire*, amounting to the open acknowledgment of a power independent of Jehovah. Hence, too, the great veneration in which he commanded that his name and attributes should be held, even in ordinary conversation. It is the breach of this last law, to which the term *blasphemy*, in its more restricted sense, has usually been applied;* but originally the command evidently extended to every word or act, directly in derogation of the sovereignty of Jehovah, such as speaking in the name of another god,†

under the earth: Thou shalt not bow down thyself to them, nor serve them: for I the Lord thy God *am* a jealous God, visiting the iniquity of the fathers upon the children unto the third and fourth *generation* of them that hate me; And shewing mercy unto thousands of them that love me, and keep my commandments. Thou shalt not not take the name of the Lord thy God in vain: for the Lord will not hold him guiltless that taketh his name in vain.

* Lev. xxiv. 11–16. And the Israelitish woman's son blasphemed the name *of the Lord*, and cursed; and they brought him unto Moses (and his mother's name *was* Shelomith, the daughter of Dibri, of the tribe of Dan): And they put him in ward, that the mind of the Lord might be shewed them. And the Lord spake unto Moses, saying, Bring forth him that hath cursed without the camp, and let all that heard *him* lay their hands upon his head, and let all the congregation stone him. And thou shalt speak unto the children of Israel, saying, Whosoever curseth his God shall bear his sin. And he that blasphemeth the name of the Lord, he shall surely be put to death, *and* all the congregation shall certainly stone him: as well the stranger, as he that is born in the land, when he blasphemeth the name *of the Lord*, shall be put to death. See A. Clarke on Matt. ix. 3.

† Deut. xiii. 6–10. If thy brother, the son of thy mother, or thy son, or thy daughter, or the wife of thy bosom, or thy friend, which *is* as thine own

or omitting, on any occasion that required it, to give to Jehovah the honour due to his own name.* Thus, when Moses and Aaron, at the command of God, smote the rock in Kadesh, that from it waters might flow to refresh the famishing multitude, but neglected to honour him as the source of the miraculous energy, and arrogated it to themselves, saying, "Hear now, ye rebels, must *we* bring you water out of this rock?"† this omission drew on them his severe displeasure. "And the Lord spake unto Moses and Aaron, Because ye believed me not, to sanctify *me* in the eyes of the children of Israel, therefore *ye* shall not bring this congregation into the land which I have given them." Accordingly, both Moses and Aaron died before the Israelites entered into the promised land.‡ No other deity was permitted to be invoked; no miracle must be wrought, but in the name of God alone. "I am Jehovah; that is my name; and my glory will I not give to another, neither my praise to graven images."§ This was ever a cardinal principle of his law, neither newly announced by Isaiah, nor by Moses. Its promulgation on Mount Sinai was merely declaratory of

soul, entice thee secretly, saying, Let us go and serve other gods, which thou hast not known, thou, nor thy fathers; *Namely*, of the gods of the people which *are* round about you, nigh unto thee, or far off from thee, from the *one* end of the earth even unto the *other* end of the earth; Thou shalt not consent unto him, nor hearken unto him; neither shall thine eye pity him, neither shalt thou spare, neither shalt thou conceal him: But thou shalt surely kill him; thine hand shall be first upon him to put him to death, and afterwards the hand of all the people. And thou shalt stone him with stones that he die; because he had sought to thrust thee away from the Lord thy God, which brought thee out of the land of Egypt from the house of bondage. Deut. xviii. 20. But the prophet, which shall presume to speak a word in my name, which I have not commanded him to speak, or that shall speak in the name of other gods, even that prophet shall die.

* It is true that in the Mishna it is written—"Blasphemus non tenetur, nisi expressit Nomen." Mishna, Pars iv. p. 242. Tractatus de Synedriis, cap. 7, § 5. But these traditions were not written until 150 years after the time of our Saviour; and the passage, moreover, seems properly to refer to that form of blasphemy which consists in evil speaking of the Supreme Being, in a direct manner, rather than to the other forms in which this offence, in its larger acceptation, might be committed. See Michælis, Comm. Art. 251. Vol. 4, p. 67-70.

† Numb. xx. 10, 12.

‡ Numb. xx. 24. Deut. i. 37, and xxxiv. 4, 5.

§ Is. xlii. 8, and xlviii. 2.

what had been well understood at the beginning, namely, that God alone was the Lord of all power and might, and would be expressly acknowledged as such, in every exertion of superhuman energy or wisdom. Thus Joseph, when required to interpret the dream of Pharaoh, replied, "It is not in me: God shall give Pharaoh an answer of peace."* And Moses, in all the miracles previously wrought by him in Egypt, expressly denounced them as the judgments of God, by whose hand alone they were inflicted.† After the solemn re-enactment of this law on Mount Sinai, its signal violation by Moses and Aaron deserved to be made as signal an example of warning; and this judgment of Jehovah may be said to constitute the leading case under this article of the law; forming a rule of action and of judgment for all cases of miracles which might be wrought in all coming time. The same principle was afterwards expressly extended to prophesying. "The prophet—that shall speak in the name of other gods, even that prophet shall die."‡ His character of prophet, and even his inspiration, shall not authorize him to prophesy but in the name of the Lord. He shall not exercise his office in his own name, nor in any name but that of Jehovah, from whom his power was derived.

That such was understood to be the true meaning of this law of God, is further evident from the practice of the prophets, in later times, to whom was given the power of working miracles. These they always wrought in his name, expressly acknowledged at the time. Thus, the miracle of thunder and rain in the season of the wheat-harvest, called for by Samuel, he expressly attributed to the Lord.§ So did Elijah, when he called fire from heaven to consume his sacrifice, in refutation of the claims of Baal.‖ So did Elisha, when he divided the waters of Jordan, by smiting

* Gen. xli. 16, 25, 28. † Exod. viii. ix. x. per tot.

‡ Deut. xviii. 20.

§ "Now, therefore, stand and see this great thing, which the LORD will do before your eyes." 1 Sam. xii. 16–18.

‖ "And it came to pass, at the time of the offering of the evening sacrifice, that Elijah the prophet came near and said, Lord God of Abraham, Isaac, and of Israel, let it be known this day that *thou art God in Israel*," &c. 1 Kings xviii. 36–38.

them with the mantle of Elijah;* and again, when he miraculously multiplied the loaves of bread, for the people that were with him;† and again, when he caused the young man's eyes to be opened, that he might behold the hosts of the Lord around him, and smote his enemies with blindness.‡ And even the angel Gabriel, when sent to interpret to Daniel the things which should befall his people in the latter days, explicitly announced himself as speaking in Jehovah's name.§

The same view of the sinfulness of exercising superhuman power without an express acknowledgment of God as its author, and of any usurpation of his authority, continued to prevail, down to the time of our Saviour. Thus, when he said to the sick of the palsy, "Son, be of good cheer, thy sins be forgiven thee," certain of the Scribes said within themselves, "This man blasphemeth. Who can forgive sins, but God alone?"‖ And again, when the Jews, on another occasion, took up stones to stone him, and Jesus, appealing to his good works done among them, asked for which of them he was to be stoned; they replied, "For a good work we stone thee not, but for blasphemy, and because that thou, being a man, makest thyself God."¶ Yet Jesus had on no occasion mentioned the *name* of Jehovah, but with profound reverence.

Thus it appears that the law of blasphemy, as it was understood among the Jews, extended not only to the offense of impiously using the name of the Supreme Being, but to every usurpation of his authority, or arrogation, by a created being, of the honour and power belonging to him alone.** Like the crime of treason among men, its essence

* "And he took the mantle of Elijah that fell from him, and smote the waters, and said, *Where is the Lord God of Elijah?*" &c. 2 Kings ii. 14.

† "For *thus saith the Lord*, they shall eat and shall leave thereof," &c. 2 Kings iv. 43.

‡ See 2 Kings vi. 16, 17, 18, 20. In some other places, where there is no express reference to the power of God, the omission may be attributed to the brevity of the narrative; but even in those cases, such reference is plainly implied.

§ Dan. ix. 21, 23, and x. 11, 12. See further, 2 Kings xviii. 30–35, and xix. 1–3. ‖ Matt. ix. 2, 3. Luke, v. 20, 21. ¶ John x. 31–33.

** This view of the Jewish law may seem opposed to that of Dr. Campbell, in his Preliminary Dissertations on the Gospels, (Vol. 2, Diss. ix. Part

consisted in acknowledging or setting up the authority of another sovereign than one's own, or invading the powers pertaining exclusively to him; an offence, of which the case of Moses, before cited, is a prominent instance, both in its circumstances and in its punishment. Whether a false god was acknowledged or the true one denied, and whether the denial was in express terms, or by implication, in assuming to do, by underived power, and in one's own name, that which God only could perform, the offence was essentially the same. And in such horror was it held by the Israelites, that in token of it every one was obliged, by an early and universal custom, to rend his garments, whenever it was committed or related in his presence.* This sentiment was deeply felt by the whole people, as a part of their religion.

Such being the general scope and spirit of the law, it would seem to have been easy to prove that Jesus had re-

2); but it is evident, on examination, that he is discussing the *word blasphemy*, and the propriety of its application, taken in its more restricted sense of intentional and direct malediction of Jehovah; and not whether the assumption of his attributes and authority was or was not a violation of his law. That this assumption was a heinous transgression, seems universally agreed. The question, therefore, is reduced to this—whether the offence was properly *termed* blasphemy. For the *act*, by whatever name it were called, was a capital crime. The Jewish judges of that day held it to amount to blasphemy; and in so doing, they do not appear to have given to their law a construction more expanded and comprehensive than has been given by judges in our own times, to the law of treason, or of sedition.

* This was judicially and solemnly done by the members of the Sanhedrim, rising from their seats, when the crime was testified to. Only one witness was permitted to repeat the words; the others simply stating that they heard the same which he had related. The practice is thus described in the Mishna: "Exactis omnibus, interrogant vetustissimum testium, dicendo,—*Edissere, quodcumque audivisti expresse.* Tum ille hoc refert. Judices autem stant erecti, vestesque discerpunt, non resarciendas. Dein secundus tertiusque ait,—*Ego idem, quod ille, audivi.*" Mishna, Pars 4. Tractat. de Synedriss, cap. 7, § 8. Upon which, Cocceius remarks:—"Assurgunt reverentiæ causa. Mos discendarum vestium probatur ex 2do Regum, xviii. 37. Hinc nata est regula,—*Qui blasphemiamaudit, vel ab ipso auctore vel ex alio, tenetur vestem discerpere.* Ratio est, ut semper ob oculos et animum versetur mæroris aut indignationis mnemosynon." Coccej. in loc. § 11, 12. The custom is fully explained, with particular reference to the high priest at the trial of Jesus by Hedenus, *De Scissione Vestium*, 38, 42. (In Ugolini Thesauro, tom. xxix. fol. 1025, &c.)

peatedly incurred its penalties. He had performed many miracles, but never in any other name than his own. In his own name, and without the recognition of any higher power, he had miraculously healed the sick, restored sight to the blind and strength to the lame, cast out devils, rebuked the winds, calmed the sea, and raised the dead. In his own name, also, and with no allusion to the Omniscient, no, "Thus saith the Lord," he had prophesied of things to come. He had by his own authority forgiven sins, and promised, by his own power, not only to raise the dead, but to resume his own life, after he should, as he predicted, be put to death. Finally, he had expressly claimed for himself a divine origin and character, and the power to judge both the quick and the dead.[1] Considered as a man, he had usurped the attributes of God. That he was not arrested at an earlier period, is to be attributed to his great popularity, and the astounding effect of his miracles. His whole career had been resplendent with beneficence to the thousands who surrounded him. His eloquence surpassed all that had been uttered by man. The people were amazed, bewildered, and fascinated, by the resistless power of his life. It was not until his last triumphal visit to Jerusalem, after he had openly raised Lazarus from the dead, when the chief priests and elders perceived that "the world was gone after him," that they were stricken with dismay and apprehension for their safety, and under this panic resolved upon the perilous measure of his destruction.

The only safe method in which this could be accomplished, was under the sanction of a legal trial and sentence. Jesus, therefore, upon his apprehension, was first brought before the great tribunal of the Sanhedrim, and charged with the crime of blasphemy. What were the specifications

* That the Jews understood Jesus to make himself equal with God, is maintained by Mr. Salvadore, himself a Jew, in his Histoire des Institutions de Moise et du Peuple Hebreu, Liv. iv. ch. 3, p. 81, of which chapter a translation is given at the end of this article. Mr. Noah, also a Jew, seems to be of opinion, that Jesus was brought to trial under the law in Deut. xiii. 1-11. See his Discourse on the Restoration of the Jews, p. 19. But whether he was charged with a blasphemous usurpation of the attributes of Deity, or with sedition, in inciting the people to serve another god, meaning himself, the difference is of no importance; the essence of the offence in both cases being the same.

under this general charge, or whether any were necessary, we are not informed. But that this was the offence charged, is manifest both from the evidence adduced and from the judgment of conviction.* Such was the estimation in which he was held, that it was with great difficulty that witnesses could be found to testify against him; and the two who at last were procured, testified falsely, in applying his words to the temple of Solomon, which he spake of the temple of his body. When, upon the occasion of his scourging the money-changers out of the temple, the Jews demanded by what authority he did this, Jesus replied, alluding to his own person, "Destroy *this* temple, and in three days I will raise it up.† But though the witnesses swore falsely in testifying that he spake of the Jewish temple, yet his words, in either sense, amounted to a claim of the power of working miracles, and so brought him within the law. The high priest, however, still desirous of new evidence, which might justify his condemnation in the eyes of the people, proceeded to interrogate Jesus concerning his character and mission. "I adjure thee, by the living God, that thou tell us whether thou be the Christ, the Son of God. Jesus saith unto him, Thou hast said: nevertheless, I say unto you, hereafter ye shall see the Son of Man sitting on the right hand of power, and coming in the clouds of heaven. Then the high prist *rent his clothes*, saying He hath *spoken blasphemy;* what *further* need have we of witnesses? Behold, now *ye have heard* his *blasphemy*. What think ye? They answered and said, *He is guilty of death.*" ‡ We may suppose the multitude standing without the hall of judgment, able, through its avenus and windows, to see, but not to hear, all that was transacting within. It became important, therefore, to obtain some reason upon which the high priest might rend his clothes in their sight, thus giving to the people, by this expressive and awful sign, the highest evidence of blasphemy, uttered by Jesus in the presence of that august assembly. This act turned the tide of popular

* Matt. xxvi. 69–65. This view of the nature of the offence with which Jesus was charged,, is confirmed by the learned jurist, Chr. Thomasius, in his Dissertatio de injusto Pilati judicio, § 11, 12, and by the authors whom he there cites. Dissert. Thomasii. vol. 1, p. 5.

† John ii. 13–22.

‡ Matt. xxvi. 63–66.

indignation against him, whose name, but a short time before, had been the theme of their loudest hosannas. There was now no need to go into the past transactions of his ministry, for matter of accusation. His friends might claim for him on that score all that the warmest gratitude and love could inspire; and all this could be safely conceded. But here, his accusers might say, was a new and shocking crime, just perpetrated in the presence of the most sacred tribunal; a crime so shocking, and so boldly committed, that the high priest rent his clothes with horror, in the very judgment seat, in the presence of all the members of the Sanhedrim, who, with one accord, upon that evidence alone, immediately convicted the offender and sentenced him to death.

If we regard Jesus simply as a Jewish citizen, and with no higher character, this conviction seems substantially right in point of law, though the trial were not legal in all its forms. For, whether the accusation were founded on the first or second commands in the decalogue, or on the law, laid down in the thirteenth chapter of Deuteronomy, or on that in the eighteenth chapter and twentieth verse, he had violated them all, by assuming to himself powers belonging alone to Jehovah. And even if he were recognized as a prophet of the Lord, he was still obnoxious to punishment, under the decision in the case of Moses and Aaron, before cited. It is not easy to perceive on what ground his conduct could have been defended before any tribunal, unless upon that of his superhuman character. No lawyer, it is conceived, would think of placing his defence upon any other basis.

The great object of exciting the people against Jesus being thus successfully accomplished, the next step was to obtain legal authority to put him to death. For though the Sanhedrim had condemned him, they had not the power to pass a capital sentence; this being a right which had passed from the Jews by the conquest of their country, and now belonged to the Romans alone. They were merely citizens of a Roman province; they were left in the enjoyment of their civil laws, the public exercise of their religion, and many other things relating to their police and municipal regulations; but they had not the power of life and death.

This was a principal attribute of soveregnity, which the Romans always took care to reserve to themselves in order to be able to reach those individuals who might become impatient of the yoke, whatever else might be neglected. *Apud quos (Romanos), vis imperii valet; inania transmittuntur.** The jurisdiction of capital cases belonged ordinarily to the governor general or *Præses* of a province, the *Procurator* having for his principal duty only the charge of the revenue and the cognizance of revenue causes. But the right of taking cognizance of capital crimes was, in some cases, given to certain *Procurators*, who were sent into small provinces, to fill the places of governors, (*Vice Præsides*,) as clearly appears from the Roman laws. The government of all Syria was at this time under a governor general, or *Præses;* of which Judea was one of

* Tacit. Annal. xv. 31. See M. Dupin's Trial of Jesus, p. 57–59, (Amer. Ed.) Chr. Thomasius, Dissertatio de injusto Pilati judicio, § 12, 60. The want of this power was admitted by the Jews, in their reply to Pilate, when he required them to judge Jesus according to their own law, and they replied, "It is not lawful for us to put any man to death." John xviii. 31.

This point has been held in different ways by learned men. Some are of opinion that the Sanhedrim had power to inflict death for offences touching religion, though not for political offences; and that it was with reference to the charge of treason that they said to Pilate what has just been cited from St. John. They say that, though the Sanhedrim had convicted Jesus of blasphemy, yet they dared not execute that sentence, for fear of a sedition of the people:—that they therefore craftily determined to throw on Pilate the odium of his destruction, by accusing him of treason; and hence, after condemning him, they consulted further, as stated in Matt. xxvii. 1, 2. Mark xv. 1, how to effect this design:—that when Pilate found no fault in him, and directed them to take and crucify him, some replied, "We have a law, and by our law he ought to die," (John xix. 7,) to intimate to Pilate that Jesus was guilty of death by the Jewish law also, as well as the Roman, and that therefore he would not lose any popularity by condemning him. See Zorrius, His. Fisci Judaici, ch. 2, § 2, (in Ugolini Thesaur. tom. 26, col. 1001–1003.) The same view is taken by Deylingius, De Judœorum Jure Gladii, § 10, 11, 12, (in Ugolin. Thesaur. tom. 29, col. 1189–1192.) But he concludes that in all capital cases, there was an appeal from the Sanhedrim to the Prætor; and that without the approval of the latter, the sentence of the Sanhedrim could not be executed. Ibid. § 15, col. 1196. Molinæus understood the Jewish law in the same manner. See his Harmony of the Gospels, note on John xviii. 31. C. Molinæi Opera, tom. 5, pp. 603, 604. But this opinion is refuted by what is said by M. Dupin, Trial, &c., § 8, and by Thomasius, abo e cited.

the lesser dependencies, under the charge of Pilate as *Vice Præses*, with capital jurisdiction.*

It could not be expected that Pilate would trouble himself with the cognizance of any matter, not pertaining to the Roman law ; much less with an alleged offence against the God of the Jews, who was neither acknowledged nor even respected by their conquerors. Of this the chief priests and elders were fully aware; and therefore they prepared a second accusation against Jesus, founded on the Roman law ; as likely to succeed with Pilate, as the former had done with the people. They charged him with attempting to restore the kingdom of Israel, under his own dominion as king of the Jews. "We found this fellow, said they, perverting the nation, and forbidding to give tribute to Cæsar, saying, That he himself is Christ, a King."†

It was a charge of high treason against the Roman state and emperor ; a charge which was clearly within Pilate's cognizance, and which, as they well knew, no officer of Tiberius would venture lightly to regard. Pilate accordingly forthwith arraigned Jesus, and called upon him to answer this accusation. It is worthy of note, that from the moment when he was accused of treason before Pilate, no further allusion was made to the previous charge of blasphemy ; the Roman Governor being engaged solely with the charge newly preferred before himself. The answer of Jesus to this charge satisfied Pilate that it was groundless, the kingdom which he set up appearing plainly to be not a kingdom of this world, but his spiritual reign in righteousness and holiness and peace, in the hearts of men. Pilate therefore acquitted him of the offence. "He went out again unto the Jews, and saith unto them, *I find in him no fault*

* See M. Dupin's Trial of Jesus, pp. 55–62. His authorities are Loiseau-Godefroy, and Cujas, the two latter of whom he cites as follows:—"Procurator Cæsaris *fungens vice præsidis* potest cognoscere *de causis criminalibus*. Godefroy, in his note (letter S) upon the 3rd law of the code, *Ubi causæ fiscales*, &c. And he cites several others, which I have verified, and which are most precise to the same effect. See particularly the 4th law of the Code, *Ad. leg. fab. de plag.*, and the 2nd law of the Code, *De Pœnis.*—Procuratoribus Cæsaris data est jurisdictio in causis fiscalibus pecuniariis, non in criminalibus, nisi quum fungebantur *vice præsidum;* ut Pontius Pilatus fuit procurator Cæsaris *vice præsidis* in Syria. Cujas, Observ. xix. 13."

† Luke xxiii. 2.

at all."* Here was a sentence of acquittal, judicially pronounced, and irreversible, except by a higher power, upon appeal; and it was the duty of Pilate thereupon to have discharged him. But the multitude, headed now by the priests and elders, grew clamorous for his execution; adding, "He stirreth up the people, teaching throughout all Jewry, beginning from Galilee to this place."† Hearing this reference to Galilee, Pilate seized the opportunity, thus offered, of escaping from the responsibility of a judgment, either of acquittal or of condemnation, by treating the case as out of his jurisdiction, and within that of Herod tetrarch of Galilee, who was then in Jerusalem on a visit. He therefore sent Jesus and his accusers to Herod; before whom the charge was vehemently renewed and urged. But Herod, too, perceived that it was utterly groundless, and accordingly treated it with derision, arraying Jesus in mock habiliments of royalty, and remanding him to Pilate.‡ The cause was then solemnly re-examined by the Roman governor, and a second judgment of acquittal pronounced. For "Pilate, when he had called together the chief priests and the rulers, and the people, said unto them, Ye have brought this man unto me, as one that perverteth the people; and behold, I having examined him before you, have found no fault in this man, touching those things whereof ye accuse him: No, nor yet Herod: for I sent you to him; and lo, nothing worthy of death is done unto him. I will therefore chastise him and release him."§

It may seem strange to us that after a judgment of acquittal thus solemnly pronounced, any judge, in a civilized country, should venture to reverse it, upon the same evidence, and without the pretence of mistake or error in the proceedings. Probably, in the settled jurisprudence of the city of Rome, it could not have been done. But this was in a remote province of the empire, under the administration not of a jurist, but a soldier; and he, too, irresolute

* John xviii. 38. † Luke xxiii. 5. ‡ Luke xxiii. 10, 11.

§ Luke xxiii. 13, 14, 15. I regard this judgment as conclusive evidence of the innocence of the accused. Pilate's strenuous endeavours to release him instead of Barabbas, and his solemn washing his own hands of the guilt of his blood, though they show the strength of his own convictions, yet add no legal force to the judgment itself.

and vacillating ; fearful for his office, and even for his life, for he served the "dark and unrelenting Tiberius." As soon as he proposed to release Jesus, "the Jews cried out, saying, If thou let this man go, *thou art not Cæsar's friend. Whosoever maketh himself a king speaketh against Cæsar.*"* Whereupon "Pilate gave sentence that it should be as they required."† That Jesus was executed under the pretence of treason, and that alone, is manifest from the tenor of the writing placed over his head, stating that he was king of the Jews ; such being the invariable custom among the Romans, in order that the public might know for what crime the party had been condemned.‡ The remaining act in this tragedy is sufficiently known.

In the preceding remarks, the case has been considered only upon its general merits, and with no reference to the manner which the proceedings were conducted. But M. Dupin, in his tract on the Trial of Jesus before the Sanhedrim, in reply to Mr. Salvador's account of it, has satisfactorily shown that throughout the whole course of that trial the rules of the Jewish law of procedure were grossly violated, and that the accused was deprived of rights, belonging even to the meanest citizen. He was arrested in the night, bound as a malefactor, beaten before his arraignment, and struck in open court during the trial ; he was tried on a feast day, and before sunrise ; he was compelled to criminate himself, and this, under an oath of solemn judicial adjuration ; and he was sentenced on the same day of the conviction. In all these particulars the law was wholly disregarded.§

* John xix. 12. † Luke xxiii. 24.

‡ See M. Dupin's Trial of Jesus, pp. 82–84.

§ Ibid, pp. 7–15 John's Bibl. Ant. § 246.

THE JEWISH

ACCOUNT OF THE TRIAL OF JESUS.

BY MR. SALVADOR.

MR. JOSEPH SALVADOR, a physician and a learned Jew, a few years ago published at Paris, a work, entitled, "Histoire des Institutions de Moise et due Peuple Hebreu," in which, among other things, he gives an account of their course of criminal procedure, in a chapter on "The Administration of Justice;" which he illustrates, in a succeeding chapter, by an account of the trial of Jesus. As this is the recent work of a man of learning, himself a Jew, it may be regarded as an authentic statement of what is understood and held by the most intelligent and best informed Jews, respecting the claims of our Lord, the tenor of his doctrines, the nature of the charge laid against him before the Sanhedrim, and the grounds on which they condemned him. The following translation of the last-mentioned chapter will therefore not be unacceptable to the reader. It will be found in Book IV. chapter iii., entitled, "The Trial and Condemnation of Jesus." The reader will bear in his mind, that it is the language of an enemy of our Saviour, and in justification of his murderers.

"According to this exposition of judicial proceedings," says the Jew, "I shall follow out the application of them in the most memorable trial in history, that of Jesus Christ. I have already explained the motives which have directed me, and the point of view in which I have considered the subject; I have already shown, that among the Jews no title was a shelter against a prosecution and sentence. Whether the law or its forms were good or bad, is not the object of my present investigation; neither is it to ascertain whether we ought to pity the blindness of the Hebrews in not discovering a Diety in Jesus, or to be astonished that a God personified could not make himself comprehended when he desired it. But since they regarded him only as a citizen, did they not try him according to their law and its existing forms? This is my question, which can admit of no equivocation. I shall draw all my facts from the Evangelists themselves, without inquiring whether all this history was developed after the event, to serve as a form to a new doctrine, or to an old one which had received a fresh impulse.

Jesus was born of a family of small fortune; Joseph, his supposed father, perceived that his wife was big before they had come together. If he had brought her to trial, in the ordinary course of things, Mary, according to the 23rd verse of the 22nd chapter of Deuteronomy, would have been condemned, and Jesus, having been declared illegitimate, could never, according to the 2nd verse of the 23rd chapter, have been admitted to a seat in the Sanhedrim.* But Joseph, who, to save his wife from disgrace, had taken the resolution of sending her away privately, soon had a dream which consoled him.†

After having been circumcised, Jesus grew like other men, attended the solemn feasts, and early displayed surprising wisdom and sagacity. In the assembly on the Sabbath, the Jews, eager for the disputes to which the interpretation of the law gave rise, loved to hear him. But he soon devoted himself to more important labours; he pronounced censures against whole towns, Capernaum, Chorazin and Bethsaida.‡ Recalling the times of Isaiah and Jeremiah, he thundered against the chiefs of the people with a vehemence which would in our day be terrific.§ The people then regarded him as a prophet;‖ they heard him preach in towns and country without opposition; they saw him sur-

* Deut. xxii. 22, and xxiii, 2. Selden De Synedriis, lib. 3 cap. 4, 5.

† Matt. i. 19, 20.

‡ Matt. xi. 20–24. Luke iv. &c.

§ Matt. xxiii. per tot.

‖ Matt. xxi. 11–46. John vii. 40.

rounded with disciples according to the custom of the learned men of the age; whatever may have been the resentment of the chief men, they were silent as long as he confined himself to the law.

But Jesus, in presenting new theories, and in giving new forms to those already promulgated, speaks of himself as God; his disciples repeat it; and the subsequent events prove in the most satisfactory manner, that they thus understood him.* This was shocking blasphemy in the eyes of the citizens: the law commands them to follow Jehovah alone, the only true God; not to believe in gods of flesh and bone, resembling men or women; neither to spare nor listen to a prophet who, even doing miracles, should proclaim a new god, a god neither they nor their fathers had known.†

Jesus having said to them one day: "I have come down from heaven to do these things," the Jews, who till then had listened to him, murmured and cried: "Is not this Jesus, the son of Joseph and of Mary? we know his father, his mother, and his brethren; why then does he say that he has come down from heaven?"‡ On another day, the Jews, irritated from the same cause, took stones and threatened him. Jesus said unto them, "I have done good works in your eyes by the power of my Father, for which of these works would you stone me?" "It is for no good work," replied the Jews, who stated the whole process in few words, "but because of thy blasphemy; for being a man,§ thou makest thyself God."‖

His language was not always clear. Often his disciples

* The expression *son of God* was in common use among the Jews, to designate a man of remarkable wisdom and piety. It was not in this sense that Jesus Christ used it; for in that case it would have occasioned no great sensation. Besides, if we should assume, in order to make it a subject of accusation against these Jews, that Jesus did not expressly declare himself to be God, we should be exposed to this rejoinder: Why then do you believe in him?

† See Deut. iv. 15, and xiii. per tot.

‡ John xi. 39–42. Matt. xiii. 55.

§ This fact is as clearly established as possible; and we must observe that till then there had been neither opposition nor enmity in the minds of this people, since they had listened to him with the greatest attention, and did not hesitate to acknowledge in him all that the public law permitted them to do viz., a prophet, a highly inspired man.

‖ John x. 30–33.

themselves did not comprehend him. Among his maxims, some of which showed the greatest mildness, there were some which the Hebrews, who were touched only through their natural sense, thought criminal. "Think not that I am come to send peace on earth ; I came not to send peace, but a sword. For I am come to set a man at variance against his father, and the daughter against her mother, and the daughter-in-law against her mother-in-law. And a man's foes shall be they of his own household. He that loveth father or mother more than me, is not worthy of me."* Finally, if he wrought miracles before certain of the people, his replies to the questions of the doctors were generally evasive.†

In regard to political relations, he caused dissensions.‡ A great number of disorderly persons whom he had the design of reclaiming, but who inspired dread in the national council, attached themselves to him,§ his discourse flattered them inasmuch as he pronounced anathemas against riches. "Know," said he, "that it is easier for a camel to go through the eye of a needle, than for a rich man to enter the kingdom of heaven."‖ In this state of affairs, the council deliberates ; some are of opinion that he should be regarded as a madman,¶ others say that he seeks to seduce the people.** Caiaphas, the high priest, whose dignity compels him to defend the letter of the law, observes that these dissensions would furnish an excuse to the Romans for overwhelming Judea, and that the interests of the whole nation must outweigh those of a single individual ; he constitutes himself the accuser of Jesus.††

The order is given to seize him. But let us pause here upon a fact of the highest importance. The senate did not begin by actually seizing Jesus, as is now the practice ; they begin by giving, after some debate, an order that he should be seized.‡‡ This decree is made public ; it is known to all, especially to Jesus. No opposition is offered to his passing the frontier : his liberty depends entirely

* Matt. x. 34. Mark x. 29. † Matt. xvi. 1–4. John viii. 13–18.
‡ John vii. 43. Luke xxiii. 5.
§ Matt. ix. 10. Mark ii. 15. Luke xv. 1.
‖ Matt. xix. 24. ¶ John x. 20. ** John vii. 12.
†† John xi. 47–50. ‡‡ Matt. xxvi. 4. John xi. 53, 54.

upon himself. This is not all; the order for his arrest was preceded by a decree of admonition. One day, Jesus having entered the temple, took upon himself authority contrary to the common law; then he preached to the people, and said: "That those who should believe in him should be able to do all things, so that if they should say to a mountain, remove thyself and cast thyself into the sea, it would obey." Then the chief priest and senators went to find him and said to him, "By what authority doest thou things? who gave thee this power?"*

Meanwhile a traitor discloses the place whither the accused had retired; the guards, authorized by the high priest and by the elders,† hasten to seize him. One of his disciples, breaking into open rebellion, with a stroke of his sword cuts off the ear of one of them, and brings upon himself the reproof of his master.‡ As soon as Jesus is arrested, the zeal of his apostles is extinguished; all forsake him.§ He is brought before the grand council, where the priests sustain the accusation. The witnesses testify, and they are numerous; for the deeds of which he is accused were done in the presence of all the people. The two witnesses whom St. Matthew and St. Mark accuse of perjury, relate a discourse which St. John declares to be true, with regard to the power which Jesus arrogates to himself.‖ Finally, the high priest addresses the accused, and says: "Is it true that thou art Christ, that thou art the Son of God?" "I am he," replies Jesus; "you shall see me hereafter at the right

* Matt. xxi. 23.

† It will be recollected, that the senate held its sessions in one of the porticos of the temple. At this time the high priest presided over the senate, so that the guards of the high priest, of the elders and the temple, were no other than the legal militia.

‡ John xviii. 10, 11.

§ Mark xiv. 50. Matt. xxvi. 56.

‖ Matt. xxvi. 60, 61. And the last came two false witnesses, and said, This fellow said, I am able to destroy the temple of God, and to build it in three days. Mark xiv. 57, 58. And there arose certain and bare false witness against him, saying, We heard him say, I will destroy this temple that is made with hands, and within three days I will build another made without hands. John ii. 19, 21, 22. Jesus answered and said unto them, Destroy this temple, and in three days I will raise it up. But he spake of the temple of his body. When, therefore, he was risen from the dead, his disciples remembered that he said this unto them; and they believed the scripture, and the word which Jesus had said.

hand of the majesty of God, who shall come upon the clouds of heaven." At these words, Caiaphas rent his garments in token of horror.* "You have heard him." They deliberate. The question already raised among the people was this: Has Jesus become God? But the senate having adjudged that Jesus, son of Joseph, born at Bethlehem, had profaned the name of God by usurping it to himself, a mere citizen, applied to him the law of blasphemy, and the law in the 13th chapter of Deuteronomy, and the 20th verse in chapter 18, according to which every prophet, even he who works miracles, must be punished, when he speaks of a god unknown to the Jews and their fathers:† the capital sentence was pronounced. As to the ill-treatment which followed the sentence, it was contrary to the spirit of the Jewish law; and it is not in the course of nature, that a senate composed of the most respectable men of a nation, who, however, they might have been deceived, yet intended to act legally, should have permitted such outrages against him whose life was at their disposal. The writers who have transmitted to us these details, not having been present at the trial, have been disposed to exaggerate the picture, either on account of their prejudices, or to throw greater obloquy on the judges.

One thing is certain, that the council met again on the morning of the next day or the day following that,‡ as the law requires, to confirm or to annul the sentence: it was confirmed. Jesus was brought before Pilate, the procurator that the Romans had placed over the Jews. They had retained the power of trying according to their own laws, but the executive power was in the hands of the procurator alone: no criminal could be executed without his consent: this was in order that the Senate should not have the means of reaching men who were sold to foreigners.§ Pilate, the

* I repeat that the expression *Son of God*, includes here the idea of God himself; the fact is already established, and all the subsequent events confirm it. Observe, also, that I quote the narrative of only one of the parties to this great proceeding.

† Deut. xxviii. 20. But the prophet, which shall presume to speak a word in my name, which I have not commanded him to speak, or that shall speak in the name of other gods, even that prophet shall die.

‡ Matt. xxvii. 1. Mark xv. 1.

§ The duties of Pilate were to inform himself whether the sentences given did or did not affect the interests of Rome; there his part ended.

Roman, signed the decree. His soldiers, an impure mixture of diverse nations, were charged with the punishment. These are they who brought Jesus to the judgment hall, who stripped him before the whole cohort, who placed upon his head a crown of thorns, and a reed in his hand, who showed all the barbarity to which the populace in all ages is disposed; who finally caused him to undergo a punishment common at Rome, and which was not in use among the Jews.* But before the execution, the governor had granted to the condemned an appeal to the people, who, respecting the judgment of their own council, would not permit this favour, couching their refusal in these terms: "We have a law; and by our law he ought to die, because he made himself the Son of God."† Then Pilate left them the choice of saving Jesus, or a man accused of murder in a sedition; the people declared for the latter; saying that the other would scatter the seeds of discord in the bosom of the nation, at a time when union was most necessary.‡

Jesus was put to death. The priests and elders went to the place of punishment; and as the sentence was founded upon this fact, that he had unlawfully arrogated to himself the title of Son of God, God himself, they appealed to him thus: "Thou wouldst save others; thyself thou canst not save. If thou art indeed the king of Israel, come down into the midst of us, and we will believe in thee; since thou hast said, I am the Son of God, let that God who loves thee come

Thus it is not astonishing that this procurator, doubtless little acquainted with the Jewish laws, signed the decree for the arrest of Jesus, although he did not find him guilty. We shall see hereafter that there were then many parties among the Jews, among whom were the Herodians or serviles, partisans of the house of Herod, and devoted to the foreign interests. These are they who speak continually of Cæsar, of rendering to Cæsar the tribute due to Cæsar; they also insist that Jesus called himself *king of the Jews:* but this charge was reckoned as nothing before the senate, and was not of a nature alone to merit capital punishment.

* See Matt. xxvii. 27. Mark xv. 16. John xix. 2.

† John xix. 7.

‡ The sending back of Jesus to Herod, which, according to the Gospel of St. Luke, Pilate would have done, is not stated by the other Evangelists, and does not at all change the judicial question. Herod Antipas, tetrarch of Galilee, and of Perea, had no authority in Jerusalem. Upon his visit to this city, Pilate, according to St. Luke, would, out of respect, have caused Jesus to appear before this ally of the Romans, because Jesus was surnamed

now to thine aid.* According to the Evangelist, these words were a mockery; but the character of the persons who pronounced them, their dignity, their age, the order which they had observed in the trial, prove their good faith. Would not a miracle at this time have been decisive?"

the Galilean, though originally from Judea. But to whatever tribe he belonged, the nature of the accusation would still have required, according to the Hebrew law, that he should be judged by the senate of Jerusalem.

* Matt. xvii. 42, 43.

THE

TRIAL OF JESUS

BEFORE

CAIAPHAS AND PILATE.

BEING A REFUTATION OF MR. SALVADOR'S CHAPTER ENTITLED

"THE TRIAL AND CONDEMNATION OF JESUS."

By M. DUPIN,

ADVOCATE AND DOCTOR OF LAWS.

"If thou let this man go, thou art not Cæsar's friend."—*John* xix. 12.

TRANSLATED FROM THE FRENCH

By JOHN PICKERING, LL.D.,

COUNSELLOR-AT-LAW, AND PRESIDENT OF THE AMERICAN ACADEMY OF ARTS AND SCIENCES.

PREFACE.

A few years ago, Mr. Joseph Salvador, a physician—and a descendant of one of those Jewish families, whom the intolerance of Ferdinand the Catholic expelled, in a body, from Spain, about the year 1492—published at Paris a learned work, entitled "Histoire des Institutions de Moise et du Peuple Hebreu," or History of the Institutions of Moses and the Hebrew People; and in one chapter of his work he gives an account of the *Administration of Justice* among the Hebrews. To that chapter he has subjoined an account of the "Trial and Condemnation of Jesus;" in the course of which he expresses his opinion, that the trial, considered merely as a *a legal proceeding*, was conformable to the Jewish laws.

The author of the following little work, M. Dupin, who is one of the most eminent lawyers of the French Bar, immediately called in question the correctness of Mr. Salvador's opinion, and entered upon an analysis of this portion of his work, with a view to examine its soundness; and the present volume contains the result of that examination, conducted with great legal skill and extensive learning.

It appears, that he had, many years before, in a little work, entitled "*The Free* Defense of Accused Persons," published in 1815, taken the same views of this great trial; which, as he observes, has been justly called "the *Passion* or *Suffering* of our Saviour; for he did in truth *suffer*, and had not a trial."

The author's attention, however, had been withdrawn from this subject for several years, when it was again brought under his notice by the work of Mr. Salvador, a copy of which was sent to him by that writer, with a request that M. Dupin would give some account of it. Accordingly, says the latter, "it is in compliance with *his request*, and not from a spirit of hostility, that I have made this examination of his work;" and he gives ample proof of his good feeling towards Mr. Salvador, with whom, he says, he is personally acquainted and for whose talents he has a great respect.

With this friendly spirit he enters upon his examination; which is conducted with an ability, learning, animation, and interest, that leave nothing to be desired. As an argument, his work is unanswerable,—he has demolished that of his adversary; and, for intense interest, we do not know any publication of the present day to be compared with it.

The introductory *Analysis* of Mr. Salvador's chapter on the Administration of Justice according to the Jewish Law will be highly instructive and interesting, and those persons, who hrve not been accustomed to read the Bible with particular reference to the *Law*, will find many new and striking views of that portion of the Scriptures. They cannot fail to be particularly struck with the extraordinary care taken to secure by law the personal liberty and rights of the citizen.

According to Mr. Salvador's view, "the fundamental division into *castes* is the principal basis of the oriental theocracies." Moses, on the contrary, took for his basis the *unity* of the people. In his system of legislation the people are every thing; and the author shows us, that every thing, eventually, is done for them, by them, and with them. The tribe of Levi was established, only to supply a secondary want; and that tribe was very far from obtaining all the powers which we are apt to attribute to it; it did not make, nor develop the laws; it does not judge or govern; all its members, even the high priest himself, were subject to the control of the Elders of the nation, or of a Senate legally assembled.

Intimately connected with these rights of the people was the *liberty of speech;* and Mr. Salvador, in his chapter on the *Public Orators and Prophets*, maintains, and in the opinion of M. Dupin, proves clearly, that in no nation was the liberty of speech ever so unlimited, as among the Hebrews. Accordingly he observes—"What an additional difference was this between the Israelites and the Egyptians! Among the latter, the mass of the people did not dare, without incurring the hazard of the most terrible punishment, to utter a word on affairs of state; it was Harpocrates, the god of silence with his finger on his closed lips, who was their God; in Israel, it was *the right of speech.*"

But we forbear any further reflections, and submit this remarkable performance to our readers. Those, who are familiar with the animated tone of French writers, will perhaps discover in this translation some loss of the fire and intensity of the original; but the translator's purpose will be effected, if his version shall be found to be a faithful one.

September 3, 1839.

ANALYSIS

OF THE CHAPTER OF MR. SALVADOR, ENTITLED "THE ADMINISTRATION OF JUSTICE" AMONG THE JEWS.*

MR. SALVADOR has discussed with particular care whatever relates to the *administration of justice* among the Jewish people. We shall dwell upon this chapter, which undoubtedly will most interest our readers.

Judicare and *judicari*, to judge and to be judged, express the rights of every Hebrew citizen; that is, no one could be condemned without a judgment, and every one might, in his turn, be called upon to sit in judgment upon others. Some exceptions to this principle are explained; but they do not affect the rule. In matters of mere interest each party chose a judge, and these two chose a third person. If a discussion arose as to *the interpretation of a law*, they carried it to the lower council of Elders, and from thence to the Great Council at Jerusalem. Each town of more than one hundred and twenty families was to have its lower council, consisting of twenty-three members; and these had jurisdiction in criminal cases.

The expressions, *he shall die*, *he shall be cut off from the people*, which are so often used in the Mosaic law, embrace three very different significations, which we are accustomed to confound. They indicate the suffering of death as a punishment, civil death, and that premature death, with which an individual is naturally threatened, who departs from those rules which are useful to the nation and to the

* This Analysis first appeared in the *Gazette des Tribunaux*.

individual himself. Civil death is the last degree of *separation*, or *excommunication;* it is pronounced, as a judicial punishment, by the assembly of the judges.

There were three kinds of separation; which Mr. Salvador compares to the three degrees of civil excommunication provided for in the French Penal Code, and which condemn the criminal to hard labour either for life or for a term of years, or to certain correctional punishments. But the Hebrew excommunication had this advantage, that the party *never lost all hope of regaining his original standing.*

The Hebrew lawyers, in relation to the punishment of death, maintained opinions, which deserve to be quoted:—

"A tribunal, which condemns to death *once in seven years*, may be called *sanguinary*."—"It deserves this appellation, says Doctor Eliezer, when it pronounces a like sentence once in seventy years."—"If we had been members of the high court, say the doctors Tyrphon and Akiba, we should never have condemned a man to death." Simeon, the son of Gamaliel, replied—"Would not that be an abuse? Would you not have been afraid of multiplying crimes in Israel?" Mr. Salvador answers—"No, certainly; far from lessening their number, the severity of the punishment increases it, by giving a more resolute character to the men who are able to brave it; and, at the present day, how many intelligent minds range themselves on the side of Akiba and Tyrphon! How many consciences refuse to participate, in any manner, in the death of a man! The flowing of blood, the multitude excited by an unbecoming curiosity, the victim dragged in triumph to the horrible altar, the impossibility of repairing a mistake, (from which human wisdom is never exempt), the dread of one day seeing a departed shade rising up and saying, '*I was innocent*,' the facility which modern nations have of expelling from among them the man whose presence pollutes them—the influence of general depravity on the production of crimes—and finally the absurd contrast of the whole of society, while in possession of strength, intelligence, and arms, opposing itself to an individual wretch (who has been drawn on by want, by passion, or by ignorance) and yet finding no other means of redress than by exceeding him in cruelty—all these things, and many others, have so deeply penetrated the minds of all ranks of people, that there will one day proceed from them the most striking proof of the power of morals over the laws; for the law will be changed by the simple fact, that we shall not find any person who will consent to apply it."

I feel honored in having maintained the same opinion in my *Observations on Criminal Legislation;* but I solicit those, who wish to see this question discussed in its whole extent, to read the profound reflections which the Duke de Broglie has just published on the subject, in the last number of the *Revue Francaise* (for October, 1828.)

The whole criminal procedure in the Pentateuch rests upon three principles, which may be thus expressed; publicity of the trial, entire liberty of defence allowed to the accused; and a guaranty against the dangers of testimony. Acccording to the Hebrew text *one* witness is no witness; there must be at least two or three who know the fact. The witness, who testifies against a man, must swear that he speaks the truth; the judges then proceed to take exact information of the matter; and, if it is found that the witness has sworn falsely, they compel him to undergo the punishment to which he would have exposed his neighbour. The discussion between the accuser and the accused is conducted before the whole assembly of the people. When a man is condemned to death, those witnesses whose evidence decided the sentence inflict the first blows, in order to add the last degree of certainty to their evidence. Hence the expresssion—*Let him among you who is without sin, cast the first stone.*

If we pursue their application of these fundamental rules in practice, we shall find that a trial proceeded in the following manner.

On the day of the trial, the executive officers of justice caused the accused person to make his appearance. At the feet of the Elders were placed men who, under the name of *auditors*, or *candidates*, followed regularly the sittings of the Council. The papers in the case were read; and the witnesses were called in succession. The president addressed this exhortation to each of them: "It is not conjectures, or whatever public rumour has brought to thee, that we ask of thee ; consider that a great responsibility rests upon thee : that we are not occupied by an affair, like a case of pecuniary interest, in which the injury may be repaired. If thou causest the condemnation of a person unjustly accused, his blood, and the blood of all the posterity of him, of whom thou wilt have deprived the earth, will fall upon thee ; God will demand of thee an account, as he demanded of Cain an account of the blood of Abel. Speak."

A woman could not be a witness, because she would not have the courage to give the first blow to the condemned person ; nor could a child, that is irresponsible, nor a slave, nor a man of bad character, nor one whose infirmities prevent the full enjoyment of his physical and moral faculties. *The simple confession of an individual against himself*, or the declaration of a prophet, however renowned, would not decide a condemnation. The Doctors say—" We hold it as fundamental, that *no one shall prejudice himself.* If a man accuses himself before a tribunal, we must not believe him, unless the fact is attested by two other witnesses ; and it is proper to remark, that the punishment of death inflicted upon Achan, in the time of Joshua* was an exception, occasioned by the nature of the circumstances ; for our law does not condemn upon the simple confession of the accused, nor upon the declaration of one prophet alone."

" The witnesses were to attest to the identity of the party, and to depose to the month, day, hour, and circumstances of the crime. After an examination of the proofs, those judges who believed the party innocent stated their reasons ; those who believed him guilty spoke afterwards, and *with the greatest moderation.* If one of the *auditors*, or *candidates*, was entrusted by the accused with his defence, or if he wished in his own name to present any elucidations in favour of innocence, he was admitted to the seat, from which he addressed the judges and the people. But this liberty was not granted to him, if his opinion was in favour of condemning. Lastly ; when the accused person himself wished to speak, they gave the most profound attention. When the discussion was finished, one of the judges recapitulated

* Joshua vii. 19, &c.

the case; they removed all the spectators; two scribes took down the votes of the judges; one of them noted those which were in favour of the accused, and the other, those which condemned him. Eleven votes, out of twenty-three, were sufficient to acquit; but it required thirteen to convict. If any of the judges stated that they were not sufficiently informed, there were added two more Elders, and then two others in succession, till they formed a council of sixty-two, which was the number of the Grand Council. If a majority of votes acquitted, the accused was discharged *instantly;* if he was to be punished, the judges postponed pronouncing sentence till the third day; during the intermediate day they could not be occupied with anything but the cause, and they abstained from eating freely, and from wine, liquors, and everything which might render their minds less capable of reflection.

On the morning of the third day they returned to the judgment seat. Each judge, who had not changed his opinion, said, *I continue of the same opinion and condemn;* any one, who at first condemned, might at this sitting acquit; but he who at once acquitted was not allowed to condemn. If a majority condemned, two *magistrates* immediately accompanied the condemned person to the place of punishment. The Elders did not descend from their seats; they placed at the entrance of the judgment hall an officer of justice with a small flag in his hand; a second officer, on horseback, followed the prisoner, and constantly kept looking back to the place of departure. During this interval, if any person came to announce to the elders any new evidence favourable to the prisoner, the first officer waved his flag, and the second one, as soon as he perceived it, brought back the prisoner. If the prisoner declared to the *magistrates*, that he recollected some reasons which had escaped him, they brought him before the *judges* no less than five times. If no incident occurred, the procession advanced slowly, preceded by a herald who, in a loud voice, addressed the people thus: "This man (stating his name and surname) is led to punishment for such a crime; the witnesses who have sworn against him are such and such persons; if any one has evidence to give in his favour, let him come forth quickly."

It was in consequence of this rule that the youthful Daniel caused the procession to go back, which was leading Susanna to punishment, and he himself ascended the seat of justice to put some new questions to the witnesses.

At some distance from the place of punishment, they urged the prisoner to confess his crime, and they made him drink a stupefying beverage, in order to render the approach of death less terrible.*

By this mere analysis of a part of Mr. Salvador's work we may judge of the extreme interest of the whole. His principal object has been, to make apparent the mutual aids which history, philosophy, and legislation afford in explaining the institutions of the Jewish people. His book is a scientific work, and at the same time a work of taste. His notes indicate vast reading ; and in the choice of his citations he gives proofs of his critical skill and discrimination. Mr. Salvador belongs, by his age, to that new generation, which is distinguished as much by its application to solid studies, as by elevation and generosity of sentiment.

* By this, says Father Lamy, we may understand what the mixture of wine and myrrh was, which they presented to Jesus on the cross, and which he would not drink. *Introd. to the reading of the Holy Scriptures*, chap. vi. (*Note of Mr. Salvador*, Book iv. ch. 2.)

TRIAL OF JESUS.

REFUTATION OF THE CHAPTER OF MR. SALVADOR, ENTITLED "THE TRIAL AND CONDEMNATION OF JESUS."

THE chapter, in which Mr. Salvador treats of *the Administration of Justice among the Hebrews*, is altogether theoretical. He makes an exposition of *the law*—that things, in order to be *conformable to rule*, must be transacted in a certain mode. In all this I have not contradicted him, but have let him speak for himself.

In the subsequent chapter the author announces: "That according to this *exposition of judicial proceedings* he is going to follow out the application of them to the most memorable trial in all history, that of Jesus Christ." Accordingly the chapter is entitled: *The Trial and Condemnation of Jesus.*

The author first takes care to inform us under what point of view he intends to give an account of that accusation: "That we ought to lament the blindness of the Hebrews for not having recognized a God in Jesus, is a point which I do not examine." (There is another thing also, which he says he shall not examine.) "But, when they discovered in him *only a citizen*, did they try him *according to existing laws and formalities?*"

The question being thus stated, Mr. Salvador goes over all the various aspects of the accusation; and his conclusion is, that the procedure was perfectly regular, and the condemnation perfectly appropriate to the act committed. "Now," says he, (p. 87,) "the Senate, having adjudged that Jesus, the son of Joseph, born in Bethlehem, had profaned the name of God by usurping it himself, though a simple citizen, applied to him the law against blasphemy, the law in the 13th chapter of Deuteronomy, and verse 20, chapter 18th, conformably to which every prophet, even one that performs miracles, is to be punished when he speaks of a God unknown to the Hebrews or their fathers."

This conclusion is formed to please the followers of the Jewish law; it is wholly for their benefit, and the evident object is, to justify them from the reproach of *deicide.*

We will, however, avoid treating this grave subject in a theological point of view. As to myself, Jesus Christ is the *Man-God;* but it is not with arguments drawn from my religion and my creed, that I intend to combat the statement and the conclusion of Mr. Salvador. The present age would charge me with being intolerant; and this is a reproach which I will never incur. Besides, I do not wish to give to the enemies of Christianity the advantage of making the outcry, that we are afraid to enter into a discussion with them, and that we wish to crush rather than to convince them. Having thus contented myself with declaring my own faith, as Mr. Salvador has let us clearly understand his, I shall also examine the question under a merely *human* point of view, and proceed to inquire, with him, "Whether Jesus Christ, considered as a *simple citizen,* was tried according to the existing laws and formalities."

The Catholic religion itself warrants me in this; it is not a mere fiction; for God willed, that Jesus should be clothed in the forms of humanity (*et homo factus est*), and that he should undergo the lot and sufferings of humanity. The son of *God,* as to his moral state and his holy spirit, he was also, in reality, the *Son of Man,* for the purpose of accomplishing the mission which he came upon earth to fulfil.

This being the state of the question, then, I enter upon my subject; and I do not hesitate to affirm, because I will prove it, that, upon examining all the circumstances of this great trial, we shall be very far from discovering in it the application of those legal maxims, which are the safeguard of the rights of accused persons, and of which Mr. Salvador, in his chapter *On the Administration of Justice,* has made a seductive exposition.

The accusation of Jesus, instigated by the hatred of the

priests and the Pharisees, and presented at first as a charge of *sacrilege*, but afterwards converted into *political* crime and an *offence against the state*, was marked, in all its aspects, with the foulest acts of violence and perfidy. It was not so much a *trial* environed with legal forms, as a real *passion*, or prolonged suffering, in which the imperturbable gentleness of the victim displays more strongly the unrelenting ferocity of his persecutors.

When Jesus appeared among the Jews, that people was but the shadow of itself. Broken down by more than one subjugation, divided by factions and irreconcilable sects, they had in the last resort been obliged to succumb to the Roman power and surrender their own sovereignty. Jerusalem, having become a mere appendage to the province of Syria, saw within its walls an imperial garrison; Pilate commanded there, in the name of Cæsar; and the late people of God were groaning under the double tyranny of a conqueror, whose power they abhorred and whose idolatry they detested, and of a priesthood that exerted itself to keep them under the rigorous bonds of a religious fanaticism.

Jesus Christ deplored the misfortunes of his country. How often did he weep for Jerusalem! Read in Bossuet's *Politics drawn from the Holy Scriptures*, the admirable chapter entitled, *Jesus Christ the good citizen.* He recommended to his countrymen *union*, which constitutes the the strength of states. "O Jerusalem, Jerusalem (said he,) thou that killest the prophets and stonest them which are sent unto thee, how often would I have gathered thy children together, even as a hen gathereth her chickens under her wings, and ye would not!"

He was supposed to be not favorable to the Romans; but he only loved his own countrymen more. Witness the address of the Jews, who, in order to induce him to restore to the centurion a sick servant that was dear to him, used as the most powerful argument these words—that he was worthy for whom he should do this, for he loveth our nation. And Jesus went with them. Luke vii. 4, 5.

Touched with the distresses of the nation, Jesus comforted them by holding up to them the hope of another life; he alarmed the great, the rich, and the haughty, by the prospect of a final judgment, at which every man would be judged not according to his rank, but his works. He was desirous of again bringing back man to his original dignity; he spoke to him of his *duties*, but at the same time of his *rights*. The people heard him with avidity, and followed him with eagerness; his words affected them; his hand healed their diseases, and his moral teaching instructed them; he preached, and practised one virtue till then unknown, and which belongs to him alone—*charity*. This celebrity, however, and these wonders excited envy. The partisans of the *ancient theocracy* were alarmed at the *new doctrine;* the chief priests felt that their power was threatened; the pride of the Pharisees was humbled; the scribes came in as their auxiliaries, and the destruction of Jesus was resolved upon.

Now, if his conduct was reprehensible, if it afforded grounds for a *legal accusation*, why was not that course taken openly? Why not try him for the acts committed by him, and for his public discourses? Why employ against him subterfuges, artifice, perfidy, and violence? for such was the mode of proceeding against Jesus.

Let us now take up the subject, and look at the narratives which have come down to us. Let us, with Mr. Salvador, open the books of the Gospels; for he does not object to that testimony; nay, he relies upon it: "It is by the Gospels themselves," says he, "that I shall establish *all the facts*."

In truth, how can we (except by contrary evidence, of which there is none) refuse to place confidence in an historian, who tells us, as Saint John does, with affecting simplicity: "He that saw it bare record, and his record is true; and he knoweth that he saith true, that ye might believe." John xix. 35.

SECTION I.—Spies, or Informers.

Who will not be surprised to find in this case the odious practice of employing *hired informers?* Branded with infamy, as they are in modern times, they will be still more so when we carry back their origin to the trial of Christ. It will be seen presently, whether I have not properly characterized by the name of *hired informers*, those emissaries, whom of the chief priests sent out to be about Jesus.

We read in the evangelist Luke chap. xx. 20: *Et observantes miserunt insidiatores, qui se justos simularent, ut caperent eum in sermone, et traderent illum principatui et potestati præsidis.* I will not translate this text myself, but will take the language of a translator whose accuracy is well known, Mr. De Sacy: "As they only sought occasions for his destruction, they sent to him *apostate persons* who *feigned themselves just men*, in order to *take hold* of his words, that they might deliver him unto the magistrate and into the power of the governor." And Mr. De Sacy adds —"if there should escape from him the least word against the public authorities."

This first article has escaped the sagacity of Mr. Salvador.

SECTION II.—The Corruption and Treachery of Judas.

According to Mr. Salvador, the senate, as he calls it, did not commence their proceedings by arresting Jesus, as would be done at the present day; but they began by passing a preliminary decree, that he should be arrested; and he cites, in proof of his assertion, St. John xi. 53, 54, and St. Matthew xxvi. 4, 5.

But St. John says nothing of this pretended decree. He speaks, too, not of a public sitting, but of a consultation held by the chief priests and the *Pharisees*, who did not, to my knowledge, constitute a judicial tribunal among the Jews. "Then gathered the chief priests and the Pharisees a council, and said, What do we? for this man *doeth many miracles*." John xi. 47. They add: "If we let him thus alone, all men will believe on him,"—which imported also, in their minds, *and they will no longer believe in us*. Now, in this, I can readily perceive the fear of seeing the morals and doctrines of Jesus prevail; but where is the preliminary *judgment*, or decree? I cannot discover it.

"And one of them named Caiaphas, being the high priest that same year, said unto them, Ye know nothing at all, nor consider, that it is expedient for us, that one man should die for the people . . . . . . and he *prophesied*, that Jesus should die for the nation of the Jews." But to *prophesy* is not to *pass judgment;* and the *individual* opinion of Caiaphas, who was only *one* among them, was not the opinion of all, nor a *judgment of the senate.* We, therefore, still find a *judgment* wanting; and we only observe, that the priests and Pharisees are stimulated by a violent hatred of Jesus, and that "from that day forth they took counsel together for *to put him to death; ut interficerent eum.*" John xi. 53.

The authority of St. John, then, is directly in contradiction of the assertion, that there was an *order of arrest* previously passed by a regular tribunal.

St. Matthew, in relating the same facts, says, that the chief priests assembled at the palace of the high priest, who was called Caiaphas, and there held counsel together. But what counsel? and what was the result of it? Was it to issue an *order of arrest* against Jesus, that they might hear him and then pass sentence? Not at all; but they held counsel together, "that they might take Jesus *by subtilty*, or *fraud*, and *kill him; concilium fercerunt, ut Jesum* DOLO *tenerent et* OCCIDERENT. Matt. xxvi. 5. Now in the Latin language, a language perfectly well constituted in everything relating to terms of the law, the words *occidere* and *interficere* were never employed to express the act of passing *sentence* or *judgment of death*, but simply to signify *murder* or *assassination.**

This *fraud*, by the aid of which they were to get Jesus into their power, was nothing but the bargain made between the chief priests and Judas.

Judas, one of the twelve, goes to find the chief priests,

* As was that of Stephen, whom the same priests caused to be massacred by the populace, without a previous sentence of the law. OCCIDERE: Non occides, thou shalt not kill. *Deut.* v. 17. Veneno homines occidere. Cic. pro Roscio, 61. Virginiam filiam sua manu occidit Virginius. Cic. de Finib. 107. Non hominem occidi. Horat. I. Epist. 17, 10. Inermem occidere. Ovid. ii. Fast. 139. INTERFICERE: Feras interficere. Lucret. lib. v. 251. Interfectus in acie. Cic. de Finib. 103. Cæsaris interfectores. Brutus Ciceroni, 16, 8. Interfectorem Gracchi. Cic. de Claris Orrato. 66.

and says to them, What will ye give me, and I will deliver him unto you? Matt. xxvi. 14, 15. And they covenanted with him for thirty pieces of silver! Jesus, who foresaw his treachery, warned him of it mildly, in the midst of the Last Supper, where the voice of his master, in the presence of his brethren, should have touched him and awakened his reflections! But not so; wholly absorbed in his reward, Judas placed himself at the head of a gang of servants, to whom he was to point out Jesus; and, then, by a *kiss* consummated his treachery!*

Is it thus that a *judicial decree was to be executed*, if there had really been one made for the arrest of Jesus?

SECTION III.—Personal Liberty.—Resistance to an Armed Force.

The act was done in the *night time*. After having celebrated the Supper, Jesus had conducted his disciples to the Mount of Olives. He prayed fervently; but they fell asleep.

Jesus awakes them, with a gentle reproof for their weakness, and warns them that the moment is approaching. "Rise, let us be going; behold he is at hand that doth betray me." Matt. xxvi. 46.

Judas was not alone; in his suite there was a kind of ruffian band, almost entirely composed of servants of the high priest, but whom Mr. Salvador honours with the title of the *legal soldiery*. If in the crowd there were any Roman *soldiers*, they were there as spectators, and without having been legally called on duty; for the Roman commanding officer, Pilate, had not not yet heard the affair spoken of.

* Will it be believed, that Tertullian and St. Irenæus were obliged to refute seriously some writers of their day, who considered the conduct of Judas not only excusable, but worthy of admiration and highly meritorious, "because (as they said) of the immense service which he had rendered to the human race by *preparing their redemption!*" In the same manner, at a certain period, we have seen plunderers of the public money make a merit of their conduct, because in that way they had weakened the usurpation and prepared the way for the triumph of legitimacy.

This personal seizure of Jesus had so much the appearance of a forcible arrest, an illegal act of violence, that his disciples made preparation to repel by force.

Malchus, the insolent servant of the high priest, having show himself the most eager to rush upon Jesus, Peter, not less zealous for his own master, cut off the servant's right ear.

This resistance might have been continued with success, if Jesus had not immediately interfered. But what proves that Peter, even while causing bloodshed, was not resisting a *legal order*, a *legal judgment* or decree, (which would have made his resistance an act of *rebellion by an armed force against a judicial order*,) is this—that he was not arrested, either at the moment or afterwards, at the house of the high priest, to which he followed Jesus, and where he was most distinctly recognized by the maid servant of the high priest, and even by a relative of Malchus.

Jesus alone was arrested; and although he had not individually offered any active resistance, and had even restrained that of his disciples, they bound him as a malefactor; which was a criminal degree of rigour, since for the purpose of securing a single man by a numerous band of persons armed with swords and staves it was not necessary. "Be ye come out as against a thief with swords and staves?" Luke xxii. 52.

SECTION IV.—Other Irregularities in the Arrest.—Seizure of the Person.

They dragged Jesus along with them; and, instead of taking him directly to the proper magistrate, they carried him before Annas, who had no other character than that of being *father-in-law to the high priest.* John xviii. 13. Now, if this was only for the purpose of letting him be seen by him, such a curiosity was not to be gratified; it was a vexatious proceeding, an irregularity.

From the house of Annas they led him to that of the high priest; all the time being *bound.* John xviii. 24. They placed him in the court yard; it was cold, and they made a fire; it was in the night time, but by the light of the light of the fire Peter was recognised by the people of the palace.

Now the Jewish law prohibited *all proceedings by night;* here, therefore, there was another infraction of the law.

Under this state of things, his person being forcibly seized and detained in a private house, and delivered into the hands of servants, in the midst of a court, how was Jesus treated? St. Luke says, the men that held Jesus *mocked* him and *smote* him; and when they had blindfolded him, they struck him on the face, and asked him, saying, Prophesy, who is it that smote thee? And many other things blasphemously spake they against him. Luke xxii. 63, 64, 65.

Will it be said, as Mr. Salvador does, that all this took place out of the presence of the senate? Let us wait, in this instance, till the senate shall be called up, and we shall see how far they protected the accused person.

SECTION V.—Captious Interrogatories.—Acts of Violence towards Jesus.

Already had the cock crowed! But it was not yet day. The elders of the people and the chief priests and the scribes came together, and, having caused Jesus to appear before their council, they proceeded to interrogate him. Luke xxii. 66.

Now, in the outset, it should be observed, that if they had been less carried away by their hatred, they should, as it was the *night time*, not only have postponed, but put a stop to the proceedings, because it was *the feast of the Passover*, the most solemn of all festivals; and according to their law no *judicial procedure* could take place on a feast-day, under the penalty of being null.* Nevertheless, let us see who proceeded to interrogate Jesus. This was that same Caiaphas, who, if he had intended to remain a *judge*, was evidently liable to objection; for in the

* See, as to these two grounds of nullity, the Jewish authors cited by Prost de Royer, tome 2, p. 205, *verbo* Accusation.

preceding assemblage he had made himself the *accuser* of Jesus.* Even before he had seen or heard him, he declared him to be *deserving of death.* He said to his colleagues, that "it was *expedient* that one man should die for all." John xviii. 14. Such being the opinion of Caiaphas, we shall not be surprised, if he shows partiality.

Instead of interrogating Jesus respecting *positive acts done*, with their circumstances, and respecting *facts personal to himself*, Caiaphas interrogates him respecting *general facts*, respecting his disciples (whom it would have been much more simple to have called as witnesses), and respecting his *doctrine*, which was a mere abstraction so long as no external acts were the consequence of it. "The high priest then asked Jesus of his disciples and of his doctrine." John xviii. 19.

Jesus answered with dignity: "I spake openly to the world; I ever taught in the synagogue and in the temple, whither the Jews always resort; and in secret have I said nothing." Ib. 20.

"Why asketh thou me? Ask them which heard me, *what I have said unto them;* behold, they know what I said." Ib. 21.

"And when he had thus spoken, one of the officers which stood by struck Jesus with the palm of his hand, saying, Answerest thou the high priest so?" Ib.

Will it here be still said, that this violence was the individual act of the person who thus struck the accused? I answer, that on this occasion the fact took place in the presence and under the eyes of the whole council; and, as the high priest who presided did not restrain the author of it, I come to the conclusion, that he became an accomplice, especially when this violence was committed under the pretence of avenging the alleged affront to his dignity.

But in what respect could the answer of Jesus appear offensive? "If I have spoken evil," said Jesus, "bear witness of the evil; but if well, why smitest thou me?" † John xviii. 23.

* Mr. Salvador admits this: "Caiaphas," says he, "made himself his accuser." p. 85.

† Ananias, a chief priest, having given orders to strike Paul upon the face, Paul said to him: God shall smite thee, thou whited wall; for sittest

There remained no mode of escaping from this dilemma. They accused Jesus; it was for those, who accused, to prove their accusation. An accused person is not obliged to criminate himself. He should have been convicted by proofs; he himself called for them. Let us see what witnesses were produced against him.

SECTION VI.—WITNESSES.—NEW INTERROGATORIES.—THE JUDGE IN A PASSION.

"AND the chief priests and all the council sought for witness against Jesus to put him to death; and found none." Mark xiv. 55.

"For many bare *false witness* against him, but their witness agreed not together." Ib. 56.

"And there arose certain, and bare false witness against him, saying, We heard him say, I will destroy this temple that is made with hands, and within three days I will build another made without hands." Ib. 57, 58.

"But (to the same point still) neither so did their witness agree together." Ib. 59.

Mr. Salvador, on this subject, says, p. 87: "The two witnesses, whom St. Matthew and St. Mark charge with *falsehood*, narrate a discourse which St. John declares to be *true*, so far as respects the power which Jesus Christ attributes to himself."

This alleged contradiction among the Evangelists does not exist. In the first place, St. Matthew does not say that the discourse was had by Jesus. In chapter xxvi. 61, he states the depositions of the witnesses, but saying at the same time that they were *false witnesses;* and in chapter xxvii. 40, he put the same declaration into the mouth of those who insulted Jesus at the foot of the cross; but he does not put it into the mouth of Christ. He is in accordance with St. Mark.

St. John, chapter ii. 19, makes Jesus speak in these words: "Jesus answered and said unto them, Destroy this

thou to judge me after the law, and commandest me to be smitten, *contrary to the law?*" Acts xxiii. 3.

temple, and in three days I will raise it up." And St. John adds: "He spake of the temple of his body.

Thus Jesus did not say in an affirmative and somewhat menacing manner, *I will destroy this temple*, as the witnesses *falsely* assumed; he only said, hypothetically, *Destroy this temple*, that is to say, suppose this temple should be destroyed, I will raise it up in three days. Besides, they could not dissemble, that he referred to a temple altogether different from theirs, because he said, I will raise up another in three days, *which will not be made by the hands of man.*

It hence results, at least, that the Jews did not understand him, for they cried out, "Forty and six years was this temple in building, and wilt thou rear it up in three days?"

Thus, then, the witnesses did not agree together, and their declarations had nothing conclusive. Mark xiv. 59. We must, therefore, look for other proofs.

"Then the high priest, (we must not forget that he is still the accuser,) the high priest stood up in the midst, and asked Jesus, saying, Answerest thou nothing? what is it, which these witness against thee? But he held his peace, and answered nothing." Mark xiv. 60. In truth, since the question was not concerning the temple of the Jews, but an ideal temple, not made by the hand of man, and which was alone in the thoughts of Jesus, the explanation was to be found in the very evidence itself.

The high priest continued: "I adjure thee, by the living God, that thou tell us, whether thou be the Christ, the Son of God." Matt. xxvi. 63. I adjure thee, I call upon thee on oath! a gross infraction of that rule of morals and jurisprudence, which forbids our placing an accused person between the danger of perjury and the fear of inculpating himself, and thus making his situation more hazardous. The high priest, however, persists, and says to him: Art thou the Christ, the Son of God?* Jesus answered, *Thou hast said.* Matthew xxvi. 64; *I am.* Mark xiv. 62.

* Mr. Salvador, in his note to p. 82., admits, that "the expression *Son of God* was in common use among the Hebrews, to signify a man of great wisdom, or of deep piety. But adds, "*It was not in this sense*, that it was used by Jesus Christ; it would not have caused so strong a sensation."

"Then the high priest rent his clothes, saying, *He hath spoken blasphemy; what further need have we of witnesses?* behold, now *ye have heard his blasphemy.* What think ye? They answered and said, He is guilty of death." Matt. xxvi. 66.

Let us now compare this scene of violence with the mild deduction of principles, which we find in the chapter of Mr. Salvador *On the Administration of Justice;* and let us ask ourselves, if, as he alleges, we find a just *application* of them in the proceedings against Christ?

Do we discover here that *respect* of the Hebrew judge towards the party accused, when we see that Caiaphas permitted him to be struck, in his presence, *with impunity?*

What was this Caiaphas, at once an accuser and judge?* A passionate man, and too much resembling the odious portrait which the historian Josephus has given us of him! † A judge, who was irritated to such a degree, that he rent his clothes; who imposed upon the accused a most solemn oath, and who gave to his answers the criminal character, that *he had spoken* blasphemy! And, from that moment, he wanted no more witnesses, notwithstanding the law required them. He would not have an inquiry, which he perceived would be insufficient; he attempts to supply it by captious questions. He is desirous of having him condemned *upon his own declaration alone,* (interpreted, too, as he chooses to understand it,) though that was forbidden by the laws of the Hebrews! And, in the midst of a most violent transport of passion, this accuser himself, a high priest, who means to speak in the name of the living God, is the first to pass sentence of death, and carries with him the opinions of the rest!

In this hideous picture I cannot recognise that justice of the Hebrews, of which Mr. Salvador has given a fine view in *his theory!*

Thus, then, by *construction* and changing the words from their usual meaning, an article of accusation is formed against Jesus.

* That is, he usurped the functions of a judge; for we shall see, in the next section, that the *Council* of the Jews had not jurisdiction of capital cases.

† Antiq. Judaic. lib. 18. cap. 3 & 6.

SECTION VII.—Subsequent Acts of Violence.

Immediately after this kind of sacerdotal verdict rendered against Jesus, the acts of violence and insults recommenced with increased strength; the fury of the judge must have communicated itself to the bystanders. St. Matthew says: "Then did they spit in his face, and buffeted him; and others smote him with the palms of their hands, saying, Prophesy unto us, thou Christ; who is he that smote thee?" Matt. xxvi. 67, 68.

Mr. Salvador does not contest the truth of this ill treatment. In page 88 he says, "It was contrary to the spirit of the Hebrew law, and that it was not according to the order of nature, that a senate composed of the most respectable men of a nation,—that a senate, which might perhaps be mistaken, but which thought it was acting mildly, should have permitted such outrages against him whose life it held in its own hands. The writers, who have transmitted these details to us, not having been present themselves at the trial, were disposed to overcharge the picture, either on account of their own feelings, or to throw upon their judges a greater odium."

I repeat; this ill treatment was entirely contrary to the spirit of the law. And what do I want more, since my object is to make prominent *all the violations of law.*

"It is not in nature to see a body, which respects itself, authorize such attempts." But of what consequence is that, when the fact is established? "The historians, it is said, were not present at the trial." But was Mr. Salvador there present himself, so that he could give a flat denial of their statements? And when even an able writer, who was not an eye-witness, relates the same events after the lapse of more than eighteen centuries, he ought at least to bring opposing evidence, if he would impeach that of contemporaries; who, if they were not in the very hall of the council, were certainly on the spot, in the vicinity, perhaps in the court yard, inquiring anxiously of every thing that was happening to the man whose disciples they were.* Besides, the

* Peter followed him afar off unto the high priest's palace, and went in and sat with the servants to see the end. Matt. xxvi. 58. So also the

learned author whom I am combating says, in the outset (p. 81), "it is from the Gospels themselves that he will take all his facts." He must then take the whole together, as well those which go to condemn, as those which are in palliation or excuse.

Those gross insults, those inhuman acts of violence, even if they are to be cast upon the servants of the high priest and the persons in his train, do not excuse those individuals, who, when they took upon themselves the authority of judges, were bound at the same time to throw around him all the protection of the law. Caiaphas, too, was culpable as the master of the house (for every thing took place in his house), even if he should not be responsible as high priest and president of the council for having permitted excesses, which, indeed were but too much in accordance with the rage he had himself displayed upon the bench.

These outrages, which would be inexcusable even towards a man irrevocably condemned to punishment, were the more criminal towards Jesus, because, legally and judicially speaking, there had not yet been any sentence properly passed against him according to the public law of the country; as we shall see in the following section, which will deserve the undivided attention of the reader.

SECTION VIII.—The Position of the Jews in respect to the Romans.

We must not forget, *that Judea was a conquered country*. After the death of Herod—most inappropriately surnamed *the Great*—Augustus had confirmed his last will, by which that king of the Jews had arranged the division of his dominions between *his* two sons: but Augustus did not continue their title of *king*, which their father had borne.

Archelaus, on whom Judea devolved, having been recalled on account of his cruelties, the territory, which was at first intrusted to his command, was united to the province of Syria. (*Josephus*, Antiq. Jud. lib. 17, cap. 15.)

young man spoken of by St. Mark, xiv. 51: And there followed him a certain young man, &c.

Augustus then appointed particular officers for Judea. Tiberius did the same; and at the time of which we are speaking, Pilate was one of those officers. (*Josephus*, lib. 18, cap. 3 & 8.)

Some have considered Pilate as governor, by title, and have given him the Latin appellation *Præses*, president or governor. But they have mistaken the force of the word. Pilate was one of those public officers, who were called by the Romans, *procuratores Cæsaris*, Imperial procurators.

With this title of *procurator*, he was placed under the superior authority of the governor of Syria, the true *præses*, or governor of that province, of which Judea was then only one of the dependencies.

To the governor (*præses*) peculiarly belonged the right of taking cognizance of *capital* cases.* The *procurator*, on the contrary, had, for his principal duty, nothing but the collection of the revenue, and the trial of revenue causes. But the right of taking cognizance of *capital* cases did, in some instances, belong to certain *procurators*, who were sent into small provinces to fill the places of governors (*vice præsides*), as appears clearly from the Roman laws.† Such was *Pilate* at Jerusalem.‡

The Jews, placed in this political position—notwithstanding they were left in the enjoyment of their civil laws, the public exercise of their religion, and many things merely relating to their police and municipal regulations—the Jews, I say, had had not the *power of life and death*; this was a principal attribute of sovereignty, which the Romans always took great care to reserve to themselves, even if they neglected other things. *Apud Romanos, jus valet gladii; cætera transmittuntur.* TACIT.

What then was the right of the Jewish authorities in

* *De Crimine* præsidis cognitio est. Cujas, xix. Observ. 13.

† Procurator Cæsaris *fungens vice præsidis* potest cognoscere *de causis criminalibus*. Godefroy, in his note (letter S) upon the 3rd law of the Code, *Ubi causæ fiscales*, &c. And he cites several others, which I have verified, and which are most precise to the same effect. See particularly the 4th law of the Code, *Ad leg. fab. de plag.*, and the 2nd law of the Code, *De Pœnis*.

‡ Procuratoribus Cæsaris data est jurisdictio in causis fiscalibus pecuniariis, non in criminalibus, nisi quum fungebantur *vice præsidum*; ut Pontius Pilatus fuit procurator Cæsaris *vice præsidis* in Syria. Cujas, Observ. xix. 13.

regard to Jesus? Without doubt the scribes, and their friends the Pharisees, might well have been alarmed, as a body and individually, at the preaching and success of Jesus; they might be concerned for their worship; and they might have interrogated the man respecting his creed and his doctrines,—they might have made a kind of preparatory proceeding,—they might have declared, in point of fact, that those doctrines, which threatened their own, were contrary to their law, as understood by themselves.

But this law, although it had not undergone any alteration as to the affairs of religion, had no longer any coercive power as to the external or civil regulations of society. In vain would they have undertaken to pronounce sentence of death under the circumstances of the case of Jesus; the council of the Jews had not the power to pass a *sentence of death;* it only would have had power to make *an accusation* against him before the governor, or his deputy, and then deliver him over to be tried by him.

Let us distinctly establish this point; for here I entirely differ in opinion from Mr. Salvador. According to him, (p. 88), "the Jews had *reserved the power of trying, according to their law;* but it was in the hands of the *procurator* alone, that the executive power was vested; every culprit must be put to death by *his* consent, in order that the senate should not have the means of reaching persons that were sold to foreigners."

No; the Jews had not reserved *the right of passing sentence of death.* This right had been transferred to the Romans by the very act of conquest; and this was not merely that the senate should not have the means of reaching persons who were sold to foreign countries; but it was done, in order that the conqueror might be able to reach those individuals who should become *impatient of the yoke;* it was, in short, for the equal protection of all, as all had become Roman subjects; and to Rome alone belonged the highest judicial power, which is the principal attribute of sovereignty. Pilate, as the representative of Cæsar in Judea, was not merely an agent of the *executive authority*, which would have left the *judiciary* and *legislative* power in the hands of the conquered people—he was not simply an officer appointed to give an *exequatur* or mere approval (*visa*) to sentences passed by *another aathority*, the *authority of the Jews.* When the matter in question was a *capital* case, the Roman authorities not only ordered the *execution* of a sentence, but also took cognizance (*cognitio*) of the crime; it had the right of jurisdiction *a priori*, and that of *passing judgment in the last resort.* If Pilate himself had not had this power by special delegation, *vice præsidis*, it was vested in the governor, within whose territorial jurisdiction the case occurred; but in any event we hold it to be clear, that the Jews had lost the right of *condemning to death* any person whatever, not only so far as respects the *execution* but the *passing* of the sentence. This is one of the best settled points in the provincial law of the Romans.

The Jews were not ignorant of this; for when they went before Pilate, to ask of him the condemnation of Jesus, they themselves declared, that it was not permitted to them to put any person to death: "It is not lawful for us to put any man to death." John xviii. 31.

Here I am happy to be able to support myself by the opinion of a very respectable authority, the celebrated Loiseau, in his treatise on *Seigneuries*, in the chapter on the administration of *justice belonging to cities*. "In truth," says he, "there is some evidence, that the *police*, in which the people had the sole interest, was administered by officers of the people; but I know not upon what were founded the concessions of power to some cities of France to exercise criminal jurisdiction; nor why the Ordinance of Moulins left that to them rather than civil cases; for the criminal jurisdiction is the *right of the sword*, the *merum imperium*, or absolute sovereignty. Accordingly, by the Roman law, the administration of justice was so far prohibited to the officers of cities, that they could not punish even by a simple fine. *Thus it is doubtless that we must understand* that passage of the Gospel, where the Jews say to Pilate, *It is not lawful for us to put any man to death;* for, after they were subjected to the Romans, they had not jurisdiction of crimes."

Let us now follow Jesus to the presence of Pilate.

SECTION IX.—THE ACCUSATION MADE BEFORE PILATE.

AT this point I must entreat the particular attention of the reader. The irregularities and acts of violence, which I have hitherto remarked upon, are nothing in comparison with the unbridled fury, which is about to display itself before the *Roman Judge*, in order to extort from him, against his own conviction, a sentence of death.

"And straightway in the morning the chief priest held a consultation with the elders, and scribes, and the whole council, and bound Jesus, and carried him away, and delivered him to Pilate." Mark xv. 1.

As soon as the morning was come; for, as I have observed already, every thing which had been done thus far against Jesus was done *during the night.*

They then led Jesus from Caiaphas unto the Hall of Judgment of Pilate.* It was early; and they themselves went not into the judgment hall, lest *they should be defiled;* but that they might eat the passover. John xviii. 28.

Singular scrupulousness! and truly worthy of the Pharisees! They were afraid of *defiling themselves on the day of the passover* by entering *the house of* a heathen! And, yet, the same day, only some hours before presenting themselves to Pilate, they had, in contempt of their own law, committed the outrage of *holding a council* and deliberating upon *an accusation of a capital crime.*

As they would not enter, "Pilate went out to them." John xviii. 29. Now observe his language. He did not say to them, *Where is the sentence you have passed;* as he must have done, if he was only to give them his simple *exequatur*, or permission to execute the sentence; but he takes up the matter from the beginning, as would be done by one who had *plenary jurisdiction;* and he says to them: What accusation bring ye against this man? Ib.

They answered, with their accustomed haughtiness: If he were not a *malefactor* we would not have delivered him up to thee. John xviii. 30. They wished to have it understood that, being a question of *blasphemy*, it was the *cause*

* "To carry one from Caiaphas to Pilate" has since become a proverb.

of their religion, which they could appreciate better than any others could. Pilate, then, would have been under the necessity of believing them *on their word*. But this Roman, indignant at their proposed course of proceeding, which would have restricted his jurisdiction by making him the passive instrument of the wishes of the Jews, answered them in an ironical manner: Well, since you say he has sinned against your law, take him yourselves and judge him according to your law. John xviii. 31. This was an absolute mystification to them, for they knew their own want of power to condemn him to death. But they were obliged to yield the point, and to submit to Pilate himself their *articles of accusation*.

Now what were the grounds of this accusation? Were they *the same* which had hitherto been alleged against Jesus—the charge of *blasphemy*—which was the only one brought forward by Caiaphas before the council of the Jews? Not at all; despairing of obtaining from the Roman judge a sentence of *death* for a *religious* quarrel, which was of no interest to the Romans,* they suddenly changed their plan; they abandoned their first accusation, the charge of blasphemy, and substituted for it a *political* accusation, an *offence against the state*.

Here we have the very crisis, or essential incident, of the passion; and that which makes the heaviest accusation of guilt on the part of the informers against Jesus. For, being fully bent on destroying him in any manner whatever, they no longer exhibited themselves as the avengers of *their religion*, which was alleged to have been outraged, or of their worship, which it was pretended was threatened; but, ceasing to appear as Jews, in order to affect sentiments belonging to a foreign nation, those hypocrites held out the appearance of being concerned for the interests of *Rome;* they accused their own countryman of an intention to restore the kingdom of Jerusalem, to make himself *king* of the *Jews*, and to make an insurrection of the people against their conquerors. Let us hear them speak for themselves:

"And they began to *accuse* him, saying, We found this

* Lysias thus wrote to Felix the Governor, in relation to Paul: Whom I perceived to be accused of questions of their law, but to have nothing laid to his charge worthy of death or bonds. Acts xxiii. 29.

fellow perverting the nation, and forbidding to give tribute to Cæsar, saying, that he himself is Christ a *king*." Luke xxiii. 2.

What a calumny! Jesus forbidding to give tribute to Cæsar! when he had answered the Pharisees themselves, in presence of the whole people, by showing them the image of Cæsar upon a Roman piece of money, and saying, Give unto Cæsar the things which are Cæsar's. But this accusation was one mode of interesting Pilate in respect to his jurisdiction; for, as an imperial *procurator*, he was specially to superintend the collection of the revenue. The second branch of the accusation still more directly affected the sovereignty of the Romans: "He holds himself up for a *king*."

The accusation having thus assumed a character purely *political*, Pilate thought he must pay attention to it "Then Pilate entered into the judgment hall, (the place where justice was administered,) and having *summoned Jesus to appear* before him, he proceeds to his Examination, and says to him: "Art thou the king of the Jews?" John xviii. 33.

This question, so different from those which had been addressed to him at the house of the high priest, appears to have excited the astonishment of Jesus; and, in his turn, he asked Pilate: "Sayest thou this thing of thyself, or did others tell it thee of me?" Ib. 24. In reality, Jesus was desirous of knowing, first of all, the authors of this new accusation—Is this an accusation brought against me by the *Romans* or by the *Jews?*

Pilate replied to him—"Am I a Jew? Thine own nation and the chief priests have delivered thee unto me; what hast thou done?" Ib. 35.

All the particulars of this procedure are important; I can not too often repeat the remark, that in no part of the transactions before Pilate is there any question at all respecting a previous sentence, a judgment already passed—a judgment, the execution of which was the only subject of consideration; it was a case of a capital accusation; but an accusation which was then just beginning; they were about the preliminary *interrogatories* put to the accused, and Pilate says to him, "What hast thou done?"

Jesus, seeing by the explanation what was the source of the *prejudging* of his case, and knowing the secret thoughts which predominated in making the accusation, and that his enemies wanted to arrive at the same end by an artifice, answered Pilate—"*My kingdom is not of this world;* if my kingdom were of this world, then would my servants fight, that I should not be delivered to the Jews;" (we see, in fact, that Jesus had forbidden his people to resist) but, he added, "now is my kingdom not from hence." John xviii. 36.

This answer of Jesus is very remarkable; it became the foundation of his religion, and the pledge of its universality, because it detached it from the interests of all governments. It rests not merely in assertion, in doctrine; it was given in *justification*, in *defence* against the accusation of intending to make himself *King of the Jews.* Indeed, if Jesus had affected a *temporal* royal authority, if there had been the least attempt, on his part, to usurp *the power of Cæsar*, he would have been guilty of treason in the eyes of the magistrate. But, by answering twice, my *kingdom is not of this world*, my kingdom *is not from hence*, his justification was complete.

Pilate, however, persisted and said to him: "Art thou a king then?" Jesus replied, Thou sayest that I am a king. To this end was I born, and for this cause came I into the world, that I should bear witness unto the truth. Every one that is of the truth heareth my voice. John xviii. 37.

Pilate then said to him: *What is the truth?*

This question proves that Pilate had not a very clear idea of what Jesus called *the truth.* He perceived nothing in it but *ideology;* and, satisfied with having said (less in the manner of a question than of an exclamation) "*What is the truth,*" he went out to the Jews (who remained outside) and said to them, "*I find in him no fault at all.*" John xviii. 38.

Here, then, we see Jesus absolved from the accusation by the declaration of the Roman judge himself.

But the accusers, persisting still farther, added—"*He stirreth up the people, teaching* throughout all Jewry, beginning from Galilee to this place." Luke xxiii. 5.

"He stirreth up the people!" This is a charge of sedition; and for Pilate. But observe, it was *by the doctrine which he teaches;* these words comprehended the real complaint of the Jews. To them it was equivalent to saying—He *teaches* the people, he instructs them, he enlightens them; he preaches *new doctrines* which are not *ours.* "He stirs up the people!" This, in their mouth signified—the people hear him willingly; the people follow and become attached to him; for he preaches a doctrine that is friendly and consolatory to the people; he unmasks our pride, our avarice, our insatiable spirit of domination!

Pilate, however, does not appear to have attached much importance to this new turn given to the accusation; but he here betrays a weakness. He heard the word *Galilee;* and he makes that the occasion of shifting off the responsibility upon another public officer, and seizes the occasion with avidity. He says to Jesus—you are a *Galilean* then? and, upon the answer being in the affirmative, considering Jesus as belonging to the jurisdiction of Herod-Antipas, who, by the good pleasure of Cæsar, was then tetrarch of Galilee, he sent him to Herod. Luke xxiii. 6, 7.

But Herod, who, as St. Luke says, had been long desirous of *seeing Jesus* and had hoped to see *some miracle* done by him, after satisfying an idle curiosity and putting several questions to him, which Jesus did not deign to answer,—Herod notwithstanding the presence of the priests, (who had not yet gone off, but stood there with their scribes,) and notwithstanding the pertinacity with which they continued to accuse Jesus, perceiving nothing but what was merely chimerical in the *accusation of being a king*, made a mockery of the affair, and sent Jesus back to Pilate, *after having arrayed him in a gorgeous robe*, in order to show that he thought this pretended royalty was a subject of ridicule rather than of apprehension. Luke xxiii. 8, &c., and De Sacy. Ib.

SECTION X.—The Last Efforts before Pilate.

No person, then, was willing to condemn Jesus; neither Herod, who only made the case a subject of mockery, no. Pilate, who had openly declared that he found nothing criminal in him.

But the hatred of the priests was not disarmed; so far from it, that the chief priests, with a numerous train of their partisans, returned to Pilate with a determination to force him to a decision.

The unfortunate Pilate, reviewing his proceedings in their presence, said to them again: "Ye have brought this man unto me as one that perverteth the people; and behold, I, having examined him before you, *have found no fault in this man touching those things whereof ye accuse him:* No, nor yet Herod; for I sent you to him, and lo, *nothing worthy of death is done unto him.* I will therefore chastise him and release him. Luke xxiii. 14, 15.

After "chastising" him! And was not this a piece of cruelty, when he considered him to be innocent?* But this was an act of condescension by which Pilate hoped to quiet the rage with which he saw they were agitated.

"Then Pilate therefore took Jesus and scourged him." John xix. 1. And, supposing that he had done enough to disarm their fury, he exhibited him to them in that pitiable condition; saying to them at the same time, Behold the man! *Ecce homo.* John xix. 5.

Now, in my turn, I say, here is indeed a decree of Pilate; and an unjust decree; but it is not the pretended decree alleged to have been made by the Jews. It is a decision wholly different; an unjust decision, it is true; but sufficient to avail as *a legal bar* to any new proceedings against Jesus for the same act. *Non bis in idem*, no man shall be put twice in jeopardy, &c., is a maxim, which has come down to us from the Romans.

* Gerhard makes the following unanswerable dilemma upon this point. "Be consistent with thyself, Pilate; for, if Christ is innocent, why dost thou not send him away acquitted? And if thou believest him deserving of chastisement with rods, why dost thou proclaim him to be innocent?" *Gerh. Harm.* ch. 193, p. 1889.

Accordingly, "from thenceforth Pilate sought to *release* Jesus." John xix. 12.

Here, now, observe the deep perfidy of his accusers. "If thou let this man go, thou art not Cæsar's friend; whosoever maketh himself a *king* speaketh against Cæsar." Ib.

It does not appear that Pilate was malignant; we see all the efforts he had made at different times to save Jesus. But he was a *public officer*, and was attached to *his office;* he was intimidated by the outcry which called in question his *fidelity to the emperor;* he was afraid of a *dismissal;* and he yielded. He immediately reascended the judgment seat; (Matt. xxvii. 19) and, as new light had thus come upon him, he proceeded to make a second decree!

But being for a moment stopped by the voice of his own conscience, and by the advice which his terrified wife sent to him—"*Have thou nothing to do with that just man*"—(Matt. xxvii. 19)—he made his last effort, by attempting to influence the populance to accept of Barabbas instead of Jesus. "But the chief priests moved the people, that he should rather release Barabbas unto them." Mark xv. 11. Barabbas! a murderer! an assassin!

Pilate spoke to them again: *What will ye then that I should do with Jesus?* And they cried out, *Away with him, crucify him.* Pilate still persisted: *Shall I crucify your king?* thus using terms of raillery, in order to disarm them. But here showing themselves to be more truly Roman than Pilate himself, the chief priests hypocritically answered: *We have no king but Cæsar.* John xix. 15.

The outcry was renewed—Crucify him, crucify him! and the clamour became more and more threatening; "and the voices of them and of the chief priests prevailed." Luke xxiii. 23.

At length Pilate, *being desirous of pleasing the multitude*, proceeds to speak. But can we call it a legal adjudication, a *judgment*, that he is about to pronounce? Is he, at the moment, in that free state of mind which is necessary for a judge, who is about to pass a *sentence of death?* What new witnesses, what proofs have been brought forward to change his conviction and opinion which had been so energetically declared, of the innocence of Jesus?

"When Pilate saw that he could prevail nothing, but

that rather a tumult was made, he took water and washed his hands before the multitude, saying, *I am innocent of the blood of this just person*; see ye to it. Matt. xxvii. 24. And Pilate gave sentence, that it should be as they required. Luke xxiii. 24. And he delivered him to them to be crucified." Matt. xxvii. 26.

Well mayest thou wash thy hands, Pilate, stained as they are with innocent blood! Thou hast authorized the act in thy weakness; thou art not less culpable, than if thou hadst sacrificed him through wickedness! All generations, down to our own time, have repeated that the *Just One* suffered *under Pontius Pilate*. Thy name has remained in history, to serve for the instruction of all public men, all pusillanimous judges, in order to hold up to them the shame of *yielding contrary to one's own convictions*. The populace, in its fury, made an outcry at the foot of the judgment-seat, where, perhaps, thou thyself didst not sit securely! But of what importance was that? Thy *duty* spoke out; and in such a case, better would it be to suffer death, than to inflict it on another.*

We will now come to this conclusion.

The *proof* that Jesus was not, as Mr. Salvador maintains, put to death for the crime of blasphemy or sacrilege, and for having preached a new religious worship in contravention of the Mosaic law, results from *the very sentence*, pronounced by Pilate; a sentence, in pursuance of which he was led to execution by Roman soldiers.

There was among the Romans a custom, which was borrowed from their jurisprudence, and which is still followed, of placing over the head of a condemned criminal a writing containing *an extract from his sentence*, in order that the

* We will cite here the words of one of the finest laws of the Romans: Vanæ voces populi non sunt audiendæ, quando aut noxium crimine absolvi, aut innocentem condemnari desiderant—The idle clamour of the populace is not to be regarded, when they call for a guilty man to be acquitted, or an innocent one to be condemned. *Law* 12, *Code de Pænis.* Pilate might also have read in Horace: Justum et tenacem, &c.—

"The man in conscious virtue bold,
Who dares his secret purpose hold,
Unshaken hears the *crowd's* tumultuous cries,
And the impetuous *tyrant's* angry brow defies."

public might know *for what crime* he was condemned. This was the reason why Pilate put on the cross a label, on which he had written these words: *Jesus Nazarenus Rex Judæorum,* (Jesus of Nazareth, King of the Jews), which has since been denoted by the initials J. N. R. J. This was the alleged cause of his condemnation. St. Mark says —"And the superscription of his *accusation* was written over—*The King of the Jews.*" Mark xv. 26.

This inscription was first in *Latin*, which was the legal language of the *Roman* judge; and it was repeated in *Hebrew* and *Greek,* in order to be understood by the people of the nation and by foreigners.

The chief priests, whose indefatigable hatred did not overlook the most minute details, being apprehensive that people would take it to be literally a fact affirmed, that Jesus *was the King of the Jews*, said to Pilate: "Write not *King of the Jews*, but that *he said* I am king of the Jews." But Pilate answered: "What I have written I have written." John xix. 21, 22.

This is a conclusive answer to one of the last assertions of Mr. Salvador, (p. 88,) that "the Roman Pilate signed the sentence;" by which he always means that Pilate did nothing but sign a sentence, which he supposes to have been passed by the Sanhedrim; but in this he is mistaken. Pilate did not merely *sign* the sentence, or decree, but *drew it up;* and, when his draft was objected to by the priests, he still adhered to it, saying, what I have written shall remain as written.

Here, then we see the true cause of the condemnation of Jesus? Here, we have the "*judicial and legal* proof." Jesus was the victim of a *political* accusation! He was put to death for the imaginary crime of having aimed at the power of Cæsar, by calling himself *King of the Jews!* Absurd accusation; which Pilate never believed, and which the chief priests and the Pharisees themselves did not believe. For they were not authorized to arrest Jesus on that account; it was a new, and totally different, accusation from that which they first planned—a sudden accusation of the moment, when they saw that Pilate was but little affected by their *religious* zeal, and they found it necessary to arouse *his zeal for* Cæsar.

"*If thou let this man go, thou art not Cæsar's friend!*" This alarming language has too often, since that time, reverberated in the ears of timid judges, who, like Pilate, have rendered themselves criminal by delivering up victims through want of firmness, whom they would never have condemned if they had listened to the voice of their own consciences.

Let us now recapitulate the case, as I have considered it from the beginning.

It is not evident, contrary to the conclusion of Mr. Salvador, that Jesus considered merely as *a simple citizen*, was not tried and sentenced either *according to law, or agreeably to the forms of legal proceedings then existing?*

God, according to his eternal design, might permit the just to suffer by the malice of men; but he also intended, that this should at least happen by a disregard of all laws, and by a violation of all established rules, in order that the entire contempt of forms should stand as the first warning of the violation of law.

Let us not be surprised then, that in another part of his work, Mr. Salvador (who, it is gratifying to observe, discusses his subject dispassionately) expresses some regret in speaking of the *unfortunate sentence against Jesus.*" Vol. i. p. 59. He has wished to excuse the Hebrews; but, one of that nation, in giving utterance to the feelings of his heart, still says—in language which I took from his his own mouth: "We should be very cautious of condemning him at this day."

I pass over the excesses which followed the order of Pilate; as, the violence shown to Simon, the Cyrenian, who was made in some degree a sharer in the punishment, by being compelled to carry the cross; the injurious treatment which attended the victim to the place of the sacrifice,* and even the cross, where Jesus still prayed for his brethren and his executioners!

To the heathen themselves I would say—You, who have gloried in the death of Socrates, how much must you be struck with wonder at that of Jesus! Ye, censors of the

* "To the sufferings of those who were put to death were added mockery and derision." TACIT. *Ann.* xv. 44.

Areopagus, how could you undertake to excuse the Synagogue, and justify the sentence of the Hall of Judgment? Philosophy herself has not hesitated to proclaim, and we may repeat with her—" Yes, if the life and death of *Socrates* were those of a sage, the life and death of *Jesus* were those of a divinity."

www.ingramcontent.com/pod-product-compliance
Lightning Source LLC
LaVergne TN
LVHW021059110826
845150LV00001B/119

* 9 7 8 1 4 2 5 5 6 6 3 0 2 *